To my wife Bonni – it's a privilege to share my l

Philip Yaeger, PhD, MBA, CPA, CGMA   Owner, Editor-in-chief
Megan Lewczyk, MAcc, CPA   Production Editor

This book was set in Calibri font designed by Lucas de Groot.
Cover Design: Larissa Jaster Design Studio
Cover Photography: Travis Rieth

The following items, copyright © the American Institute of Certified Professional Accountants, Inc., New York, NY 10036, are reprinted and/or adapted with permission:

1. Material from Uniform CPA Exam Selected Questions and Unofficial Answers © 2000–2017
2. Definitions, examples, etc. from The Code of Professional Conduct
3. Material from the Preparation, Compilation and Review Standards
4. Material from the Clarified Statements on Auditing Standards
5. Material from the AICPA Audit Guide over Audit Sampling

Material from the Certified Management Accountant Examinations, copyright © 2011–2014 by the Institute of Certified Management Accountants, Montvale, New Jersey 07645, are reprinted and/or adapted with permission.

The FASB material is copyrighted by the Financial Accounting Foundation, 401 Merritt 7, Norwalk, CT 06856, and is used with permission.

The information disclosed in this document, including all designs and related materials, is the property of Yaeger CPA Review. Yaeger CPA Review and/or its licensors, as appropriate, reserve all patent, copyright and other proprietary rights to this document, including all design, reproduction, use, and sales rights thereto. You may not reproduce or transmit in any form or by any means, electronic or mechanical, including photocopying, recording, and storage in an information retrieval system, nor may you modify or create derivative works based on the text of any file, or any part thereof, without the prior written permission of Yaeger CPA Review.

Limit of Liability/Disclaimer of Warranty: While the content development team has used their best efforts in preparing this book, they make no representations or warranties with respect to the accuracy or completeness of the contents of this book and specifically disclaim any implied warranties of merchantability or fitness for a particular purpose. No warranty may be created or extended by sales representatives or written sales materials. The advice and strategies contained herein may not be suitable for your situation. You should consult with a professional where appropriate. Neither the publisher nor author shall be liable for any loss of profit or any other commercial damages, including but not limited to special, incidental, consequential, or other damages.

Solicitation or disclosure of CPA Examination questions and answers is strictly prohibited.

ISBN: 978-0-9987002-4-3   *Yaeger CPA Review 2018 - Auditing and Attestation*
        978-0-9987002-5-0   *Yaeger CPA Review 2018 - Business Environment and Concepts*
        978-0-9987002-6-7   *Yaeger CPA Review 2018 - Regulation*
        978-0-9987002-7-4   *Yaeger CPA Review 2018 - Financial Accounting and Reporting*

Copyright © 2018 Yaeger CPA Review. ALL RIGHTS RESERVED.

Second Edition: December 2017 (Version 2.8)

For additional information on our other products or for customer service, please call 1.800.824.2811.

Introduction:
Preparing for the CPA Exam

A. Message from Phil Yaeger

On behalf of YAEGER CPA REVIEW, I thank you for purchasing our program, and I wish you the best success with the CPA EXAM! If you have questions during your studies, I will be very happy to speak with you personally at any time. I am here to help you and motivate you during your journey.

With warmest regards,

Philip S. Yaeger

B. CPA Exam Basics

The CPA (Certified Public Accountant) exam is a computer-based exam that according to the American Institute of Certified Public Accountants (AICPA), tests the knowledge and skills typically possessed by a person with two years of accounting experience, to protect the public interest. Experience requirements may be obtained before or after passing the CPA exam with some time limitations dependent on your state. Even though many students take the CPA Exam after graduating college, the AICPA has stated that this should not, and will not, impact the standard established regarding required knowledge and skills necessary for licensure as a CPA.

The CPA Exam must be passed to qualify for licensure as a CPA. The licensure can be obtained in any of the 55 U.S. jurisdictions, which includes all 50 states, Puerto Rico, Guam, District of Columbia, Commonwealth of Northern Mariana Islands, and the U.S. Virgin Islands.

Apply to take the exam through your state board of accountancy or NASBA (nasba.org), as applicable. It is best to apply to take the exam when you have met the educational requirements of the jurisdiction you plan to apply for the exam in. It is recommended to check the jurisdiction you plan to take the exam in to ensure you have met the requirements before commencing your CPA Exam preparation. Most states offer a self-assessment education evaluation worksheet which you can complete to determine your status.

The Uniform CPA Exam consists of four sections: Auditing and Attestation(AUD), Business Environment and Concepts (BEC), Financial Accounting and Reporting (FAR), and Regulation (REG). Each exam section is four hours, for a total of 16 hours of testing.

Examination Structure by Section				
Section	Item Type	Item Weighting	Testlet and Time Allocation Recommendation	
Auditing and Attestation (AUD)	72 MCQs 8 TBSs	50% 50%	No.1 36 MCQs - 1 hour No.2 36 MCQs - 1 hour No.3 2 TBSs - 30 min. No.4 3 TBSs - 45 min. No.5 3 TBSs - 45 min.	Time to complete – 4 hours
Business Environment and Concepts (BEC)	62 MCQs 4 TBSs 3 Written Communications	50% 35% 15%	No.1 31 MCQs - 1 hour No.2 31 MCQs - 1 hour No.3 2 TBSs - 30 min. No.4 2 TBSs - 30min. No.5 3 Written Communications - 60 min.	Time to complete – 4 hours

Financial Accounting and Reporting (FAR)	66 MCQs 8 TBSs	50% 50%	No.1 33 MCQs - 1 hour No.2 33 MCQs - 1 hour No.3 2 TBSs - 30 min. No.4 3 TBSs - 45 min. No.5 3 TBSs - 45 min.	Time to complete – 4 hours
Regulation (REG)	76 MCQs 8 TBSs	50% 50%	No.1 38 MCQs - 1 hour No.2 38 MCQs - 1 hour No.3 2 TBSs - 30 min. No.4 3 TBSs - 45 min. No.5 3 TBSs - 45 min.	Time to complete – 4 hours

Sections may be taken in any order; however, you must complete all four sections within 18 months of passing the first section. The passing score is 75 for each section.

The exam is administered at Prometric testing centers in the USA (and some international locations): https://www.prometric.com/en-us/clients/cpa/Pages/landing.aspx. The exam can be physically sat for in a different state to that in which you apply for your license in. Some states allow for candidates to sit the exam internationally in Japan, Brazil, Bahrain, Kuwait, Lebanon and the United Arab Emirates. Check your state board for more information.

Testing "windows" represent available months when a candidate can take the exam. The testing windows are the first two months of each calendar quarter (e.g., January and February). To accommodate candidate demand for more opportunities to take the exam, the testing windows have been extended through the 10th of the third month of each testing window and are applicable for all testing windows through December 2018. Additional information will be posted as it is announced by the AICPA.

Types of questions on the CPA Exam include:
1) **Multiple-choice questions**: These questions are in all four sections and are based on the content/topics outlined in the AICPA blueprint (discussed below).

2) **Task-based simulations:** These questions utilize the type of activities that replicate real-life work situations. The simulations may include tasks such as editing a document, searching databases, or completing worksheets. Task-based simulations appear in all four sections of the exam.

   Document Review Simulations (DRS) and *Research* simulations are two specialized types of task-based simulations. A *DRS* will present a primary document, as well as related source materials, for the candidate to review. Highlighted words, phrases, sentences or paragraphs in the DRS document may or may not be correct, requiring the candidate to select appropriate edits based on relevant source materials.

   Research simulations require candidates to locate authoritative guidance to answer the prompt and cite the location where he/she found the information.

3) **Written communications tasks**: Written Communication questions are found only in the BEC sections. They are like a case study that includes a writing skill exercise. The candidate must review a description of a situation and will then be asked to write a constructed response relating to the situation. The instructions will require that the CPA candidate write a letter or a memorandum providing the correct information about the situation in a clear, complete, and professional manner.

C. **CPA Candidate Checklist**
   ☐ **Complete your state's education requirements to sit for the CPA Exam**
   ☐ **Start studying with YAEGER CPA REVIEW**
   ☐ **Apply for your exam:**

   Option A (NASBA-supported state – see NASBA.org):
   ☐ Apply at https://cpacentral.nasba.org/ to sit for the exam
   ☐ Your application, fees, and transcripts must be sent to NASBA
   ☐ NASBA will send your authorization to test (ATT) to the National Candidate Database (NCD)
   ☐ If approved by NCD, you will receive a notice to schedule (NTS)

   Option B (non NASBA-supported state):
   ☐ Apply to your State Board of Accountancy directly to sit for the exam
   ☐ Your application, fees, and transcripts must be sent to the State Board
   ☐ The State Board will send your ATT to the NCD
   ☐ If approved by NCD, NCD will issue a Payment Coupon to notify you of remaining exam fees that must be paid to NASBA if you only were required to send the application fee to the State Board
   ☐ Once all fees are paid, you will receive your NTS

   After you receive your NTS:
   ☐ **Visit www.prometric.com to schedule your exam**
   ☐ **Sit for the scheduled exam** (*you MUST bring NTS and two forms of ID or you can't take exam*)
   ☐ **Wait patiently and receive your scores**
   ☐ **Complete the experience requirements for your state and submit application for licensure to state board**

D. **Exam Day**

	Testlet 1	Testlet 2	Testlet 3	Scheduled 15 Minute Break	Testlet 4	Testlet 5
AUD	36 MCQ	36 MCQ	2 TBS		3 TBS	3 TBS
BEC	31 MCQ	31 MCQ	2 TBS		2 TBS	3 WC
FAR	33 MCQ	33 MCQ	2 TBS		3 TBS	3 TBS
REG	38 MCQ	38 MCQ	2 TBS		3 TBS	3 TBS

Candidates must work each testlet in order and complete/submit the current testlet before access to the next testlet is permitted. Once you submit, you are **not** permitted to return and reopen a completed/submitted testlet.

E. **Current Version of the CPA Exam**

Beginning April 1 2017, an updated version of the CPA Exam will be administered to CPA candidates. According to the AICPA, professional content knowledge will remain fundamental to protecting the public interest. Also, the candidates must be competent in the following skills:
- Remembering and understanding: The perception and comprehension of the significance of an area utilizing knowledge gained.
- Application: The use of demonstration of knowledge, concepts or techniques.

- Analysis: The examination and study of the interrelationships of separate areas in order to identify causes and find evidence to support inferences.
- Evaluation: Examination of assessment of problems and use of judgment to draw conclusions.

To test these competencies, the new CPA Exam has increased the number of task-based simulations and the length of the CPA Exam increased from 14 to 16 hours (four hours for each section).

The material that the candidate should learn is now based on the **AICPA Blueprints**. In 2018, the CPA Exam is no longer based on content specification outlines (CSOs). The AICPA Blueprints can be found at https://www.aicpa.org/becomeacpa/cpaexam/examinationcontent.html

These are the maps that tell the candidate the areas that are tested and what tasks are required for the candidate to master the information. *If you just follow the blueprints, you will know exactly the required information to be successful on the exam.*

There are hundreds of specific "representative tasks" that indicate what a new CPA would typically be responsible for performing on the job.

> **Hint: At a glance -- what is the AICPA blueprint?**
> - Serves as an essential study tool for CPA candidates
> - Replaces OLD Content Specific Outline (CSO)
> - Demonstrates what is tested on exams (including specific tasks)
> - Outlines skills and knowledge needed for licensure (typically possessed by a person with two years of experience)

YAEGER CPA REVIEW textbooks, and all videos, follow the AICPA Blueprints. Each blueprint is mentioned, and the relevant material is discussed, along with any relevant journal entries. Not all courses in CPA REVIEW follow the blueprints, but YAEGER DOES!

YAEGER CPA REVIEW has aligned its review content with the blueprints and shows each representative task with this icon:

CPA Exam
Blueprint
Representative
Task

For example, below is a representative task from the AUDITING AND ATTESTATION (AUD) section blueprint, under:
- Area I — Ethics, Professional Responsibilities and General Principles
- Content Group/Topic: A. NATURE AND SCOPE
- 1. Nature and scope: audit engagements
- Representative Task: Identify the nature, scope and objectives of the different types of audit engagements, including issuer and nonissuer audits.

In the auditing and attestation YAEGER CPA REVIEW book, this representative task will look like this:

 | Identify the nature, scope and objectives of the different types of audit engagements, including issuer and nonissuer audits.

F. **Exam Schedule**
The CPA Exam schedule for 2018 will be posted on the AICPA website when announced. The AICPA website is www.aicpa.org. Candidates should **definitely** visit this site before scheduling their exam for the most recent updates and information.

G. AICPA Tutorial and Sample Tests

On the AICPA website (https://www.aicpa.org/becomeacpa/cpaexam/forcandidates/tutorialandsampletest.html) candidates can experience the user interface that they will see on exam day. It is also the best place to see AICPA constructed examples of multiple-choice and task-based simulations with full functionality. YAEGER CPA REVIEW highly recommends all CPA candidates complete the sample test prior to taking their exam.

H. Access to Professional Literature

A commonly tested task-based simulation involves answering a research question, where the candidate must search through professional literature databases to answer the question.

Candidates who have applied to take the exam and have received their NTS can access a **free six-month subscription to the professional literature** used in the computerized CPA Exam. The professional literature includes the AICPA Professional Standards, FASB Original Pronouncements, and FASB Accounting Standards Codification. Access to this authoritative literature will familiarize candidates with the use of online accounting resources with full search functionality. Candidates should test the use of the keyword search to make the best use of their time in the exam.

The following link will take you to the National Association of State Boards of Accountancy (NASBA) website where you can apply for the free six-month subscription to the professional literature package: https://nasba.org/proflit/

I. Examination Scoring

A score of 75 is required to pass each section of the exam. A score of 75, however, is not indicative of the percent of correct answers. Rather, the score represents the weighted combination of multiple-choice questions, task-based simulations and written communications (for BEC only). Each section uses a scoring scale from 0 to 99. The scaled scores take into consideration whether the question was answered correctly and the level of difficulty of each question. The CPA exam score was obtained using Item Response Theory (IRT) scoring and was calculated as a whole, taking into account all of your responses.

Fifty percent of a candidate's score in the AUD, FAR, and REG sections comes from multiple-choice questions with the remaining 50% from task-based simulations. In the BEC section, 50% of a candidate's score comes from multiple-choice questions, 35% comes from task-based simulations, and 15% from written communication tasks.

A Candidate Performance Report will be provided if you receive a non-passing score. An example of this report is below.

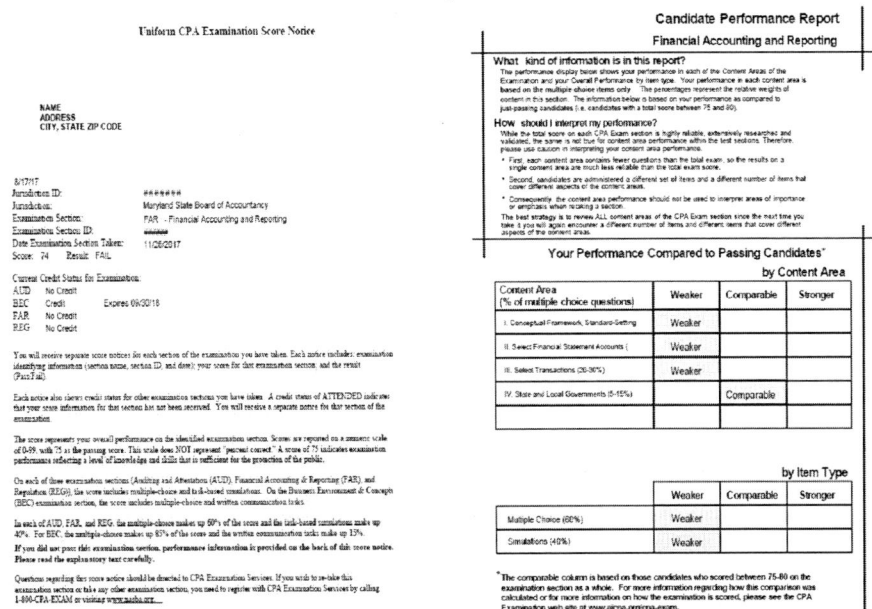

The Candidate Performance Report helps you determine what areas to focus on when you prepare to re-take an exam section. The Candidate Performance Report shows performance in each of the content areas of the exam and overall performance by item type and provides a comparison of your exam results to candidates who passed with a score between 75 and 80. According to the AICPA:

> *The relative performance scale (stronger, comparable, weaker) on the Candidate Performance Report is derived from the range between one-half of one standard deviation above and below the average score of candidates who earned scores between 75 and 80. Performance within the range is considered "comparable," below the range "weaker," and above the range "stronger."*

Candidates who received a weaker assessment for a particular content area should not focus only on that area when reviewing the material. It is always best to study everything. As no two exams are identical, if a candidate only studies their areas of weakness, they may do better in those areas, but worse on others when re-testing.

J. Yaeger's AdaptaPASS Technology

Since 1977, YAEGER CPA REVIEW has been following the philosophy that conceptual learning trumps memorization every time. And today is no different! YAEGER CPA REVIEW takes learning to the next level. With the most advanced technology in the CPA Exam Review industry, YAEGER CPA REVIEW combines traditional teaching and learning with an adaptive technology that determines what learning style works best for each individual CPA Exam candidate.

What is AdaptaPASS? It is an adaptive learning program that YAEGER developed to determine what learning style works best for each CPA candidate. Some students are visual learners, or auditory learners; others prefer to read and work a great deal of multiple-choice and/or simulation problems to reinforce a concept. Some have more time than others to prepare. It makes no difference. AdaptaPASS accounts for all different learning styles and creates a study program just for each individual candidate! The candidate begins by answering a few qualifying questions, then AdaptaPASS will deliver the optimal learning environment. This will include a blend of all study formats and content served in a way that takes the guesswork out of how the candidate is doing and what study method/format works best for them to succeed.

AdaptaPASS is not a "results" based platform like all others in the market. AdaptaPASS is the only program that creates a prescribed learning environment that adapts simultaneously with the candidate's progress. Proactively, the candidate will benefit from the "best" learning environment for them. Fully utilize the study plan that you will establish with YAEGER CPA REVIEW to stay on track for success on the CPA Exam.

K. Partnership with Dr. Marc Schoen

YAEGER CPA REVIEW is very excited to partner with Dr. Marc Schoen, a UCLA professor and leading performance psychologist to bring his expertise to you with a customized program designed specifically for CPA candidates.

The Performance under Pressure Audio Bundle teaches you how to properly control your fear response when faced with CPA Exam stress to boost your test score! Perform at your very best on exam day and tap into your brain's ability to problem solve with higher-order processing.

How? Using a gentle, but powerful technique that will reshape the way your brain responds to pressure. Train both your mind and body for CPA Exam success with an integrated study experience. Be reminded while using our AdaptaPASS software when to practice these research-based techniques founded in cutting-edge neuroscience.

We look forward to helping you on your CPA Exam journey. Best wishes for CPA Exam success from YAEGER CPA REVIEW!

Note: Permission has been received from the Institute of Certified Management Accountants to use questions and/or unofficial answers from past CMA examinations.

BEC 1 – Corporate Governance

A. Internal Control Frameworks   1A-1 – 1A-16
     1. COSO Internal Control – Integrated Framework (COSO IC)   1
     2. Corporate Governance Structure   8

B. Enterprise Risk Management Frameworks   1B-1 – 1B-9
     1. COSO Enterprise Risk Management — Integrated Framework (COSO ERM)   1
     2. COSO Guidance on Monitoring Internal Control Systems (2009)   8

C. Other Regulatory Frameworks and Provisions   1C-1 – 1C-4
     1. Sarbanes-Oxley Act of 2002 (Sarbanes-Oxley)   1
     2. Dodd-Frank Wall Street Reform and Consumer Protection Act of 2010 (Dodd-Frank)   3
     3. JumpStart Our Business Startups Act of 2012 (JOBS Act)   4

Glossary: Corporate Governance   Glossary 1-1 – 1-2

Multiple Choice – Questions   MCQ 1-1 – 1-5

Multiple Choice – Solutions   MCQ 1-6 – 1-13

Corporate Governance

Modern corporate governance promises accountability and transparency. By definition, corporate governance is a monitoring mechanism that provides assurance that management's actions properly align with the best interests of the entity's stakeholders. Recall the saying, "power tends to corrupt, and absolute power corrupts absolutely." Management is in a position of power due to the enormous amount of discretion afforded to them by the entity's owners regarding business dealings. Corporate governance exists to subdue the potential conflicts of interest inherent in the corporate entity by keeping management's power in check. Individuals in charge of governance are in a position to evaluate, direct, and monitor the organization to ensure stakeholder needs are met (e.g., ensuring benefits delivery, risk optimization, resource optimization, and stakeholder transparency).

This chapter dissects the current corporate governance landscape within the United States, post the Sarbanes-Oxley Act of 2002 (Sarbanes-Oxley) and the Dodd-Frank Wall Street Reform and Consumer Protection Act of 2010 (Dodd-Frank). Also contained in this chapter are descriptions of internal control and enterprise risk management, specifically the accompanying COSO frameworks. Due to the nature of corporate governance, there is overlap between REG, AUD, and BEC.

COSO – Internal Control Framework (IC) 2012	COSO Enterprise Risk Management (ERM) – Integrated Framework 2004	[Eligible for testing Q2 2018] COSO ERM – Integrating Strategy and Performance 2017
Components	**Components**	**Components**
1. Control Environment	1. Internal Environment	1. Governance and Culture
	2. Objective Setting	2. Strategy and Objective-Setting
	3. Event Identification	3. Performance
2. Risk Assessment	4. Risk Assessment	4. Review and Revisions
	5. Risk Response	5. Information, Communication, and Reporting
3. Control Activities	6. Control Activities	
4. Information and Communication	7. Information and Communication	
5. Monitoring	8. Monitoring	
Entity Objectives	**Entity Objectives**	
Operations	Operations	
Reporting	Reporting	
Compliance	Compliance	
	Strategic	

Note: Please refer to this chart while learning the similarities and differences between the COSO IC and COSO ERM frameworks.

A. Internal Control Frameworks
1. COSO Internal Control – Integrated Framework (COSO IC)
   COSO IC (updated in 2013) is recognized as a leading, broadly-accepted set of concepts and practices that provide structure for an organization's internal control governance. It was developed by the Committee of Sponsoring Organizations of the Treadway Commission (COSO).

   COSO defines internal control as a process, effected by an entity's board of directors, management, and other personnel, designed to provide reasonable assurance regarding the achievement of objectives relating to operations, reporting, and compliance.

Define internal control within the context of the COSO Internal Control framework including the purpose, objectives and limitations of the framework.

a. Purpose and objectives
The purpose of the Internal Control framework under COSO is to provide reasonable assurance that objectives in the three areas of operations, reporting, and compliance are met.

COSO differentiates aspects of internal control into objectives over operations, reporting, and compliance. Operations objectives pertain to operational and financial performance goals, measuring efficiency and effectiveness. Safeguarding assets is a focus. Reporting objectives relate to internal and external reporting, highlighting reliability, timeliness, and transparency. Compliance objectives concern an entity's adherence to regulations. Effective Internal controls should change to adhere to changing processes of an entity.

> *Hint*: COSO has also published an expanded framework to provide a comprehensive enterprise-wide approach to managing risk, called the Enterprise Risk Management – Integrated Framework or COSO ERM framework. This complementary, partially overlapping framework is an extension of the COSO Internal Control – Integrated Framework.

b. Limitations of internal control
The concept of an invincible, foolproof internal control structure is inherently unrealistic, even idealistic. Certain actions and circumstances (e.g., collusion, management override, human judgment, faulty decision-making, and human error) limit even the most effective internal control systems.

Controls may simply not be designed properly to meet the control objectives; or, individuals responsible for the control might not be executing the control procedure properly. Management might also interfere with the control's operation or circumvent a control entirely.

Unfortunately, many of these conditions cannot be completely eliminated. Internal controls provide only reasonable assurance, not absolute assurance that the entity will achieve their control objectives. No system is perfect, and every system has the possibility of errors.

Multiple Choice
BEC 1-Q1 through BEC 1-Q3

c. Components and principles

Identify and define the components, principles and underlying structure of the COSO Internal Control framework.

The components of the COSO framework recognize how an organization can design, implement, and address internal control. The five integrated components are (1) control environment, (2) risk assessment, (3) control activities, (4) information and communication, and (5) monitoring.

Each element is associated with a set of principles. There are seventeen principles in total, split among the five components. The framework also addresses the entity's organizational structure (e.g., entity, division, operating unit, and function) as dimensions for consideration, segmenting the enterprise into smaller components to make implementation more manageable.

The CPA candidate must learn each of the elements and their associated principles.

1) Control environment
The control environment provides a foundation for internal control in an organization. The organizational structure, culture of integrity and ethical decision-making, and performance measurement criteria each play a role in the control environment. The board of directors and senior management establish the tone at the top, and the board of directors is responsible for oversight.

The following COSO internal control principles are associated with an entity's control environment:
1. *The organization demonstrates a commitment to integrity and ethical values.*
   a. Senior management should set the "tone" and be an example through their own behavior and other actions including, policies that encourage and support this commitment.
2. *The board of directors demonstrates independence from management and exercises oversight of the development and performance of internal control.*
3. *Management establishes, with board oversight, structures, reporting lines, and appropriate authorities and responsibilities in the pursuit of objectives.*
4. *The organization demonstrates a commitment to attract, develop, and retain competent individuals in alignment with objectives.*
5. *The organization holds individuals accountable for their internal control responsibilities in the pursuit of objectives.*
   a. Individuals should have performance measures related to internal control accountability as part of their annual goals and incentives.

2) Risk assessment
A risk assessment evaluates the likelihood that risks will occur and the effects that the risks will have on the organization. Risk assessment is an iterative process and risks are considered relative to an organization's tolerance for risk.

The following COSO internal control principles are associated with risk assessment:
1. *The organization specifies objectives with sufficient clarity to enable the identification and assessment of risks relating to objectives.*
2. *The organization identifies risks to the achievement of its objectives across the entity and analyzes risks as a basis for determining how the risks should be managed.*
3. *The organization considers the potential for fraud in assessing risks to the achievement of objectives.*
4. *The organization identifies and assesses changes that could significantly impact the system of internal control.*

Every organization must determine their control objectives to respond to a variety of risks; risk acceptance, risk avoidance, risk reduction, and risk sharing are all potential responses. Each of these responses is expanded on in the COSO ERM framework (see the Risk Responses component in the COSO ERM framework below on page 1B-4).

3) Control activities
Control activities help mitigate risks across all levels of the organization, including over the entity's information system.

The following COSO internal control principles are associated with control activities:
1. *The organization selects and develops control activities that contribute to the mitigation of risks to the achievement of objectives to acceptable levels.*
2. *The organization selects and develops general control activities over technology to support the achievement of objectives.*
3. *The organization deploys control activities through policies that establish what is expected and procedures that put policies into action.*

Control activities include segregation of duties (e.g., separating recordkeeping, authorization, custody, and reconciliation responsibilities to reduce the risk of error and fraud); authorization and approval; reconciliation; information matching and verification; access administration, and supervisor review. See example risk and control consideration scenarios below for an illustration of each type of control.

4) Information and communication
Relevant internal and external information is necessary to achieve objectives, and timely communication supports the function of internal control.

The following COSO internal control principles are associated with information and communication:
1. *The organization obtains or generates and uses relevant, quality information to support the functioning of internal control.*
2. *The organization internally communicates information, including objectives and responsibilities for internal control, necessary to support the functioning of internal control.*
3. *The organization communicates with external parties regarding matters affecting the functioning of internal control.*

Information must be communicated both internally and externally. Internal communication is heavily reliant on the entity's information system. The quality and reliability of information depend on policies and procedures that are used to collect and transmit it to appropriate parties.

External communication, about internal control, is important for regulatory compliance. Two-way communication with external parties supports internal control functioning. External parties are more objective and able to provide unbiased recommendations.

5) Monitoring activities
Evaluations determine if each of the five components of internal control are present and functioning properly. Findings are evaluated and deficiencies, if any are identified, are communicated to management and the board of directors.

The following COSO internal control principles are associated with monitoring activities:
1. *The organization selects, develops, and performs ongoing and/or separate evaluations to ascertain whether the components of internal control are present and functioning.*
2. *The organization evaluates and communicates internal control deficiencies in a timely manner to those parties responsible for taking corrective action, including senior management and the board of directors, as appropriate.*

Monitoring activities include both ongoing evaluations and separate evaluations. Ongoing evaluations create constant awareness of the operating effectiveness of controls to support risk management. Separate evaluations (e.g., internal audits), offer a periodic determination of the functionality of the internal control. The COSO Guidance on Monitoring Internal Control Systems examines monitoring in greater detail (see page 1B-8).

Multiple Choice

BEC 1-Q4 through BEC 1-Q6

d. Example risk and control consideration scenarios

> Apply the COSO internal control framework to identify:
> - entity and transaction level risks (inherent and residual) related to an organization's compliance, operations and reporting (internal and external, financial and non-financial) objectives.
> - risks related to fraudulent financial and non-financial reporting, misappropriation of assets and illegal acts, including the risk of management override of controls.
> - controls to meet an entity's compliance, operations and reporting (internal and external, financial and non-financial) objectives, throughout an entity's structure, from entity-wide through sub-units, down to the transactional level.
> - an appropriate mix of automated and manual application controls, (e.g., authorization and approval, verifications, physical controls, controls over standing data, reconciliations and supervisory controls) to prevent and detect errors in transactions.

Aside from corporate governance regulations (e.g., Sarbanes-Oxley), an organization's desire to respond to risk is the catalyst for developing an internal control structure. First, risks are identified by the organization. Next, control objectives are created to address the specific risks. Third, controls are created to satisfy each control objective. The following chart outlines example risks and control considerations, control objectives, and controls.

Note: Be aware that this chart is not comprehensive and should not be memorized. Every organization is unique and will have a different set of internal controls. The controls below are for illustration only. Be prepared to identify internal controls for a given risk scenario.

Risk Scenario	Control objective	Controls
Revenue cycle (sales and cash receipts)		
Inaccurate or incomplete sales order Invalid or illegitimate sales orders	Controls provide reasonable assurance sales orders are complete and accurate.	Automated input controls validate data and alert personnel of input errors. Sales order requires a valid customer ID.
Theft of deposits	Controls provide reasonable assurance cash transactions are processed accurately and recorded timely.	Duties related to deposits are appropriately segregated (e.g., A mail clerk opens mail and logs checks received daily. A supervisor endorses checks and deposits them at the bank daily. Accounts receivable clerk updates ledger using log.) Alternatively, a lockbox payment system is maintained where the bank receives, processes, and deposits all receivables.
Shipping errors (wrong quantity, failure to ship order) Failure to invoice customer	Controls provide reasonable assurance all sales orders are accurately processed and goods are sent to customers completely and accurately.	A matching sales order, packing slip, and invoice is required prior to the shipment of goods. The system-generated report identifying gaps in document numbering is reviewed regularly.
Sales order is inappropriately modified	Controls provide reasonable assurance only authorized employees enter transactions.	The information system restricts the ability to create, change, or delete sales orders to authorized personnel only.
Inaccurate records of customer payments	Controls provide reasonable assurance payments are recorded completely and accurately.	Customers are provided with a serially numbered receipt of payments.

Risk Scenario	Control objective	Controls
Expenditure and disbursement cycle (purchase goods and services)		
Receipt of unordered goods Receipt unauthorized purchases	Controls provide reasonable assurance that expenditures are authorized, properly calculated, and recorded accurately and timely.	Purchase order and related vendor invoices are reviewed and approved. Reconciliations of purchase order, receiving report, and vendor invoice, are prepared and reviewed. Discrepancies are identified and resolved. Reconciliations of accounts payable subsidiary ledgers and related bank accounts are prepared, reviewed and approved.
Payment for goods or services not ordered	Controls provide reasonable assurance payments are only disbursed for authorized and approved purchase orders.	Invoices, purchase orders and receiving reports must match prior to payment. Duties related to invoice processing, invoice approval, and check signing are adequately segregated. Cash disbursements are reviewed and approved.
Investing and financing cycle (issue stock, pay debt, borrow)		
Interest payment is not properly calculated	Controls provide reasonable assurance interest payments are properly calculated and recorded accurately and timely.	Cash disbursements for interest are reviewed and approved. Officer periodically reviews compliance with debt provisions.
Payment of unauthorized dividends	Controls provide reasonable assurance transactions dividends paid are authorized, properly calculated, and recorded accurately and timely.	Dividends are declared by the board of directors prior to payment. Equity accounts are periodically reviewed by an appropriate officer.
Conversion cycle (purchase inventory)		
Request unnecessary inventory / Excess inventory Out of stock	Controls provide reasonable assurance inventory is recorded are completely and accurately.	Material requisitions and purchase orders for inventory are properly authorized. Inspect inventory weekly to check for losses and accuracy of records. Reconciliation of physical inventory and accounting records performed weekly and discrepancies are identified and resolved.
IT general controls*		
Passwords do not meet policies for syntax and expiration. Users are added to the system prior to approval from a supervisor. System access not removed timely after employee termination.	Controls provide reasonable assurance logical access to system programs and data is restricted to authorized personnel.	Passwords are configured to conform to organization policies for syntax and expiration. User access to the system is granted after approval from an appropriate supervisor. User access for terminated employees is removed from the system in a timely manner. Privileged user access is authorized and limited to appropriate personnel.

Risk Scenario	Control objective	Controls
Privileged user access not limited to appropriate personnel.		
System changes are not documented appropriately. Unauthorized system changes are migrated to production. Testing on program changes not completed prior to implementation.	Controls provide reasonable assurance changes to existing systems (or applications) are authorized, tested, approved, properly implemented, and documented.	Change requests are submitted and documented according to policy. Changes are authorized, tested, and approved prior to implementation.
New systems are installed prior to testing.	Controls provide reasonable assurance new systems are authorized, tested, approved, properly implemented, and documented.	System development projects require project authorization and senior-management approval.
Batch processing fails and no action to resolve is performed.	Controls provide reasonable assurance job processing is authorized, scheduled, and deviations from scheduled processing are identified and resolved.	Job processing issues are addressed and resolved according to procedures over incident management.
System failure causes unanticipated data loss and downtime.	Controls provide reasonable assurance programs, files, and data are backed up periodically.	A system backup is performed daily.
Malicious or accidental damage to computer equipment.	Controls provide reasonable assurance access to facilities that house processing equipment and storage media is restricted to appropriate personnel.	Card readers ensure physical access to computers is restricted to appropriate personnel only.
IT application controls*		
Incomplete and inaccurate data processing is not identified.	Controls provide reasonable assurance batch processing transactions for critical financial data are accurate and inaccuracies are identified and resolved.	Batch processing reconciliations are performed daily and reviewed by a supervisor.
Inappropriate access to input adjusting entries. Unauthorized adjusting journal entries Inaccurate adjusting journal entries.	Controls provide reasonable assurance adjusting journal entries are approved and are complete and accurate.	Access to perform adjusting journal entries is restricted to appropriate personnel. Adjusting journal entries are reviewed and approved by an authorized individual and agree with supporting documentation.

*Please refer to chapter BEC 4 – Information Technology for a detailed description of IT general and application controls.

Multiple Choice

BEC 1-Q7 through BEC 1-Q10

e. Classification of internal controls
   Internal controls can be classified as preventive, detective, or corrective.

   1) Preventive – controls aim to deter the occurrence of errors and fraudulent activities and are designed to stop unauthorized acts before they happen (e.g., controls over security, access administration).
   2) Detective – controls help identify errors and fraud that have previously occurred within the organization when preventive controls fail to stop an undesirable act. Detective controls are in place to discover and communicate issues promptly (e.g., reconciliation of account balances).
   3) Corrective – controls correct errors and irregularities discovered after the fact. This type of control not only identifies an issue but plays an active role in alleviating the issue and restoring functionality (e.g., user access review to remove inappropriate access).

2. Corporate Governance Structure

> **Describe the corporate governance structure within an organization (tone at the top, policies, steering committees, oversight, etc.).**

a. Tone at the top
   Tone at the top is a crucial element of ethical operations and decision-making within an organization and establishes the control environment. Tone at the top is defined as the ethical climate or atmosphere within an entity that cascades from leadership (i.e., the board of directors and executives) to frontline employees. The climate, or tone, set by leaders and managers is effective in encouraging and discouraging certain behaviors. For instance, a heavy emphasis on aggressive financial performance measures has the potential to create a climate for fraud. Employees might feel the need to employ creative (read: fraudulent) accounting techniques to meet management's unrealistic expectations. Conversely, if the tone at the top encourages morality, it may manifest itself as a values-driven workforce that is quick to report unethical behavior. For this type of climate to exist in an organization, leadership must set reasonable expectations, focus on performance measurement factors beyond only financial measurements, and reward employees who demonstrate ethical behavior and proper conduct. Leadership must also impose appropriate punishment for incidents involving fraudulent behavior.

   1) Measuring tone at the top
      While the concept of tone at the top is relatively straightforward, it is difficult to measure. Simply asking employees about their experiences and their perception of the tone at the top is a great place to start. Data gathering techniques include anonymous employee surveys, focus group discussions, and exit interviews. Next, to support or refute the findings obtained via inquiry, it is helpful to inspect actual messages from leadership (e.g., emails) to interpret the tone of their communication with employees.

      Another way to obtain corroborative evidence about tone is to examine incident records involving fraudulent behavior. Many organizations employ an anonymous incident reporting and whistleblower hotline to provide a secure way to report fraudulent behavior and protect employees against retaliation. How leadership handles the reports of unethical actions, and other incidents is a strong indicator of the entity's tone at the top. Repeatedly ignoring certain wrongdoings might be a red flag, especially if the incidents were reported through appropriate channels.

      Externally, a company can gauge their tone at the top based on their online reputation using social media (e.g., Twitter) and company review websites (e.g., Glassdoor.com).

b. Corporate formation policies
Incorporators (e.g., owners) of fledgling corporations need to file articles of incorporation and draft a set of bylaws to commence operations.

1) Articles of incorporation (or corporate charter)
Articles of incorporation (also called a corporate charter) is the document that a corporation's founders must submit to the secretary of a U.S. state government in order to establish a corporate legal entity. The information that states require to form a corporation include:
   i. *Corporate name.* It must contain "Corporation", "Incorporated", Company", "Limited", or corresponding abbreviation (e.g., "Corp.", "Inc.", "Co.", or "Ltd.")
   ii. *Corporate address.* Physical location of the business.
   iii. *Purpose.* The nature of the business, including the object or purpose.
   iv. *Shares.* The number of shares which the corporation will have the authority to issue (e.g., authorized shares), any share class designations (e.g., Class A), and the par value per share.
   v. *Registered agents.* The name and street address of the initial registered agents.
   vi. *Incorporators.* The name and address of each incorporator.

Changes or amendments must be filed with the state of incorporation and often require a processing fee.

2) Bylaws
Bylaws are the most important legal document maintained by a corporation. The bylaws outline the high-level rules over how the corporation is to operate on a day-to-day basis. Typical topics include the guidelines about how the board of directors and/or officers are elected, the duties of directors and officers, the schedule of required meetings, the procedure for how these meetings are to be conducted, and the process for settling disputes. Bylaw amendments can occur at any point by a vote of the board of directors and can occur with no fee.

c. Corporate stakeholders, steering committees, and oversight
Basic corporate stakeholders include owners (e.g., investors or shareholders), management, employees, customers, and suppliers. The community and government agencies are also often key stakeholders. This discussion considers the owners (shareholders), officers, board of directors with respect to corporate governance.

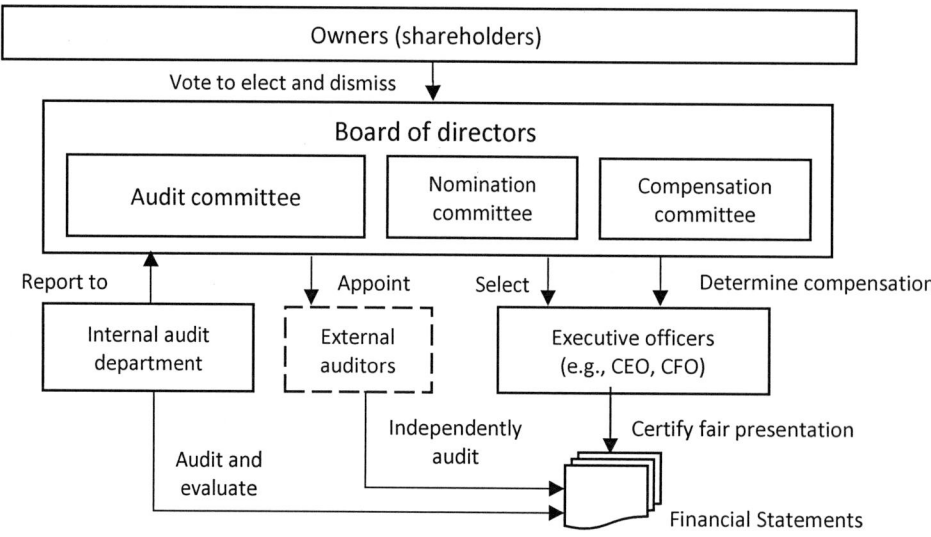

1) Owners (shareholders)
   Owners, namely common shareholders in a basic corporate structure, provide the capital necessary for the organization to conduct business. When a company is successful, the shareholders will partake in the profitability of the corporate entity. It is generally understood that the primary goal of a corporation is to maximize shareholder wealth. Equally, the corporation does not guarantee that invested capital will produce a return on investment. The shareholder accepts a calculated level of risk in exchange for the potential return on their investment.

   i. Rights of shareholders
      While shareholders are not active participants in the management of a corporation, they have some rights including:
      a) Economic rights – right to receive dividends as are declared by the corporation's board of directors (note, the right to dividends starts at the point dividends are declared, and if no dividends have been declared, no right exists) and the right to sell shares
      b) Control rights – right to vote on important matters relating to the business, such as electing directors, approving mergers and acquisitions, and granting approval for other actions (e.g., amending the articles of incorporation by changing the corporation's name)
      c) Information rights – right to inspect the corporation's books and records and to review basic documents (e.g., articles of incorporation, bylaws, list of shareholders, board meeting minutes)
      d) Litigation rights (derivative rights) – judicial enforcement of other rights under certain circumstances (e.g., nonpayment of declared dividends, illegal declaration of dividends, officer fraud)
      e) Pre-emptive right – right of common shareholders to purchase new issuances first so that they can maintain their proportionate share of outstanding shares of common stock and their ownership is not diluted

   Arguably, the two most fundamental rights of the shareholder are: (1) the right to sell shares and (2) the right to elect directors. The right to sell shares at will, assuming no restrictions have been imposed (e.g., insider trading restrictions, poison pill takeover defenses), is a means for obtaining a potentially large return on investment or exiting if dissatisfied with management's decisions.

   The right to elect directors is a component of corporate governance, acting as a check and balance to distribute the power within the corporation. Shareholders have a cumulative voting right that is based on the number of shares they own, one vote for each share. For example, assume the shareholder has 500 shares. The shareholder can allocate the 500 votes, 1 vote per share, in any ratio to the candidates (e.g., 500 to a single candidate). Shareholders are also permitted to vote to remove a director.

   Only shareholders that hold an additional role in the corporation (e.g., managers, employees) are involved in management or operation of the corporation.

Multiple Choice

BEC 1-Q10 through BEC 1-Q12

2) Officers
The executive management team, or officers, are in charge of directing day-to-day business operations. Their leadership is pivotal to the success or failure of the business.

  i. Agency relationship
  Officers are entrusted with a substantial amount of power with regard to the corporation. As an agent, a single officer has the authority and ability to bind the corporation in a contractual agreement legally. No other party, individually, has this authority. Directors only have the authority to contractually bind the corporation if the board votes in favor of signing the contract. An individual director is not permitted to act as the corporation's agent unless also serving as an officer.

  ii. Officer duties and responsibilities
  Officers have a long list of duties and responsibilities, ranging from decision-making to operational oversight. The number of people on the executive management team varies based on the entity's size and purpose. The specific duties of each officer also vary. Several universal duties and responsibilities have particular importance about corporate governance including the officers' fiduciary duty to stakeholders, the responsibility to fairly present the entity's financial statements, and the duty for the CEO and CFO to certify the financial statements.

    a) Fiduciary duty
    Officers have an obligation to act in the best interest of the corporation's stakeholders. This obligation is called a fiduciary duty.

    If an officer makes a questionable decision, which is potentially not in the corporation's best interest, the business judgment rule is applicable. The business judgment rule is a legal standard based on case law that stipulates if officers act in good faith, with reasonable care, they cannot be held liable for an error in judgment.

    b) Fair presentation of the financial statements
    An entity's management team is responsible for the financial statements and establishing accounting policies that conform to generally accepted accounting principles (GAAP). Officers also are responsible for establishing and monitoring internal controls that support their financial statement assertions.

    c) CEO/CFO certification of financial statements
    Both the CEO and CFO of a publicly traded company must certify with the SEC that the financial statements fairly present, in all material respects, the operations and financial condition of the company. This requirement, outlined in Sarbanes-Oxley Sec. 302, applies to issuers required to file reports under Securities Exchange Act of 1934. Sarbanes-Oxley Sec. 906 imposes penalties for the failure of corporate officers to certify financial reports.

  In some instances, officers may also serve on the board of directors so long as the board as a whole meets the stipulations over board independence (note, this is not as stringent as auditor independence). Officers are permitted to own shares of the corporation that they manage, assuming no illegal insider trading actions occur during ownership. Ownership by officers is not required.

Multiple Choice

BEC 1-Q13

3) Directors
Corporations establish a board of directors to oversee operations. The shareholders elect directors through a majority vote. It is the primary duty of the board of directors to consider stakeholder interests, particularly the relationship between owners and managers, and to provide independent guidance and strategic advice.

   i. Board of directors' duties and responsibilities
      a) Selecting and appointing officers
      b) Declaring dividends
      c) Determining management compensation
      d) Appoint external auditors
      e) Resolve disagreements between management and external auditors
         Directors must act as mediators to resolve conflicts (e.g., accounting treatment disputes) between management and auditors.
      f) Fiduciary duty
         Directors have an obligation to act in the best interest of the corporation's stakeholders. As long as a director acts in good faith and within the scope of their authority, s(he) cannot be held liable for errors in judgment in accordance with the business judgment rule. This is equivalent to the business judgment rule applicable to executive officers. However, in contrast to officers, directors have no individual power to bind the corporation.
      g) Duty of loyalty
         The director's duty of loyalty requires the director to place priority of the corporation's interest before his or her own interest. Therefore, if a director is presented with a corporate opportunity, the director should first offer the opportunity to the corporation; if the corporation declines, then the director may pursue the opportunity.

Multiple Choice

BEC 1-Q14 through BEC 1-Q16

   ii. Board of directors' committees
   The board of directors often delegate important matters to committees (e.g., audit, compensation, nominating/corporate governance).

      a) Audit committee
         The audit committee, arguably the most important committee, oversees the corporation's accounting function, external auditor, and matters pertaining to regulatory compliance (e.g., adequate internal control). The committee is also responsible for the oversight and performance of the internal audit department. Audit committee independence is defined by Sarbanes-Oxley Sec. 301.

      b) Compensation committee
         The independent compensation committee determines the CEO's compensation, typically submitting their recommendation to the full board for approval. Executive compensation can include a base salary, bonuses for performance, stock options, stock grants, and executive perquisites (perks) such as the use of corporate assets. The committee also sets the CEO's performance goals (e.g., balanced score card metrics) and monitors goal achievement.
         Using an independent body to determine management compensation is a way to override the inherent agency problem of self-serving decision-making that fails to consider the long-term interests of shareholders. The compensation committee must be mindful of the potential for earnings management, especially if

compensation is directly tied to financial performance when determining an appropriate compensation structure.

With the implementation of Dodd-Frank, corporations are also required to hold a shareholder vote to approve the compensation structure (called a "say-on-pay" vote) every three years, with a vote on the frequency of the say-on-pay vote every six years. This vote acts as an additional oversight measure. Dodd-Frank Sec. 952 also requires the compensation committee to be independent, with the same criteria as the audit committee. Per the JOBS Act, emerging growth companies (EGCs) are exempt from the say-on-pay vote.

c) Nominating/corporate governance committee
The nominating/corporate governance committee is responsible for nominating candidates to serve on the board, to be voted on by shareholders. This committee also is in charge of determining the governance standards and frameworks (e.g., COSO) to be used by the corporation.

iii. Financial expert requirement
Sarbanes-Oxley Sec. 407 requires a company to disclose if it has at least one audit committee financial expert, the expert's name, and if s(he) is independent of management. If a company does not have an expert, it must disclose this fact and explain why.

The financial expert classification is intentionally broad. The expert must be familiar with financial statements and generally accepted accounting principles (GAAP). This understanding must be at a level that is sufficient to assess the application of GAAP, especially with respect to accounting for estimates, accruals, and reserves. Additionally, s(he) must have previous or concurrent experience with the preparation and evaluation of financial statements, including audits, for other companies that are comparable regarding complexity to the current company.

S(he) must also have an understanding of internal controls over financial reporting and the role of the audit committee. An audit committee financial expert is not required to be a CPA.

Multiple Choice

BEC 1-Q17 through BEC 1-Q18

iv. Director independence requirements
An effective director can evaluate the company they serve impartially, exercising independent judgment while performing their duties. To limit the possibility of conflicting interests, the majority of the board of directors are required to be independent. Plus, all audit committee members are required to be independent. These requirements for director independence are outlined in the New York Stock Exchange (NYSE) and NASDAQ listing standards and Sarbanes-Oxley (which emphasizes audit committee independence).

> *Hint:* The requirements for director independence differ greatly from the requirements for auditor independence (i.e., they are substantially less stringent). To signify the less extensive criteria, remember that directors are independent with a lowercase "i" (rather than a capital "I").

The NYSE and NASDAQ listing standards require all listed companies to have a majority of independent directors. The board must have an entirely independent audit committee (consisting of at least three members), an independent compensation committee, and an independent nominating/corporate governance committee.

Per the NYSE/NASDAQ listing standards, directors are not independent if they are currently employed, or have been in the last three years, by the company. Additionally, the director cannot accept more than $120,000 of direct compensation within a consecutive twelve-month period during the three proceeding years.

Audit committees of listed companies must meet the general NYSE/NASDAQ requirements in addition to the requirements enumerated in Sarbanes-Oxley Sec. 301. The following is the Sarbanes-Oxley criteria for determining the independence of audit committee members:
   a) Audit committee members are prohibited from accepting any consulting, advisory, or another compensatory fee from the issuer (other than in the member's capacity as a member of the board of directors)
   b) The audit committee member may not be an affiliated person (i.e., someone with the power to direct management) of the issuer or any subsidiary of the issuer apart from his or her capacity as a member of the board and any board committee.

Dodd-Frank Sec. 952 also defines equivalent independence requirements for the compensation committee and stipulates the guidelines over hiring a compensation consultant and other independent advisers. An issuer must disclose when advice is obtained and if any conflicts of interest.

4) Additional oversight
   i. Internal auditors
   Corporations rely on internal auditors to monitor operations and give ongoing recommendations concerning internal control, enterprise risk management, and corporate governance activities. The NYSE requires listed companies to have an internal audit function. (The NASDAQ proposed a similar requirement in 2013, but the proposal has since been withdrawn.)

   Internal auditors typically administer assurance services (e.g., audits) and report their findings directly to the company's board of directors. For example, an internal auditor may conduct a quasi-independent (i.e., objective) assurance engagement to evaluate control procedures, providing constructive feedback about the design and operating effectiveness of controls. Areas for improvement are communicated to the audit committee of the board of directors in addition to management.

   The independence rules applicable to external auditors do not apply to internal auditors, and they are not prohibited from providing consulting and advisory services. Consequently, it is permissible for internal auditors to offer the company advice regarding enterprise risk management procedures and other corporate governance matters.

   Certified Internal Auditors (CIA) are members of the Institute of Internal Auditors (IIA), a professional organization that issues the International Standards for Professional Practice of Internal Auditing and oversees licensing (e.g., administering the CIA examination).

ii. External auditors

External auditors (e.g., CPA firms) provide independent audit and attestation services to evaluate a company's financial statement assertions and internal control structure, if applicable. Firms that conduct audits of issuers, or entities that issue or propose to issue securities under the Security and Exchange Act of 1934, must follow the audit standards promulgated by the Public Company Accounting Oversight Board (PCAOB). Issuers are also referred to as publicly-traded companies. Otherwise, firms that audit non-issuers must adhere to the generally accepted auditing standards (GAAS) established by the American Institute of CPAs (AICPA).

The requirement of an auditor's attestation over a company's internal control depends on the client's status as an accelerated filer. Only auditors of accelerated filers and large accelerated filers must attest to management's report on internal control as a component of an integrated audit engagement.

External auditors are appointed by the audit committee of the board of directors and external auditors, much like internal auditors, report directly to the audit committee. Significant audit findings are other issues are first discussed with management. Meanwhile, the board of directors is kept abreast of audit findings communicated to management (e.g., material misstatements or internal control deficiencies) and any disagreements or difficulties that arose during the audit.

iii. Other external monitoring

Corporations are more likely to adhere to legal and ethical standards when an outside party is observing their actions. Likewise, when a corporation is required to disclose information (e.g., tax return, 10-K) it provides an opportunity for scrutiny and oversight by outside parties. While their role in corporate governance is subtle, external parties often play a part in monitoring. Since the corporation must be forthcoming and transparent, untrue or misleading information is likely to raise red flags.

External parties that have monitoring relationships with corporations (whether subtle or overt) include the Internal Revenue Service (IRS), the Securities and Exchange Commission (SEC), creditors, credit rating agencies, security analysts, and attorneys.

d. Relevant corporate classifications
The following corporate classifications are for reference as we discuss the governance of the corporate entity.

1) Categorization of SEC filers
The categories of SEC filers are large accelerated filer, accelerated filer, and non-accelerated filer pursuant to 240.12b–2 of title 17, Code of Federal Regulations. They are differentiated based on the corporation's amount of market capitalization (called public float), or the aggregate worldwide market value of voting and non-voting common equity held by non-affiliates of the issuer. Accelerated filer and large accelerated filers must adhere to shorter filing deadlines for periodic reports (e.g., 10-K).

	$74,999,999	$75 M — $75,000,000 - $699,999,999	$700 M — $700,000,000+
Category of filer	Non-accelerated filer	Accelerated filer	Large accelerated filer
	Less than **$75 million** in market capitalization	Greater than or equal to **$75 million**, but less than **$700 million** in market capitalization	Greater than or equal to **$700 million** in market capitalization
Deadlines for filing periodic reports	Form 10-K: **90 days** From 10-Q: **45 days**	Form 10-K: **75 days** From 10-Q: **40 days**	Form 10-K: **60 days** From 10-Q: **40 days**

2) Emerging growth company (EGC) status
An EGC is defined as a company with gross revenues of less than a billion dollars that has already completed an initial public offering (IPO), the first time issuing common stock, and the IPO occurred after December 18, 2011.

Achieving EGC status:
- Gross revenues < $1 billion
- IPO occurred after 12/18/2011

Benefits of EGC status:
- Confidential review by the SEC.
- Implement FASB standards as a "private company", even though the company is public. Typically, the company gets another year to for implementation.
- No mandatory disclosures for compensation and say-for-pay requirements (part of Dodd-Frank Act).

The company can retain emerging growth status until the company's total annual gross revenues are $1 billion or more, the company becomes a large accelerated filer, the company issues greater than $1 billion in non-convertible debt over three years, or until five years have passed after the IPO. If any one of these occurs, the company is no longer eligible for emerging growth company status.

Retain EGC status until:
- Gross revenues >= $1 billion
- It becomes an accelerated filer
- Issue > $1 billion in non-convertible debt over 3 years
- 5 years after IPO

B. Enterprise Risk Management (ERM) Frameworks

1. COSO Enterprise Risk Management —Integrating with Strategy and Performance (COSO ERM)
   The Enterprise Risk Management framework is the second framework by COSO that complements the Internal Control framework. It does not supersede that COSO Internal Control – Integrated Framework.

   > **Hint:** COSO updated the 2004 COSO ERM framework in September 2017. The updated 2017 ERM framework is titled "Enterprise Risk Management – Integrating with Strategy and Performance." The updated framework is **eligible for testing beginning in Q2 2018.**
   >
   > The primary changes are:
   > - Updated title – adds the phrase "Strategy and Performance" to the title
   > - Greater emphasis on strategy and integrating ERM with decision-making (i.e., ERM is not a risk inventory or siloed, discrete function or isolated exercise performed periodically)
   > - Adopts a components and principles structure
   >   - Eight (8) components to five (5) updated components
   >   - 20 principles in total
   > - Simplifies the definition of ERM – ERM is "the culture, capabilities, and practices, integrated with strategy-setting and its execution, that organizations rely on to manage risk in creating, preserving, and realizing value."

   > Define ERM within the context of the COSO ERM framework, including the purpose and objectives of the framework.

   a. Purpose and objectives
      Enterprise risk management (ERM) is defined as a process to identify events that may affect an entity and manage risk to provide reasonable assurance the entity can achieve its objectives. To put it another way, ERM helps an entity achieve its objectives while avoiding surprises along the way.

      The COSO ERM framework guides entities as they navigate uncertainty and challenges with balancing risk and opportunities (e.g., return). An optimal balance hinges on the level of risk an entity chooses to accept. Considering risk is critical, albeit difficult. The ERM framework conceptualizes this challenging task in eight (2004) or five (2017) interrelated components.

      The COSO ERM frameworks expand upon, rather than supersede, the COSO IC framework. COSO ERM (2004) modifies the control environment component, substituting internal environment. The expanded framework also adds a new objective, **strategic**, to objectives over operations, reporting, and compliance. COSO ERM (2017) deviates from the terminology of components of the COSO IC framework, and instead follows the steps of ERM (1) defining the mission, vision, and values, (2) strategy development, (3) business objective formulation, (4) implementation and performance, (5) enhanced value. These activities each align with one of the five components of the framework.

   Enterprise Risk Management

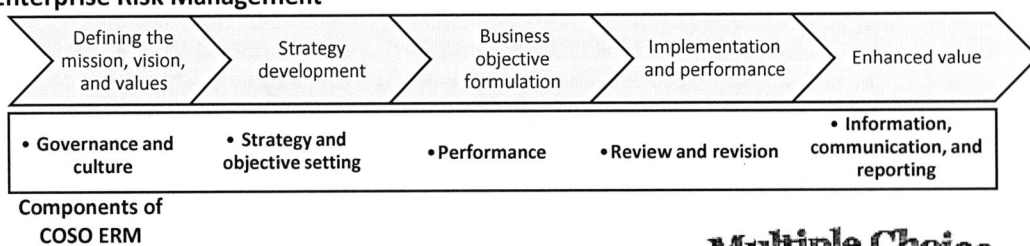

   Components of COSO ERM

   Multiple Choice

   BEC 1-Q21

b. Limitations of COSO ERM
COSO ERM is subject to several limitations including uncertainty, imperfect information resulting in poor human judgment, unforeseen circumstances, and willing disregard for risk management policies and procedures.

Primarily, the framework deals with the topic of risk, which is inherently uncertain. This uncertainty means that no risk management initiative can provide absolute assurance, or even reasonable assurance, that the organization will meet its objectives (e.g., generate profit). There is no guarantee that an organization's chosen risk management model will not break down due to some unforeseen circumstance.

Additionally, cost-benefit constraints limit risk assessment activities. As a result, the determinations over risk response must be made using imperfect information. Even if the near-perfect information did exist concerning a particular risk, humans often find it difficult to judge the consequences of a decision (e.g., the impact of accepting a risk). There are simply too many uncertain variables to consider, and it is possible that an individual will simply forget to include an important consideration.

Lastly, collusion and management override might also result in the personnel disregarding the organization's stated policies on risk appetite and risk tolerance. Management override is any time that management disregards policies or procedures for illegitimate purposes (e.g., personal gain or inflated financial condition). For instance, managers might bypass approval and invest in a speculative forward contract to inflate short-term earnings.

c. Components and principles

> Identify and define the components, principles, and underlying structure of the COSO Enterprise Risk Management framework.

COSO ERM (2004): The eight interrelated components are: (1) internal environment, (2) objective setting, (3) event identification, (4) risk assessment, (5) risk response, (6) control activities, (7) information and communication, and (8) monitoring.

COSO ERM (2017) [Eligible for testing Q2 2018]: There are five components: (1) governance and culture, (2) strategy and objective setting, (3) performance, (4) review and revision, (5) information, communication, and reporting.

COSO ERM (2004):
1) Internal environment
An entity's internal environment is its foundation for understanding risk and supporting ERM activities. Risk is any occurrence that impedes or otherwise adversely affects the achievement of objectives. An entity's risk management philosophy, influenced by their culture regarding risk, sets the tone for the organization.

The level of risk an organization is willing to accept is called its risk appetite. The organization's risk philosophy dictates their risk appetite, and it is embedded in both long-term strategic decisions and short-term day-to-day activities.

Risk appetite defines the maximum risk an organization can handle. Risk tolerance, a related concept, is the range of risk variation an entity is willing to accept to meet a specific objective.

An organization's board of directors should oversee management's risk philosophy and risk appetite. It is their job to raise red flags if the organization is taking on significant levels of risk contrary to their philosophy and appetite. Additionally, the entity's people at every level should exhibit integrity and ethical values. These traits factor into the application of management's risk philosophy on a day-to-day basis.

Other items that play a role in the internal environment are the entity's commitment to competence, organizational structure, assignment of authority, and human resource standards.

2) Objective setting
Establishing direction by setting objectives is the first step. Every organization should have a process in place to set objectives, and those objectives should align with the entity's mission and risk appetite.

There are four categories of objectives, each distinct but overlapping:
  i. *Strategic* – objectives relating to high-level goals in support of the entity's mission
  ii. *Operations* – objectives relating to efficient and effective resource use
  iii. *Reporting* – objectives relating to the reliability of financial reporting
  iv. *Compliance* – objectives relating to compliance with applicable laws and regulations

Strategic objectives cascade down to operations, reporting, and compliance objectives. Starting with high-level strategic objectives promotes cohesive entity-level objectives.

3) Event identification
Each day, an entity's experiences internal and external events that have both positive and negative influence on the fulfillment of their objectives. External events are influenced by economic, natural environment, political, social, and technological factors; while; internal events include infrastructure, personnel, process, and technology factors.

Event identification focuses on pinpointing potential events before their occurrence, allowing the organization to reduce surprises and be poised to seize opportunities.

When considering potential events, organizations must distinguish between events that represent risks, opportunities, or both. An opportunity is the opposite of a risk or an event with a positive effect on the achievement of an entity's objectives.

Techniques that can be used to identify events include event inventories (e.g., industry benchmark listings), internal analysis (e.g., staff meetings), escalation or threshold triggers (e.g., continuous monitoring with a trigger notification), facilitated workshops and interviews (e.g., accounting department workshop), and process flow analysis (e.g., process flowcharting), leading event indicators (e.g., monitoring correlation data), and loss event data methodologies (e.g., root cause analysis).

4) Risk Assessment
After event identification, an entity must analyze risks and determine a basis for risk management. Involved in this process is consideration of the likelihood and impact of a event and its potential to impede the achievement of an entity's objectives.

Each event has a certain level of inherent risk, or risk absent management action or other mitigating factors. The residual risk is the amount of risk that remains after considering management's response.

Risk can be evaluated using both quantitative and qualitative assessment techniques. Quantitative techniques include benchmarking (e.g., likelihood and impact of risk across an industry), probabilistic models (e.g., simulated value/earnings at risk using quantified assumptions), and non-probabilistic models (e.g., sensitivity measures, scenario analysis). Qualitative assessment is appropriate when quantitative techniques are not appropriate or sufficient quantitative data is unavailable.

Management should use risk assessment to determine resource allocation related to internal control activities, focusing on critical areas or controls that would be significant to financial recording.

5) Risk Response
Management must consider the likelihood and impact of each risk in line with their risk philosophy. The entity then selects an appropriate action based on their risk appetite and risk tolerance.

There are four possible responses to risk:
   i. *Avoidance* – exit the activity
   ii. *Reduction* – mitigate the risk
   iii. *Sharing* – transfer a portion of the risk (e.g., hedging derivatives or insurance)
   iv. *Acceptance* (retention) – do nothing

The organization may use a cost-benefit analysis to determine appropriate deployment of capital resources. Each risk should be evaluated in the context of the portfolio or entity-wide risk appetite. If composite risk acceptance is lower than the risk appetite, management may encourage personnel to accept more risk. The opposite is also true. If the organization has recently accepted a substantial risk, from a portfolio perspective, management might encourage reducing or sharing other potential risks to keep their risk within their overall risk appetite.

6) Control activities
Typically, risk response involves implementing a control activity. Control activities are the policies and procedures that are preventive, detective, or corrective in nature. They provide reasonable assurance that the risk responses are executed appropriately and timely.

7) Information and Communication
Personnel should be aware of the importance of ERM. Within the organization, personnel should speak a common language regarding risk. All roles and responsibilities should be clearly defined and communicated. Information systems are often utilized in capturing the responsibilities and timeframe for risk response.

8) Monitoring
Monitoring confirms that risk management is functioning properly and not deteriorating over time. Staying vigilant allows an entity to proactively modify its risk response if it becomes necessary. Both ongoing and separate evaluations may be used to help monitor ERM activities. Deficiencies are reported to management, the board of directors, or both, depending on the severity of the issue.

Multiple Choice

BEC 1-Q22 through BEC 1-Q29

COSO ERM (2017) [**Eligible for testing Q2 2018**]: There are five components: (1) governance and culture (2) strategy and objective setting, (3) performance, (4) review and revision, (5) information, communication, and reporting.

1) Governance and culture
   Governance considers the organization's tone at the top and oversight of enterprise risk management. Culture includes the organization's core values.

   Principles of governance and culture:
   1. *Exercises Board Risk Oversight—The board of directors provides oversight of the strategy and carries out governance responsibilities to support management in achieving strategy and business objectives.*
   2. *Establishes Operating Structures—The organization establishes operating structures in the pursuit of strategy and business objectives.*
   3. *Defines Desired Culture—The organization defines the desired behaviors that characterize the entity's desired culture.*
   4. *Demonstrates Commitment to Core Values—The organization demonstrates a commitment to the entity's core values.*
   5. *Attracts, Develops, and Retains Capable Individuals—The organization is committed to building human capital in alignment with the strategy and business objectives.*

2) Strategy and objective setting
   This component determines if the mission and vision are in alignment with the entity's strategy to drive value for the organization.

   Principles of strategy and objective setting:
   6. *Analyzes Business Context—The organization considers potential effects of business context on risk profile.*
   7. *Defines Risk Appetite—The organization defines risk appetite in the context of creating, preserving, and realizing value.*
   8. *Evaluates Alternative Strategies—The organization evaluates alternative strategies and potential impact on risk profile.*
   9. *Formulates Business Objectives—The organization considers risk while establishing the business objectives at various levels that align and support strategy.*

3) Performance
   Risks must be identified, prioritized, and addressed with consideration for the strategy and business objectives.

   Principles of performance:
   10. *Identifies Risk—The organization identifies risk that impacts the performance of strategy and business objectives.*
   11. *Assesses Severity of Risk—The organization assesses the severity of risk.*
   12. *Prioritizes Risks—The organization prioritizes risks as a basis for selecting responses to risks.*
   13. *Implements Risk Responses—The organization identifies and selects risk responses.*
   14. *Develops Portfolio View—The organization develops and evaluates a portfolio view of risk.*

4) Review and revision
   The functionality of the entity's ERM components is evaluated and revised, as needed, in light of changes and diminishing effectiveness.

   Principles of review and revision:
   15. *Assesses Substantial Change*—The organization identifies and assesses changes that may substantially affect strategy and business objectives.
   16. *Reviews Risk and Performance*—The organization reviews entity performance and considers risk.
   17. *Pursues Improvement in Enterprise Risk Management*—The organization pursues improvement of enterprise risk management.

5) Information, communication, and reporting
   Information sharing, internally and externally, is key to an effective and efficient ERM system.

   Principles of Information, communication, and reporting:
   18. *Leverages Information Systems*—The organization leverages the entity's information and technology systems to support enterprise risk management.
   19. *Communicates Risk Information*—The organization uses communication channels to support enterprise risk management.
   20. *Reports on Risk, Culture, and Performance*—The organization reports on risk, culture, and performance at multiple levels and across the entity

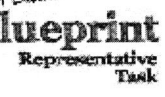

Understand the relationship among risk, business strategy and performance within the context of the COSO ERM framework.		
Mission	**Vision**	**Strategy**
WHAT is the organization's propose?	**WHY** is the mission important?	**HOW** will the company accomplish the mission?

The term business strategy is a set of principles that guide focused decision-making, helping companies prioritize and allocate resources. A deliberate strategy ("HOW") must be in place to realize the mission ("WHAT") and vision ("WHY") without comprising core values. Strategy selection is about making choices and accepting trade-offs. The strategy is a blueprint for business objectives. Generic strategies include growth, product differentiation, cost-leadership.

Example: Assume an airline operates Boeing 787, servicing destinations throughout the U.S. and Canada.

Mission	To transport people to their destinations with the highest level of customer service, with a wide range of destinations, and consistently on-time departures and arrivals.
Vision	Our airline will be a profitable transportation provider of choice and be known for providing reliable transportation without the hassle.
Core values	Our values are to treat our passengers, pilots, and our flight attendants with respect, honesty, compassion, and accountability.
Strategy	• Maximize value for our passengers by increasing the number of non-stop destination • Seek opportunities to manage fuel costs • Integrate operating efficiency and cost-management initiatives • Manage airplane maintenance issue and reduce delays whenever possible

Business strategy in the context of COSO ERM is very important, and the 2017 COSO ERM elevates the discussion of strategy, making it sure that strategy aligns with the mission, vision, and values.

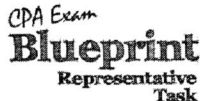

> Apply the COSO Enterprise Risk Management framework to identify risk/opportunity scenarios in an entity.

COSO ERM can be used to identify risk and opportunities in an entity. After gaining an understanding of the mission, vision, values, and strategy, both risks and opportunities can be considered and addressed in the context of this broad view of the company.

Examples of risks that result from internal or external changes include:
- The entity adopts a new strategy
- Changes in consumer preferences
- Regulation changes
- Discovery of unknown or unanticipated product or service shortcomings (e.g., BPA-free water bottles)

Risks that are likely to disrupt operations include:
- Emerging technology impacting existing products or services
- Expanding role of big data and using structured and unstructured data
- Depleting natural resources and increasing costs to obtain them
- Rise of virtual entities impacting traditional entities
- Mobility of workforces (e.g., rise of remote workers)
- Skilled labor shortages
- Shifts in preferences, lifestyle, and demographics

Example: Rollermania Co. manufactures and sells roller skates. It has adopted a cost-leadership strategy, and its mission is to sell skates that anyone can afford. Its vision is that all kids have the chance to roller skate, regardless of their socioeconomic background.

In the context of COSO ERM, Rollermania is ready to *identify risks* (COSO ERM, principle 10). Some of the questions that the company could ask are:
- Have we accurately forecasted our customer demand?
- Will our supply chain deliver on time?
- Will we go over budget?
- Will new competitors emerge that can undercut us on price?
- Is our manufacturing infrastructure up to the task?
- Is our technology up to date and secure?

For instance, Rollermania may determine that their supply chain is not able to handle the potential demand if their demand projections are inaccurate. This could lead to reputation issues or problems with quality if management determines that the pace of the production line must speed up to meet demand. The company determines that this risk is severe reduces the risk by finding a second, outsourced manufacturer to processes overflow orders.

Over time opportunities may arise such as if the outsourced manufacturer does such a nice job that the company determines to discontinue their in-house manufacturing operations. By doing so, it can cut costs, which is in alignment with the company's cost leadership strategy. It also satisfies the company's vision and mission if prices can be reduced as a result of the change.

> *Hint:* A common misconception is ERM is a risk inventory exercise to address current organizational risk factors. But, ERM should not stop with the risk response. It is still important for the organization to monitor, learn, and improve, as demonstrated by the COSO ERM component *Review and Revision*.
>
> ERM also goes beyond internal controls, encompassing topics such as strategy-setting, governance, communication, and measuring performance.

2. COSO Guidance on Monitoring Internal Control Systems (2009)
   In 2009, COSO released supplementary monitoring guidance to increase clarity and understanding of monitoring activities by elaborating on the principles outlined in COSO IC (i.e., ongoing and separate evaluations, reporting deficiencies). It encourages an organization to establish a foundation for monitoring, design and execute monitoring procedures, and assess and report results.

   a. Establish a foundation for monitoring
      The prompt identification of ineffective controls starts out with a supportive foundation, consistent with the COSO IC framework's control environment component. An organization's tone at the top, organizational structure, and baseline understanding of control effectiveness (e.g., control baseline, change identification, change management, and control revalidation/update) create a stable footing for monitoring.

      A proactive and long-term mindset about internal controls must be communicated consistently by the organization's leadership and embedded in the organizational structure. Additionally, individuals who are in charge of monitoring must be competent (e.g., able to recognize a deficiency) and objective (e.g., willing to report findings regardless of the consequences). In this context, these individuals are called evaluators.

      Control systems fail because of (1) poor system design from the start, (2) an original design and/or implementation that is no longer appropriate due to environmental changes, or (3) an original design and/or implementation that is no longer effective (e.g., no longer mitigates applicable risks) due to changes in control operation.

   b. Design and execute monitoring procedures
      When a stable foundation is in place, the COSO monitoring guidance recommends utilizing a risk-based evaluation approach to develop internal controls. In line with COSO ERM, a risk assessment is the first step to identifying key controls. Key controls are high-risk controls based on their significance to the organization and consequences to financial reporting objectives (e.g., control failure will materially impact the financial statements).

      After prioritizing risks and identifying key controls, the next step is to identify persuasive information which will be used to determine the overall effectiveness of the internal control system. Persuasive information is made up of direct (e.g., observation and re-performance of controls) and indirect (e.g., performance indicators, statistics, industry benchmarks) information.

      The final step is to implement and monitor the controls. Key controls are given priority, and monitoring is likely to occur frequently, if not continuously. Continuous monitoring is the most effective monitoring technique, often involving embedded data-collecting procedures that alert the evaluator of abnormalities (e.g., programmed validity checks). Conversely, evaluators may choose to monitor relatively low risks controls less frequently (e.g., annually) and the evaluation procedures may be less extensive.

   c. Assess and report results
      When monitoring is designed and implemented appropriately, evaluators can quickly identify exceptions. Persuasive information, especially regarding control deficiencies, must be reported to

appropriate parties (e.g., the board of directors' audit committee, management) and receive prompt corrective action.

1) Ongoing evaluations and self-assessment
   Ongoing self-assessment prepares management to report on the effectiveness of internal controls confidently. The information gathered during the self-assessment process is also helpful for decision-making and improves the reliability of financial reporting.

   Management cannot "set it and forget it" when it comes to internal control. Controls can easily become obsolete due to a continuously changing operational environment. Evaluators are more likely to be aware of procedure changes if they are required to participate in ongoing monitoring activities. Continuous monitoring increases the timely identification of controls that may need updates.

2) Periodic evaluation
   Periodic evaluation should be the second line of defense against control deficiencies. Internal auditors and/or external auditors have the potential to supplement ongoing self-assessment initiatives, especially if deficiencies exist and they have not been identified during ongoing self-assessment.

C. Other Regulatory Frameworks and Provisions

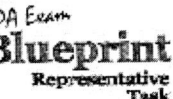

> Identify and define key corporate governance provisions of the Sarbanes-Oxley Act of 2002 and other regulatory pronouncements.

> Identify regulatory deficiencies within an entity by using the requirements associated with the Sarbanes-Oxley Act of 2002.

1. Sarbanes-Oxley Act of 2002 (Sarbanes-Oxley)
   In 2002, as the dust settled on the financial devastation caused by the demise of Enron and Arthur Andersen, Congress voted to enact Sarbanes-Oxley to bolster confidence in the financial reporting and improve corporate governance. The act has directly changed the corporate governance and regulatory environment for public companies in the United States. Sarbanes-Oxley requires greater separation between the external auditors and corporate officers (Sec. 301), increases corporate responsibility for financial reports (Sec. 302), emphasizes the importance of internal control with enhanced disclosure requirements (Sec. 404), proposes whistleblower protection (Sec. 806), and creates criminal penalties for corporate fraud (Sec. 802, 804, 906).

   a. Title III, Corporate responsibility
      1) Sec. 301, Public company audit committees
         An issuer establishes an audit committee amongst the board of directors to oversee financial statement audits and consider accounting policies and procedures. The members of the committee are independent of the company, except for their roles as board members, and cannot be associated with the external audit firm. Audit committee members are prohibited from accepting any consulting, advisory, or another compensatory fee from the issuer and may not be an affiliated person to the issuer or any of its subsidiaries.

         In addition to appointing an external audit firm, the committee is responsible for addressing complaints and concerns regarding questionable accounting or auditing matters brought to their attention.

      2) Sec. 302, Corporate responsibility for financial reports
         Phony financial reports have no place in a bustling capital market, and someone must be held ultimately responsible for a financial statement's content. Sarbanes-Oxley puts accountability on the CEO and CFO, or equivalent signing officer.

         It is the CEO and CFO's job to affirm that the report does not contain misleading omissions or untrue statements of material fact. Based on the officer's knowledge, their signature certifies that the report fairly presents, in all material respects, the financial condition of the issuer for the periods presented in the report. Both the CEO and CFO must make a certification statement regarding internal control systems on a Form 10-K.

   b. Title IV, Enhanced financial disclosures
      1) Sec. 404, Management assessment of internal controls
         The requirement for management to assess the effectiveness of corporation's internal controls over financial reporting is arguably one of the most difficult and costly requirements of Sarbanes-Oxley. Management is responsible for maintaining an adequate internal control structure.

         If applicable, the design and operating effectiveness of the internal controls must also be evaluated by an independent auditor. Accelerated filers are required to include an independent auditor's attestation over management's report on internal control in their financial statements. Material weaknesses due to internal control deficiencies must be disclosed.

SEC legislation subsequent to Sarbanes-Oxley has modified the entities required to comply with Sec. 404. Both non-accelerated filers, per Dodd-Frank in 2010, and emerging growth companies (EGCs), per the JOBS Act in 2012, are exempt.

c. Title VIII, Corporate and criminal fraud accountability
1) Sec. 802, Criminal penalties for altering documents
Companies and auditors are held accountable under Sarbanes-Oxley for destroying, altering, or falsifying records and could face either a fine, incarceration, or both if found guilty. A corporate officer (e.g., CEO, CFO) can be fined up to $5 million and could spend up to 20 years in prison.

Additionally, an auditor found guilty of altering client documents or failing to retain working papers for the required retention period (i.e., 7 years) could receive a sentence of up to 10 years in prison, a fine, or both.

2) Sec. 804, Statute of limitations for securities fraud
The statute of limitations for securities fraud is the earlier of 2 years after the discovery of the facts constituting the violation; or 5 years after such violation.

3) Sec. 806, Protection for employees of publicly traded companies who provide evidence of fraud
Sarbanes-Oxley establishes whistleblower protection to prevent retaliatory discrimination (e.g., termination, demotion, suspension, harassment) against employees who lawfully provide information to aid in an investigation by law enforcement, federal regulators, members of Congress, or other individuals with supervisory authority.

Remedies for such retaliatory discrimination against the whistleblower include compensatory damages such as reinstatement, back pay with interest, and compensation for damages arising from the discrimination (e.g., litigation costs, attorney fees).

Whistleblower protection is further strengthened by the Dodd-Frank Wall Street Reform and Consumer Protection Act of 2010.

d. Title IX, White-collar crime penalty enhancements
1) Sec. 906, Corporate responsibility for financial reports
If a CEO or CFO fails to certify the accuracy of financial reports, (s)he can be held criminally liable under Sarbanes-Oxley. Fines and imprisonment vary from $1 million to $5 million and 10 to 20 years, respectively, depending on the officer's willingness to deceive the public. An officer that willfully certifies a statement knowing it is misleading is subject to the stricter punishment of up to a $5 million fine, 20 years in prison, or both.

2) Sec. 907, Criminal penalties for defrauding shareholders of publicly traded companies
Individuals who perpetrate securities fraud can receive a sentence of up to 25 years in prison, a fine, or both.

Crime	Defendant	Maximum Prison Sentence	Fine
Willingly altering or falsifying records	Executive Officer (e.g., CEO / CFO)	20 years	Yes $5 million max*
Willingly failing to retain working papers	Auditor	10 years	Yes $5 million max*
Failure to certify the accuracy of financial reports	Executive Officer	10 years or 20 years	Yes 10 years, $1 million max 20 years, $5 million max
Willingly committing securities fraud	Executive Officer	25 years	Yes $5 million max*

*$25 million max if other than a natural person (e.g., corporate entity)

Multiple Choice

BEC 1-Q30

2. Dodd-Frank Wall Street Reform and Consumer Protection Act of 2010 (Dodd-Frank)
The stated purpose of Dodd-Frank is "to promote the financial stability of the United States by improving accountability and transparency in the financial system, to end 'too big to fail,' to protect the American taxpayer by ending bailouts, to protect consumers from abusive financial services practices, and for other purposes."

   a. Title IX, Investor protections and improvements to the regulation of securities
      1) Sec. 922, Whistleblower protection
      Whistleblowers, although protected under Sarbanes-Oxley, are protected and rewarded under Dodd-Frank. If a whistleblower's original information results in sanctions of $1 million or more, then s(he) is entitled to 10% to 30% of the total collected monetary sanctions. This reward is meant to act as an incentive for individuals to come forward with information that could assist judicial or administrative action brought against a corporation. A whistleblower is also permitted to provide tips anonymously.

      Those not eligible for the monetary incentive include auditors performing an audit of a corporation's financial statements, employees of the Department of Justice, members of the Public Company Accounting Oversight Board (PCAOB), and members of law enforcement.

      2) Sec. 951, Shareholder vote on executive compensation disclosures
      Dodd-Frank requires shareholders to vote on matters involving executive compensation. First, shareholders must vote on executive compensation (or "say-on-pay" vote) at least every three years. Second, shareholders must also vote on the frequency of the say-on-pay vote once every six years. This will determine if going forward the say-on-pay vote occurs yearly, once every two years, or once every three years. Finally, shareholders must vote to approve golden parachutes, or compensation arrangements with executive officers in connection with merger transactions, when it is applicable.

3) Sec. 972, Disclosures regarding chairman and CEO structures
Corporations must disclose a justification as to why (or why not) the Chairman of the board of directors is also the CEO. This disclosure must be included in the annual proxy statement.

3. JumpStart Our Business Startups Act of 2012 (JOBS Act)
The JumpStart Our Business Startups Act stimulates the United States economy by encouraging more companies to go public to reverse the trend of declining initial public offerings (IPOs). A key feature is that it simplifies the offering process by creating special rules and exemptions for emerging growth companies (EGC). It also permits crowdfunding (smaller amounts of capital sourced from a large number of individuals to finance a new business).

   a. Title I, Reopening American capital markets to emerging growth companies (EGC)
   The JOBS Act scales down disclosures thought to deter companies from going public and ultimately treats EGCs more like private companies for the first five years after their IPO, assuming the company does not lose EGC status for any reason other than the passage of time (e.g., gross revenues exceed $1 billion, the company becomes a large accelerated filer, the company issues greater than $1 billion in non-convertible debt over three years).

   As a result of the JOBS Act, an EGC may submit a draft IPO registration statement to the SEC for a confidential review by SEC staff prior to the company's IPO date.

   The JOBS Act also modifies the requirements for qualifying EGCs regarding the content of the IPO registration statement outlined in Securities Act of 1933. Accordingly, only two fiscal years of audited financial statements (compared to three years) are required for EGCs.

   Lastly, with regard to IPOs, the JOBS Act removes restrictions on gauging the market's interest in the offering with qualified institutional buyers (QIBs), sometimes called test-the-waters communications.

   Qualifying EGCs are also exempt from auditor attestations of internal control over financial reporting (i.e., Sarbanes-Oxley Sec. 404) and the executive compensation disclosures (i.e., Item 402 of Regulation S-K as amended by Dodd-Frank) within the five year period following their IPO.

   Hint: If a company does not qualify as an EGC or other exception, Item 402 of Regulation S-K requires the amounts, and types executive compensation be disclosed to the public in registration statements, proxy statements, and annual reports. As amended by Dodd-Frank, it also requires the company to disclose to the public the ratio of the CEO's compensation to median compensation paid to the company's employees.

Multiple Choice
BEC 1-Q31 through BEC 1-Q34

Glossary: Corporate Governance

A
Accelerated filer – entity with greater than or equal to $75 million, but less than $700 million in market capitalization
Agent – individual with the power to bind the principal in a contractual obligation
Articles of incorporation – document required to establish a corporate legal entity; contains corporate name, corporate address, purpose, shares, and registered agents
Audit committee – independent committee of directors that oversees the corporation's accounting function, external auditor, and matter about regulatory compliance

B
Board of directors – corporate oversight body that provides independent guidance and strategic advice
Business judgment rule – legal standard based on case law that stipulates if officers act in good faith, with reasonable care, they cannot be held liable for an error in judgment
Bylaws – document that outlines the high-level rules over how the corporation is to operate on a day-to-day basis

C
Compensation committee – independent committee of directors that determines the CEO's compensation
Continuous monitoring – ongoing evaluation to evaluations to determine if the components of internal control exist and are functioning properly
Corporate charter – see articles of incorporation
Corporate governance – monitoring mechanism that provides assurance that management's actions properly align with the best interests of the entity's stakeholders
Corrective control – control that corrects an error or irregularity discovered after the fact
Cumulative voting right – right for an individual shareholder to cast multiple votes based on the number of shares s(he) owns, one vote for each share

D
Detective control – control that identifies error or fraud that has previously occurred
Dodd-Frank Wall Street Reform and Consumer Protection Act of 2010 (Dodd-Frank) – legislation to improve accountability and transparency in the financial system
Duty of loyalty – requirement for a director to place the corporation's interest before his or her own individual interest

E
Emerging growth company (EGC) – a company with gross revenues of less than a billion dollars that has already completed an initial public offering and this event occurred after December 18, 2011
Enterprise risk management (ERM) – a process to identify events that may affect an entity and manage risk to provide reasonable assurance the entity can achieve its objectives.
Evaluators – competent and objective individuals in charge of monitoring activities

F
Fiduciary duty – agent's obligation to act in the best interest of a principal

G
Golden parachutes – compensation arrangements with executive officers in connection with merger transactions

H

I
Inherent risk – risk absent management action or other mitigating factors
Initial public offering (IPO) – the first time a corporation issues common stock
Internal auditors – employees that monitor operations and give ongoing recommendations concerning internal control, enterprise risk management, and corporate governance activities

J

K
Key controls – high-risk controls are typically considered significant to the organization

L
Large accelerated filer – entity with greater than or equal to $700 million in market capitalization

M

Management override – illegitimate disregard of policies or procedures by management (e.g., personal gain, inflated financial condition)

Market capitalization – aggregate worldwide market value of voting and non-voting common equity held by non-affiliates of the issuer

N

Nominating/corporate governance committee – committee of directors responsible for nominating candidates to serve on the board, to be voted on by shareholders

Non-accelerated filer – entity with less than $75 million in market capitalization

O

Officers – executive management team in charge of directing day-to-day business operations

Owners – individuals who provide the capital necessary for the organization to conduct business

P

Poison pill – a strategy to prevent a hostile takeover by selling stock at a discount when one shareholder exceeds a certain percentage of ownership

Preemptive right – right of common shareholders to purchase new issuances first so that they can maintain their proportionate share of outstanding shares of common stock and their ownership is not diluted

Preventive control – a control to deter the occurrence of errors and fraudulent activity

Public float – see market capitalization

Q

R

Residual risk – the risk of an event after considering management's response

Risk – occurrence that impedes or otherwise adversely impacts the achievement of objectives

Risk appetite – amount of risk an entity is willing to accept

Risk assessment – likelihood that risks will occur and the effects that the risks will have on the organization

Risk tolerance – range of risk variation an entity is willing to accept with respect to a particular objective

Regulation S-K – a federal regulation defining the standard instructions for filing forms under Securities Act of 1933 and Securities Exchange Act of 1934

S

Sarbanes-Oxley Act of 2002 (Sarbanes-Oxley) – legislation to bolster confidence in the financial reporting and improve corporate governance

Stakeholders – an individual or group of individuals that are affected by or has an interest in an entity (e.g., owners, management, employees, customers, suppliers, local community, government agencies)

T

Test-the-waters communications – gauging the market's interest in an initial public offering (IPO) with qualified institutional buyers (QIBs) prior to the IPO date

Tone at the top – ethical climate or atmosphere within an entity that cascades from leadership (i.e., the board of directors and executives) to frontline employees

U

Uncertainty – inability to predict future outcome and impact of a decision or action

V

W

Whistleblower – individuals to original information that could assist in judicial or administrative action against a corporation

Whistleblower hotline – secure, anonymous way to report fraudulent behavior and protect employees against retaliation

X

Y

Z

Multiple Choice – Questions

BEC 1-Q1 B1147. According to COSO, an executive's deliberate misrepresentation to a banker who is considering whether to make a loan to an enterprise is an example of which of the following internal control limitations?

A. Costs versus benefits
B. Management override.
C. Break down.
D. Collusion.

BEC 1-Q2 B1148. Internal controls are likely to fail for any of the following reasons, **except**
A. They are not designed and implemented properly at the outset.
B. They are designed and implemented properly as static controls, but the environment in which they operate changes.
C. They are designed and implemented properly, but their operation changes in some way.
D. They are designed and implemented properly, and their design changes as processes change.

BEC 1-Q3 B16. According to COSO, which of the following is a compliance objective?

A. To maintain adequate staffing to keep overtime expense within budget.
B. To maintain a safe level of carbon dioxide emissions during production.
C. To maintain material price variances within published guidelines.
D. To maintain accounting principles that conform to GAAP.

BEC 1-Q4 B32. According to COSO, which of the following is the most effective method to transmit a message of ethical behavior throughout an organization?

A. Demonstrating appropriate behavior by example.
B. Strengthening internal audit's ability to deter and report improper behavior.
C. Removing pressures to meet unrealistic targets, particularly for short-term results.
D. Specifying the competence levels for every job in an organization and translating those levels to requisite knowledge and skills.

BEC 1-Q5 B33. Within the COSO Internal Control—Integrated Framework, which of the following components is designed to ensure that internal controls continue to operate effectively?

A. Control environment.
B. Risk assessment.
C. Information and communication.
D. Monitoring.

BEC 1-Q6 B34. According to COSO, an effective approach to monitoring internal control involves each of the following steps, **except**

A. Establishing a foundation for monitoring.
B. Increasing the reliability of financial reporting and compliance with applicable laws and regulations.
C. Designing and executing monitoring procedures that are prioritized based on risks to achieve organizational objectives.
D. Assessing and reporting the results, including following up on corrective action where necessary.

BEC 1-Q7 B6. A company's new time clock process requires hourly employees to select an identification number and then choose the clock-in or clock-out button. A video camera captures an image of the employee using the system. Which of the following exposures can the new system be expected to change the least?

A. Fraudulent reporting of employees' own hours.
B. Errors in employees' overtime computation.
C. Inaccurate accounting of employees' hours.
D. Recording of other employees' hours.

BEC 1-Q8 B1218. Employees of an entity feel peer pressure to do the right thing; management appropriately deals with signs that problems exist and resolves the issues; and dealings with customers, suppliers, employees, and other parties are based on honesty and fairness. According to COSO, the above scenario is indicative of which of the following?

A. Strategic goals.
B. Operational excellence.
C. Reporting reliability.
D. Tone at the top.

BEC 1-Q9 B1217. Which of the following statements is true regarding internal control objectives of information systems?

A. Primary responsibility of viable internal control rests with the internal audit division.
B. A secure system may have inherent risks due to management's analysis of trade-offs identified by cost-benefit studies.
C. Control objectives primarily emphasize output distribution issues.
D. An entity's corporate culture is irrelevant to the objectives.

BEC 1-Q10 B1241. According to COSO, a primary purpose of monitoring internal control is to verify that the internal control system remains adequate to address changes in

A. Risks.
B. The law.
C. Technology.
D. Operating procedures.

BEC 1-Q11 B166. Which of the following statements best states the purpose of cumulative voting?

A. To assure the continuance of incumbent directors.
B. To allow minority shareholders to gain representation on the board of directors.
C. To allow for the election of one-third of the board of directors each year.
D. To assure that a majority of shares voted elects the entire board of directors.

BEC 1-Q12 B270. Which of the following corporate actions is subject to shareholder approval?

A. Election of officers.
B. Removal of officers.
C. Declaration of cash dividends.
D. Removal of directors.

BEC 1-Q13 B212. Hughes and Brody start a business as a closely-held corporation. Hughes owns 51 of the 100 shares of stock issued by the firm and Brody owns 49. One year later, the corporation decides to sell another 200 shares. Which of the following types of rights would give Hughes and Brody a preference over other purchasers to buy shares to maintain control of the firm?

A. Shareholder derivative rights.
B. Pre-emptive rights.
C. Cumulative voting rights.
D. Inspection rights.

BEC 1-Q14 B368. Smith was an officer of CCC Corp. As an officer, the business judgment rule applied to Smith in which of the following ways?

A. Because Smith is not a director, the rule does not apply.
B. If Smith makes, in good faith, a serious but honest mistake in judgment, Smith is generally not liable to CCC for damages caused.
C. If Smith makes, in good faith, a serious but honest mistake in judgment, Smith is generally liable to CCC for damages caused, but CCC may elect to reimburse Smith for any damages Smith paid.
D. If Smith makes, in good faith, a serious but honest mistake in judgment, Smith is generally liable to CCC for damages caused, and CCC is prohibited from reimbursing Smith for any damages Smith paid.

BEC 1-Q15 B81. In order to comply with a director's duty of loyalty to a corporation, what action(s) should a director take when presented with a corporate opportunity?

A. Reject the opportunity and not offer it to the corporation.
B. Accept the opportunity and not offer it to the corporation.
C. Accept the opportunity and disclose the acceptance to the corporation.
D. Offer the opportunity to the corporation and accept it if the corporation rejects it.

BEC 1-Q16 B119. Which of the following positions best describes the nature of the Board of Directors of XYZ Co.'s relationship to the company?

A. Agent.
B. Executive.
C. Fiduciary.
D. Representative.

BEC 1-Q17 B1146. A company officer who is **not** a director is authorized to perform which of the following duties?

A. Terminate the company's external audit firm.
B. Remove a director for failure to exercise reasonable supervision.
C. Declare dividends to shareholders.
D. Enter into a contract with a vendor of computers for the company.

BEC 1-Q18 B162. According to the Sarbanes-Oxley Act of 2002, which of the following statements is correct regarding an issuer's audit committee financial expert?

A. The issuer's current outside CPA firm's audit partner must be the audit committee financial expert.
B. If an issuer does not have an audit committee financial expert, the issuer must disclose the reason why the role is not filled.
C. The issuer must fill the role with an individual who has experience in the issuer's industry.
D. The audit committee financial expert must be the issuer's audit committee chairperson to enhance internal control.

BEC 1-Q19 B118. Which of the following is necessary to be an audit committee financial expert according to the criteria specified in the Sarbanes-Oxley Act of 2002?

A. A limited understanding of generally accepted auditing standards.
B. Education and experience as a certified financial planner.
C. Experience with internal accounting controls.
D. Experience in the preparation of tax returns.

BEC 1-Q20 B75. In a large public corporation, evaluating internal control procedures should be the responsibility of

A. Accounting management staff who report to the CFO.
B. Internal audit staff who report to the board of directors.
C. Operations management staff who report to the chief operations officer.
D. Security management staff who report to the chief facilities officer.

BEC 1-Q21 B1219. According to COSO, which of the following identifies the group directly responsible for the implementation and development of the enterprise risk management framework?

A. Management.
B. The board of directors.
C. External auditors.
D. Internal auditors.

BEC 1-Q22 B76. Which of the following items is one of the eight components of COSO's enterprise risk management framework?

A. Operations.
B. Reporting.
C. Monitoring.
D. Compliance.

BEC 1-Q23 B96. Each of the following is a limitation of enterprise risk management (ERM), except

A. ERM deals with risk, which relates to the future and is inherently uncertain.
B. ERM operates at different levels with respect to different objectives.
C. ERM can provide absolute assurance with respect to objective categories.
D. ERM is as effective as the people responsible for its functioning.

BEC 1-Q24 B97. A manufacturing firm identified that it would have difficulty sourcing raw materials locally, so it decided to relocate its production facilities. According to COSO, this decision represents which of the following responses to the risk?

A. Risk reduction.
B. Prospect theory.
C. Risk sharing.
D. Risk acceptance.

BEC 1-Q25 B117. According to COSO, the use of ongoing and separate evaluations to identify and address changes in internal control effectiveness can best be accomplished in which of the following stages of the monitoring-for-change continuum?

A. Control baseline.
B. Change identification.
C. Change management.
D. Control revalidation/update.

BEC 1-Q26 B163. According to COSO, which of the following components of enterprise risk management addresses an entity's integrity and ethical values?

A. Information and communication.
B. Internal environment.
C. Risk assessment.
D. Control activities.

BEC 1-Q27 B1243. According to COSO, which of the following differences relevant to the risk-assessment process is most likely to exist between a large entity and a small entity?

A. The CEO of a small entity is more likely than the CEO of a large entity to be attuned to risks arising from internal factors through hands-on involvement with all levels of personnel.
B. The risk-assessment process in a small entity is more structured than in a large one because of the nature of some of the internal control components in a small entity.
C. An owner-manager of a small entity will not normally learn about risks arising from external factors through direct contact with customers, suppliers, and other outsiders, whereas in large entities this process is part of the entity's primary way of identifying new risk.
D. Risk assessment in a small entity, as opposed to that in a large entity, can be problematic to implement because the in-depth involvement of the CEO and other key managers is a conflict of interest that must be addressed separately in the internal control assessment process.

BEC 1-Q28 B1244. According to COSO, the presence of a written code of conduct provides for a control environment that can

A. Override an entity's history and culture.
B. Encourage teamwork in the pursuit of an entity's objectives.
C. Ensure that competent evaluators are implementing and monitoring internal controls.
D. Verify that information systems are providing persuasive evidence of the effectiveness of internal controls.

BEC 1-Q29 B1242. The materials manager of a warehouse is given a new product line to manage with new inventory control procedures. Which of the following sequences of the COSO internal control monitoring-for-change continuum is affected by the new product line?

A. Control baseline but not change management.
B. Change management but not control baseline.
C. Neither control baseline nor change management.
D. Both control baseline and change management.

BEC 1-Q30 B74. According to the Sarbanes-Oxley Act of 2002, a chief executive officer or chief financial officer who misrepresents the company's finances may be penalized by being

A. Fined, but **not** imprisoned.
B. Imprisoned, but **not** fined.
C. Removed from the corporate office and fined.
D. Fined and imprisoned.

BEC 1-Q31 B1220. Which of the following organizations was established by the Sarbanes-Oxley Act of 2002 to control the auditing profession?

A. Information Systems Audit and Control Foundation (ISACF).
B. IT Governance Institute (ITGI).
C. Public Company Accounting Oversight Board (PCAOB).
D. Committee of Sponsoring Organizations (COSO).

BEC 1-Q32 B1221. Which of the following situations most clearly illustrates a breach of fiduciary duty by one or more members of the board of directors of a corporation?

A. A corporation previously has distributed 50% of its earnings as dividends. This year, it has annual earnings per share of $2, and the board of directors voted 4 to 1 against paying any dividend to finance growth.
B. A director of a corporation who co-owns a computer vendor negotiated the purchase of a computer system by the corporation from the vendor, making a disclosure to the corporation and the other board members. The purchase price was competitive, and the board (absent the vendor co-owner) unanimously approved the purchase.
C. Two directors of a corporation favor business expansion, two oppose it, and the fifth did not attend the meeting. During the five years that the fifth person has been a director, the individual did not attend two other meetings.
D. A director who learned that the corporation is thinking of buying retail space in a city personally purchased a vacant building in the same city that would have been suitable for use by the corporation.

BEC 1-Q33 B1245. Which of the following statements is correct regarding the requirements of the Sarbanes-Oxley Act of 2002 for an issuer's board of directors?

A. Each member of the board of directors must be independent from management influence, based on the member's prior and current activities, economic and family relationships, and other factors.
B. The board of directors must have an audit committee entirely composed of members who are independent from management influence.
C. The majority of members of the board of directors must be independent from management influence.
D. The board of directors must have a compensation committee, a nominating committee, and an audit committee, each of which is entirely composed of independent members.

BEC 1-Q34 B1213. For qualifying emerging growth companies, the content of their initial public offering registration statement may contain only two fiscal years of audited financial statements, compared to the three year requirement, is part of the

A. Dodd-Frank Wall Street Reform and Consumer Protection Act of 2010
B. Securities Act of 1933
C. JumpStart Our Business Startups Act of 2012
D. Sarbanes-Oxley Act of 2002

This page is intentionally left blank.

Multiple Choice – Solutions

BEC 1-Q1 B1147. The correct answer is B. This is an example of management override where management has overruled a policy or procedure for personal gain or advantage.

Answer A is incorrect because costs versus benefit consider the costs of implementing specific controls compared to the overall value to the Company.

Answer C is incorrect because even well designed internal controls can break down if prescribed procedures and policies are not followed.

Answer D is incorrect because individuals acting collectively can alter financial data or other management information in a manner that cannot be identified by control systems.

BEC 1-Q2 B1148. The correct answer is D. For internal controls to be effective they must be designed and implemented properly and must be able to change as processes changes.

Answer A is incorrect because if the controls are not designed and implemented properly at the outset, they will fail.

Answer B is incorrect because if controls do not change in the environment in which they operate they will become ineffective and fail.

Answer C is incorrect because if the operation of a control changes it will make the control ineffective and fail.

BEC 1-Q3 B16. The correct answer is B. The compliance objective is to comply with applicable laws, rules, and regulations. Maintaining a safe level of carbon dioxide emissions during production is a compliance objective because it is an example of compliance with safety, health, and environmental regulations. Choices A and C are not correct because they are examples of maintaining efficiency and effectiveness, which is the operations objective. Choice D is not correct because it is an example of the reporting objective.

BEC 1-Q4 B32. The correct choice is A. As part of the control environment component, management must demonstrate a commitment to integrity and ethical values. By demonstrating appropriate behavior by example, this would set the tone at the top and would be the most effective method of transmitting a message of ethical behavior throughout an organization because others in the organization would observe management's behavior and adopt it as their own behavior.

Choices B, C and D are not correct because, although these actions support principles related to the control environment, they are not as visible to others and therefore do not carry the same weight as management's appropriate behavior by example.

BEC 1-Q5 B33. The correct choice is D. The five components of the COSO integrated framework for internal control are: control environment, risk assessment, control activities, information and communication, and monitoring. The monitoring component helps to ensure that the internal control activities associated with the other four components have been implemented and are working effectively and efficiently.

Choice A is not correct because the control environment component helps to set the overall framework for the internal control program through standards, processes, and organizational structure.

Choice B is not correct because the risk assessment component helps management to identify, analyze, and react to risks that may prevent the organization from achieving its objectives.

Choice C is not correct because information and communication, both internal and external to the organization, helps to support the activities of the other four components by informing and communicating the requirements of the internal control program and each party's responsibilities.

BEC 1-Q6 B34. The correct answer is B. The requirement is to find the exception that does not implement the monitoring component of internal control. The COSO definition of internal control is: "A process, effected by the entity's board of directors, management, and other personnel designed to provide reasonable assurance regarding the achievement of objectives relating to operations, reporting, and compliance." Therefore, the exception is "increasing the reliability of financial reporting and compliance with applicable laws and regulations" because reporting is an objective of the overall internal control framework and all five components of the internal control framework work together to achieve this objective.

Choices A, C, and D are not correct because these activities are effective approaches for implementing the monitoring component.

BEC 1-Q7 B6. The correct choice is B. The calculation of overtime is outside the time-clock process because overtime calculations are done by the payroll department by comparing an employee's weekly hours versus the maximum number of hours allowed for regular time pay before overtime pay is paid for the hours in excess of regular time hours. Choice A is not correct because the internal controls of the video camera, employee identification number, and time clock would help to prevent fraudulent reporting of an employee's own hours. Choice C is not correct because the time clock internal control would help to prevent inaccurate accounting of employees' hours. Choice D is not correct because the controls of the video camera and employee identification number would help to prevent recording of other employees' hours.

BEC 1-Q8 B1218. The correct answer choice is D. According to COSO, the control environment provides a foundation for internal control in an organization. One of the COSO internal control principles associated with an entity's control environment is the "tone" at the top. Tone at the top is defined as the ethical climate or atmosphere within an entity that cascades from leadership (i.e., the board of directors and executives) to frontline employees. The climate, or tone, set by leaders and managers is effective in encouraging and discouraging certain behaviors. In this question, management established guidelines and leads by example, to set the tone at the top. They foster a culture where employees feel peer pressure to do the right thing; where management appropriately deals with signs that problems exist and resolves the issues; and dealings with customers, suppliers, employees, and other parties are based on honesty and fairness.

Choices A, B and C are incorrect because they are not part of the COSO internal control framework.

BEC 1-Q9 B1217. The correct answer choice is B. Risk assessment evaluates the likelihood that risks will occur and the effects that the risks will have on the organization. Cost-benefit constraints limit risk assessment activities. A secure system may have inherent risks due to management's analysis of trade-offs identified by cost-benefit studies. As a result, the determinations over risk response must be made using imperfect information. Even if near perfect information did exist concerning a particular risk, humans often find it difficult to judge the consequences of a decision (e.g., impact of accepting a risk). There are simply too many uncertain variables to consider and it is possible that an individual will simply forget to include an important consideration.

Choice A is incorrect because the primary responsibility of viable internal control rests with management, with oversight by the board of directors.

Choice C is incorrect because control objectives emphasize input, processing, and output controls.

Choice D is incorrect because the organizational structure, the type of culture related to integrity and ethical decision-making, and performance measurement criteria each play a role in the internal control objectives.

BEC 1-Q10 B1241. The correct answer choice is A. The monitoring of internal controls includes evaluations that determine if the internal controls are functioning as they were designed and are effective in addressing risks. Over time, business risks change and through the monitoring process, it can be determined if the controls currently in place are still effective and relevant related to the changing risks, and are at an acceptable level.

Choices B, C and D are incorrect because an effective system of internal controls, through the monitoring process, will provide the ability to contain risks at an acceptable level to ensure effective and efficient operations on an ongoing basis, and enable management to deal with changes in internal and external factors such as applicable laws and regulations, technology and operating procedures.

BEC 1-Q11 B166. The correct choice is B. The following example illustrates cumulative voting: If a shareholder owns five shares and there are five directors to be elected, then cumulative voting would allow for 5 shares x 5 directors = 25 votes. The shareholder could then assign all 25 votes to one director instead of all five directors; this would help the director to get elected and help to allow minority shareholders to gain representation on the board of directors.

Choices A, C, and D are not correct because they do not describe cumulative voting.

BEC 1-Q12 B270. The correct choice is D. Because the shareholders vote to elect the directors on the board of directors, shareholders may also vote to remove directors.

Choice A is not correct because the shareholders do not have a right to manage the corporation unless they are also officers or directors on the board of directors; therefore, shareholders cannot elect officers.

Choice B is not correct because the shareholders do not have a right to manage the corporation unless they are also officers or directors on the board of directors; therefore, shareholders cannot remove officers.

Choice C is not correct because it is the directors on the board of directors that vote to declare cash dividends. However, once the cash dividends are declared, the shareholders have a right to receive the cash dividends.

BEC 1-Q13 B212. The correct choice is B. The shareholder preemptive right is the right of current shareholders to purchase new issuances of common stock so that they may maintain their percentage ownership in the corporation and their ownership is not diluted.

Choice A is not correct because the shareholder derivative right is the right to sue the management and directors of the corporation on the behalf of the corporation.

Choice C is not correct. The following example illustrates cumulative voting: If a shareholder owns five shares and there are five directors to be elected, then cumulative voting would allow for 5 shares x 5 directors = 25 votes. The shareholder could then assign all 25 votes to one director instead of all five directors; this would help the director to get elected and help to allow minority shareholders to gain representation on the board of directors.

Choice D is not correct because inspection rights are the right that a shareholder has to inspect the books and records of the corporation, assuming that the inspection is for a valid purpose.

BEC 1-Q14 B368. The correct choice is B. The business judgment rule applies to both directors and officers. The business judgment rule is based on case law; the rule, in general, is that as long as the director or officer acts in good faith and within the scope of their authority then they cannot be held liable for errors in judgment.

Choice A is not correct because the business judgment rule applies to both directors and officers.

Choices C and D are not correct because the business judgment rule, in general, is that as long as the director or officer acts in good faith and within the scope of their authority then they cannot be held liable for errors in judgment.

BEC 1-Q15 B81. The correct choice is D. The director's duty of loyalty requires the director to place priority of the corporation's interest before his or her own interest. Therefore, if a director is presented with a corporate opportunity, the director should first offer the opportunity to the corporation; if the corporation declines, then the director may pursue the opportunity.

Choices A, B and C are not correct because the director's duty of loyalty requires the director to place priority of the corporation's interest before his or her own interest. Therefore, the director must present the opportunity to the corporation first and the director may pursue the opportunity after the corporation declines the opportunity.

BEC 1-Q16 B119. The correct choice is C. The Board of Directors' (BOD) duty is to act as a fiduciary to oversee the management of the corporation on behalf of and in the interest of the shareholders. The BOD helps establish the mission, vision, and strategy of the corporation and approves dividends to the shareholders.

Choice A is not correct because it is management of the corporation that may act as an agent of the corporation within management's authority.

Choice B is not correct because it is management (the executives) of the corporation that may act as an agent of the corporation within management's authority.

Choice D is not correct because the BOD's duty is to act as a fiduciary to oversee the management of the corporation on behalf of and in the interest of the shareholders. The BOD is not a representative of the corporation.

BEC 1-Q17 B1146. The correct answer is D. Officers are in charge of directing day-to-day business operations. One of the duties of an officer is to enter into contracts with vendors on behalf of the Company.

Answer A is incorrect because an officer does not have authority to terminate the Company's external audit firm.
Only the audit committee can terminate the Company's external audit firm.

Answer B is incorrect because an officer does not have authority to remove a director.

Answer C is incorrect because only the directors of the Company have the authority to declare and pay dividends.

BEC 1-Q18 B162. The correct choice is B. The Sarbanes-Oxley Act (SOX) provides that at least one Director on the audit committee should be a financial expert. If the audit committee has no financial expert, then the issuer must explain why.

Choice A is not correct because the CPA firm auditing the issuer must be independent of the issuer and therefore the partner cannot be a member of the audit committee.

Choice C is not correct because SOX does not require the financial expert to have experience in the issuer's industry. SOX provides that the financial expert should understand GAAP, internal control, financial statements and financial reporting, and the roles, responsibilities, and operations of the audit committee; and have experience in dealing with financial statements that are comparable to the issuer's financial statements in terms of complexity.

Choice D is not correct because SOX does not require the financial expert to be the chairperson of the audit committee.

BEC 1-Q19 B118. The correct choice is C. Under the Sarbanes-Oxley Act (SOX), the financial expert is required to have an understanding of financial statements and U.S. GAAP; internal controls and financial statement audits; and the role of the audit committee. The financial expert must also have financial reporting experience with similar characteristics in terms of complexity of the corporation's financial reporting.

Choice A is not correct because under the SOX, the financial expert must have an understanding of internal controls and financial statement audits.

Choice B is not correct because under SOX, the financial expert is not required to have experience as a certified financial planner.

Choice D is not correct because under SOX, the financial expert is not required to have experience in the preparation of tax returns.

BEC 1-Q20 B75. The correct choice is B. The internal audit function in a large public corporate corporation evaluates internal control procedures.

Choices A, C, and D are not correct because the accounting management staff, operations management staff, and security management staff implement internal control procedures.

BEC 1-Q21 B1219. The correct answer choice is A. Management is responsible for the financial statements and establishing accounting policies that conform to GAAP; in addition to being responsible for establishing, implementing and monitoring internal controls, enterprise risk management, and corporate governance, in support of the financial statement.

Choice B is incorrect because the board of directors is a corporate oversight body that provides independent guidance and strategic advice. They are not responsible for the implementation and development of the enterprise risk management framework.

Choice C is incorrect because external auditors provide independent audit and attestation services to evaluate a company's financial statement assertions, internal control structure and the enterprise risk management assertions. They are not responsible for the implementation and development of the enterprise risk management framework.

Choice D is incorrect because internal auditors monitor operations and give ongoing recommendations concerning internal control, enterprise risk management, and corporate governance activities to management and the board of directors. They are not responsible for the implementation and development of the enterprise risk management framework.

BEC 1-Q22 B76. The correct choice is C. A helpful way to remember the five components of the COSO internal control framework and the eight components of the COSO Enterprise Risk Management (ERM) framework is to compare the two frameworks in a table like the one presented below:

COSO Internal Control	COSO Enterprise Risk Management
1. Control Environment	1. Internal Environment
2. Risk Assessment	2. Objective Setting
	3. Event Identification
	4. Risk Assessment
	5. Risk Response
3. Control Activities	6. Control Activities
4. Information and Communication	7. Information and Communication
5. Monitoring	8. Monitoring

Choices A, B, and D are not correct because they are not one of the eight components of the COSO ERM framework.

BEC 1-Q23 B96. The correct choice is C. The question asked for the item which is not a limitation of ERM. A limitation of ERM is that it provides reasonable assurance that the entity will achieve its objectives, not absolute assurance.

Choices A, B and D are not correct because these items are examples of the limitations of ERM.

BEC 1-Q24 B97. The correct choice is A. An entity reduces its risk by taking action to eliminate or reduce the risk. Relocating the production facilities nearer to the source of the raw materials helps to reduce the risk associated with difficulty in obtaining the raw materials.

Choice B is not correct because prospect theory assumes that decision makers base their decisions on the relative gain or loss associated with each possible outcome rather than the outcome itself and choose the option according to their perception of the greatest gain or least loss.

Choice C is not correct because an entity shares its risk by taking actions to transfer the risk through outsourcing the risky activity or through sharing the risk with others through hedging or insurance contracts.

Choice D is not correct because an entity accepts the risk for a particular activity and takes no action.

BEC 1-Q25 B117. The correct choice is B. The COSO monitoring-for-change continuum consists of four stages: control baseline, change identification, change management, and control revalidation/update. The change identification stage helps to identify changes that must be made to adapt to changes in the internal control environment (e.g., changes in the industry, economy, or regulation).

Choice A is not correct because the control baseline stage provides a starting point for comparative purposes.

Choice C is not correct because the change management stage effects the changes needed to arrive at the new baseline.

Choice D is not correct because the control revalidation/update stage revalidates the new baseline even though management is not aware of any changes in the internal control environment.

BEC 1-Q26 B163. The correct choice is B. The eight components of the COSO's enterprise risk management (ERM) are internal environment, objective setting, event identification, risk assessment, risk response, control activities, information and communication, and monitoring. The internal environment is the component which addresses the entity's integrity and ethical values. This is similar to COSO's internal control framework where the control environment addresses an entity's integrity and ethical values.

Choice A is not correct because the information and communication component addresses the identification and accumulation of information needed to communicate the risk management policies of the entity to its employees at all levels of the entity so that the employees understand their roles and responsibilities within the entity's ERM program.

Choice C is not correct because the risk assessment component addresses the probability and effect of events that have been identified in the event identification component.

Choice D is not correct because the control activities component addresses the policies and procedures that management has put in place to implement management's actions in the risk response component.

BEC 1-Q27 B1243. The correct answer choice is A. The risk assessment component of COSO helps management to identify, analyze, and react to risks that may prevent the organization from achieving its objectives. These are equally applicable to both small entities and large entities, however the implementation approaches between to the two can be different. Small entity management will usually have more of a hands-on approach, with a broader span of control, and perform a lot of the ongoing monitoring through more direct interactions with key employees, creditors and vendors. Therefore, a CEO of a small entity is more likely than the CEO of a large entity to be attuned to risks arising from internal factors through hands-on involvement with all levels of personnel.

Choice B is incorrect because the risk-assessment process in a small entity tends to not be more structured than in a large one. Often the hands-on approach of management of a small entity lends itself to having controls that are less formal, without diminishing the quality and effectiveness of the controls.

Choice C is incorrect because due to their hands-on nature of management, a small entity will normally learn about risks arising from external factors through direct contact with customers, suppliers.

Choice D is incorrect because the in-depth involvement of the small entity CEO and other key managers in internal control management does not itself create a conflict of interest that must be addressed separately in the internal control assessment process.

BEC 1-Q28 B1244. The correct answer choice is B. An entity's code of conduct provides a guide for acceptable behaviors, activities and decisions. The COSO control environment provides a foundation for internal control. The organizational structure, culture of integrity and ethical decision-making, and performance measurement criteria each play a role in the control environment. According to the COSO internal control principles associated with the control environment, management establishes, with board oversight, structures, reporting lines, and appropriate authorities and responsibilities in the pursuit of objectives. The presence of a written code of conduct provides for a control environment that can encourage teamwork in the pursuit of an entity's objectives, because all employees are following the same principles included in the code.

Choice A is incorrect because the written code of conduct should typically reflect an entity's historical perspective and overall culture of how it operates and is not meant to override it.

Choice C is incorrect because ensuring that competent evaluators are implementing and monitoring internal controls is not part of a written code of conduct, as they are part of the overall management of an entity's system of internal control.

Choice D is incorrect because verifying that information systems are providing persuasive evidence of the effectiveness of internal controls is not part of a written code of conduct, as they are part of the overall management of an entity's system of internal control.

BEC 1-Q29 B1242. The correct answer choice is D. The COSO internal control monitoring-for-change continuum is made up of four sequences: control baseline, change identification, change management, and control revalidation/ update. In this question, there is a new product line with new inventory control procedures to manage. This will result in a change in the operation of controls, which will impact both the control baseline and change management sequences. The control baseline sequence is the starting point to provide a benchmark on the internal control system design and whether or not those controls will fulfill the internal control objectives of the company. The change management sequence effects the changes needed to ensure the internal controls system will address the new inventory control procedures related to the new product line.

Choices A, B and C are incorrect because both the control baseline and change management sequences are affected by the new product line and new inventory control procedures.

BEC 1-Q30 B74. The correct choice is D. In the Sarbanes-Oxley Act of 2002 (SOX), a CEO or CFO who misrepresents the company's finances may be fined up to $5 million and imprisoned for 10 to 20 years. Choices A, B, and C are not correct because in SOX a CEO or CFO who misrepresents that company's finances may be both fined and imprisoned.

BEC 1-Q31 B1220. The correct answer choice is C. The Public Company Accounting Oversight Board (PCAOB) is a not-for-profit organization established by the Sarbanes–Oxley Act of 2002. The PCAOB's mission is to oversee public company audits in preparation of accurate and independent audit reports.

Choice A is incorrect because the Information Systems Audit and Control Association (ISACA) is a not-for-profit organization that began in 1969 as a way to fulfill the need of sourcing auditing controls for computer systems. The Information Systems Audit and Control Foundation (ISACF) is part of the ISACA and it was established in 1976 to work on research in IT governance and control, for the education of the profession.

Choice B is incorrect because the IT Governance Institute (ITGI) was formed by the Information Systems Audit and Control Association (ISACA) to assist companies in learning the importance of aligning IT goals with business goals.

Choice D is incorrect because the Committee of Sponsoring Organizations (COSO) was established in 1985 by five professional accounting associations, as an independent group to research situations that can cause fraudulent financial reporting and to establish recommendations based on their findings. The five accounting associations that formed COSO were:
1) American Accounting Association (AAA),
2) American Institute of Certified Public Accountants (AICPA),
3) Financial Executives International (FEI),
4) Institute of Internal Auditors (IIA), and
5) Institute of Management Accountants (IMA)

BEC 1-Q32 B1221. The correct answer choice is D. The primary duty of the board of directors is to consider stakeholder interests, particularly the relationship between owners and management, and to provide independent guidance and strategic advice. Directors have a fiduciary duty to act in the best interest of the corporation's shareholders. In this question, by personally purchasing a vacant building that would have been suitable for use by the corporation, the director placed their own interest above that of the shareholders and did not act in their best interest, thereby breaching the director's fiduciary duty.

Choice A is incorrect because part of the board of directors' duties and responsibilities is to vote on whether to declare or not declare the payment of dividends. There is no breach of fiduciary duty by voting against paying a dividend.

Choice B is incorrect because the director acted in the best interest of the shareholders by disclosing their ownership in the computer vendor to the corporation and the other board members. Also, the purchase price was competitive and the director did not participate in the vote. This director did not breach their fiduciary duty.

Choice C is incorrect because by not attending the latest board meeting and missing another two board meetings in the last five years; the fifth board member did not breach their fiduciary duty. Often, companies have board of director meeting attendance policies, so that all directors can be treated fairly and consistently, and the board can address attendance matters as they arise.

BEC 1-Q33 B1245. The correct answer choice is B. The audit committee of a board of directors oversees an issuer's (public company's) accounting function, external auditor, internal auditor and matters pertaining to regulatory compliance (e.g., adequate internal control). The audit committee must be independent from management influence per the Sarbanes-Oxley Act of 2002.

Choice A is incorrect because each and every member of a board of directors does not have to be independent from management influence, based on the member's prior and current activities, economic and family relationships, and other factors. For example, the Chief Executive Officer (CEO) of an entity is typically a member of the board of directors and often is also the chairperson of the board.

Choice C is incorrect because a majority of members are not required to be independent from management influence, although it is often viewed that corporate governance is enhanced when a board of directors is made up of more independent members that are not influenced as management.

Choice D is incorrect because there are two committees that must be made up entirely of independent board members and they are the audit committee and the compensation committee.

BEC 1-Q34 B1213. The correct answer is C. For qualifying emerging growth companies (EGC), the content of their initial public offering registration statement may contain only two fiscal years of audited financial statements, compared to the three year requirement, is part of the JumpStart Our Business Startups Act of 2012 (JOBS Act).

Answers A, B and D are incorrect because they do not contain provisions for required number of years of audited financial statements for EGCs.

BEC 2 – Economic Concepts and Analysis

A. Economic and Business Cycles - Measures and Indicators   2A-1 – 2A-21

     1. Demand   1
     2. Supply   5
     3. Business cycles   7
     4. Gross Domestic Product (GDP)   8
     5. Cyclical and non-cyclical businesses   11
     6. Aggregate demand and supply   11
     7. Economic indicators and measures   14

B. Market Influences on Business   2B-1 – 2B-15

     1. Market equilibrium   1
     2. Production costs and profits   3
     3. Market structure   7
     4. Economic theories   8
     5. International trade   8

C. Financial Risk Management   2C-1 – 2C-14

     1. Market, interest rate, currency, liquidity, credit, price and other risks   1
     2. Means for mitigating/controlling financial risks   9

Glossary: Economic Concepts and Analysis   Glossary 2-1 – 2-5

Multiple Choice – Questions   MCQ 2-1 – 2-8

Multiple Choice – Solutions   MCQ 2-9 – 2-19

Economic Concepts and Analysis

While there are many definitions of economic theory, in general, economics is concerned with how the market process operates related to the production and consumption of goods, the allocation of scarce resources, and the transfer of wealth in a market. Economics attempts to explain how people, businesses, and the government behave in various circumstances.

There are two broad categories of economics, microeconomics, and macroeconomics. Microeconomics is concerned with how individuals or individual firms make decisions in choosing among alternative goods, such as the interactions between buyers and sellers. Macroeconomics is concerned about the economy as a whole and examines the economic activity for an entire marketplace or an entire country.

Business-related economics, which is the theoretical underpinning for the field of finance, refers to management applying both microeconomic and macroeconomic principles in analyzing and making business decisions. These decisions can include the type of product to produce, how much to produce, and the appropriate sales price. These require an analysis of demand and supply, among other economic principles.

A. Economic and Business Cycles - Measures and Indicators

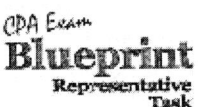

> Identify and define business cycles (trough, expansion, peak, recession) and conditions and government policies that impact an entity's industry or operations.

Demand and supply of goods and services are used to determine many factors within economics (i.e., the market price of goods and services). To begin a review in economics for the CPA exam, an overview of demand and supply will establish a basis for the other areas covered in this chapter.

1. Demand
   The downward sloping demand curve indicates that for specific levels of the quantity demanded; there is an inverse relationship (where other demand variables are constant) to the corresponding price that people are willing to pay. The demand curve is shown as:

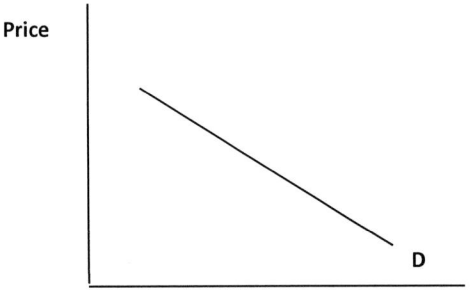

   a. A **change in the price** of goods and services will cause a **movement along the demand curve** (change in quantity demanded). For price increases, there will be a corresponding movement up the demand curve, indicating lower demand. The opposite is true for price decreases. For movements along the demand curve, the price will change first, and the change in demand will follow.

   b. A **change in demand, not resulting from a price change**, will cause a **shift in the demand curve** (change in demand). This shift in demand takes place, causing consumers to purchase more or less of the goods and services, even though the price stays the same.

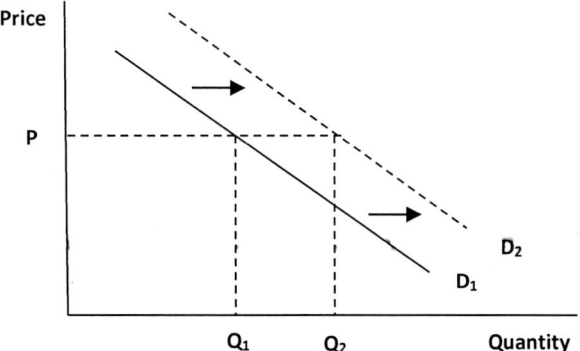

With a shift in the demand curve, the demand changes first and it is not a result of a price change. As shown in the graph above, as the demand increased, it causes a shift in the demand curve to the right (from D1 to D2), and the price (P) does not change. The opposite would occur if demand decreased, causing the demand curve to shift to the left.

Shifts in the demand curve (due to changes other than price) are caused by factors including: the availability of substitute products (related products that replace the original product, i.e. Pepsi to Coke) or complimentary products (related products that are used in conjunction with the original product, i.e., potato chips) and changes in income or consumer preferences.

Further, the concepts of normal goods, inferior goods, and luxury goods also affect the demand curve as well. Normal goods or services experience increases in quantity demanded as the real income of an individual or economy rises. Food staples and clothing are examples of normal goods. Inferior goods and services, on the other hand, includes goods and services that people only purchase because they can't afford higher-quality substitutes such as off-brand goods. Lastly, luxury goods, as the name implies, suggest an increase in demand for an increase in income. Examples would include HD televisions, Rolex watches, etc. The following table describes these relationships.

Determinants (other than price) that shift demand curve	Relationship of shift in demand curve	Result
Disposable income	Normal goods: Direct Inferior goods: Inverse Luxury goods: Direct+	• For normal goods, an increase in disposable income tends to cause the demand curve to shift to the right as consumers will pay more for these goods than they did with lower disposable income. • With an increase in disposable income, demand for inferior goods (i.e., instead of taking public transportation, which is the inferior good, you purchase a car and drive yourself) would decrease and shift the demand curve to the left. • For luxury goods, an increase in income causes a bigger percentage increase in demand. This results in an upward sloping demand curve.
Consumer preferences (tastes)	Direct	• As consumer preferences change so does the demand relative to the preference for the product.
Prices of other goods that are substitutes	Direct	• If the price of coffee increases, the demand for tea will increase.
Prices of other goods that are complements	Inverse	• If the price of ice cream decreases, the demand for chocolate syrup and toppings will increase.
Size of market	Direct	• Demand will increase and shift the demand curve to the right when there is an increase in market size because there are more people to purchase the product.
Anticipated price changes	Direct	• Demand will increase and shift the demand curve to the right when there is an expected future increase in the price of a product and consumers will buy at the lower price now.

c. **Substitution effect and income effect**
   1) With the **substitution effect**, if there is an increase in the price of a product, the product becomes more expensive than its substitute (alternative/similar) products, which will cause people to purchase the alternative/similar product. For example, if a consumer always buys Skippy peanut butter and the price of Jif peanut butter decreases, it becomes a substitute for Skippy, and the consumer will buy Jif.
   2) With the **income effect**, where income remains constant, if there is a decrease in the price of a good, people will either buy more of that product, or due to the decrease in the price of that product, would buy more of other goods because their real income has technically increased (they have more money to spend due to the price decrease).

d. The **law of diminishing marginal utility** states that as a consumer increases consumption of a product, there is a reduction in the marginal utility (satisfaction) that the consumer gets out of consuming each additional amount. For example, even for chocolate lovers, the candy will be less and less appetizing, as a consumer eats more of it.

e. The **price elasticity (sensitivity) of demand** is a measurement that considers a change in quantity demanded to a change in price. The formula is:

$$E_D = \frac{\%\text{ change in quantity demanded}}{\%\text{ change in price}}$$

> *Hint:* Think of this formula as the percent change in the "run" (X-axis) over the "rise" (Y-axis) in the demand curve graph.

   1) **Arc elasticity** a method of calculating the price elasticity as a percentage change between two points using the relationship between the average price and quality to find the curve's average elasticity. This shows the arc of the curve between the points.

   The formula is:

   $$E_D = \frac{\text{Change in quantity demanded}}{\text{Average quantity}} \div \frac{\text{Change in price}}{\text{Average price}}$$

   2) A product is **elastic** if a small change in price results in a large change in quantity demanded. A product is **inelastic** if a large change in price results in small change in quantity demanded.

   If $E_D > 1$, then elastic (sensitive to price changes)
   If $E_D = 1$, then unitary (neither sensitive nor insensitive)
   If $E_D < 1$, then inelastic (insensitive to price changes)

   A high price elasticity of demand indicates that customers can switch between products due to the availability of substitutes. For example, if a product with a high price elasticity of demand decreases in price, then consumers will switch that product as an acceptable substitute, and therefore, demand will increase even greater than the decrease in price.

   3) Price elasticity of demand is important in determining the relationship of **how revenue will change as a result of price changes** and the related change in quantity demanded. Price elasticity of demand is used by firms in product pricing to assist in determining the sales impact on pricing decisions. For, example a firm will charge lower prices if demand for their product is elastic.

Change in Price	$E_D > 1$	$E_D = 1$	$E_D < 1$
	Elastic	Unitary	Inelastic
Price increases ↑	Revenue decreases ↓	No change in revenue	Revenue increases ↑
Price decreases ↓	Revenue increases ↑	No change in revenue	Revenue decreases ↓

4) Some of the factors that affect how much the quantity demanded changes as a result of a change in price include:
   i. The number of close substitutes because demand is more elastic with more substitutes on the market.
   ii. If it is a luxury as opposed to necessities because necessities have inelastic demand and luxury goods tend to be more elastic.

Multiple Choice

BEC 2-Q1

f. The **income elasticity of demand** describes how demand changes relative to changes in income per the following formula:

$$E_I = \frac{\% \text{ change in quantity demanded}}{\% \text{ change in income}}$$

Where:
$E_I > 0$ for normal goods, where the demand will increase as income increases (i.e., steak).

$E_I < 0$ for inferior goods, where the demand will decrease as income increases (i.e., hot dogs).

(NOTE: There is another concept called "Superior Goods" which is similar to Normal Goods but has the added characteristic that its share of income also goes up. $E_I > 1$)

g. The **cross elasticity of demand** measures the rate of change for a product, relative to a change in the price of another competing or similar product.

$$E_{XY} = \frac{\% \text{ change in quantity demanded of product X}}{\% \text{ change in price of product Y}}$$

Where:
$E_{XY} > 0$, the products are substitutes. For example, if the cross elasticity of demand for Skippy peanut butter in relation to Jif peanut butter was .9, then a 4% increase in the price of Skippy would translate into a 3.6% (4% x .9) increase in demand for Jif).

$E_{XY} = 0$, the products are unrelated goods
$E_{XY} < 0$, the products are complements. For example, if the price of hotdogs increases, the demand for hot dog relish will decrease.

h. The **consumption function** shows the relationship of consumption and disposable income, holding constant factors such as wealth, price level, and future income prospects that could also impact consumption. The formula is:

$$C = C_0 + C_1 Y_D$$

Where:
C = Consumption for the period
Y_D = Disposable income for the period
C_0 = Constant
C_1 = Slope of consumption function (Marginal propensity to consume, MPC)

i. For every dollar that a consumer earns, they can either spend it or save it. The **marginal propensity to consume (MPC)** measures the change in spending as income changes. The **marginal propensity to save (MPS)** measures the change in savings as income changes.

$$MPC + MPS \text{ must equal } 1$$

In economics, if a consumer does not spend the money earned, it is considered to be saved. For example, if MPC is .7, then MPS would be .3, and for every dollar of income, $0.70 is spent, and $0.30 is saved.

j. **Market demand** is the total of all individual demand curves within the marketplace. It is a downward sloping demand curve, where price and quantity demanded are inversely related. The market demand curve shows the quantity demanded by everyone in the market for every price point.

2. Supply
The upward sloping **supply curve** indicates that for specific levels of the quantity supplied; there is a direct relationship to the corresponding price of the goods or service. The supply curve is shown as:

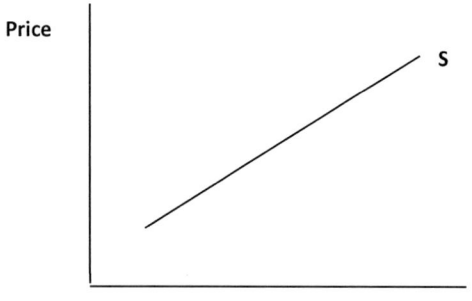

a. A **change in the price** of goods and services will cause a **movement along the supply curve** (change in quantity supplied). For price increases, there will be a corresponding movement up the supply curve, indicating a higher amount supplied. The opposite is true for price decreases. For movements along the supply curve, the price will change first, and the change in supply will follow.

b. A **change in supply, not resulting from a price change**, will cause a **shift in the supply curve** (change in supply). This shift in supply takes place, causing suppliers to produce more or less of the goods and services, even though the price stays the same.

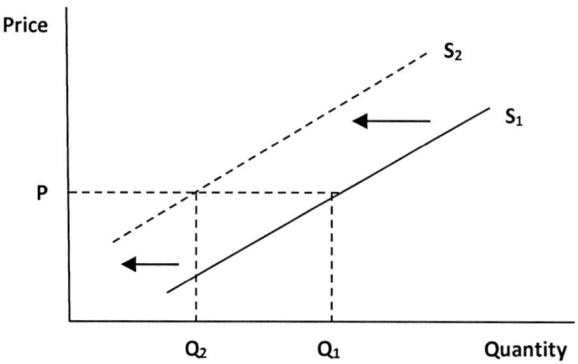

With a shift in the supply curve, the supply changes first and it is not a result of a price change. As shown in the graph above, if the cost of producing the goods increases, the amount supplied will decrease, causing the supply curve to shift to the left (from S_1 to S_2). The opposite would occur if the cost of producing the goods decreased, causing the supply curve to shift to the right.

Shifts in the supply curve (due to changes other than price) are caused by factors such as the cost to produce the product, regulatory or governmental actions, and prices of other goods, as shown in the chart below:

Determinants (other than price) that shift supply curve	Relationship of shift in supply curve	Result
Demand or prices of other goods	Inverse	• If demand for one of their products decreases, a supplier will change focus to increase the supply of a product that is more in demand. • If a supplier can produce other products that are more profitable, they will shift resources toward supplying the more lucrative the product.
Change in production costs	Inverse	• If production costs increase, a supplier will produce less of the product.
Technological advances	Direct	• Technological advances often lead to more efficiencies and lower costs of production, causing the supply curve to shift to the right, increasing supply.
Anticipated price changes	Direct	• If a supplier expects the price of the goods to increase in the future, they will produce more now in anticipation of the price increase.
Government taxes	Inverse	• An increase in taxes will reduce income and result in lower demand for the goods due to less consumer disposable income. The supplier will decrease the supply of the product.
Government subsidies	Direct	• An increase in subsidies will lead a supplier to produce more goods because the subsidy can be used to offset some of the production costs.

c. The **elasticity of supply** is a measurement that considers a change in quantity supplied compared to a change in the price of the product. The formula is:

$$Es = \frac{\% \text{ change in quantity supplied}}{\% \text{ change in price}}$$

1) A product is **elastic** if a small change in price results in a large change in quantity supplied. A product is **inelastic** if a large change in price results in a small change in quantity supplied.

If Es > 1, then elastic (sensitive to price changes)
If Es = 1, then unitary (neither sensitive nor insensitive)
If Es < 1, then inelastic (not sensitive to price changes)

d. When a supplier does not face the threat of substitute products, they can influence or control buyers. Even if the supplier increases prices or decreases the quality of the product or service, buyers have no substitutes for the product or service and must accept whatever the supplier produces or go without it.

e. In macroeconomics, **Market supply** is the total of all individual supply curves within the marketplace. It is an upward sloping supply curve, where price and quantity supplied are directly related. The market supply curve shows the quantity supplied by all suppliers in the market for every price point.

Multiple Choice

BEC 2-Q2

3. Business cycles
   Over time, the economy will go through a series of economic expansions and contractions. A business cycle follows fluctuations in economic activity over a period of time. Business cycles can be graphically shown as follows:

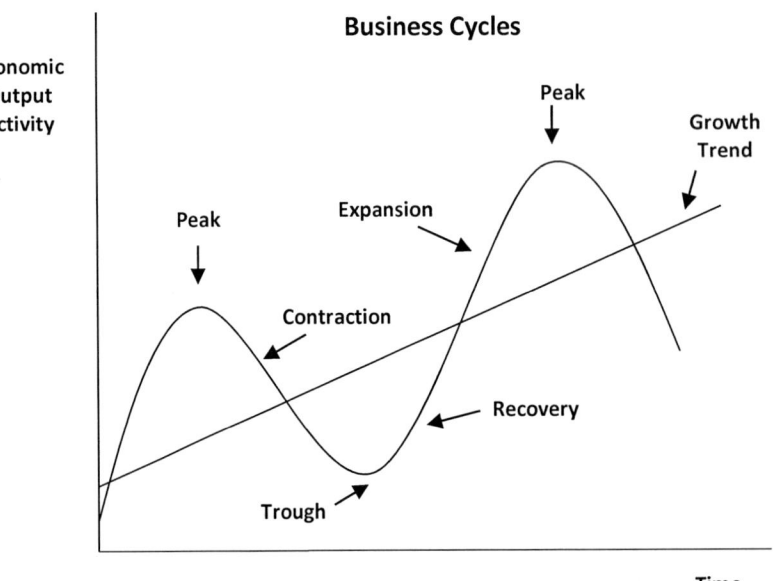

a. The growth trend line shown in the business cycle graph indicates the long-term movement of the economy. At any point along this growth line, the economy will be in one of four "phases": peak, contraction, trough, or expansion. These four phases occur at irregular intervals and can extend for different lengths of time.
   1) **Peak**: The highest point of economic activity, which can indicate there may be production capacity constraints and shortages, leading to higher production costs and prices for goods. In the past, some peaks are labeled with the term "irrational exuberance" which means that the market is considered somewhat overvalued.
   2) **Contraction**: Following a peak, the economy begins to slow. It can include lower corporate growth and profits. Economic activity will go lower than the long-term growth line.
   3) **Trough**: Lowest point in the economic activity which can indicate excess production capacity and inventory that result in cost-cutting and higher unemployment, leading to a recession.
      i. **Recession**: Defined as two consecutive quarters, or six months of declining gross domestic product (GDP, covered later in this section).
      ii. **Depression**: Defined as a prolonged and excessive recession which lasts for two or more years.
   4) **Expansion**: Economy begins to expand and grow (periods of economic prosperity). Economic activity will go higher than the long-term growth trend line.

> *Hint*: Some economists categorize business cycles via five phases in this order:
> 1) Expansion, 2) Peak, 3) Recession, 4) Trough, and 5) Recovery

b. The variations between business cycle phases are related to the duration and intensity of each cycle. Each phase and each phase's timeframe within a business cycle is measured by the U.S. Department of Commerce Bureau of Economic Analysis (BEA). The BEA's national economic statistics provide a comprehensive view of U.S. production, consumption, investment, exports and imports, and income and saving. These statistics are best known by summary measures such as gross domestic product (GDP), corporate profits, personal income and spending, and personal saving.

c. A CPA performing an audit must understand the nature of the entity's business, including business cycles and reasons for business fluctuations. This understanding assists auditors to be able to accurately interpret fluctuations in financial statement elements such as fluctuations in sales revenue, net income, cash and other monetary assets. In addition, it would assist the auditor in understanding the cash flow mixes from operating, investing, and financing activities.

Multiple Choice

BEC 2-Q3 through BEC 2-Q4

4. Gross Domestic Product (GDP)
Gross domestic product (GDP) is the total output of goods and services produced in the domestic economy during a particular time period. For U.S. GDP, the goods and services produced are ones that have been produced within the U.S. borders, regardless of ownership of the resources to produce the goods and services. For example, the production done in the U.S. from both foreign companies and U.S. companies are combined to determine the U.S. GDP. The production done by U.S. companies in foreign countries is not included in the U.S. GDP. (That situation would be part of the Gross National Product (GNP) which is defined as the total value of all products/services produced by a country's means of production during a specific period). Since the GDP includes all sectors of the economy, GDP is one of the best and most common measurements of the overall condition of the economy.

The main components of the economy that are *not* included in the calculation of GDP are:
- Barter transactions: Represent the trading of one good or service for another. For example, firm A gives its available advertising space to firm B in exchange firm A receives a certain amount of goods produced by firm B.
- Unpaid labor: Examples include volunteers and homemakers.
- Black market: Examples include stolen goods and other illegal activities.

According to the National Income and Product Accounts (NIPA), the total economic output of four sectors; 1) consumers, 2) business entities, 3) federal, state and local governments and 4) foreign activity, make up the components of GDP. There are also various terms related to GDP, including:

a. **Nominal GDP**: The unadjusted GDP measures the total amount of goods and services produced at the prices that were in effect when they were produced. Nominal GDP is stated at current prices and is considered unadjusted because it has not been adjusted for inflation.
b. **Real (actual) GDP**: The adjusted GDP that measures the total amount of goods and services produced by using the price index (constant dollar) to eliminate the effects of inflation.
c. **GDP Deflator**: The price index used to convert nominal GDP to real GDP. The price index is derived from all the goods and services that are included in GDP. Using the GDP deflator, real GDP is calculated using the following formula:

$$\text{Real GDP} = \frac{\text{Nominal GDP}}{\text{GDP Deflator}} \times 100$$

d. **Potential GDP**: The maximum amount of goods and services produced at a constant inflation rate, with ideal production and high employment levels.

e. **GDP Gap:** Calculated as the difference between real GDP (actual output of the economy) and the potential GDP (full capacity). The GDP gap is often used as a measurement of unemployment and the inefficiencies of government and business, because real GDP will seldom equal potential GDP. The formula for determining GDP gap is:

GDP gap = Real GDP – Potential GDP

A **positive gap** is when the actual output is greater than the potential output (or full capacity). It indicates the economy is in an expansionary phase, and the demand is increasing faster than supply. This means the economy is at full employment and there is still a demand for more workers. A **negative gap** value indicates that the economy is operating without utilizing all available resources (e.g., high unemployment or spare capacity). This could also indicate a recession or weak demand.

Neither a positive gap or negative gap is ideal, both indicating inefficiencies.

Multiple Choice

BEC 2-Q5

f. There are two ways to calculate GDP, the **income (output) approach,** and the **expenditure (input) approach**.
  1) The income (output) approach combines all business profits (corporations and proprietors) and includes such items as wages, rents, dividends and interest. GDP, using the income approach is calculated as follows:

	Compensation to Employees
+	Corporate Profits
+	Net Interest
+	Proprietor's Income
+	Rental Income of Persons
=	National Income
+	Indirect Taxes
–	Other, Including Statistical Discrepancy
=	Net National Product
+	Consumption of Fixed Capital
=	Gross National Product
+	Payments of Factor Income to Other Countries
–	Receipts of Labor Income from Other Countries
=	Gross Domestic Product

  2) The expenditure (input) approach combines all the amounts to purchase goods and services from government purchases, net exports, personal consumption, domestic fixed investment and changes in inventories. Calculate GDP using the income approach as follows:

	C	Personal consumption expenditures
+ or –	I	Gross private domestic fixed investment (business & residential, including changes in business inventories, which may be + or –)
+	G	Government Purchases (federal, state, & local)
+ or –	N	Net exports of goods and services (may be + or –)
=	GDP	Gross Domestic Product

> **Hint:** For the expenditure approach, use the following equation:
>
> $$GDP = C + I + G + N$$
>
> Where:
> - C = Personal consumption expenditures
> - I = Gross private domestic fixed investment
> - G = Government purchases
> - N = Net exports (gross exports – gross imports)

Multiple Choice

BEC 2-Q6

g. Spending by consumers, businesses, and the government
In general, for the year 2016, expenditures that comprise GDP are approximately 70% from consumer spending, 16 % from business investment (i.e., inventory and property, plant, and equipment), an 18 % from federal, state, and local government spending and a -4% from net imports.

h. During the expansion phase of a business cycle, GDP rises and unemployment decreases. Likewise, the reverse is true in a contraction phase. When economic activity is shown above the growth trend line, typically unemployment will decrease. This can be explained by Okun's Law, which states that there is a relationship between GDP and unemployment. This relationship varies by country. In the U.S., Okun's law estimates that for each 2% increase in GDP, unemployment will fall by 1%. Conversely, if unemployment increases by 1% in the U.S., the country's GDP would decline by 2%. Keep in mind is that these are estimates and economists do not universally accept the actual percentages.

i. The **multiplier effect** is the effect that spending (consumer, business, and government) has on gross domestic product (GDP). The multiplier effect shows that an increase in spending will lead to an even greater increase in economic activity (i.e., $1 increase in government spending leads to $1.10 increase in real GDP). The multiplier effect calculation is derived from MPC + MPS = 1, which was covered earlier in part A of this chapter. Under the multiplier effect, MPC is always less than 1 because there is a part of consumers' income which is saved. The multiplier formula is:

$$\text{Multiplier} = \frac{1}{(1 - MPC)}$$

The resulting impact on real GDP is then calculated as:

Real GDP change = Multiplier x Spending change

For example, if MPC is .6 and the change in spending is $50, the real GDP change is calculated as:

Real GDP change = [(1 / (1 - .6)] x $50 = $125

j. The **accelerator effect** relates to the increase of a firm's investments in production that are done to meet the rate of growth in demand of goods. As consumer spending increases, firms will meet this increase in demand through additional investment.

> **Hint:** The multiplier effect is about changes in GDP and the accelerator effect is about changes in investment.

5. Cyclical and non-cyclical businesses
   a. A **cyclical business** is sensitive to business cycles. Revenues for cyclical businesses are typically higher during economic expansion and lower in economic contractions. During an economic expansion, businesses expand and build new property, plant, and equipment and hire more workers. As a result, people have more disposable income and are usually willing to spend more money. Examples of cyclical businesses include:
      - Airlines
      - Automobile manufacturers
      - Homebuilders

      When economic activity contracts, cyclical businesses will tend to produce less in the contractionary phase, which will lead to reductions in compensation and increased layoffs.

   b. A **non-cyclical business** is not affected by business cycles because demand for their products continues, regardless of the economic phase. The products produced by non-cyclical businesses are typically products necessary for daily life such as food, water, electricity, soap, and toothpaste. These are products that no matter what phase the economy is in, consumers will still purchase them. Examples of non-cyclical businesses include:
      - Utilities
      - Healthcare
      - Appliances
      - Personal and household products

      A defensive business is another term used for non-cyclical businesses that are not sensitive to business cycles.

BEC 2-Q7

6. Aggregate demand and supply
   a. **Aggregate demand** (AD) is the total of all goods and services in the entire economy that is demanded at any given price and any given period. Aggregate demand is the demand for real GDP of an entire country. The aggregate demand curve depicts the relationship between price levels and the output that companies will produce. The two are inversely related as demonstrated by a downward sloping line

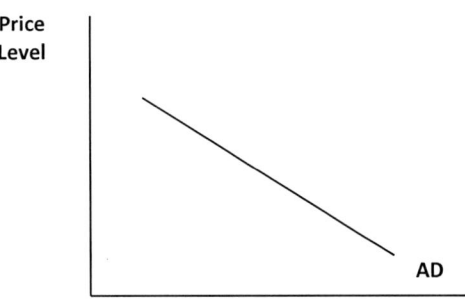

   b. **Aggregate supply** (AS) is the total of all goods and services in the entire economy that firms are willing to produce at any given price and any given period. The short-run aggregate supply curve (SRAS) is upward sloping and depicts the relationship between price levels and the output that companies will produce. Production costs such as raw materials, labor wages, subsidies, and taxes affect the aggregate supply curve. The price level and output quantity are directly related, where higher prices will lead firms to produce more due to the increase in aggregate demand.

The long-run aggregate supply curve (LRAS) depicts the potential output level in the economy. The long-run aggregate supply curve is vertical because, in the long run, the only way to increase production is for firms to increase their spending on labor and capital. Therefore, in the long run, the aggregate supply curve is impacted only from labor and capital and not from the price level. The LRAS is affected by activity that changes the potential production of the entire economy. The LRAS curve is at the intersection of AD and SRAS. The LRAS curve does not change if the general price level changes.

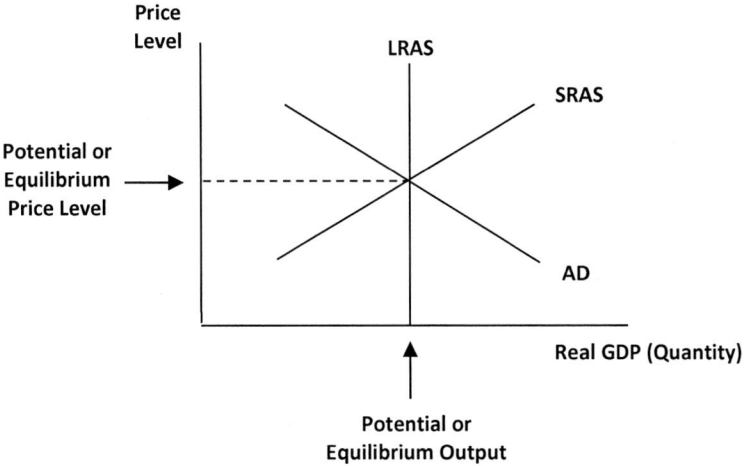

c. Aggregate demand and aggregate supply effect on business cycles
Business cycles occur due to shifts in the AD and the SRAS. **LRAS does not impact business cycles because it relates to long-term economic conditions.**

The following chart summarizes the result of shifts in the aggregate demand and aggregate supply curves.

Shifts in Aggregate Demand and Aggregate Supply Curves		
Aggregate demand increase: AD Curve shifts to right	• AD increases • GDP increases • Price increases	• Lower excess firm capacity • Increase in firm profits • Business cycle expansion
Aggregate demand decrease: AD curve shifts to left	• AD decreases • GDP decreases • Price decreases	• Excess firm capacity • Decrease in firm profits • Business cycle contraction • Risk of recession
Aggregate supply increase: SRAS curve shifts to right	• SRAS increases • GDP increases • Price decreases	• Increased production • Lower unemployment • Increase in firm profits • Business cycle expansion
Aggregate supply decrease: SRAS curve shifts to left	• SRAS decreases • GDP decreases • Price increases	• Excess firm capacity • Decrease in firm profits • Business cycle contraction • Risk of recession

d. Factors that cause shifts in aggregate demand and aggregate supply curves

Factors that cause Aggregate Demand to Increase (AD Curve shifts to right)	
Interest rate effect: Decrease in real interest rates	• Borrowing increases • Spending increases
Consumer confidence* effect: Increase in consumer confidence increases	• Spending increases
Wealth effect: Increase in wealth	• Spending increases
Foreign currency effect: Domestic price level decreases compared to foreign prices	• Exports increase • Imports decrease
Tax Effect: Decrease in consumer taxes	• Spending increases
Government spending effect: Increase in government spending	• National output increases

Factors that cause Aggregate Demand to decrease (AD Curve shifts to left)	
Interest rate effect: Increase in real interest rates	• Borrowing decreases • Spending decreases
Consumer confidence* effect: Decrease in consumer confidence increases	• Spending decreases
Wealth effect: Decrease in wealth	• Spending decreases
Foreign currency effect: Domestic price level increases compared to foreign prices	• Exports decrease • Imports increase
Tax Effect: Increase in consumer taxes	• Spending decreases
Government spending effect: decrease in government spending	• National output decreases

*The consumer confidence index is a measure of consumer optimism with the general economy's performance, based on consumer behavior with regard to savings and spending.

Factors that cause Aggregate Supply to Increase (SRAS Curve shifts to right)	
Supply shock effect: Increase in material for production	• Output increases
Cost of production input effect: Cost decreases (i.e. raw material, labor, taxes)	• Output increases

Factors that cause Aggregate Supply to Decrease (SRAS Curve shifts to left)	
Supply shock effect: decrease in material for production	• Output decreases
Cost of production input effect: Cost increases (i.e. raw material, labor, taxes)	• Output decreases

7. Economic indicators and measures

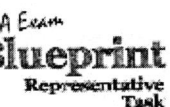

Use appropriate inputs to calculate economic measures and indicators (e.g., Nominal and Real GDP, Consumer Price Index, Aggregate Demand Curve, Money Supply, etc.) and apply leading, coincident and lagging indicators (e.g., bond yields, new housing starts, personal income, unemployment, etc.).

Use economic measures and indicators to explain the impact on an entity's industry and operations due to changes in:
- government fiscal policy, monetary policy, regulations, trade controls and other actions.
- business cycles and economic conditions, caused by factors such as exchange rates, inflation, productivity, state of the global economy, unemployment levels, etc.

a. Economic indicators
Economists continually predict economic activity using **economic indicators**. The Conference Board, a private independent research organization, developed and maintains a list of economic indicators, classified as leading indicators, lagging indicators and coincident indicators, as follows:

1) Leading indicators
Indicators that predict or signal future economic events are called leading indicators.
- Average weekly hours (manufacturing)
- Average new weekly jobless claims for unemployment insurance
- Manufacturer's new orders for consumer goods/materials
- New order index (compares vendors with increased orders and decreased orders each month)
- Manufacturer's new orders for non-defense capital goods (excluding aircraft)
- Building permits for new private housing units
- Stock prices, (e.g., Standard & Poor's 500 stock index)
- Leading credit index (e.g., LIBOR less 3-month treasury bill yield spread)
- Interest rate spread (e.g., 10-year treasury bonds less federal funds)
- Index of consumer expectations

2) Lagging indicators
Indicators that follow economic events are called lagging indicators.
- Average duration of unemployment
- Inventories-to-sales ratio (manufacturing and trade)
- Labor cost per unit of output (manufacturing)
- Average bank prime rate
- Commercial and industrial loans outstanding
- Consumer installment credit to personal income ratio
- Consumer price index (CPI) for services

3) Coincident indicators
Indicators that occur at about the same time as economic events are called coincident indicators.
- Employees on nonagricultural payrolls
- Personal income less transfer payments
- Industrial production
- Manufacturing and trade sales

Hint: CPA candidates don't need to memorize this list but be familiar the indicators which are utilized to gauge the economy as a whole. These indicators predict economic performance and may be used by businesses to make informed decisions. Typically, businesses are not so concerned with lagging indicators, and much more concerned with leading indicators as a way to forecast future demand.

b. Economic measures related to GDP

As previously mentioned, GDP is the most used economic measurement of the economy's production and performance. Other measures that are related to GDP include Gross National Product (GNP), Net Domestic Product (NDP), Net National Product (NNP), National Income (NI), Personal Income (PI), and Disposable Income (DI).

1) **Gross National Product (GNP)** represents the total amount of all final goods and services produced by citizens of a country over a specific time period, regardless of their location (even if they were located in a foreign country) during the period.

Goods and Services Produced by...	U.S. GDP	U.S. GNP
U.S. companies in foreign countries	Excluded	Included
Foreign companies in the U.S.	Included	Excluded

2) **Net Domestic Product (NDP)** is calculated by taking GDP and subtracting depreciation. This depreciation represents the amount required to replace the depreciated assets and is also called a capital consumption allowance (accounting depreciation).

```
   Gross Domestic Product
 − Depreciation (Capital Cost Allowance)
 = Net Domestic Product
```

3) **Net National Product (NNP)** represents the amount of all final goods and services produced by a country's citizens (regardless if they are in the U.S. or a foreign country), minus the economic depreciation. Economic depreciation is different from depreciation used in accounting. Economic depreciation is the amount of GNP required for the purchase of new goods and services due to the usage, obsolescence, or decline in value of the nation's fixed capital assets.

```
   Gross National Product
 − Economic Depreciation
 = Net National Product
```

> *Hint*: Be sure to remember the following distinction:
>
> Accounting depreciation — Systematic allocation of fixed asset cost over its estimated useful life, with periodic charges to expense.
>
> Economic depreciation — Decline in value of capital assets, taking into account its productivity and other factors affecting it. For example, a piece of property declines in value due to a major road that is constructed next to it.

4) **National Income (NI)** is calculated by taking NNP and subtracting business sales taxes.

5) **Personal Income (PI)** is the total income received by households and non-corporate businesses. The income may or may not be earned from productive activities. It measures the actual amount of income paid out. After adjusting for income taxes, personal income is the basis for consumption expenditures in GDP.

6) **Personal Disposable Income (PDI)** is calculated by taking personal income and subtracting income taxes. After adjusting for income taxes, personal income is the basis for consumption expenditures in GDP.

c. Unemployment measures
The unemployment rate is calculated as the percent of unemployed people divided by the total labor force (includes all 16+-year-old, non-institutionalized labor). There are three types of unemployment: structural unemployment, frictional unemployment, and cyclical unemployment.

1) **Structural unemployment** occurs when there is not a match-up of worker skills with job requirements due to things like technological advances, or if the workers who are not employed do not live near the job opportunities. Often, workers in this category will acquire new skills to find a new job.

2) **Frictional unemployment** is considered normal in the economy. It results from temporary worker transitions as they move from one job to another. Workers could be in transition due to voluntarily changing jobs, or being laid off.

3) **Cyclical unemployment** results from decreases in real GDP. Cyclical unemployment would increase in recessionary phases and decrease in expansionary phases.

Real GDP	Unemployment
Increases	Decreases
Decreases	Increases

4) **Full employment** occurs when there is no cyclical unemployment. Periods of full employment can occur even with remaining structural and frictional unemployment as full employment does not mean 100% employed.

d. Inflationary measures
Inflation is an increase over time of the general or aggregate price level in the economy, causing an increase in the prices of goods and services. Inflation equates to an increase in the cost of living, which is a decline in the purchasing power of money. The Federal Reserve (the U.S.'s central bank) controls inflation by tightening or loosening the money supply (money allowed into the market). Tightening the money supply generally reduces the risk of inflation. Loosening the money supply generally increases the risk of inflation.

1) **Deflation** is the opposite of inflation and comes about when there is a decrease in the general or aggregate price level in the economy. Deflation causes a decrease in the prices of goods and services as well as, a general decline in interest rates. During a deflationary time, businesses will be reluctant to purchase new property, plant, and equipment because the cost of the equipment is expected to continue to decline. Businesses will also be reluctant to borrow money because they do not want to pay back the borrowed funds in the future with money that, due to deflation, has more purchasing power than the principal did when borrowed.

Multiple Choice

BEC 2-Q8

2) **Hyperinflation** occurs when the price of goods and services sharply increase (usually 50%+ per month).

3) **Consumer Price Index (CPI)** is the measurement used to gauge inflation (i.e., the inflation rate) by taking the percentage change in the CPI from one period, over another period. CPI is defined as the current prices paid by consumers for a fixed basket of goods and services, relative to those prices during the same period in a previous year. Keep in mind, however, that the weight of the individual goods, as well as the basket makeup, can change from month to month. The inflation rate formula is:

$$\text{Inflation Rate (Change in CPI)} = \frac{\text{CPI current period} - \text{CPI previous period}}{\text{CPI previous period}} \times 100$$

The CPI is calculated by the U. S. Bureau of Labor Statistics on a monthly basis.

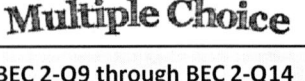

BEC 2-Q9 through BEC 2-Q14

4) **Producer Price Index (PPI)** is defined as the current wholesale prices for a fixed basket of goods and services produced by firms, relative to those prices during the same period in a previous year.

5) The **Phillips Curve** shows the inverse relationship between inflation and unemployment. When unemployment is high, inflation usually decreases, and when unemployment is low, inflation usually increases.

6) The **causes of inflation** can be broken down into two main types, Demand-Pull and Cost-Push.

   i. **Demand-Pull Inflation**: Inflation caused by excess aggregate demand which is greater than normal output (supply) at full employment, usually when the economy is growing too fast. This occurs at the peak of a business cycle when real GDP is greater than potential GDP. Prices will typically increase due to labor shortages. Demand-Pull inflation can be caused by:
      a) Decreases in taxes
      b) Increased consumer confidence from having more wealth (i.e., from tax decreases)
      c) Increased government spending
      d) Increases in money supply

   ii. **Cost-Push Inflation**: Inflation caused by a shortage of output (supply) which drives up prices for those goods and services. The demand typically remains constant but, with less output, producers increase the price. Examples include:
      a) Wage increases that firms pass on to consumers in the way of higher prices for their goods and services
      b) Increase in gasoline prices

7) Monetary and non-monetary assets and liabilities
The purchasing power of money decreases with inflation (the two are inversely related). Inflation affects both monetary and non-monetary assets and liabilities.

Monetary assets and liabilities are either already cash or, can be readily converted into cash. Monetary items include cash, accounts receivable, notes receivable, investments, accounts payable, notes payable, sales taxes payable, and other accrued expenses. Fixed interest rate monetary assets lose their value as inflation increases (e.g., corporate bonds). Conversely, holding fixed interest rate monetary liabilities (e.g., mortgages or corporate debt) in periods of inflation make it easier to pay back the debt with devalued (or inflated) dollars.

Non-monetary assets and liabilities include inventory, fixed assets, warranties payable, and deferred income tax credits. Nonmonetary items cannot be easily converted to cash and do not have a precise dollar value (e.g., the dollar value may fluctuate).

In periods of inflation, it is better to invest in non-monetary assets, which will hold their value because their prices will also increase with inflation.

Multiple Choice

BEC 2-Q15

8) **Money supply** is categorized into three groups; M1, M2, and M3.

M1	Includes currency, demand deposits and travelers checks. It does not include CDs or savings accounts. (Money in Circulation)
M2	Equals M1 plus savings accounts, mutual fund accounts, CDs less than $100,000 and short-term (i.e., 24 hour) money market accounts. (Near Money)
M3	Equals M2 plus CDs greater than $100,000 and other large time deposits. (Near, Near Money)

Shown another way:

$$\begin{aligned}
& \text{Currency} \\
+\ & \underline{\text{Demand Deposits}} \\
=\ & M_1 \\
+\ & \text{Savings Accounts} \\
+\ & \underline{\text{Small Time Deposits } (< \$100{,}000)} \\
=\ & M_2 \\
+\ & \underline{\text{Large Time Deposits } (\geq \$100{,}000)} \\
=\ & M_3
\end{aligned}$$

9) Interest rates
Interest rates are expressed as a percentage and represent what is charged or paid for the use of money. Changes in interest rates are often the result of actions by the Federal Reserve, or inflation. The main difference between the **nominal interest rate** and the **real interest rate** is how the inflation rate affects each one.
   i. The nominal interest rate is not adjusted for inflation and is the rate of interest charged by a lender and paid by the borrower in loan transactions. It is calculated as the real interest rate, plus the inflation rate. Credit risk (the risk that the borrower will not pay the loan interest and principal) will often make the rate charged for a loan higher than the nominal rate. Nominal interest rates are the rates quoted in financial newspapers and banks.
   ii. The real interest rate is an inflation-adjusted interest rate. For example, if a business takes out a loan at 6% nominal interest and the inflation rate is 2%, the effective real interest rate on the loan is 4%.

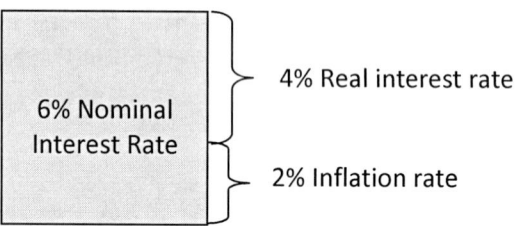

   iii. Nominal interest rates and inflation have a direct relationship. When the inflation rate decreases, the nominal rate decreases by the same amount and the opposite holds true for increases in the inflation rate.

The demand for cash is inversely related to interest rates. For example, if interest rates increase, the holder of money would be better off investing the money to earn the higher rate of interest.

Multiple Choice

BEC 2-Q16

10) Federal government **budget surpluses and deficits**
A budget deficit occurs when tax revenue does not cover governmental spending. When a deficit occurs, the government could put more money into the supply (print more) but, that will increase inflation. Usually, the government issues treasury bonds to borrow funds to finance a deficit. Interest rates are affected by the amount of governmental borrowings. An increase in the supply of money generally lowers interest rates, which stimulates consumer spending and increases production by firms.

A budget surplus is the opposite of a budget deficit and occurs when tax revenue, in total, is greater than governmental spending.

e. Monetary policy
Monetary policy relates to the Federal Reserve's programs to influence the amount of money and credit in the economy. The goal of monetary policy is to manage long-term economic growth, keep inflation under control, maximize employment, and maintain price stability. The three Federal Reserve tools of monetary policy are open market operations, reserve requirements, and the discount rate.

1) **Open market operations** are the most frequently used tools of monetary policy and refer to the Federal Reserve buying and selling government securities, such as treasury bonds and treasury bills, to manage the money supply and influencing short-term interest rates.

Purchases of government securities (expansionary measure)	↑ money supply	Stimulates growth	↓ firm's cost of capital (interest rates) Results in: ↑ firm investment in new equipment ↑ production ↑ aggregate demand ↑ in real GDP ↑ prices ↓ unemployment
Sales of government securities (contractionary measure)	↓ money supply	Slows the economy and inflation	↑ firm's cost of capital (interest rates) Results in: ↓ firm investment in new equipment ↓ aggregate demand ↓ real GDP ↓ prices ↑ unemployment

   i. Purchases of government securities increase the money supply, stimulate growth, and put downward pressure on short-term interest rates. This causes a firm's cost of capital to be lower, which results in additional investment in new equipment, an increase production, increase aggregate demand, increase in real GDP, increase in prices and a decrease in unemployment (expansionary measure).
   ii. Sales of government securities decrease the money supply and curtail the expansion of credit. The decrease in the money supply will increase interest rates, decrease firm investment, decrease aggregate demand, decrease real GDP, decrease prices, and cause unemployment to increase (contractionary measure).

2) The Federal Reserve establishes **reserve requirements** on banks, which represents the percentage of money in demand deposit accounts that must be held in reserve. These reserves are either held in their vaults or on deposit at the Federal Reserve. Reserve requirement changes are seldom done.
   i. If the reserve requirement increases, banks have less money to lend, which decrease the money supply.
   ii. If the reserve requirement decreases, banks have more money to lend, increasing the money supply.

3) The **discount rate** is the interest rate that the Federal Reserve charges depository banks on a short-term basis. The Federal Reserve lending at the discount rate goes along with open market operations in managing the target federal funds rate. The federal funds rate is the interest rate charged by the banks and credit unions to lend reserve balances (funds maintained at the Federal Reserve) to other banks and depository institutions overnight. Effectively, banks are borrowing from each other. In June 2017, the rate was between 1% and 1.25%.

i. If the Federal Reserve reduces the discount rate, banks that do not maintain adequate reserves would be able to borrow at a lower interest rate to boost their reserves to the minimum level. Lowering the discount rate (decreasing rates) will influence other rates charged by banks and will encourage bank lending (increasing the money supply) and consumer spending.
ii. Increasing the discount rate (increasing rates) would discourage lending (decreasing the money supply) and consumer spending.
iii. The prime rate is the interest rate that financial institutions lend to their most creditworthy customers.

To counteract a recession, the Federal Reserve would most likely decrease the discount rate it charges to banks for loans. When the Federal Reserve decreases the discount rate, banks will also decrease their interest rates. A decrease in interest rates will then increase consumer demand for capital investments that require financing (e.g., purchases of homes and automobiles).

In periods of deflation (price declines), demand decreases because consumers are less likely to buy in the short-term if they believe that prices may decline further. By increasing the money supply, more money will be available in the economy, but the level of goods and services will remain the same.

Multiple Choice

BEC 2-Q17 through BEC 2-Q19

f. Fiscal policy
Fiscal policy relates to actions taken by the government related to government spending, taxes, and subsidies. The effects of the increases and decreases in government spending, taxes, and subsidies will influence aggregate demand and inflation. Fiscal expansion is often called a "loose fiscal policy," and a fiscal contraction is often called a "tight fiscal policy."

1) **Fiscal expansion**
   i. Government spending increases, taxes decrease, or both.
   ii. Aggregate demand will increase.
   iii. Consumer spending increases because of additional disposable income.
   iv. Any increased government spending will increase the budget deficit and often leads to increased government borrowings.

2) **Fiscal contraction**
   i. Government spending decreases, taxes increase, or both.
   ii. Aggregate demand will decrease.
   iii. Consumer spending decreases because there is less disposable income.
   iv. Any decrease in government spending will decrease the budget deficit and reduce government borrowings.

B. Market Influences on Business

> Identify and define the key factors related to the economic marketplace (e.g., competition, currencies, globalization, supply and demand, trade, etc.) and how they generally apply to a business entity.

> Identify and define market influences (e.g., economic, environmental, governmental, political, legal, social and technological, etc.).

> Determine the impact of market influences on:
> - the overall economy (e.g., consumer demand, labor supply, market prices, production costs, volatility, etc.).
> - an entity's business strategy, operations and risk (e.g., increasing investment and financial leverage, innovating to develop new product offerings, seeking new foreign and domestic markets, undertaking productivity or cost-cutting initiatives, etc.).

In the section below, the various market factors and market influences are discussed regarding how each applies to the business entity, as well as the market itself. Businesses must take into account each of these factors and influences in determining the optimal business strategy.

1. Market equilibrium
   Market equilibrium is where demand is equal to supply. The **equilibrium price** and the **equilibrium supply** are at the intersection of the demand curve and the supply curve.

   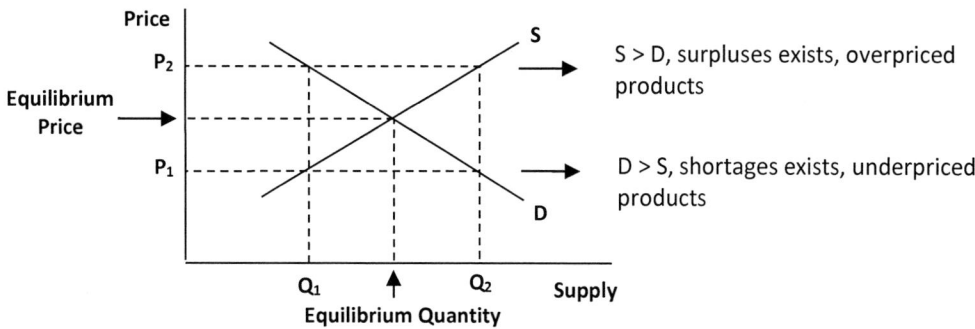

   a. **Government intervention** in the marketplace includes two scenarios that change the equilibrium price: 1) price ceilings and 2) price floors.
      1) A **price ceiling** is the highest price that is established for a good. If it is set below the equilibrium price (P_1), demand (Q_2) will be greater than supply (Q_1). In this case, firms will shift their production to other more profitable goods.
      2) A **price floor** is the minimum price that is established for a good. If it is set above the equilibrium price (P_2), supply (Q_2) will be greater than demand (Q_1). In this case, firms will continue to produce the good and surpluses will exist.

   b. There are other factors, called **externalities** that affect price. Externality is a term used to describe components of economic activity that affects parties who are not directly involved. When externalities exist, not everyone will benefit from a firm producing a good or service. Pollution is a good example of a **negative externality**, where consumers purchase electricity from the utility company, whose power plant is dumping production waste in the local river. That pollution will cause harm to others, which is not included in the price of the product. If there is government intervention that requires the utility to reduce pollutants, the cost of the additional equipment and processes would be passed along to the utility's customers in the form of a price increase. A positive externality, on the other hand, creates a benefit to a third party. As an example, a farmer who grows apple trees provides a benefit to a beekeeper. The beekeeper gets a good source of nectar to help make more honey.

c. Factors that impact market equilibrium and their potential impact on overall economy and individual entities

Demand increases (shifts to right) can be caused by a decrease in real interest rates, increase in consumer confidence, increase in wealth, decrease in domestic price level compared to foreign prices, decrease in consumer taxes, or Increase in government spending. In general, when the demand curve shifts to the right, this creates more opportunity for an entity to sell more products and/or services.

Demand decreases (shifts to the left) can be caused by increase in real interest rates, decrease in consumer confidence increases, decrease in wealth, increases in domestic price level compared to foreign prices, increase in consumer taxes, or decrease in government spending. When the demand curve shifts left, this will generally cause the entity to sell less products and/or services.

Short-run aggregate supply (SRAS) curve increases (shift to the right) can be caused by increase in material for production, cost decreases (i.e. raw material, labor, taxes). Supply curve decreases (shift to the left) can be caused by decrease in material for production and cost increases (i.e., raw material, labor, taxes).

Demand and supply shifts effect an entity's sales and production costs, as demonstrated in the chart below.

Demand Curve Shift	Supply Curve Shift	Equilibrium Price	Quantity Purchased	Potential Economic Impact				Entity Impact
				Borrowing	Spending	Exports	Imports	
↑ Increase (shift to right)	↑ Increase (shift to right)	Indeterminate	↑	↑	↑	↑	↓	Increases in sales Decrease in production costs
↓ Decrease (shift to left)	↓ Decrease (shift to left)	Indeterminate	↓	↓	↓	↓	↑	Decrease in sales Increase in production costs
↑ Increase	No change	↑	↑	↑	↑	↑	↓	Increases in sales No change in costs
↓ Decrease	No change	↓	↓	↓	↓	↓	↑	Decreases in sales No change in costs
No change	↑ Increase	↓	↑	Indeterminate				Decrease in production costs
No change	↓ Decrease	↑	↓	Indeterminate				Increase in production costs
↑ Increase	↓ Decrease	↑	Indeterminate	↑	↑	↑	↓	Increases in sales Increase in production costs
↓ Decrease	↑ Increase	↓	Indeterminate	↓	↓	↓	↑	Decrease in sales Increase in production costs

Multiple Choice

BEC 2-Q20

2. Production costs and profits
   Firms have both variable and fixed production costs.
   - Variable costs will vary with output and usually increase at a constant rate relative to labor and capital. Examples of variable costs include materials and labor.
   - Fixed costs remain constant (within a relevant range). Examples of fixed costs include rent and insurance.

   In economics, there are variable costs and fixed costs in the short-run. However, in the long-run, all production costs are considered variable costs because a firm can change the dynamics of costing in the long-run (i.e., increase capacity, new facilities).

   a. **Short-run costs**
      There are four short-run cost inputs: average variable costs, average fixed costs, average total costs, and marginal costs.
      1) The average variable costs (AVC) formula is:

      $$AVC = \frac{\text{Total variable costs}}{\text{Total units produced}}$$

      2) The average fixed cost (AFC) formula is:

      $$AFC = \frac{\text{Total fixed costs}}{\text{Total units produced}}$$

      3) The average total cost formula (ATC) is:

      $$ATC = \frac{\text{Total costs}}{\text{Total units produced}}$$

      Also, ATC = AVC + AFC

      4) The marginal cost (MC) represents the additional cost of producing one more unit of goods. Another term for marginal cost is incremental cost. Fixed costs are constant in the total and therefore, not relevant (if there excess capacity). It is dependent on variable costs only. The marginal cost formula is:

      $$MC = \frac{\text{Change in total costs}}{\text{Change in total units produced}}$$

      The **law of diminishing returns** states that continually increasing inputs in the production process, while all other inputs remain constant, will lead to a point at which the additional inputs will result in smaller (diminishing) increases in output.

      For example, if a factory hires more and more workers and all other factors of production are held constant, there is a point at which each additional worker would produce a smaller amount of output than the previously hired worker.

The following graph visualizes the concept:

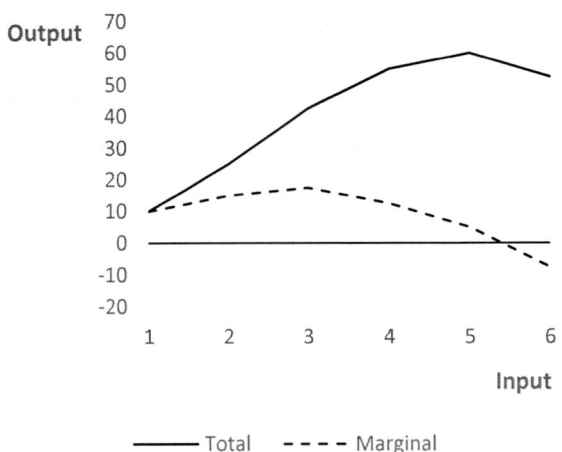

The short run costs are shown on a graph as follows:

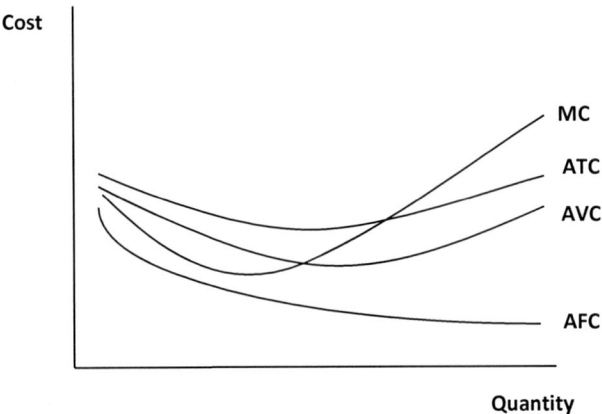

b. **Profit** is calculated by taking total revenues and subtracting total costs. Calculations of revenue include:

1) Total revenue (TR):

$$TR = Price (P) \times Total\ units\ produced$$

2) Average revenue (AR) is the revenue received by a firm for each unit of production (output):

$$AR = \frac{Total\ Revenue}{Total\ units\ produced}$$

3) Marginal revenue (MR) is the change in the total revenue from each additional unit of production:

$$MR = \frac{Change\ in\ total\ revenue}{Change\ in\ total\ units\ produced}$$

In economics, firms ignore fixed and sunk costs and will make decisions based on marginal revenue and marginal cost, in the short run as fixed costs need to be considered in the future. To maximize profits, firms will continue to add more units of production, until the cost of adding a unit becomes greater than the revenue derived from it, or where MR − MC = 0. Profits will be maximized in the long run when MR = MC. This is because a firm should produce and sell goods as long as the marginal cost is less than or equal to the marginal revenue. Profits will be maximized in the short run where price equals the marginal revenue and the marginal cost (P = MR = MC).

c. **Economic profit** is the profit remaining after subtracting implicit costs from accounting profit.

$$\text{Economic profit} = \text{Accounting profit (Revenue} - \text{Explicit costs)} - \text{Implicit (opportunity) costs}$$

Explicit costs are recognizable accounting expenses (e.g., rent, labor) that result from actual transactions. Accountants are familiar with explicit costs since GAAP only deals with explicit costs, disregarding implicit costs in most situations.

Implicit costs quantify the benefits foregone when choosing one alternative over another alternative, also known as opportunity costs. Implicit costs do not involve a payment or transaction but decrease economic profit. Accounting costs do not include opportunity costs. In other words, it is not recorded on any general ledger. So, an **Opportunity Cost** is the cost of benefits foregone when choosing one alternative versus another alternative.

Examples of implicit costs include the potential salary an owner could earn if he or she chose to work outside the company rather than run the company. Or, the interest that could be earned if capital currently held as inventory was instead invested in securities. Again, accountants do not recognize implicit costs in financial statements.

Due to the structure of the equation, economic profit is typically less than accounting profit. Economic loss (or negative economic profit) occurs when implicit costs are greater than the accounting profit. For instance, assume a company earns accounting profit (or net income) of $10,000 during the period. If the company had purchased equity securities rather than inventory, it could have generated earnings of $15,000 during the same period.

The result is an economic loss of $5,000 ($10,000 - $15,000 = -$5,000). Purchasing inventory in this example is not economically lucrative, even though the company is profitable from an accounting standpoint. Economists argue that owners will ultimately leave the marketplace to invest in securities rather than operating the business (i.e., purchasing inventory) if they experience consistent economic losses. The bottom line is that economic profits and accounting profits are not the same.

d. Long-run costs
In economics, all costs are variable in the long run because firms can adjust all costs and production capacity (i.e., build a new plant to increase capacity) in the long run. This is different than in the short-run, where firms can affect prices through only changes made in production levels. This is why fixed costs are not considered in the short run as explained earlier but are considered in the long-run.

An increase in the resources available within the economy increases the inputs available for production and a corresponding increase in the output of production. This will happen only if there is sufficient production capacity to accommodate the increases in inputs.

In the long run, the term "returns to scale" indicates what happens when production increases and all costs are considered variable.

1) **Increasing returns to scale** (IRS): An increase in units of production result in a decrease in the average cost per unit. Firms experience economies of scale in this situation.
2) **Constant returns to scale** (CRS): An increase in units produced results in no change in the average cost per unit.
3) **Diminishing returns to scale** (DRS): An increase in units of production results in an increase in the average cost per unit. Firms experience diseconomies of scale in this situation.

The graph below illustrates the term returns to scale:

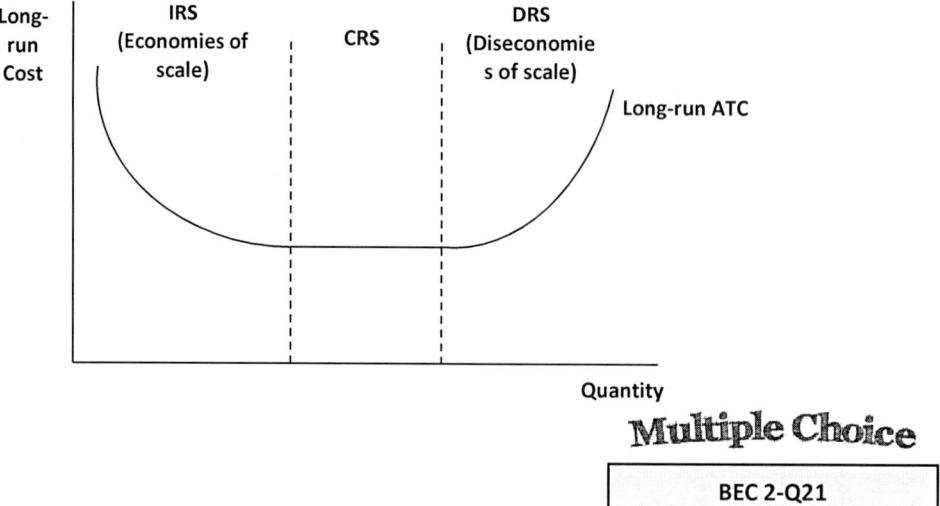

Multiple Choice

BEC 2-Q21

3. Market structure
Firms operate under four main market structures. Their ranking from most competitive to least competitive is as follows:

Perfect competition — Most Competitive
Monopolistic competition
Oligopoly
Monopoly — Least Competitive

The following chart compares each of the market structures:

	Perfect Competition	Monopolistic Competition	Oligopoly	Monopoly
Number of firms	Lots of firms	Lots of firms	Few firms	One firm
Degree of competition	Highly competitive	Highly competitive	Moderately competitive	None
Barriers to entry	No barriers	Few barriers	Many barriers (i.e., technology)	N/A – No entry due to controls or restrictions
Average firm size	Small	Small to medium	Large	Very large
Demand curve	Perfectly elastic, demand curve is horizontal, firms are price takers (accepts market price)	Highly elastic, demand curve is downward sloping	Inelastic, demand curve is affected by competition	Inelastic, demand curve is downward sloping
Product differentiation	None	Some	Various types of differentiation	None, product is unique and/or a necessity
Existence of substitute products	Many differentiated substitutes	Some differentiated substitutes	Many differentiated substitutes	None
Buyer demand	Almost unlimited, depends on availability of supply	Demand is dependent on competitor's differentiated products	Buyer controls the type of product and quantity to purchase	When demand is elastic, firms will produce more
Firm's control over quantity and price	Has control over quantity, market sets price	Has some control over quantity, market mostly sets price	Has control over quantity and price	Has control over quantity and price
Price strategy	None, no single firm is able to affect price. Takes market price $P = MR = MC$	Some pricing control, $P > MR = MC$	Looks to maximize $P > MR = MC$	Firms have the most control over price, looks to maximize $P > MR = MC$
Long-term profit potential	No economic profit	No economic profit	Some economic profit	Large economic profit
Government intervention	Very little intervention	Small amount of intervention (i.e., permits)	Intervention may be introduced to control market manipulation	Can have high intervention such as taxes
Nature of competition	Price only	Price and marketing features and benefits	Price and marketing features and benefits	Advertising
Examples	Produce, gold, milk	Fast food restaurants, movies	TVs, golf balls	Utilities

Multiple Choice

BEC 2-Q22

4. Economic theories

Classical economics states that there should be minimal government intervention, which would result in markets functioning at their best. It does not believe that fiscal policy should be used to grow the economy. Its assumptions include that prices for goods and wages are flexible, markets are self-regulating, supply will create its own demand, and there is equality between savings and investments.

Monetarist economics is the economics of the money supply, prices and interest rates, and their repercussions on the economy. It focuses on the monetary and other financial markets, the determination of the interest rate, the extent to which these influence the behavior of the economic units and the implications of that influence in the macroeconomic context. It also studies the formulation of monetary policy, usually by the central bank or "the monetary authority," concerning the supply of money and manipulation of interest rates, in terms both of what is actually done and what would be optimal.

Under **Keynesian economics**, the market is imperfect and not self-regulating. At equilibrium, negative growth and unemployment could exist. The government should intervene (fiscal policy) when economic growth is slowing. Consumer income will stimulate demand and result in economic growth. Keynesian economics says that optimal economic performance could be achieved, and economic contraction prevented, by influencing aggregate demand by government intervention. It is an economic theroy that focuses mainly on government spending and demand.

Supply-side economics assumptions include that income levels reflect the ability to supply more goods and services people demand and that economic growth cannot be achieved without expansion in output (supply). The way supply-side economics accomplishes this is by less government intervention and reduced taxes (especially for wealthy individuals and businesses). By reducing taxes, there will be increases in employment, savings and investment. Supply-side economics is also known as trickle-down economics and Reaganomics. The Laffer curve is used extensively in promoting this policy.

Neo-Keynesian (or New Keynesian) economics, as the name suggests, is based on classical Keynesian economics. The theories differ because Neo-Keynesian economics assumes that there is imperfect competition, resulting in prices and wages do not adjust to economic conditions immediately. This means that prices and wages may appear "sticky" when short-term market fluctuations occur, holding relatively constant. This theory justifies government intervention to minimize the impact of market failures (e.g., failure to reach full employment). Policies may include increasing or decreasing taxes or government spending to stimulate the economy.

5. International trade

> Determine the business reasons for, and explain the underlying economic substance of, significant transactions (e.g., business combinations and divestitures, product line diversification, production sourcing, public and private offerings of securities, etc.)

Some of the reasons companies acquire or merge with other companies, also known as legal business combinations, include: to become more competitive, to utilize more efficient means of production, to become more cost-efficient, and to diversify products, and to bolster revenue streams. The opposite of a merger or acquisition is a divestiture, which occurs when a company sells a division or subsidiary. Economic business cycles tend to affect the volume of merger, acquisition, and divestiture activity in the economy.

To understand the business reasons for these significant transactions, it is necessary to understand some background information on international economics.

Economists usually divide the various types of economic systems around the world into traditional economies, centrally restricted (command) economies, and market economies.

- **Traditional economies** follow long-standing traditions of allocating resources based on family inheritance. The goods produced do not change very much from generation to generation and are typically obtained through farming or hunting. Examples are the Australian aborigines and Canadian Inuit.
- **Centrally restricted (command) economies** are based on government control of all economic activities, including distribution of resources, production, prices, and wages. Socialism and communism are examples of this type of economy.
- **Market economies** are based on individuals and the choices they make in producing goods, selling goods, and purchasing goods. Interactions between individuals and companies determine the resource allocation. Consumer behavior and the market trends will dictate what a business produces and its price. The U.S. is an example of a market economy.

a. Expanding globally
Businesses expand into foreign markets for a variety of reasons including:
- Increasing sales
- Lowering costs
- Diversifying market and customer base
- Creating Economies of scale
- Obtaining Competitive advantage
- Extending product life-cycle
- Tax Arbitraging

1) Absolute advantage and comparative advantage
Absolute advantage is the ability for a country (or business) to produce goods that require a smaller amount of "inputs" (i.e., low-cost labor or more efficient production process) than any other country (or business) producing the same good.

Comparative advantage is the ability of a country (or business) to produce goods at lower opportunity costs when compared to another country. A country (or business) with a comparative advantage should consider **specializing** in producing those goods where they have a comparative advantage and export such goods, especially if it also has an absolute advantage. Likewise, a country (or business) should import goods where it has a comparative disadvantage.

> *Hint:* Absolute advantage refers to differences in input productivity. Comparative advantage refers to differences in opportunity costs.

> *Example:* Country A and Country B both produce violins and bicycles. Assuming all other factors of production are the same, the number of labor hours to produce each product is shown below:
>
> | Country | Violin | Bicycle |
> |---|---|---|
> | A | 21 hrs. | 7 hrs. |
> | B | 8 hrs. | 4 hrs. |
>
> Absolute advantage
> Country B has the absolute advantage for both violins and bicycles because it can produce those goods with a lower amount of inputs (labor hours).

> *Continued from last page.*
> <u>Comparative advantage</u>
> To determine which countries have a comparative advantage, the opportunity cost (amount given up of one good to produce another) for each country producing each good is determined as shown below:
>
> To produce 1 violin:
> Country A's opportunity cost is 3 (21/7) bicycles
> Country B's opportunity cost is 2 (8/4) bicycles → Has comparative advantage
>
> To produce 1 bicycle:
> Country A's opportunity cost is .333 (7/21) violins → Has comparative advantage
> Country B's opportunity cost is .50 (4/8) violins

2) The *Diamond of National Advantage* by Michael Porter explains how some countries are more competitive than others and how some industries within those countries are more competitive than others. A country can utilize more of its factor endowments (for example, skilled labor and natural resources), which will contribute to the country's comparative advantage.

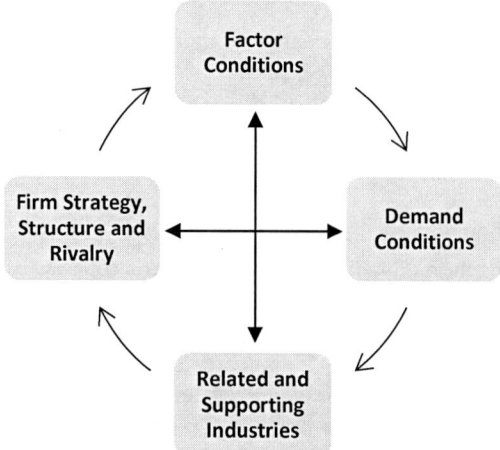

Factor conditions: A country can create its own factors of production such as infrastructure, technology, or skilled labor. Any disadvantages of factors will incentivize businesses to innovate.
Demand conditions: More local market demand will lead to a comparative advantage because additional attention and resources are expended to satisfy the demand.
Related and supporting industries: A comparative advantage will result when local industries' competitive opportunity costs are lowered from innovation and efficiencies.
Firm strategy, structure, and rivalry: A fiercely competitive industry within a country will lead to a comparative advantage for the country when competing internationally.

3) Barriers to trade
Governments typically are responsible for establishing **barriers to trade**. Barriers to trade are often referred to as **protectionism**, which is a government's economic policy of limiting trade between their country and foreign countries. The opposite of protectionism is **free-trade**, where governments decrease as many barriers to trade as they can. In general, economists agree that protectionism results in a negative impact on economic growth because it results in trading activity in less protective industries.

Examples of barriers to entry include:
- **Tariffs** are the most common barrier to trade. Tariffs represent a tax on imports, which raise the price of imported goods, compared to domestic goods. The goal of a tariff is to reduce demand for imported goods and raise domestic revenue. Threshold limits (trigger prices) are placed on import prices, and when the price is below a certain amount, the tariff will begin.
- An **embargo** is the most restrictive barrier to trade and represents a full or partial prohibition of the ability for a foreign country to import or export.
- An import **quota** represents a restriction on a number of goods that can be imported.
- **Foreign exchange controls** are put in place by a government to restrict or stop foreign currency purchases or sales by the government's citizens, or on the purchase or sale of local currency by nonresidents. Foreign exchange controls include:
    - Establishing fixed exchange rates
    - Restricting the use of currency exchange to only exchanges approved by the government
    - Banning the use of any foreign currency
    - Prohibiting flight of capital
    - Compensating Agreements- a type of bartering between two nations whereby the net of the two will be zero. No gain, no loss.

Other activities that governments undertake to combat trade imbalances include:
- **Export subsidies** provide incentives to producers to export more of a certain type of good. It can have the effect of raising prices for foreign countries and cause further trade imbalances.
- **Countervailing duties** represent an import tax on goods to stop dumping or counter export subsidies.
- **Dumping** is where a country sells products in a foreign country at prices below its cost or below what those products sell for in the home market. This is a type of predatory pricing.

4) Balance of (international) payments
The **balance of payments** is a summary of all economic transactions between one country and the rest of the world's economies, or just between two countries. The summary includes all transactions made by the country's government, businesses, and individuals. Freely fluctuating exchange rates allow exchange rates to reach an equilibrium based on market factors of supply and demand for the currency used in imports and exports.
- A **trade surplus** arises when one country exports more than it imports.
- A **trade deficit** arises when one country imports more than it exports.
- Total goods exported minus total goods imported equals the **balance of trade** for a country.

The balance of payments is separated into three accounts: a) the current account, b) the capital account, and c) the financial account.
- The current account is used to mark the inflow and outflow of goods and services into a country. Earnings on investments, both public and private, are also put into the current account.
- The capital account is where all international capital transfers are recorded. This refers to the acquisition or disposal of non-financial assets (for example, a physical asset such as land) and non-produced assets, which are needed for production but have not been produced, like a mine used for the extraction of diamonds.

- The financial account is where international monetary flows related to investment in business, real estate, bonds, and stocks are documented. Also included are government-owned assets such as foreign reserves, gold, special drawing rights (SDRs) held with the International Monetary Fund (IMF), private assets held abroad and direct foreign investment. Assets owned by foreigners, private and official, are also recorded in the financial account.

Theoretically, the balance of payments should always equal zero when the current account is added to the capital account and the financial account. For example, if a country's imports exceed their exports, it will have a trade deficit. The deficit can be counterbalanced in any one of a number of ways, including borrowing from other countries or by using central bank reserves.

> **Example:** Assume a country had a current account deficit of $5 billion. The capital account and financial account would total $5 billion to offset the current account, netting the balance of payments to zero.

When the U. S. dollar changes in value, import prices, and export prices move in the opposite direction. For example, if the dollar depreciates, any imports will be more expensive, and exports will be less expensive.

Multiple Choice

BEC 2-Q23 through BEC 2-Q24

b. Foreign exchange rates
In conducting business internationally, **foreign exchange rates** are a very important consideration because exchange rates between countries are always changing and affect both individual/corporate transactions and financial statement reporting. The **spot rate** is the exchange rate "on the spot," or at the moment of the foreign exchange activity. The **forward rate** is the exchange rate at a future date.

If Country A's currency is higher relative to Country B, Country B's exports will be more expensive, and its imports will be less expensive for County B. Country B's higher exchange rate will lower the balance of trade.

When the U.S. dollar becomes weaker compared to the foreign competitor's currency, U.S. goods become cheaper for U.S. consumers relative to foreign goods and the U.S. companies will have an advantage in the U.S. market. Likewise, when a foreign competitor's currency becomes weaker compared to the U.S. dollar, foreign goods become cheaper relative to U.S. goods for U.S. consumers and the foreign company will have an advantage in the U.S. market.

> **Example**: Assume the euro has a spot rate of €1 to $1.2. To determine amount of U.S. dollars for a given number of euros, multiple the foreign currency price times the U.S. dollar per foreign currency (the exchange rate ratio). In this example, the equivalent U.S. dollar amount for €500 is calculated as follows:
>
> €500 * ($1.2 / €1) = $600

> **Hint**: If you make the exchange rate ratio into a fraction (€1 / $1.2), the units that you're looking for, in this case U.S. dollars, **go on the top**. This effectively cancels the other unit of currency.

Factors influencing exchange rates include:
1) **Interest rates**: If interest rates increase in a country relative to another country, it will attract foreign investors and cause the exchange rate to increase due to a decrease in demand for home country's currency.
2) **Inflation**: Countries with higher inflation will have the value of their currency deflated as the currency has less purchasing power.
3) **Trade terms** are related to the balance of payments: If a country's price for exports increases by a larger amount than its imports, that country's trade terms are better. This will result in increased revenues on exports and an increase in the country's currency.
4) **Economic performance**: Foreign investors who are willing to invest are attracted to countries with strong economic performance. More investment in strong economies will lessen the incentive to invest in other weaker economies because the investors in the stronger economies will receive a greater return.
5) **Government intervention**: Central banks play a key role in exchange rates by selling and purchasing foreign exchange market money.

c. Forward premium and discount
The difference between spot rate and the forward rate represents either a premium or discount.

Forward rate > Spot rate → Expectation is that value of currency will increase
Forward rate < Spot rate → Expectation is that value of currency will decrease

The formula to calculate the premium or discount is as follows:

$$\frac{\text{Forward rate} - \text{Spot rate}}{\text{Spot rate}} \times \frac{\text{Months (or days) in year}}{\text{Months (or days) in forward period}} \times 100$$

Usually, the central bank of a country will establish programs, called **exchange rate regimes**, to manage how its currency compares to currencies of other countries. Exchange rate regimes are closely tied to a country's monetary policy. The various exchange rate regimes in use include:
1) **Pegged exchange rate regime**: Rates are maintained at or close to the central bank's targeted rate. A crawling peg rate is a rate that is periodically adjusted by the central bank.
2) **Fixed exchange rate regime**: Rates are tied to another country's rate or the rates of a set grouping of other countries.
3) **Floating exchange rate regime**: Rates are allowed to fluctuate with the market.

Multiple Choice

BEC 2-Q25 through BEC 2-Q29

d. Mergers, acquisitions, and divestitures
There are two ways for companies to grow, either organically (i.e., increasing existing company sales) or, through a business combination via acquisition or merger. These activities are also known in financial reporting as significant transactions.

Economic business cycles tend to affect the volume of merger, acquisition and divestiture activities.

1) Mergers
A **merger** occurs when two companies agree to combine into one "new" company. For example, Daimler-Benz merged with Chrysler to form DaimlerChrysler.

Company A + Company B = Company C

i. **Horizontal merger**: Both companies, usually competitors, are in the same line of business (i.e., Exxon and Mobil).
ii. **Vertical merger**: Both companies are in supply chain relationship (i.e., Pixar and Disney).
iii. **Congeneric (concentric) merger**: Both companies are in the same general industry but do not have the same customers.
iv. **Conglomerate merger**: Both companies are in unrelated businesses (i.e., ABC and Disney).

2) Acquisitions

An **acquisition** occurs when one company buys another (target) company. For example, company A buys company B:

$$\text{Company A} + \text{Company B} = \text{Company A}$$

The company buying the other company will typically purchase the outstanding stock of the company it is acquiring while simultaneously exchanging its stock for the target company's stock.

i. A **friendly takeover** is where the target company endorses the offer and is willing to accept it.
ii. A **hostile takeover** is where the target company does not support and objects the offer. Hostile takeovers are usually done through direct offerings to the shareholders.

3) Divestitures

A **divestiture** occurs when a company sells or disposes of a division or subsidiary. Reasons for a divestiture include: a) poor financial performance, b) change of strategic focus, c) cash flow needs of the parent company, d) divestiture is worth more to another company, and e) division/ subsidiary could perform better as a stand-alone company.

Divestitures can also be done through government intervention. For example, in 1982, because of an antitrust lawsuit, AT&T, which had a monopoly on telephone service in the U.S., had to split itself into separate competing companies called Regional Bell Operating Companies.

After a series of mergers and acquisition activity, a company may become over-diversified and will decide to divest some assets to remain focused on more of their core business. For example, Ford Motor Company acquired Aston Martin, Jaguar, Land Rover and Volvo starting in the late 1980s and by early 2010, had sold them all to other companies to concentrate on their core products.

Forms of divestiture include:
i. **Outright sale** of all the assets to another company.
ii. **Liquidation** of the division or subsidiary by breaking it up and selling the parts separately.
iii. **Spin-off** as a separate entity, where the parent's shareholders receive stock.
iv. **Carve-out** as a partial divestiture, by retaining some ownership and selling a partial equity stake to another company.

4) Business cycle impact
   Merger and acquisition activity tend to track along with business cycles, with more of them occurring during expansionary phases, as the business cycle moves toward peaking, and less so in contractionary phases.

   i. As the economy recovers and expands, companies typically spend more to fund internal products while seeing an increase in sales. As the company increases its cash and its internally developed products have provided a return, the pipeline for additional organic growth may begin to wane causing management to look at business combinations for additional opportunities.

   ii. In a contractionary phase heading toward a trough in the business cycle, company sales and profits generally decrease. Companies tend to explore ways to preserve cash, reduce costs, focus more on sales, and reduce business combination activity. During this phase, there are few companies that want to sell at depressed values and few companies willing to buy due to less available funding options.

C. Financial Risk Management

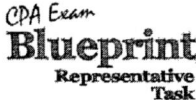

> Calculate and use ratios and measures to quantify risks associated with interest rates, currency exchange, liquidity, prices, etc. in a business entity.

1. Market, interest rate, currency, liquidity, credit, price and other risks
   Risk refers to the uncertainty of a return and the potential for financial loss. Return is the actual gain or loss from an investment for a particular period. There is a risk-return tradeoff, where the potential return will increase with an increase in risk. In general, the more risk an investor takes on, the greater the potential for a higher return (or loss).

   a. Risk preference behaviors
      Risk preference represents a person's tendency for risk tolerance. The main risk preference behaviors are risk adverse, risk seeking, and risk neutral.
      1) **Risk adverse**: This is the most common risk preference behavior and describes a reluctance to take on risk. A person who is risk adverse will take on additional risk only in exchange for a potentially higher return.
      2) **Risk seeking**: A person who takes risks and is willing to accept the potential of a lesser return to take on more risk.
      3) **Risk neutral**: Someone who is neither risk averse or risk seeking, and indifferent to risk when making a decision. If risk preference is a continuum, risk neutral is in the middle.

   b. Return
      Investment returns are typically shown as a percentage. Actual returns are calculated by taking the profit or loss from a change in the value of an investment, plus any cash distributions, and dividing it by the value of the asset at the beginning of the period. This calculation will provide the return on an investment (ex-post, or based on information after the fact).

   c. Estimating expected return
      When estimating the **expected return on an investment**, actual returns from prior periods can be used to predict the future return (ex-ante, or based on predictions). There are three ways to calculate expected returns, the arithmetic average return, the geometric average return, and the holding period return.

      1) **Arithmetic average return**: Add up each return for every period and divide by the number of periods. For example, a $100 stock investment that an investor held for two years and had returns of 50% for year one and -50% for year two would have an arithmetic average return of 0% [(.5 + -.5)/2].

         However, while not intuitive, the investor cannot assume he or she will have the same $100 because there would only be $75 left of the original $100 after two years:

Initial investment	$100.00
Add: Year 1, 50% return	(50.00)
Balance of investment	$150.00
Less: Year 2, -50% return	(75.00)
Balance of investment	$75.00

         To arrive at a more accurate estimate of expected return, the geometric average return calculation is preferred.

2) **Geometric average return**: Due to the fluctuations (volatility) of actual investment returns over time, the geometric average return provides an accurate estimate based on the compounded annual returns. To arrive at the geometric average return, add 1 to each of the actual returns for each period (this removes any negative return numbers), multiply them by each other and raise that product by the power of 1 divided by the number of periods. Lastly, subtract the result from 1. Here is the calculation using the same returns from above ($100 stock investment that was held for 2 years and had returns of 50% for year one, -50% for year two):

$$[(1.50 \times .50)^{1/2}] - 1 = -13.4\%$$

Here is the proof: The 13.4% geometric average return still results in the $75 balance at the end of year 2:

Initial investment	$100.00
Add: Year 1, -13.4% return	(13.40)
Balance of investment	$86.60
Less: Year 2, -13.4% return	(11.60)
Balance of investment	$75.00

The geometric average annual return (-13.4%) is an accurate estimate of expected return because it considers the volatility of the returns and the arithmetic average return (0%) does not. Also, due to the effect of compounding, the geometric average return will always be lower than the arithmetic average return.

3) **Holding period return**: The return over a period of time, either that has actually elapsed or is expected for a future period. The holding period return is calculated as income (dividend cash flow) plus price increase/decrease during the period, divided by the investment's cost.

$$\text{Holding Period Return} = (P_1 + D - P_0) / P_0$$

P_1 = Ending value of investment
P_0 = Beginning value of investment
D = Dividend Cash Flow

> **Example**: On October 10, 20X7, Dodgeball Inc. paid $10 per share for 120 shares. On October 10, 20X9, the stock is worth $15 per share. Over the past two years, the stock paid 8 equal quarterly dividend payments worth $0.05 per share. What is the holding period return for the investment? (Dividend cash flow = $0.05 * 8 payments = $0.40)
>
> Holding period return = ($15 + $0.40 - $10) / $10 = 0.54 or 54%

4) The **expected estimated return of a portfolio** of investments is calculated by taking the weighted average of the expected returns of each investment in the portfolio.

Multiple Choice

BEC 2-Q30 through BEC 2-Q37

d. Estimating risk
Whenever risk is estimated, most of the time the returns will follow a normal distribution (bell-shaped curve). If the distribution happens to be normal, about 95% of the returns that that one can expect to get on the investments will fall within the range of plus or minus, two standard deviations from the mean. For 99% of the returns, it would be three standard deviations from the mean.

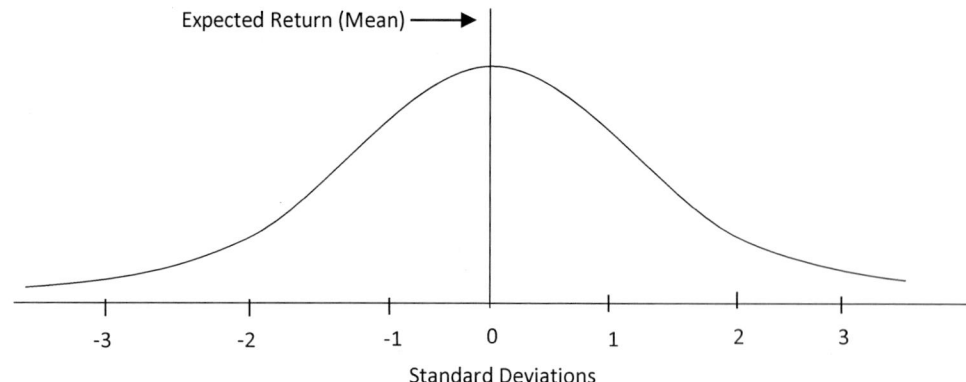

Volatility is represented in the graph above as the fluctuation of the price around the mean, or the standard deviation. The standard deviation is applied to an investment's annual rate of return to measure the investment's volatility.

e. Coefficient of variation
The **coefficient of variation** is a measurement of one type of risk and indicates the degree of variation among investments with means that are different from one another. A lower coefficient indicates less risk. The formula for calculating the coefficient of variation is:

$$\frac{\text{Standard Deviation}}{\text{Expected (mean) Return}}$$

Example: Acme Corporation currently only operates in the U.S. and is risk adverse, with a mean return of 18% and a standard deviation of 16%. Acme is evaluating two investment proposals to expand into either foreign country A, or foreign country B. After the investment, Acme will have 50% of their operations in the U.S. and 50% of their operations in one of the foreign countries. Based on this information, Acme determined that the portfolio risk and return of each alternative were as follows:

Proposed Investment	Mean Return	Standard Deviation
U.S. & Country A	19%	4%
U.S. & Country B	22%	18%

Since Acme is risk averse, the company would ideally want the proposal that has the highest return and the lowest risk. Unfortunately, that might not always occur and therefore, one would need to use the Coefficient of Variance to determine the "biggest bang with the least risk." Using the coefficient of variance to measure risk, Acme can compare their results with the two proposed investments.

Coefficient of variance = Standard deviation / expected mean return

> *(continued from previous page)*
> **Acme (U.S only):**
> Coefficient of variance = .16 / .18 = .89
>
> **U.S. & Foreign Country A:**
> Coefficient of variance = .04 / .19 = .21
>
> **U.S. & Foreign Country B:**
> Coefficient of variance = .18 / .22 = .82
>
> The coefficient of variance for both U.S. & Foreign Country A (.21) and U.S. & Foreign Country B (.82) are below Acme's coefficient of variance of .89, which makes either one an attractive proposition because they reduce risk. However, Acme wants the highest return with the lowest risk and would choose to invest in U.S. & Foreign Country A.
>
> Acme's decision so far would be based on quantitative information, but part of management's overall decision should also be based on qualitative factors. If one of Acme's major competitors was starting operations in Foreign Country B, they should consider an alternative to selecting the U.S. & Foreign Country B proposal to mitigate a major competitive threat.

f. Systematic risk and unsystematic risk
    1) **Systematic risk**: Relates to factors for an entire market or entire market segment that cannot be avoided simply by diversifying a portfolio of investments. Sources of systematic risk include recessions, changes in interest rates, and GDP fluctuations. Systematic risk is sometimes referred to as market risk or undiversifiable risk in that it cannot be diversified away.
    2) **Unsystematic risk**: Relates to the risk for a specific company (stock), or a group of similar companies in an industry that are in a portfolio of investments. An example of a source of unsystematic risk is a labor strike. Unsystematic risk can be reduced through diversification, and it is sometimes referred to as diversifiable risk or specific risk.

g. Risk factors
    Businesses must assess some risk factors when considering whether to either borrow money or lend money. The main risks include credit (default) risk, interest rate risk, market risk, liquidity risk, management risk, and foreign exchange risk.

    1) **Credit (default) risk**: The risk that the debtor will not be able to repay the principal and/or interest that is due on their indebtedness.
    2) **Interest rate risk**: The risk that the value of an investment will change as interest rates change. For example, the risk that a bond's yield will increase due to a decrease in its price after it was bought. As an example, this occurs because, with a fixed interest rate, when interest rate in the market increases, the value of that investment will decrease.
    3) **Market risk**: The risk that is caused by factors outside a company's control affecting all securities in the market in the same manner. Market risk cannot be diversified away and is sometimes called systematic risk.
    4) **Liquidity risk**: The risk associated with having funds invested in long-term assets that cannot be easily converted into cash (sold) within a necessary timeframe or, the inability to meet payment obligations as they come due.
    5) **Management risk**: The risk that management will make incorrect decisions about future outcomes.
    3) **Foreign exchange risk**: There are three types of foreign exchange risk: a) foreign currency transaction risk, b) foreign currency translation risk, and c) economic risk.

- **Foreign currency transactions** relate to purchases (accounts payable) or sales (accounts receivable) of goods or services in a foreign currency. **Foreign currency transaction risk** is the possibility of losses resulting from changes in exchange rates resulting from the purchase or sale.
- **Foreign currency translations** relate to converting entire financial statements, reported in a foreign currency, into U.S. dollars. For example, a U.S. company may have a foreign subsidiary with financial statements using a foreign currency. Translation into U.S. dollars is necessary to make the financial statements more useful but also to comply with US GAAP. Exchange rates typically change between financial statement reporting periods and cause **foreign currency translation risk.**
- **Economic risk** is the risk to a company's present value of future cash flows related to fluctuations in foreign exchange rates.

Multiple Choice

BEC 2-Q38

h. Portfolio variance

The variance of a portfolio is a measurement of the fluctuations (standard deviation) of actual returns of a group of investments in a portfolio. The variance (standard deviation) of a portfolio also indicates how the returns on the investment vary together. Another factor in determining portfolio variances is the weight of each investment in the portfolio relative to the portfolio total. There are two measures of how the returns on a pair of investments vary together; that is, the correlation coefficient and the covariance. The lower the correlation between investments in a portfolio, the lower the portfolio variance.

Portfolio variances can be reduced by selecting investments with low, or negative correlation (i.e., stocks and bonds), which will diversify the portfolio and reduce risk.

i. Volatility, systematic risk, and investment portfolios

The volatility of an individual investment should be analyzed within that portfolio of investments to determine how the risk of an individual investment affects the risk of the portfolio. The measurement to determine whether an investment is more or less volatile than the portfolio is called the **beta** coefficient. Beta is used to determine the implications of portfolio risk as a result of adding or decreasing individual investments.

1) **Beta <1:** Stock is less volatile than the portfolio. For example, if the value of the portfolio decreases, an individual stock in the portfolio with a negative beta would increase in value. This helps to diversify the portfolio and reduce risk, even if the return is low. The portfolio is less risky because the negative beta helps to balance out other risky stocks in the portfolio. Utility stocks usually have a beta less than 1.
2) **Beta = 1:** Stock's value moves with the portfolio.
3) **Beta >1:** Stock is more volatile than the portfolio. For example, an individual stock with a beta of 1.3 is 30% more volatile than the portfolio. So, if the value of the portfolio decreased $1, that individual stock would decrease $1.30. A positive beta provides little diversification and indicates more risk. Many high-tech stocks can have a beta greater than 1 because while generating higher returns, they also carry more risk.

An **efficient (optimal) portfolio** is one that provides an investor with the highest expected return, given that investor's level of risk, (risk-return trade-off) and is the lowest risk for a given expected return. On a larger scale, the **efficient frontier** represents the groupings of efficient portfolios that offer the highest expected return for a specific level of risk or the lowest risk for a given level of expected return.

Example: Spruce Corporation has the following investment portfolio:

Investment	Expected return	Amount	Beta
A	17%	$200,000	1.4
B	11%	$200,000	-0.7
C	7%	$400,000	1.8
D	9%	$300,000	-1.0

The expected return of the portfolio is determined by taking the expected returns for each investment, times its weight within the portfolio, which totals $1,100,000.

Investment A: .17 x $200,000/$1,100,000 = .0310
Investment B: .11 x $200,000/$1,100,000 = .0200
Investment C: .07 x $400,000/$1,100,000 = .0255
Investment D: .08 x $300,000/$1,100,000 = .0218
Expected return of the portfolio   .0983 or 9.83%

If Spruce decided to sell one of the investments, ideally, they would sell the one with the highest beta and lowest return, which in this case would be investment C. The high beta of 1.8 means that investment C's return is correlated to move with the portfolio's return, which increases the risk of the portfolio.

Investment A: The expected return is 17%, and it has a beta of 1.4. The positive beta provides little diversification and indicates more risk. In comparing Investment A to the other negative beta in the portfolio (Investment C), Investment A appears to be a better investment, because Investment C has an even higher beta of 1.8 and the expected return is only 7%.

Investment B: The expected return is 11%, and it has a beta of -0.7. The negative beta provides for diversification which means that it makes the portfolio less risky because it balances out the risks of other investments.

Investment C: The expected return is 7%, and the beta is 1.8. While the return is relatively low, the beta is high which can result in substantial losses or gains. Overall, since the return is relatively low, and the beta is positive as well, so it does not reduce risk.

Investment D: The expected return is 9%, but it has a beta of -1.0, which provides diversification in the portfolio. That means if the value of the portfolio goes down, that investment is going to go up.

Therefore, Spruce would likely sell investment C, because it has a very high beta of 1.8, it provides very little diversification and therefore, more risky. It also has a low expected return of 7%, especially compared to the other positive beta in the portfolio (investment A).

j. Interest rates and risk

As mentioned earlier, an interest rate represents what is charged (or paid) for the use of money. There are various names associated with interest rates. For example, a bond may contain a contract interest rate of 8%.

- The contract rate represents the interest rate contained in a financial instrument. It represents the rate that bondholders receive periodic interest payments from the bond issuer (contract rate x face amount of bond). The contract rate is calculated as **simple interest**, which is determined by multiplying the contract rate by the original principal and by the number of periods. Simple interest calculations do not take into account compounding or the time value of money.
- The market rate of interest is the rate of interest for similar types of investments (i.e., bonds) that are available in the market. The market rate of interest is used to determine the periodic interest expense recorded on the books of the bond issuer (market rate x carrying value of the bond). Some of the other terms used for contract rate and market rate are shown below:

Commonly Used Terms for Contract Rate of Interest and Market Rate of Interest	
CONTRACT RATE	**MARKET RATE**
Stated Rate	Yield to Maturity
Coupon Rate	Real Rate
Bond Rate	Yield
Nominal Rate	
Face Rate	

k. Stated interest rate compared to the effective annual interest rate

Annual percentage rate (APR): The term APR has multiple definitions, but assume that APR is referring to nominal APR unless otherwise specified. Nominal APR is the periodic interest rate on a loan or other instrument.

> *Example*: A company has a loan that accrues 2% interest each month. The nominal APR on the loan is calculated by multiplying 2% per month by 12 months, or 24%.

Effective annual percentage rate (annual percentage yield): The effective APR considers compound interest or the accrual of interest on any unpaid amounts of previously accrued interest. Compounding can occur daily, weekly, monthly, or quarterly.

When comparing the stated rate to the **effective annual interest rate**, the effective rate considers the effect of compounding and the stated rate does not. The effective annual interest rate is determined by taking the stated rate and adjusting for the number of compounding periods (i.e., month or year). The stated rate will always be less than the effective annual interest rate, and the effective annual interest rate indicates a more accurate determination of the payments. It is sometimes called the APR (annual percentage rate). The formula for the APR is:

$$\text{Effective APR} = [(1 + \text{periodic rate})^{\text{number of compounding periods}} - 1]$$

> *Example:* Maple Corporation secured a $200,000 one-year 6% term loan, with interest compounded quarterly. Maple's effective annual interest rate (APR) for the loan is calculated as follows:
>
> $$\text{Effective APR} = [1 + (.06/4)]^4 - 1$$
> $$= .0614 \text{ or } 6.14\%$$
>
> Note that the stated, nominal rate (6%) will always be less than the effective APR (6.14%) as a result of compounding.

Multiple Choice
BEC 2-Q39

I. Yield curve

The **yield curve** depicts interest rates for different lengths of time-to-maturity and interest rates (costs of borrowing). This relationship between short-term and long-term interest rates is called the **term structure of interest rates**. The theory behind the yield curve is that lenders will want a higher interest rate as the length of the maturity increases because a) the difficulty of predicting future economic activity (i.e., inflation) and b) greater potential for default issues. The yield curve indicating this is called a **normal yield curve** and is upward sloping. It usually relates to signs of economic growth and the potential for inflation. The normal yield curve is shown as follows:

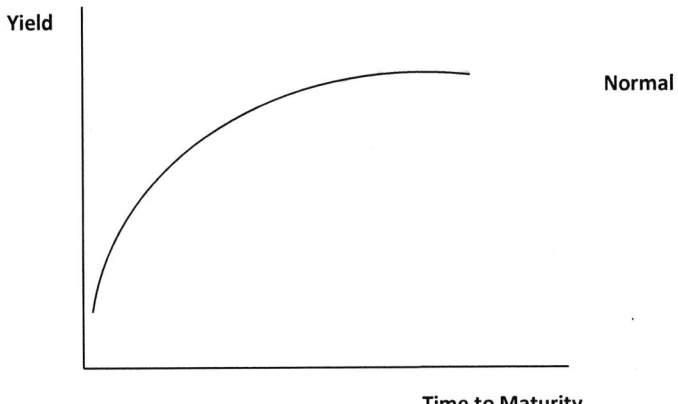

Other forms of yield curves include:
- **Flat yield curve**: Short and long-term yields are the same and typically imply uncertainty in the market.
- **Inverted yield curve**: Downward sloping curve caused by long-term yields that are lower than short-term yields. Economists often see this as an indicator of a pending recession.
- **Humped yield curve**: Long-term yields are the same as short-term yields, and medium (in-between intermediate) yields are higher than both of them.

The term, structure of interest rates, indicates market expectations for future interest rate changes related to monetary policy. Three theories have been developed based on the yield curve.
1) **Market segmentation theory**: Explains the humped yield curve whereby the shape of the yield curve is dependent on the various market segments and their individual preference for investments and maturities. For example, insurance companies may prefer longer terms and

bank lenders might prefer shorter terms. This will result in a yield curve showing what the market segments prefer versus the overall market's expectations.

2) **Liquidity preference theory:** As interest rates increase, the value of a fixed rate investment decreases. Investors should be compensated for holding securities for longer terms, and therefore, long-term rates should be higher than short-term rates which represent a premium.

3) **Expectations theory**: Theory that long-term rates can forecast future expected short-term rates. It assumes that the total interest on a one-year bond purchased today, plus a second, successive one-year bond purchased one year from now would equal the interest on a two-year bond purchased today. Since this theory is reliant on market expectations, it doesn't always hold true.

m. Bond valuations

When bonds are issued, the contract or coupon rate represents the amount of interest the bondholders will be paid by the bond issuer. At issue date, a bond can be issued with a contract rate that is either below, equal to, or higher than the market rate of interest.

- If the **contract rate is below the market rate, the bond will sell at a discount** (less than its face amount) because investors will want to pay less than the face amount of the bond to compensate them for accepting a lower rate in the market for similar types of securities.
- If the **contract rate is higher than the market rate, the bond will sell at a premium** (more than its face amount) because investors would be willing to pay more than the face amount of the bond due to the bond paying a higher interest rate in the market for similar types of securities.
- If the **contract rate equals the market rate, the bond will sell at its face amount**.

> *Hint:* Overall, in order for a business to manage through various business cycles and interest rate movements, it is important to utilize both short term and long term financial strategies when determining the proper mix of debt and equity financing.

2. Means for mitigating/controlling financial risks

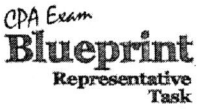

> Identify strategies to mitigate financial risks (market, interest rate, currency, liquidity, etc.) and quantify their impact on a business entity.

There are two ways to mitigate risk -- diversification and hedging.

a. Diversification

Diversification occurs when management takes action to mitigate risk through management's selection among alternatives. Those alternatives include acquiring a new business, selling part of an existing operation, or selling new products. By doing such, companies are looking to diversify.

There are two types of diversification -- related diversification and unrelated diversification.

1) Related diversification is where a business offers new products that are similar to the current products. McDonald's is an example of related diversification, where it expanded its product offerings from the original hamburgers to include additional products such as chicken McNuggets and McCafe coffee.

2) Unrelated diversification is where a business offers new products that are unrelated to its current products to penetrate new market segments. For example, a company that produces toys may diversify by starting a perfume product line.

Unsystematic risks, relating to a specific company or set of similar companies, can be reduced through diversification. For example, the risk of a labor strike may be mitigated through diversifying the means of production such as increasing automation instead of labor-intensive production.

Multiple Choice

BEC 2-Q40

b. Derivatives

A **derivative** is a type of financial instrument whose value is dependent (derived) from another financial instrument, or multiple financial instruments (called the underlying instrument or instruments). A derivative is formed as a contract between two or more parties. A derivative gets its value from the underlying instrument(s). An underlying instrument can be a commodity, foreign currency, stock, bond, or another asset. For example, in a derivative contract for 1 million barrels of oil, the underlying instrument is the oil. For accounting purposes, derivatives are recorded at their fair value on the balance sheet.

The four main types of derivatives categories are futures contracts, forward contracts, options, and swaps.

1) **Futures contracts** are standardized contracts to buy or sell an asset at a specified price and future date. Futures are standardized to facilitate trading (e.g., pre-set quantities and settlement dates), and, as such, can be traded on an exchange. Traded futures indicate the quality and quantity of the commodity agreed-upon, as applicable.
2) **Forward contracts** are contracts developed for a specific purpose between two parties, where one party agrees to purchase or sell an asset at a specified price and date in the future. A forward can be written for any commodity at any quantity and can be settled in cash or by delivery. Forwards are over-the-counter instruments, and are not traded on an exchange. Often, forward contracts are associated with commodities or currencies. In a forward contract, both parties to the agreement are obligated to satisfy the terms of the agreement (unlike an option). Forward contracts are arranged for large dollar contracts or multiple transactions (i.e., transactions of a subsidiary).
3) **Options** grant the right, but not the obligation, to buy (i.e., call) or sell (i.e., put) an underlying asset, with a specified exchange or "strike," or "exercise" price and with a date-based expiration. The option's value is mostly dependent on the market price of the underlying security. Options can be bought and sold on an exchange or over-the-counter.
4) **Swaps** (unlike the first three types of derivatives) are actually made up of two agreements where one party agrees to exchange a stream of cash flows with the expectation of another stream of cash flows at a future date. Typically, it is a fixed stream of cash flows exchanged for a variable stream of cash flows. Typically, the principal is not exchanged in a swap, and no entry is required when the contract is signed since there is not typically any up-front payment due to either party. One party often would like to swap their fixed cash flow with one that is variable (based on a floating interest rate, e.g., LIBOR). Swaps are a popular form of hedging, and if used in as a hedge the U.S. GAAP over hedging takes precedence.
    i. **Interest rate swaps** are forward type contracts where the two parties agree to exchange payments (in the same currency) related to party-specific interest rates, at a specified time period. For example, party A agrees to pay party B a predetermined, fixed rate of interest and party B agrees to make their payments using a variable interest rate.
    ii. **Currency swaps** are forward based type contracts where the two parties agree to exchange payments, in different currencies, for a specified time period.
    iii. **A swaption** is an option to enter into an interest rate swap or some another type of swap. It grants the holder the right (not an obligation) to enter into the swap in exchange for an option premium.

iv. Swaps are valued using the **zero coupon method**, which is similar to the net present value method of the estimated future cash flows. Swaps are worth nothing on the date initiated, but their value will change over time. The estimated future cash flows represent the amount of net settlement that is required when the future interest rate is equal to the current yield. The discount rate and timing of the cash flows are components of the calculation with the zero coupon method.

Multiple Choice

BEC 2-Q41 through BEC 2-Q42

c. Hedging
There are two uses for derivatives, one used for **speculative** reasons and the other for **hedging** purposes. Speculative reasons represent investors who "gamble" on market price changes. Hedging is used to mitigate risks as a defensive strategy.

One hedging approach uses investments to minimize the threat of losses by taking offsetting positions in related derivatives. For example, the value of that related derivative would change inversely with respect to that investment. In general, hedging involves paying third parties to take on some of the risk exposure. Usually, a hedging strategy is only for the protection of risk. The risks that a hedge can protect against include interest rates and foreign currency exchange risks. A hedge is considered a **highly effective hedge** if the fair value or cash flow of the hedged item and the hedging derivative offset each other by a large percentage (80% to 125%).

Hint: Under the new ASC 815 for Hedge Accounting, the guidance eliminates the requirement to separately measure and report hedge ineffectiveness.

1) Types of hedging activities
   i. **Fair value hedges** are used to hedge exposures to changes in the fair value of an asset or liability, including unrecognized firm commitments (i.e., purchase order).
   ii. **Cash flow hedges** are used to hedge the exposure to changes in expected future cash flows.
   iii. **Foreign currency hedges** are used to reduce the risk of adverse movements in the future exchange rate.

2) Recall that there are three types of foreign currency exchange risks: foreign currency exchange transaction risk, foreign currency exchange translation risk, and economic risk.

   i. Mitigating foreign currency *transaction* risk
   Foreign currency transactions relate to purchases (accounts payable) or sales (accounts receivable) of goods or services where the money that changes hands is not in U.S. dollars. Foreign currency transaction risk is the possibility of losses resulting from changes in exchange rates resulting from the purchase or sale.

   Purchase (accounts payable): If the domestic currency weakens compared to the foreign currency, it will take a more domestic currency to settle the account payable. This risk of a foreign currency transaction loss can be mitigated by the domestic entity entering a **futures hedge contract to buy** the foreign currency at a specified price, at the time the accounts payable is due.

   Sale (accounts receivable): If the domestic currency strengthens compared to the foreign currency, the domestic entity will have less currency to spend when the foreign entity pays the accounts receivable. This risk of a foreign currency transaction loss can be mitigated by the domestic entity entering a **futures hedge contract to sell** the foreign currency at a specified price, at the time the accounts receivable is due.

Foreign currency transaction risk can also be mitigated with **money market hedges,** in which a domestic entity "locks in" the current foreign currency exchange rate (spot rate) in advance of a foreign currency transaction.
- For a purchase (accounts payable) transaction, the domestic entity will then settle the accounts payable at the exchange rate they want to pay.
- For a sales (accounts receivable) transaction, the domestic entity could factor the receivables with a foreign financial institution, such as a bank. The domestic entity could also borrow in the foreign currency and after converting the amount to domestic currency, invest it until the accounts receivable due date. The loan can be paid off with the money received from the settlement of the accounts receivable.

ii. Mitigating foreign currency *translation* risk
Foreign currency translations relate to converting entire financial statements, reported in a foreign currency, into U.S. dollars. For example, a U.S. company may have a foreign subsidiary with financial statements using the currency of the foreign country. Translation into U.S. dollars is necessary to make the financial statements more useful and comparable with a common currency unit. Exchange rates typically change between financial statement reporting periods and cause foreign currency translation risk, which means the changes in exchange rates could lead to translation adjustments.

Forward contracts can be used to create an offsetting asset and liability in the foreign currency, thereby potentially reducing translation risk. Also, a company can adjust the planned cash flows to or from domestic operations to foreign subsidiaries to minimize translation risk.

iii. Mitigating *economic* risk
Economic risk is the risk to a company's present value of future cash flows related to fluctuations in foreign exchange rates. To mitigate the risk, management may analyze various cash inflows and outflows scenarios compared to exchange rate and assess the results. Depending on the risk exposure from the assessment, management can shift operational emphasis to reduce exchange rate sensitive cash flows.

Multiple Choice

BEC 2-Q43 through BEC 2-Q44

d. Mitigating liquidity risk
Liquidity risk is the risk associated with having funds invested in long-term assets that cannot be easily converted into cash (sold) within a necessary timeframe or, the inability to meet payment obligations as they come due. Managing liquidity to reduce the risk includes assessing the need for funds to meet both current and future obligations and ensuring there is enough cash or collateral to fulfill those needs when payment obligations arise. The risk mitigation process may also include:
- Funding strategy established as part of the budget process.
- Developing alternative scenarios to assess the level of liquidity needed, including crisis situations.

This page is intentionally left blank.

Glossary: Economic Concepts and Analysis

A

Absolute advantage – the ability for a country (or business) to produce goods that require a smaller amount of "inputs" (i.e. low cost labor or more efficient production process) than any other country (or business) producing the same good

Accelerator effect – relates to the increase of a firm's investments in production that are done to meet the rate of growth for demand of goods

Acquisition – when one company buys another (target) company

Aggregate demand (AD) – the total of all goods and services in the entire economy that are demanded at any given price and at any given period

Aggregate supply (AS) – the total of all goods and services in the entire economy that firms are willing to produce at any given price and at any given period

Arc elasticity – a method of calculating the price elasticity as a percentage change between two points using the relationship between the average price and quality to find the curve's average elasticity. This shows the arc of the curve between the points

Average revenue (AR) – the revenue received by a firm for each unit of production (output)

B

Balance of payments – a summary of all economic transactions between one country and the rest of the world's economies, or just between two countries

Balance of trade – total goods exported minus total goods imported

Barriers to trade – a government's economic policy of limiting trade between their country and foreign countries

Beta – the measurement to determine whether an investment is more or less volatile than the portfolio

Budget deficit – occurs when tax revenue does not cover governmental spending

Budget surplus – occurs when tax revenue, in total, is greater than governmental spending

Business cycle – fluctuations in economic activity over a period of time

C

Coefficient of variation – measurement of risk and indicates the degree of variation among investments with means that are different from one another

Coincident indicators – indicators that occur at about the same time as economic events

Comparative advantage – the ability of a country (or business) to produce a good at a lower opportunity cost when compared to another country

Constant returns to scale (CRS) – an increase in units produced results in no change in the average cost per unit

Consumer confidence index – measure of consumer optimism with the general economy's performance, based on consumer behavior with regard to savings and spending

Consumer price index (CPI) – the current prices paid by consumers for a fixed basket of goods and services, relative to those prices during the same period in a previous year

Consumption function – relationship of consumption and disposable income, holding constant factors such as wealth, price level, and future income prospects that could also impact consumption

Contraction – following a peak in the business cycle where the economy begins to slow

Cost-push inflation – inflation caused by a shortage of output (supply) drives up prices for those goods and services

Countervailing duties – Represent an import tax on goods to stop dumping or counter export subsidies

Cross elasticity of demand – Measures the rate of change for a product, relative to a change in price of another competing or similar product

Cyclical business – sensitive to business cycles, where revenues for cyclical businesses are typically higher during economic expansion and lower in economic contractions

Cyclical unemployment – results from decreases in real GDP, where it is less than potential GDP

D

Deflation – represents a decrease in the general or aggregate price level in the economy

Demand curve – is downward sloping and indicates that for specific levels of the quantity demanded, there is an inverse relationship (where other demand variables are constant) to the corresponding price that people are willing to pay

Demand-pull inflation – inflation caused by excess aggregate demand which is greater than normal output (supply) at full employment
Depression – a prolonged and excessive recession which lasts for two or more years
Derivative – a type of financial instrument whose value is dependent (derived) from another financial instrument, or multiple financial instruments (called the underlying instrument or instruments)
Diminishing returns to scale (DRS) – an increase in units of production results in an increase in the average cost per unit. Firms experience diseconomies of scale in this situation
Diversification – where management takes action to mitigate risk through management's selection among alternatives
Divestiture – when a company sells or disposes a division or subsidiary
Dumping – occurs when a country sells products in a foreign country at prices below its cost or below what those products sell for in the home market

E

Economic depreciation – the amount of GNP required for the purchase of new goods and services in order to maintain existing stock
Economic indicators – developed by economists to predict economic activity
Economic profit – the profit remaining after subtracting implicit costs from accounting profit
Elastic – where a small change in price results in a large change in quantity demanded
Elasticity of demand – measurement that considers a change in quantity demanded compared to a change in the price of the product
Elasticity of supply – measurement that considers a change in quantity supplied compared to a change in the price of the product
Embargo – the most restrictive barrier to trade and represents a full or partial prohibition of the ability for a foreign country to import or export
Expansion – economy begins to expand and grow (periods of economic prosperity)
Expenditure (input) approach of calculating GDP – combines all the amounts to purchase goods and services from government purchases, net exports, personal consumption, domestic fixed investment and changes in inventories
Explicit costs – recognizable accounting expenses (e.g., rent, labor) that result from a transaction.
Export subsidies – incentives to producers to export more of a certain type of good.
Externality – term used to describe components of economic activity that affects parties who are not directly involved

F

Fiscal contraction – a tight fiscal policy
Fiscal expansion – a loose fiscal policy
Fiscal policy – represent actions taken by the government related to government spending, taxes, and subsidies
Fixed costs – costs that remain constant (within a relevant range)
Fixed exchange rate regime – rates are tied to another country's rate or the rates of a set grouping of other countries
Floating exchange rate regime – rates are allowed to fluctuate with the market
Foreign exchange controls – a government restricts or stop foreign currency purchases or sales by the government's citizens, or on the purchase or sale of local currency by nonresidents
Foreign exchange rate – the amount (rate) that the currency of one country can be exchanged for another country's currency
Forward rate – the exchange rate at a future date
Free trade – where governments decrease as many barriers to trade as they can
Frictional unemployment – considered normal in the economy and results from temporary worker transitions as they move from one job to another
Full employment – occurs when there is no cyclical unemployment

G

GDP Deflator – the price index used to convert nominal GDP to real GDP
GDP Gap – difference between real GDP (actual output of the economy) and the potential GDP (full capacity)
Gross domestic product (GDP) – total output of goods and services produced in the domestic economy during a particular time period

Gross national product (GNP) – represents the total amount of all final goods and services produced by citizens of a country over a specific time period

H

Hedging – uses an investment to minimize the threat of losses by taking an offsetting position in a related derivative

Hyperinflation – occurs when the price of goods and services sharply increase

I

Implicit costs – quantify the benefits forgone when choosing one alternative over another alternative, also known as opportunity costs. Also known as opportunity costs

Income (output) approach of calculating GDP – combines all business profits (corporations and proprietors), and includes such items as wages, rents, dividends and interest

Income effect – where income remains constant, if there is a decrease in the price of a good, people will either buy more of that product, or buy more of all goods because their real income has increased (they have more money to spend due to the price decrease)

Income elasticity of demand – describes how demand changes relative to changes in income

Increasing returns to scale (IRS) – an increase in units of production result in a decrease in the average cost per unit. Firms experience economies of scale in this situation

Inelastic product – a product is inelastic if a large change in price results in small change in quantity demanded

Inelastic – where a large change in price results in small change in quantity demanded

Inflation – an increase in the cost of living which is a decline in the purchasing power of money

Interest rates – what is charged or paid for the use of money and is represented as a percentage

J

K

L

Lagging indicators – indicators that follow economic events

Law of diminishing marginal utility – states that as a consumer increases consumption of a product, there is a reduction in the marginal utility (satisfaction) that the consumer gets out of consuming each additional amount

Law of diminishing returns – states that continually increasing inputs in the production process, while all other inputs remain fixed, will lead to a point at which the additional inputs will result in smaller (diminishing) increases in output

Leading indicators – indicators that predict or signal future economic events

M

M1 money supply – includes currency, demand deposits and travelers checks. It does not include CDs or savings accounts

M2 money supply – equals M1 plus savings accounts, mutual fund accounts, CDs less than $100,000 and short-term (i.e., 24 hour) money market accounts

M3 money supply – equals M2 plus CDs greater than $100,000 and other large time deposits

Marginal cost (MC) – represents the additional cost of producing one more unit of goods

Marginal propensity to consume (MPC) – measures the change in spending as income changes

Marginal propensity to save (MPS) – measures the change in spending as income changes

Marginal revenue (MR) – the change in the total revenue from each additional unit of production

Market demand – the total of all individual demand curves within the marketplace

Market equilibrium – where demand is equal to supply

Market supply – the total of all individual supply curves within the marketplace

Merger – when two companies agree to combine into one "new" company

Monetary assets and liabilities – items that either are already cash or, can be readily converted into cash, includes cash, accounts receivable, notes receivable, investments, accounts payable, and notes payable

Monetary items – items that are either already cash or, can be readily converted into cash

Monetary policy – the Federal Reserve's programs to influence the amount of money and credit in the economy

Multiplier effect – the effect that spending (consumer, business, and government) has on gross domestic product (GDP)

N

National Income (NI) – net national product less business sales taxes

Net Domestic Product (NDP) – calculated as GDP minus depreciation

Net National Product (NNP) – represents amount of all final goods and services produced by a country's citizens (regardless if they are in the U.S. or in a foreign country), minus the economic depreciation

Nominal GDP – the unadjusted GDP which measures the total amount of goods and services produced at the prices that were in effect when they were produced

Nominal interest rate – the rate of interest charged by a lender and paid by the borrower in loan transactions

Non-cyclical business – not affected by business cycles because demand for a company's products continues, regardless of the economic phase

Non-monetary assets and liabilities – nonmonetary items cannot be easily converted to cash and do not have a precise dollar value (e.g., the dollar value may fluctuate) such as inventory, fixed assets, warranties payable, and deferred income tax credits.

O

Open market operations – a monetary policies and represents the Federal Reserve buying and selling government securities, such as treasury bonds and treasury bills, for the purpose of managing the money supply and influencing short-term interest rates

Opportunity cost – the cost of benefits forgone when choosing one alternative versus another alternative

P

Peak – highest point of economic activity in the business cycle

Pegged exchange rate regime – where rates are maintained at or close to the central bank's targeted rate

Personal Disposable Income (PDI) – personal income minus income taxes

Personal Income (PI) – the total income received by households and non-corporate businesses

Phillips Curve – represents the inverse relationship between inflation and unemployment

Potential GDP – the maximum amount of goods and services produced at a constant inflation rate, with ideal production and high employment levels

Price ceiling – highest price that is established for a good

Price elasticity (sensitivity) of demand – measurement that considers a change in quantity demanded to a change in price

Price floor – minimum price that is established for a good

Producer Price Index (PPI) – the current wholesale prices for a fixed basket of goods and services produced by firms, relative to those prices during the same period in a previous year

Profit – calculated by taking total revenues and subtracting total costs

Q

Quota – represents a restriction to the amount of goods that can be imported

R

Real (actual) GDP – the adjusted GDP that measures the total amount of goods and services produced by using the price index (constant dollar) to eliminate the effects of inflation

Real interest rate – represents an inflation adjusted interest rate

Recession – defined as two consecutive quarters, or six months of declining gross domestic product

Reserve requirements – the Federal Reserve establishes the percentage of money in demand deposit accounts that banks must hold in reserve

Risk-adverse – a reluctance to take on risk; a person who is risk-adverse will take on risk only if they will be compensated for it in the form of a higher return

Risk-neutral – describes a person who in not concerned about risk and would take a higher risk option, regardless of the risk

Risk-seeking – describes a person who likes to take risks and is willing to accept the potential of a lesser return in order to take on more risk

S

Spot rate – the exchange rate "on the spot", or at the moment of the foreign exchange activity

Structural unemployment – Occurs when there is not a match-up of worker skills with job requirements due to things like technological advances, or if the workers who are not employed do not live near the job opportunities

Substitution effect – if there is an increase in the price of a product, the product becomes more expensive than its substitute (alternative/similar) products, which will cause people to purchase the alternative/similar product

Supply curve – an upward sloping curve which indicates for specific levels of the quantity supplied, there is a direct relationship to the corresponding price of the goods or service

Systematic risk – relates to factors for an entire market or entire market segment that cannot be avoided simply by diversifying a portfolio of investments

T

Tariffs – represent a tax on imports, which raise the price of imported goods, compared to domestic goods

Term structure of interest rates – the relationship between short-term and long-term interest rates

Trade deficit – arises when one county imports more than it exports

Trade surplus – arises when one country exports more than it imports

Trough – lowest point in the economic activity of the business cycle

U

Unemployment rate – calculated as the percent of unemployed people divided by the total labor force

Unsystematic risk – relates to the risk for a specific company (stock), or a group of similar companies in an industry that are in a portfolio of investments

V

Variable costs – costs that vary with output and usually increase at a constant rate relative to labor and capital

W

X

Y

Yield curve – depicts interest rates for different lengths of time-to-maturity and interest rates (costs of borrowing)

This page is intentionally left blank.

Multiple Choice – Questions

BEC 2-Q1 B181. Which of the following characteristics would indicate that an item sold would have a high price elasticity of demand?

A. The item has many similar substitutes.
B. The cost of the item is low compared to the total budget of the purchasers.
C. The item is considered a necessity.
D. Changes in the price of the item are regulated by governmental agency.

BEC 2-Q2 B361. Under which of the following conditions is the supplier most able to influence or control buyers?

A. When the supplier's products are **not** differentiated.
B. When the supplier does **not** face the threat of substitute products.
C. When the industry is controlled by a large number of companies.
D. When the purchasing industry is an important customer to the supplying industry.

BEC 2-Q3 B90. Variations between business cycles most likely are attributable to which of the following factors?

A. The law of diminishing returns.
B. Comparative advantage.
C. Duration and intensity.
D. Opportunity costs.

BEC 2-Q4 B362. An auditor is required to obtain an understanding of the entity's business, including business cycles and reasons for business fluctuations. What is the audit purpose most directly served by obtaining this understanding?

A. To enable the auditor to accurately identify reportable conditions.
B. To assist the auditor to accurately interpret information obtained during an audit.
C. To allow the auditor to more accurately perform tests of controls.
D. To decide whether it will be necessary to perform analytical procedures.

BEC 2-Q5 B299. Gross domestic product includes which of the following measures?

A. The size of a population that must share a given output within one year.
B. The negative externalities of the production process of a nation within one year.
C. The total monetary value of all final goods and services produced within a nation in one year.
D. The total monetary value of goods and services including barter transactions within a nation in one year.

BEC 2-Q6 B297. All of the following are components of the formula used to calculate gross domestic product **except**

A. Household income.
B. Foreign net export spending.
C. Government spending.
D. Gross investment.

BEC 2-Q7 B363. Which of the following segments of the economy will be **least** affected by the business cycle?

A. Commercial construction industry.
B. Machinery and equipment industry.
C. Residential construction industry.
D. Healthcare industry.

BEC 2-Q8 B122. Which of the following economic terms describes a general decline in prices for goods and services and in the level of interest rates?

A. Expansion.
B. Inflation.
C. Deflation.
D. Recession.

BEC 2-Q9 B57. A hospital is comparing last year's emergency rescue services expenditures to those from 10 years ago. Last year's expenditures were $100,500. Ten years ago, the expenditures were $72,800. The CPI for last year is 168.5 as compared to 121.3 ten years ago. After adjusting for inflation, what percentage change occurred in expenditures for emergency rescue services?

A. 38.0% increase.
B. 13.8% increase.
C. 0.6% decrease.
D. 18.1% decrease.

BEC 2-Q10 B123. The primary purpose of the consumer price index (CPI) is to

A. Establish a cost-of-living index.
B. Identify the strength of an economic recovery.
C. Help determine the Federal Reserve Bank's discount rate.
D. Compare relative price changes over time.

BEC 2-Q11 B177. What does the consumer price index measure?

A. Cost of capital.
B. Average household income.
C. Rate of inflation.
D. Prime rate of interest.

BEC 2-Q12 B261. Which of the following is correct regarding the consumer price index (CPI) for measuring the estimated decrease in a company's buying power?

A. The CPI is measured only once every 10 years.
B. The products a company buys should differ from what a consumer buys.
C. The CPI measures what consumers will pay for items.
D. The CPI is skewed by foreign currency translations.

BEC 2-Q13 B369. The federal government measures inflation with which of the following indicators?

A. Dow Jones index.
B. Consumer price index.
C. Consumer confidence index.
D. Corporate profits.

BEC 2-Q14 B371. Which of the following concepts compares the price of goods in a given year to a base year?

A. Consumer Price Index.
B. Consumer Confidence Index.
C. Gross National Product.
D. Net National Product.

BEC 2-Q15 B58. If a CPA's client expected a high inflation rate in the future, the CPA would suggest to the client which of the following types of investments?

A. Precious metals.
B. Treasury bonds.
C. Corporate bonds.
D. Common stock.

BEC 2-Q16 B72. The following information is available on market interest rates:

The risk-free rate of interest	2%
Inflation premium	1%
Default risk premium	3%
Liquidity premium	2%
Maturity risk premium	1%

What is the market rate of interest on a one-year U.S. Treasury bill?

A. 3%
B. 5%
C. 6%
D. 7%

BEC 2-Q17 B171. Which of the following Federal Reserve policies would increase money supply?

A. Change the multiplier effect.
B. Increase reserve requirements.
C. Reduce the discount rate.
D. Sell more U.S. Treasury bonds.

BEC 2-Q18 B354. To address the problem of a recession, the Federal Reserve Bank most likely would take which of the following actions?

A. Lower the discount rate it charges to banks for loans.
B. Sell U.S. government bonds in open-market transactions.
C. Increase the federal funds rate charged by banks when they borrow from one another.
D. Increase the level of funds a bank is legally required to hold in reserve.

BEC 2-Q19 B359. Which of the following actions is the acknowledged preventive measure for a period of deflation?

A. Increasing interest rates.
B. Increasing the money supply.
C. Decreasing interest rates.
D. Decreasing the money supply.

BEC 2-Q20 B265. A city ordinance that freezes rent prices may cause

A. The demand curve for rental space to fall.
B. The supply curve for rental space to rise.
C. Demand for rental space to exceed supply.
D. Supply of rental space to exceed demand.

BEC 2-Q21 B320. Which of the following statements is correct if there is an increase in the resources available within an economy?

A. More goods and services will be produced in the economy.
B. The economy will be capable of producing more goods and services.
C. The standard of living in the economy will rise.
D. The technological efficiency of the economy will improve.

BEC 2-Q22 B142. Which of the following is an assumption in a perfectly competitive financial market?

A. No single trader or traders can have a significant impact on market prices.
B. Some traders can impact market prices more than others.
C. Trading prices vary based on supply only.
D. Information about borrowing/lending activities is only available to those willing to pay market prices.

BEC 2-Q23 B377. What is the effect on prices of U.S. imports and exports when the dollar depreciates?

A. Import prices and export prices will decrease.
B. Import prices will decrease and export prices will increase.
C. Import prices will increase and export prices will decrease.
D. Import prices and export prices will increase.

BEC 2-Q24 B180. Freely fluctuating exchange rates perform which of the following functions?

A. They automatically correct a lack of equilibrium in the balance of payments.
B. They make imports cheaper and exports more expensive.
C. They impose constraints on the domestic economy.
D. They eliminate the need for foreign currency hedging.

BEC 2-Q25 B143. A country's currency conversion value has recently changed from 1.5 to the U.S. dollar to 1.7 to the U.S. dollar. Which of the following statements about the country is correct?

A. Its exports are less expensive for the United States.
B. Its currency has appreciated.
C. Its imports of U.S. goods are more affordable.
D. Its purchases of the U.S. dollar will cost less.

BEC 2-Q26 B277. What is the effect when a foreign competitor's currency becomes weaker compared to the U.S. dollar?

A. The foreign company will have an advantage in the U.S. market.
B. The foreign company will be disadvantaged in the U.S. market.
C. The fluctuation in the foreign currency's exchange rate has no effect on the U.S. company's sales or cost of goods sold.
D. It is better for the U.S. company when the value of the U.S. dollar strengthens.

BEC 2-Q27 B372. A company manufactures goods in Esland for sale to consumers in Woostland. Currently, the economy of Esland is booming and imports are rising rapidly. Woostland is experiencing an economic recession, and its imports are declining. How will the Esland currency, $E, react with respect to the Woostland currency, $W?

A. The $E will remain constant with respect to the $W.
B. The $E will increase with respect to the $W.
C. The $E will decline with respect to the $W.
D. Changes in imports and exports will **not** affect currency changes.

BEC 2-Q28 B1250. A company considers investing $20 million in a foreign company whose local currency is under pressure. The company suspects that the exchange rate may fluctuate soon. The exchange rate at the time of the investment is 2.57 to $1.00. After the investment, the exchange rate changes to 3.15 to $1.00. What is the change in the value of the company's investment in U.S. dollars?

A. 18.4% increase.
B. 18.4% decrease.
C. 22.6% increase.
D. 22.6% decrease.

BEC 2-Q29 B1226. A U.S.-based company decides to invest capital in an emerging market operation that has a lower expected return rate compared to the expected return for an alternative domestic operation. Which of the following statements correctly supports this decision?

A. Management expects the U.S. dollar to decline in value relative to the foreign location's currency.
B. Management expects inflation to increase in the emerging market compared to the U.S. inflation rate.
C. Management expects inflation to decrease in the U.S. compared to the foreign location's inflation rate.
D. Management expects the U.S. dollar to strengthen in value relative to the foreign location's currency.

BEC 2-Q30 B647.* Johnson Software has developed a new software package. Johnson's sales manager has prepared the following probability distribution describing the relative likelihood of monthly sales levels and relative income (loss) for the company's new software package.

Monthly Sales In Units	Probability	Income (Loss)
10,000	0.2	$(4,000)
20,000	0.3	10,000
30,000	0.3	30,000
40,000	0.2	60,000

If Johnson decides to market its new software package, the expected value of additional monthly income will be

A. $23,200.
B. $24,000.
C. $24,800.
D. $25,000.

---

* CMA adapted.

BEC 2-Q31 B648.* According to recent focus sessions, Norton Corporation has a "can't miss" consumer product on its hands. Sales forecasts indicate either excellent or good results, with Norton's sales manager assigning a probability of .6 to a good results outcome. The company is now studying various sales compensation plans for the product and has determined the following contribution margin data.

	Contribution Margin
If sales are excellent and	
Plan 1 is adopted	$300,000
Plan 2 is adopted	370,000
If sales are good and	
Plan 1 is adopted	240,000
Plan 2 is adopted	180,000

On the basis of this information, which of the following statements is correct?

A. Plan 2 should be adopted because it is $10,000 more attractive than Plan 1.
B. Plan 1 should be adopted because it is $8,000 more attractive than Plan 2.
C. Plan 1 should be adopted because of the sales manager's higher confidence in good results.
D. Either Plan should be adopted, the decision being dependent on the probability of excellent sales results.

BEC 2-Q32 B650.* Scarf Corporation's controller has decided to use a decision model to cope with uncertainty. With a particular proposal, currently under consideration, Scarf has two possible actions, invest or not invest in a joint venture with an international firm. The controller has determined the following.

Action 1: Invest in the Joint Venture
Events and Probabilities:
Probability of success = 60%.
Cost of investment = $9.5 million.
Cash flow if investment is successful = $15.0 million.
Cash flow if investment is unsuccessful = $2.0 million.
Additional costs to be paid = $0
Costs incurred up to this point = $650,000.

Action 2: Do Not Invest in the Joint Venture
Events:
Costs incurred up to this point = $650,000.
Additional costs to be paid = $100,000.

Which one of the following alternatives correctly reflects the respective expected values of investing versus not investing?

A. $300,000 and $(750,000)
B. $(350,000) and $(100,000)
C. $300,000 and (100,000)
D. $(350,000) and $(750,000)

BEC 2-Q33 B651.* Allbee Company has three possible investment opportunities. The controller calculated the payoffs and probabilities, as follows.

	Probabilities		
Payoffs	Investment A	Investment B	Investment C
$(20,000)	.3	.2	.3
(10,000)	.1	.2	.1
30,000	.3	.2	.2
70,000	.2	.2	.3
100,000	.1	.2	.1

The cost of investments A, B, and C are the same. Using the expected-value criterion, which one of the following rankings of these investments, from highest payoff to lowest payoff, is correct?

A. A, B, C
B. B, A, C
C. C, A, B
D. B, C, A

---

* CMA adapted.

BEC 2-Q34 B652.* The sales manager of Serito Doll Company has suggested that an expanded advertising campaign costing $40,000 would increase the sales and profits of the company. He has developed the following probability distribution for the effect of the advertising campaign on company sales.

Sales increase (units)	Probability
15,000	.10
30,000	.35
45,000	.10
60,000	.25
75,000	.20

The company sells the dolls at $5.20 each. The cost of each doll is $3.20. Serito's expected incremental profit, if the advertising campaign is adopted, would be

A. $6,500.
B. $46,500.
C. $53,000.
D. $93,000.

BEC 2-Q35 B653.* Stock X has the following probability distribution of expected future returns.

Probability	Expected Return
.10	-20%
.20	5%
.40	15%
.20	20%
.10	30%

The expected rate of return on stock X would be

A. 10%.
B. 12%.
C. 16%.
D. 19%.

BEC 2-Q36 B654.* Which one of the following four probability distributions provides the highest expected monetary value?

	Alternative #1		Alternative #2	
Prob.	Cash Inflows	Prob.	Cash Inflows
10%	$50,000	10%	$50,000
20%	75,000	20%	75,000
40%	100,000	45%	100,000
30%	150,000	25%	150,000

	Alternative #3		Alternative #4	
Prob.	Cash Inflows	Prob.	Cash Inflows
10%	$50,000	10%	$150,000
20%	75,000	20%	100,000
40%	100,000	40%	75,000
30%	125,000	30%	50,000

A. Alternative #1.
B. Alternative #2.
C. Alternative #3.
D. Alternative #4.

---

* CMA adapted.

BEC 2-Q37 B655.* The Lions Club is planning to sell pretzels at a local football game and has estimated sales demand as follows.

Sales demand	8,000	10,000	12,000	15,000
Probability	10%	40%	30%	20%

The cost of the pretzels varies with the quantity purchased as follows.

Purchase quantity	8,000	10,000	12,000	15,000
Cost per unit	$1.25	$1.20	$1.15	$1.10

Any unsold pretzels would be donated to the local food bank. The calculated profits at the various sales demand levels and purchase quantities are as follows.

Expected Profits at Various Purchase Quantity Levels

Sales Demand	8,000	10,000	12,000	15,000
8,000	$6,000	$4,000	$2,200	$(500)
10,000	6,000	8,000	6,200	3,500
12,000	6,000	8,000	10,200	7,500
15,000	6,000	8,000	10,200	13,500

Which one of the following purchase quantities would you recommend to the Lions Club?

A. 8,000
B. 10,000
C. 12,000
D. 15,000

BEC 2-Q38 B278. Which of the following factors is inherent in a firm's operations if it utilizes only equity financing?

A. Financial risk.
B. Business risk.
C. Interest rate risk.
D. Marginal risk.

BEC 2-Q39 B1135. * The Texas Corporation is considering the following opportunities to purchase an investment at the following amounts and discounts.

Term	Amount	Discount
90 days	$ 80,000	5%
180 days	75,000	6%
270 days	100,000	5%
360 days	60,000	10%

Which opportunity offers the Texas Corporation the highest annual yield?

A. 90-day investment.
B. 180-day investment.
C. 270-day investment.
D. 360-day investment.

BEC 2-Q40 B94. Which of the following types of risk can be reduced by diversification?

A. High interest rates.
B. Inflation.
C. Labor strikes.
D. Recessions.

BEC 2-Q41 B47. A company has several long-term floating-rate bonds outstanding. The company's cash flows have stabilized, and the company is considering hedging interest rate risk. Which of the following derivative instruments is recommended for this purpose?

A. Structured short-term note.
B. Forward contract on a commodity.
C. Futures contract on a stock.
D. Swap agreement.

BEC 2-Q42 B79. A put is an option that gives its owner the right to do which of the following?

A. Sell a specific security at fixed conditions of price and time.
B. Sell a specific security at a fixed price for an indefinite time period.
C. Buy a specific security at fixed conditions of price and time.
D. Buy a specific security at a fixed price for an indefinite time period.

---

* CMA adapted.

BEC 2-Q43 B178. Platinum Co. has a receivable due in 30 days for 30,000 euros. The treasurer is concerned that the value of the euro relative to the dollar will drop before the payment is received. What should Platinum do to reduce this risk?

A. Buy 30,000 euros now.
B. Enter into an interest rate swap contract for 30 days.
C. Enter into a forward contract to sell 30,000 euros in 30 days.
D. Platinum cannot effectively reduce this risk.

BEC 2-Q44 B313. An American importer expects to pay a British supplier 500,000 British pounds in three months. Which of the following hedges is best for the importer to fix the price in dollars?

A. Buying British pound call options.
B. Buying British pound put options.
C. Selling British pound put options.
D. Selling British pound call options.

Multiple Choice – Solutions

BEC 2-Q1 B181. The correct choice is A. The elasticity of demand is determined by how demand for a product changes according to changes in price. Demand that is elastic means that demand for a product will increase to a greater extent if there is a decrease in price; higher elasticity will have more pronounced effects. A high price elasticity of demand indicates that customers can switch between products due to the availability of substitutes. So, if a product with a high price elasticity of demand decreases in price, then consumers will switch to it as an acceptable substitute and demand will increase to a greater extent than the decrease in price.

Choice B is not correct because when an item has a low cost as compared to the total budget of the purchasers, changes in prices would have less influence on purchasers' spending patterns and therefore a lower price elasticity of demand.

Choice C is not correct because items that are a necessity have a low price elasticity of demand; a necessity has no available substitute.

Choice D is not correct because regulated prices occur in a monopoly regulated by a governmental agency. The product or service in a monopoly has only one supplier and is a necessity. Because the prices are controlled, their demand is less variable.

BEC 2-Q2 B361. The correct choice is B. When the supplier does not face the threat of substitute products, then the supplier is able to influence or control buyers. Even if the supplier increases prices or decreases the quality of the product or service, buyers have no substitutes for the product or service and must accept what the supplier produces. Therefore, the supplier is able to influence or control buyers.

Choice A is not correct because when a supplier's products are not differentiated, then a buyer can purchase the same product from a different buyer; therefore, the supplier is not able to influence or control buyers.

Choice C is not correct because when the industry is controlled by a large number of companies, then a supplier has many competitors for the same or similar product or service and buyers may switch from one supplier to another supplier; therefore, the supplier is not able to influence or control buyers.

Choice D is not correct because in the case where a customer is important to the supplier, then it is the customer that may have control and influence over the supplier; therefore, the supplier is not able to influence or control buyers.

BEC 2-Q3 B90. The correct choice is C. The variations between business cycles are most likely attributable to the duration and intensity of the current business cycle. For example, if the current business cycle is a deeper and longer recession (trough), then it may take longer to progress to the next business cycle of recovery (expansion), which in turn may take longer to progress to the next business cycle of optimum economic activity (peak).

Choice A is not correct because the law of diminishing returns recognizes that due to the limits of a firm's productive capacity, at a certain point, additional input does not yield the proportionate additional output and the output begins to decrease after the point of diminishing returns.
Choice B is not correct because comparative advantage recognizes that a producer has a lower opportunity cost for producing a particular product relative to another producer's opportunity cost for producing that product. Therefore, producers should concentrate on producing the product with the least opportunity cost relative to the opportunity cost of other producers.

Choice D is not correct because opportunity cost is the cost of benefits forgone when choosing one alternative versus another alternative.

BEC 2-Q4 B362. The correct choice is B. An auditor is required to obtain an understanding of the entity's business, including business cycles and reasons for business fluctuations; this understanding assists the auditors to accurately interpret fluctuations in financial statement elements, e.g., fluctuations in sales revenue, net income, cash and other monetary assets, and cash flows from operating activities, which may increase during expansionary/growth cycles in the entity's business or decrease during contractionary cycles in the entity's business.

Choice A is not correct because identifying reportable conditions occurs during tests of controls in an audit; the poor design or operation of a control results in a significant deficiency when the likelihood is more than inconsequential that a material misstatement in the financial statements will not be prevented or detected.

Choice C is not correct because obtaining an understanding of the entity's internal control allows the auditor to more accurately perform tests of controls.

Choice D is not correct because performing analytical procedures (e.g., analyzing financial statement ratios) are necessary in planning and performing the audit.

BEC 2-Q5 B299. The correct choice is C. Gross Domestic Product (GDP) is defined as the market value of the goods and services produced by labor and property located in that nation; therefore, GDP is the total monetary value of all final goods and services produced within a nation in one year.

Choice A is not correct because population size is not considered in GDP.

Choice B is not correct because negative externalities (e.g., pollution) are not considered in GDP.

Choice D is not correct because GDP does not include the monetary value of goods and services in barter transactions.

BEC 2-Q6 B297. The correct choice is A. The expenditure approach (input approach) formula for calculating gross domestic product (GDP) is:

Personal Consumption Expenditures
+ Gross Private Domestic Fixed Investment (Business & Residential)
+ Government Purchases (Federal, State & Local)
+ Net Exports [may be a (+) or a (−) number]
= Gross Domestic Product

Therefore, choice A for household income is not included in the GDP formula above.

Choice B is not correct because foreign net export spending is included in "Net Exports [may be a (+) or (−) number]" and would be included in GDP.

Choice C is not correct because government spending is included in "Government Purchases (Federal, State & Local)" and would be included in GDP.

Choice D is not correct because gross investment is included in "Gross Private Domestic Fixed Investment (Business & Residential)" and would be included in GDP.

BEC 2-Q7 B363. The correct choice is D. The segment of the economy that would be least affected by the business cycle is the healthcare industry because the demand for health care is dependent upon consumers' essential health needs and these needs have priority over the needs for non-essential products and services.

Choices A, B, and C are not correct because investment in capital assets, such as construction of commercial buildings, manufacture of machinery and equipment, and construction of residential buildings and homes, requires substantial commitments of resources and financing over multiple years (e.g., borrowing and paying interest), and the demand for these investments increases during an expansionary/growth business cycle and decreases during a contractionary/recessionary business cycle.

BEC 2-Q8 B122. The correct choice is C. Deflation describes a general decline in prices for goods and services, as well as a general decline in the level of interest rates.

Choice A is not correct because an economic expansion creates demand that typically puts upward pressure on prices for goods and services and an increase in interest rates.

Choice B is not correct because inflation describes a general increase in prices for goods and services, as well as a general increase in the level of interest rates.

Choice D is not correct because an economic recession is defined as a decline in gross domestic product for two consecutive quarters; a recession typically creates lower demand for goods and services.

BEC 2-Q9 B57. The correct choice is C. In order to make comparisons, you must first render last year's amount of $100,500 comparable to the amount from ten years ago of $72,800. We can do this by using the CPI indexes as described below.

Last year's cost comparable to cost, 10 years ago = $100,500 x (121.3 CPI, 10 years/168.5 CPI, 1 year)

Last year's cost comparable to cost, 10 years ago = $100,500 x 0.72 approximately

Last year's cost comparable to cost, 10 years ago = $72,360

Then compare the $72,360 as adjusted vs. $72,800 = $440 decrease

Then calculate the change, which is $440 decrease/$72,800 = (0.00604) or 0.6% decrease

BEC 2-Q10 B123. The correct choice is D. The CPI adjusts current price levels to the price levels of a base year; the CPI is applied to a basket of goods and services to make prices of the basket of goods and services comparable across periods.

Choice A is not correct because the cost-of-living index is a measure of how prices for goods and services have increased due to inflation.

Choice B is not correct because the CPI is not an economic indicator that helps identify the strength of an economic recovery.

Choice C is not correct because the CPI does not help determine the Federal Reserve Bank's (FRB) discount rate. The discount rate is a tool used by the FRB to implement monetary policy.

BEC 2-Q11 B177. The correct choice is C. The CPI adjusts current price levels to the price levels of a base year; the CPI is applied to a basket of goods and services to make prices of the basket of goods and services comparable across periods. Therefore, the CPI is a measure of inflation.

Choice A is not correct because the cost of capital is the cost entities pay in order to finance their assets.

Choice B is not correct because average household income is not included in the consumer price index.

Choice D is not correct because the prime rate of interest is the interest rate at which banks lend to their most creditworthy customers.

BEC 2-Q12 B261. The correct choice is B. The consumer price index (CPI) adjusts current price levels to the price levels of a base year; the CPI is applied to a basket of goods and services to make the price of the basket of goods and services comparable across periods. If the CPI measures the estimated decrease in a company's buying power, then the basket of goods and services to which the CPI is applied should be different for a company versus the basket of goods and services for a consumer.

Choice A is not correct because the CPI is measured more frequently than once every 10 years. For example, the Bureau of Labor Statistics of the U.S. Department of Labor publishes CPIs by state by month.

Choice C is not correct because the CPI adjusts current price levels to the price levels of a base year; the CPI is applied to a basket of goods and services to make the price of the basket of goods and services comparable across periods. The CPI is a measure of what consumers will pay for a basket of goods and services in the base year's dollars. Current prices measure what consumers will pay for items.

Choice D is not correct because in U.S. GAAP, foreign currency translation is the conversion of financial statements that are denominated in non-U.S. dollars into financial statements that are denominated in U.S. dollars. The CPI is based on a basket of goods and services, not financial statements.

BEC 2-Q13 B369. The correct choice is B. The consumer price index (CPI) adjusts current price levels to the price levels of a base year. The CPI is applied to a basket of goods and services to make the price of the basket of goods and services comparable across periods. Therefore, the federal government measures inflation with the CPI.

Choice A is not correct because the Dow Jones index (the Dow Jones Industrial Average) is a measure based on 30 significant stocks traded on the New York Stock Exchange and the Nasdaq. The index is a measure of overall market performance.

Choice C is not correct because the consumer confidence index is a measure of consumer optimism in the general economy's performance based on consumer behavior with regard to saving and spending.

Choice D is not correct because corporate profits are a measure of earnings as reported in financial statements prepared in accordance with U.S. GAAP or IFRS.

BEC 2-Q14 B371. The correct choice is A. The consumer price index (CPI) adjusts current price levels to the price levels of a base year; the CPI is applied to a basket of goods and services to make the price of the basket of goods and services comparable across periods. The CPI is a measure of what consumers will pay for a basket of goods and services in the base year's dollars.

Choice B is not correct because the consumer confidence index is a measure of consumer optimism in the general economy's performance based on consumer behavior with regard to saving and spending.

Choice C is not correct because gross national product (GNP) is a measure of all goods and services produced by a country's residents in terms of labor and capital investment.

Choice D is not correct because net national product (NNP) is gross national product (GNP) less depreciation on capital investment. GNP is a measure of all goods and services produced by a country's residents in terms of labor and capital investment.

BEC 2-Q15 B58. The correct choice is A. If a high inflation rate is expected, it is better to invest in non-monetary assets which will hold their value because their prices will also increase with inflation. Therefore, precious metals are a non-monetary asset which will better hold their value in an economy with high inflation.

Choices B and C are not correct because the fixed rates of return (expressed as an interest rate) of these monetary assets will not increase with inflation; this will cause these monetary assets to decline in value in an economy with high inflation.

Choice D is not correct because common stock of a publicly traded company (whose value may increase in an economy with high inflation), will also be affected by market factors and other factors specific to that company (e.g., effects of market share or competition).

BEC 2-Q16 B72. The correct choice is A. The market rate of interest on a one-year U.S. Treasury bill is the 2% Risk-free rate of interest and the 1% Inflation premium for a total of 3%.
The 3% default risk premium is not included because a one-year U.S. Treasury bill has no default risk. The 2% liquidity risk premium is not included because a one-year U.S. Treasury bill is liquid and may be easily sold. The 1% maturity risk premium is not included because a one-year U.S. Treasury bill matures within a relatively short period of time.

BEC 2-Q17 B171. The correct choice is C. The Federal Reserve (the Fed) is the central bank of the United States. The Fed effects monetary policy through the following tools: open market operations (the most common tool), changing the discount rate (a common tool), and changing reserve requirements (a tool rarely used). By reducing the discount rate, banks that do not maintain adequate reserves may borrow at a lower interest rate in order to boost their reserves to the minimum level. The lower discount rate may encourage banks to lend more because it becomes cheaper to borrow. When banks lend more, this increases the money supply.

Choice A is not correct because the multiplier effect is the effect that spending (consumer, business, and government) has on gross domestic product (GDP). For example, an additional $1 spent will have a multiplied effect on GDP throughout the economy as others earn the additional $1 over and over and also spend the $1 over and over. The Fed's monetary policy does not target the GDP multiplier.

Choice B is not correct because changing the reserve requirements is a tool rarely used by the Fed; however, increasing reserve requirements would contract the money supply, not increase the money supply.

Choice D is not correct because selling more U.S. Treasury bonds removes money from the money supply and therefore contracts the money supply; however, open market operations (purchases and sales of U.S Treasury securities) are the most common tool used by the Fed to affect monetary policy.

BEC 2-Q18 B354. The correct choice is A. The Federal Reserve Bank (the central bank of the United States) most likely would decrease the discount rate it charges to banks for loans in order to address the problem of a recession. When the Federal Reserve decreases the discount rate, banks will also decrease their interest rates. A decrease in interest rates will increase consumer demand for capital investments that require financing (e.g., purchases of homes and automobiles). The increase in demand will address the problem of a recession.

Choice B is not correct because the sale of U.S. government bonds in open-market transactions will decrease the money supply and help to increase interest rates. However, lowering the discount rate the Federal Reserve charges to banks for loans is a more direct method of decreasing interest rates and increasing demand.

Choice C is not correct because increasing the federal funds rate would tend to increase interest rates. An increase in interest rates will decrease consumer demand for capital investments that require financing (e.g., purchases of homes and automobiles); the decrease in demand would make a recession worse.

Choice D is not correct because the Federal Reserve rarely changes the reserve requirements for banks.

BEC 2-Q19 B359. The correct choice is B. Deflation is a period of declining prices. Deflation depresses demand because consumers are less likely to buy in the short-term if they believe that prices may decline further. By increasing the money supply, more money will be available in the economy, but the amount of goods and services will remain the same; this will increase prices and prevent deflation.

Choice A is not correct because increasing interest rates decreases the demand for goods that are financed through borrowing (e.g., capital-intensive assets such as homes and automobiles) and will make a period of deflation worse because deflation also results in a decrease in demand.

Choice C is not correct because decreasing interest rates increases the demand for goods and services that are financed through borrowing (e.g., capital-intensive assets such as homes and automobiles) and will increase demand for capital-intensive goods and services. However, decreasing interest rates is not a preventive measure for deflation; it is a preventive measure for recession.

Choice D is not correct because by decreasing the money supply, less money will be available in the economy, but the amount of goods and services will remain the same; this will decrease prices and will make a period of deflation worse because deflation also results in a decrease in demand.

BEC 2-Q20 B265. The correct choice is C. A freeze on rent prices will cause the demand for rental space to exceed the supply of rental space. This is because the market for rental space is not allowed to reach equilibrium between supply and demand. For example, if rent prices are frozen below the equilibrium price, then landlords will switch to selling condominiums instead of renting apartments in order to generate a return; this will cause the supply of rental apartments to decrease and demand will exceed supply.

Choice A is not correct because the demand curve in general is downward sloping and a freeze on rent prices will increase demand, which will be a movement upward to the left along the demand curve.

Choice B is not correct because the supply curve in general is upward sloping and a freeze on rent prices will decrease supply, which will be a movement downward and to the left along the supply curve.

Choice D is not correct because a freeze on rent prices will have the opposite effect: the demand for rental space will exceed the supply of rental space. For example, if rent prices are frozen below the equilibrium price, then landlords will switch to selling condominiums instead of renting apartments in order to generate a return; this will cause the supply of rental apartments to decrease and demand will exceed supply.

BEC 2-Q21 B320. The correct choice is B. If there is an increase in the resources available within the economy, the economy will be capable of producing more goods and services. Because the inputs to production have increased, then this may increase the output of production if there is sufficient production capacity to accommodate the increase in inputs.

Choice A is not correct because although an increase in the resources available within the economy will increase the inputs available for production, a corresponding increase in the output of production will occur only if there is sufficient production capacity to accommodate the increase in inputs.

Choice C is not correct because the standard of living in the economy will rise if the quality of goods and services increases and/or the quantity of goods and services increases relative to the purchasing power of consumers.

Choice D is not correct because an increase in the resources available in the economy does not increase the technological efficiency of the economy. An increase in technological efficiency will produce more goods and services given the same amount of inputs; produce goods and services of a higher quality given the same amount of inputs; produce goods and services faster; and/or produce goods and services for a lower cost.

BEC 2-Q22 B142. The correct choice is A. In a perfectly competitive market, there are many sellers of a particular product or service; because of the large number of sellers, no single seller is able to affect the price of the product or service.

Choice B is not correct because in a perfectly competitive market, there are many sellers of a particular product or service; because of the large number sellers, no single seller is able to affect the price of the product or service. If a particular seller is able to influence market prices more than other sellers, then this seller is likely the price leader in an oligopolistic market.

Choice C is not correct because, in a monopsony, there is only one buyer for all sellers' goods and services (e.g., the Federal government is the only buyer of aircraft carriers). Therefore, prices of goods and services are based on the competition between suppliers to sell to the only buyer.

Choice D is not correct because, in a perfectly competitive market, there is "perfect information," meaning that information (e.g., information about borrowing/lending activities) is publicly available and all have access to the information.

BEC 2-Q23 B377. The correct choice is C. When the dollar depreciates, it makes U.S. imports more expensive and U.S. exports less expensive. Therefore, import prices will increase, and export prices will decrease.

Choices A and D are not correct because when the dollar changes in value, import prices and export prices move in opposite directions, not in the same direction.

Choice B is not correct because this choice describes the effect of the dollar appreciating in value, not depreciating in value. When the dollar appreciates in value, it makes U.S. imports less expensive and U.S. exports more expensive.

BEC 2-Q24 B180. The correct choice is A. The balance of payments is a system of accounts for goods and services imported and exported between two countries. Freely fluctuating exchange rates allow exchange rates to reach an equilibrium based on market factors of supply and demand for the currency used in imports and exports.

Choice B is not correct because exchange rate regimes that increase the value of the domestic currency relative to foreign currencies result in cheaper imports and more expensive exports.

Choice C is not correct because various factors impose constraints on the domestic economy, such as regulations on working conditions and the environment; taxation is also a factor.

Choice D is not correct because freely fluctuating exchange rates are determined by market factors, which may increase the need for foreign currency hedging.

BEC 2-Q25 B143. The correct choice is A. If a foreign country's currency conversion to the U.S. dollar increased 0.2, then it would take 0.2 additional foreign currency units to purchase one U.S. dollar. This would make the value of the foreign currency lower and make its products cheaper (e.g., its exports) relative to U.S. products.

Choice B is not correct because if the foreign currency appreciated in value relative to the U.S. dollar, then the conversion would go the other direction, e.g., from 1.5 foreign currency units to one

U.S. dollar to 1.3 foreign currency units to one U.S. dollar.

Choice C is not correct because the foreign country's imports of U.S. goods would become more expensive since something that previously cost 1.5 foreign currency units would now cost 1.7 foreign currency units.

Choice D is not correct because the purchases of U.S. dollars would cost more in terms of foreign currency units since it would now take 1.7 foreign currency units (instead of 1.5 foreign currency units) to purchase one U.S. dollar.

BEC 2-Q26 B277. The correct choice is A. When a foreign competitor's currency becomes weaker compared to the U.S. dollar, then for U.S. consumers the foreign goods become cheaper relative to U.S. goods; therefore, the foreign company will have an advantage in the U.S. market.

Choice B is not correct because when a foreign competitor's currency becomes weaker compared to the U.S. dollar, then for U.S. consumers the foreign goods become cheaper relative to U.S. goods; therefore, the foreign company will have an advantage in the U.S. market, not a disadvantage in the U.S. market.

Choice C is not correct because fluctuations in the foreign currency's exchange rate will make the foreign competitor's currency weaker or less weak compared to the U.S. dollar, meaning that for U.S. consumers the foreign goods will become cheaper or less cheap relative to U.S. goods; therefore, there is an effect.

Choice D is not correct because it is better for the U.S. company when the value of the U.S. dollar becomes weaker compared to the foreign competitor's currency. When the U.S. dollar becomes weaker, for U.S. consumers the U.S. goods become cheaper relative to the foreign goods; therefore, the U.S. company will have an advantage in the U.S. market.

BEC 2-Q27 B372. The correct choice is C. Because Woostland is experiencing a recession and its imports are declining, there is less demand for $E currency that Woostland needs to pay for Esland's goods. Therefore, because the demand for $E is decreasing, the $E will decline in value with respect to the value of $W.

Choice A is not correct because as long as each country's demand for the other country's goods is not at equilibrium, then the value of each country's currency will not be at equilibrium and will not remain constant with respect to each other's currency.

Choice B is not correct because Woostland is experiencing a recession and its imports are declining, so there is less demand for $E currency that Woostland needs to pay for Esland's goods; therefore, because the demand for $E is decreasing, the $E will decline in value instead of increase in value.

Choice D is not correct because changes in imports and exports change the demand for countries' currencies and therefore affect currency values.

BEC 2-Q28 B1250. The correct answer choice is B. The exchange rates in the question are stated as the foreign currency price to the U.S. dollar (i.e. 2.57 to $1). To determine the change in the value of the company's investment in U.S. dollars, multiple the foreign currency price times the U.S. dollar per foreign currency, for the two periods. The U.S. dollar per foreign currency is calculated as follows:

At the time of the investment: $1/2.57 = $.3891
After the investment: $1/3.15 = $.3175

The difference in the U.S. dollar per foreign currency for the two periods is a $.0716 ($.3891 - $.3175) decrease. The change in the value of the company's investment in U.S. dollars would be an 18.4% decrease ($.0716/.3891).

BEC 2-Q29 B1226. The correct answer is choice A. Emerging markets typically do not have established standards that are as advanced and strict as more advanced markets, such as the United States. Emerging markets tend to have lower per capita income, experience better than average GPD growth, and high volatility due to typically an unstable political environment. The better than average growth in GDP is achieved from the exposure of their economies to global capital and investment. As emerging market's economic growth increases, investors try to tap into the momentum to experience higher returns. When the U.S. dollar declines in value relative to the foreign location's emerging market currency, goods produced in the U.S. become less expensive, resulting in U.S. made goods being more competitive compared to goods produced in foreign countries. The result is an increase in U.S. exports and the company will be able to fully utilize the emerging market operations in producing goods.

Choice B is incorrect because there is an inverse relationship between the value of currency and inflation. For example, a decline in currency will lead to inflation because the price of goods produced locally increase. To support the decision for a U.S.-based company who decides to invest capital in an emerging market operation that has a lower expected return rate compared to the expected return for an alternative domestic operation; management would expect inflation to decrease in the emerging market compared to the U.S. inflation rate.

Choice C is incorrect because to support the decision for a U.S.-based company who decides to invest capital in an emerging market operation that has a lower expected return rate compared to the expected return for an alternative domestic operation; management would expect inflation to increase in the U.S. compared to the foreign location's inflation rate.

Choice D is incorrect because when the U.S. dollar strengthens in value relative to the foreign location's currency, goods produced in the U.S. become more expensive, resulting in U.S. made goods being less competitive compared to goods produced in foreign countries. The result is a decrease in U.S. exports.

BEC 2-Q30 B647. The correct answer is A. Expected value is a weighted average of all possible outcomes and calculates the average return from a decision that is repeatedly made. It is determined by multiplying the value of each possible outcome by the probability of that outcome and totaling the results.

If Johnson decides to market its new software package, the expected value of the additional monthly income is calculated as follows:

Expected value = (.2 x $60,000) + (.3 x $30,000)
$\quad\quad\quad\quad\quad\quad$ + (.3 x $10,000) − (.2 x $4,000)
$\quad\quad\quad\quad$ = $12,000 + $9,000 + $3,000 - $800
$\quad\quad\quad\quad$ = $23,200

BEC 2-Q31 B648. The correct answer is B. This question is about expected value, which is a weighted average of all possible outcomes and calculates the average return from a decision that is repeatedly made. It is determined by multiplying the value of each possible outcome by the probability of that outcome and totaling the results.

To answer this question, determine the expected value of both Plan 1 and 2. Then, compare them to see which plan adds greater value.

Plan 1 expected value
($300,000 x .4) + ($240,000 x .6)
$264,000

Less: Plan 2 expected value
($370,000 x .4) + ($180,000 x .6)
(256,000)
$ 8,000

Plan 1 is more attractive than Plan 2 by $8,000 so, Plan 1 should be adopted.

BEC 2-Q32 B650. The correct answer is C. Expected value is a weighted average of all possible outcomes and calculates the average return from a decision that is repeatedly made. It is determined by multiplying the value of each possible outcome by the probability of that outcome and totaling the results. In this question, the $650,000 cost incurred to date is a sunk cost and should not be considered.

Expected value of investing
= .6 ($15.0 mil - $9.5 mil) + .4 ($2.0 mil - $9.5 mil)
= $3.3 mil - $3.0 mil
= $300,000

Value of not investing
= ($100,000) for the additional costs to be paid

BEC 2-Q33 B651. The correct answer is D. Expected value is a weighted average of all possible outcomes and calculates the average return from a decision that is repeatedly made. It is determined by multiplying the value of each possible outcome by the probability of that outcome and totaling the results. The rankings of the investments are as follows:

Investment A = .3 (-$20,000) + .1 (-$10,000) + .3 ($30,000) + .2 ($70,000) + .1 ($100,000)
= ($6,000) + ($1,000) + $9,000 + $14,000 + $10,000
= $26,000

Investment B = 2 (-$20,000) + .2 (-$10,000) + .2 ($30,000) + .2 ($70,000) + .2 ($100,000)
= ($4,000) + ($2,000) + $6,000 + $14,000 + $20,000
= $34,000

Investment C = .3 (-$20,000) + .1 (-$10,000) + .2 ($30,000) + .3 ($70,000) + .1 ($100,000)
= ($6,000) + ($1,000) + $6,000 + $21,000 + $10,000
= $30,000

From highest to lowest, the rankings are: B: $34,000, C: $30,000, A: $26,000

BEC 2-Q34 B652. The correct answer is C. This question is based on expected value. Expected value is a weighted average of all possible outcomes and calculates the average return from a decision that is repeatedly made. It is determined by multiplying the value of each possible outcome by the probability of that outcome and totaling the results.

Increased units sold
= .1 (15,000) + .35 (30,000) + .1 (45,000) + .25 (60,000) + .2 (75,000)
= 1,500 + 10,500 + 4,500 + 15,000 + 15,000
= 46,500 units

Increased profit
= [46,500 x ($5.20 - $3.20)] - $40,000
= $93,000 - $40,000
= $53,000

BEC 2-Q35 B653. The correct answer is B. Expected rate of return (value) is a weighted average of all possible outcomes and calculates the average return from a decision that is repeatedly made. It is determined by multiplying the value of each possible outcome by the probability of that outcome and totaling the results. The expected return is calculated as follows:

Expected return = .1 (-.20) + .2 (.05) + .4 (.15) + .2 (.20) + .1 (.30)
= (.02) + .01 + .06 + .04 + .03
= 12%

BEC 2-Q36 B654. The correct answer is A. Expected value is a weighted average of all possible outcomes and calculates the average return from a decision that is repeatedly made. It is determined by multiplying the value of each possible outcome by the probability of that outcome and totaling the results. The expected value of each alternative is as follows:

Alternative 1
= .1($50,000) + .2($75,000) + .4($100,000) + .3($150,000)
= $105,000

Alternative 2
= .1($50,000) + .2($75,000) + .45($100,000) + .25($150,000)
= $102,500

Alternative 3
= .1($50,000) + .2($75,000) + .4($100,000) + .3($125,000)
= $97,500

Alternative 4
= .1($150,000) + .2($100,000) + .4($75,000) + .3($50,000)
= $80,000

Alternative 1 has the highest expected value.

BEC 2-Q37 B655. The correct answer is C. Expected value (demand) is a weighted average of all possible outcomes and calculates the average return from a decision that is repeatedly made. It is determined by multiplying the value of each possible outcome by the probability of that outcome and totaling the results.

The question is asking for the recommended purchase quantities, which is determined by calculating the expected demand based on estimated sales as follows:

Expected demand = .1(8,000) + .4(10,000) + .3(12,000) + .2(15,000) = 11,400 units. The closest purchase quantity level to 11,400 would be 12,000.

BEC 2-Q38 B278. The correct choice is B. If a firm uses only equity financing, then business risk is inherent in a firm's operations because if the firm performs poorly, then its stock price will decline and the firm may have difficulty obtaining additional financing by issuing additional shares of common stock.

Choice A is not correct because financial risk is a type of risk that encompasses multiple types of risk, such as business risk, interest rate risk, risk that customers or other debtors will default, and foreign currency exchange risk; therefore, financial risk is more general and not specific about risk for a firm that uses only equity financing.

Choice C is not correct because interest rate risk is the risk that interest rates will increase and increase the cost of borrowing. Because the firm uses equity financing exclusively, the firm has no interest-bearing debt and therefore no interest rate risk.

Choice D is not correct because marginal risk is the amount of risk contributed to the overall portfolio risk when adding one additional investment to the portfolio of investments. Marginal risk is a risk associated with investing, not financing.

BEC 2-Q39 B1135. The correct answer is A. To calculate the annual yield, first annualize the dollar amount of the discount and divide it by the amount invested. The 90-day investment has the highest yield and Texas Corporation should purchase it based on the calculations as follows:

90-day: Discount ($80,000 x .05)	$4,000
Annualized amount of discount ($4,000/(90/360))	$16,000
Annual yield ($16,000/$80,000)	20% [highest annual yield]
180-day: Discount ($75,000 x .06)	$4,500
Annualized amount of discount ($4,500/(180/360))	$9,000
Annual yield ($9,000/$75,000)	12%
270-day: Discount ($100,000 x .05)	$5,000
Annualized amount of discount ($5,000/(270/360))	$6,667
Annual yield ($6,667/$100,000)	6.7%
360-day: Discount ($60,000 x .10)	$6,000
Annualized amount of discount ($6,000/(360/360))	$6,000
Annual yield ($6,000/$60,000)	10%

BEC 2-Q40 B94. The correct choice is C. Diversification occurs when management takes action to mitigate risk through management's selection among alternatives. The risk of labor strikes may be mitigated through diversifying the means of production (e.g., the use of automated means of production instead of labor-intensive means of production) or by taking steps to prevent a labor strike from occurring (e.g., good management-labor relationships).

Choices A, B and D are not correct because they are examples of risks due to macroeconomic factors (and are also examples of systematic risks) and are difficult to diversify; management cannot prevent or control these macroeconomic factors.

BEC 2-Q41 B47. The correct choice is D. Because the corporation has several long-term floating rate bonds, there is the risk that the market interest rate may increase, causing the floating rate to increase and the corporation to incur higher interest costs; furthermore, the variability in interest rates will cause variability in the future payments for interest, making it more difficult for the corporation to plan in the intermediate- and long-term and will also increase the variability of its reported expenses and earnings. To reduce these risks, the corporation may purchase a swap agreement whereby the cash flows from the variable interest rates will be swapped for cash flows from long-term interest rates.

Choice A is not correct because a structured short-term note will not eliminate the risk that the market interest rate may increase and when the corporation refinances the note, the higher interest rate will result in higher interest costs.

Choice B is not correct because a forward contract on a commodity would be more useful in hedging risks from the variability of prices in that commodity.

Choice C is not correct because a futures contract on a stock would be more useful in hedging risks from the variability of prices in that stock.

BEC 2-Q42 B79. The correct choice is A. A put option is an option to sell a security at fixed conditions of price and time.

Choice B is not correct because a put option is an option to sell a security at fixed conditions of price and time instead of an indefinite time period.

Choice C is not correct because this is a description of a call option, not a put option.

Choice D is not correct because this is an incorrect description of a call option; a call option is an option to buy a security at fixed conditions of price and time instead of an indefinite time period.

BEC 2-Q43 B178. The correct choice is C. This problem is an example of a foreign currency transaction, which is where a U.S. company either purchases (and has an account payable) or sells (and has an account receivable) goods or services and the money exchanging hands is NOT U.S. dollars. In this case, Platinum Co. made a sale and has an A/R and the value of the A/R is decreasing because of the decreasing value of the euros. Platinum needs to get rid of the euros once they are collected, so in order to mitigate the foreign currency transaction risk, Platinum could lock in the sales price for the euros by entering into a forward contract to sell the euros in the future.

Choice A is not correct because buying euros may be an appropriate action to mitigate foreign currency transaction risk for an account payable instead of an account receivable.

Choice B is not correct because an interest rate swap is an appropriate action to mitigate foreign currency transaction risk for a change in interest rates.

Choice D is not correct because Platinum can reduce the foreign currency transaction risk by entering into a forward contract to sell euros, thereby locking in the price.

BEC 2-Q44 B313. The correct choice is A. The American importer has an accounts payable where the importer must pay 500,000 British pounds. The importer must obtain the 500,000 British pounds and mitigate any risk in the exchange rate between U.S. dollars and British pounds, whereby more U.S. dollars are required to purchase the 500,000 pounds. Therefore, purchasing a call option (an option to buy) will enable the importer to acquire the 500,000 British pounds at a fixed amount of U.S. dollars and mitigates the exchange rate risk.

Choice B is not correct because a put option is an option to sell the British pounds at a fixed amount of U.S. dollars and would be a strategy to use in the case of an accounts receivable in British pounds.

Choices C and D are not correct because a firm that specializes in selling derivatives such as put options and call options would sell the options; the American importer would purchase the call options from this firm.

This page is intentionally left blank.

BEC 3 – Financial Management

A. Capital Structure   3A-1 – 3A-13
     1. Debt and equity terminology refresher   1
     2. Cost of capital, debt, and equity   5
     3. Leverage   7

B. Working Capital   3B-1 – 3B-14
     1. Fundamentals and key metrics of working capital management   1
     2. Strategies for managing working capital   5

C. Financial Valuation Methods and Decision Models   3C-1 – 3C-29
     1. Financial valuation methods   1
     2. Asset structure and asset management   6
     3. Accounting estimates   6
     4. Present value   9
     5. Capital budgeting   14
     6. Lease versus buy decisions   27

Glossary: Financial Management   Glossary 3-1 – 3-5

Multiple Choice – Questions   MCQ 3-1 – 3-14

Multiple Choice – Solutions   MCQ 3-15 – 3-31

Financial Management

This chapter focuses on financial management, that is, the decisions necessary to manage the monetary resources of an entity. For the CPA exam, candidates are expected to have an understanding of a variety of relevant topics including: (A) evaluating the optimal corporate capital structure, (B) understanding the fundamentals of working capital management (including strategies for inventory, accounts payable, and financing), and (C) utilizing basic financial valuation methods and decision models.

Since financial management is a formula intensive topic, it is important for candidates to spend time memorizing and understanding the calculations discussed in this chapter. CPA candidates are usually less familiar with financial management calculations when compared to the many ratios emphasized in college accounting curriculum. These topics are usually covered in managerial finance courses at the undergraduate level. Extra care should be applied to this chapter.

A. Capital Structure

> Describe an organization's capital structure and related concepts, such as cost of capital, asset structure, loan covenants, growth rate, profitability, leverage and risk.

The term **capital**, in this context, refers to the monetary resources that finance a company's assets. The concepts and terms in this blueprint are explained throughout this section.

Capital structure decisions relate to *how* a company decides to finance its assets; be it with liabilities, equity, or a combination of both. Excluding off-balance-sheet financing (e.g., operating leases), these are the only two ways a company can obtain assets to initiate and sustain business operations. (Note that off-balance-sheet financing is becoming more restricted due to changes in U.S. GAAP for leases and variable-interest entities). The basic accounting equation, assets equal liabilities plus stockholders' equity, clearly represents both ways of acquiring capital.

Selecting a capital structure is one of a company's most significant financial decisions. A company must determine: (1) the proper mix of liabilities to equity and (2) the types of liabilities to use. These capital structure decisions have a direct effect on the company's cost of capital, profitability, leverage, and risk.

The **optimal capital structure** is the mix of debt and equity that maximizes an entity's share price, increasing shareholder wealth. The primary technique used to select the optimal capital structure for a particular company is to minimize the company's weighted-average cost of capital (WACC), discussed below. First, this chapter starts by reviewing terminology that pertains to debt and equity financing.

1. Debt and equity terminology refresher
   a. Types of debt financing
      Companies can issue a variety of debt instruments to raise capital. Debt instruments are contractual obligations between a borrower (the company) and lender (outside party). Forms of debt include notes, bonds, certificates and other more complex debtor-creditor relationships.

      Debt can be either secured or unsecured. **Secured** debt is a promise to pay guaranteed by collateral. Secured debt is less risky for the lender; if the borrower defaults, then the collateral asset is forfeited to the lender. Borrowers can obtain lower interest rates on secured debt. **Unsecured** debt does not require any form of collateral but has higher interest rates when compared to similar secured debt options. Higher interest rates are the result of higher risk.

Some examples of debt financing are as follows:
1) Short-term borrowing
    Short-term borrowing is ideal to provide immediate funding for working capital to avoid business constraints that are caused by illiquidity. To be considered short-term, the principal payment must be due to the lender within one year.

    i. Factoring – sale of accounts receivables to a third party (called a factor) for immediate cash.
    ii. Chattel mortgage – a loan secured by moveable personal property (called chattel).
    iii. Bankers' acceptances – a time draft promising a stated future payment on a specific date; the payment is guaranteed by a bank.
    iv. Line of credit – amount of credit extended by a bank to a borrower with a set maximum and no specific purpose. This can also be called revolving credit due to its renewable nature. Lines of credit are ideal to provide capital for a business that has seasonal fluctuations. Large companies in the financial reports usually categorize this under the section labeled Credit Facilities.
    v. Commercial paper – short-term unsecured promissory note issued by large corporations to meet immediate obligations (e.g., payroll) with a fixed maturity, typically within one month, but extending no more than 270 days. These are issued to avoid SEC registration.

2) Bonds
    A **bond** is a debt instrument that obligates the issuer to repay the lender (bondholder) a specified sum of money (the bond's face value) at a future maturity date. During the duration of the bond, periodic interest (coupon) payments are due to the bondholder. Bonds are sold at either a premium or discount depending on whether a variation exists between the stated coupon rate printed on the bond and the prevailing market rate. Bonds are rated by an independent rating service (Standard & Poor's, Moody's) to evaluate the issuer's risk of default. In general, low risk, investment grade bonds receive high ratings (AAA, AA, A, or BBB) and high risk, non-investment grade bonds receive a low rating (BB, B, CCC, CC, or C) due to their vulnerability for nonpayment.

    There are a number of different attributes that can be associated with bonds:
    i. Mortgage bond – a bond secured by a mortgage of one or more assets that, in the event of default, entitles the bondholder claim to the underlying asset subject to the lien (e.g., real estate or equipment).
    ii. Income bond – a bond with coupon payments that are only paid if the issuer generates earnings above a threshold amount.
    iii. Debenture – an unsecured bond (e.g., no underlying collateral) issued by a company with a reputation for creditworthiness.
    iv. Subordinated debenture – an unsecured bond that is paid after superior, higher priority debt is paid, if the issuer defaults or declares bankruptcy.
    v. Zero-coupon – a bond that does not pay interest during the term of the bond and is bought at a large discount. Investors pay significantly less than the face value of the bond (value at maturity). When the zero-coupon bond matures, the investor receives one lumps sum equal to the initial investment plus imputed interest; also called an accrual bond.
    vi. Floating-rate – a bond with a variable coupon payment based on a periodically updated market rate (e.g., LIBOR, which is a benchmark rate on international market funds).
    vii. Callable – a bond provision that grants the issuer the option to redeem (repay) the bond prior to stated maturity date.
    viii. Convertible – a bond that can be traded for a pre-determined number of shares of the issuing company's common stock.

ix. Junk – a high-risk bond (e.g., rated BB or lower by Standard & Poor's) that offer investors a premium to entice them to purchase a bond with a greater than normal default risk.
x. Sinking fund – a custodial account the borrower (issuer) establishes to periodically deposits funds into that are used to retire a bond over time by buying it back or pay in full at maturity.
xi. Serial bond – a bond that has a series of successive maturities that retire portions of the bond over the term of the bond
xii. Loan covenant (or debt covenants) – covenants are agreements between the borrower and the lender that the borrower will maintain certain financial statement ratios (e.g., debt-to-equity ratio, current ratio) or the borrower will restrict its ability to incur additional debt (limiting the percentage of financing with long-term debt when compared to total financing). The entity needs to consider all of this before determining the optimal capital structure.

Multiple Choice

BEC 3-Q1 through BEC 3-Q5

b. Types of equity financing
Equity securities represent ownership in a company. Equity is most often used to finance long-term projects rather than short-term liquidity or working capital needs.

1) Common stock
Common shareholders purchase a stake in a company to have rights to a company's earnings, which are either retained or distributed as dividends. In exchange for their capital contribution, shareholders have an ownership interest in the company and voting rights. In the event of a liquidation, common stockholders are the last in line for liquidating distributions.

   i. Dividend – At the discretion of the company, earnings that are not retained to sustain operations are distributed to shareholders as a dividend. It could consist of cash, stock, or combination of both. The dividend policy of a company might depend on the company's target payout ratio (percentage of income paid as cash dividends) and patterns of past dividend payments.
   ii. Stock dividend – Rather than receiving a cash payment, shareholders receive additional shares of stock as a dividend.
   iii. Preemptive right – a right given to common shareholders requiring a company to offer the current common shareholders the right to purchase the additional shares first, if the corporation issues additional shares of common stock, giving common shareholders the ability to maintain their proportionate share of outstanding shares of common stock.
   iv. Appraisal right – the right of minority shareholders to receive an equitable value for their shares as determined by an independent party in the event of a merger or other transaction that transfers control of the corporation.

2) Preferred stock
Preferred stock is a form of equity security that typically has no voting rights and entitles the shareholder to priority stipulated dividend payments, before common shareholders. While deemed equity, stock analysts tend to view preferred stock more akin to debt.

   i. Callable preferred stock – If the preferred stock is callable, then the corporation has the right to buy back the stock usually at a premium.

ii. Cumulative preferred stock – Preferred stock that provides shareholders with a cumulative claim to preferred dividends. If preferred dividends are not declared in a particular year, they are dividends in arrears and must be paid with the next declared dividend on preferred stock, before the commons shareholders receiving a dividend.

Multiple Choice
BEC 3-Q6 through BEC 3-Q10

c. Debt or equity

The decision to issue debt or equity has many positive and negative implications. Attributes of both debt and equity are summarized in the following table:

	Debt	Equity
Advantages	<ul><li>Increases creditworthiness (within limits)</li><li>Interest paid is tax deductible by corporation</li><li>Issuance costs are less when compared to equity</li><li>Can enhance return on equity</li><li>No dilution of ownership</li></ul>	<ul><li>No fixed charges over time</li><li>No maturity date or repayment required</li></ul>
Disadvantages	<ul><li>Obligation to pay fixed interest payments</li><li>Debt covenants may place restrictions on corporation</li><li>Principal repayment due at maturity date</li><li>A greater amount of debt puts increased risk on equity shareholders and may decrease stock price</li></ul>	<ul><li>Requires current owners to share ownership interest (i.e., potential to dilute ownership)</li><li>Dividends are not tax deductible by corporations.</li><li>Issuance costs are typically more than issuing debt</li><li>Preferred stock typically sells at a higher yield basis than bonds</li></ul>

Multiple Choice
BEC 3-Q11 through BEC 3-Q13

d. Target capital structure

A company's capital structure is analyzed using solvency ratios (e.g., debt to equity) to measure its ability to meet long-term financial obligations. Most companies identify a target capital structure within a range usually within overall industry averages and/or company's comfort zone. Examples would be 58%-63% debt to 42-37% equity, summing to 100%. If the ratio starts to shift out of the target range, managers take action. Debt is adjusted by issuing new debt or repaying outstanding debt, and equity can be increased by selling additional shares or repurchasing outstanding shares to hold as treasury stock.

Multiple Choice
BEC 3-Q14 through BEC 3-Q17

2. Cost of capital, debt, and equity
   a. Cost of capital

| Calculate the cost of capital for a given financial scenario. |

The cost of capital is the return that lenders (debt) and owners (equity) expect to receive for providing financing to a business. A company's **weighted-average cost of capital (WACC)** is the average after-tax cost of its unique combination of debt and equity financing. Each category of financing is weighted proportionately according to the entity's market value of its targeted capital structure and then added to equal the firm's single WACC. A company's WACC is utilized in capital budgeting, and investment decisions, including specifically the economic value added (EVA) formula (discussed in "Capital Budgeting" later in this chapter).

$$WACC = w_d [(r_d)*(1-t)] + w_e (r_e)...$$

Where:
w_d = percentage of debt
r_d = cost of debt
t = tax rate
w_e = percentage of equity
r_e = cost of equity

Hint: Depending on the complexity of the company's capital structure, the weighted-average cost of capital (WACC) could include the weighted cost of debt, weighted cost of new common equity, weighted cost of existing common equity, and weighted cost of preferred equity. In total, all percentages used to weight the cost of each item should add to 100%.

Example: Assume a company has the following target capital structure and the tax rate is 30%. The company does not anticipate issuing any new stock.

Debt – 7% interest rate	45%
Preferred equity – 8% yield	30%
Common equity – 12% cost of equity	25%
	100%

To calculate the weighted-average cost of capital (WACC):

Bonds	0.45 (0.07) (1 – 0.30)	= 0.022
Common stock	0.30 (0.08)	= 0.024
Preferred stock	0.25 (0.12)	= 0.030
Weighted-average cost of capital		= 0.076 or 7.6%

| Compare and contrast the strategies for financing new business initiatives and operations within the context of an optimal capital structure, using statistical analysis where appropriate. |

An important part of a company's strategy is determining financing options for new business initiatives. The type of company, as well as its risk tolerance, help determine the strategy chosen with regard to capital structure. Incurring more debt leads to higher returns on equity, but it also increases risk. Because of the mandatory principal and interest payments associated with debt financing, cash flows regarding their certainty, timing, and amounts represent a business risk in capital structure decisions. While a steady income may work for many companies, a startup company may not have income for several years, and therefore must select equity financing. The appropriate mix is different for every company.

Minimizing the weighted average cost of capital (WACC) is desirable because it maximizes the difference between the cost of capital percentage and the return on investment (ROI) percentage. The larger this spread, the greater the increase in shareholder wealth. Statistical analysis can determine the optimal WACC.

Multiple Choice

BEC 3-Q18 through BEC 3-Q27

b. Cost of debt
   The cost of debt is the interest rate on a debt instrument (e.g., a bank loan).

   1) Cost of debt (after-tax)
      The interest on debt is tax deductible. Therefore, the cost of debt is reduced by the tax savings from deductible interest.

      $$\text{Cost of debt (after-tax)} = \text{Interest Rate} \times (1 - \text{Tax Rate})$$

      Hint: If no tax rate is provided, assume that the cost of debt is already after-tax.

      Hint: A compensating balance reduces the amount available, thereby increasing the effective interest rate. The effective interest rate of the loan is calculated below. If a compensating balance is present, the effective interest rate is used in the after-tax cost of debt calculation.

      $$\text{Effective interest rate} = \frac{\text{Interest expense}}{\text{Amount available, net of compensating balance}}$$

      Hint: When a debt instrument is sold at a discount, this temporarily increases the effective interest rate because the discount is subtracted up front from the available amount of the borrowing.

Multiple Choice

BEC 3-Q28 through BEC 3-Q30

   2) Cost of debt (before-tax)

      $$\text{Cost of debt (before-tax)} = \frac{\text{Interest payment}}{\text{Debt Price} - \text{Floatation Cost}}$$

c. Cost of preferred equity

   $$\text{Cost preferred equity} = \frac{\text{Preferred dividend}}{\text{Preferred Stock Issue Price}}$$

Multiple Choice

BEC 3-Q31 through BEC 3-Q32

d. Cost of new common equity
The cost of equity is the percentage yield on equity. The cost of equity considers both new common equity (e.g., initial public offering), existing common equity (e.g., common stock outstanding), and retained earnings. The cost of new common equity is determined by dividing the next expected dividend in relation to the current stock price, considering the effects of a constant growth rate and floatation costs. The calculation is:

$$k_s = \frac{D_1}{P_0 - F} + g$$

Where k_s = cost of new common equity
D_1 = next expected dividend
P_0 = current stock price
g = growth rate in earnings
F = floatation cost per share (new common equity)

Floatation costs include:
- Cost of Issuing a prospectus
- Investment banking fees
- Cost for having audited financial statements prepared
- Legal fees

Hint: The growth rate in earnings is the annualized rate at which a company experiences increases to earnings. It is typically calculated by determining the percentage change in earnings per share (EPS) from one year to the next.

Existing common equity and retained earnings require the use of a valuation approach to determine their cost. See BEC 3C, *Financial Valuation Methods and Decision Models* later in this chapter for alternative valuation models.

Multiple Choice

BEC 3-Q33 through BEC 3-Q37

3. Leverage
There are two types of leverage in business: (1) **operating leverage** and (2) **financial leverage**.

a. Operating leverage
Operating leverage measures the extent a company incurs fixed operating costs in relation to variable operating costs. A company with a large amount of operating leverage (i.e., highly leveraged) will use a relatively high amount of fixed operating costs and a relatively low amount of variable operating costs. The choice of having either a highly leveraged or low leveraged structure depends on corporate philosophy. A highly leveraged operation will result in superior financial performance during prosperous times and worse performance during hardships.

A company can measure its operating leverage through a ratio known as the **degree of operating leverage (DOL)**. There are two ways to define DOL. The DOL is equal to (1) the percentage change in earnings before interest and taxes (EBIT) divided by the percentage change in sales or (2) the contribution margin divided by operating income (OI).

$$DOL = \frac{\%\Delta \text{ EBIT}}{\%\Delta \text{ Sales}}$$

Where:
Δ = change in

OR

$$DOL = \frac{CM}{OI}$$

> **Hint**: The lower the variable operating costs, the higher the contribution margin. Recall, contribution margin (CM) is equal to sales minus variable costs. Once the company covers all its fixed costs, the additional contribution margin increases operating income dollar for dollar. When sales increase in a highly leveraged company, the operating income will increase more quickly due to this relationship.

The percentage change in sales multiplied by the degree of operating leverage equals the percentage change in operating income.

$$\%\Delta \text{ sales} \times DOL = \%\Delta \text{ operating income}$$

Where:
Δ = change in

Multiple Choice

BEC 3-Q38

Example 1: High degree of operating leverage

Assume a company has the following contribution format operating income statement:

ABC Corporation
Contribution Format Income Statement
For the Year Ended December 31, 20XX

	100%	110%
Production level		
Sales	$1,000,000	$1,100,000
Variable costs	400,000	440,000
Contribution margin	600,000	660,000
Fixed costs	500,000	500,000
Operating income	$ 100,000	$ 160,000

ABC Corporation has a degree of operating leverage of 6 times ($600,000 / $100,000). Therefore, if its sales increase by 10 percent, its operating income will increase by 60 percent (10% x 6).

(continued from previous page) Operating income increased by $60,000 when sales increased by $100,000. The variable costs increased by 10 percent to $440,000 while fixed costs remained the same. The change in operating income was indeed 60 percent [($160,000 − $100,000) / $100,000] as predicted by the formula using the degree of operating leverage.

ABC Corporation has a degree of operating leverage of 4.125 ($660,000 / $160,000) at the higher level of sales. The degree of operating leverage is not constant. It reacts inversely to a change in contribution margin. The degree of operating leverage goes down as contribution margin goes up, and it goes up as contribution margin goes down.

Example 2: Low degree of operating leverage

Assume a company has the following contribution format operating income statement.

XYZ Corporation
Contribution Format Income Statement
For the Year Ended December 31, 20XX

Production level	100%	110%
Sales	$1,000,000	$1,100,000
Variable costs	775,000	852,500
Contribution margin	225,000	247,500
Fixed costs	75,000	75,000
Operating income	$150,000	$172,500

XYZ Corporation has a degree of operating leverage of 1.5 times ($225,000 / $150,000). If its sales increase by 10 percent, its operating income will increase by 15 percent (10% x 1.5).

Operating income increased by $22,500 ($172,500 − $150,000) when sales increased by $100,000. The variable costs increased by 10 percent to $852,500 while fixed costs remained the same. The change in operating income was indeed 15 percent [($172,500 − $150,000) / $150,000] as predicted by the formula using the degree of operating leverage.

b. Financial leverage
Financial leverage is the use of debt or capital leases, usually with a fixed interest rate, with the objective of earning a higher rate of return on the borrowed funds than their interest cost. Earning a higher rate of return than the interest rate on borrowed funds leads to a higher return on stockholders' equity.

1) Obligation for repayment
A debtor has a legal obligation to pay interest on debt and to repay its principal at maturity or in required installment payments. A company has no obligation to pay dividends or to repurchase common stock or preferred stock (except for redeemable preferred stock).

2) Benefits of financial leverage
Financial leverage has the potential to increase net income and earnings per share. Interest expense is deductible for tax purposes whereas dividends and the implicit cost of equity capital are not deductible for tax purposes. Lastly, if interest rates drop, a company may be able to refinance its debt to reduce interest expense and its risk of default.

> *Example:* A company issued $10,000,000 of bonds outstanding with an annual interest rate of 10%. The company is earning 16% on its assets. The company is using leverage wisely because it is earning six (6) percentage points more on its assets than it has to pay to its bondholders. This is the interest rate spread.

3) Risks of financial leverage
Financial leverage is a double-edged sword. It can help to increase the return on equity. However, it can also increase losses and reduce earnings per share when the company is suffering a financial setback, such as during a recession. Debt also increases the risk of default and bankruptcy.

4) Degree of financial leverage
The **degree of financial leverage (DFL)** is equal to the percentage change in earnings per share (EPS) divided by the percentage change in earnings before interest and taxes (EBIT).

$$DFL = \frac{\%\Delta \text{ EPS}}{\%\Delta \text{ EBIT}}$$

One can transform this equation to calculate the percentage change in earnings per share by multiplying both sides of the equation by the percentage change in EBIT:

$$\%\Delta \text{ EPS} = \%\Delta \text{ EBIT} \times DFL$$

Another way to calculate the DFL is to divide the EBIT and taxes by the difference between EBIT and interest expense (I):

$$DFL = \frac{EBIT}{EBIT - I}$$

Multiple Choice

BEC 3-Q39 through BEC 3-Q42

Example 1: *Financial leverage with net income*
For the two sample companies below, what is each company's degree of financial leverage (DFL)?

	Company A ($000,000)	Company B ($000,000)
Debt (10% interest rate)	$40	$10
Common stock ($10 par value)*	50	80
Retained earnings	10	10
Total equities	$100	$100
Earnings before interest and taxes (EBIT)	$20	$20
Interest expense (10%)	(4)	(1)
Net income before tax	$16	$19
Tax expense (40%)	(6.4)	(7.6)
Net income	$9.6	$11.4
Earnings per share (EPS)**	$1.920	$1.425

*Shares outstanding: Company A has 5,000,000 ($50,000,000 / $10 per share) shares outstanding.
Company B has 8,000,000 ($80,000,000 / $10 per share) shares outstanding.

**EPS calculation: Company A = $9,600,000 / 5,000,000 = $1.920
Company B = $11,400,000 / 8,000,000 = $1.425

> **Hint:** Although Company A has a lower net income, it has higher earnings per share than does Company B. The reason is Company A has issued fewer shares because it has more debt than does Company B.

$$DFL = \frac{EBIT}{EBIT - I}$$

Company A
DFL = $20,000,000 / ($20,000,000 − $4,000,000)
DFL = $20,000,000 / $16,000,000
DFL = 1.25 or for every 1% change in EBIT, EPS will change by 1.25%

Company B
DFL = $20,000,000 / $20,000,000 − $1,000,000)
DFL = $20,000,000 / $19,000,000
DFL = 1.053 or for every 1% change in EBIT, EPS will change by 1.053%.

What if EBIT increases by one percentage point for each of the two companies?
The EBIT increase would be $200,000 ($20,000,000 x 1%). Taxes expense would increase by $80,000 ($200,000 x 40%). The net income would increase by $120,000 ($200,000 − $80,000). Company A would have a net income of $9,720,000 ($9,600,000 + $120,000) and an EPS of $1.944 ($9,720,000 / 5,000,000). Company B would have a net income of $11,520,000 ($11,400,000 + $120,000) and an EPS of $1.440 ($11,520,000 / 8,000,000).

Change in EPS	Company A	Company B
EPS with 1% increase in EBIT	$1.944	$1.440
Previous EPS	1.920	1.425
Change in EPS	$0.024	$0.015
Percentage Change in EPS	1.25%	1.053%

Company A = ($0.024 / $1.92) x 100% = 1.25%
Company B = ($0.015 / $1.425) x 100% = 1.053%

Example 2: *Financial leverage with a net loss*
For the two sample companies below, what is each company's degree of financial leverage (DFL)?
Note that the capital structure did not change from the previous example.

	Company A ($000,000)	Company B ($000,000)
Debt (10% interest rate)	$40	$10
Common stock ($10 par value)*	50	80
Retained earnings	10	10
Total equities	$100	$100
Earnings before interest and taxes (EBIT)	$10	$10
Interest expense (10%)	(4)	(1)
Net income before tax	($14)	($11)
Tax benefit (40%)	5.6	4.4
Net loss	$8.4	$6.6
Earnings per share (EPS)**	($1.680)	($0.825)

*Shares outstanding: Company A has 5,000,000 ($50,000,000 / $10 per share) shares outstanding.
Company B has 8,000,000 ($80,000,000 / $10 per share) shares outstanding.
**EPS calculation: Company A = ($8,400,000 / 5,000,000 = ($1.680)
Company B = $6,600,000 / 8,000,000 = ($0.825)

Financial leverage helped Company A to increase its EPS more than the EPS for Company B increased when EBIT increased. However, when EBIT shows a loss, the company with the lower financial leverage shows less of a loss per share. Comparing these two scenarios shows how financial leverage is a double-edged sword.

Example 3: *Comparison of high financial leverage and low financial leverage*
Company X and Company Y both have equal total assets, but Company X has a high degree of financial leverage, and Company Y has a low degree of financial leverage.

	Company X ($000)	Company Y ($000)
Total assets	$10,000	$10,000
Current liabilities	0	0
Long-term debt (10% interest rate)	8,000	1,000
Stockholders' equity	2,000	9,000

Scenario 1: If each of the two companies had earnings before interest and taxes of $1,500,000, the net income for each company and the return on equity (net income divided by stockholders' equity) is:

	Company X	Company Y
Earnings before interest and taxes (EBIT)	$1,500	$1,500
Interest expense (10%)	800	100
Net income before tax	$700	$1,400
Tax expense (40%)	(280)	(560)
Net income	420	840
Return on equity	$420 / $2,000	$1,140/ $9,000
	21.00%	9.33%
DFL	$1,500 / $700	$1,500 / $1,400
	2.143	1.071

(continued from previous page)
Company Y has a higher net income because of its lower interest expense. However, Company X has a higher degree of financial leverage. Company X also has a much higher return on equity than does Company Y.

Scenario 2: What if earnings before interest and taxes increased by doubled to $3,000,000 for each company with the debt and interest expense for each company remaining the same?

Earnings before interest and taxes (EBIT)	$3,000	$3,000
Interest expense (10%)	800	100
Net income before tax	$2,200	$2,900
Tax expense (40%)	(880)	(1,160)
Net income	$1,120	$1,740
Return on equity	$1,120 / $2,000	$1,740 / $9,000
	56.00%	19.33%

Each company would have a higher net income and a higher return on equity. However, Company X would have a much greater return on equity because it has a higher degree of financial leverage.

Scenario 3: What if earnings before interest and tax declined to $750,000 for each company?

Earnings before interest and taxes (EBIT)	$750	$750
Interest expense (10%)	800	100
Net income (loss) before tax	($50)	$650
Tax expense or benefit (40%)	20	260
Net income	($30)	$390
Return on equity	($20) / $2,000	$390 / $9,000
	(1.00%)	4.33%

Company X would have a net loss and a negative return on equity. Company Y would still have net income and a positive return on equity. Financial leverage helps return on equity to increase rapidly when earnings before interest and taxes increase. However, financial leverage can cause the return on equity to go down rapidly when earnings before interest and taxes decrease.

B. Working Capital
1. Fundamentals and key metrics of working capital management

Calculate the metrics associated with the working capital components, such as current ratio, quick ratio, cash conversion cycle, inventory turnover and receivables turnover.

Working capital management is the practice of determining the appropriate amount of cash, marketable securities, accounts receivable, and inventory necessary for a company to operate efficiently. Successful managers can minimize their financing costs while still being able to pay their short-term obligations when they become due.

The term **working capital** refers to the current operating liquidity (current assets less current liabilities). The concept is said to date back to the era when traveling salesmen sold inventory as quickly as possible to repay short-term bank notes that financed the goods. If a salesman was unable to sell his wares promptly, the bank would refuse additional borrowings. In this scenario, the net working capital equals the salesman's inventory and other cash on hand less the outstanding short-term banknote.

Hint: In conversation, "working capital" can sometimes refer to gross working capital, or the company's current assets only. For the CPA exam, assume working capital means net working capital (current assets minus current liabilities) since it is more meaningful in terms of liquidity.

a. Working capital components
The amount of net working capital a company has on hand is calculated by subtracting current liabilities from current assets.

$$\text{Net Working capital} = \text{Current assets} - \text{Current liabilities}$$

Here are items commonly included in both current assets and current liabilities:

Current assets	Current liabilities
Reasonably expect to convert to cash in one year (or the operating cycle) or less	Due within one year (or the operating cycle)
Cash and cash equivalents	Accounts payable
Short-term investments	Short-term notes payable
Marketable securities, current portion	Accrued expenses
Accounts receivable, net	Accrued payroll and benefits
Inventories	Current portion of long-term debt
Prepaid expenses	Unearned revenue
	Income taxes payable

Hint: Sometimes analysts exclude the current portion of long-term debt and interest-bearing notes payables to determine the net operating working capital. This is important for calculating a company's free cash flow. (This is one approach of many to calculate a company's free cash flow.)

$$\text{Net Operating Working capital} = \text{Current assets} - (\text{Current liabilities} - \text{Notes Payable})$$

Multiple Choice

BEC 3-Q43

The following cash flow timeline is helpful to understand the elements that impact working capital:

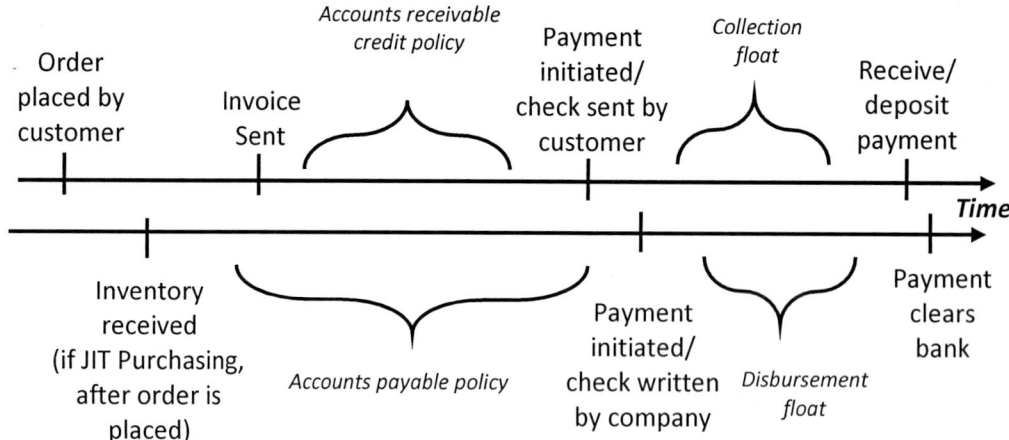

Management of cash accounts, and short-term investments, inventory, accounts receivable, and accounts payable are all important components that play a role in the management of working capital.

Another key concept in working capital management is called **float**. Float is the time that an incoming (outgoing) payment is in the process of collection (disbursement). Even with computerized payment technology, float cannot be eliminated completely as there is an inherent lag involved between the time payment is initiated (e.g., the check is signed) and the time the payment clears the bank.

b. Key working capital metrics
The key working capital metrics (i.e., current ratio, quick ratio, cash conversion cycle, inventory turnover and receivables turnover) are helpful to determine if a company's managers are efficiently and effectively utilizing working capital within the organization. While there are many variations of these formulas, the ones presented are the most common and will be tested on the CPA exam.

1) Current ratio (working capital ratio)

$$\text{Net Working capital} = \text{Current assets} - \text{Current liabilities}$$

$$\text{Current ratio} = \frac{\text{Current assets}}{\text{Current liabilities}}$$

The current ratio illustrates the number of times a company's current assets would cover its current liabilities. A ratio of less than 1 is a red flag, indicating the company may be unable to pay its short-term debt as it is due.

2) Quick ratio (acid-test ratio)

$$\text{Quick ratio} = \frac{\text{Cash and cash equivalents} + \text{Marketable securities} + \text{A/R, net}}{\text{Total current liabilities}}$$

The quick ratio (or acid-test) is a gauge of a company's ability to fulfill its short-term obligations with liquid or near liquid assets. Compared to the current ratio, by excluding inventories and other current (albeit less liquid) assets, the quick ratio is more conservative.

Multiple Choice

BEC 3-Q44

3) Cash conversion cycle
The cash conversion cycle is the length of time between when the company makes payments (cash outflow) to when it receives payment from customers (cash inflow).

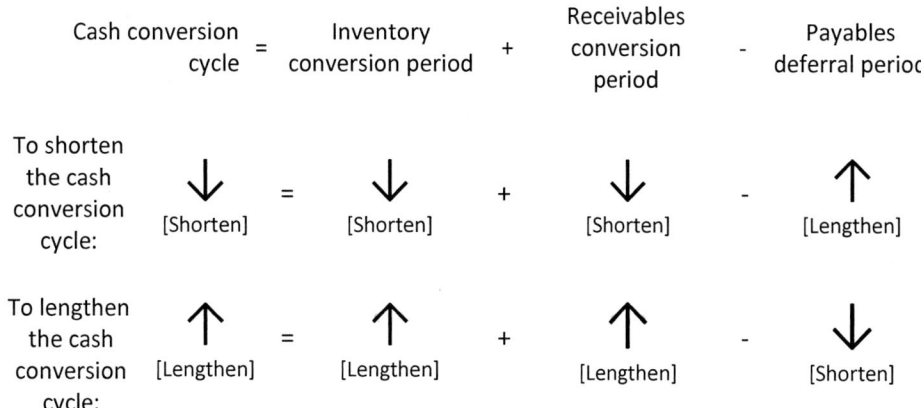

Ideally, the time it takes customers to pay for a good or service will be shorter than the time the company uses to pay its suppliers. That way, the cash is on hand for the longest period of time possible.

i. Inventory conversion period: Number of days of sales in inventory

$$\text{Inventory Conversion Period} = \frac{\text{Average Inventory}}{\text{COGS per day}}$$

ii. Receivable conversion (collection) period: Number of days of sales outstanding

$$\text{Receivables Conversion Period} = \frac{\text{Average Accounts Receivable}}{\text{Credit Sales per day}}$$

iii. Payables deferral period:

$$\text{Payables Conversion Period} = \frac{\text{Average Accounts Payable}}{\text{COGS per day}}$$

4) Inventory turnover

$$\text{Inventory turnover} = \frac{\text{Cost of goods sold}}{\text{Average inventory}}$$

This ratio is an asset utilization measurement to judge how efficient a company is at managing their inventory.

```
    Net sales
  − COGS
    Gross profit or gross margin
```

```
    Inventory, beginning balance
  + COGS purchase
    Cost of goods available for sale
  − Inventory, ending balance
    COGS
```

```
    Gross purchases
  − Purchase discounts
  − Returns and allowances
    Net purchases
  + Freight-in or transportation-in
    COGS purchases
```

5) Receivable turnover

$$\text{Receivables turnover} = \frac{\text{Net credit sales}}{\text{Average accounts receivable, net}}$$

Managers use this ratio to evaluate how efficiently accounts receivable are collected and how well working capital is managed by the company.

A higher ratio is favorable, indicating receivables are more liquid and credit sales convert quickly to cash. A lower ratio could signal a collection problem.

```
    Accounts receivable, gross
  − Allowance for doubtful accounts
    Accounts receivable, net
```

$$\text{Average accounts receivable, net} = \frac{(\text{Beginning Balance} + \text{Ending Balance})}{2}$$

> **Hint**: If the question does not distinguish between the credit sales and the total sales and there is not enough information provided to determine credit sales – it is appropriate to use total sales to calculate receivables turnover.

i. Average collection period

$$\text{Average collection period in days} = \frac{365 \text{ days}}{\text{Accounts receivable turnover}}$$

This measure is also called days sales outstanding.

Multiple Choice

BEC 3-Q45 through BEC 3-Q46

c. Working capital fluctuations

> Detect significant fluctuations or variances in the working capital cycle using working capital ratio analyses.

Fluctuations and variances in the working capital cycle can always be explained by pinpointing what has changed in the entity's environment, both internally and externally. Managers can also use the information gleaned from ratio analysis to adjust and fine-tune the company's working capital cycle. By managing working capital, the company can use its capital more efficiently and generate the most value for the firm.

Managers should pay attention to their inventory management processes (inventory planning) and accounts payable management (purchase discounts, payment periods) to anticipate changes to the company's working capital. Additionally, establishing appropriate credit and collection policies (which impacts the accounts receivable balance and collection float, respectively) help companies predict when cash from customers will be collected and plan their working capital requirements accordingly.

2. Strategies for managing working capital
    a. Inventory management processes

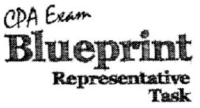

> Compare inventory management processes, including pricing and valuation methods, to determine the effects on the working capital of a given entity.

Economic Order Quantity (EOQ)	$$EOQ = \sqrt{\frac{2aD}{k}}$$ Where a = Cost to place order D = Annual demand in units k = Carrying cost for 1 unit in inventory for 1 year
Reorder Point	**Reorder point =** **(Average Daily Usage x Purchasing Lead Time) + Safety Stock** Full Safety Stock = (Maximum Daily Usage – Average Daily Usage) x Purchasing Lead Time Reorder Point with Full Safety Stock = Maximum Daily Usage x Lead Time
Economic Production Run (EPR)	$$EPR = \sqrt{\frac{2aD}{k}}$$ Where a = Cost to set up an order D = Annual demand in units K = Cost to carry 1 unit in inventory for 1 year

1) Inventory costs
   A company incurs costs to both order and carry inventory. The more units in each order, the lower the yearly ordering costs since the company does not need to place as many orders. However, if a company orders inventory less frequently, it must maintain a larger average inventory. Larger inventories mean higher carrying costs for the year.

   Carrying costs behave the opposite from ordering costs. The fewer orders the company places per year, the more units the company will have on hand. The more units a company has on hand, the higher will be its carrying costs. The costs of carrying inventory include interest costs from borrowing, spoilage, insurance, warehouse space, and security costs. An increase in the cost of carrying inventory would cause management to reduce its average inventory to decrease the carrying costs.

Ordering Costs	Carrying Costs
- Preparing a purchase requisition - Preparing a purchase order - Transmitting the purchase order by mail, telephone, or electronically - Inspecting the goods on arrival - Comparing the purchase order to the invoice - Preparing a receiving report - Comparing the receiving report to the invoice - Preparing a debit memo for goods on the invoice not received or damaged	- Property insurance on the inventory - Property taxes on the inventory - Storage costs such as rent or depreciation on the warehouse or store, utilities, and depreciation on the shelves - Securing the inventory including security guards and electronic security systems - Spoilage and theft loss - Opportunity cost of the money invested in the inventory

   Multiple Choice

   BEC 3-Q47 through BEC 3-Q48

   i. Reducing non-value-added inventory costs
      A non-value-added cost is a cost for which a customer would not willingly pay, therefore, absorbed by the company. Another name for non-value-added cost is waste. Management should strive to minimize the non-value-added costs of ordering and carrying inventory.

      > **Example**: Management could change from ordering inventory by switching from using printed forms and its mailing of purchases order electronically to ordering inventory.
      >
      > Management can also reduce the non-value-added carrying costs of spoilage and theft by installing better security systems and by keeping inventory at the proper temperature.

      The goal of management is to reduce the sum of ordering costs and carrying costs via some balance as these costs behave inversely. Management through the use of the economic order quantity (EOQ) model can minimize the sum of ordering costs and carrying costs.

2) Economic order quantity (EOQ)
   Economic order quantity (EOQ) determines the optimal amount of inventory to order by balancing the cost of placing an order for inventory with the costs of carrying the inventory. EOQ is the point where carrying costs equal restocking costs. The objective is to minimize the total cost of ordering and carrying inventory.

The EOQ is equal to the square root of the product of two times and the cost per order and the annual demand in units divided by the annual carrying cost per unit.

$$EOQ = \sqrt{\frac{2aD}{k}}$$

Where a = Cost to place order
D = Annual demand in units
k = Carrying cost for 1 unit in inventory for 1 year

> **Example**: Assume that the cost to place an order is $20, the annual demand is 40,000 units, and the annual carrying cost for one unit is $10. What is the EOQ?
>
> EOQ = $\sqrt{(2 \times \$20 \times 40{,}000) \div \$10 \text{ per unit}}$
> EOQ = $\sqrt{(\$1{,}600{,}000) \div \$10 \text{ per unit}}$
> EOQ = $\sqrt{160{,}000 \text{ units}}$
> EOQ = 400 Units

> **Hint**: The calculator provided for the CPA exam includes the square root function.

   i. Minimum order requirement
   If the supplier has a minimum order quantity, the company would order the greater of the EOQ or the minimum order.

> **Example (continued)**: In the example above, the EOQ is 400 units. If the supplier had a minimum order of 500 units, the company would order 500 units. The company could seek to negotiate a lower minimum order or find a different supplier that would allow the company to order 400 units.

Multiple Choice
BEC 3-Q49 through BEC 3-Q54

3) Reorder Point
The **reorder point** is the point managers need to order additional inventory to prevent a stockout, or insufficient inventory for the customers' demand.

   i. With no safety stock
   If a company does not maintain a safety stock, it will order the number of units determined by the EOQ when the inventory level is less than or equal to the average daily usage, multiplied by the number of days of purchasing lead time. The lead time is the number of days from the date the company places an order until it receives the order.

> **Example (continued)**: Continuing with the information from the examples above, the company operates 365 days a year. Therefore, its average daily usage is 110 units (40,000 units ÷ 365 days). If the purchasing lead time is five days, the company will place an order for the EOQ of 400 units when its inventory is down to 550 units (110 units per day x 5 days).

4) Safety Stock

   Safety stock is the number of units of inventory a company keeps in stock to avoid losing sales if its sales are higher than average. Maintaining a safety stock increases the company's carrying costs, but it reduces potential stockout cost. The profit a company loses for not having adequate inventory is stockout cost.

   The company must be willing to accept a level of risk if it does not have a safety stock. Using average daily usage to determine the reorder point could cause the company to lose sales if demand is higher than average. The lost sales could lead to greater loss of sales in the future if the company loses customers because the company did not have the products on hand the customers wanted.

   i. **Stockout cost** is the opportunity cost of the profit lost from lost sales due to lack of inventory. To reduce stockout cost, the company should maintain a safety stock.

      Examples of situations that result in stockout costs include: (1) lost contribution margin (sales revenue minus variable costs) from not having the item on hand the customer wanted to buy, (2) lost future sales because the customer decided not to do business with the company again, (3) lost sales to new customers because the disappointed customer informed potential new customers of their bad experience with the company.

   ii. **Full safety stock** is the difference between the maximum daily inventory usage and the average daily inventory usage multiplied by the lead time.

       Full Safety Stock = (Maximum Daily Usage – Average Daily Usage) x Purchasing Lead Time

       Management adds the safety stock to the reorder point without safety stock to determine the reorder point with safety stock.

       The calculation of the reorder point with full safety stock is:

       Reorder point = (Average Daily Usage x Purchasing Lead Time) + Safety Stock

       Maintaining a safety stock increases carrying costs. Therefore, management must consider the tradeoff between stockout cost and carrying costs when deciding on the number of units of safety stock.

       > *Example: Reorder point with full safety stock*
       > Assume a company has a maximum daily usage of 500 units and an average daily usage of 420 units. The lead time is six days.
       >
       > The company's full safety stock would be 480 units [(500 – 420) x 6]. The company's reorder point without safety stock is 2,520 units (420 units per day x 6 days). Adding the safety stock of 480 units will result in a reorder point of 3,000 units (2,520 + 480). If the company wants a full safety stock, it will order the number of units determined by the economic order quantity when its inventory is down to 3,000 units.

       A quicker way to determine the reorder point when a company wants a full safety stock is to multiply the maximum daily usage by the lead time.

       Reorder Point with Full Safety Stock = Maximum Daily Usage x Lead Time

> **Example (continued):** If the maximum daily usage is 500 units and the lead time is six days, the reorder point with a full safety stock would be 3,000 units (500 units per day x 6 days).

In certain circumstances, such as economic downturn or other financial situation that would require liquidity, management could decide to maintain a safety stock less than a full safety stock. This decision would decrease the reorder point in units.

> **Example (continued):** *Reorder point with less than full safety stock*
>
> Management could decide to maintain a safety stock of 250 units instead of the full safety stock of 480 units. In that case, the reorder point would be 2,770 units [(420 x 6) + 250)].

5) Economic Production Run (EPR)

A manufacturing company can adapt the EOQ formula to determine the optimal number of units to produce in each production run. The optimal number of units to produce is called the **economic production run (EPR)** or the economic production quantity (EPQ). The EPR minimizes the sum of setup costs and carrying costs.

The EPR is equal to the square root of two multiplied by the setup cost per production run and the annual production requirement in units all divided by the annual cost to carry one unit in inventory.

$$EPR = \sqrt{\frac{2aD}{k}}$$

Where a = Cost to set up an order
       D = Annual demand in units
       K = Cost to carry 1 unit in inventory for 1 year

> **Example:** *A manufacturing company needs to produce 50,000 units per year. The cost to set up the machinery to produce one run is $1,210. The cost to carry one unit in inventory is $16 per year.*
>
> The company calculates its EPR as follows:
> $$EPR = \sqrt{(2 \times \$1,210 \times 50,000) \div \$16 \text{ Per Unit}}$$
> $$EPR = \sqrt{\$121,000,000 \div \$16 \text{ Per Unit}}$$
> $$EPR = \sqrt{7,562,500 \text{ Units}}$$
> $$EPR = 2,750 \text{ Units}$$
>
> Therefore, the company would produce 2,750 units during each production run.

6) Just-in-time (JIT) purchasing

Just-in-time, or JIT, systems obtain and deliver goods exactly as-needed, delivering no more or less than the quantity demanded. JIT principles can be applied to purchasing (procurement) and manufacturing (production).

In a JIT purchasing system, the suppliers (vendors) deliver materials or merchandise just in time for the merchant to sell it or deliver raw materials to a manufacturing company just in time for the materials to enter into production.

Companies that might be interested in JIT purchasing include those in manufacturing and merchandising. It has also been determined that many companies that adopt JIT purchasing also choose to adopt JIT manufacturing.

A JIT system is a demand-pull system; therefore, the purchasing and the manufacturing processes are initiated only when a customer orders a product. This is opposite of a production-push system, where inventory is purchased based on a manager's forecast of future demand. In a more traditional system, a merchandising company maintains large quantities of inventory and attempt to sell it to customers.

	JIT Purchasing
Benefits	<ul><li>Reduction in inventory carrying costs</li><li>Reduction in ordering costs through the use of long-term contracts with vendors and technology</li><li>Rapid identification of quality problems and improved quality</li><li>Reduced lead times</li><li>Reduced setup times for manufacturing companies</li><li>Freed up space that the company would otherwise use to store inventory (another benefit of having inventory carrying costs reduced)</li><li>Reduced probability of inventory becoming obsolete</li></ul>
Risks	Stockout and stockout costs due to:<ul><li>Higher than expected demand by customers</li><li>Strikes by transportation companies</li><li>Inability of vendors to meet delivery requirements</li><li>Failures of technology used to order inventory</li><li>Acquisition of main suppliers by competitors and other parties</li></ul>

b. Accounts payable management

Compare accounts payable management techniques, including usage of discounts, factors affecting discount policy, uses of electronic funds transfer as payment methods and determination of an optimal vendor payment schedule in order to determine the effects on the working capital of a given entity.

1) Usage of discounts
Companies, if funds are available, are wise to take advantage of **discounts** to reduce the amount due to a vendor by paying early. The discount is written like a fraction, with the discount percentage (e.g., 2%) on the top and the last day the discount is valid on the bottom. As such, a 2% discount that is due 10 days from the receipt of the invoice is a "2/10" discount. The term "net" often follows the discount terms to indicate the length of time before payment is required or considered delinquent. A 30-day payment window is written "net 30," or simply "n30" and together with the payment discount, it is written "2/10, n30" on the invoice.

The operating cycle (or selling cycle) of the company is the main factor that affects the discount policy. If the company is operating with limited working capital, prompt payment from customers is needed for the company to be able to pay its current liabilities.

2) Electronic fund transfer
Electronic funds transfer (EFT) is an electronic transmission of funds-related transactions using a computer-based system that does not require either party to execute a physical exchange of a financial instrument (e.g., cash, checks). Some examples of EFTs include automatic teller machine (ATM) transactions, wire transfers, debit payments, and payroll direct deposits. EFT is a technique to decrease the amount of collection float, or the time that an incoming payment is in the process of collection.

3) Optimal vendor payment schedule
The modern understanding of working capital is that excessive cash reserves and liquidity can hinder financial performance as the funds are not employed in earning assets such as plant and equipment. The optimal vendor payment schedule manages disbursements to achieve a minimum working capital, reducing current assets that are not generating a high yield (ROA) and paying liabilities with the proceeds from operations rather than cash reserves. Typically, it is beneficial for a company to pay vendors on the last day of the payment window (e.g., on day 30 if payment terms are "net 30"), assuming no discount is available.

c. Corporate banking arrangements

> Distinguish between corporate banking arrangements, including establishment of lines of credit, borrowing capacity and monitoring of compliance with debt covenants in order to determine the effects on the working capital of a given entity.

A company may need temporary (or stop-gap) working capital due to fluctuations in seasonal business demands or for short-term, revenue-generating projects. Corporate banking arrangements are a popular solution for temporary working capital requirements. Common financing vehicles and its various terms are as follows:

1) A **line of credit** is an amount of credit extended by a bank to a borrower with a set maximum and no specific purpose. This can also be called revolving credit due to its renewable nature.

2) A **discount note** is a short-term debt instrument issued by a bank at a discount but requires repayment of the face value.

3) A **term loan** is a short-term borrowing agreement where the bank loans the borrower a specific amount, which must be repaid according to an agreed-upon repayment schedule.

4) A loan is considered **self-liquidating** when the borrower finances revenue generating activities using the loan proceeds and then promptly repays the loan with the revenues generated with the debt.

5) A company's **borrowing capacity** is the maximum amount a company can obtain from a bank given its current financial standing and credit rating.

6) Creditors may impose requirements on the company called **debt covenants** until the company repays its outstanding debt. The debt covenants may limit the ability of the company to borrow additional funds and require the company to maintain certain financial ratios. If the company defaults on the debt covenants, the creditors may be able to impose a higher interest rate or call the loan before maturity. Audits are usually the means for verification.

7) A **compensating balance** is a specified sum of money deposited into a restricted, non-interest bearing account, providing surety (a guarantee) the loan will be repaid. In effect, it is a form of collateral.

A compensating balance raises the effective interest rate of a loan (i.e., the borrower pays interest on a stated face value larger than the amount it can use) and decreases the net working capital available compared to a loan without a compensating balance requirement.

8) A **zero balance account** is a bank account where funds are transferred in to cover checks that are presented for payment. Companies can then keep most of their money in a master account, allowing them more opportunity to use larger sums of money for investment purposes.

9) **Concentration banking** is used by companies to pool or concentrate collections from multiple locations into a single bank account. When a company uses a concentration account, money can be deposited at a local bank branch but, as a way to simplify the process, the money is then moved from all local bank branches to the company's primary bank account. The bank doesn't need to keep track of multiple bank accounts since the money is deposited into one central account regardless of the branch location.

Multiple Choice

BEC 3-Q55 through BEC 3-Q60

d. Credit management policies

CPA Exam Blueprint Representative Task

> Interpret the differences between the business risks and the opportunities in an entity's credit management policies to determine the effects on the working capital of a given entity.

Credit management policies are instituted by a company to make sure outstanding balances due from customers are paid promptly. Bad debt arising from delinquent payments have the potential to cause a company to run out of working capital, which leads to risks pertaining to failure to pay current liabilities and may impact the company's ability to borrow in the future.

Accounts receivable credit policies should be established by the organization addressing the amount of credit granted each customer based on their default risk, the standard credit terms (i.e., payment due after 15 days), cash discount policies, and delinquent accounts collection procedures.

A more generous credit policy will increase sales. A tighter credit policy will yield fewer sales. Therefore, the company must select an optimal credit policy maximizing sales but minimizing uncollectable accounts.

1) Lockbox
A **lockbox** is a way to manage customer payments using a post office box managed by a bank, rather than the company receiving payment directly. Customers send payments made by check through the mail to the company's lockbox. Each day, a courier picks up the collections and brings them directly to the bank to be deposited into the company's account.

The bank's customer purchases the lockbox service because it decreases the time that is needed for checks to clear the customer's bank account and the cash collected is available sooner; therefore, lockbox services are a form of accounts receivable (A/R) management. It also decreases internal processing costs.

The bank's customer also has improved internal control over its A/R collections because the lockbox service avoids handling of collections by the customer's employees. However, it can be risky since lockboxes are rarely supervised and could create an opportunity for fraud.

Multiple Choice

BEC 3-Q61 through BEC 3-Q62

2) **Payment discounts** are a deduction from the amount due by the customer that is granted for early or prompt payment. The calculation of the cost of credit (annual cost not electing to discount) is:

$$\text{Nominal annual cost of discount} = \frac{(\text{Discount \%})}{(100\% - \text{Discount \%})} \times \frac{360}{\text{Allowed payment days} - \text{discount days}}$$

> *Example:* The company offers a credit term of 3/10, net 30 (i.e., a 3% discount is deducted from the total due if payment is made within 10 days).
>
> The cost of credit for the payment discount is:
>
> $$\text{Nominal annual cost of discount} = \frac{3\%}{97\%} \times \frac{360}{30 \text{ days} - 10 \text{ days}}$$
>
> Nominal annual cost of discount = 0.0309 x 18
> Nominal annual cost of discount = **55.62%**

> *Hint:* Compared to a typical cost of capital (e.g., 5%-10%), offering discounts is expensive, and many companies do not think the trade-off for prompt payment is worth the cost of the discount. However, if roles are reversed and the company can utilize a discount on a payable, it is smart to take advantage of it due to the high annual percentage rate (APR) yield.

Multiple Choice

BEC 3-Q63 through BEC 3-Q71

e. Short-term and long-term financing

Analyze the effects on working capital caused by financing using long-term debt and/or short-term debt.

There are both advantages and disadvantages associated with a company's decision to use either short-term or long-term debt financing. Liquidity concerns and interest rates are two key factors.

1) Short-term
   Short-term financing refers to a financial obligation that is due in one year or less. Depending on the situation, short-term financing is favored because it allows a firm to be more liquid and can lower the firm's financing cost (i.e., short-term rates are lower than long-term rates).

   The primary disadvantage of a short-term arrangement is that interest rates can shift favorably or unfavorably if the company must refinance. Also, the creditor has the option to deny the firm's refinancing request without recourse.

2) Long-term financing
   Long-term financing is due in over one year and is classified on the balance sheet as a non-current liability. Long-term financing is preferable for permanent working capital, due to the nature of permanent working capital (see the definition below). The extended nature of the obligation lowers interest rate risk since refinancing is not required within the year.

   The primary disadvantage of long-term financing is that long-term rates are higher than short-term rates, resulting in higher financing costs.

   > *Hint*: The above statements assume a normal yield curve and not an inverted yield curve. A normal yield curve has lower **yields** than long-term debt instruments of the same credit quality. Inverted yield curves have the opposite relationship.

   > *Hint:* Permanent working capital (also called fixed working capital) is the minimum amount of working capital a company must maintain throughout the year to sustain operations.

Multiple Choice

BEC 3-Q72

C. Financial Valuation Methods and Decision Models
1. Financial valuation methods

> **Identify and define the different financial valuation methods and their assumptions, including but not limited to fair value, Black-Scholes, Capital Asset Pricing Model and Dividend Discount Model.**

Financial valuations assist management in determining such things as 1) asset worth 2) offering price of a new security, and 3) expected returns. Once a valuation is done, management can use the information to determine where to invest, how to fund it, and its expected return.

a. Cost of newly issued common stock
The cost of newly issued stock is higher than the cost of previously issued stock due to flotation costs. The formula for the cost of newly issued common stock is as follows:

$$K_S = \frac{D_1}{P_0 - F} + \text{Expected G}$$

Where:
D_1 = Expected dividend payment
P_0 = Current price of stock
G = Growth rate in earnings
F = Flotation cost per share

Example: A company has the following information related to its issuance of new common stock:
Flotation costs per share $3.00
Common stock price per share $30.00
Expected dividend payment per share $2.00
Earnings growth rate 3%

The company's cost of newly issued common stock is:

$$[\$2 / (\$30 - \$3)] + .03 = 10.4\%$$

> *Hint*: The dividend-yield-plus-growth approach method of dividend valuation estimates an investor's expected yield on their investment. The formula for the dividend-yield-plus-growth approach is the same as the cost of newly issued stock, except that it does not include flotation costs.

b. Capital Asset Pricing Model
Securities typically have some level of risk associated with them. The more risk that a security has, the more an investor expects to be compensated for taking on the risk. The capital asset pricing model (CAPM) determines the expected return of a security (estimate of the cost of equity capital) in relation to its risk. The formula for the CAPM is as follows:

Expected Return = Risk free rate + [Beta x (Market rate – Risk free rate)]

Where:
Risk-free rate = The short-term U.S. Treasury Bill rate or the U.S. Treasury Bond rate.
Beta = It is the price volatility of a single investment compared to the price volatility of the market. The beta will be different depending upon how the market is defined. For instance, IBM's beta would be different if comparing it to the S&P 500 versus the Wilshire 5000 Total Market Index.

Beta <1: A stock is less volatile (less risky) than the market.
Beta = 1: Stock's value moves with the market.
Beta >1: A stock is more volatile (riskier) than the market.

Market rate = The expected return for similar securities, with similar risk and is applicable to systematic risk. Market Risk can also be labeled systematic risk or undiversifiable risk.

With CAPM, a security's expected return equals the risk-free rate, plus a risk premium. If the expected return is not equal to or greater than the required rate of return, the security should not be invested in.

Example: A company has the following information related to its capital structure:
Risk-free rate of return   3%
Equity risk premium   2%
Beta value   1.2

The company's expected return using the CAPM is:

Expected Return = Risk free rate + [Beta x (Market rate − Risk free rate)]
= 0.03 + (1.2 x 0.02) = 5.4%

Hint: The risk-free rate is an interest rate that has no risk of loss. Any interest rate over the risk-free rate amount indicates that the investor could experience a loss on the investment. In practice, a risk-free government bond or U.S. Treasury bill interest rate is used. More specifically, to be classified as a risk-free asset, there must have no default risk and no reinvestment risk.

c. Arbitrage pricing model (or arbitrage pricing theory)
The CAPM addresses only systematic risk, which is one of the two types of risk. The other type of risk is unsystematic risk.

1) Systematic risk: Relates to factors for an entire market or entire market segment that cannot be avoided simply by diversifying a portfolio of investments. Also known as market risk or undiversifiable risk.
2) Unsystematic risk: Relates to the risk for a specific security, or a group of similar securities that are in a portfolio of investments. Unsystematic risk can be reduced through diversification, and it is sometimes referred to as diversifiable risk or specific risk.

The arbitrage pricing model is a technique for valuation that includes both systematic risk and unsystematic risk. The arbitrage pricing model shows that a security's return may be predicted by utilizing the relationship between that security and many common systematic risk factors. Systematic risk can be impacted by many (macroeconomic) factors such as economic growth, exchange rates, and interest rates. The formula for the arbitrage pricing model is as follows:

$$r_p = b_1(k_1 - k_{rf}) + b_2(k_2 - k_{rf}) + (b_3(k_3 - k_{rf})...$$

Where:
r_p = Risk premium for the security.
k_{rf} = Risk-free interest rate.
$b_{1,2,3}$ = Beta for the various risk factors (i.e., economic growth, exchanges rates and interest rates indicated above).
$k_{1,2,3}$ = Market rate for each risk factor.

> *Hint:* Some analysts feel that the arbitrage pricing model is superior to CAPM because the arbitrage pricing model contains many risk factors, versus one risk factor in the CAPM. However, this belief is not universal as over the last several years, the performance of CAPM was equally, if not stronger than APM. This conclusion was a result of the many inaccuracies in quantifying the variables used in APM.

d. Bond-yield-plus approach

The bond-yield-plus approach is based on the theory that a company's equity is riskier than its debt and that the cost of both of these moves together. The bond-yield-plus approach formula is as follows:

$$\text{Required rate of return on equity} = \text{Before-tax cost of debt} + \text{Risk premium}$$

> *Hint:* This is not viewed as a very accurate model.

e. Dividend Discount Model

For common stock shareholders, their cash flows are represented by the dividends received while they own the stock and the price received when the stock is sold. The dividend discount model takes into account an investor's expectation that the future selling price reflects the present value of the dividends expected after the sale. There can be any number of holding periods (i.e., years) selected for the dividend discount model. For each holding period, the investor will need to determine the dividend projections, in addition to the expected price of the stock when it is sold (at the end of the holding period).

The formula for the value of stock using the dividend discount model for one holding period is as follows:

$$V_0 = \frac{D_1 + P_1}{1 + K_E}$$

Where:
V_0 = Value per share at time 0 (today)
D_1 = Expected dividend (assumes it is paid at the end of the year)
P_1 = Expected price of stock at time 1
K_E = Required return on equity

Example for one holding period: In one year, a company's common stock is expected to trade at $40 per share and is expected to pay a $1.00 dividend per common share. If an investor requires a 12% rate of return on the company's stock, the value per share today is calculated as follows:

$$V_0 = \frac{\$41}{1.12}$$

$$= \$36.61$$

If the company's share price is lower than $36.61, the investor would want to invest in the stock because it appears to be undervalued. Likewise, if the company's share price was higher than $36.61, the investor would probably not invest because the stock appears to be overvalued. When more than one holding period is used, needs to include a hypothetical stock sale. The formula for the value of stock using the dividend discount model for multiple holding periods is as follows (assume 3 periods):

$$V_0 = \frac{D_1}{1 + K_E} + \frac{D_2}{(1 + K_E)^2} + \frac{D_3 + P_3}{(1 + K_E)^3}$$

> *Hint*: The present value of $1 formula is part of the dividend discount model. The present value of $1 formula is:
>
> $$PV = \frac{\$1}{(1+i)^n}$$

Example for multiple holding periods: The same investor from the previous example expects another company to pay dividends over the next three years of $2.00, $2.50 and $3.00. The investor expects the stock price to be $95.00 at the end of the third year. If an investor requires a 10% rate of return on the company's stock, the value per share today is calculated as follows:

$$V_0 = \frac{D_1}{1+K_E} + \frac{D_2}{(1+K_E)^2} + \frac{D_3 + P_3}{(1+K_E)^3}$$

$$V_0 = \frac{\$2.00}{1.10} + \frac{\$2.50}{(1.10)^2} + \frac{\$3.00 + \$95}{(1.10)^3}$$

$$V_0 = \$1.82 + \$2.07 + \$73.63 = \$77.00$$

f. **Black-Scholes Model**

The Black-Scholes model is used to determine the estimated price of options. The assumptions incorporated into the Black-Scholes model include:
- Transaction costs (i.e., commissions) are ignored.
- The risk-free interest rate is known and constant over the option's life.
- Stock returns are normally distributed (i.e., bell-shaped curve). Technically, lognormal distributed.
- The volatility of the underlying stock's returns is known and constant over the option's life.
- The options call can only be exercised at expiration (called European options).
- The underlying asset does not generate cash flows (dividends).

Changes in option value result from the changes in the 5 inputs used in the Black-Scholes model calculation.

5 Inputs of Black-Scholes Model	
Input	**Impact on Option Value**
1. Exercise price	• As exercise price increases, calls are worth less; puts are worth more. • As exercise price decreases, calls are worth more; puts are worth less.
2. Underlying stock price	• As the price of underlying stock increases, the value of call option increases (put option decreases). • As the price of underlying stock decreases, the value of call option decreases (put option increases).
3. Time to option expiration	• The longer the time to option expiration, the higher the value of the call or put option.
4. Price volatility of underlying stock	• The greater the expected volatility of the underlying stock's return, the more the put and call option is worth.
5. Risk-free interest rate	• Increase in interest rate usually results in an increase in call option prices and a decrease in put option prices.

> *Hint:* The CPA Exam does not require any further analysis of the Black-Scholes model, but keep in mind that these assumptions are from the original, developed model and that newer versions which have modified the limiting assumptions addressed above.

g. Asset valuation

Calculate the value of an asset using commonly accepted financial valuation methods.

Asset valuations are performed using various methods such as discounted cash flow valuations (or income method), relative valuations (or multiples), and fair value measurements (or market method).

1) Discounted cash flow valuations are done by taking the expected future cash flows of an asset and discounting them back to its present value, using a discount rate that reflects the riskiness of the expected future cash flows. Usually starting with the cost of capital and adding some additional risk premium. For example, if an asset has an expected useful life of 4 years and has expected cash flows of $100,000 in year 1, $125,000 in year 2, $140,000 in year 3 and $150,000 in year 4, the value of this asset, using discount cash flows at a discount rate of 6%, is calculated as follows:

   Year 1: $100,000 / (1+.06) $106,000
   Year 2: $125,000 / (1+.06)^2 $140,449
   Year 3: $140,000 / (1+.06)^3 $166,742
   Year 4: $150,000 / (1+.06)^4 $\underline{\$189,372}$
   Present value of asset $\underline{\$602,563}$

Present value and additional discounting methods are covered in the present value and capital budgeting sections of this chapter.

2) Relative valuations, also known as comparable valuation or multiples, value assets by using observing the value of comparable assets (e.g., P/E ratio, or Price to Book). Since these assets are similar, but not exactly the same, relative valuation should account for differences by making appropriate adjustments to the valuation.

3) Fair value measurements estimate the price at which an orderly transaction to sell an asset or to transfer the liability, would take place between market participants at the measurement date, under current market conditions. For fair value measurement (FASB ASC 820, Fair Value Measurement), there are three types of inputs for applying the fair value measurement, which are Level 1, Level 2, or Level 3 inputs (fair value hierarchy).

Level	Estimation Description	Measure of Fair Value
1	Observable information (direct, unadjusted inputs) for identical assets. The market approach is an applicable valuation technique.	Best
2	Observable information for similar, comparable assets in active or inactive markets.	↓
3	Unobservable inputs, not derived from the market, and used when either the market doesn't exist or are the market is illiquid. Level 3 is highly subjective.	Least

The hierarchy gives the highest priority to unadjusted quoted prices in active markets for identical assets and liabilities (Level 1 measurements) and the lowest priority to unobservable inputs (Level 3 measurements).

4) The value of an entire company (enterprise) can be determined by taking the market value of equity and debt, and netting them with liquid assets.

    Market capitalization (common shares outstanding x market price per share)
+ Market value of preferred stock (preferred shares outstanding x price per share)
+ Market value of debt (if traded, otherwise historical cost is sometimes used)
- <u>Cash equivalents and short-term investments</u>
= Enterprise value

Often, the enterprise value is considered the buyout value of the company.

> *Hint:* On a side note, firm value is simply the market value of debt and equity without subtracting out the cash and short-term investments.

2. Asset structure and asset management

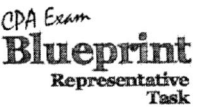

Identify and define the different financial decision models and assumptions involved in making decisions relating to asset and investment management, debt, equity and leasing.

a. Asset structure
Just as there is an optimal capital structure, there is also an optimal asset structure for every company. The term **asset structure** refers to the mix of capitalized assets on the balance sheet, including short-term and long-term assets.

b. Asset management
Asset and investment managers determine the most appropriate financial instruments or capital assets to invest the company's resources in to generate earnings. This includes determining the debt financing or leasing arrangement that would be the best in each unique situation.

Typically, asset managers try to match the life of the asset to the term of the financing arrangement. This helps mitigate the risk that the company will be unable to meet its financial obligations when they come due. This is called Maturity Matching.

c. Asset effectiveness and/or efficiency
Asset utilization ratios are critical in determining whether assets are being used efficiently and effectively. Asset utilization ratios include receivable turnover, inventory turnover, and total asset turnover.

3. Accounting estimates

Identify the sources of data and factors that management considers in forming the assumptions used to prepare an accounting estimate.

Accounting estimates are inherent in any business and are often subjective, requiring management assumptions related to this uncertainty. Additional reading for the CPA candidate to further understand the impact of accounting estimates is contained in Public Accounting Oversight Board (PCAOB) AS 2501: Auditing Accounting Estimates and the AICPA's AU-C 540: Auditing Accounting

Estimates, including Fair Value Accounting Estimates, and Related Disclosures. These pronouncements provide a basis for this section on accounting estimates.

Some accounting estimates arise from management's need to forecast an outcome or outcomes of one or more transactions, events or conditions. Other accounting estimates may be required by the applicable financial reporting framework. For example, the applicable financial reporting framework may require fair value measurement based on an assumed hypothetical current transaction between knowledgeable, willing parties (i.e., market participants) in an arm's length transaction. Fair value measurement represents the price that would be received to sell an asset or paid to transfer a liability in an orderly transaction between market participants at the measurement date. Like other accounting estimates, fair value measurements may be based on subjective and/or objective information and generally involve measurement uncertainty.

> *Hint*: Accounting estimates and fair value measurements involving a high degree of subjectivity and judgment and as such, may be more susceptible to misstatement of financial statements. These types of situations would require more auditor focus during an audit.

a. Management is responsible for making the accounting estimates included in the financial statements. Estimates are based on subjective and objective factors requiring substantial judgment. Management's judgment is normally based on its knowledge and experience about past and current events and its assumptions about conditions it expects to exist along with courses of action it expects to take. Examples of accounting estimates include:
   1) Allowance for doubtful accounts
   2) Warranty obligations
   3) Useful life of assets
   4) Depreciation method
   5) Costs arising from litigation settlements and judgments
   6) Going concern assessment
   7) Outcome of long-term contracts

b. Sources of accounting estimates include:
   1) Historical results.
   2) Budgets.
   3) Use of outside specialists with experience and competence necessary to recommend estimates.
   4) Commonly used industry standards and practices accepted by regulators and compliance personnel.

c. Management should have a process in place to develop and manage accounting estimates.

> Describe the process and framework within which management exercises its responsibilities over the review and approval of accounting estimates.

The typical management process in developing accounting estimates include:
1) Identifying situations for which accounting estimates are required.
2) Identifying the relevant factors that may affect the accounting estimate.
3) Accumulating relevant, sufficient, and reliable data on which to base the estimate.
4) Developing assumptions that represent management's judgment of the most likely circumstances and events with respect to the relevant factors.
5) Determining the estimated amount based on the assumptions and other relevant factors.
6) Determining that the accounting estimate is presented in conformity with applicable accounting principles and that disclosure is adequate.

7) In addition, management should ensure the:
   i. Need for proper accounting estimates, where appropriate, is communicated within the company.
   ii. Preparation of the accounting estimates by qualified personnel.
   iii. Management bias is removed from the process, in order to arrive at a validated estimate.
   iv. Adequate review and approval of the accounting estimates by appropriate levels of authority, including:
      a) Review of sources of relevant factors.
      b) Review of development of assumptions.
      c) Review of the reasonableness of assumptions and resulting estimates.
      d) Consideration of the need to use the work of specialists.
      e) Consideration of changes in previously established methods to arrive at accounting estimates.
   v. Comparison of prior accounting estimates with subsequent results to assess the reliability of the process used to develop estimates.
   vi. Consideration by management of whether the resulting accounting estimate is consistent with the operational plans of the entity.

> *Hint*: The risk of material misstatement of the financial statements from accounting estimates normally varies with the complexity and subjectivity associated with the process, the availability and reliability of relevant data, the number of significant assumptions that are made, and the degree of uncertainty associated with the assumptions.

Besides management's responsibility of accounting estimates, an audit committee's role is vital to proper oversight. The audit committee should:
1) Understand the process for establishing accounting estimates.
2) Evaluate significant accounting estimates and the judgments made to arrive at them.
3) Carefully weigh any issues with management bias in developing estimates.
4) Benchmark the company's accounting estimate disclosures with those of other companies in the same industry.

Management disclosures related to accounting estimates are shown in the Management Discussion and Analysis (MD&A) section of financial statements. The SEC continues to emphasize the importance of disclosures regarding critical accounting estimates. Also, the SEC Division of Enforcement recently began analyzing MD&A's for appropriateness using data analytics.

> *Example of an accounting estimate disclosure in the MD&A from a General Electric Corporation 2006 annual report (one excerpt is shown):*
>
> *Accounting estimates and assumptions discussed in this section are those that we consider to be the most critical to an understanding of our financial statements because they inherently involve significant judgments and uncertainties. For all of these estimates, we caution that future events rarely develop exactly as forecast, and the best estimates routinely require adjustment. Also see Summary of Significant Accounting Policies, which discusses accounting policies that we have selected from acceptable alternatives.*
>
> *LOSSES ON FINANCING RECEIVABLES are recognized when they are incurred, which requires us to make our best estimate of probable losses inherent in the portfolio. Such estimate requires consideration of historical loss experience, adjusted for current conditions, and judgments about the probable effects of relevant observable data, including present economic conditions such as delinquency rates, financial health of specific customers and market sectors, collateral values*

> *(continued from previous page) and the present and expected future levels of interest rates. Our risk management process, which includes standards and policies for reviewing major risk exposures and concentrations, ensures that relevant data are identified and considered either for individual loans or leases, or on a portfolio basis, as appropriate.*
>
> *Our lending and leasing experience and the extensive data we accumulate and analyze facilitate estimates that have proven reliable over time. Our actual loss experience was in line with expectations for 2006, 2005 and 2004. While prospective losses depend to a large degree on future economic conditions, we do not anticipate significant adverse credit development in 2007.*

4. Present value

   The basis of present value theory (time value of money) is that a dollar in hand today is worth more than a dollar to be received in the future because the dollar today could be invested and result in more than a dollar in the future unless in times of deflation. The value today of a dollar to be received in the future is called the **present value** (PV) of the dollar. Present value is an important concept and is used in a number of calculations in accounting, including determining the value of bonds and in capital budgeting decisions.

   The process, of determining how much an amount to be received in a certain number of periods in the future at a certain interest rate is called discounting. The interest rate used to determine the present value is called the discount rate. The higher the discount rate, the lower will be the present value. The longer the number of periods until the company receives the cash payment, the lower the present value.

   a. **Present value of a single amount (PV of $1)**
      1) The present value of a single amount is single amount is how much a dollar in the future is worth today at a specified interest rate. The formula to calculate the present value of a single amount is as follows:

         $$PV = \frac{FV}{(1+i)^n}$$

         Where:
         FV = the cash to be received at one point in the future
         i = interest rate at which to discount the cash to be received in the future (known as the discount rate)
         n = number of periods in the future until the company will receive the cash

      2) Present value tables (shown below) are also used to determine the "factor" for PV calculations. The present value of a single amount factor is where the interest rate and number of periods intersect. To calculate the present value of a single amount to be received in the future, multiply the amount to be received in the future by the present value of a single amount factor:

         PV = amount to be received x PV factor

      3) For example, a company expects to receive $5,000 at the end of 3 years for an investment of $3,000 today, and the discount rate is 10%.

         The present value of the $5,000 to be received in 3 years is calculated as follows:

         PV = $5,000 x 0.751 = $3,756.00

Present value factors of a single amount

Periods	4%	6%	8%	10%
1	0.962	0.943	0.926	0.909
2	0.925	0.890	0.857	0.826
3	0.889	0.840	0.794	0.751
4	0.855	0.792	0.735	0.683
5	0.822	0.747	0.681	0.621

b. **Present value of an annuity**

An **annuity** is a series of equal cash flows at equal intervals. There are two kinds of annuities in future value and present value calculations: (1) an ordinary annuity and (2) an annuity due. The only difference is when the payments are made.

- For an **ordinary annuity**, or annuity in arrears, the series of equal payments are made at the END of the period.
- For an **annuity due**, or annuity in advance, the series of equal payments are made at the BEGINNING of the period.

> *Hint*: Most questions related to annuities on the CPA are on ordinary annuities.

1) The present value of an annuity is the sum of the present value of the single, equal amounts for each period the company will receive cash in the future. Even though adding up the present value of the single amounts for each period will provide the annuity factor, the most efficient way to determine the annuity is to use the present value of an annuity table.

2) Using the present value of an annuity table (shown below), the present value of an ordinary annuity is calculated by multiplying the cash payment made each period, by the present value of an ordinary annuity factor. The present value of an ordinary annuity factor is the number where the interest rate intersects the number of periods for which the payment will be received.

   PV = payment x present value of an ordinary annuity factor

3) Present value of an ordinary annuity example:

   For example, a company will receive a payment of $7,000 per year at the end of each of the next 3 years at a discount rate of 8%. The present value of the annuity is calculated as follows:

   i. Using the sum of the present values for each period from the present value of a single amount table:

      $7,000 x 0.926 = $6,482.00
      $7,000 x 0.857 = $5,999.00
      $7,000 x 0.794 = $5,558.00
      Present value $18,039.00

   ii. Using the present value of an ordinary annuity factor from a table:

      $7,000 x 2.577 = $18,039.00

   Using the present value of an ordinary annuity table is a much more efficient way to calculate the present value of an ordinary annuity.

> *Hint*: If you sum up the three single amount factors in the above example, it will add up to the PV of the annuity factor of 2.577.

> **Hint**: Although it is important to understand the PV formulas, the CPA exam questions typically provide the PV factors or, tables of PV factors to use in present value calculations.

Present value factors of an ordinary annuity

Periods	4%	6%	8%	10%
1	0.962	0.943	0.926	0.909
2	1.886	1.833	1.783	1.736
3	2.775	2.673	2.577	2.487
4	3.630	3.465	3.212	3.170
5	4.452	4.212	3.993	3.791

4) Present value of an annuity due example:
A company will receive a lease payment of $7,500 at the beginning of this year and for each of the next 4 years for a total of 5 payments. The interest rate is 10%. The present value of the annuity due is calculated using the factor from the table (shown below) as follows:

PV = Annual payment x present value of an annuity due factor
PV = $7,500 x 4.170
PV = $31,275.00

Present value of an annuity due

Periods	4%	6%	8%	10%
1	1.000	1.000	1.000	1.000
2	1.862	1.943	1.926	1.909
3	2.886	2.833	2.783	2.736
4	3.775	3.673	3.577	3.487
5	4.630	4.465	4.312	4.170

c. **Future value of a single amount (FV of $1)**
The amount that an investment made today will be worth at a specified number of periods in the future, at a specified interest rate, is called the future value of the amount. A simple example of the use of future value is a savings account. The higher the interest rate, the higher will be the future value. The longer the number of periods the amount is invested, the higher the future value. The reinvestment of the interest earned is called compounding. Future value is used to determine the future value of an investment such as a bond sinking fund. It is the reciprocal of the PV formula and concepts.

1) The formula for calculating future value is as follows:

$$FV = PV \times (1 + i)^n$$

Where:
FV = Future Value
PV = Present Value
i = interest rate the investment will earn
n = number of periods of the investment

> **Hint**: The CPA exam will provide the possible factors and tables of factors to use in future value calculations.

Using the FV factors, the future value of a single amount is calculated as follows:

FV = amount x future value of a single amount factor

2) For example, an amount to be invested today is $9,000. It will be invested for 4 years at an interest rate of 10%. Using the future value of a single amount table (shown below), the future value factor is where 10% intersects 4 periods. That factor is 1.4641. The future value is calculated as follows:

FV = PV x future value of a single amount factor
FV = $9,000 x 1.464
FV = $13,176.00

Future value of a single amount

Periods	4%	6%	8%	10%
1	1.040	1.060	1.080	1.100
2	1.082	1.124	1.166	1.210
3	1.125	1.191	1.260	1.331
4	1.170	1.262	1.360	1.464
5	1.217	1.338	1.469	1.611

d. **Future value of an ordinary annuity**
The future value of an ordinary annuity is the amount available in a specified number of periods in the future, as the result of a payment made at the end of each period. To calculate the future value of an ordinary annuity, multiply the payment by the future value of an ordinary annuity factor. The future value of an ordinary annuity factor is the number where the interest rate insects the number of periods.

FV = payment x future value of ordinary annuity factor

1) For example, a company will invest $6,000 at the end of each of the next 4 years. The interest rate is 10%. The future value of the ordinary annuity is calculated as follows:

PV = $6,000 x 4.641
PV = $27,846.00

Future value of an ordinary annuity

Periods	4%	6%	8%	10%
1	1.000	1.000	1.000	1.000
2	2.040	2.060	2.080	2.100
3	3.122	3.184	3.246	3.310
4	4.427	4.375	4.506	4.461
5	5.416	5.637	5.867	6.105

e. **Future value of an annuity due**
To calculate the future value of an annuity due, multiply the payment by the future value of an annuity due factor from the table (shown below). The future value of an annuity due factor is the number where the interest rate insects the number of periods of payments on a future value of an annuity due table.

1) For example, a company will deposit into a bond sinking fund, $10,000 on the first day of each year for 5 years. The interest rate is 8% compounded annually. The future value of an annuity due factor where 5 periods intersects 8% is 6.336. The future value of an annuity due is calculated as follows:

$$FV = \$10,000 \times 6.336 = \$63,360$$

Future value of an annuity due

Periods	4%	6%	8%	10%
1	1.040	1.060	1.080	1.100
2	2.122	2.184	2.246	2.310
3	3.247	3.375	3.506	3.641
4	4.416	4.637	4.867	5.105
5	5.633	5.975	6.336	6.716

Hint: To change from an ordinary annuity (OA) to an annuity due (AD) Factor, use the following formula:

$$\text{OA Factor} \times (1 + i) = \text{AD Factor}$$

To change from an Annuity Due (AD) factor to an ordinary annuity (OA) factor, use the following formula:

$$\text{AD Factor} / (1 + i) = \text{OA Factor}$$

f. **Compounding**
Many calculations involving present value or future value assume that the cash flows are compounded or discounted annually at the stated interest rate.

1) If the cash flows are compounded or discounted at a more frequent interval, and the interest rate is stated on an annual basis, the number of periods must be increased proportionately, and the interest rate must be decreased proportionately.

For example, assume someone is going to invest $10,000 for 3 years at an annual interest rate of 12%, compounded quarterly. The interest rate to use in the future value calculation is determined by taking the 12% annual interest rate and dividing it by 4 to arrive at a quarterly interest rate of 3%. The number of periods to use in the future value calculation is determined by multiplying 4 quarters per year times 3 years to arrive at 12 periods. Using the future value of a single amount table, the future value factor is where 3 percent intersects 12 periods. That factor is 1.4258 rounded to four decimal places. The future value is calculated as follows:

$$FV = PV \times \text{future value of a single amount factor}$$
$$FV = \$10,000 \times 1.4258$$
$$FV = \$14,258$$

Hint: For continuous compounding, the formula is:
$$A = Pe^{rt}$$
Where
A = Amount
P = Principal
e = 2.718 (the mathematical constant)
r = rate of interest
t = time in years

5. Capital budgeting

CPA Exam Blueprint Representative Task

Compare investment alternatives using calculations of financial metrics (payback period, net present value, economic value added, cash flow analysis, internal rate of return etc.), financial modeling, forecasting, projection and analysis techniques.

Capital budgeting is a management and financial planning process by which management decides whether or not to invest in projects from available alternatives. Capital budgeting includes evaluating potential long-term investments in fixed assets, capital leases, businesses, and intangible assets such as patents. The primary focus of capital budgeting is usually on fixed assets. A company invests in fixed assets to generate additional revenues and reduce costs via efficiencies. The fixed assets should provide the company with cash flows that help increase the value of the company. These would include the following:

- Land
- Buildings
- Vehicles
- Furniture
- Machinery
- Equipment

An organization usually plans its capital expenditures budget for 5 to 10 years. The capital expenditures budget is not a part of the annual master budget. However, there is a nexus to the annual master budget to the extent the company plans to purchase fixed assets in the next year.

A company buys fixed assets to generate cash flows or to reduce cash outflows. For example, a company could buy a new machine that will produce the same product and generate the same revenues as a current machine, but the company expects the new machine to cost far less to operate. The reduction in operating costs will reduce the company's outflow of cash for operating the machine. Saving cash flows is the equivalent to generating cash inflows. For example, a company might evaluate the purchase of a new computer system to process its business transactions. The computer system will generate no cash inflows, however, in making their investment decision, management will compare the cash outflows of the new computer system to the cash outflows of the current computer system.

a. **Stages of the capital budgeting process**
1) Identification
Management identifies the types of projects that will help achieve the organization's goals and objectives.
2) Search
Management specifies the alternative capital investments that could meet the company's goals and objectives.
3) Information acquisition
Management obtains information on the various investments such as their costs and benefits.
4) Selection
Management selects the investments the company will acquire based on an evaluation of them using one or more of the capital budgeting techniques. Much of the capital budgeting process focuses on this stage.
5) Financing
Management decides how the company will pay for the investment. The company could pay cash for the investment, finance it in part or in full with debt, or acquire the asset through a capital lease. The financing decision is not relevant to the selection decision.

6) **Implementation and control**
   Management should monitor how well the asset is meeting the company's goals and objectives. One aspect of this stage is a post-investment audit. Management seeks to determine how well the projections made in the capital budgeting process match the actual results. Management uses this feedback to improve the capital budgeting process for future projects. If the asset is not performing close to the planned results, management might decide to dispose of the asset and acquire a different one.

b. **Capital rationing**
   Finance theory suggests that a company should invest in all assets the company expects to provide a return greater than the cost of capital. As a practical matter, companies must ration the capital they plan to spend for the purchase of fixed assets. Capital rationing is the process of deciding how much capital to spend for the purchase of fixed assets. Management often uses the net present value method to provide the initial ranking of possible capital investments.

c. **Risks in capital budgeting**
   A company incurs risk in capital budgeting because the fixed asset might not generate the cash flows the company expects. The present value of the cash flows might be less than the cost of the investment. Management can address the issue of risk in several ways. The first way is to use judgment to evaluate the risk of a project. Another way to compensate for risk is to use a risk-adjusted discount rate or hurdle rate by adding percentage points to it. While not a highly recommended method, companies may use the payback period method as a secondary capital budgeting method to assess the risk of investments with similar net present values or internal rates of return. Another way to analyze risk is sensitivity analysis.

   Sensitivity analysis is subjecting the capital budgeting decisions to changes in assumptions. Accountants may use sensitivity analysis to compensate for risk by calculating an expected range for each of the variables used to rank possible capital investments. These variables include the amount of the expected cash flows, the discount rate, and the tax rate.

   > *Hint*: The hurdle rate is the expected (target) rate of return that is established by management, which is the minimum acceptable rate. Examples include the company's cost of capital or returns earned for similar investments in the industry. Nevertheless, the cost of capital is the minimum rate.

d. **Investment decision**
   Capital budgeting is an investment decision. How the company pays for the fixed assets is a financing decision. The company should not include the cash flows associated with financing a fixed asset in the capital budgeting process. For example, if a company plans to borrow money to buy a fixed asset, it should not include the cash paid for interest, cash paid on the principal of the debt, or the cash flows used to evaluate the investment.

e. **Mutually inclusive projects**
   Mutually inclusive projects require the company to purchase one or more secondary projects if it supports the purchase of a primary project. For example, a company is considering new computer hardware for its factory. If the company buys the computer hardware, it would also need to purchase the related software. In evaluating mutually inclusive projects, the company should consider the cost and cash flows of all the related projects.

f. **Mutually exclusive projects**
   If projects are mutually exclusive, management will select one project and reject the other projects under consideration. Choosing from among several possible new machines to replace an old machine

is an example of mutually exclusive projects. Selecting one of the new possible machines will result in management rejecting the other machines.

g. **Independent projects**

Projects are independent if the selection of one project does not affect the selection of another project. For example, a company is choosing from among several possible new vehicles to replace an old vehicle. The company is also evaluating several new printers for purposes of replacing an old printer. The vehicles are mutually exclusive to each other as are the printers. However, the vehicle project and the printer project are independent of each other.

h. **Cash flows and income**
   1) Difference

   One of the main differences between cash flows and net income is depreciation. Net income reflects depreciation expense. However, depreciation expense does not affect cash flows except to the extent that depreciation reduces the cash outflow for taxes. The depreciation expense for tax purposes is usually different from the depreciation for book purposes.

   2) Effect of depreciation on income taxes and cash flow

   The payment of taxes because of the additional income generated by a capital investment is a relevant cash outflow in calculating the net cash flow generated by the investment. Depreciation is an expense, but it does not require the outflow of cash. However, depreciation is relevant in calculating the cash outflow for taxes because depreciation is deductible for income taxes. Therefore, depreciation reduces the outflow of cash for income taxes. This effect is known as the depreciation tax shield.

   3) How to calculate after-tax cash flow

   One way to calculate the after-tax cash flow from a capital investment is to calculate the cash generated by the investment before taxes and then subtract the taxes paid. Depreciation is a reduction in taxable income in calculating the taxes paid. Another way to calculate the after-tax cash flow from a capital investment is first to calculate the net income. The net income includes a subtraction for depreciation and income tax expense. As a result, the depreciation is added back because it does not require any outflow of cash. The result is the after-tax cash flow from the investment.

   > **Example**: An investment will cost $140,000. It will have a life of seven years and have no salvage value. It will generate cash flows before depreciation and taxes of $30,000 a year for each of the next seven years. The depreciation for book and tax purposes is assumed to be the same. The tax rate is assumed to be a flat 40 percent.
   >
   > The depreciation is $20,000 per year ($140,000 / 7). If it were not for depreciation, the company would have to pay $12,000 ($30,000 x 40%) in additional income taxes each year. However, depreciation shields $20,000 of the income from depreciation and thereby saves the company $8,000 ($20,000 x 40%) per year in income taxes. The annual tax expense is $4,000 [($30,000 – $20,000) x 40%]. The after-tax cash flow is calculated as follows:
   >
   > | | |
   > |---|---:|
   > | Cash generated by the investment before taxes | $30,000 |
   > | Less: depreciation | (20,000) |
   > | Taxable income | $10,000 |
   > | Less: tax expense ($10,000 x 40%) | (4,000) |
   > | After-tax income | $6,000 |
   > | Add: depreciation | 20,000 |
   > | After-tax cash flow | $26,000 |

> Although a company will usually generate cash flows from an investment throughout the year, capital budgeting methods that use cash flows generally assume that the company receives the cash flow from the investment each year on the last day of the year. While this assumption is not realistic, it simplifies the calculations. The numbers used in capital budgeting are estimates. Thus, the company should not treat the numbers as though they are precise. The results of the capital budgeting process are inputs from the management team.

> *Hint*: Don't forget the following calculation.
>
> After-tax cash inflows [Calculated as pretax cash flows x (1 - tax rate)]
> + Depreciation or amortization expense tax shield [Calculated as the expense x tax rate]
> After-tax cash flow

i. **Importance of salvage value (residual value)**
Salvage value is the amount management expects to receive for a sale of the asset at the end of its useful life. Salvage value is also known as residual value.

> *Hint*: While sometimes these terms are used interchangeably, they are technically not the same. Disposal value does not have to be the amount at the end of the asset's life. It is the amount when the asset is sold which could be prior to the end of its useful life.

Management should attempt to estimate salvage value as accurately as possible. In particular, management should not assume that salvage value is zero simply because it makes the calculations easier. Underestimating the salvage value can bias the company against making marginal investments in assets. Failing to invest in assets that would otherwise be acceptable if management estimated the salvage value accurately puts the company at a disadvantage.

j. **Effects of changes in required working capital**
Sometimes investment in a new asset requires an increase in working capital. Working capital equals current assets minus current liabilities. Current assets include cash, marketable securities, accounts receivable, notes receivable, inventory, supplies, and prepaid expenses. The current assets most likely to increase because of the purchase of a capital investment are accounts receivable and inventory. Current liabilities are generally debts due within one year. The current liability most likely to increase because of the purchase of a capital investment is accounts payable. A company should treat the required increase in working capital as an additional cash outflow for the investment in the project at the time of its purchase. At the end of the asset's useful life, the release of the working capital is an additional cash inflow similar to salvage value.

k. **Advantages of capital budgeting**
- A useful planning tool to make long-term strategic investments.
- Assists management in controlling the amount of money used for investment in long-term projects.
- When comparing investment alternatives, it helps management choose the best option.
- Various capital budgeting techniques can be used to determine the most appropriate investment.

l. **Disadvantages of capital budgeting**
   - Investment decisions are for long-term projects and are usually difficult to reverse in the future, once they are implemented.
   - Capital budgeting techniques include estimates, which inherently contain uncertainty.
   - Investment risk and discounting are subject to management's interpretation.

m. **Capital budgeting techniques**
   There are several discounted cash flow capital budgeting techniques that companies can employ such as:
   - Net present value(NPV) method
   - Economic value added (EVA) – Note: Uses NOPAT as a surrogate for Cash Flow
   - Internal rate of return (IRR) method
   - Profitability index (PI) method
   - Discounted payback method

   The capital budgeting techniques that do not use discounted cash flows are the:
   - Payback method
   - Accounting rate of return (ARR) method (uses net income rather than cash flows)

   > *Hint:* Any significant capital budgeting decision must be made using discounted cash flow techniques.

   1) **Payback method**
      The payback method, as the name implies, is the length of time required to recover the initial cost or cash outflow of an investment. A company will typically establish an acceptable payback period in which an investment should be able to repay the initial cost. When evaluating investment opportunities, payback periods that are too long are rejected. Investment alternatives within the parameters of the acceptable payback range are evaluated by the fastest payback.

      The formula for calculating the payback period is as follows:

      $$\text{Payback Period} = \frac{\text{Investment}}{\text{Annual cash inflow}}$$

      Where:
      Annual cash inflow (Before depreciation, amortization, and taxes)
      Less: Depreciation and amortization expense
      = Net income before taxes
      Less: taxes
      = Net income after taxes
      Add: Depreciation and amortization expense
      = Annual cash inflow (net of taxes)

      > *Hint*: This formula assumes an annuity whereby every year the cash flow is the same. If the cash flows are not the same each year, one must subtract every cash flow from the investment outlay. See example below for non-annuity cash flows.

      The payback method is a simple but, rather crude measure of risk. The shorter the payback period, the less is the perceived risk of the investment in the asset. Another weakness is that payments received after the payback period cutoff is disregard which can be a major mistake.

Example payback method (illustration of potential for misuse):

Project 1: Initial Investment $1,000		Project 2: Initial Investment $1,000	
Year	Net Cash Flow	Year	Net Cash Flow
1	$500	1	$100
2	$500	2	$200
3	$0	3	$100
4	$0	4	$600
5	$0	5	$100,000

Is Project 1 really better since it has a shorter payback period? Of course not.

Differing payback periods and estimating cash flows are important considerations in payback analysis.

    i.   Different payback periods for different types of investments

A company might establish a maximum payback period for different types of capital investments. The payback period for equipment would be lower than the payback period for a building. For example, a company could establish a policy of payback period for equipment of five years or less and a payback period for buildings of 20 years or less.

    ii.   Estimated cash flows

Management must estimate the amounts and timing of the cash flows the investment in the asset will generate or that the asset will save the company compared to not investing in the asset.

> **Example (payback method with equal cash flows):** A company buys a machine for $54,000. The company estimates the machine will generate production that will provide the company with $12,000 in additional net cash flows each year for 10 years. The payback period is calculated as follows:
>
> Payback period = $54,000 / $12,000 per year = 4.5 years
>
> If management's policy is that equipment purchases must have a payback of five years or less, the investment in the equipment would be acceptable. If management's policy is that equipment purchases must have a payback of four years or less, the purchase of the equipment would not be acceptable.

    iii.   Payback method with unequal cash flows

If the company does not expect equal cash flows each year, the payback period is the number of years from the date of the purchase of the asset until the company has received cash flows equal to its cost.

> **Example (payback method with unequal cash flows)**: A company is considering the purchase of a machine that will cost $40,000. The company expects the machine to generate additional cash flows as follows:
>
> | | Cash Flows | Unrecovered Cost |
> |---|---|---|
> | Year 1 | $10,000 | $30,000 |
> | Year 2 | $8,500 | $21,500 |
> | Year 3 | $7,500 | $14,000 |
> | Year 4 | $7,000 | $7,000 |
> | Year 5 | $5,000 | $2,000 |
> | Year 6 | $4,000 | $ -0- |
> | Year 7 | $2,000 | $ -0- |
>
> The payback period would be 5.5 years assuming that the company expects to receive cash flows in Year 6 evenly throughout the year. The company would need half of year 6 to realize the $2,000 in cash flows needed to recover the $10,000 investment fully. The payback period ignores the cash flows expected to be received in the second half of Year 6 and the cash flows expected to be received in Year 7.

    iv.   Advantages of the payback method
- Emphasizes liquidity because management will typically want shorter payback periods to recoup principal.
- Simple calculations, easy to use and understand.

    v.   Disadvantages of the payback method
- Does not consider the time value of money unless one uses the discounted cash flow method.
- Does not consider cash flows that continue after the payback period.
- Does not consider a company's desired rate of return.

Multiple Choice
BEC 3-Q73 through BEC 3-Q78

2) **Discounted payback method**
The discounted payback method overcomes one of the problems with the payback method in that the discounted payback method discounts the cash flows expected to be received or saved to their present values. The discounted payback period is the number of years required until the discounted cash flows equal the cost of the investment. The discounted payback method ignores the cash flows expected to be received or saved after the payback period just as does the payback method. In all other respects, the discounted payback method is the same as the payback method. Nevertheless, the opinion in the marketplace suggests that if one is using a discounted cash flow technique, might as well use Discounted Cash Flow and/or Internal Rate of Return.

> **Example:** A company is considering the purchase of a machine that will cost $50,000. The discount rate is 12 percent. The company expects the machine to generate additional cash flows as follows:
>
> | | Cash Flows | PV Factor of $1 at 12% | PV of Cash Flows | Unrecovered Cost |
> |---|---|---|---|---|
> | Year 1 | $15,000 | .89286 | $13,392.90 | $36,607.10 |
> | Year 2 | $13,500 | .79719 | $10,762.07 | $25,845.04 |
> | Year 3 | $12,000 | .71178 | $ 8,541.36 | $17,303.68 |
> | Year 4 | $11,000 | .63552 | $ 6,990.72 | $10,312.96 |
> | Year 5 | $10,000 | .56743 | $ 5,674.30 | $ 4,638.66 |
> | Year 6 | $8,000 | .50663 | $ 4,953.04 | $ 585.62 |
> | Year 7 | $5,000 | .45235 | $ 2,261.75 | $-0- |
> | Year 8 | $4,000 | .40388 | $1,615.52 | $-0- |
>
> The discounted payback period would be 6.25 years ($585.62 / $2,261.75 = .258) assuming that the company expects to receive cash flows in Year 7 evenly throughout the year. The discounted payback period ignores the cash flows expected to be received in the remainder of Year 7 and the cash flows expected to be received in Year 8.

3) **Accounting rate of return method**
The accounting rate of return method is the only capital budgeting method that uses net income rather than cash flows. The main difference, but not the only difference, between cash flows and net income is depreciation. Depreciation reduces net income, but depreciation has no direct effect on cash flows. The depreciation claimed for tax purposes reduces the outflow of cash for taxes. The depreciation amount claimed for tax purposes is usually different from the depreciation deduction for book purposes.

The accounting rate of return measures the percentage of the return on investment each year. The formula to calculate the accounting rate of return is as follows:

$$\text{Accounting rate of return} = \frac{\text{Average net income}}{\text{Average investment}}$$

The average net income should be the average net income from the investment in the asset. Thus, it should be the addition to net income resulting from the investment in the asset. The average investment in the asset is calculated as follows:

$$\frac{\text{Cost of investment + salvage value}}{2}$$

The cost of the investment should include all costs necessary to get the asset in place and ready for use and the additional investment in working capital required, if any, because of the investment in the asset. Some companies would use the initial investment rather than the average investment in the denominator. Management would compare the accounting rate of return of the investment to the company's desired rate of return.

> **Example**: A company is considering an investment in a machine that will cost $100,000 and have a salvage value of $20,000. Management expects it to last five years and generate the following expected net income after tax:
>
> | Year | Expected Income |
> |---|---|
> | 1 | $20,000 |
> | 2 | $18,000 |
> | 3 | $15,000 |
> | 4 | $12,000 |
> | 5 | $10,000 |
> | Total | $75,000 |
> | Divided by number of years | ÷ 5 |
> | Average income | $15,000 |
>
> Average investment = ($100,000 + $20,000) / 2
> = $120,000 / 2
> = $60,000
>
> Accounting rate of return = ($15,000 / $60,000) x 100%
> = 0.25 x 100%
> = 25%
>
> Management would consider the investment to be acceptable if its required rate of return was 25% or less.

> **Hint:** Both the payback period and the accounting rate of return methods ignore the time value of money.

Advantages of the accounting rate of return
- Simple and straightforward to calculate from existing accounting information.
- Focuses on the profitability of an investment.

Disadvantages of the accounting rate of return
- Does not use the time value of money.
- Uses accounting net income and not cash flows of the project.
- Does not consider reinvesting the profits.
- ARR will not stay constant over an investment's life, resulting in the investment appearing more attractive in one period versus another.

> **Hint:** The ARR is not highly regarded in the field of finance.

4) Net present value (NPV) method

The net present value method assists management in determining the initial investment that is required for the purchase of a fixed asset and ascertains whether this investment will provide a return that is greater than management's hurdle (target) rate of return. The net present value method estimates the amounts and timing of the cash flows associated with a capital investment. The discount rate should at least be the company's cost of capital. Private companies will often use the weighted average cost of capital. Public companies may use the weighted average cost of capital and add a premium.

The net present value method assumes that the company reinvests the cash flows received at the end of each period at a rate of return equal to the discount rate. This is a conservative assumption because finance theory states that if management cannot invest assets at a rate of return greater than or equal to the cost of capital, management should then return the money to the shareholders. The formula for net present value is as follows:

NPV = PV of future net cash flows − Required investment

> **Remember**: With NPV, the discount rate is calculated in advance in order to discount the future cash flows to their present value.

> **Example**: A company is considering the purchase of a machine that will cost $50,000 and have an expected salvage value of $8,000. The useful life is five years. Management expects the machine to generate net after-tax cash flows of $12,000 for each of the next five years. The discount rate is 10 percent. The net present value is calculated as follows:
>
> Present value of an annuity of $12,000 for 5 years at 10%
> $12,000 x 3.79079 $45,489.48
> Add: Present value of $8,000 salvage value in 5 years
> $8,000 x 0.62092 $ 4,967.36
> Total present value of future cash flows $50,456.84
> Less: Cost of the machine   (50,000.00)
> Net present value $456.84
>
> Because the machine has a positive net present value, the investment would be acceptable. However, the net present value is rather small and very sensitive to the assumptions made, especially the salvage value. If salvage value were less, the net present value would likely be negative.

PV	NPV Result
PV of Investment > PV of investment benefits	NPV is negative, and this would be a poor investment
PV of Investment < PV of investment benefits	NPV is positive, and this would be a good investment
PV of Investment = PV of investment benefits	NPV is zero and management would be indifferent. This is also called the Internal Rate of Return (see below).

Advantages of net present value
- Typically considered the best capital budgeting technique.
- Includes the time value of money.
- Include all the cash flows for the life of the project.

Disadvantages of net present value
- Can be difficult to calculate.
- Does not provide the actual rate of return on the investment but only whether the investment will achieve the discount rate.
- It does not consider the dollar amounts (investment size) of each alternative in comparing NPVs.

> *Hint*: Net present value calculations:
>   After-tax cash inflows [Calculated as pretax cash flows x (1 - tax rate)]
> + Depreciation or amortization expense tax shield [Calculated as the expense x tax rate]
>   After-tax cash flow
> x PV factor of annuity of $1
>   Net present value

Multiple Choice

BEC 3-Q79 through BEC 3-Q83

5) Economic Value Added
Economic value added (EVA) is a performance measurement based on the accrual basis of accounting and does not take into account the time value of money. It is concerned with economic profits and not so much accounting profits. It is a capital budgeting technique that is actually trademarked. EVA is calculated as:

$$EVA = NOPAT - (k - Capital)$$

Where:
NOPAT = Net Operating Profit after Taxes
k = WACC
Capital = Equity plus Long-Term Debt

6) Profitability index (PI)
The profitability index (also called benefit-cost ratio) is the ratio of the present value of the future cash flows from the investment divided by the cost of the investment. The formula is as follows:

$$\text{Profitability index} = \frac{\text{PV of future net cash flows}}{\text{Initial investment}}$$

If the PI is equal to, or greater than 1, management should invest because the investment's return is at least equal to, or greater than the required rate of return. If the profitability index is less than 1.0, the investment is not acceptable.

Example: A potential investment would cost $80,000 and have projected future cash flows with a present value of $100,000. The profitability index is calculated as follows:
$$\$100,000 / \$80,000 = 1.25$$

Because the investment in the example has profitability index of 1.25, it would be acceptable. Often, with limited funds available, companies will prioritize projects in order of the highest PI to the lowest PI, which can lead to very detailed analysis.

Advantages of the profitability index
- Includes the time value of money.
- Includes all cash flows for the life of the project.
- Relative profitability allows comparison of two investments irrespective of their amount of investment. (This is the main usage of the PI.)

Disadvantages of the profitability index
- Is dependent on projections of future cash inflows that can require detailed analysis.
- Can be difficult to assess PI results for investments with different useful lives.
- Investments having different investment amounts can result in the same PI.

Multiple Choice
BEC 3-Q84 through BEC 3-Q86

7) **Internal rate of return (IRR)**
The internal rate of return method is a discounted cash flow method. It assumes that a company invests the cash flows received each period at the internal rate of return. The internal rate of return is the rate of return that, when used as the discount rate in the net present value formula, causes the net present value to be exactly zero. The formula for the internal rate of return is as follows:

$$\text{IRR Factor (to be used in PV Table)} = \frac{\text{Cost of investment}}{\text{Annual net cash flow}}$$

Hint: This model assumes an annuity oriented cash flows. If amounts differ each year, one must calculate the IRR as if calculating the NPV.

Management then compares the internal rate of return to the company's required rate of return as a percentage. The required rate of return is known as the hurdle rate. The investment is acceptable if its internal rate of return is equal or greater than the hurdle rate. Some companies use its weighted average cost of capital (WACC) to compare to the internal rate of return. In that case, the WACC is the hurdle rate.

Relationship between NPV and IRR		
NPV	IRR	Investment Decision
NPV > 0	IRR > Hurdle rate or WACC	Make investment
NPV = 0	IRR = Hurdle rate or WACC	Management is indifferent
NPV < 0	IRR < Hurdle rate or WACC	Do not make investment

> **Hint:** Due to its complexity, most professionals would use a calculator or excel to calculate the IRR. For educational purposes, one tends to uses PV tables to calculate both NPV and IRR.

> **Example:** A company is considering an investment that costs $76,000. Management expects it will generate net after-tax annual cash flows of $20,000. Management expects the useful life to be five years and that the asset will have no salvage value.
>
> The internal rate of return is best solved using a computer or a financial calculator, especially if the annual cash flows differ. However, one can solve for the internal rate of return using tables, especially when the annual cash flows are the same. The internal rate of return factor is equal to the cost of the investment divided by the annual cash flow, as long as the cash flow is the same each year.
>
> $$IRR = \frac{\text{Cost of investment}}{\text{Annual net cash flow}} = \frac{\$76,000}{\$20,000} = 3.8$$
>
> This number is the same as the payback period in years. The next step is to find where the factor 3.8 is closest to the interest rate on the present value of an ordinary annuity table for five periods. The factor for 5 periods at an interest rate of 10 percent is 3.79079. The factor for 5 periods at an interest rate of 9 percent is 3.88965. So, the internal rate of return is between 9 and 10 percent, but it is much closer to 10 percent. To calculate a more exact answer requires interpolation and that type of calculation is not likely to be on the CPA exam.

Advantages of the internal rate of return method:
- Includes the time value of money.
- Includes all the cash flows for the life of the project.
- Determines the return on the initial investment.

Disadvantages of the internal rate of return method:
- Investment alternatives are based on IRR achieved and does not include investment profitability.
- Because estimates are used, the risk of higher or lower rates may result.
- Assumes cash flows generated from the investment are reinvested at the IRR, which tends to be unrealistic.
- For example, if a company can earn a high rate of return on one project, it does not necessarily mean the company can reinvest the annual cash flows at the same high rate of return.
- If management expects the signs of the cash flows to change during the life of the investment, it is mathematically possible for the investment to have multiple internal rates of return. For example, the cash paid for an overhaul of a machine in a future year could be expected to exceed the cash flows generated that year. Thus, the overhaul would cause the cash flows to be negative that year. However, management would expect the cash flows to turn positive again the next year.

> *Hint*: For actual decision-making, the NPV is preferable to the IRR. In case one gets differing recommendations from the NPV versus IRR, one selects based on the NPV. This however, will not be tested on the CPA exam.

Multiple Choice
BEC 3-Q87 through BEC 3-Q90

n. **Post investment audit**
A post investment audit is a part of the control function of management. It compares the results predicted during the capital budgeting process to the actual results. It not only provides insight on how well the projects are performing, but also can provide insight on how good its inputs were. Management can then take action to improve the process for the future.

Multiple Choice
BEC 3-Q91

6. **Lease versus buy decisions**

CPA Exam Blueprint Representative Task: Compare options in a lease vs. buy decision scenario.

Before a determination is made on whether to lease or buy equipment, management would have already decided to invest in the equipment. During the investment decision, a capital budgeting technique such as NPV would have been performed, with a resulting outcome greater than a Profitability Index greater than one. Once the decision to invest in the equipment is made, management will need to make the financing decision on whether to lease or purchase the asset. A discounted cash flow analysis is used to determine whether leasing or buying is the most appropriate choice.

In a lease or buy analysis, there are typically three relevant cash flows to consider in buying and two cash flows to consider in leasing.

Buying: Relevant cash flows to include:
1) Purchase price
2) Depreciation tax savings
3) Salvage value

Leasing: Relevant cash flows to include:
1) Lease payments
2) Tax savings on lease payments

In making the decision, one must not consider irrelevant costs and items such as 1) production activity (output) and 2) rate of inflation.

The discount rate to use in determining the present value of cash flows is the after-tax cost of borrowing (debt), which is calculated as follows:

After-tax cost of borrowing = Loan interest rate x (1-tax rate)

The company's cost of capital is usually not used in lease versus buy analysis because the cost of capital includes irrelevant issues such as operational risk and the cash flows that are not used in the buy versus lease decision.

The depreciation tax savings (shield) is calculated as follows:

$$\text{Depreciation tax savings} = \text{Depreciation expense} \times \text{Tax rate}$$

Lease payment tax savings are calculated similarly by taking the lease payment and multiplying it by the tax rate. The cash flow benefits from depreciation and lease payment tax savings is shown in the subsequent year analysis because taxes are paid one year in arrears.

The discounted cash flow analysis of whether to lease or buy is set up as NPV calculations, one for leasing and one for buying. The analysis will result in negative NPVs because only relevant costs are included in the analysis. The selection is the one with the smallest negative NPV number, which indicates the lowest cost.

> *Hint*: Sometimes, the method is called Net Present Cost since there are no cash inflows from the transaction other than cost savings.

Other factors to consider:
- A lease may contain such items as maintenance programs and licensing agreements as part of the lease. To make the lease versus buy analysis comparable, an estimate of the maintenance costs and licensing agreement costs and their related tax savings should be included in the buy NPV analysis.

Advantages of leasing:
- No large initial payment.
- Lower monthly payments.
- More flexibility to upgrade equipment.
- Little, if any financial restrictions.
- Ability to spread payments over longer periods.
- Protection against the risk of equipment obsolescence.
- If the lessee is in bankruptcy, the lessor claims to the equipment are more restricted than general creditors.
- Certain leases can be classified as operating leases and are not recorded as debt on the company's balance sheet.

Disadvantages of leasing:
- The lessee does not own the equipment.
- No recognition of salvage value.
- Difficult to cancel a lease.
- Could cost more due to loss of some tax savings (i.e., depreciation).

Advantages of buying:
- Buyer owns the equipment and records it as an asset on the balance sheet.
- Potentially greater tax advantages due to depreciation and investment tax credits.

Disadvantages of buying:
- Buyer's loan covenants may contain financial restrictions.
- Buyer eventually owns the old obsolete equipment.

Example: On January 1, 20X7, Crown Company has determined to invest in new equipment for its factory. Management is considering whether to buy or to lease the equipment. The equipment is expected to decrease operating costs by $12,000 per year. Crown's tax rate is 40%.

If Crown decides to buy the equipment, its cost is $200,000, and it has a useful life of 4 years, with a salvage value of $20,000. Crown uses 200% double declining balance method of depreciation. Crown would obtain a $200,000, 4-year loan to purchase the equipment at an interest rate of 10%.

If Crown decides to lease the equipment, they will pay 4 annual lease payments of $33,000, payable in advance at the beginning of each year. After 4 years the equipment is returned to the leasing company.

"Buy" analysis:

Depreciation and related tax savings calculations				
Year	Equipment Carrying Value (beginning of year)	Depreciation (straight-line rate x 2)	Equipment Carrying Value (end of year)	Depreciation Tax Savings (Depreciation x tax rate)
20X7	$200,000	$100,000	$100,000	$40,000
20X8	$100,000	$50,000	$50,000	$20,000
20X9	$50,000	$25,000	$25,000	$10,000
20X0	$25,000	$5,000	$20,000 (salvage value)	$2,000

After-tax cost of borrowing = Loan interest rate x (1-tax rate)
= 10% x (1- 40%)
= 6%

Present Values of Cash Flows to Buy Equipment					
Year	20X7	20X8	20X9	20X0	20X1
Initial Cost	($200,000)				
Depreciation Tax Savings	$40,000	$20,000	$10,000	$2,000	
Salvage Value					$20,000
Net Cash Flows	($160,000)	$20,000	$10,000	$2,000	$20,000
PV of $1 Factor at 6%	1	0.943	0.890	0.840	0.792
PV of Cash Flows	($160,000)	$18,860	$8,900	$1,680	$15,840
NPV of Buying Equipment					($114,720)

"Lease" analysis:

Present Values of Cash Flows to Lease Equipment					
Year	20X7	20X8	20X9	20X0	20X1
Lease Payment	($33,000)	($33,000)	($33,000)	($33,000)	
Lease Payment Tax Savings*		$13,200	$13,200	$13,200	$13,200
Net Cash Flows	($33,000)	($19,800)	($19,800)	($19,800)	$13,200
PV of $1 Factor at 6%	1	0.943	0.890	0.840	0.792
PV of Cash Flows	($33,000)	($18,671)	($17,622)	($16,632)	$10,454
NPV of Leasing Equipment					($75,471)

*$33,000 x 40% = $13,200

Crown should **lease** the equipment because the NPV of leasing the equipment is less than the cost of buying it.

This page is intentionally left blank.

Glossary: Financial Management

A

Accounting estimates – subjective valuations requiring management assumptions related to uncertainty

Accounting rate of return method – the percentage of the return on investment each year of a capital budgeting project a capital investment

Acid-test – see quick ratio

Annuity – a series of equal cash flows at equal intervals

Annuity due – a series of equal payments are made at the *BEGINNING* of the period; also called annuity in advance

Annuity in advance – see annuity due

Annuity in arrears – see ordinary annuity

Appraisal right – the right of minority shareholders to receive an equitable value for their shares as determined by an independent party in the event of a merger or other transaction that transfers control of the corporation

Arbitrage pricing models – a security's return predicted by utilizing the relationship between that security and many common systematic risk factors

Asset structure – the mix of capitalized assets on the balance sheet, including short-term and long-term assets

B

Bankers' acceptances – a time draft promising a stated future payment on a specific date; the payment is guaranteed by a bank

Black-Scholes model – calculation used to determine the estimated price of options

Bond – a debt instrument that obligates the issuer to repay the lender (bondholder) a specified sum of money (the bond's face value) at a future maturity date

Bond-yield-plus approach – required rate of return on equity equal to the before-tax cost of debt plus risk premium

Borrowing capacity – is the maximum amount a company can obtain from a bank given its current financial standing and credit rating

C

Callable bond – a bond provision that grants the issuer the option to redeem (repay) the bond prior to stated maturity date

Callable preferred stock – the corporation has the right to buy back the stock, but usually must pay the preferred stockholder a premium (e.g., a liquidating premium, sometimes called a "sweetener").

Capital – the monetary resources that finance a company's assets

Capital asset pricing model (CAPM) – the expected return of a security (estimate of the cost of equity capital) in relation to its risk

Capital budgeting – management planning process by which management decides to whether or not to invest in projects from available alternatives

Capital rationing – process of deciding how much capital to spend for the purchase of fixed assets

Capital structure – how a company decides to finance its assets; be it with liabilities, equity, or a combination of both

Cash conversion cycle – the length of time between when the company makes payments (cash outflow) to when it receives payment from customers (cash inflow)

Chattel mortgage – a loan secured by moveable personal property (called chattel)

Commercial paper – short-term unsecured promissory note issued by large corporations to meet immediate obligations (e.g., payroll) with a fixed maturity, typically within one month, but extending no more than 270 days

Compensating balance – a specified sum of money deposited into a restricted, non-interest bearing account, providing surety (a guarantee) debt will be repaid; a form of collateral

Convertible bond – a bond that can be traded for a pre-determined number of shares of the issuing company's common stock

Cost of debt – interest rate on a debt instrument (e.g., a bank loan)

Cost of equity – percentage yield on equity (e.g., common stock outstanding)

Cost of newly issued stock – cost of external equity

Credit management policies – guidelines instituted by a company to make sure outstanding balances due from customers are paid in a timely manner

Current ratio – the number of times a company's current assets would cover its current liabilities

D

Debenture – an unsecured bond (e.g., no underlying collateral) issued by a company with a reputation for creditworthiness

Debt covenants – requirements a company must adhere to until it repays its outstanding debt

Degree of financial leverage (DFL) – the percentage change in earnings per share (EPS) divided by the percentage change in earnings before interest and taxes (EBIT)

Degree of operating leverage (DOL) – the percentage change in earnings before interest and taxes (EBIT) divided by the percentage change in sales; or, the contribution margin divided by operating income (OI)

Discount – reduction of the amount due to a vendor by paying early (e.g., 2/10, n30)

Discount note – a short-term debt instrument issued by a bank at a discount but requires repayment of the face value

Discounted payback period – the number of years required until the discounted cash flows equal the cost of the investment

Dividend – a nonguaranteed cash payment of earnings not retained to sustain business operations distributed to shareholders

Dividend discount model – value of equity calculation that takes into account an investor's expectation that the future selling price reflects the present value of the dividends expected after the sale

Dividend-yield-plus-growth approach method – dividend valuation that estimates an investor's expected yield on their investment

E

Economic order quantity (EOQ) – the optimal amount of inventory to order by balancing the cost of placing an order for inventory with the costs of carrying the inventory

Economic production quantity (EPQ) – see economic production run

Economic production run (EPR) – the optimal number of units to produce in each production run to minimizes the sum of setup costs and carrying costs

Economic value added (EVA) – a performance measurement based on the accrual basis of accounting and does not take into account the time value of money

Electronic funds transfer (EFT) – an electronic transmission of funds-related transactions using a computer-based system that does not require either party to execute a physical exchange of a financial instrument (e.g., cash, checks)

Excess present value index – see profitability index

F

Factor – third party who purchases accounts receivable from a company for cash and assumes the responsibility of collecting the receivable from the customer

Factoring – sale of accounts receivables to a third party (called a factor) for immediate cash

Fair value measurements – estimate of the price at which an orderly transaction to sell an asset or to transfer the liability, would take place between market participants at the measurement date, under current market conditions

Financial leverage – the use of debt or capital leases with the objective of earning a higher rate of return on the borrowed funds than their interest cost

Fixed working capital – see permanent working capital

Float – the time that an incoming (outgoing) payment is in the process of collection (disbursement)

Floating-rate bond – a bond with a variable coupon payment based on a periodically updated market rate (e.g., LIBOR)

Full safety stock – the difference between the maximum daily inventory usage and the average daily inventory usage multiplied by the lead time

Future value of a single amount – amount that an investment made today will be worth at a specified number of periods in the future, at a specified interest rate

Future value of an annuity – amount available in a specified number of periods in the future, as the result of a payment made at the end of each period

G

H

Hurdle rate – the expected (target) rate of return that is established by management, which is the minimum acceptable rate

I

Income bond – a bond with coupon payments that are only paid if the issuer generates earnings above a threshold amount

Independent – if the selection of one project has no effect on the selection of another project

Internal rate of return – the rate of return that when used as the discount rate in the net present value formula causes the net present value to be exactly zero

Internal rate of return method – a discounted cash flow method for capital budgeting that assumes a company invests the cash flows received each period and earns the same rate as the internal rate of return

Inventory conversion period – time it takes to produce and sell inventory

Inventory turnover – ratio is an asset utilization measurement to judge how efficient a company is at managing their inventory

J

Junk bond – a high-risk bond (e.g., rated BB or lower by Standard & Poor's) that offer investors a premium to entice them to purchase a bond with a greater than normal default risk

Just-in-time (JIT) – obtain and deliver goods exactly as-needed, delivering no more or less than the quantity demanded; a demand-pull manufacturing system

K

L

Line of credit – amount of credit extended by a bank to a borrower with a set maximum and no specific purpose. This can also be called revolving credit due to its renewable nature. Lines of credit are ideal to provide capital for business that have seasonal fluctuations

LIBOR – Stands for the London Interbank Offered Rate, which is a benchmark rate on international market funds.

Lockbox – method to managing payment of accounts receivable using a post office box rented by a bank

Long-term financing – a financial obligation due in over one year and is classified on the balance sheet as a non-current liability

M

Mortgage bond – a bond secured with a mortgage of one or more assets that, in the event of default, entitles the bondholder claim to the underlying asset subject to the lien (e.g., real estate or equipment)

Mutually exclusive – management decisions that require a company to select one project and reject the other projects under consideration

Mutually inclusive – management decisions that require a company to purchase one or more secondary projects if it purchases a primary project

N

O

Operating leverage – the extent a company incurs fixed operating costs in relation to variable operating costs

Optimal capital structure – mix of debt and equity that maximizes an entity's share price, increasing shareholder wealth

Ordinary annuity – a series of equal payments are made at the *END* of the period; also called annuity in arrears

P

Payable deferral period – time the company uses to pay its suppliers

Payback method – the length of time required to recover the initial cost or cash outflow of an investment

Payment discounts – deduction from the amount due by the customer that is granted for early or prompt payment

Permanent working capital – the minimum amount of working capital a company must maintain throughout the year to sustain operations

Preemptive right – a right given to common shareholders requiring a company offer the current common shareholders the right to purchase the additional shares first, if the corporation issues additional shares of common stock, giving common shareholders the ability to maintain their proportionate share of outstanding shares of common stock

Present value (PV) – value today of a dollar to be received in the future

Present value method – technique to determine which investment will provide a return that is greater than management's hurdle (target) rate of return by estimating the amounts and timing of the cash flows associated with the investment
Present value of a single amount – how much a dollar to be received for one time only at a specified time in the future is worth today at a specified interest rate
Present value of an annuity – the sum of the present value of the single, equal amounts for each period the company will receive cash in the future
Profitability index – the ratio of the present value of the future cash flows from the investment divided by the cost of the investment; also called excess present value index

Q

Quick ratio – a gauge of a company's ability to fulfill its short-term obligations with liquid or near liquid assets

R

Receivables collection period – time it takes customers to pay for a good or service
Receivables turnover – ratio to evaluate how efficiently accounts receivable are collected and how well working capital is managed by the company
Reorder point – the point managers need to order additional inventory to prevent a stockout

S

Safety stock – the number of units of inventory a company keeps in stock to avoid losing sales if its sales are higher than average
Salvage value – the amount management expects to receive for a sale of the asset at the end of its useful life; also see residual value
Secured debt – a promise to pay guaranteed by an asset (collateral)
Self-liquidating loan – a financing vehicle where the borrower finances revenue generating activities using the loan proceeds and then promptly repays the loan with the revenues generated with the debt
Serial bond – a bond that has a series of successive maturities that retire portions of the bond over the term of the bond
Short-term borrowing – a promise to pay with a principal payment that is due to the lender within one year
Short-term financing – a financial obligation that is due in one year or less
Sinking fund – a custodial account the borrower (issuer) established to periodically deposits funds into that are used to retire a bond over time by buying it back, rather than paying in full at maturity
Stock dividend – shareholders receive additional shares of stock rather than a cash payment
Stockout – insufficient inventory for the customers' demand
Stockout cost – the opportunity cost of the profit lost from lost sales due to lack of inventory
Subordinated debenture – an unsecured bond that is paid after superior, higher priority debt if the issuer defaults or declares bankruptcy
Systematic risk – risk factors for an entire market or entire market segment that cannot be avoided simply by diversifying a portfolio

T

Term loan – a short-term borrowing agreement where the bank loans the borrower a specific amount, which must be repaid according to an agreed-upon repayment schedule

U

Unsecured debt – a promise to pay that does not require any form of collateral but has higher interest rates when compared to similar secured debt options
Unsystematic risk – diversifiable risk or specific risk related to a specific security, or a group of similar securities

V

W

Weighted-average cost of capital (WACC) – the after-tax average cost of a company's unique combination of debt and equity financing
Working capital – a company's current operating liquidity; current assets less current liabilities
Working capital management – the practice of determining the appropriate amount of cash, marketable securities, accounts receivable, and inventory necessary for a company to operate efficiency

Z
Zero-coupon bond – a bond that does not pay interest during the term of the bond, bought at a large discount. When the zero-coupon bond matures, the investor receives one lumps sum equal to the initial investment plus imputed interest; also called an accrual bond

This page is intentionally left blank.

Multiple Choice – Questions

BEC3-Q1 B184. Which of the following types of bonds is most likely to maintain a constant market value?

A. Zero-coupon.
B. Floating-rate.
C. Callable.
D. Convertible.

BEC 3-Q2 B322. At the beginning of year 1, $10,000 is invested at 8% interest, compounded annually. What amount of interest is earned for year 2?

A. $800.00
B. $806.40
C. $864.00
D. $933.12

BEC 3-Q3 B1034.* The call provision in some bond indentures allows

A. The issuer to exercise an option to redeem the bonds.
B. The bondholder to exchange the bond, at no additional cost, for common shares.
C. The bondholder to redeem the bond early by paying a call premium.
D. The issuer to pay a premium in order to prevent bondholders from redeeming bonds.

BEC 3-Q4 B1038.* Which one of the following statements concerning debt instruments is correct?

A. The coupon rate and yield of an outstanding long-term bond will change over time as economic factors change.
B. A 25-year bond with a coupon rate of 9% and one year to maturity has more interest rate risk than a 10-year bond with a 9% coupon issued by the same firm with one year to maturity.
C. For long-term bonds, price sensitivity to a given change in interest rates is greater the longer the maturity of the bond.
D. A bond with one year to maturity would have more interest rate risk than a bond with 15 years to maturity.

BEC 3-Q5 B1040.* Which one of the following is a debt instrument that generally has a maturity of ten years or more?

A. A bond
B. A note
C. A chattel mortgage
D. A financial lease

BEC 3-Q6 B121. Which of the following is considered a corporate equity security?

A. A shareholder's preemptive right.
B. A shareholder's appraisal right.
C. A callable bond.
D. A share of callable preferred stock.

BEC 3-Q7 B346. Which of the following decreases stockholder equity?

A. Investments by owners.
B. Distributions to owners.
C. Issuance of stock.
D. Acquisition of assets in a cash transaction.

BEC 3-Q8 B248. Which of the following statements is correct regarding the declaration of a stock dividend by a corporation having only one class of par value stock?

A. A stock dividend has the same legal and practical significance as a stock split.
B. A stock dividend increases a stockholder's proportionate share of corporate ownership.
C. A stock dividend causes a decrease in the assets of the corporation.
D. A stock dividend is a corporation's ratable distribution of additional shares of stock to its stockholders.

BEC 3-Q9 B1043.* Preferred stock may be retired through the use of any one of the following except a

A. Conversion.
B. Call provision.
C. Refunding.
D. Sinking fund.

---

* CMA adapted.

BEC 3-Q10 B1044.* All of the following are characteristics of preferred stock except that

A. It may be callable at the option of the corporation.
B. It may be converted into common stock.
C. Its dividends are tax deductible to the issuer.
D. It usually has no voting rights.

BEC 3-Q11 B264. Bander Co. is determining how to finance some long-term projects. Bander has decided it prefers the benefits of no fixed charges, no fixed maturity date and an increase in the credit-worthiness of the company. Which of the following would best meet Bander's financing requirements?

A. Bonds.
B. Common stock.
C. Long-term debt.
E. Short-term debt.

BEC 3-Q12 B1039.* Which one of the following situations would prompt a firm to issue debt, as opposed to equity, the next time it raises external capital?

A. High breakeven point.
B. Significant percentage of assets under capital lease.
C. Low fixed-charge coverage.
D. High effective tax rate.

BEC 3-Q13 B1045.* Which one of the following describes a disadvantage to a firm that issues preferred stock?

A. Preferred stock dividends are legal obligations of the corporation.
B. Preferred stock typically has no maturity date.
C. Preferred stock is usually sold on a higher yield basis than bonds.
D. Most preferred stock is owned by corporate investors.

BEC 3-Q14 B301. The benefits of debt financing over equity financing are likely to be highest in which of the following situations?

A. High marginal tax rates and few noninterest tax benefits.
B. Low marginal tax rates and few noninterest tax benefits.
C. High marginal tax rates and many noninterest tax benefits.
D. Low marginal tax rates and many noninterest tax benefits.

BEC 3-Q15 B291. Which of the following statements is correct regarding both debt and common shares of a corporation?

A. Common shares represent an ownership interest in the corporation, but debt holders do **not** have an ownership interest.
B. Common shareholders and debt holders have an ownership interest in the corporation.
C. Common shares typically have a fixed maturity date, but debt does **not**.
D. Common shares have a higher priority on liquidation than debt.

BEC 3-Q16 B375. Which of the following items represents a business risk in capital structure decisions?

A. Contractual obligations.
B. Management preferences.
C. Cash flow.
D. Timing of information.

___
* CMA adapted.

BEC 3-Q17 B970. * The capital structure of four corporations is as follows.

	Corporation			
	Sterling	Cooper	Warwick	Pane
Short-term debt	10%	10%	15%	10%
Long-term debt	40%	35%	30%	30%
Preferred stock	30%	30%	30%	30%
Common equity	20%	25%	25%	30%

Which corporation is the most highly leveraged?

A. Sterling
B. Cooper
C. Warwick
D. Pane

BEC3-Q18 B48. A company uses its company-wide cost of capital to evaluate new capital investments. What is the implication of this policy when the company has multiple operating divisions, each having unique risk attributes and capital costs?

A. High-risk divisions will over-invest in new projects and low risk divisions will under-invest in new projects.
B. High-risk divisions will under-invest in high-risk projects.
C. Low-risk divisions will over-invest in low-risk projects.
D. Low-risk divisions will over-invest in new projects and high risk divisions will under-invest in new projects.

BEC 3-Q19 B91. A company has the following target capital structure and costs:

	Proportion of capital structure	Cost of capital
Debt	30%	10%
Common stock	60%	12%
Preferred stock	10%	10%

The company's marginal tax rate is 30%. What is the company's weighted-average cost of capital?

A. 7.84%
B. 9.30%
C. 10.30%
D. 11.20%

BEC 3-Q20 B126. Which of the following statements is correct regarding the weighted-average cost of capital (WACC)?

A. One of a company's objectives is to minimize the WACC.
B. A company with a high WACC is attractive to potential shareholders.
C. An increase in the WACC increases the value of the company.
D. WACC is always equal to the company's borrowing rate.

BEC 3-Q21 B157. The target capital structure of Traggle Co. is 50% debt, 10% preferred equity, and 40% common equity. The interest rate on debt is 6%, the yield on the preferred is 7%, the cost of common equity is 11.5%, and the tax rate is 40%. Traggle does not anticipate issuing any new stock. What is Traggle's weighted-average cost of capital?

A. 6.50%
B. 6.77%
C. 7.10%
D. 8.30%

BEC 3-Q22 B187. A company with a combined federal and state tax rate of 30% has the following capital structure:

Weight	Instrument	Cost of capital
40%	Bonds	10%
50%	Common stock	10%
10%	Preferred stock	20%

What is the weighted-average after-tax cost of capital for this company?

A. 3.3%
B. 7.7%
C. 8.2%
D. 9.8%

---

* CMA adapted.

BEC 3-Q23 B193. A company has the following financial information:

Source of capital	Proportion of capital structure	Cost of capital
Long-term debt	60%	7.1%
Preferred stock	20%	10.5%
Common stock	20%	14.2%

To maximize shareholder wealth, the company should accept projects with returns greater than what percent?

A. 7.1%
B. 9.2%
C. 10.6%
D. 14.2%

BEC 3-Q24 B255. The optimal capitalization for an organization usually can be determined by the

A. Maximum degree of financial leverage (DFL).
B. Maximum degree of total leverage (DTL).
C. Lowest total weighted-average cost of capital (WACC).
D. Intersection of the marginal cost of capital and the marginal efficiency of investment.

BEC 3-Q25 B1046.* Which of the following, when considered individually, would generally have the effect of increasing a firm's cost of capital?

I. The firm reduces its operating leverage.
II. The corporate tax rate is increased.
III. The firm pays off its only outstanding debt.
IV. The Treasury bond yield increases.

A. I and III
B. II and IV
C. III and IV
D. I, III and IV

BEC 3-Q26 B1047.* An accountant for Stability Inc. must calculate the weighted average cost of capital of the corporation using the following information.

		Interest Rate
Accounts payable	$35,000,000	-0-
Long-term debt	10,000,000	8%
Common stock	10,000,000	15%
Retained earnings	5,000,000	18%

What is the weighted average cost of capital of Stability?

A. 6.88%.
B. 8.00%.
C. 10.25%.
D. 12.80%.

BEC 3-Q27 B1049.* Following is an excerpt from Albion Corporation's balance sheet.

- Long-term debt (9% interest rate) $30,000,000
- Preferred stock (100,000 shares, 12% dividend) $10,000,000
- Common stock (5,000,000 shares outstanding) $60,000,000

Albion's bonds are currently trading at $1,083.34, reflecting a yield to maturity of 8%. The preferred stock is trading at $125 per share. Common stock is selling at $16 per share, and Albion's treasurer estimates that the firm's cost of equity is 17%. If Albion's effective income tax rate is 40%, what is the firm's cost of capital?

A. 12.6%.
B. 13.1%.
C. 13.9%.
D. 14.1%.

---

* CMA adapted.

BEC 3-Q28 B148. Larson Corp. issued $20 million of long-term debt in the current year. What is a major advantage to Larson with the debt issuance?

A. The reduced earnings per share possible through financial leverage.
B. The relatively low after-tax cost due to the interest deduction.
C. The increased financial risk resulting from the use of the debt.
D. The reduction of Larson's control over the company.

BEC 3-Q29 B182. A company has an outstanding one-year bank loan of $500,000 at a stated interest rate of 8%. The company is required to maintain a 20% compensating balance in its checking account. The company would maintain a zero balance in this account if the requirement did not exist. What is the effective interest rate of the loan?

A. 8%.
B. 10%.
C. 20%.
D. 28%.

BEC 3-Q30 B292. The capital structure of a firm includes bonds with a coupon rate of 12% and an effective interest rate is 14%. The corporate tax rate is 30%. What is the firm's net cost of debt?

A. 8.4%.
B. 9.8%.
C. 12.0%.
D. 14.0%.

BEC 3-Q31 B92. A company recently issued 9% preferred stock. The preferred stock sold for $40 a share with a par of $20. The cost of issuing the stock was $5 a share. What is the company's cost of preferred stock?

A. 4.5%
B. 5.1%
C. 9.0%
D. 10.3%

BEC 3-Q32 B1052.* Cox Company has sold 1,000 shares of $100 par, 8% preferred stock at an issue price of $92 per share. Stock issue costs were $5 per share. Cox pays taxes at the rate of 40%. What is Cox's cost of preferred stock capital?

A. 8.00%
B. 8.25%
C. 8.70%
D. 9.20%

BEC 3-Q33 B46. The stock of Fargo Co. is selling for $85. The next annual dividend is expected to be $4.25 and is expected to grow at a rate of 7%. The corporate tax rate is 30%. What percentage represents the firm's cost of common equity?

A. 12.0%.
B. 8.4%.
C. 7.0%.
D. 5.0%.

BEC 3-Q34 B1050.* Thomas Company's capital structure consists of 30% long-term debt, 25% preferred stock, and 45% common equity. The cost of capital for each component is shown below.

Long-term debt 8%
Preferred stock 11%
Common equity 15%

If Thomas pays taxes at the rate of 40%, what is the company's after-tax weighted average cost of capital?

A. 7.14%.
B. 9.84%.
C. 10.94%.
D. 11.90%.

---

* CMA adapted.

BEC 3-Q35 B1051.* Joint Products Inc., a corporation with a 40% marginal tax rate, plans to issue $1,000,000 of 8% preferred stock in exchange for $1,000,000 of its 8% bonds currently outstanding. The firm's total liabilities and equity are equal to $10,000,000. The effect of this exchange on the firm's weighted average cost of capital is likely to be

A. No change, since it involves equal amounts of capital in the exchange and both instruments have the same rate.
B. A decrease, since a portion of the debt payments are tax deductible.
C. A decrease, since preferred stock payments do not need to be made each year, whereas debt payments must be made.
D. An increase, since a portion of the debt payments are tax deductible.

BEC 3-Q36 B1054.* The Hatch Sausage Company is projecting an annual growth rate for the foreseeable future of 9%. The most recent dividend paid was $3.00 per share. New common stock can be issued at $36 per share. Using the constant growth model, what is the approximate cost of capital for retained earnings?

A. 9.08%
B. 17.33%
C. 18.08%
D. 19.88%

BEC 3-Q37 B1055.* The management of Old Fenske Company (OFC) has been reviewing the company's financing arrangements. The current financing mix is $750,000 of common stock, $200,000 of preferred stock ($50 par) and $300,000 of debt. OFC currently pays a common stock cash dividend of $2. The common stock sells for $38, and dividends have been growing at about 10% per year. Debt currently provides a yield to maturity to the investor of 12%, and preferred stock pays a dividend of 9% to yield 11%. Any new issue of securities will have a flotation cost of approximately 3%. OFC has retained earnings available for the equity requirement. The company's effective income tax rate is 40%. Based on this information, the cost of capital for retained earnings is

A. 9.5%
B. 14.2%
C. 15.8%
D. 16.0%

BEC 3-Q38 B972.* A degree of operating leverage of 3 at 5,000 units means that a

A. 3% change in earnings before interest and taxes will cause a 3% change in sales.
B. 3% change in sales will cause a 3% change in earnings before interest and taxes.
C. 1% change in sales will cause a 3% change in earnings before interest and taxes.
D. 1% change in earnings before interest and taxes will cause a 3% change in sales.

BEC 3-Q39 B971.* A summary of the Income Statement of Sahara Company is shown below.

Sales	$15,000,000
Cost of sales	9,000,000
Operating expenses	3,000,000
Interest expense	800,000
Taxes	880,000
Net income	$1,320,000

Based on the above information, Sahara's degree of financial leverage is

A. 0.96
B. 1.36
C. 1.61
D. 2.27

BEC 3-Q40 B973.* Firms with high degrees of financial leverage would be best characterized as having

A. High debt-to-equity ratios
B. Zero coupon bonds in their capital structures
C. Low current ratios
D. High fixed-charge coverage

---

* CMA adapted.

BEC 3-Q41 B974.* The use of debt in the capital structure of a firm

A. Increases its financial leverage
B. Increases its operating leverage
C. Decreases its financial leverage
D. Decreases its operating leverage

BEC 3-Q42 B975.* A financial analyst with Mineral Inc. calculated the company's degree of financial leverage as 1.5. If net income before interest increases by 5%, earnings to shareholders will increase by

A. 1.50%
B. 3.33%
C. 5.00%
D. 7.50%

BEC 3-Q43 B960. * Shown below are selected data from Fortune Company's most recent financial statements.

Marketable securities	$10,000
Accounts receivable	60,000
Inventory	25,000
Supplies	5,000
Accounts payable	40,000
Short-term debt payable	10,000
Accruals	5,000

What is Fortune's net working capital?

A. $35,000
B. $45,000
C. $50,000
D. $80,000

BEC 3-Q44 B956.* Birch Products Inc. has the following current assets.

Cash	$250,000
Marketable securities	100,000
Accounts receivable	800,000
Inventories	1,450,000
Total current assets	$2,600,000

If Birch's current liabilities are $1,300,000, the firm's

A. Current ratio will decrease if a payment of $100,000 cash is used to pay $100,000 of accounts payable.
B. Current ratio will not change if a payment of $100,000 cash is used to pay $100,000 of accounts payable.
C. Quick ratio will decrease if a payment of $100,000 cash is used to purchase inventory.
D. Quick ratio will not change if a payment of $100,000 cash is used to purchase inventory.

BEC 3-Q45 B281. The CFO of a company is concerned about the company's accounts receivable turnover ratio. The company currently offers customers terms of 3/10, net 30. Which of the following strategies would most likely improve the company's accounts receivable turnover ratio?

A. Pledging the accounts receivable to a finance company.
B. Changing customer terms to 1/10, net 30.
C. Entering into a factoring agreement with a finance company.
D. Changing customer terms to 3/20, net 30.

BEC 3-Q46 B1075.* Locar Corporation had net sales last year of $18,600,000 (of which 20% were installment sales). It also had an average accounts receivable balance of $1,380,000. Credit terms are 2/10, net 30. Based on a 360-day year, Locar's average collection period last year was

A. 26.2 days
B. 26.7 days
C. 27.3 days
D. 33.4 days

---

* CMA adapted.

BEC 3-Q47 B127. An increase in which of the following should cause management to reduce the average inventory?

A. The cost of placing an order.
B. The cost of carrying inventory.
C. The annual demand for the product.
D. The lead time needed to acquire inventory.

BEC 3-Q48 B1124.* All of the following are carrying costs of inventory except

A. Storage costs
B. Insurance
C. Freight-out shipping costs
D. Opportunity costs

BEC 3-Q49 B169. Which of the following assumptions is associated with the economic order quantity formula?

A. The carrying cost per unit will vary with quantity ordered.
B. The cost of placing an order will vary with quantity ordered.
C. Periodic demand is known.
D. The purchase cost per unit will vary based on quantity discounts.

BEC 3-Q50 B366. Which of the following inventory management approaches orders at the point where carrying costs equate nearest to restocking costs in order to minimize total inventory cost?

A. Economic order quantity.
B. Just-in-time.
C. Materials requirements planning.
D. ABC.

BEC 3-Q51 B1129.* Carnes Industries uses the Economic Order Quantity (EOQ) model as part of its inventory control program. An increase in which one of the following variables would increase the EOQ?

A. Carrying cost rate.
B. Purchase price per unit.
C. Ordering costs.
D. Safety stock level.

BEC 3-Q52 B1130.* Which one of the following is not explicitly considered in the standard calculation of Economic Order Quantity (EOQ)?

A. Level of sales.
B. Fixed ordering costs.
C. Carrying costs.
D. Quantity discounts.

BEC 3-Q53 B1131.* Which one of the following statements concerning the economic order quantity (EOQ) is correct?

A. The EOQ results in the minimum ordering cost and minimum carrying cost.
B. Increasing the EOQ is the best way to avoid stockouts.
C. The EOQ model assumes constantly increasing usage over the year.
D. The EOQ model assumes that order delivery times are consistent.

BEC 3-Q54 B1132.* Moss Products uses the Economic Order Quantity (EOQ) model as part of its inventory management process. A decrease in which one of the following variables would increase the EOQ?

A. Annual sales
B. Cost per order
C. Safety stock level
D. Carrying costs

BEC 3-Q55 B1058.* All of the following can be utilized by a firm in managing its cash outflows except

A. Zero-balance accounts
B. Centralization of payables
C. Controlled disbursement accounts
D. Lock-box system

---

* CMA adapted.

BEC 3-Q56 B317. What would be the primary reason for a company to agree to a debt covenant limiting the percentage of its long-term debt?

A. To cause the price of the company's stock to rise.
B. To lower the company's bond rating.
C. To reduce the risk for existing bondholders.
D. To reduce the interest rate on the bonds being sold.

BEC 3-Q57 B1136.* Which of the following financing vehicles would a commercial bank be likely to offer to its customers?

I. Discounted notes
II. Term loans
III. Lines of credit
IV. Self-liquidating loans

A. I and II.
B. III and IV.
C. I, III and IV.
D. I, II, III and IV.

BEC 3-Q58 B1142.* Keller Products needs $150,000 of additional funds over the next year in order to satisfy a significant increase in demand. A commercial bank has offered Keller a one-year loan at a nominal rate of 8%, which requires a 15% compensating balance. How much would Keller have to borrow, assuming it would need to cover the compensating balance with the loan proceeds?

A. $130,435.
B. $172,500.
C. $176,471.
D. $194,805.

BEC 3-Q59 B1035.* Protective clauses set forth in an indenture are known as

A. Provisions
B. Requirements
C. Addenda
D. Covenants

BEC 3-Q60 B1036.* A requirement specified in an indenture agreement which states that a company cannot acquire or sell major assets without prior creditor approval is known as a

A. Protective covenant
B. Call provision
C. Warrant
D. Put option

BEC 3-Q61 B1059.* Powell Industries deals with customers throughout the country and is attempting to more efficiently collect its accounts receivable. A major bank has offered to develop and operate a lock-box system for Powell at a cost of $90,000 per year. Powell averages 300 receipts per day at an average of $2,500 each. Its short-term interest cost is 8% per year. Using a 360-day year, what reduction in average collection time would be needed in order to justify the lock-box system?

A. 0.67 days
B. 1.20 days
C. 1.25 days
D. 1.50 days

BEC 3-Q62 B285. Which of the following effects would a lockbox most likely provide for receivables management?

A. Minimized collection float.
B. Maximized collection float.
C. Minimized disbursement float.
D. Maximized disbursement float.

BEC 3-Q63 B684.* Granite Company sells products exclusively on account, and has experienced the following collection pattern: 60% in the month of sale, 25% in the month after sale, and 15% in the second month after sale. Uncollectible accounts are negligible. Customers who pay in the month of sale are given a 2% discount. If sales are $220,000 in January, $200,000 in February, $280,000 in March, and $260,000 in April, Granite's accounts receivable balance on May 1 will be

A. $107,120
B. $143,920
C. $146,000
D. $204,000

---

* CMA adapted.

BEC 3-Q64 B686.* Brown Company estimates that monthly sales will be as follows.

January	$100,000
February	150,000
March	180,000

Historical trends indicate that 40% of sales are collected during the month of sale, 50% are collected in the month following the sale, and 10% are collected two months after the sale. Brown's accounts receivable balance as of December 31 totals $80,000 ($72,000 from December's sales and $8,000 from November's sales). The amount of cash Brown can expect to collect during the month of January is

A. $76,800.
B. $84,000.
C. $108,000.
D. $133,000.

BEC 3-Q65 B688.* Bootstrap Corporation anticipates the following sales during the last six months of the year.

July	$460,000
August	500,000
September	525,000
October	500,000
November	480,000
December	450,000

20% of Bootstrap's sales are for cash. The balance is subject to the collection pattern shown below.

Percentage of balance collected in the month of sale	40%
Percentage of balance collected in the month following sale	30%
Percentage of balance collected in the second month following sale	25%
Percentage of balance uncollectible	5%

What is the planned net accounts receivable balance as of December 31?

A. $279,300
B. $294,000
C. $360,000
D. $367,500

BEC 3-Q66 B693.* ANNCO sells products on account, and experiences the following collection schedule.

In the month of sale	10%
In the month after sale	60%
In the second month after sale	30%

At December 31, ANNCO reports accounts receivable of $211,500. Of that amount, $162,000 is due from December sales, and $49,500 from November sales. ANNCO is budgeting $170,000 of sales for January. If so, what amount of cash should be collected in January?

A. $129,050
B. $174,500
C. $211,500
D. $228,500

BEC 3-Q67 B1023.* A change in the estimate for bad debts should be

A. Treated as an error.
B. Handled retroactively.
C. Considered as an extraordinary item.
D. Treated as affecting only the period of the change.

BEC 3-Q68 B1061.* Dexter Products receives $25,000 worth of merchandise from its major supplier on the 15th and 30th of each month. The goods are sold on terms of 1/15, net 45, and Dexter has been paying on the net due date and foregoing the discount. A local bank offered Dexter a loan at an interest rate of 10%. What will be the net annual savings to Dexter if it borrows from the bank and utilizes the funds to take advantage of the trade discount?

A. $525
B. $1,050
C. $1,575
D. $2,250

* CMA adapted.

BEC 3-Q69 B1069.* Northville Products is changing its credit terms from net 30 to 2/10, net 30. The least likely effect of this change would be a(n)

A. Increase in sales
B. Shortening of the cash conversion cycle
C. Increase in short-term borrowings
D. Lower number of days sales outstanding

BEC 3-Q70 B1062.* The Rolling Stone Corporation, an entertainment ticketing service, is considering the following means of speeding cash flow for the corporation.

- Lock Box System. This would cost $25 per month for each of its 170 banks and would result in interest savings of $5,240 per month.
- Drafts. Drafts would be used to pay for ticket refunds based on 4,000 refunds per month at a cost of $2.00 per draft, which would result in interest savings of $6,500 per month.
- Bank Float. Bank float would be used for the $1,000,000 in checks written each month. The bank would charge a 2% fee for this service, but the corporation will earn $22,000 in interest on the float.
- Electronic Transfer. Items over $25,000 would be electronically transferred; it is estimated that 700 items of this type would be made each month at a cost of $18 each, which would result in increased interest earnings of $14,000 per month.

Which of these methods of speeding cash flow should Rolling Stone Corporation adopt?

A. Lock box and electronic transfer only.
B. Bank float and electronic transfer only.
C. Lock box, drafts, and electronic transfer only.
D. Lock box, bank float, and electronic transfer only.

BEC 3-Q71 B1072.* Consider the following factors affecting a company as it is reviewing its trade credit policy.

I. Operating at full capacity.
II. Low cost of borrowing.
III. Opportunity for repeat sales.
IV. Low gross margin per unit.

Which of the above factors would indicate that the company should liberalize its credit policy?

A. I and II only
B. I, II and III only
C. II and III only
D. III and IV only

BEC 3-Q72 B253. Why would a firm generally choose to finance temporary assets with short-term debt?

A. Matching the maturities of assets and liabilities reduces risk.
B. Short-term interest rates have traditionally been more stable than long-term interest rates.
C. A firm that borrows heavily long term is more apt to be unable to repay the debt than a firm that borrows heavily short term.
D. Financing requirements remain constant.

BEC 3-Q73 B170. Which of the following statements about investment decision models is true?

A. The discounted payback rate takes into account cash flows for all periods.
B. The payback rule ignores all cash flows after the end of the payback period.
C. The net present value model says to accept investment opportunities when their rates of return exceed the company's incremental borrowing rate.
D. The internal rate of return rule is to accept the investment if the opportunity cost of capital is greater than the internal rate of return.

---

* CMA adapted.

BEC 3-Q74 B147. Which of the following statements is correct regarding the payback method as a capital budgeting technique?

A. The payback method considers the time value of money.
B. An advantage of the payback method is that it indicates if an investment will be profitable.
C. The payback method provides the years needed to recoup the investment in a project.
D. Payback is calculated by dividing the annual cash inflows by the net investment.

BEC 3-Q75 B284. A project has an initial outlay of $1,000. The projected cash inflows are:

Year 1	$200
Year 2	200
Year 3	400
Year 4	400

What is the investment's payback period?

A. 4.0 years.
B. 3.5 years.
C. 3.4 years.
D. 3.0 years.

BEC 3-Q76 B309. Harvey Co. is evaluating a capital investment proposal for a new machine. The investment proposal shows the following information:

Initial Cost	$500,000
Life	10 years
Annual net cash inflows	$200,000
Salvage Value	$100,000

If acquired, the machine will be depreciated using the straight-line method. The payback period for this investment is

A. 3.25 years.
B. 2.67 years.
C. 2.5 years.
D. 2 years.

BEC 3-Q77 B312. In considering the payback period for three projects. Fly Corp. gathered the following data about cash flows:

Cash Flows by Year

	Year 1	Year 2	Year 3	Year 4	Year 5
Project A	($10,000)	$3,000	$3,000	$3,000	$3,000
Project B	($25,000)	$15,000	$15,000	($10,000)	15,000
Project C	($10,000)	$5,000	$5,000		

Which of the projects will achieve payback within three years?

A. Projects A, B, and C.
B. Projects B and C.
C. Project B only.
D. Projects A and C.

BEC 3-Q78 B367. Which of the following statements is true regarding the payback method?

A. It does **not** consider the time value of money.
B. It is the time required to recover the investment and earn a profit.
C. It is a measure of how profitable one investment project is compared to another.
D. The salvage value of old equipment is ignored in the event of equipment replacement.

BEC 3-Q79 B64. The discount rate is determined in advance for which of the following capital budgeting techniques?

A. Payback.
B. Accounting rate of return.
C. Net present value.
D. Internal rate of return.

BEC 3-Q80 B66. An investment in a new product will require an initial outlay of $20,000. The cash inflow from the project will be $4,000 a year for the next six years. The payment will be received at the end of each year. What is the net present value of the investment at 8% using the correct factor from below?

Present value of $1 to be received after six periods	0.63017
Present value of an ordinary annuity of $1 per period for six periods	4.62288
Present value of an ordinary annuity due of $1 per period for six periods	4.99271
Future value of $1 at the end of six periods	1.58687

A. ($4,875.92)
B. ($1,508.48)
C. ($29.16)
D. $18,084.88

BEC 3-Q81 B84. A corporation is considering purchasing a machine that costs $100,000 and has a $20,000 salvage value. The machine will provide net annual cash inflows of $25,000 per year and has a six-year life. The corporation uses a discount rate of 10%. The discount factor for the present value of a single sum six years in the future is 0.564. The discount factor for the present value of an annuity for six years is 4.355. What is the net present value of the machine?

A. ($2,405)
B. $8,875
C. $20,155
D. $28,875

BEC 3-Q82 B144. Salem Co. is considering a project that yields annual net cash inflows of $420,000 for years 1 through 5, and a net cash inflow of $100,000 in year 6. The project will require an initial investment of $1,800,000. Salem's cost of capital is 10%. Present value information is presented below:

Present value of $1 for 5 years at 10% is 0.62.
Present value of $1 for 6 years at 10% is 0.56.
Present value of an annuity of $1 for 5 years at 10% is 3.79.

What was Salem's expected net present value for this project?

A. $ 83,000
B. ($108,200)
C. ($152,200)
D. ($442,000)

BEC 3-Q83 B259. Net present value as used in investment decision-making is stated in terms of which of the following options?

A. Net income.
B. Earnings before interest, taxes, and depreciation.
C. Earnings before interest and taxes.
D. Cash flow.

BEC 3-Q84 B86. Which of the following is a limitation of the profitability index?

A. It uses free cash flows.
B. It ignores the time value of money.
C. It is inconsistent with the goal of shareholder wealth maximization.
D. It requires detailed long-term forecasts of the project's cash flows.

BEC 3-Q85 B125. What is the formula for calculating the profitability index of a project?

A. Subtract actual after-tax net income from the minimum required return in dollars.
B. Divide the present value of the annual after-tax cash flows by the original cash invested in the project.
C. Divide the initial investment for the project by the net annual cash inflow.
D. Multiply net profit margin by asset turnover.

BEC 3-Q86 B341. The profitability index is a variation on which of the following capital budgeting models?

A. Internal rate of return.
B. Economic value-added.
C. Net present value.
D. Discounted payback.

BEC 3-Q87 B69. Which of the following phrases defines the internal rate of return on a project?

A. The number of years it takes to recover the investment.
B. The discount rate at which the net present value of the project equals zero.
C. The discount rate at which the net present value of the project equals one.
D. The weighted-average cost of capital used to finance the project.

BEC 3-Q88 B87. Which of the following metrics equates the present value of a project's expected cash inflows to the present value of the project's expected costs?

A. Net present value.
B. Return on assets.
C. Internal rate of return.
D. Economic value-added.

BEC 3-Q89 B167. Which of the following rates is most commonly compared to the internal rate of return to evaluate whether to make an investment?

A. Short-term rate on U.S. Treasury bonds.
B. Prime rate of interest.
C. Weighted-average cost of capital.
D. Long-term rate on U.S. Treasury bonds.

BEC 3-Q90 B356. A multi-period project has a positive net present value. Which of the following statements is correct regarding its required rate of return?

A. Less than the company's weighted average cost of capital.
B. Less than the project's internal rate of return.
C. Greater than the company's weighted average cost of capital.
D. Greater than the project's internal rate of return.

BEC 3-Q91 B186. Which of the following limitations is common to the calculations of payback period, discounted cash flow, internal rate of return, and net present value?

A. They do **not** consider the time value of money.
B. They require multiple trial and error calculations.
C. They require knowledge of a company's cost of capital.
D. They rely on the forecasting of future data.

Multiple Choice – Solutions

BEC 3-Q1 B184. The correct choice is B. Market values of bonds fluctuate due to changes in interest rates. Because the interest rate on a bond is typically fixed, if market interest rates rise above the bond rate, the bond will decrease in value; if market interest rates fall below the bond rate, the bond will increase in value. Therefore, a floating rate bond, whose rate adjusts to a rate similar to the market rate, is more likely to maintain a constant market value.

Choices A, C, and D are not correct because they are bonds that typically have fixed rates of interest. If market interest rates rise above the bond rate, the bond will decrease in value; if market interest rates fall below the bond rate, the bond will increase in value.

BEC 3-Q2 B322. The correct choice is C. Compounding interest means earning interest on (principal + interest already earned). Compounding may occur daily, monthly, quarterly, semi-annually, or annually. In this question, compounding occurs annually. The amount of interest earned for Year 2 is calculated below.

Year 1: $10,000 x 1.08 = $10,800 balance to compound in Year 2
Year 2: $10,800 x 1.08 = $11,664 balance to compound in Year 3

The amount of interest earned in Year 2 is
$11,664 – $10,800 = $864

BEC 3-Q3 B1034. The correct answer is A. A call provision in a bond indenture allows the issuer to redeem all of the outstanding bonds. The terms and details (i.e. before maturity at a fixed price) of the provision is also part of the bond indenture.

BEC 3-Q4 B1038. The correct answer is C. The longer the duration (maturity) of the bond, the greater the price fluctuation associated with a given change in market required return.

Answer A is incorrect because even though a bond's yield changes over time, the coupon rate is fixed when the bond is issued.

Answer B is incorrect because both of these bonds, with the same coupon rates and identical remaining maturities, bear equal interest rate risk.

Answer D is incorrect because the shorter the bond's term, the lower the interest rate risk.

BEC 3-Q5 B1040. The correct answer is A. A bond is a long-term debt instrument with maturities being 10 years or more.

Answer B is incorrect because a note is a short-term debt instrument with a maturity of 90 days or less.

Answer C is incorrect because a chattel mortgage is a debt instrument secured by transportable property (i.e. inventory) and it does not have to have a maturity of 10 years or longer, if the collateral has a shorter life.

Answer D is incorrect because financial leases may have a term that is less than 10 years.

BEC 3-Q6 B121. The correct choice is D. Preferred stock is a form of equity security in a corporation. If the preferred stock is callable, then the corporation has the right to buy back the stock, but usually must pay the preferred stockholder a premium (e.g., a liquidating premium, sometimes called a "sweetener").

Choice A is not correct because the preemptive right is a right given to the common shareholders. When the corporation issues additional shares of common stock, the corporation must offer the current common shareholders the right to purchase the additional shares first, which allows the current common shareholders the ability to maintain their proportionate share of outstanding shares of common stock.

Choice B is not correct because the appraisal right is the right of shareholders to receive an equitable value for their shares as determined by an independent party in the event of a merger or other transaction that transfers control of the corporation.

Choice C is not correct because a callable bond is a liability of a corporation.

BEC 3-Q7 B346. The correct choice is B. Distributions to owners decrease stockholder equity. The most common distribution to owners is the declaration of dividends; the journal entry is:
Dr. Retained Earnings $XX
    Cr. Dividends Payable $XX

Choice A is not correct because investments by owners increase stockholder equity, not decrease stockholder equity. The most common investment by owners is the sale of common stock for cash; the journal entry is:
Dr. Cash $XX
    Cr. Common Stock $XX
    Cr. Add'l Paid-in Capital $XX

Choice C is not correct because the issuance of stock increases stockholder equity, not decreases stockholder equity. The most common issuance of stock is the sale of common stock for cash; the journal entry is:
Dr. Cash $XX
    Cr. Common Stock $XX
    Cr. Add'l Paid-in Capital $XX

Choice D is not correct because the acquisition of assets in a cash transaction does not affect stockholder equity because it substitutes one asset for another asset. The journal entry is:
Dr. Asset $XX
    Cr. Cash $XX

BEC 3-Q8 B248. The correct choice is D. A stock dividend distributes additional shares to the stockholders, but in a manner that maintains each stockholder's relative percentage of ownership. For example, if a corporation grants a 10 percent stock dividend, then all stockholders are granted the 10 percent stock dividend (which is an additional number of shares that is 10 percent of the number of shares they already own), which maintains their current ownership percentage relative to the other stockholders.

Choice A is not correct because a stock dividend does not have the same legal and practical significance as a stock split. The journal entry to record a stock dividend decreases retained earnings and increases paid-in capital. A stock split typically requires a memorandum entry only to decrease the par value per share of common stock and increase the number of shares of common stock. For example, a 2-for-1 stock split will decrease the par value to one-half, but double the number of shares.

Choice B is not correct because a stock dividend does not increase a stockholder's proportionate share of corporate ownership. For example, if a corporation grants a 10 percent stock dividend, then all stockholders are granted the 10 percent stock dividend (which is an additional number of shares that is 10 percent of the number of shares they already own), which maintains their current ownership percentage relative to the other stockholders.

Choice C is not correct because a stock dividend does not decrease the assets of the corporation. The journal entry to record a stock dividend decreases retained earnings and increases paid-in capital; the assets are unaffected.

BEC 3-Q9 B1043. The correct answer is C. Preferred stock cannot be refunded because it is an equity security. Only debt can be refunded.

Answers A and B are incorrect because preferred stock can be issued with both of these choices.

Answer D is incorrect because a sinking fund can be set up for preferred stock.

BEC 3-Q10 B1044. The correct answer is C. Dividends are not tax deductible to the issuer for tax purposes.

Answers A, B and D are incorrect because preferred stock can be issued with these choices.

BEC 3-Q11 B264. The correct choice is B. Common stock has no fixed charges because common stock does not have to pay a dividend; common stock has no fixed maturity date; and as the credit-worthiness of the company increases, the value of the common stock will increase and this increases shareholder wealth. By financing long-term projects with common stock now, this leaves Bander with more options in the future to finance with debt.

Choices A and C are not correct because bonds and long-term debt have fixed charges (in the form of interest) and fixed maturity dates (in the form of principal); Bander Co. prefers the benefits of no fixed charges and no fixed maturity date.

Choice D is not correct because short-term debt has fixed charges (in the form of interest) and fixed maturity dates (in the form of principal), but to a greater degree than bonds and long-term debt because short term debt is renewed more frequently. Short-term debt also has greater risk that interest rates will increase by the next maturity date.

BEC 3-Q12 B1039. The correct answer is D. A firm would likely issue debt instead of equity when the effective tax rate is high, because the interest expense associated with debt reduces income and reduces tax expense.

Answer A is incorrect because a high breakeven point indicates the firm is highly leveraged.

Answers B and C are incorrect because both choices are irrelevant to the decision of using debt or equity.

BEC 3-Q13 B1045. The correct answer is C. A disadvantage of preferred stock to the issuer is that it generally sells on a higher yield basis than bonds. This is because preferred stock is a more risky investment than bonds, so investors want to be paid a premium for the risk.

Answer A is incorrect because dividends do not represent legal obligations of the corporation until they are declared.

Answer B is incorrect because preferred stock is considered equity (i.e. ownership) and not having a maturity date is an advantage for the issuer.

Answer D is incorrect because it is typically irrelevant to the corporation whether its preferred stock is owned by corporate investors or individuals.

BEC 3-Q14 B301. The correct choice is A. Debt financing involves the payment of interest, which is a tax deductible expense. When marginal tax rates are high, the tax savings from interest expense are higher. When there are few alternative tax deductible expenses other than interest expense, there is an incentive to use debt because of the tax deductibility of the interest expense.

Choice B is not correct because low marginal tax rates do not create an incentive for debt financing. Debt financing involves the payment of interest, which is a tax deductible expense. When marginal tax rates are low, the tax savings from interest expense are lower, and there is less incentive to finance with debt.

Choice C is not correct because if there are many alternative tax deductible expenses other than interest expense, then there is less incentive to use the tax deductible interest expense from debt financing for its tax benefits.

Choice D is not correct because low marginal tax rates do not create an incentive for debt financing. Debt financing involves the payment of interest, which is a tax deductible expense. When marginal tax rates are low, the tax savings from interest expense are lower, and there is less incentive to finance with debt. Furthermore, if there are many alternative tax deductible expenses other than interest expense, then there is less incentive to use the tax deductible interest expense from debt financing for its tax benefits.

BEC 3-Q15 B291. The correct choice is A. Common shares are shareholders' equity and represent the stockholders' ownership interest, whereas debt represents the creditors' interest in the company. Creditors are not owners and therefore do not have an ownership interest in the corporation.

Choice B is not correct because debt represents the creditors' interest in the company; creditors are not owners and therefore do not have an ownership interest in the company.

Choice C is not correct because shares of common stock (which are shareholders' equity) do not have a fixed maturity date, whereas debt has a fixed maturity date.

Choice D is not correct because, in a liquidation of a corporation, debtors have a higher priority than shareholders of common stock. In a liquidation of a corporation, the shareholders of common stock are paid the residual after all creditors and preferred stockholders are paid.

BEC 3-Q16 B375. The correct choice is C. Capital structure decisions relate to the proper mix between equity and debt financing. Because of the mandatory principal and interest payments associated with debt financing, cash flows in terms of their certainty, timing, and amounts represent a business risk in capital structure decisions.

Choice A is not correct because contracts require a meeting of the minds between the two parties to the contract and management may structure its contracts in a manner that minimizes business risk. Furthermore, contractual obligations are not typically associated with capital structure decisions, except for contractual obligations to bondholders.

Choice B is not correct because management's preferences in capital structure decisions may or may not minimize business risk, depending on management's self-interests.

Choice D is not correct because the timing of information is a business risk associated with making all business decisions, not just capital structure decisions.

BEC 3-Q17 B970. The correct answer is A. The corporation that is the most highly leveraged is Sterling, because it has the greatest percentage of debt/financing with a fixed interest expense (50% = 10% short-term debt + 40% long-term debt).

BEC 3-Q18 B48. The correct choice is A. When a company-wide cost of capital is used to evaluate new capital projects, the same cost of capital (expressed as an interest rate) is applied to both high-risk projects and low-risk projects; however, the cost of capital interest rate should be commensurate with the level of risk, so high-risk projects should have higher cost of capital rates and low-risk projects should have lower cost of capital rates. Otherwise, low-risk projects will be evaluated as higher risk and high risk projects will be evaluated as lower risk; this will lead to inappropriate choices of projects.

Answer B is not correct because high-risk divisions will over-invest in high-risk projects.

Answer C is not correct because low-risk divisions will under-invest in low risk projects.

Answer D is not correct because low-risk divisions will under-invest in new projects and high-risk divisions will over-invest in new projects.

BEC 3-Q19 B91. The correct choice is C. The WACC of capital is calculated as follows:

Debt:
Weight 0.30 x cost of capital 0.10 x (1 – 0.30)
= 0.30 x 0.10 x 0.70
= 0.021

C/S:
Weight 0.60 x cost of capital 0.12
= 0.072

P/S:
Weight 0.10 x cost of capital 0.10
= 0.01

WACC = Debt 0.021 + C/S 0.072 + P/S 0.01
WACC = 0.103 or 10.3%

BEC 3-Q20 B126. The correct choice is A. The WACC is the cost the company incurs to invest in new projects. If a company minimizes its WACC, the company increases the difference between the lower WACC and the higher Return on Investment (ROI) generated by projects; the greater difference between the lower WACC and the higher ROI increases shareholder wealth to a greater extent.

Choice B is not correct because a high WACC is not attractive to potential shareholders. A higher WACC decreases the difference between the WACC and the ROI generated by projects; the smaller difference between the WACC and the ROI will result in a smaller increase in shareholder wealth.

Choice C is not correct because an increase in WACC will decrease the value of the company. An increase in WACC decreases the difference between the WACC and the ROI generated by projects; the smaller difference between the WACC and the ROI will result in a smaller increase in shareholder wealth and a lower value for the company.

Choice D is not correct because the WACC is based on the weighted-average cost of capital for common stock, preferred stock, borrowing (net of tax), and internally generated earnings.

BEC 3-Q21 B157. The correct choice is C. The weighted-average cost of capital (WACC) is calculated below.

0.50 weight for Debt x (0.06 x [1 – 0.40 Tax Rate])	= 0.018
+ 0.10 weight for Preferred Stock x 0.07	= 0.007
+ 0.40 weight for Common Stock x 0.115	= 0.046
= WACC	0.0710 or 7.10%

BEC 3-Q22 B187. The correct choice is D. The weighted-average cost of capital is calculated below.

Bonds	0.40 (0.10)(1 − 0.30)	= 0.028
Common Stock	0.50 (0.10)	= 0.05
Preferred Stock	0.10 (0.20)	= 0.02
Weighted-Average Cost of Capital		= 0.098
		or 9.8%

BEC 3-Q23 B193. The correct choice is B. To maximize shareholder wealth, the company should accept projects with returns greater than its weighted-average cost of capital (WACC). The WACC is calculated as follows:

Long-term Debt	0.60 × 0.071 = 0.0426
(this assumes that the 7.1% is already net of tax)	
Preferred Stock	0.20 × 0.105 = 0.021
Common Stock	0.20 × 0.142 = 0.0284
Weighted-average Cost of Capital	= 0.092 or 9.2%

Note that we assumed the long-term debt cost of capital of 7.1% is already net of tax because no tax rate was provided.

BEC 3-Q24 B255. The correct choice is C. The weighted-average cost of capital (WACC) weights each form of financing used in the organization, i.e., debt, common stock, preferred stock, and internal financing through retained earnings. The lowest total WACC represents the most efficient mix among the forms of financing and increases the difference between total WACC and the return on investment (ROI). The larger the difference between the lowest total WACC and ROI, the greater the increase to shareholder wealth.

Choice A is not correct because the maximum degree of financial leverage is the greatest level of debt financing and lowest level of equity financing that is achievable in the organization's capital structure. This mix of capitalization may not lead to the lowest total WACC and does not optimize the increase to shareholder wealth.

Choice B is not correct because the maximum degree of total leverage combines the maximum degree of financial leverage (based on capital structure) and the maximum degree of operating leverage (based on the mix between the use of fixed assets [a fixed cost] versus labor [a variable cost]). The maximum degree of financial leverage is the greatest level of debt financing and lowest level of equity financing that is achievable in the organization's capital structure. The maximum degree of operating leverage is the greatest use of fixed assets that is achievable in the organizations operating structure. The maximum degree of financial leverage and the maximum degree of operating leverage is a combination that may not optimize the increase to shareholder wealth.

Choice D is not correct because the intersection of the marginal cost of capital and the marginal efficiency of investment is the point at which the organization should stop making investments; at this point, the cost of earning the return equals the return itself. Once the cost of capital exceeds the earnings from the investment, shareholder wealth will decrease, not increase.

BEC 3-Q25 B1046. The correct answer is C. Choices III and IV would generally have the effect of increasing a firm's cost of capital. Cost of capital is the weighted average cost of debt (after tax), preferred stock, common stock and retained earnings. Generally, the cost of debt is lower than the cost of equity because the interest on debt is tax deductible and debt is senior to equity in a firm's capital structure (in bankruptcy or liquidation, debt holders get paid before equity holders). When a firm pays off debt, the more expensive capital (preferred stock and common stock) remains in the firm's capital structure, resulting in an increase in the cost of capital. Likewise, Treasury bond yield increases would generally result in an increase to the overall required rate of return, causing an increase in the cost of capital.

Choice I and II would generally have the effect of decreasing a firm's cost of capital. A firm that reduces its operating leverage will have less business risk and therefore, lower cost of capital. For debt, the cost of capital (interest), is tax-deductible. If the corporate tax rate is increased, the firm's cost of capital is decreased since a higher tax rate resulted in a larger tax shield.

BEC 3-Q26 B1047. The correct answer is D. Stability's cost of capital is 12.80% and is calculated as follows:

Long-term debt:		
$10,000,000	40% × 8%	3.20%
Common stock:		
10,000,000	40% × 15%	6.00%
Retained earnings:		
5,000,000	20% × 18%	3.60%
$25,000,000		12.80%

BEC 3-Q27 B1049. The correct answer is B. The cost of capital for a firm is the weighted-average cost of its debt and equity financing components.
- The cost of debt = debt interest rate x (1-tax rate).
- The cost of preferred equity is determined by dividing the preferred dividend amount by the issue price of the stock.
- The cost of common stock is given as 17%.

Albion's cost of capital is calculated as follows:

Capital	Market value (000)	% of Total	Cost of capital	Weighted cost
Long-term debt (30,000 bonds x $1,083.34)	$32,500	26%	[.08 x (1 - .4)] = .048	1.25%
Preferred stk. (100,000 x $125)	12,500	10%	1,200 (dividend) / 12,500 (market value) = .096	0.96%
Common stk. (5,000,000 x $16)	80,000	64%	.17	10.88%
	125,000	100%		13.09%

BEC 3-Q28 B148. The correct choice is B. The interest on the debt is tax deductible, which reduces the after-tax cost of debt. The after tax cost of debt is calculated as

Debt interest rate x (1 – Tax Rate)

Choice A is not correct because interest expense of the long-term debt will reduce net income and reduce earnings per share; this is a disadvantage.

Choice C is not correct because the increased financial risk is a disadvantage when issuing long-term debt. The debt payments are a fixed cost that must be paid regardless of Larson's economic performance; this increases the risk that Larson will default, which increases financial risk.

Choice D is not correct because Larson issues its long-term debt to bondholders or other creditors and they do not have voting rights; therefore, Larson's issuance of long-term debt does not reduce control over the company.

BEC 3-Q29 B182. The correct choice is B. A compensating balance reduces the amount available, thereby increasing the effective interest rate. The effective interest rate of the loan is calculated below.

Effective interest rate = Interest expense/Amount available, net of compensating balance
Effective interest rate = ($500,000 x 0.08)/[$500,000 x (1 – 0.20)]
Effective interest rate = $40,000/($500,000 x 0.8)
Effective interest rate = $40,000/$400,000
Effective interest rate = 0.1 or 10%

BEC 3-Q30 B292. The correct choice is B. The effective interest rate should be used to calculate the firm's net cost of debt because the effective interest rate is used to calculate the interest expense under the accrual basis of accounting; the coupon rate (which is used to calculate the interest payments) would reflect the cash basis of accounting. The firm's net cost of debt is calculated as follows:

Cost of debt (after-tax) = Effective Interest Rate (1 – Tax Rate)
Cost of debt (after-tax) = 0.14 (1 – 0.30)
Cost of debt (after-tax) = 0.14(0.70)
Cost of debt (after-tax) = 0.098 or 9.8%

BEC 3-Q31 B92. The correct choice is B. The cost of preferred equity is calculated as

Preferred Dividend/(Preferred Stock issue price – Floatation cost)
Numerator: P/S par value $20 x 0.09 P/S dividend = $1.80
Denominator: P/S issue price $40 – Floatation cost $5 = $35
Cost of preferred equity = $1.80/$35
Cost of preferred equity = 0.051 or 5.1%

BEC 3-Q32 B1052. The correct answer is D. The cost of preferred equity is determined by dividing the preferred dividend by the issue price of the stock. Cox's cost of preferred stock capital is calculated as follows:

Cost of preferred stock = Stated annual dividend / (Market price – cost of issue)
= $8 / ($92 - $5)
= 9.20%

BEC 3-Q33 B46. The correct choice is A. The cost of common equity may be calculated using the Dividend-Yield-Plus-Growth-Rate approach; the formula is:

$$k_s = (D_1/P_0) + g$$

Where
k_s = cost of existing common equity
D_1 = next expected dividend
P_0 = current stock price
g = growth rate in earnings
and is calculated below.

k_s = ($4.25/$85.00) + 0.07
k_s = 0.05 + 0.07
k_s = 0.12 or 12%

BEC 3-Q34 B1050. The correct answer is C. Weighted average cost of capital is determined by taking the cost of the various types of financing (debt, preferred equity, common equity, etc.) and weighting each by the actual or proposed percentage to the total capital. Thomas' cost of capital is calculated as follows:

Long-term debt	(.08 x (1 - .4)) x .30	1.44%
Preferred stock	.11 x .25	2.75%
Common stock	.15 x .45	6.75%
		10.94%

BEC 3-Q35 B1051. The correct answer is D. If Joint Products exchanges debt for equity, the firm's cost of capital is likely to increase. This is due to the fact that the cost of debt is lower than the cost of equity because the interest on debt is tax deductible and debt is senior to equity in a firm's capital structure (in bankruptcy or liquidation, debt holders get paid before equity holders).

BEC 3-Q36 B1054. The correct answer is C. The cost of retained earnings is the return that shareholders require on the firm's common stock. The cost of capital for Hatch's retained earnings, using the constant growth model, is calculated as follows:

Required rate of return
= (Dividend next period / Market value) + Growth rate
= (($3 x 1.09) / $36) + .09
= .0908 + .09
= 18.08%

BEC 3-Q37 B1055. The correct answer is C. The retained earnings cost of capital is equal to the required rate of return on OFC's common stock and is calculated as follows:

Required rate of return
= (Dividend next period ÷ Market value) + Growth rate

= (($2 x 1.10) ÷ $38) + .10
= 15.8%

BEC 3-Q38 B972. The correct answer is C. Operating leverage represents a company's fixed costs as a percentage of its total costs. Operating leverage is used to evaluate the likely profit levels on individual sales and the breakeven point of a business. Operating leverage can be calculated using the following formulas:

Change in operating income (or, EBIT)/change in sales, or
Contribution margin/operating income, or
(Sales – variable costs)/(sales – variable costs – fixed costs), or
Contribution margin percentage/operating margin

The degree of operating leverage measures the percent change in EBIT caused by a percent change in sales. The degree of operating leverage of 3 indicates that a 1% change in sales will cause a 3% change in EBIT.

BEC 3-Q39 B971. The correct answer is B. The degree of financial leverage represents the proportional change in net income caused by a change in a corporation's capital structure. The degree of financial leverage is used to evaluate the amount of debt that a corporation is obligated to repay. The formula for the degree of financial leverage is as follows:

Earnings before interest and taxes (EBIT)
Earnings before taxes

Sahara's degree of financial leverage is calculated as follows:
Earnings before interest and taxes (EBIT)
Earnings before taxes

($1,320,000 + $880,000 + $800,000)
($1,320,000 + $880,000)

Degree of financial leverage = 1.36

BEC 3-Q40 B973. The correct answer is A. The degree of financial leverage represents the proportional change in net income caused by a change in a corporation's capital structure. Stated another way, financial leverage is defined as the use of financing with a fixed charge, such as interest. The degree of financial leverage is used to evaluate the amount of debt that a corporation is obligated to repay. Firms with a high degree of financial leverage make significant use of debt and therefore, have high debt-to-equity ratios.

BEC 3-Q41 B974. The correct answer is A. The degree of financial leverage represents the proportional change in net income caused by a change in a corporation's capital structure. Stated another way, financial leverage is defined as the use of financing with a fixed charge, such as interest. The degree of financial leverage is used to evaluate the amount of debt that a corporation is obligated to repay. Since debt is financing with a fixed charge, the use of debt in the capital structure of a firm increases financial leverage.

BEC 3-Q42 B975. The correct answer is D. The degree of financial leverage represents the proportional change in net income caused by a change in a corporation's capital structure. Stated another way, financial leverage is defined as the use of financing with a fixed charge, such as interest. The degree of financial leverage is used to evaluate the amount of debt that a corporation is obligated to repay. Firms with a high degree of financial leverage make significant use of debt and therefore, have high debt-to-equity ratios.

If net income before interest and taxes (EBIT) increases by 5%, earnings to shareholders will increase by 7.5% as follows:

Degree of financial leverage
= % change in net income/% change in EBIT
1.5 = % change in net income/5%
% change in net income = 7.5%

BEC 3-Q43 B960. The correct answer is B. Net working capital calculated by taking total current assets and subtracting total current liabilities. Fortune's net working capital is calculated as follows:

($10,000 + $60,000 + $25,000 +5,000) – ($40,000 + $10,000 + $5,000) = $45,000

BEC 3-Q44 B956. The correct answer is C. The quick (acid test) ratio is:

Quick (acid test) ratio = (Current assets – Inventory) / Current liabilities

Another way of stating the quick ratio is:

Quick (acid test) ratio = (Cash + Cash Equivalents + Marketable equity securities) / Current liabilities

If $100,000 is used to purchase inventory, the firm's quick ratio will decrease. Since inventory is not included in the calculation of current assets for the quick ratio, current assets will decrease while liabilities remain unchanged.

BEC 3-Q45 B281. The correct choice is C. The accounts receivable (A/R) turnover ratio is calculated as:
A/R Turnover = Net Sales (or net credit sales)/Average Accounts Receivable, net

By reducing the level of accounts receivable, net through factoring (the sale of A/R and the removal of A/R from the balance sheet), this action would decrease the balance of A/R, net and increase the A/R turnover ratio.

Choice A is not correct because pledging the A/R is using the A/R as collateral to secure a note payable. In pledging, the A/R is not removed from the balance sheet; therefore, the A/R, net balance will not decrease and there would be no effect on the A/R turnover.

Choice B is not correct because changing the credit terms from 3/10, net 30 to 1/10, net 30 would give customers the incentive to pay at 30 days instead of 10 days; this is because the reward/savings for paying early has decreased from 3 percent to 1 percent of the invoice amount. Decreasing the credit terms from 3/10, net 30 to 1/10, net 30 would likely increase the A/R, net balance and cause the A/R turnover to get worse.

Choice D is not correct because changing the credit terms from 3/10, net 30 to 3/20, net 30 would give customers the incentive to pay at 20 days instead of 10 days; this is because the reward/savings for paying early has increased an additional 10 days (from 10 days to 20 days). The change from credit terms of 3/10, net 30 to 3/20, net 30 would likely increase the A/R, net balance and cause the A/R turnover to get worse.

BEC 3-Q46 B1075. The correct answer is B. Locar's average collection period is calculated as follows:

Average collection period
= (Receivables x Annual days) / Credit sales
= ($1,380,000 x 360) / $18,600,000
= 26.7 days

BEC 3-Q47 B127. The correct choice is B. The costs of carrying inventory include interest costs from borrowing, spoilage, insurance, warehouse space, and security costs. An increase in the cost of carrying inventory would cause management to reduce its average inventory in order to decrease the carrying costs.

Choice A is not correct because an increase in the cost of placing an order would cause management to reduce its number of orders, thereby increasing the number of units per order and increasing the average inventory.

Choice C is not correct because an increase in the annual demand for the product would cause management to increase its average inventory in order to prevent a stockout due to increased sales.

Choice D is not correct because an increase in the lead time needed to acquire inventory would cause management to increase its average inventory in order to prevent a stockout due to the longer lead times between the order and receipt of inventory.

BEC 3-Q48 B1124. The correct answer is C. The cost of carrying (holding) inventory includes:

- Invoice price paid on inventory purchases.
- Storage costs such as, warehouse rent or deprecation (if applicable).
- Insurance cost, property taxes and utility costs.
- The funding for inventory, including the cost of capital and opportunity cost of the funds.
- Cost of obsolescence.
- Freight-in shipping costs.

Carrying costs are sometimes calculated as a percentage of the total inventory cost.

In this question, storage costs, insurance, and opportunity costs are all costs of carrying inventory. Freight-out shipping costs relate to inventory sales and the related cost of shipping the goods to the customers.

BEC 3-Q49 B169. The correct choice is C. The economic order quantity (EOQ) formula is:

$$EOQ = \sqrt{\frac{2aD}{k}}$$

Where:
a = ordering cost per order
D = Annual demand
k = carrying cost for 1 unit for 1 year

Therefore, D, the annual demand is a known periodic demand in the EOQ formula.

Choice A is not correct because, k, the carrying cost for 1 unit for 1 year, does not vary with quantity ordered in the EOQ formula.

Choice B is not correct because a, the ordering cost per order, does not vary with the quantity ordered in the EOQ formula.

Choice D is not correct because the purchase cost per unit is not considered in the EOQ formula.

BEC 3-Q50 B366. The correct choice is A. The economic order quantity (EOQ) determines the optimal amount of inventory to order by balancing the cost of placing an order for inventory with the costs of carrying the inventory. Therefore, EOQ is the point where carrying costs equal restocking costs; this minimizes the total cost of ordering and carrying inventory.

Choice B is not correct because just-in-time (JIT) inventory methods implement activity-based costing (ABC) principles to reduce the non-value added costs of inventory. JIT works by shortening the time between ordering, receiving, and putting into production raw materials in order to minimize raw materials inventory; this requires a close relationship with vendors/suppliers. JIT also works by shortening the time between manufacturing and shipping finished goods in order to minimize finished goods inventory; this requires a close relationship with customers.

Choice C is not correct because materials requirements planning (MRP) uses computerized systems to manufacture finished goods based on forecasted sales. Once sales have been forecasted, this automatically triggers the other production processes, such as producing production schedules and ordering raw materials.

Choice D is not correct because ABC (activity-based costing) implements just-in-time (JIT) inventory methods in order to reduce the non-value added costs of inventory.

BEC 3-Q51 B1129. The correct answer is C. The EOQ model is useful in determining the combination of orders and units purchased per order, which will result in the lowest combined cost for ordering and carrying inventory. When ordering costs increase, the EOQ model would increase the order quantity.

Purchase price and safety stock do not affect the EOQ model. When carrying cost increase, the EOQ model would decrease the order quantity.

BEC 3-Q52 B1130. The correct answer is D. The EOQ is used to determine the combination of orders and units purchased per order, which will result in the lowest combined cost for ordering and carrying inventory. Since quantity discounts affect the overall purchase price, they are not considered in the EOQ calculation because purchase price is not part of the EOQ.

BEC 3-Q53 B1131. The correct answer is D. The EOQ model is useful in determining the combination of orders and units purchased per order, which will result in the lowest combined cost for ordering and carrying inventory. In calculating the EOQ, it is assumed that order delivery times are consistent and lead times do not vary.

BEC 3-Q54 B1132. The correct answer is D. The EOQ is used to determine the combination of orders and units purchased per order, which will result in the lowest combined cost for ordering and carrying inventory. A decrease in carrying costs would result in an increase in the EOQ as it would be less costly to store units. A decrease in sales or ordering costs would decrease EOQ while the EOQ is unaffected by safety stock.

BEC 3-Q55 B1058. The correct answer is D. A lock-box system is used for cash inflow management instead of cash outflow management.

BEC 3-Q56 B317. The correct choice is D. A debt covenant is an agreement between the borrower and the lender (the bondholders) that the borrower will maintain certain financial statement ratios (e.g., debt-to-equity ratio, current ratio) or the borrower will restrict its ability to incur additional debt (limiting the percentage of financing with long term debt when compared to total financing). When a borrower agrees to a debt covenant, this reduces the lender's risk and the reduced risk is reflected in a lower interest rate on the debt.

Choice A is not correct because there are many factors that cause the price of the company's stock to rise and these factors may be unrelated to debt or debt covenants.

Choice B is not correct because when a borrower agrees to a debt covenant, this reduces the lender's (the bondholders') risk and would tend to improve the company's bond rating, not lower the company's bond rating. Furthermore, there are many factors that cause the borrower's bond rating to change and these factors may be unrelated to debt or debt covenants.

Choice C is not correct because a debt covenant on a borrower's new debt reduces the risk for the new bondholders and only indirectly reduces the risk for existing bondholders.

BEC 3-Q57 B1136. The correct answer is D. A commercial bank would typically provide its customers with all 4 of these financing options.

BEC 3-Q58 B1142. The correct answer is C. With compensating balance requirements, the total borrowings equals the funds needed divided by one minus the compensating balance percentage. The formula is:

Funds needed / (1-compensating balance %)
$150,000 / (1 - .15)
$176,471

BEC 3-Q59 B1035. The correct answer is D. Protective clauses or restrictions in bond indentures and loan agreements are known as covenants. The covenants can include items such as working capital requirements and capital expenditure limitations.

Answer A is incorrect because not all indenture provisions are protective.

Answers B and C are incorrect because the terms requirements and addenda do not have any meaning in this situation.

BEC 3-Q60 B1036. The correct answer is A. Protective clauses (also known as restrictive covenants) in bond indentures are known as covenants. The covenants can include items such as working capital requirements and capital expenditure limitations. A trustee is sometimes appointed to oversee the process.

Answer B is incorrect because a call provision allows the bond issuer the option to redeem the bonds before the maturity date.

Answer C is incorrect because warrants represent certificates to purchase stock at certain price within a certain period.

Answer D is incorrect because put options are not part of bond indentures.

BEC 3-Q61 B1059. The correct answer is D. The reduction in the average collection time needed in order to justify the lock-box system is calculated as follows:

Daily collections (300 x $2,500)	$750,000
Daily interest ($750,000 x .08)	$60,000
Reduction in days ($90,000 / $60,000)	1.5 days

BEC 3-Q62 B285. The correct choice is A. A lockbox is a post office box rented by a bank to receive payments made by check through the mail. Each day, a courier picks up the collections and brings them directly to the bank. The bank's customer purchases the lockbox service because it decreases the time that is needed for checks to clear the customer's bank account and the cash collected is available sooner; therefore, lockbox services are a form of accounts receivable (A/R) management. The bank's customer also has improved internal control over its A/R collections because the lockbox service avoids handling of collections by the customer's employees.

Choice B is not correct because using lockbox services reduces the firm's collection float.

Choices C and D are not correct because lockbox services are used in collections, not disbursements.

BEC 3-Q63 B684. The correct answer is C. Granite's accounts receivable balance on May 1 is calculated as follows:

Receivables applicable to sales in March ($280,000 x 15%)	$42,000
Receivables applicable to sales in April ($260,000 x 40%)	104,000
Account receivable balance, May	$146,000

BEC 3-Q64 B686. The correct answer is C. The amount of cash Brown can expect to collect during the month of January is calculated as follows:

From November sales	$8,000
From December sales (($72,000/.6) x .5)	60,000
From January sales ($100,000 x .4)	40,000
January cash collections	$108,000

BEC 3-Q65 B688. The correct answer B. Planned net accounts receivable balance as of December 31 is calculated as follows:

November ($480,000 x .8 x .25)	$ 96,000
December ($450,000 x .8 x .55)	198,000
Accounts receivable at 12/31	$ 294,000

BEC 3-Q66 B693. The correct answer is B. ANNCO's January cash collections are calculated as follows:

November sales collections	$49,500
December sales collections ($162,000 ÷ .9 x .6)	108,000
January sales collections ($170,000 x .1)	17,000
Total cash collections	$174,500

BEC 3-Q67 B1023. The correct answer is D. A change in estimate for bad debts is accounted for as affecting the period of the change. Changes in estimates for bad debt are considered normal recurring corrections and retrospective treatment must not be taken.

BEC 3-Q68 B1061. The correct answer is B. The net annual savings to Dexter if it borrows from the bank and utilizes the funds to take advantage of the trade discount is calculated as follows:

Savings from trade discount
(1% x $25,000 x 24) $6,000
Less: Interest to bank
(10% x $24,750 / 12 x 24)   (4,950)
Net savings $1,050

BEC 3-Q69 B1069. The correct answer is C. Changing the credit terms from net 30 to 2/10, net 30 will shorten the cash conversion cycle and would likely reduce the need for short-term borrowings.

BEC 3-Q70 B1062. The correct answer is D. Rolling Stone should use of all of the methods except for the drafts, because it results in a loss as follows:

Lockbox cost
($25 x 170) = $4,250
Savings
($5,240 - $4,250) = $990

Drafts cost
(4,000 x $2) = $8,000
Loss
($6,500 - $8,000) = ($1,500)

Bank Float
($1,000,000 x .02) = $20,000
Savings
($22,000 - $20,000) = $2,000

Electronic Transfer
(700 x $18) = $12,600
Savings
($14,000 - $12,600) = $1,400

BEC 3-Q71 B1072. The correct answer is C. A company should consider easing its credit policy if it has a low cost of borrowing and the potential for repeat sales. Customers would be attracted by a liberal credit policy and if the company needs to borrow funds because of slower than expected payments, the cost would not be too high. Factors I and IV have no relationship to the company's credit policy.

BEC 3-Q72 B253. The correct choice is A. In general, matching the maturities of assets and liabilities reduces risk because as liabilities come due, the maturing assets become available to liquidate the liabilities at the same time.

Choice B is not correct because short-term interest rates have more risk; when the short-term debt matures, the new interest rate is less predictable and may have increased. However, long-term debt, which typically has higher interest rates than short-term debt, is more predictable because the interest rate remains fixed in the long-term and management has time to plan and adjust to changes in interest rates.

Choice C is not correct because a firm that borrows heavily in the long term has a longer time to plan and adjust to future payments of interest and principle which increases the firm's ability to repay the debt. However, a firm that borrows heavily in the short-term has less time to plan and adjust and is more likely to be unable to repay the debt.

Choice D is not correct because the financing requirements of a firm do not remain constant; financing requirements change based on changes in management's strategic objectives in the short-term and long-term.

BEC 3-Q73 B170. The correct choice is B. The payback rule (also known as the payback period method) calculates the number of years needed before an investment "pays back" its cost. Once the cost is paid back, the payback rule ignores the future net cash inflows that occur after the payback period.

Choice A is not correct because the discounted payback rate (also known as the discounted payback period) is similar to the traditional payback period method in that once the cost is paid back, the discounted payback rate ignores future net cash inflows that occur after the payback period.

Choice C is not correct because the net present value (NPV) model says to accept investment opportunities when they have a positive NPV, meaning that the discounted future net cash inflows exceed the investment's cost.

Choice D is not correct because the internal rate of return rule (IRR) is the interest rate which renders the investment's cost equal to the future net cash inflows of the investment. The IRR rule is to accept the investment opportunity if the IRR generated by the investment is greater than the required rate of return, which may also be called the opportunity cost of capital or the weighted-average cost of capital.

BEC 3-Q74 B147. The correct choice is C. The payback period is a capital budgeting technique used to calculate the number of years needed to recoup an investment. Management may prefer to invest in projects that "pay back" sooner (this would be a lower payback period).

Choice A is not correct because the payback period ignores the time value of money, which is one of the major disadvantages of the payback period technique.

Choice B is not correct because the payback period only calculates the number of years needed to recoup an investment and ignores the cash flows that occur after the payback point; the cash flows after the payback point will produce a profit.

Choice D is not correct because the payback period is calculated as:

Net Investment/Annual Net Cash Inflow

BEC 3-Q75 B284. The correct choice is B. The payback period is calculated below. Note that the payback period formula of

Payback period = Investment/Annual Cash Inflow (net of tax)

cannot be used because the cash flows are not equal amounts. Also note that because information about taxes is not included in the question, we assume that the cash flows are net of tax effect.

$1,000	Investment	
(200)	Year 1 Cash Inflow	
800	Subtotal after Year 1	
(200)	Year 2 Cash Inflow	
600	Subtotal after Year 2	
(400)	Year 3 Cash Inflow	
200	Subtotal after Year 3	
(200)	$200 out of the $400 of Year 4 cash inflow, which is 0.5	
0	Payback period is 3.5 years	

BEC 3-Q76 B309. The correct choice is C. The payback period is calculated as the investment cost divided by the future net cash inflow:

Payback Period = Investment/Future net cash inflow
Payback Period = $500,000/$200,000
Payback Period = 2.5 years

BEC 3-Q77 B312. The correct choice is B. Only Projects B and C achieve a payback within three years.

Payback period for Project A:
Investment/Annual Net Cash Inflow = $10,000/$3,000 = 3.33 years. Project A does not pay back within 3 years because 3.33 exceeds 3.0.

Payback period for Project B:

$25,000	Investment
− 15,000	Year 1 Net Cash Inflow
$10,000	Subtotal
− 10,000	Year 2 Net Cash Inflow ($10,000 out of $15,000, which is two-thirds or 0.67)
$ 0	Subtotal

Project B pays back between 1 and 2 years, which is 1.67 years. Therefore, Project B pays back within 3 years.

Payback period for Project C:

Investment/Annual Net Cash Inflow = $10,000/$5,000 = 2.0 years. Therefore, Project C pays back within 3 years.

BEC 3-Q78 B367. The correct choice is A. The payback method is a capital budgeting technique used to calculate the number of years needed to recoup an investment. The payback method divides the investment by the future net cash flow; the cash flow is not discounted so the payback method does not consider the time value of money.

Choice B is not correct because the payback method calculates the number of years needed to recoup the investment; but, the number of years in the payback method does not consider the time required to earn a profit.

Choice C is not correct because the payback period measures the number of years needed to recoup an investment; the payback method is not a measure of profitability. When comparing investments, management may prefer the investment with a shorter payback period.

Choice D is not correct because the payback method divides the investment by the future net cash inflow; the salvage value of old equipment would be a cash inflow, so the salvage value would be considered when replacing equipment.

BEC 3-Q79 B64. The correct choice is C. In order to calculate the NPV, the discount rate must be determined in advance so that the future cash flows may be discounted to calculate their present value; then, the cost of the project is subtracted to calculate the NPV.

Choices A and B are not correct because the payback period and the accounting rate of return do not consider the time value of money, so a discount rate is not needed.

Choice D is not correct because the IRR calculates the discount rate which makes the present value of the future cash flows exactly equal the cost of the project, making the NPV equal to zero; therefore, a discount rate is not needed in advance.

BEC 3-Q80 B66. The correct choice is B. The future cash flows will be received at the end of each year for six years, making this an ordinary annuity (also called an annuity in arrears). If the future cash flows were received at the beginning of each year, then this would be an annuity due (also called an annuity in advance). The NPV of the investment at 8% is calculated below.

NPV = PV of future cash flows – Cost
NPV = ($4,000 future cash flows x PV of the ordinary annuity of $1 at 8% for 6 periods 4.62288) – $20,000
NPV = $18,491.52 – $20,000.00
NPV = ($1,508.48)

BEC 3-Q81 B84. The correct choice is C. The Net Present Value (NPV) is calculated as the present value (PV) of the future cash inflows, less the cost. In this question, there are two future cash inflows: the annuity of $25,000 each year for the next 6 years and the single sum payment of $25,000 at the end of six years.

First, calculate the PV of the future cash inflows:
  $25,000 annuity x 4.355 PV of the ordinary annuity of $1, six periods, 10% = $108,875

  $20,000 single sum x 0.564 PV of $1, six periods, 10% = $11,280
  Total PV of the future cash inflows = $120,155
Second, subtract the cost of $100,000
NPV = $120,155 – $100,000
NPV = $20,155

BEC 3-Q82 B144. The correct choice is C. The calculation of Net Present Value (NPV) is presented below:

PVA of $1 for 5 periods, 10% 3.79 x future net cash inflows $420,000	$1,591,800
+ PV of $1 for 6 periods, 10% 0.56 x $100,000	56,000
= Total PV of future net cash inflows	$1,647,800
– Investment (cost)	(1,800,000)
= Net Present Value (a negative NPV in this case)	($152,200)

BEC 3-Q83 B259. The correct choice is D. The net present value (NPV) is the present value of the future net cash inflows less the cost of the investment. Therefore, NPV is based on cash flows.

Choices A, B, and C are not correct because net income, earnings before interest, taxes and depreciation, and earnings before interest and taxes are based on the accrual basis of accounting. Net present value (NPV) is the present value of the future net cash inflows less the cost of the investment. Therefore, NPV is based on cash flows.

BEC 3-Q84 B86. The correct choice is D. The Profitability Index is calculated as follows:

Profitability Index = (PV of future cash inflows/Initial Investment) x 100

In an environment where there is a limit on the funds available to invest, management may prioritize projects accordingly from highest to lowest profitability index; this invests scarce resources in those projects with the highest return and maximizes shareholder wealth.

Therefore, a limitation of the profitability index is that it requires projections of future cash inflows that may require detailed analysis for the long-term.

Choice A is not correct because free cash flow is calculated as:

  Net Operating Profit After Taxes (NOPAT)
  + Depreciation Expense or Amortization Expense
  – Capital Expenditures
  – Change in Working Capital Expenditures
  = Free Cash Flow

Free cash flow is not included in the calculation of Profitability Index.

Choice B is not correct because the Profitability Index uses the time value of money when discounting the future cash inflows.

Choice C is not correct because in an environment where there is a limit on the funds available to invest, management may prioritize projects accordingly from the highest to lowest profitability index; this invests scarce resources in those projects with the highest return and maximizes shareholder wealth.

BEC 3-Q85 B125. The correct choice is B. The formula for the profitability index is:

Present Value of Future Net Cash Inflows/Initial Investment

The index may or may not be multiplied by 100 to convert to a percentage.

Choice A is not correct because this formula describes in dollars the change in shareholders' wealth.

Choice C is not correct because this formula describes the payback period.

Choice D is not correct because this formula describes the Return on Assets (also known as the Return on Investment).

BEC 3-Q86 B341. The correct choice is C. The profitability index is a variation of the net present value (NPV) capital budgeting model. The profitability index is calculated as net present value (NPV) divided by the investment, and then multiplied by 100 to express the index as a percentage.

Choice A is not correct because the internal rate of return (IRR) is the discount rate at which the present value of the future cash flows from the project exactly equals the cost of the project; the IRR is not used in calculating the profitability index.

Choice B is not correct because the economic value-added (EVA) is calculated as:

EVA = NOPAT − [WACC x (Total Assets − Current Liabilities)]

Where:
  NOPAT = Net Operating Profit After Taxes
  WACC = Weighted-Average Cost of Capital

The EVA is not used in calculating the profitability index.

Choice D is not correct because the discount payback is calculated as the amount of the investment less the present value of each of the future net cash inflows per year until the investment is paid back; the year in which the investment is paid back is the discounted payback period. The discounted payback is not used in calculating the profitability index.

BEC 3-Q87 B69. The correct choice is B. The internal rate of return is the discount rate at which the present value of the future cash flows from the project exactly equals the cost of the project. When the PV of the future cash flows exactly equals the cost, the NPV is zero.

Choice A is not correct because the number of years it takes to recover the investment describes the payback period.

Choice C is not correct because an NPV of one means that the PV of the future cash flows from the project only slightly exceeds the cost of the project, but the IRR means that the PV of the future cash flows exactly equals the cost and the NPV is zero.
Choice D is not correct because the weighted-average cost of capital used to finance a project is the discount rate used in calculating NPV.

BEC 3-Q88 B87. The correct choice is C. The Internal Rate of Return (IRR) is the interest rate at which, when discounted, the present value (PV) of the project's future cash inflows exactly equals the cost of the project. Typically, the cost of the investment occurs at the project's inception and the PV of the cost is the cost at the time of investment and does not need discounting. If there are future costs, then the future cash outflows would be netted against the future cash inflows to arrive at the net future cash inflows.

Choice A is not correct because the Net Present Value (NPV) is the PV of the project's future cash inflows less the cost of the project.

Choice B is not correct because Return on Assets (ROA) is a performance measurement based on the accrual basis of accounting and does not take into account the time value of money. ROA is calculated as:

ROA = Net Income/Average Investment

Choice D is not correct because the Economic Value Added (EVA) is a performance measurement based on the accrual basis of accounting and does not take into account the time value of money. EVA is calculated as:

EVA = NOPAT − [WACC x (Total Assets − Current Liabilities)]

Where:
  NOPAT = Net Operating Profit After Taxes
  WACC = Weighted-Average Cost of Capital

BEC 3-Q89 B167. The correct choice is C. The internal rate of return (IRR) of an investment is the interest rate which renders the investment's cost equal to the future net cash inflows of the investment. The IRR may be compared to the weighted-average cost of capital (WACC) because when

IRR > WACC, then the net present value (NPV) will be positive and the company earns a return in excess of its cost of capital, increasing shareholder wealth;

IRR < WACC, then NPV will be negative and the company earns a return below its cost of capital, which would decrease shareholder wealth; and

IRR = WACC, then NPV will be zero and the company earns a return equal to its cost of capital, which would not change shareholder wealth.

Choices A and D are not correct because interest rates on U.S. Treasury securities are used as examples of interest rates on investments that have no risk of default.

Choice B is not correct because the prime rate of interest is the interest rate at which banks lend to their most creditworthy customers. The prime rate is often used as a benchmark interest rate and determines interest rates charged to the bank's customers, e.g., an interest rate of prime + 2 percent.

BEC 3-Q90 B356. The correct choice is B. The internal rate of return (IRR) calculates the discount rate which makes the present value of the future cash flows exactly equal to the cost of the project; when this occurs, the net present value (NPV) equals zero. If the NPV is greater than zero, then the IRR is greater than the discount rate used in the NPV; if the NPV is less than zero, then the IRR is less than the discount rate used in the NPV. Therefore, if the NPV is positive (greater than zero), then the required rate of return (used in the project's NPV) is less that the project's IRR.

Choices A and C are not correct because the discount rate used in calculating the net present value is called the required rate of return; the required rate of return may also be the same rate as the company's weighted average cost of capital. Therefore, the required rate of return and the weighted average cost of capital may be the same rate.

Choice D is not correct because if the net present value (NPV) is positive (greater than zero), then the required rate of return (used in the project's NPV) is less than the project's internal rate of return (IRR), not greater than the project's IRR.

BEC 3-Q91 B186. The correct choice is D. The payback period, discounted cash flow, internal rate of return, and net present value all rely on forecasting future net cash inflows.

Choice A is not correct because only the payback period does not consider the time value of money. The discounted cash flow, internal rate of return, and net present value consider the time value of money.

Choice B is not correct because only the internal rate of return may require multiple trial and error calculations. The payback period, discounted cash flow, and net present value do not require multiple trial and error calculations; a single calculation is made.

Choice C is not correct because the payback period does not require knowledge of the company's cost of capital. The discounted cash flow and net present value use the company's cost of capital as the discount rate when discounting future net cash inflows; the internal rate of return of a project is compared to the company's cost of capital when evaluating a project.

This page is intentionally left blank.

BEC 4 – Information Technology

A. Information Technology Governance		**4A-1 – 4A-15**
1.	Vision and strategy	2
2.	Organization	4
3.	Risk Assessment	10
B. Role of Information Technology in Business		**4B-1 – 4B-9**
1.	Big data and data analytics	1
2.	Integrated systems	2
3.	Data interfaces	2
4.	Transaction processing alternatives – online, real-time processing vs. batch processing	3
5.	Transaction processing alternatives – centralized vs. distributed processing	4
6.	Electronic commerce	5
7.	Opportunities for business process reengineering	7
8.	Roles of internet evolution on business operations and organization cultures	7
9.	Cryptocurrencies	8
10.	Automation	9
C. Information Security/Availability		**4C-1 – 4C-10**
1.	Protection of information	1
2.	IT general controls (including logical and physical access controls)	5
3.	System disruption/resolution	9
D. Processing Integrity (Input/Processing/Output) Controls		**4D-1 – 4D-3**
1.	IT application controls	1
2.	Testing control design and operational effectiveness	3
E. System Development and Maintenance		**4E-1 – 4E-4**
1.	System development lifecycle	1
2.	Segregation of duties	3
F. IT Terminology and Concept Refresher		**4F-1 – 4F-17**
1.	Hardware	1
2.	Software	4
3.	Programming languages	5
4.	Databases	6
5.	Networks	10
6.	Virtualization	14

7.	Internet	14
8.	Firewalls	15
9.	Virtual private networks (VPNs)	16
10.	Artificial intelligence information systems	16

Glossary: Information Technology — Glossary 4-1 – 4-10

Multiple Choice – Questions — MCQ 4-1 – 4-10

Multiple Choice – Solutions — MCQ 4-11 – 4-29

Information Technology

A CPA's understanding of information technology is essential to appropriately utilizing and properly auditing accounting information systems. Given the role of technology in accounting systems today, we believe it is no longer possible to effectively assess controls and risks in an internal control structure without assessing the risks and controls associated with the company's IT environment.

The term information technology encompasses all of the software and hardware that an organization uses to manage and analyze accounting records for decision-making and financial reporting. Over the last several decades, reliance on these systems has increased both computational power and efficiency. However, increased system complexity has also increased organizational risk. Understanding the delicate balance of efficiency and risk is key to effectively using and evaluating a company's use of information technology.

> *Hint:* The IT content area is subject to constant evolution as the nature, role, risks, and impact of technological change. The AICPA has identified the following areas eligible for testing, which will be discussed throughout this chapter:
> - Automation
> - Big Data, data analytics, and data visualizations
> - Blockchain and cryptocurrencies (e.g., Bitcoin, Ethereum)
> - Cloud operations and data storage
> - Cybersecurity
> - Digital business models
>
> Be sure to stay up to date on emerging trends on each of these topics prior to your exam.

A. Information Technology Governance

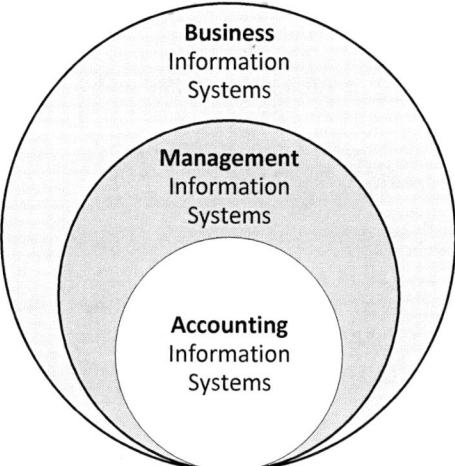

In an organization, the information that is critical for decision-making must be organized methodically for effective communication. The purpose of a business information system (BIS) is to organize and integrate information. An organization's people, information technology infrastructure, software, procedures, data, and business strategy all play a valuable role. Each component of the system, or subsystem, depends upon, and interrelates, with other components. A system's formal procedures create structure and clarity about how to collect data, process and transform it into usable information, and distribute it to users.

When categorizing information systems, the business information system category is the broadest. Within this larger category are more specific types of information systems including both management information systems and accounting information systems. A management information system processes both financial and nonfinancial data and provides past, present, and future information about an organization. It focuses on summarizing data to plan and monitor an organization's operations. Management information systems help managers see patterns and relationships hidden in large quantities of data.

A management information system often compiles data about transactions and events that are not stored or processed by an accounting information system. For example, the system stores information about production, distribution, human resources, and marketing. While some of this information may not be required for financial statement reporting, it is useful for internal decision-making.

The narrowest category is reserved for the accounting information system. An accounting information system supports only financial information about transactions. Some of the most common subsystems of an accounting information system include: the transaction processing system (TPS), the general ledger and financial reporting system, and the management reporting system. The TPS processes routine transactions that impact sales, accounts receivable, and accounts payable. The reporting systems produce financial statements and reports for external and internal use, respectively.

1. Vision and strategy

> **Identify the role that the Information Technology function plays in determining/supporting an organization's vision and strategy.**

Business strategy and information technology strategy must properly align. If synergy exists, it will enable the organization to reduce costs by improving efficiency, increasing productivity, improving workflow, and enhancing communication. If an organization treats information technology as an afterthought, the resulting disconnect between IT and strategy is detrimental, impeding efficient operations.

a. Data capture
The data capture function of an accounting information system enables recordkeeping. Data about financial transactions and events is input into a system and subsequently stored. Common tools used to capture data include: a mouse, a keyboard, a scanner, and a touchscreen, however, most modern accounting systems allow the import of transactions from data files or electronic interfaces (e.g., automated data feeds from services like Yodlee or Fiserv).

b. Processing
Once data is recorded (captured) in a system, processing can begin. An accounting information system processes input data into meaningful information by categorizing and summarizing the information. This information is then used to manage the organization. A computerized system is more efficient than a manual system and will result in fewer mathematical errors. Processing can occur online, real-time or in batches at a specified point in time, and the processing capability of the system can be centralized or distributed.

Multiple Choice
BEC 4-Q1

c. Reporting
Reporting, an output function, allows for human interaction with information technology. This function is necessary to view and distribute the information housed in an accounting information system. For example, an organization's financial statements and supporting schedules are key reports that the user can display digitally on a screen or the user can print out hard copies using a printer.

d. Types of management information systems
Information technology can act as a tool for strategic decision-making. Three specific types of management information systems that are used for this purpose include: executive support systems, decision support systems, and expert systems.

An executive support system is specifically designed to provide executives with timely, relevant information to make strategic decisions. For example, an executive may have access to a real-time dashboard that summarizes information about the organization. The system is also likely to incorporate information about competitors for benchmarking and comparison.

A decision support system assists users at multiple levels of the organization by providing information to support decisions about day-to-day operations. It provides valuable information about non-routine or rapidly changing factors that impact a decision. This type of system uses data modeling and statistical analysis to generate meaningful information for its users.

An expert system is a specific type of computer-based decision support system. Similar to seeking advice from a human expert, this type of system can use computer-based reasoning methods to provide recommendations when queried about a specific topic. While most computer-based decision support systems require a great deal of user involvement, an expert system is self-sufficient and could eventually replace the decision-maker altogether.

e. Data management architecture
Data management architecture represents the design of the processes and applications which control the data that is collected, stored, arranged, and accessed by an organization's computer systems. This framework of policies, rules, standards, and procedures are designed to organize the company's data for reliability so that it can be found, accessed, and utilized by internal and external stakeholders when required.

Multiple Choice

BEC 4-Q2

2. Organization

> **Describe the Information Technology (IT) governance structure within an organization (tone at the top, policies, steering committees, IT strategies, oversight, etc.).**

IT governance is a subcategory of corporate governance. As such, leading corporate governance methodologies are also applicable to an organization's IT infrastructure. The recent updates to the COSO internal control framework and the legal requirements associated with corporate governance reforms related to the Sarbanes-Oxley Act have reemphasized the importance of effective governance over information technology as part of an effective internal control structure.

   a. COSO internal control framework (COSO IC)
   Enterprise risk management is all about strategy, which dictates a balance of risk versus reward. Leading governance models define how an organization should approach internal control to manage risk best. Organizations depend on a governance framework, or a set of concepts and practices that provide structure for the organization, to direct enterprise-wide internal control objectives.

   The *COSO Internal Control – Integrated Framework*, updated in 2013, is recognized as a leading, broadly-accepted framework for internal control governance. It was developed by the Committee of Sponsoring Organizations of the Treadway Commission (COSO). This framework is referred to as the COSO internal control framework. (Note: COSO has also published an expended framework to provide a comprehensive enterprise-wide approach to managing risk, called the Enterprise Risk Management – Integrated Framework or COSO ERM framework. This complementary, partially overlapping framework is an extension of the COSO internal control framework. This discussion focuses on the narrower COSO internal control framework.)

   To best address the complex issues that arise from enterprise risk management, COSO differentiates aspects of internal control into objectives over operations, reporting, and compliance. Operations objective pertain to operational and financial performance goals, measuring efficiency and effectiveness. Safeguarding assets is a focus. Reporting objectives pertain to internal and external reporting, highlighting reliability, timeliness, and transparency. Compliance objectives pertain to an entity's adherence to regulations.

   The components of the COSO framework recognize how an organization can design, implement, and address internal control. The five integrated components are control environment, risk assessment, control activities, information and communication, and monitoring. Fundamental concepts related to each component are defined in the framework as principles, seventeen principles in total. The framework also addresses the entity's organizational structure (e.g., entity, division, operating unit, and function) as a dimension for consideration, segmenting the enterprise into smaller components to make implementation more manageable.

   1) Control environment
   The control environment provides a foundation for internal control in an organization. The organizational structure, culture of integrity and ethical decision-making, and performance measurement criteria each play a role in the control environment. The board of directors and senior management establish the tone at the top, and the board of directors is responsible for oversight.

   The following COSO internal control principles are associated with an entity's control environment:
   1. *The organization demonstrates a commitment to integrity and ethical values.*
   2. *The board of directors demonstrates independence from management and exercises oversight of the development and performance of internal control.*

3. Management establishes, with board oversight, structures, reporting lines, and appropriate authorities and responsibilities in the pursuit of objectives.
4. The organization demonstrates a commitment to attract, develop, and retain competent individuals in alignment with objectives.
5. The organization holds individuals accountable for their internal control responsibilities in the pursuit of objectives.

With regard to IT, a company should acknowledge that an organization's IT function does not operate independently and is an integrated part of the overall control environment.

2) Risk assessment
A risk assessment evaluates the likelihood that risks will occur and the effects that the risks will have on the organization. Risk assessment is an iterative process and risks are considered relative to an organization's tolerance for risk.

The following COSO internal control principles are associated with risk assessment:
1. The organization specifies objectives with sufficient clarity to enable the identification and assessment of risks relating to objectives.
2. The organization identifies risks to the achievement of its objectives across the entity and analyzes risks as a basis for determining how the risks should be managed.
3. The organization considers the potential for fraud in assessing risks to the achievement of objectives.
4. The organization identifies and assesses changes that could significantly impact the system of internal control.

IT risks such as security, availability, processing integrity, confidentiality, and privacy must be included in the risk assessment at both a company-level and an activity-level (i.e., within the system development process).

Multiple Choice

BEC 4-Q3

3) Control activities
Control activities help mitigate risks across all levels of the entity, including over the entity's information system.

The following COSO internal control principles are associated with control activities:
1. The organization selects and develops control activities that contribute to the mitigation of risks to the achievement of objectives to acceptable levels.
2. The organization selects and develops general control activities over technology to support the achievement of objectives.
3. The organization deploys control activities through policies that establish what is expected and procedures that put policies into action.

Control activities over IT are necessary to create reliable financial statements. Relevant control activities include both IT general controls and application controls.

4) Information and communication
Relevant internal and external information is necessary to achieve objectives, and timely communication supports this function of internal control.

The following COSO internal control principles are associated with information and communication:
1. *The organization obtains or generates and uses relevant, quality information to support the functioning of internal control.*
2. *The organization internally communicates information, including objectives and responsibilities for internal control, necessary to support the functioning of internal control.*
3. *The organization communicates with external parties regarding matters affecting the functioning of internal control.*

IT facilitates the retention of information and assists in timely communication to stakeholders. As the storage capacity increases, IT faces increasing demands on a company's computer resources and its IT infrastructure.

5) Monitoring activities
Evaluations determine if each of the five components of internal control are present and functioning properly. Findings are evaluated and deficiencies, if any, are identified, and communicated to management and the board of directors.

The following COSO internal control principles are associated with monitoring activities:
1. *The organization selects, develops, and performs ongoing and/or separate evaluations to ascertain whether the components of internal control are present and functioning.*
2. *The organization evaluates and communicates internal control deficiencies in a timely manner to those parties responsible for taking corrective action, including senior management and the board of directors, as appropriate.*

Monitoring activities over IT take the form of both continuous monitoring (i.e., ongoing evaluations) and separate evaluations, depending on the nature of the assessment and subject matter. Continuous monitoring, as the name suggests, maintains ongoing awareness of the operating effectiveness of controls to support risk management. Separate evaluations (e.g., internal audits), offer a periodic determination of the functionality of the internal control.

Monitoring can be performed more efficiently and with a higher level of precision as a result of technology. However, the complexity of computerized systems also adds difficulty. Monitoring using technology requires personnel with additional knowledge and expertise about the organization's system infrastructure. The benefit of the steady advancement of technology is that monitoring is no longer solely dependent on the user. Automated monitoring can alert the organization of abnormalities in processing and system errors in a timelier manner than manual monitoring.

The monitoring process is the responsibility of management but is accomplished both internally and externally. Internal monitoring involves management's review of control activities such as reconciliations, internal audit testing, and regulatory compliance. External monitoring exposes the operating effectiveness of internal controls through independent auditor examinations and regulatory reports.

b. Policies
The importance of consistently applied policies should not be understated. Organizations are responsible for documenting policies and procedures must be clear and concise. Policy documents typically consist of a written narrative and diagrams, as appropriate, to convey information.

1) Flowcharts and other diagrams

   Flowcharts are a popular tool used to visualize the design of information systems. Often, flowcharts are included in an organization's policy and procedure documents governing information systems to increase the reader's understanding. Flowcharts are particularly helpful as a way to represent how data flows through a system and can also highlight key interfaces between applications. The symbols are universally recognized in accordance with the guidance set forth by the International Organization for Standardization (ISO).

Symbol	Represents	Examples
▭	Process	Issue payment for invoice
⬓	Subprocess	Three-way match
▱	Document	Invoice Receiving report Purchase order
◇	Decision	Does three-way match exist?
⬭	Start/End	Receive invoice
▱	Data (Input/Output)	Transaction file Journal Trial balance
⌭	Database	Master file Customer list Vendor list Employee list
⎈	External Data	Import from external vendor (payroll)

   Internal control (audit) flowcharts depict how documents travel from one department to another within an organization, and any controls management has put in place to restrict the process. As an example, consider the control, "A manager must review and approve all capital expenditures." The flowchart depicting this control shows the appropriate action and next steps if a proposed capital expenditure is either accepted by management or rejected.

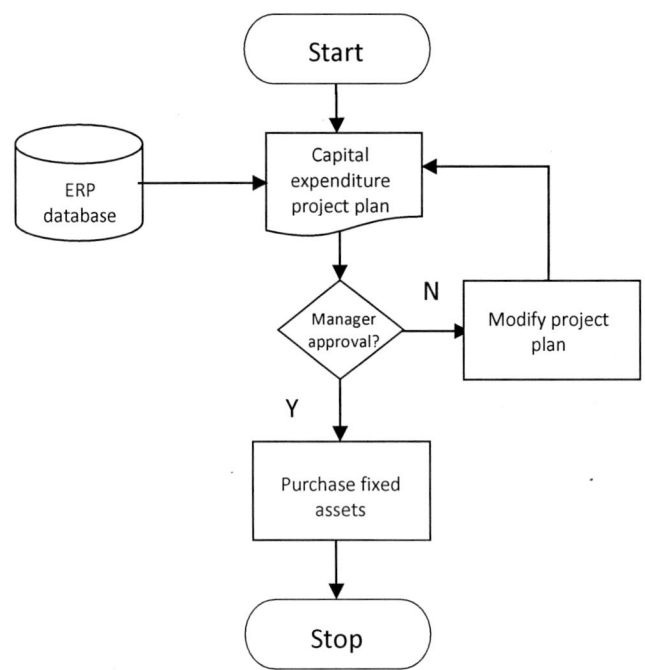

A system flowchart is a visual representation of the system environment at an organization. It highlights application interfaces and acts as a summary of the environment. A program (or application) flowchart depicts additional detail of the processing steps within a computer application.

Multiple Choice

BEC 4-Q4

A decision table is a compact way to depict all possible alternatives (called conditions), all appropriate actions, and the rules for each alternative. This example demonstrates a three-way match and indicates the action required if a particular condition combination is present. For example, if all three conditions are present (indicated by Y for "Yes" in column 1), the decision table directs the employee to inquire of the vendor, the purchasing department, and the receiving department to resolve the issue.

		Rules							
		1	2	3	4	5	6	7	8
Conditions	Invoice is missing or contains inconsistent information	Y	Y	Y	Y	N	N	N	N
	Purchase order is missing or contains inconsistent information	Y	Y	N	N	Y	Y	N	N
	Receiving report is missing or contains inconsistent information	Y	N	Y	N	Y	N	Y	N
Actions	Disburse cash to vendor								X
	Inquire of vendor	X	X	X	X				
	Inquire of purchasing department	X	X			X	X		
	Inquire of receiving department	X		X		X		X	

A data flow diagram demonstrates the passage or flow of data through an information system.

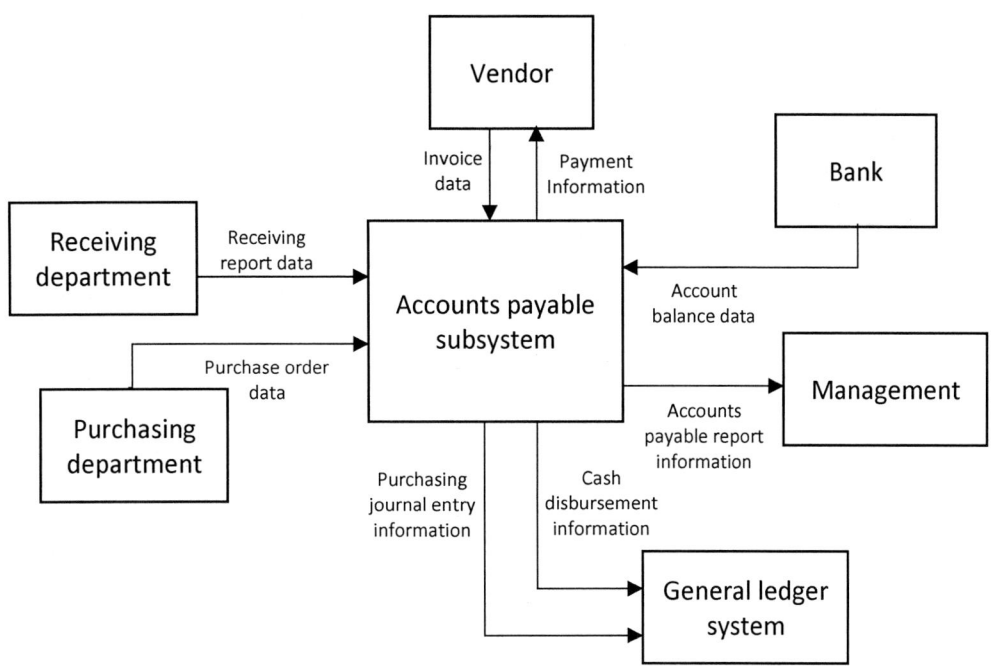

3. Risk Assessment

> Conduct an Information Technology risk assessment, identify risks and suggest mitigation strategies.

Information systems are inherently risky. Organizations use a risk assessment to evaluate the impact and likelihood that system vulnerabilities could be exploited. Information system and technology risks relate to security, availability, processing integrity, confidentiality, and privacy.

With the introduction of cloud computing and outsourcing, the responsibilities for risk mitigation shift from the user entity to its service providers. Trust is a growing factor for the user entity since it usually is heavily reliant on the service provider. Trust services, defined by the AICPA, are professional attestation services that provide assurance on the integrity of information stored in a service provider's IT-enabled systems. A trust service engagement sets out to address one or more of the system attributes related to risk, called the five Trust Services categories, and utilizes seven criteria for evaluation. The guidance for Trust Services was developed by the AICPA to enable practitioners to evaluate the design and operating effectiveness of non-financial controls for IT-enabled systems and to offer a high level of independent assurance.

Multiple Choice

BEC 4-Q5

a. AICPA's Trust Services Criteria (TSC)
The five Trust Services categories are security, availability, processing integrity, confidentiality, and privacy. Note that in 2017 the phrase "principles" was replace with "categories" to differentiate the AICPA's Trust Services from *COSO Internal Control – Integrated Framework* principles.

1) Security
The system is protected against unauthorized access, use, or modification.
2) Availability
The system is available for operation and use as committed or agreed.
3) Processing integrity
System processing is complete, accurate, timely, and authorized.
4) Confidentiality
Information designated as confidential is protected as committed or agreed.
5) Privacy
Personal information is collected, used, retained, disclosed and destroyed in conformity with the commitments in the entity's privacy notice and with criteria set forth in Generally Accepted Privacy Principles (GAPP) issued by the AICPA.

The five categories in Trust Services engagements are evaluated based on a set of criteria. Criteria are either common to all categories (excluding privacy) or applicable to a single category. The common criteria applicable to security, availability, processing integrity, and confidentiality are organized into seven subcategories: organization and management, communications, risk management and design and implementation of controls, monitoring of controls, logical and physical access controls, system operations, and change management.

1) Organization and management
Criteria pertaining to organizational structure and the accountability, integrity, ethical values and qualifications of personnel.
2) Communications
Criteria relevant to how the entity communicates its policies to responsible parties and authorized users of the system.
3) Risk management and design and implementation of controls
Criteria concerning risk identification, analysis, response, mitigation, and monitoring.

4) Monitoring of controls
Criteria over how an entity monitors its system and addresses deficiencies.
5) Logical and physical access controls
Criteria relating to restricting, provisioning, and revoking access to prevent unauthorized access to an entity's system.
6) System operations
Criteria pertaining to the execution of system procedures and the identification and mitigation of processing deviations.
7) Change management
Criteria over the initiation of system changes, the change management process, and protection from unauthorized system modification.

b. Attestation and assurance reports
The term audit is reserved for financial statement engagements concluding with the issuance of an independent audit opinion. Attestation engagements vary from audit engagements primarily based on subject matter. A system and control (SOC) report focuses on internal control environment over an IT-enabled system. The practitioner expresses an independent opinion about the subject matter against a set of criteria. The criteria used are sufficiently flexible to be tailored to the service provider's enterprise and to meet the user's requirements for the report. There are three types of SOC reports, differentiated on the basis of the control objectives and the intended users.

> *Hint*: In 2017, the AICPA changed the name underlying the acronym from "service organization control" to "system and organization controls" (SOC).

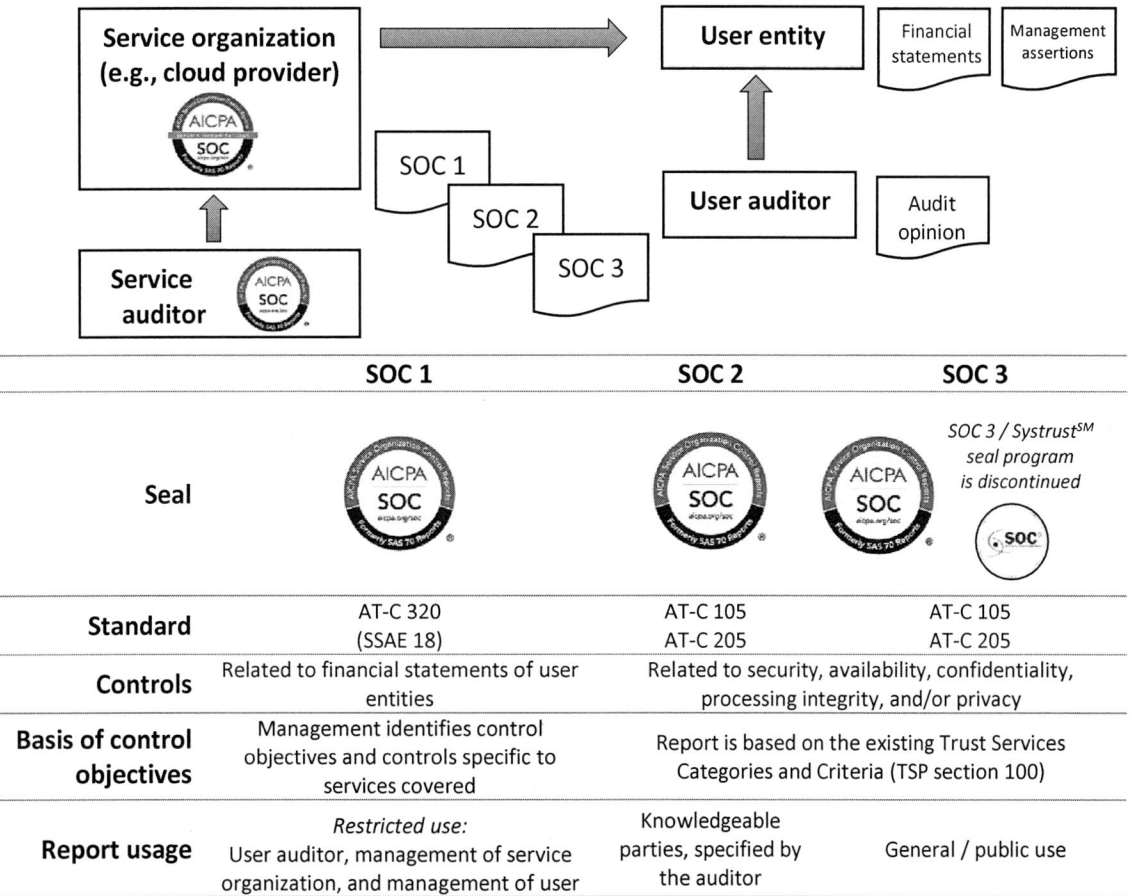

	SOC 1	SOC 2	SOC 3
Seal	AICPA SOC	AICPA SOC	AICPA SOC — SOC 3 / Systrust^{SM} seal program is discontinued
Standard	AT-C 320 (SSAE 18)	AT-C 105 AT-C 205	AT-C 105 AT-C 205
Controls	Related to financial statements of user entities	Related to security, availability, confidentiality, processing integrity, and/or privacy	
Basis of control objectives	Management identifies control objectives and controls specific to services covered	Report is based on the existing Trust Services Categories and Criteria (TSP section 100)	
Report usage	*Restricted use:* User auditor, management of service organization, and management of user	Knowledgeable parties, specified by the auditor	General / public use

1) SOC 1^{SM}
   A SOC 1 engagement is performed to evaluate the controls at a service organization relevant to a user entity's internal control over financial reporting. The engagement is performed using the guidance of AT-C 320, Reporting on an Examination of Controls at a Service Organization Relevant to User Entities' Internal Control Over Financial Reporting, based on the SSAE 18. The report includes: (1) management's description of the service organization's system, (2) a written management assertion discussing the service organization's system fairly presents the service organization's system that was designed and implemented throughout the specified period, and (3) a CPA's opinion on fairness of description, suitability of design, operating effectiveness of controls.

   > *Hint:* SSAE 16 was superseded and replaced by SSAE 18 for reports after 5/1/2017. This is eligible for testing starting in Q1 2018.

2) SOC 2^{SM}
   The SOC 2 report tests a wider scope of controls, particularly those related to security, availability, processing integrity, confidentiality, and privacy. The Trust Services criteria are used to evaluate the suitability of the design and operating effectiveness of controls. The report is more broadly distributed in comparison to the SOC 1 report. Distribution is permitted to include knowledgeable parties such as existing customers, regulators, and business partners. Since the purpose and audience of this report is distinctly different from the SOC 1, it should not be relied upon for financial statement audit support by the user entity, but instead, would be used as part of the organization's internal risk assessment process related to the activity performed by the service provider.

3) SOC 3^{SM}
   The SOC 3 report is a simplified version of the SOC 2 report, continuing to focus on the Trust Service principles and criteria and the evaluation of control effectiveness. Modified for general use, it excludes the description of the system and testing procedures. The distribution is not restricted and the service organization is free to offer the report for download to the general public. The AICPA has discontinued the seal program for SOC 3. As a replacement, the general SOC seal may be used in advertising. The SysTrust^{SM} for Service Organizations branding has also been superseded by SOC 3.

   Note that although the SysTrust seal program has been discontinued, the WebTrust seal program continues for e-commerce systems.

4) SOC for Cybersecurity^{SM}
   SOC for Cybersecurity is a framework for evaluating system and organization controls which provides a common underlying language for enterprise cybersecurity risk management reporting. This framework helps management assess the organization's cybersecurity risk management program, including the design and effectiveness of its processes and controls. This type of SOC report is typically based on the AICPA's Trust Services Criteria, but other security frameworks may be used as standards in place of the Trust Services Criteria (e.g., ISO 27001 or the NIST Cybersecurity Framework).

   ISO 27001 is an international specification for an information security management system which involves creating, documenting, and operating processes to manage the organization's security risks and controls. A company receives an ISO 27001 certification by having the documentation and operations evaluated by a third-party subject matter expert who reviews the organization's process design and documentation, and tests the operating effectiveness of the processes over a period of time.

The US National Institute of Standards and Technology (NIST) Cybersecurity Framework is a policy framework of security guidance for how private sector businesses can assess and improve their ability to prevent, detect, and respond to cyber-attacks.

The US National Institute of Standards and Technology (NIST) is part of the US Department of Commerce, and this organization's publications on information technology are often referenced in Federal and state laws and regulations and are thus *de facto* government standards for many areas of basic information security.

Multiple Choice

BEC 4-Q6

c. Audit trails

Audit trails automatically record system activity, resulting in a comprehensive log file. Increasing transparency, audit trails provide auditors with valuable information. For instance, these records allow auditors to reconstruct events, detect undocumented system modification, and identify unauthorized access. Audit trails also assist IT department personnel with problem analysis (e.g., processing errors) and improve users' individual accountability over their access and actions within the system.

d. Fraud and fraud deterrence

One of the main conditions of fraud, opportunity, is reduced as a result of duty segregation. A single individual would not be capable of perpetrating large-scale fraud only using his or her user access if user roles and permissions are properly imposed in the information system. The only way a single person could perpetrate a fraud is by colluding with an accomplice or by obtaining authorization credentials to access multiple user accounts.

When collusion is present, preventive controls such as segregation of duties, can be easily circumvented with enough effort. Detective controls are used to compensate for some of the inherent risks. Careful review of system access logs can flag unusual access (e.g., after-hours access).

Review of transaction logs can detect unauthorized changes that could be a result of fraudulent activity.

Multiple Choice

BEC 4-Q7 through BEC 4-Q8

e. COBIT

COBIT 5 is the complete framework of expert-developed, easy-to-use tools for considering IT management and governance holistically within an enterprise. Starting with the first version of COBIT created by the Information Systems Audit and Control Association (ISACA) in 1996, the current 2012 version provides generic guidance to help overcome challenges that result from IT complexity as it relates to IT management and governance. The ultimate objective, when applying COBIT 5, is to find an appropriate balance between IT benefits, risks, and resource use.

At its foundation, COBIT 5 presumes that an organization's IT function can no longer operate independently and indicates that the total integration of IT with strategy and operations is nonnegotiable. This overarching theme is evident throughout the guidance.

COBIT 5 is based on five principles and seven categories of enablers (i.e., factors that enable good governance). It has the intention to be comprehensive, integrating other models and frameworks (e.g., COSO). It is also flexible and can be adapted to any organization, large or small.

1) Five principles of COBIT 5
   Principle 1: Meeting stakeholder needs
   Stakeholder needs drive value creation and are the foundation for an enterprise's strategy. The three stakeholder needs are benefit realization, risk optimization, and resource optimization.

   i. Goal cascade or goal mapping
      COBIT 5 addresses stakeholder needs by starting with a broad view of the organization's goals and then "cascading" down to a specific, actionable level. First, stakeholder drivers (e.g., technology evolution, regulatory environment) influence stakeholder needs. Second, stakeholder needs translate into high-level enterprise goals using balanced score card (BSC) dimensions (e.g., financial, customer, internal, and learning and growth). Third, enterprise goals translate into specific IT-related goals. Fourth, IT-related goals are then mapped to enabler goals (e.g., specific processes).

      The goals cascade helps an organization define relevant and tangible goals and communicate how particular enablers are connected to the achievement of enterprise-level goals.

   Principle 2: Covering the enterprise end-to-end
   COBIT 5 considers the governance of enterprise IT an enterprise-wide endeavor. Rather than operating as a separate IT function or department, IT is considered equal to all other functions in the organization. IT governance and management extend to both internal and external stakeholders. Information is an asset, even though it is not tangible.

   Principle 3: Applying a single integrated framework
   COBIT 5 is an overarching framework that ties together and utilizes other best practice guidance into a single, integrated framework. By defining how this framework relates to other widely adopted frameworks (e.g., COSO, ISO), it simplifies some of the complexity with regard to implementation.

   Principle 4: Enabling a holistic approach
   Governance is systematic and supported by enablers. Enablers are factors that enable good governance and includes anything that can help the organization achieve its objectives. COBIT 5 identifies seven categories of enablers.

   Principle 5: Separating governance from management
   COBIT 5 distinguishes between governance and management citing that the two are entirely separate disciplines with different purposes and organizational structures. Namely, individuals in charge of governance are in a position to evaluate, direct, and monitor the organization to ensure stakeholder needs are met (e.g., ensuring benefits delivery, risk optimization, resource optimization, and stakeholder transparency).

   Conversely, management's function is to handle operations (e.g., plan, build, run, and monitor) based on the direction the governance body has set.

2) Seven enablers of COBIT 5
   i. Enablers
      a) Principles, policies, and frameworks
         Principles and policies (e.g., acceptable use policies) communicate desired behavior on a day-to-day basis. A framework (e.g., COBIT 5) is a basic conceptual structure to address complex issues.

b) Processes
Processes are a collection of activities that manipulate inputs to achieve and produce certain outputs (e.g., objectives). Processes are the result of the goals cascade and relate to SMART (specific, measurable, actionable, relevant, timely) metrics for measuring goals.

c) Organizational structure
The organization structure defines the key decision-making entities in an organization outlining the operating principles, span of control, level of authority, delegation of authority, and escalation procedures.

d) Culture, ethics, and behavior
Culture, ethics, and behavior relate to individual and collective behavior within an organization, including moral decision-making. This enabler is closely linked to the policies enabler due to the necessity that an organization communicates their corporate values, rules, and norms.

e) Information
Information is the basis for knowledge and creates value for stakeholders. The quality (e.g., accuracy, objectivity, relevance, completeness) of information is the primary goal of this enabler.

f) Services, infrastructure, and application
Service capability resources (e.g., infrastructure, applications, technology) contribute to the support of business processes.

g) People, skills, and competencies
The people component of this enabler relates to staff availability and turnover. The skills and competencies component includes the education, qualifications, technical skill, experience, and knowledge required to perform an organizational role successfully.

ii. Enabler dimensions
COBIT 5 suggests that organizations use four dimensions (e.g., stakeholders, goals, life cycle, good practices) to consider and apply enablers in practice. The four dimensions are part of the enabler performance management function and facilitate the constant achievement of enabler goals. Enabler goals are the final step in the goals cascade and consider the operation and expected outcome of each enabler. It is important to note enablers interrelate to each other, a change in one will likely impact others.

Multiple Choice

BEC 4-Q9 through BEC 4-Q10

B. Role of Information Technology in Business
  1. Big data and data analytics

> Recognize the role of big data/data analytics and statistics in supporting business decisions.

As the cost of computer storage capacity has decreased, data collection and archiving have become easier and less expensive. The increasing ease and effortlessness of data collection has resulted in the generation of gigantic stores of raw data, sometimes called big data. Big data is differentiated from other data based on its large volume, velocity (i.e., fast, continuous data generation speed), variety, and veracity (i.e., uncertain data accuracy).

The term big data refers to a large quantity of either structured and unstructured data. Structured data is data organized logically in a spreadsheet or relational database. Unstructured data is not formally organized in a database but could provide meaningful information if properly interpreted. Text (e.g., 10-Ks) and media files (e.g., photos and videos) are typically categorized as unstructured data. Unstructured data offers the greatest potential for new insight.

Creating relevant and reliable management information from this unorganized primordial soup of images, sounds, bits, and bytes require users to either create an algorithm to evaluate patterns in the data or to convert the data to a structured format. For example, a company might use a keyword scoring algorithm to convert the unstructured data of Twitter and Facebook comments into a score representing how positive or negative the stream of posts are over a period of time. This score would allow management to see at a glance the tone and volume of the posts without having to read the thousands of pages of data.

A second approach to analyzing unstructured data is to convert it to a structured data format. For example, many CPA firms use optical character recognition applications to scan paper tax forms and brokerage statements and convert the resulting unstructured data into structured formats which summarize the information for import into the tax software. This approach is designed to replace the human work of reviewing the reports, extracting the data, and keying it into the tax software.

Analysts have the opportunity to leverage big data using data analytics and predictive data processing techniques. Data analytics is the science of interpreting raw data to generate accurate, meaningful information to improve decision-making. Data analytics can be classified into the following stages:
  1) Descriptive – focuses on understanding the past
  2) Diagnostic – focuses on investigating the cause(s) of a particular result
  3) Discovery – focuses on extracting insight from data, including relationships between data
  4) Predictive – focuses on anticipating and predicting the future
  5) Prescriptive – focus on creating feedback to determine how to achieve the desired outcome

Decisions supported by data analytics are considered smarter (i.e., more informed) and more accurate. Also, analysts can more confidently forecast the impact current decisions may have in the future by leveraging and clearly understanding the results of past decisions.

  a. Data visualizations
     Data visualization help data users efficiently understand and clearly communicate information using visual graphics. Data visualizations make it easier to detect trends, data patterns, and correlations in data sets. Visualizations focus on both form and function, trying to provide aesthetically appealing graphics that are also easy to understand.

     Examples include charts/graphs (e.g., bar charts, line graphs, pie charts, scatterplots, bubble charts, tree maps, histograms), information maps or infographics, and summary dashboards. A pie chart and bubble chart are demonstrated at the top of the following page.

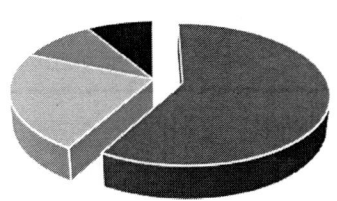
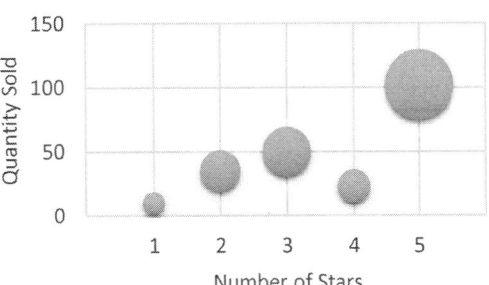

Identify the role of information systems in key business processes within an entity.

2. Integrated systems
   An enterprise resource planning (ERP) system is a robust piece of software and a type of business information system. ERP systems use a set of integrated applications to manage business activities seamlessly. A typical ERP system includes modules for the general ledger, sales, human resources management, payroll processing, accounts receivable monitoring, accounts payable automation, procurement, inventory management, fixed asset management, and vendor file management. In addition to internal data, ERPs can incorporate external data from suppliers and customers.

   When an IT enterprise uses separate software packages for each business activity, the use of manual interfaces is common and can be a hindrance to efficient operations. The main benefit of using an ERP system is that within the system and between modules few, if any, manual interfaces are needed. Once one module in the system updates, all other linked modules update automatically.

   For example, when calculating the required debit to work-in-process inventory for direct labor costs, the applicable direct labor costs can be imported directly from the payroll module, and the user is often unaware of any interaction the system is having with a different ERP module. The cohesiveness of the ERP system eliminates cumbersome manual interfaces that a separate payroll system might require for this calculation.

   Every system has a few drawbacks and ERPs are no exception. Integrated systems are, by nature, complex and therefore difficult to plan. A lot of foresight is required to create and install a system that can handle every aspect of an organization effortlessly. Due to this complexity, there are higher risks associated with implementation. And, of course, ERP systems are very costly and may be too expensive for many small- to medium-size organizations.

   Multiple Choice

   BEC 4-Q11 through BEC 4-Q13

3. Data interfaces
   A data interface transfers defined portions of data between two computer systems. It is crucial that the transfer executes completely and accurately. An interface can be either automated or performed manually. If manual, there are usually reconciliation controls in place to verify completeness and accuracy after the transfer is complete.

   a. Automated interface
      Generally, automated data transfer does not require human interaction. As such, an automated interface does not require the user to export or import data manually. One system seamlessly

transfers data to another on a schedule or when queried. Automated data validation checks the data after the transfer is complete to make sure it matches the data prior to the transfer. Data transmission errors are less likely since the program performs the interface exactly the same way every time.

    b. Manual interface
A manual interface requires the user of the system to facilitate the export and import of data from one system to another. Manual interfaces leave more potential for human error and may result in data transmission errors. A manual reconciliation, or comparison of the transferred data, is one way to detect errors and incomplete transfers.

Multiple Choice

> BEC 4-Q14

4. Transaction processing alternatives – online, real-time processing vs. batch processing
    a. Online, real-time processing
Online, real-time processing can also be referred to as direct access processing. Processing happens immediately, in real-time, as a user inputs the data into the system. Individual records update instantly in the order in which they are input by the user.

A proper internal control environment has logical access controls in place to restrict the access required to update transaction data to authorized personnel. If an error is present, the update will fail, and the user is alerted. Once alerted to an error, the user must modify the data in order continue and for the data to process properly. Two examples of systems that are known for online, real-time processing are point-of-sale retail inventory management systems and credit card authorization systems.

Online processing is grouped by either transaction or analytical processing. Online transaction processing (OLTP) records day-to-day transactions in an accounting information system and its underlying databases. The focus is operational data, such as posting journal entries. The underlying database commands are simple and repetitive (i.e., INSERT, UPDATE, and DELETE).

In online analytical processing (OLAP), a query or request for information extracts data from the system. Compared to OLTP, commands are more complex which means that the user needs fewer commands to extract useful, aggregated information. The focus is summary data, and this type of information is useful for interactive, drill-down reports and financial statements.

Multiple Choice

> BEC 4-Q15 through BEC 4-Q17

    b. Batch processing
This method collects similar transactions that occur over a specified period of time into a batch. Then, all at once, it processes each one sequentially as they appear in the batch. The result is an updated master file. When compared to online, real-time processing, it is common for batch processing to have a significant time delay. For example, a company aggregates all cash disbursements on payables for a single day and processes them together in a batch every evening. When processing is complete, the accounts payable master file is up to date. Batch processing is very efficient for high-volume transaction processing.

Typically, prior to initiating batch processing, a user, or the system, will validate that the data is accurate. Continuing the example, the system might confirm all recorded cash disbursements have a valid vendor number and a valid invoice number. If any invalid numbers are identified, the batch is unable to process. These items determine how the cash disbursement relates to company's accounts payable balance and must be accurate.

Once a batch starts processing, the data within the batch cannot be modified. If modification is necessary, the user can abort processing and restart it later. IT personnel can automate batch processing to start on a schedule or can require a user to manually start processing a batch when instructed. It is common for a batch to process daily and to start processing automatically overnight.

A benefit of using batch processing is that it typically results in an easy-to-follow audit trail. If an error is identified during batch processing, an exception report is generated for manual review.

Multiple Choice

BEC 4-Q18 through BEC 4-Q20

5. Transaction processing alternatives – centralized vs. distributed processing
   A computer's ability to process and manipulate data is called its computing or processing power. Every organization's IT infrastructure has a finite level of processing power. The total processing capacity is dependent on the system's hardware. A system's processing capabilities can be centralized or decentralized (distributed).

   a. Centralized processing
      Historically, when processing power was very expensive, it was common for an organization to use a mainframe computer for centralized processing. As the name suggests, centralized processing occurs at a single location. Terminal computers submit information to the mainframe computer and do not have any processing power of their own. Over time, processing power has become less expensive, and both decentralized processing and distributed processing have become more economical.

   b. Decentralized or distributed processing
      Distributed processing uses processing power from multiple computers in a network to process transactions at various locations. For instance, a large bank could use distributed processing to process daily deposits onsite at each branch, rather than at the main corporate office.

      It is not unusual for a complex organization to have a blended system, utilizing both centralized and decentralized processing for its systems. During system development, the organization needs to consider whether it is more appropriate to use centralized or decentralized processing. An important consideration during the decision-making process is knowing that logical and physical access controls are more difficult in a decentralized environment.

Multiple Choice

BEC 4-Q21 through BEC 4-Q22

6. Electronic commerce

Identify the role of e-commerce in key business processes within an entity.

Commerce is the term used to describe the activity of buying and selling on a macro level. Electronic commerce, or e-commerce, involves engaging in commerce remotely over a network using a computer or other technological device.

Primarily, e-commerce facilitates consumer shopping and other types of purchasing transactions. However, e-commerce is a broad category encompassing more than online shopping. It consists of marketing, sales, payment, fulfillment, procurement (e.g., acquiring inventory from suppliers), and customer service.

Historically, e-commerce began in the mid-1960s with electronic fund transfer (EFT) technology in the banking industry. It evolved in the 1970s to include electronic data interchange (EDI). In the 1990s, the 'World Wide Web' and internet technology revolutionized e-commerce and radically changed the way organizations conduct business. The implications for business, both benefits and risks, are far-reaching.

   a. Methods of electronic commerce
      1) Electronic funds transfer (EFT)
         An enduring predecessor of modern e-commerce, an EFT is an electronic transmission of funds-related transactions using a computer-based system that does not require either party to execute a physical exchange of a financial instrument (e.g., cash, checks). Some examples of EFTs include automatic teller machine (ATM) transactions, wire transfers, debit payments (also known as ACH transactions), and payroll direct deposits. EFT is a type of electronic data interchange (EDI), transferring only monetary information.

Multiple Choice

BEC 4-Q23

      2) Electronic data interchange (EDI)
         EDI extends beyond monetary transactions. It is the exchange of data electronically between trading partners based on agreed-upon message standards to ensure the data is uniformly structured. An EDI often relies on a direct connection between computers, called point-to-point, or a value-added network (VAN). VANs are privately owned networks that offer greater security than an internet connection.

         By exchanging data digitally, EDI reduces the use of paper documents and shortens the cycle time (e.g., the procure-to-pay cycle) for processing transactions. Also, due to agreed-upon message standards and formatting, there is greater assurance that data is transmitted completely and accurately. For instance, medical practitioners are required to use EDI to transmit sensitive patient data to insurance companies in accordance with the Health Insurance Portability and Accountability Act of 1996 (HIPPA).

         The risks of EDI have less to do with security (although always a factor), and more to do with system dependence and processing integrity. System downtime and processing errors can be very detrimental to entities that rely on EDI technology. Another drawback of EDI technology is the high cost of implementation.

Multiple Choice

BEC 4-Q24 through BEC 4-Q26

3) Internet-based e-commerce
By using the internet rather than a private or proprietary network, anyone, consumers and business alike, can participate in e-commerce. Private networks can be costly, and the internet is an easily-accessible, low-cost option.

The internet has created the opportunity for many 'brick-and-mortar' retailers, previously operating only at physical locations, to generate a large percentage of their sales from web-based transactions. Retailers with an online presence typically experience lower advertising costs and more adaptability when consumer trends shift. Plus, from an operations perspective, inventory procurement can be easily integrated with strategy (e.g., just-in-time inventory management).

From the consumer perspective, benefits of e-commerce can range from additional product choices, more competitive pricing, expedited product research, easier customer inquiry (e.g., requests for quotes), and quicker payments.

The primary disadvantage is that, inherently, public networks are less secure, especially when compared to EDI using private networks. Data breaches and transmission disruptions are more common over the internet. Proper design of controls and the use of encryption mitigate many of the risks associated with internet-based e-commerce; however, it remains the least secure transmission method.

b. E-commerce transaction types
E-commerce is subdivided into four transaction types, depending on the parties' involved in the transaction.

1) Business to business (B2B)
Transactions between two business organizations for goods and service, rather than the end-user or consumer (e.g., a wholesale purchase by a retailer).

2) Business to consumer (B2C)
Transactions occur between a vendor and the end-user, the consumer, of a product or service (e.g., Amazon, Rakuten).

3) Consumer to consumer (C2C)
Transactions conducted between two individuals, selling or trading products or services (e.g., eBay, Craigslist, Venmo).

4) Mobile commerce (m-commerce)
Transactions conducted in a wireless environment over mobile devices (e.g., Poshmark, Tradesy, Gilt).

c. Controls over electronic commerce
All participants in e-commerce are vulnerable to a number of universal technology risks. These risks relate to security, availability, processing integrity, confidentiality, and privacy. The data, especially while in transmission, is at the greatest risk.

Controls over e-commerce aim to mitigate risk factors. An adequate internal control environment, with well-designed IT general controls, is the foundation for risk mitigation. Special consideration is given to controls that safeguard data during transmission (e.g., encryption); prevent and minimize downtime; and fulfill legal and regulatory requirements for confidentiality and privacy.

1) Encryption for e-commerce
   Consumer confidence in e-commerce depends on secure transmission of data including sensitive financial information (e.g., credit card numbers or bank account numbers). Encryption is crucial to protect this information. Encryption secures the data as it is transmitted between trading partners in EFT, EDI, and internet-based e-commerce systems.

   EDI, inclusive of many types of EFTs, offers a high level of security using encryption via hardware, rather than software. Encryption using hardware that is physically secured generally provides better security than encryption by software. Encryption using hardware means that to circumvent the control you must first gain access to the hardware, whereas software is more easily compromised through modifying the code.

   Internet-based e-commerce depends on the public-key infrastructure (PKI) and the use of digital encryption certificates to create trust. Digital certificates are formally issued and revoked, as necessary, by Certification Authorities (CAs). Recall, CAs are third-party entities that sign digital certificates to confirm the information submitted by the entity concerning their public key is legitimate.

   Multiple Choice
   BEC 4-Q27

   i. WebTrust$^{SM/TM}$
      The WebTrust Program for Certification Authorities is a branded assurance service that assesses the adequacy and effectiveness of the controls employed by Certification Authorities (CAs).

      The program was developed jointly by the AICPA and CPA Canada. An unqualified assurance report entitles the CA to display the WebTrust seal on its website to communicate controls in place are operating effectively. The WebTrust brand is flexible by design and can its criteria can be modified to evaluate CAs that are diverse in structure and size.

7. Opportunities for business process reengineering
   The internet has challenged the old adage "if it isn't broken, don't fix it." Business process reengineering (BPR) redesigns an organization's workflow to identify inefficiency, eliminate redundancy, and optimize processes using state-of-the-art technology. By radically rethinking the way work is done, rather than just automating it, an organization can refocus on its goals and streamline operations. Proper application of BPR can increase productivity and competitiveness. The major criticism for BPR is that is can be used as the justification for downsizing. The organizational culture must be willing and receptive to change for a BPR project to be successful.

   Multiple Choice
   BEC 4-Q28

8. Roles of internet evolution on business operations and organization cultures
   The internet is a catalyst for globalization or a breakdown of cultural and geographical borders. As the brick-and-mortar paradigm shifts, the internet is making room for global e-commerce. Developments in communication have facilitated global interaction, enabling organizations to form diverse distributed teams that can work remotely from anywhere in the world. For example, many professional service firms have large offshore offices in low-cost locales, which perform a wide range of professional services using data from US companies.

The internet has created new competitive marketspaces and given rise to disruptive technologies in many established industries. Ride-sharing companies (e.g., Uber, Lyft) have rethought the way traditional cab companies operate and are revolutionizing the industry. Without the internet, these companies would not exist.

The evolution of the internet can be summarized into several stages of development.

a. Web 1.0
With its introduction in the 1990s, the 'World Wide Web' changed the relevancy of time and space. It created the opportunity for an organization to have a global, 24/7 presence. During this first stage of development, the internet was primarily read-only, and users could enjoy easily accessible, on-demand content without leaving the comfort of their own home.

b. Web 2.0
At the turn of the century, communication started to develop beyond e-mail as user-produced content, and social networking took hold. Interactive sharing of personal information using social media (e.g., Facebook, YouTube, Twitter, etc.) redefined the primary purpose of the internet.

c. Web 3.0
As the internet continues to evolve, existing technologies are becoming more personalized and are empowering the web to become more intelligent and omnipresent. For example, retailers (e.g., Amazon) are tailoring their online marketing campaigns by interfacing with social media to identify individual consumer preferences and target audiences. This stage can also be referred to as the semantic (meaning-centric) web, web of context, or the web of linked data.

d. Web 4.0 and beyond
The internet is becoming less visible and more integrated into the physical world. Humans and machines are starting to interact symbiotically, mutually dependent on one another. Hence, Web 4.0 is labeled the symbiotic web. It is anticipated that the internet will evolve into an Internet of Things (IoT), where objects (e.g., appliances) have the ability to connect to the internet, enabling object-to-object interaction without human involvement. Additionally, research is being conducted that would enable a device to perceptive human emotion, relying on artificial intelligence.

Multiple Choice

BEC 4-Q29

9. Cryptocurrencies
A cryptocurrency is a fiat digital currency that does not exist in physical form, is not backed by a government or central bank, and is not tied to any commodities or underlying assets. These currencies are built, tracked, and regulated on a blockchain skeleton, which makes them very resistant to tampering or counterfeiting. Blockchain is a public open-source, decentralized ledger system that records transactions digitally across a peer-to-peer network. Anyone can confirm transactions without a certifying authority since each block (representing a transaction) that is added to the chain is permanent and unalterable.

There are over 100 players in the Financial Technology (FinTech) industry, each offering a different cryptocurrency. The top 5 cryptocurrencies in 2017 are:
- Bitcoin (61%)
- Ethereum (14%)
- Bitcoin cash (6%)
- Ripple (4%)
- Litecoin (1.5%)

In August 2017, the FinTech industry experienced infighting between developers, causing a "hard fork" that divided Bitcoin into two. This resulted in a new currency strand called Bitcoin Cash.

Accounting for cryptocurrencies is not well defined, and current US GAAP suggests recording bitcoins and other cryptocurrencies as intangible assets, not as foreign currencies or investments.

The potential benefits of blockchain technology are increased transparency and a permanent, unalterable ledger. However, it's implementation for potential applications (such as banking, voting, and healthcare recordkeeping) are still in their infancy.

10. Automation

    Structured, repeatable tasks are easily automated and, with the advances in artificial intelligence, some seemingly complex tasks can now be automated without substantial cost or difficulty. Automation replaces a manual process with a computer-assisted process that requires little to no human intervention.

    Much of the data entry work historically performed by accounting clerks and bookkeepers is now automated. Areas where automation has or is likely to increase efficiency include:
    - Bank feeds, or other external third-party data, that automatically interface with accounting software
    - Automatic source documentation matching with the assistance of predictive technology, expediting reconciliations (e.g., invoices are matched to likely corresponding items on bank feed to expedite the bank reconciliation process)
    - Automatic, predictive account coding for transactions
    - Automatic processing of invoices and initiation of payment procedures, flagging invoices without corresponding receiving reports for follow-up
    - In auditing, the automation of testing procedures, using wizard-driven CAAT software that allows auditors to automate sample selection, evaluation, and in some cases, increase sample sizes (up to 100% testing, the entire population)

While automation will increase audit quality and save both time and money, it puts entry-level jobs at risk. However, automation results in fewer human errors and decreases fraud risk, so it is likely to be used as a tool for humans until its accuracy can be validated.

C. Information Security/Availability

> Recognize the risks and controls associated with protecting sensitive and critical information within an organization's information technology environment (the use of mobile technology, data storage devices, data transmission, cybersecurity, etc.)

1. Protection of information

    Information security is of paramount concern for modern, technology-reliant organizations. Information security is designed to defend an organization's IT infrastructure from unauthorized access and modification. When a security breach occurs, it can wreak havoc on consumer trust. Sensitive data (e.g., credit card information) is often the target of a breach. Organizations must exercise extreme vigilance; intruders are constantly seeking new vulnerabilities to exploit.

    Strong and reliable internal controls secure the information stored within a system and prevent it from falling into the wrong hands. Managing access and encrypting data are primary techniques for security management. Logical access, or a user's ability to connect to a computer system, and physical access must be carefully guarded and restricted to authorized individuals. If access controls fail, encryption ensures information is unreadable.

    Cybersecurity is a subcomponent of information security, as follows:

    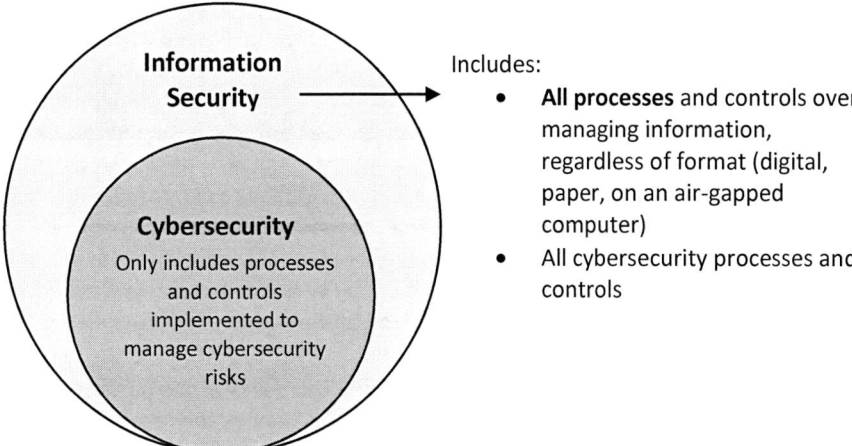

    The purpose of cybersecurity initiatives is to address cybersecurity risks that would threaten the organization (e.g., impede compliance, timely financial reporting, or unhindered operations). A security incident is an event that requires prompt action to protect data or other company assets.

    One of a company's most vulnerable assets is the personally identifiable information (PXI) it maintains about its employees and customers. PXI is used as a generic term for personally identifiable information such as name, social security number, address, and telephone number which is covered by restrictive legal or contractual compliance requirements. Types of PXI include the following:
    - PII - Personally Identifiable Information, which is the term for private data which is protected by many identify theft laws and regulations.
    - PHI - Protected Healthcare Information, which includes not only the general personally identifiable information, but also includes most healthcare information related to the subject patient or employee.
    - SPI - Sensitive Personal Information, which is a synonym for PII.

    Another acronym you are likely to see is SANS (System Administration, Audit, Network, and Security), as in SANS Institute, a provider of information security and cybersecurity training.

a. Data encryption
Data encryption is a security technique that protects data from unauthorized viewing. Encryption converts sensitive data into an unreadable form, or ciphertext, using an algorithm called a cipher. A key is needed to decrypt the ciphertext, converting back into readable data. A hacker, or other unauthorized user, is powerless to decrypt the information without the proper corresponding key.

Data is the most vulnerable when it is transmitted through a network. To increase security, data is encrypted prior to transmission by the sender and decrypted by the recipient. There are two types of encryption: public-key (asymmetrical) encryption and private-key (symmetrical) encryption.

   1) Public-key encryption

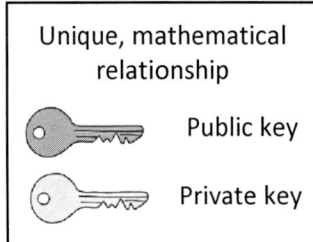

Using a pair of keys, the sender will use one key to encrypt the data, and the recipient will use another to decrypt it. It is considered asymmetrical because each key is distinct, although the keys are mathematically related. Distribution of the public key does not compromise the security of the data and enables anyone to encrypt a message. The second, private key enables only the intended recipient to decrypt the data properly. The recipient must closely guard the private key. Transmitting a private key to the recipient over a network has the potential to compromise its secrecy. If the private key must be transmitted over a potentially unsecured network, it is often broken into fragments and, as a precaution, each piece is sent separately. That way if one fragment is intercepted, the encrypted data is still safe. All the fragments would need to be intercepted and reassembled to decrypt the data.

The most common public-key encryption method is called RSA encryption, named for developers Ron Rivest, Adi Shamir, and Leonard Adleman. RSA uses a cryptographic algorithm of prime numbers.

In addition to encryption, RSA can also be used as a technique for non-repudiation, offering proof of the origin of the transmitted data. A sender digitally signs a message using a calculation based on the sender's private key. The recipient, without knowledge of the sender's private key, can confirm the calculation is accurate based on knowledge of the corresponding public key. Web browsers (e.g., Internet Explorer, Mozilla Firefox) rely on RSA or other comparable cipher algorithms for both encryption and digital signature functions. Examples are SSL/TLS protocols, identified with HTTPS prior to the domain name.

   2) Private-key encryption

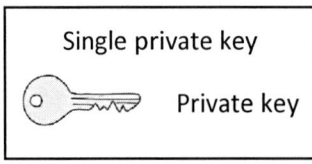
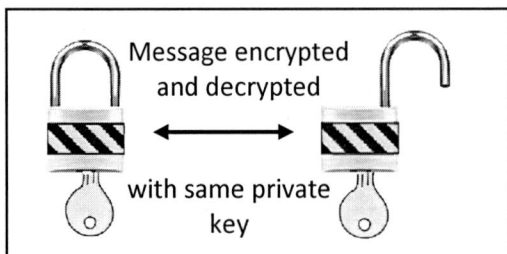

The defining feature of private-key encryption is that one key is used for both encryption and decryption. It can also be referred to as symmetric encryption. It is imperative that both the sender and receiver keep the key confidential. Unauthorized knowledge of the key can compromise the security of encrypted data.

The two most common examples of private-key algorithms are the Data Encryption Standard (DES) and Advanced Encryption Standard (AES). Of the two standards, AES is superior and preferred by the U.S. government and businesses worldwide. It supersedes DES in reputable information security guidance (e.g., National Institute of Technology and Standards [NIST]).

Multiple Choice
BEC 4-Q30 through BEC 4-Q31

b. Digital certificates
Digital certificates are essential to securely conducting electronic commerce. A digital certificate is an electronic document that communicates the genuine origin and integrity of data transmitted over the internet. It verifies the authenticity of a website and offers assurance the entity can securely transmit information online using the public-key infrastructure (PKI). The PKI provides the consistent basis for the issuance and maintenance of digital certificates and the uniform management of public-key encryption.

For an entity to obtain a digital certificate, it must first generate or purchase a corresponding public and private key. The entity submits documentation to a Certification Authority (CA) (e.g., Symantec, formerly VeriSign) or a Registration Authority (RA) to register the key pair. Either the CA or RA will perform verification procedures to confirm that the public key does, in fact, belong to the entity and, if no issues are identified, the CA will issue a signed digital certificate. Digital certificates are only valid for a finite period, usually expiring after one year.

c. Digital signatures
The digital equivalent of a handwritten signature, a digital signature authenticates a transmitted message in two ways. First, it verifies the message originated from the named sender and, second, confirms the message has not been altered during transmission. The process employs an asymmetric cryptographic algorithm such as RSA encryption. Generally, when the sender transmits a digitally signed message, the sender's private key is used to generate the digital signature and the sender's public key is used to verify the signature.

Multiple Choice
BEC 4-Q32

d. Security policies
Policies are the source of an organization's internal control structure. Outlined in writing, policies specify the rules and procedures that must be adhered to within the organization. A typical information security policy is topic-specific, addressing a single security factor or concern. Policies over encryption, acceptable use, disaster recovery, email, and passwords each cover a different security-related factor and dictate requirements for each topic. Lax policies can lead to inconsistent governance and security vulnerabilities.

1) Acceptable encryption and end-user encryption key protection policies
Policies define which encryption algorithms (e.g., DES, AES, and RSA) are acceptable for use within the organization and requirements concerning the management and confidentiality of encryption keys.

2) Acceptable use policy
The policy outlines and governs the appropriate use of technology and computer equipment at an organization. Inappropriate use exposes the organization to risk (e.g., viruses) and proper use

protects the organization's computer resources and proprietary information. Policies typically cover the general use and ownership of an organization's systems; guidelines concerning personal use; security of proprietary information; and expressly prohibited use of the system, network, email, and social media.

Multiple Choice

BEC 4-Q33

3) Disaster recovery plan policy
The policy states the requirement to have a disaster recovery plan. Depending on the scope of the policy, it may include plan content requirements (e.g., hierarchy of critical applications, responsible party contact information).

4) Digital signature acceptance policy
The policy defines the requirements for when a digital signature is permitted as a substitute for a handwritten signature, equivalent in reputability.

5) Email policy
The policy outlines the acceptable and unacceptable use of the organization's email system. Typically, the policy covers email forwarding restrictions, prohibited content (e.g., offensive or disruptive messages), monitoring, and privacy. Also, the extent of personal communication that is permissible using enterprise resources is discussed.

6) Password construction guidelines and password protection policy
The policy sets the standards for passwords syntax, change frequency, and rules over password protection and sharing.

e. Multi-factor authentication
Authentication is how a computer system verifies that a user is permitted to access a restricted system. The most common, basic form of authentication is a unique username and password. This offers a relatively low level of cybersecurity.

Multi-factor authentication is typically preferred for sensitive systems and data. Two-factor (or two-step) authentication requires each user to enter both a password and another piece of evidence that the user is who they say they are (often a physical key, ID card, or biometric scan). ATMs use two-factor authentication and require both a debit card and a PIN to withdraw cash.

Multi-factor authentication for the most sensitive systems will involve biometrics, behavior analytics, and passwords. Multi-factor authentication safeguards against data breaches that result from lax password controls.

2. IT general controls (including logical and physical access controls)

> **Identify weaknesses and mitigation strategies within an entity's IT environment in relation to logical and physical access controls.**

> **Identify weaknesses and mitigation strategies within an entity's IT environment in relation to IT general and application controls.**

General controls are relevant to an entire processing environment and all the information systems and applications within it. General control objectives focus on the overall security and reliability of the system's operations and output.

Within an organization, systems often share a common set of policies and procedures defining objectives over logical access, program change management, system development, computer operations, backup and recovery, and physical access. Controls exist to achieve management's control objectives. A collection of controls, in combination with each other, aim to create an adequate internal control structure in accordance with Sarbanes-Oxley 404. The design and operating effectiveness of a control is evaluated to determine adequacy.

Logical access to programs and data
- Policy and procedure documentation
- User authentication and password policies
- Access administration
  - New user access authorization and provisioning
  - Access modification and revokation (job change or termination)
  - Privileged user appropriateness
  - Periodic user reviews

Program change management
- Policy and procedure documentation
- Change request and authorization
- Change testing
- Migration approval
- Implementation
  - Segregation of duties
- Emergency changes

Program development and SDLC
- Methodology for system development and acquisition
  - Planning
  - Analysis
  - Design and authorization
  - Development
  - Testing
  - Implementation
  - Verification
- Data migration

Computer operations and processing
- Data Transmission
- Incident and problem management
- Environmental controls
- Backup and recovery
  - Backup
  - Incident management
  - Contingency planning

Physical access to programs and data
- Biometric devices
- Visitor logs

1) <u>Logical access to programs and data controls</u>
   Logical access is the ability a user has to connect to a computer system. The primary control objective is to provide reasonable assurance that logical access to system resources (programs and data) is restricted to authorized individuals.

   As a starting point to address this main objective, it is important for the organization to have policies over IT in place. Formal policies ensure all objectives are addressed consistently. Policy and procedure documentation communicates policy expectations to personnel. The design of most controls, not just logical access controls, can be evaluated by inspecting policies and procedure documentation.

   In most computerized systems, authentication is required for access. Authentication is a way of verifying that a user has permission to access the system. A unique username and password is the most common approach for authentication. Sensitive information may dictate the need for two-factor authentication, or a combination of a password and another component (often a physical key, ID card, or biometric scan).

If a system uses passwords for authentication, the organization should establish rules for syntax and expiration. For example, management's password policy requires passwords that are: at least 8 characters in length; include alpha, numeric, and special characters; include upper and lower-case letters; and expire after 90 days. Management has discretion as to what policies to adopt. Password policy variations are common in practice.

Once authenticated as a user, access within the processing environment is often restricted using roles, profiles, or permissions. Limitations are constructed based on job responsibilities and help systematically enforce segregation between duties.

Careful application of access administration controls is important to accomplish the primary logical access objective. When provisioning access to new users, procedures should be in place to guide how to request and approve access properly. Organizations need a rule-based authorization mechanism to provision access based on job function and prevent conflict in duty segregation. Equally, if not more important, access must be modified or revoked when a user's job function changes or employment is terminated. User accounts should be added, modified, and deleted in a timely manner.

Access management and control software support access controls in large or complex organizations. The software can control user identification and passwords for multiple applications and may permit the use of single sign-on (SSO) technology. Single sign-on allows the user to log-in once to gain access to all linked systems without additional prompts.

Privileged or superuser (e.g., an administrator in Windows, root in LINUX/UNIX, SAP_ALL in SAP, PeopleSoft Administrator in PeopleSoft, etc.) access appropriateness is a key internal control for system security. Inherently, this type of access is risky for the organization since access at this level could circumvent other system controls. Extreme care should be exercised to limit this level of access to a small, trustworthy group of individuals. Often, privileged access is granted only to a select few in the IT department such as system administrators and database administrators.

Management should perform a periodic (annually, semi-annually, or quarterly) review of user access rights to systems to verify rights are assigned appropriately based on job responsibilities. This review identifies any users with inappropriate access that might have been previously overlooked and corrects the oversight.

Multiple Choice

BEC 4-Q34 through BEC 4-Q35

2) Program change management controls
    The main control objective for program change is that adequate controls ensure that changes to existing systems (or applications) are authorized, tested, approved, properly implemented, and documented. The controls put in place by an organization for program change mirror the system development lifecycle (SDLC) steps adopted by the organization.

    Policies and procedures over program change must be documented and adhered to by management. Within the procedure documentation, the method for initiating and requesting authorization for a change is outlined (e.g., submitting a change ticket). Typically, once a change has been requested, it must be authorized, tested, and approved prior to implementation. Each step must be completed sequentially unless it is an emergency change.

In an organization with strong internal controls, an appropriate level of management will authorize every change to make certain it meets user requirements and does not exceed budgetary restrictions. Once authorization is granted, the change is made in the testing environment. A testing environment is established to determine potential issues that might result from the change in a relatively low-risk environment rather than production, which would result in higher risk.

Formal testing is performed, and sign-off is obtained from both users and information system personnel. Without sign-off, the implementation cannot proceed. Once obtained, sign-off constitutes migration approval, and the change is now ready for implementation in the production environment. A change management administrator must perform the change migration or installation as dictated by proper segregation of duties. As such, the person who developed the change should not have access to implement it.

Occasionally, the system requires an emergency change which must be implemented immediately into production. The policy for emergency changes will likely differ from normal changes, either eliminating or expediting steps. For example, an email could suffice as appropriate documentation for the change request, rather than submitting a change ticket. Also, the change may bypass standard testing procedures assuming approval from a high-level manager is granted.

3) Program development and system development lifecycle (SDLC) controls
The general objective of program development and the system development lifecycle is that adequate controls are in place to ensure new systems (or applications) are authorized, tested, approved, properly implemented, and documented.

Controls over program development are not applicable to every organization during every audit (or attestation) period. Controls over the organization's adopted SDLC can only be evaluated for effectiveness when the organization has at least one instance of program development on which to judge. When the organization is only maintaining existing technology, these controls cannot be tested and controls over program change take precedence.

In periods when the organization does have new system development or acquisition projects, strict adherence to the adopted SDLC is necessary for an adequate internal control environment to exist. As with program change, each step of the SDLC corresponds to one or more internal controls. Since the SDLC can vary from organization to organization, the controls are also likely to vary.

An example of a control for the analysis stage of the SDLC is that management prepares appropriate system documentation. Appropriate, in this case, is defined by management. Often, appropriate documentation must include a discussion of scope and budget.

Once personnel clearly define and document the project in accordance management's documentation controls, the project must be approved by senior management. This senior-management approval, or project authorization, is a control that corresponds to the design/approval stage of the SDLC.

Organizations often address the remaining stages of a typical SDLC with a single control. This control ensures systems that are either developed or acquired are authorized, tested, and approved. Sign-off by an appropriate individual is typically required for each item. Finally, a review is performed post-implementation to verify processing accuracy.

Controls over data migration safeguard data as it is converted into different file formats and ensure the data is imported into the new system completely and accurately. Completeness and accuracy are determined by comparing and reviewing legacy data files. It is best practice to maintain legacy data files for reference during the entire conversion process.

Multiple Choice

BEC 4-Q36

4) <u>Computer operations and processing controls</u>
The primary objective for computer operations and processing is that adequate controls ensure system processing is authorized, scheduled, and deviations from scheduled processing are identified and resolved.

This control objective is mainly relevant to the batch processing, data interface and transmission, and backup and recovery. Controls provide reasonable assurance that processing (often referred to as job processing) is monitored appropriately and deviations are identified and resolved. Issues are addressed and resolved according to procedures over incident management. Instructions for incident management should be documented, reviewed periodically for changes, and approved by an appropriate individual.

Backup and recovery controls provide reasonable assurance that programs, files, and data are backed up periodically. A common backup rotation scheme is a grandfather-father-son scheme. The grandfather file is a monthly full backup that makes a copy of all data files to date. The father file is a weekly differential backup, copying only data that has changed since the last full backup. The son file is a daily incremental backup file, copying the transaction activity since the last incremental backup, not including any previous activity.

Contingency planning ensures processing continuity if adverse events occur to disrupt operations. Policies and the resulting internal controls increase awareness of procedures and mitigate risk. Adverse event scenarios should be evaluated based on likelihood and risk of data loss. Highly likely or exceedingly risky scenarios should take priority for training exercises and practice drills.

Environmental controls defend against conditions that might negatively impact computer hardware. Air conditioning should be adequate in terms of both temperature and humidity. Smoke detectors and the fire suppression systems should regularly be inspected for functionality. The auxiliary power supplies (e.g., uninterruptible power sources, standby generators) should be inspected for operability. The facility should be tidy and dust-free. Equipment should be elevated to protect against water damage. Controls ensure these expectations are met.

5) <u>Physical access to programs and data</u>
Regarding physical access, the main objective is to ensure controls are in place that restrict access to facilities that house processing equipment and storage media to appropriate personnel. Care should be taken to restrict physical access to information systems, especially those relevant to financial reporting, to reduce the risk of unauthorized access, malicious or accidental damage, and other mishaps. Card readers and biometric devices may be used to ensure that physical access to computer facilities that house the financial applications and data (e.g., data centers) are restricted to appropriate personnel. Visitor logs, and the review of such logs, is used to document entry and exit of secure areas and identify unauthorized access.

Multiple Choice

BEC 4-Q37

3. System disruption/resolution

> **Describe an entity's disaster recovery/business continuity plans, including threat identification and mitigation strategies, data backup and recovery procedures, alternate processing facilities, etc.**

A natural disaster (or another unanticipated adverse event) has the potential to cause interruption to the availability of crucial systems and data. It is essential for organizations to prepare for such an event with an organization-specific disaster recovery plan. Proper preparedness can limit the potential for unanticipated system downtime, ensuring the continuity of operations.

The goal of every disaster recovery plan is to establish alternative methods for processing important information quickly. The plan should aim to minimize disruption to the organization. Since the risk is highest for critical systems, including priorities in the plan to help focus the recovery effort.

It cannot be overemphasized that careful planning of policies and procedures over disaster recovery and business continuity are extremely important. A well-crafted plan includes: identification of an alternate processing site; a roster of names, locations, and contact information for key vendors; copies of all insurance policies; a list of current hardware configurations; a list identifying critical applications and priority for recovery.

Leading practices also dictate that the plan clarifies the duties of all responsible team members. Duties of responsible parties might entail securing or activating temporary facilities, installing and configuring software, restoring saved system data from backup files, and coordinating recovery efforts. The plan should include the necessary contact information to expedite communication.

Also, to resume normal operations as quickly as possible, responsible team members should be trained to execute the recovery plan and be able to perform under emergency conditions. All responsibilities must be defined and assigned to a primary and secondary (or backup) person, if the primary person is unable to perform his or her duties.

No matter how detailed a plan, the key is to perform periodic testing of the plan to ensure it is functional and can be executed efficiently and effectively. The mock disaster exercise or drill should be taken very seriously. After each test, the lessons learned should be discussed by management and participants. Modifications should be made to improve the plan whenever possible as a result of all lessons learned from the drill.

A system revert (or rollback) is often the first technique an organization attempts to resolve a critical error or catastrophic malfunction in the operations of a computer system. The computer technician goes back to a previously saved copy of the data that functions properly without issues, in the same way, the undo button reverses the last action. If this is not possible, alternative processing might be needed.

A cost-benefit analysis is used to determine the appropriate type backup site for an organization. Generally, it is more expensive to provide the most protection against the ramifications of an information system catastrophe. Careful consideration is required to select the right approach for each organization. Three common alternatives are for backup facilities are: a hot site, a warm site, or a cold site.

	Hot Site	Warm Site	Cold Site
Key feature	Proactive	Preventive	Reactive
Relative cost	$$$	$$	$
Alternative processing facilities	✓	✓	✓
Redundant hardware	✓	✓	Delivery/installation required
Pre-installed software	✓	Installation required	Installation required
Data	Import required*	Import required	Import required

*Exception when flying-start recovery is implemented

a. Hot site (proactive) recovery
A hot site allows for an almost immediate transition from the organization's normal processing location to an alternate processing site. The backup facilities are equipped with redundant hardware and software. When necessary to restore normal operations, hot site disaster recovery procedures simply require the company to import their data. If up-to-date data is automatically mirrored at the alternative processing site, it is called a flying start site. For example, a commercial disaster recovery service that provides a turnkey facility for alternative processing will import and restore backup data on the redundant systems periodically during the day enabling a flying start with basically no downtime. An internal hot site can also allow for instantaneous cutover to the backup system.

Although it is the most expensive alternative, hot sites limit downtime in the event of a disaster. An organization must determine if the added expense is justifiable. It might be appropriate if consequences of downtime could produce a loss of revenue or decrease in customer satisfaction.

b. Warm site (preventive) recovery
A warm site is a location with pre-installed equipment and hardware. In the event of a disaster, the equipment is ready for the recovery team to import all the necessary software and data. Critical applications are not pre-loaded onto the hardware. Downtime is usually brief, and full functionality can be restored quickly.

c. Cold site (reactive) recovery
A cold site is a disaster recovery site that is a dormant shell, waiting for an emergency to occur to activate. If required, the site is ready to receive duplicate equipment; however, equipment is not at the location yet. The cold site is the least expensive option but can result in downtime.

An organization can arrange a reciprocal agreement (or mutual aid pact) to manage costs. The agreement states that either party is required to come to the other party's aid during a disaster by offering their facilities as an alternative processing site. This alternative processing site can be set up as a hot site, warm site, or cold site.

Multiple Choice
BEC 4-Q38 through BEC 4-Q46

D. Processing Integrity (Input/Processing/Output) Controls

> Describe the role of input, processing, and output controls within an entity to support completeness, accuracy and continued processing integrity.

> Determine the appropriateness of the design and operating effectiveness of application controls (authorizations, approvals, tolerance levels, input edits, etc.).

> Identify issues related to the design and effectiveness of IT control activities, including manual vs. automated controls, as well as preventive, detective and corrective controls.

1. IT application controls
   Application controls are specific to a particular process or subsystem (e.g., accounts receivable) and relate to the use of IT to initiate, record (input), process, and report (output) data. The number and scope of controls are unique to the specific processing environment and align with managements' policies.

   Generally, application controls are either automated (programmed) or manual. When a control is performed manually, it is also called a user control.

   1) Automated controls
      Automated controls are programmed to enforce organizational policies and procedures without user intervention. Due to their nature, controls of this type must be integrated into the design of the system and are not subject to breakdowns due to human failure. They are useful to help mitigate specific organizational risks ranging from fraud due to unauthorized access to routine input errors.

      i. Application access controls
         An extension of general logical access controls, application access, controls also secure access to and increase monitoring of specific processing operations and accounting tasks, such as posting adjusting journal entries. Within the general ledger application, for instance, the system is configured to require the review and approval of adjusting journal entries by a supervisor before being transferred to the general ledger. This control automatically prevents a user from posting the entry until proper approval is obtained. Additionally, the system is configured to restrict the level of access required to create adjusting journal entries in the general ledger system to appropriate personnel.

      ii. Input (validation) controls
          Programmed controls can significantly decrease the risk of input error and, by validating the data that a user inputs, it can increase data reliability. A small inaccuracy made while inputting data could lead to a much larger issue in the final financial statements. Input controls validate that the data is complete and accurate. If not, there are often warnings and error messages configured to alert users of inaccuracies and exceptions noted during data input. The user is unable to submit information without correcting the error.

          a) Preformatting forces the user to input data in a specific way, increasing consistency. A blank form is labeled to resemble a hardcopy document.
          b) Record counts keep track of the total of the number of records processed in a batch and can be used to identify incomplete data processing.
          c) A check digit, or checksum, confirms the accuracy of data input manually by comparing the check digit to the sum or product of a predefined algorithm

calculated using the other digits input by the user (e.g., 7 is the checksum for account number 1032017, 1+0+3+2+0+1=7).
d) A field check, or allowed character check, restricts the type of information (e.g., numerical data only) the user inputs into a field.
e) A validity check, like a field check, tests the input to ensure data is reasonable (valid) based on a set of programmed conditions (e.g., dates have a feasible day, month, and year).
f) A null (missing) data check prevents the user from submitting a blank field that would result in incomplete records.
g) Reasonableness tests, or limit checks, restrict values to within a certain upper and lower limit or range (e.g., billable hours per day < 12 hours)
h) An edit check compares data to criteria, such as format, and rejects inappropriate data (e.g., a nine-digit social security number must use the XXX-XX-XXX format and only contain numbers).
i) A hash total is a meaningless value that checks for completeness of the input (e.g., totaling the employees' identification numbers to ensure that all payroll records have been included in a payroll batch to be processed).
j) A redundant data check, or duplicate check, prevents duplicate identifiers (e.g., product IDs) from being recorded in the system.
k) A logic check prevents illogical input based on predefined relationships (e.g., a customer has more than one order, but an order can only have one customer).

Multiple Choice

BEC 4-Q47 through BEC 4-Q48

iii. Processing controls
Processing controls ensure data integrity exists throughout the manipulation and processing of the data by the computer. Data integrity includes accuracy, completeness, and consistency.

a) A control total is a meaningful value established prior to the processing of a batch transaction, confirming the processing was complete and accurate (e.g., total revenue).
b) A three-way match checks to make sure valid corresponding documents (e.g., invoice, purchase order, and receiving report) exist prior to generating a payment. A three-way match prevents erroneous or fraudulent cash disbursements and override would require creating a fictitious invoice, purchase order, and receiving report. Each document originates from a different source and requires a different level of system access to create. Plus, to prevent fictitious invoices, the system could require a valid customer number to be assigned to each invoice. The potential to override the control is low, especially without privileged user access, and requiring a valid customer number compensates for some of the risk if the three-way match control did not operate effectively. Controls build on one another to strengthen the internal control environment.

Multiple Choice

BEC 4-Q49 through BEC 4-Q50

2) User (manual) controls
Manual controls require user execution of the control. Regardless of the advancement of automation technology, the review of system output continues to be an important manual control. The role of the user is to follow-up on exception reports and reconciliation reports. While a computer can identify inconsistencies, fixing the issue often requires user discretion to evaluate the item and determine the next steps.

i. Output controls
   The user is often responsible for verifying the output against source documents and control totals. The user is also responsible for determining if the output is reasonable, complete, and accurate using professional judgment. Audit trails and error listings are also reviewed by the user to identify issues and initiate follow-up procedures.

Multiple Choice

BEC 4-Q51

Internal controls are designed to be preventive, detective, or corrective. The timing and nature of the control allow it to be classified in one of the three categories.

3) Preventive controls
   Preventive controls aim to deter the occurrence of errors and fraudulent activities and are designed to stop unauthorized acts before they happen. Security and access controls are typically classified as preventive. Examples consist of password policies to prevent unauthorized access and a proper request for access prior to when the access is provisioned. Physical access controls are also preventive since they deter intruders and protect an organization's data.

4) Detective controls
   Detective controls help identify errors and fraud that have previously occurred within the organization when preventive controls fail to stop an undesirable act. Detective controls are in place to discover and communicate issues in a timely manner. Examples include reconciling that organization's account balances, and the bank's balance reported on a bank statement, vouching an amount reported in the financial statements or other report to corresponding source documents, and monitoring a variance between actual and budgeted amounts.

5) Corrective controls
   Corrective controls correct errors and irregularities discovered after the fact. This type of control not only identifies an issue, but plays an active role in alleviating the issue and restoring functionality. An example of a corrective control is the removal of inappropriate user access following a user access review performed by managers.

Multiple Choice

BEC 4-Q52 through BEC 4-Q54

2. Testing control design and operational effectiveness
   As required by Section 404 of the Sarbanes-Oxley Act of 2002 (SOX 404), management must report on the company's internal control over financial reporting. Included in this report must be an assessment of the internal controls and statement regarding the framework used to determine operational effectiveness. Procedures must be sufficient to evaluate the design of the company's internal controls and to test for operating effectiveness.

   a. Test of design (TOD)
      The test of design evaluates if a control is suitably designed to prevent material misstatement or to detect it in a timely manner. The design is ineffective if implemented controls, in combination, do not meet the control objectives established by management or a key control is missing.

   b. Test of operating effectiveness (TOE)
      Operating effectiveness involves verifying if a control is operating as expected based on its design, without exceptions. An exception is an instance when the control was not performed, not performed consistently, or a criterion established by the control is not met.

E. System Development and Maintenance

| Identify different information system testing strategies. |

| Recognize the fundamental issues and risks associated with implementing new information systems or maintaining existing information systems within an entity. |

1. System development lifecycle

    The system development lifecycle (SDLC) is a multi-step process that governs the planning, implementation, and maintenance of a business information system. The typical non-agile SDLC resembles a waterfall; each step flows into the next subsequent step. An agile SDLC is more iterative and incremental. The key distinction of an agile process is that rather going step-by-step, it is permissible to jump forward and backward as needed to offer continuous planning and testing throughout the implementation phase. Agile is known for being more flexible and collaborative. However it can be more difficult to control from an internal controls perspective. This discussion will focus on the sequential steps of a typical non-agile SDLC.

    a. Non-agile SDLC

    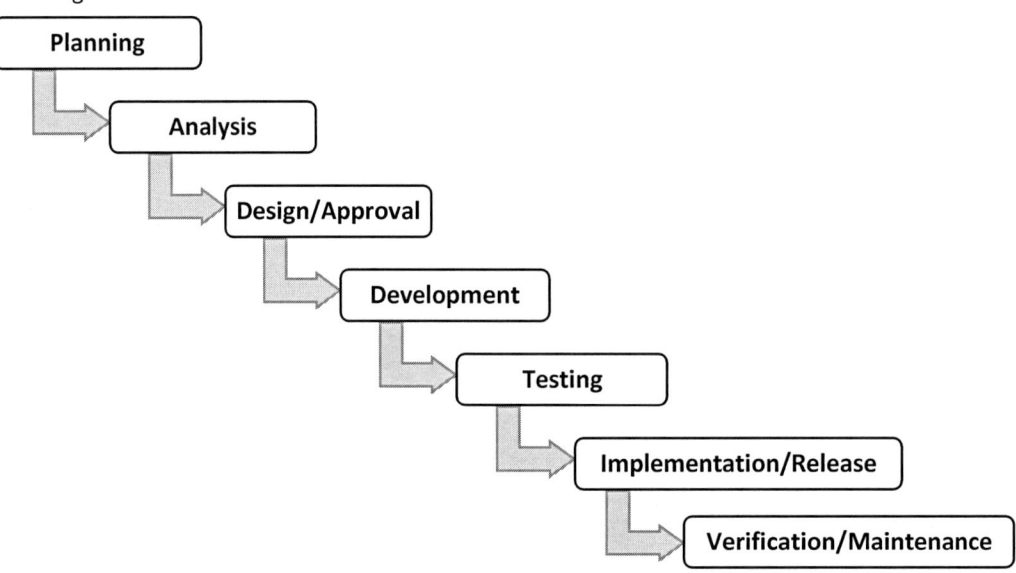

    1) Planning
       A well-designed system starts with clearly defined concept. The planning phase of the SDLC focuses on identifying problems and defining a system to appropriately address them. The plan for the system must consider and incorporate the organization's strategic goals. Defining project scope and initial feasibility are important during this phase.

    2) Analysis
       The goal of the analysis phase is to develop a deep understanding of the requirements for the proposed system or system update. Stakeholders in the analysis phase include end users, IT specialists, system analysts, and process design specialists. Early participation by end users, often through a needs assessment, ensures the system is a worthwhile investment. One technique to determine the requirements for a new or updated system is to compare the current system to the results of a needs assessment. This comparison, or gap analysis, helps establish priorities in terms of data capture, processing, and information reporting. System analysis determines what functionality end users require of the new system and the process results in a meticulously constructed system specification document.

The system specification document outlines not only the basic requirements and data elements of the system, but also details the performance level requirements, reliability, functional capabilities, and overall quality of information. The data structure and required interfaces, or interactions with existing systems, are determined at this stage. IT specialists and system analysts consider security and privacy concerns, establishing safeguards and constraints within the system to address these concerns.

3) Design/Approval
Once the analysis is complete, the system design phase aggregates the desired features into a technical blueprint for the system's architecture. System and process designers map the layout of databases, user interfaces, and reports. Consideration of automated and manual controls over the system occurs at this stage. Stakeholders approve the final design and set a budget. The approval constitutes authorization to begin development.

4) Development
Once the final plan is approved, and funding is allocated, developers start to create the proposed system using a programming language. The result is the creation of a functional system prototype.

5) Testing
It is important for every newly written piece of code to undergo testing to ensure it is operating as anticipated. Quality assurance specialists check it for errors, glitches, and bugs. Unit testing evaluates each piece of code individually for issues. System testing confirms the code is operating properly once it is functioning within the system. User acceptance testing confirms the new or updated system meets the requirements defined in the analysis phase accurately.

6) Implementation/Release
The implementation and release phase deploys approved changes into the production environment, the live system that hosts all the organization's actual data.

The following is a summary comparing the techniques organizations use to implement a system change:

	Parallel conversion	Pilot launch	Phased launch	Direct cutover or Plunge
Key feature	Operation of concurrent system	Small guinea pig group	Slow, steady rollout of changes	Immediate switch over
Relative cost	$$$	$$	$$	$
Time investment	High	Medium	Medium	Low
Risk	Minor	Moderate	Moderate	Extreme
Visual representation				

Parallel conversion involves the launch of a new system while continuing the normal operations of an existing system for a set period. Since the new system is operating concurrently, it can be compared to the existing system throughout the implementation period. This implementation method has the lowest level of risk. Risk is minimized because the existing system is protected against data processing failures and potential downtime associated with malfunctions in the new system.

Parallel conversion method is the costliest and results in the greatest amount of duplicative work. Also, the time investment can be a huge disadvantage for some organizations that are operating in fast-paced industries. The benefits of the new system (i.e., efficiency and cost savings) cannot be fully realized until an organization discontinues the use of the old system.

In a pilot launch, a portion of the organization becomes the guinea pig for the new system. That is, a part of the organization (e.g., a single department or operating division) will use the new system for a predetermined amount of time prior launching it to the rest of the organization. The pilot group identifies potential issues, isolating them only to the pilot group until they can be fixed. This method limits disruption to the organization and minimizes risk. It is less expensive than a full parallel implementation and provides many of the same benefits including protection against total system failure.

A phased launch spaces out the installation of a new system over a period by breaking the system into smaller pieces (e.g., modules) that can be installed one by one. For example, the general ledger module may be installed first, and IT specialists must prove it is fully operational in the production environment before proceeding with the implementation. Once the first module is verified, a second module may be installed, perhaps the accounts payable module, and so forth. The key requirement for this method is that both the new and existing system are compatible. Otherwise, there may be unexpected issues and errors. The risk of a large-scale malfunction is minimized using this method and reverting to the last stage of the launch is much easier. A potential advantage is that costs are incurred over a longer period.

The direct cutover or plunge implementation method basically stops the existing system and immediately shifts to the new system without any processing overlap. This method is the least expensive; but, of course, it has the highest level of risk. If the new system does not work properly, the organization may run into problems reverting to the former system. However, this may be the only option for organizations that implement a system that is incompatible with the existing system or cannot co-exist with the new system within the same IT infrastructure.

7) Verification/Maintenance
During the initial period following an implementation, the organization must verify the transactions generated by a new system. Users or IT personnel compare the actual results with the intended results and note any discrepancies. This reconciliation with intended results ensures that the processing is accurate in the modified system (i.e., updated accounting systems).

Maintenance is a continuous phase in which IT personnel monitor and support the system. When issues are identified, the organization uses a formal change management procedure to request, authorize, and test changes prior to system deployment. Organizations often set up or contract an internal or external help desk to provide technical support to users.

Multiple Choice

BEC 4-Q55 through BEC 4-Q59

2. Segregation of duties
As a precaution, no single individual should be granted full access or authority over an organization's information system. Dividing roles and responsibilities between multiple individuals reduces the risk of error and fraud. System permissions are configured to limit a single person's ability to sabotage or otherwise interfere with a critical process. Segregating duties make sure that personnel, especially those in the IT department, are restricted to perform only authorized duties commensurate with their job description.

It is beneficial to separate recordkeeping, authorization, custody, and reconciliation responsibilities in an organization. Within the IT department, the data entry, programming, operations, and library functions should be strictly segregated or compensating controls must be in place to prevent abuse. A compensating control mitigates the risk when it is impractical or impossible to enforce strict segregation of duties.

For example, when a change must be made to the system, each step should be performed by a different person. Identification of a requirement or a request for the change is the responsibility of a business analyst or user. Management outside the IT department is responsible for authorization and approval. The design and development responsibility is in the hands of a programmer or developer. Testing and approval must come from a manager (or second, separate developer.) A system administrator is responsible for implementation in production.

In small organizations, segregation of duties can be a challenge and can sometimes be impossible. To safeguard against risk, compensating controls such as periodic review of code changes and retention of system generated audit trails. With enough compensating controls in place at a small organization, even without proper segregation of duties, the control environment is still designed and operating effectively.

Multiple Choice

BEC 4-Q60 through BEC 4-Q62

a. IT department personnel
1) Systems analyst
   The role of the systems analyst is to analyze and recommend requirements necessary to modify or design existing or new systems.
2) System programmer or system engineer
   A system programmer is responsible for selecting, implementing, and maintaining system software. For instance, it is the responsibility of the system programmer to determine when the operating system requires an update or patch.
3) Application programmer or developer
   An application programmer performs programming functions in applications such as accounts payable, accounts receivable, and payroll. Therefore, coding modifications into the payroll software are appropriate duties for an application programmer.
   Programmers often use a system or application sandbox to run and test code while writing it. The sandbox is a replica of the production environment, but is non-production and has no interaction with the organization's actual, live data.
4) System administrator or computer operator
   A computer operator is responsible for maintaining control over computer operations to help ensure the completeness, accuracy, and distribution of input and output.
5) Change management administrator
   A change management administrator is responsible for migrating changes into the production environment. Their role is distinct from that of a developer.
6) Data librarian
   A data librarian maintains custody of the data, programs, and documentation. For example, this individual would manage the off-site rotation of backup media.

Multiple Choice

BEC 4-Q63 through BEC 4-Q65

F. IT Terminology and Concept Refresher

> *Hint:* While this area is not included in the AICPA blueprints, this general IT knowledge is important to understand and be familiar with for the CPA Exam. ***This area is equally important.***

1. Hardware
   Hardware refers to the tangible, physical components of a computer or other electronic device. Generally, standard computer equipment consists of a central processing unit (CPU), primary storage memory, secondary storage devices, input devices, and output devices.

   a. Central processing unit (CPU)
      All computers require a CPU or processor, a highly complex electronic circuit that is typically made up of a control unit (CU) and an arithmetic logic unit (ALU). Functioning as the brain and decision-maker for the computer, the CPU coordinates, and controls every computer operation including all input, output, and storage devices.

      To do this, the CPU repeatedly cycles through a sequence of steps called the instruction cycle or fetch-decode-execute (FDX) cycle. First, the CU (often compared to the conductor of an orchestra) fetches instructions from memory. Next, it decodes and interprets the instructions to determine the required action or operation. Finally, it directs the execution each operation with the assistance of the ALU, if necessary. The ALU performs all the required mathematical computations and logical comparisons as instructed by the CU.

      The pace and maximum processing speed of the CPU are dependent on the number of cycles (oscillations) per second of the CPU's internal clock signal that pulses at a fixed rate, called its clock speed (or alternatively, clock rate). Like a metronome, the CPU can execute a greater number of sequential instructions per second the faster the clock speed. The clock speed is measured in hertz. A high-end CPU (e.g., Intel Core i7) has approx. a 3 gigahertz (GHz) clock speed, depending on the model. It can perform at a rate of 3,000,000,000 clock cycles per second. Since more or less than one instruction can be executed per clock cycle, the CPU's performance speed is measured in millions of instructions per second (MIPS). High-end computers can execute approx. 100,000 MIPS at 3.0 GHz.

      The performance and processing capability of a CPU primarily depends on number of physical cores. A CPU is made up of at least one physical core. When more than one core is present, each core operates as an independent CPU to distribute the computer's workload and execute more than one program at a time. Multiple core CPUs (e.g., quad-core) increase the simultaneous processing power of the computer.

      Another technique for increasing the capability of the CPU is referred to as multithreading, a way to create additional virtual cores without modifying the number of physical cores. The technique uses small executable unit segments of larger processes. In a single-core CPU, multithreading creates the perception that the CPU can execute multiple threads from different processes at the same time. The CPU switches quickly from one thread to another to create this illusion. In computers with multiple cores, threads can process literally at the same time on different physical cores.

      Certain CPUs can also be configured for out-of-order execution, processing instructions as the information is available rather than in a purely serial or sequential manner. This technique allows the CPU to operate more efficiently since idle time is decreased.

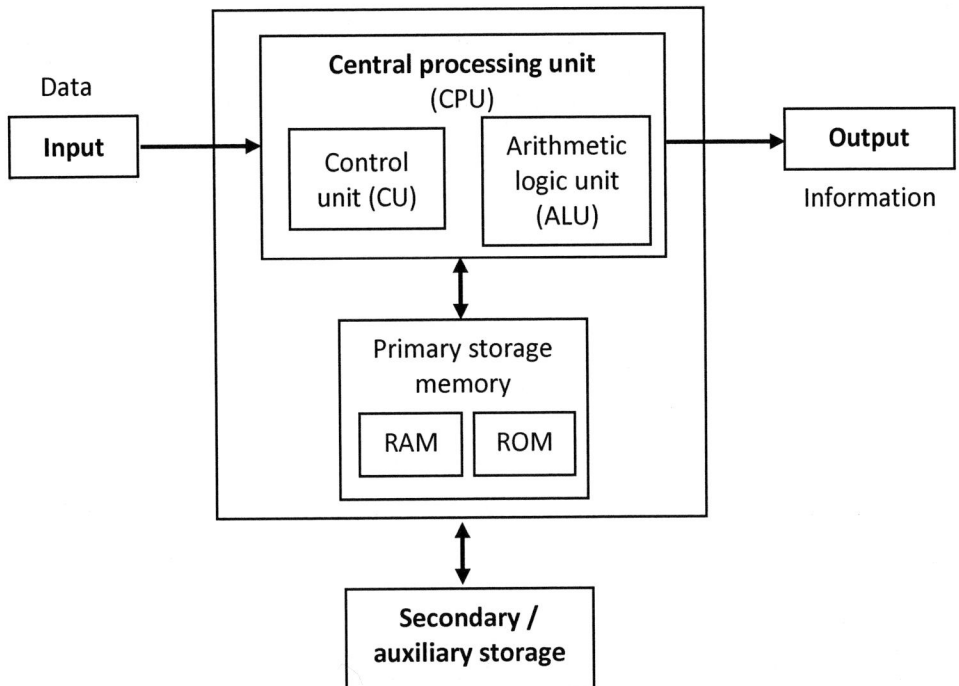

b. Primary storage memory
   The primary storage memory is divided into random access memory (RAM) and read-only memory (ROM).

   RAM, also called main memory, temporarily stores data that is currently being processed by the CPU. Once the data is done with processing, it is relocated to secondary storage or deleted. The temporary data is also erased when the device is turned off, which causes RAM to be referred to as volatile. RAM remains empty until the device is rebooted. A typical RAM is 2 gigabytes (GB) to 12 GB.

   ROM stores basic startup instructions (e.g., BIOS) and other data (e.g., firmware) that the computer needs to start-up, or boot. Since RAM is erased when the computer is off, ROM is responsible for storing permanent, non-volatile data. Basically, the computer would not remember how to reboot without this data. ROM is read-only, as the name indicates, due to the important role it plays in the computer's operation. Although updates or re-installation is rare for ROM data, if an unusual situation occurs (e.g., virus infects the system BIOS) the ROM chip can either be replaced or most modern systems have special tools to restore or update the data (e.g., BIOS update utility).

c. Secondary / auxiliary storage devices
   Secondary storage saves and retains information, even without being connected to the computer. The total capacity of an organization's IT infrastructure is limited only by budget. As such, storage devices can vary significantly in terms of both storage capacity and cost. Common storage devices include hard drives, solid state drives, optical drives, magnetic tape drives, and cloud-based storage.

   1) Hard disk drives (HDDs)
      HDDs, or hard drives, are a type of storage that features random-access to data, as opposed to sequential access, thanks to a rapidly rotating magnetic disk. If desired, data can be stored permanently, or the magnetic disk can be reused indefinitely by deleting and overwriting the previously saved data. A HDD is a staple in current computer infrastructure. HDDs often have capacities of 1 terabyte (TB) or more. A HDD can either be an internal, pre-installed component of a device or an external, auxiliary component that is connected as needed using a universal serial bus (USB) port.

One storage technique using multiple magnetic disks is called a RAID, or a redundant array of independent disks. Identical data is stored, redundantly, on several magnetic disks to prevent data loss in the event of a disk failure and to decrease latency (e.g., lag).

2) Solid state drives (SSDs)
SSDs are a type of data storage that requires no moving components to save or access data. Increasing in popularity as a fast and reliable form of secondary storage, an SSD is preferred in portable electronic devices (e.g., ultrabooks, tablets) and often used for auxiliary storage (e.g., USB drives, thumb drive, SD cards).

Compared to HDDs, SSDs can retrieve information more quickly and are less susceptible to damage due to physical shock. Cost and limited capacity have constrained their adoption as the primary storage device. Generally, an SSD is more expensive than a HDD, CD, and DVD of equal capacity.

A current trend in the electronics industry is installing both a HDD and a SSD in a computer or laptop. By mixing the two storage types, the computer capitalizes on the advantages of each one.

3) Optical drives
Optical drives use a laser beam to read compact discs (CDs), digital video disc (DVDs), and Blu-Ray discs. Discs are typically read-only if purchased commercially with pre-loaded content; but, blank discs are available for purchase and special optical drives also can both read and write discs. Blu-Ray discs offer the largest storage capacity; CDs are the most limited. Most laptops no longer have internal optical drives as a standard feature, signaling the optical drive is becoming increasingly obsolete.

4) Magnetic tape drives
Magnetic tape is an early, but enduring form of storage. Magnetic tape is commonly used for archiving data, and it remains the cheapest data storage option. Only recently has magnetic tape started to show obsolescence due to its slow speed and the decreasing cost of other high-capacity storage options.

5) Cloud-based storage
Cloud-based storage, or cloud storage, is data storage accessible via the internet, redundantly hosted at multiple off-site locations. A third-party cloud storage provider (e.g., Dropbox) is responsible for maintenance of the storage infrastructure, or cloud. Users subscribe to rent storage space on the cloud according to their storage capacity needs. Cloud storage pricing is often calculated in gigabytes per month (e.g., GB/Month). It is a service model of cloud computing called Infrastructure as a Service (IaaS).

d. Input/output devices
Simply put, input and output devices enable human-computer interaction. Input and output devices can also be called peripheral devices.

Input devices are pieces of hardware that are used to feed data into a machine. A keyboard, mouse, touchpad, microphone, webcam, and scanner are common in practically all computer systems. The collection of input devices integrated into a particular system varies depending on the user's needs and data requirements.

Specialized input devices include: controllers or joysticks, for controlling simulators or production equipment; magnetic ink card readers, for scanning checks; optical character readers, for converting printed text into digital text; bar code readers, for reading labels on products for inventory management and retail sales; and optical mark readers, for inputting assessment answer sheets that require users to fill in a bubble with a mark indicating their selection.

Output devices are computer hardware that allows users to see the electronic data and processing results in human-readable form by displaying text and graphics. The purpose of an output device is to facilitate user interaction with a computer. A monitor and a printer, inkjet or laser, are the most universal tools for output. Audio and video devices are also recognized in this category and include speakers, headphones, projectors, and flat-panel televisions.

Combination or bidirectional devices are called input/output (I/O or IO) devices. The piece of hardware can both send (input) and receive (output) information. Examples of I/O devices are touch screens, hard drives, CD-R/RW drives, DVD drives, Blu-Ray drives, SD cards, and USB flash (or thumb) drives. Most storage devices are considered I/O devices since they both store data (output) and input saved data.

Multiple Choice

BEC 4-Q66

2. Software

    The term software refers to the programs that process data, allow a computer to execute commands, and ultimately direct a computer's operation. Generally, software is categorized as either system software or application software.

    a. Operating systems (OS) and utility programs

       An operating system is a computer's master control program that schedules tasks, allocates resources, retrieves data, executes applications, and controls peripherals.

       The first widely-used OS was MS-DOS, which originally had no advanced features such as multitasking or a graphical user interface (GUI). Multitasking involves quickly switching between running applications to create the perception that the computer is executing more than one application at a time. A GUI is an aesthetically pleasing interface that allows the user to interact with a computer using menus and icons. A GUI makes the use of a mouse or touchpad possible. Both of these features are now standard.

       IBM mainframes use z/OS and rely on job control language (JCL) for operating system instructions (e.g., // EXEC for execute). Popular OSs for servers are Windows Server and UNIX. Desktops and laptops typically use Windows, Mac OS, or Linux. Smartphones and tablets use iOS, Android, Windows Phone, or Windows.

       Other system software are utility programs that manage repetitive, housekeeping tasks. Standard utility programs include a screen saver, file viewer, backup scheduler, uninstaller, and disk defragmenter.

    b. Application software

       Application software fulfills a specific user function. Functions include word processing, graphic and image editing, spreadsheets creation, email communications, and database system access. Typically, several applications are bundled and sold as a suite (e.g., Microsoft Office).

       Accounting software suitable for small organizations (e.g., Intuit QuickBooks, Sage 50 formerly Peachtree, Wave), accounting software suitable for mid-sized organizations (e.g., Deltek, Blackbaud Financial Edge), and ERP systems (e.g., SAP, Oracle formerly JD Edwards and PeopleSoft) are all applications used to support the accounting and finance function of an organization.

3. Programming languages
   In order to communicate with a computer, the programmer must use a language that the computer can understand and interpret appropriately. The programming language is defined as the vocabulary and syntax needed to instruct a computer to perform a specific task.

   Programming languages are classified into different generations, more recent (higher number) generations are more advanced and complex.

	Machine	Assembly	Object-oriented	Non-procedural, problem-oriented	Constraint-based logic
Generation	1GL	2GL	3GL	4GL	5GL
Example code	010001001000011 001101010000001 111010001000101	LOAD RX,&a LOAD RX,&a SUB AX,BX MOV CX,AX MOV DX,0	var dog = { name: "Bella", breed: poodle, bark: function () {alert("Woof!"); } };	SELECT Customer.CUSTNO, Customer.NAME, Customer.ADDR, Customer.CITY, Customer.STATE, Customer.CREDITLIM FROM Customer	change([Q,D,N,P]) :- member(Q,[0,1,2,3,4]), /*$0.25*/ member(D,[0,1,2,3,4,5,6,7,8,9,10]), /*$0.10*/ ember(N,[0,1,2,3,4,5,6,7,8,9,10,11,12,13,14,15,16,17,18,19,20]), /*$0.05*/ S is 25*Q +10*D + 5*N, S =< 100, P is 100-S. ?- change([Q,D,N,P]). ...
Example languages	Binary	Intel X86	Java, C, C++, COBOL	SQL, HTML, XML, XBRL	Prolog, OPS5, Mercury

   a. Machine languages (first generation language, abbreviated 1GL)
      Binary machine languages, 1GLs, are the basis for all other computer programming languages. 1GLs consist of a string of machine-readable code using either the numeral digit one (1) or zero (0). The code is understood directly by the computer without requiring a compiler or assembler to translate the instructions.

   b. Assembly languages (second generation, abbreviated 2GL)
      2GLs are low-level programming languages called assembly languages. Rather than numbers, the programmer uses rudimentary words and mnemonics to direct computer operations. A utility called an assembler translates the assembly language into the machine language, which is then executed by the processor.

      2GLs are specific to a certain processor (CPU) or computer architecture. Accordingly, non-portability is the primary disadvantage. As systems evolve and are replaced with newer technology, legacy assembly code is generally not compatible with the updated system and becomes obsolete.

   c. Procedural, object-oriented languages (third generation, abbreviated 3GL)
      Beginning with the 3GLs, all of the subsequent languages are classified as high-level (rather than low-level). High-level languages have more abstraction, hiding the machine language detail with a more intuitive programming language. Abstraction limits the complexity that results from using either binary code or 2GLs.

      3GLs rely on recognizable text and mathematical formulas to convey instructions and must be translated into machine language (binary) using a compiler or interpreter. Coding is less tedious compared to earlier generations, although programmers must still have a significant knowledge of the programming language to code properly.

A procedural language is a step-by-step list of executable instructions. Examples are C, Fortran, Pascal, and BASIC. An object-oriented programming language is structured to encapsulate, or neatly packaging information and instructions, as an object. Once the object is defined in the system, it can be reused over and over again, increasing efficiency. Java, C, C++, COBOL are all object-oriented languages.

3GLs are portable, operating on a number of different computers without significant modifications to the programming code.

    d. Non-procedural, problem-oriented languages (fourth generation, abbreviated 4GL)
A 4GL resembles a natural language and feasibly allows professionals without extensive computer programming knowledge to write code. Users can focus their attention on the problem or task at hand rather than losing focus to obtain the necessary skillset required for low-level programming.

Typically problem-oriented, the user specifies the desired result or inputs a what-if scenario and a compiler generates a procedure to perform the task. 4GLs are prevalent in database management systems (DBMS).

For example, structured query language (SQL) is a non-procedural programming language that generates procedures to navigate databases and extract information at the user's request. For example, a SELECT query of the Customer table will generate a list of all customers' information matching the criteria specified in the query.

Other 4GLs are HTML, (hypertext markup language) commonly used to create websites and other electronic documents; XML, (extensible markup language) a flexible data structure that is used to consistently communicate information within an industry; and XBRL, (extensible business reporting language) developed by the accounting industry to digitally report constantly in accordance with US GAAP based on reporting terms are authoritatively defined.

    e. Constraint-based logic languages (fifth generation, abbreviated 5GL)
The most technologically-advanced languages rely on constraints, rather than algorithms. A 5GL uses a compiler to generate a computer program that adheres to the defined set of constraints without a programmer painstakingly coding each step for a computer to execute. Examples include Prolog, OPS5, and Mercury. Primarily, 5GLs are used in artificial intelligence applications and expert systems. The use of 5GLs is not widespread; however, more Platform-as-a-Service (PaaS) application development tools have begun to use 5GLs.

Multiple Choice

BEC 4-Q67

4. Databases
    a. Database management system (DBMS)
A database is a collection of data stored in an organized way on a computer. A DBMS is a software application that facilitates the administration of a database. The primary functions of a DBMS include management of data storage, data dictionary (i.e., a repository of data about data, such as record quantities and field types), security, back-up and recovery, table creation and modification, transactions processing, and interfaces with other systems.

Multiple Choice

BEC 4-Q68

    b. Storage measurement
The basic building block of programming and smallest incremental unit of electronic data is called a bit. A bit, short for binary digit, is either the digit one (1) or zero (0).

A string of 8 bits is called a byte. Bytes are the unit of measure for memory and storage. A byte can store sufficient information to encode a single text character (e.g., letter or number). For example, the ASCII letter 'm' is one byte, 01101101 in ASCII binary. Character-encoding schemes (e.g., ASCII, UTF8) are standard on all device types.

Larger files are measured in byte multiples (e.g., kilobytes (KB), megabytes (MB), etc.).

1,024 bytes	2^{10}	1 kilobyte	1 KB
1,048,576 bytes	2^{20}	1 megabyte	1 MB
1,073,741,824 bytes	2^{30}	1 gigabyte	1 GB
1,099,511,627,776 bytes	2^{40}	1 terabyte	1 TB
1,125,899,906,842,624 bytes	2^{50}	1 petabyte	1 PB

c. Hierarchy of data

The hierarchy of data from smallest to largest, is bit, byte, field, record, file, and database. A field, record, and file are all important terms in the discussion of databases.

A field is a collection of bytes, the size of which can vary. A record is a group of associated fields. A file (or table) is a set of records.

Consider the following excerpt from an apparel retailer's database. One cell (e.g., 0128) is a field. A row containing all five fields (e.g., 0129, polo shirt, orange, L, $15.00) is a record. Then all rows and columns together constitute a file. This file is one of many in a database.

Product ID	product	color	size	Unit price
0128	T-shirt	Pink	M	$10.00
0129	Polo shirt	Orange	L	$15.00
0130	Dress shirt	White	S	$23.00
0131	Jacket	Black	XL	$18.00

Multiple Choice

BEC 4-Q69 through BEC 4-Q70

1) Normalization

Storing data in a flat file or spreadsheet is inefficient since it is likely to have a large amount of duplicate information. Normalization is the process of organizing data in a database to eliminate redundancy, decrease the required storage space, and simplify file maintenance.

Consider this order spreadsheet excerpt, prior to normalization:

Order ID	Customer name	Street address	City	State	Zip code	Product	Size	Color	Price	Status
1011	Bill Lumbergh	900 Atlantic Ave	Brooklyn	NY	11238	Polo shirt	L	Orange	$15.00	Sent
1012	Tom Smykowski	2033 Baseline Rd	Boulder	CO	80303	Jacket	XL	Black	$18.00	In progress
1013	Peter Gibbons	1021 Santa Monica Blvd	Beverly Hills	CA	90210	Dress shirt	S	White	$23.00	In progress
1014	Joanna Aniston	1202 Ashley River Rd	Charleston	SC	29414	T-shirt	M	Pink	$10.00	In progress
1015	Peter Gibbons	1021 Santa Monica Blvd	Beverly Hills	CA	90210	Jacket	XL	Black	$18.00	-

Notice, a duplicate customer name (e.g., Peter Gibbons) and product (e.g., jacket). Once data is in normal form, there will be little, if any, duplicate information. Data is split into separate tables (files) and relationships are communicated using cross-referencing identifiers called primary and foreign keys. In this example, transforming the data into normal form would involve separating the data into a product, order, customer, and status table.

Primary keys uniquely identify records, and one is assigned to every record. Foreign keys link the tables by cross-referencing the primary key of another table. For example, if customerID is the primary key in the customer table, it will appear as a foreign key in the order table. This relationship eliminates the need for a customer's name and address to appear in the database multiple times. By simply relying on the foreign key, the order table references the customer table for that information.

2) Database structure models
There are four database structure models, namely the hierarchical, network, relational, and object. The hierarchical and network models are the predecessors to the relational model. The object-oriented database model, defined by the Object Database Management Group (ODMG) in 2001, is the most recent addition to the group.

The hierarchical model organizes data into a tree. Relationships between data files resemble a parent-child relationship (i.e., a parent can have many children, but a child may only have one parent), also called a one-to-many relationship.

The network model resembles an interconnected web of data. Relationships are no longer limited to one-to-many, and by extending the analogy, a child file could have multiple parent files.

The limitation of using either the hierarchical or network model is that when database structures are modified, applications that rely on them may no longer function properly. As a result of this limitation, the relational model was developed by E.F. Codd in early 1970s.

The relational model organizes data into records of a table focusing on the relationships between each table (e.g., one-to-one, one-to-many, many-to-many). Each table relates to another table on the basis of primary and foreign keys, enabling normalization of the data. In practice, the relational model is widely accepted as the primary model for database structure. Examples include Oracle, Microsoft SQL Server, MySQL, and DB2.

The relatively new object model, or object-oriented model, integrates object-oriented programming languages by classifying data as objects and structuring relationships based on characteristics (e.g., attributes, operations) of object classes. Rather than focusing on only relationships between object classes, the characteristics within the object class have contextual meaning too.

Combining the benefits of both the object model and relational model, the object-relational hybrid model adds object classification to the trusted relational model. Oracle and MS SQL Server have the ability to implement this technology.

3) Database modeling
Entity-relationship diagrams (ERD) are tools to depict the data and relationships in a relational database. An ERD shows the cross-referencing between tables and how they rely on each other. For example, a customer must place an order. While many variations in format exist, tables are represented using rectangles and relationships using connecting lines. Cardinality, the constraints on relationships, connect rectangles and lines. In this example, primary keys are bold and foreign keys are italic.

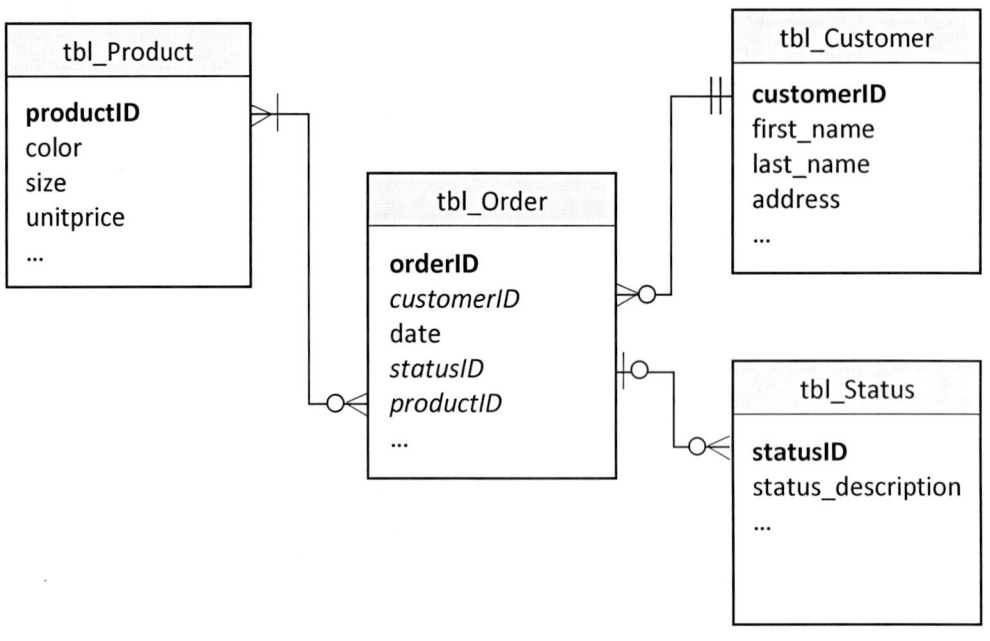

Zero-to-One	─○┼	An order can only have one status at a time, or no status.
Zero-to-Many	─○≪	A customer can have multiple orders.
One-and-Only-One	─┼┼─	An order can be associated with one and only one customer.
One-to-Many	─≪	An order can consist of one or many products.

A REA (resource-event-agent) data model demonstrates resource flows that result from engaging in business transactions (i.e., events) with agents. This model can help to clarify the structure of new relational and object-oriented database design, especially when an organization is not bound by legacy information systems (e.g., Workday). This example of a REA model shows the revenue cycle for a service-based organization.

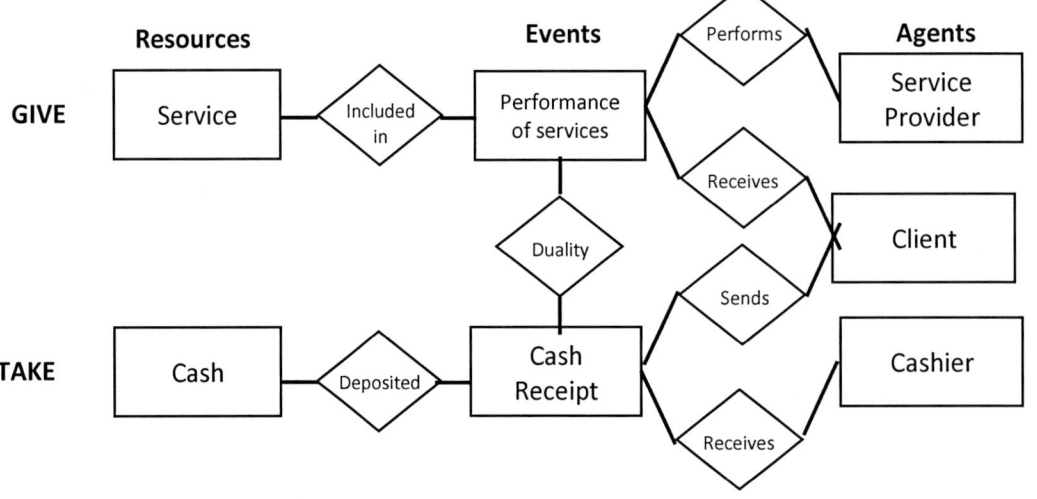

4F-9
Business Environment and Concepts (BEC)
Copyright © 2018 Yaeger CPA Review. All rights reserved.

d. Master file vs. transaction file
A master file is an aggregated collection of information that serves as a permanent record of all transactions. Traditionally in accounting, this type of file is called a ledger. An example is an inventory subsidiary ledger or control account.

Transaction files are compiled and used to update a master file. A journal, such as cash disbursement journal, is considered a transaction file.

Multiple Choice

BEC 4-Q71

5. Networks
A network is designed to link two or more computing devices. Within organizations, networks increase productivity by facilitating resource sharing, reducing hardware costs, enabling instantaneous communication and data exchange, and simplifying collaboration. Networks are typically categorized based on their scope or scale.

   a. Local area networks (LANs)
   A LAN is a privately-owned network that links multiple devices together within close proximity to each other. This is often at single geographic location (e.g., office building, home, or campus). LANs allow users to share peripheral devices such as printers and store files on a server which become easily accessible to every other device on the network. Data is transferred across a cable (e.g., Ethernet or twisted pair, coaxial, fiber optic). The typical protocol, or the rules for data transmission, is to divide the data into small protocol packets. When using an Ethernet cable, packets are encapsulated into several Ethernet frames for transmission. Each frame is sent haphazardly over the cable, without waiting until the cable is free. If a collision occurs and it is unable to reach its destination, the frame is resent. Frames are repeatedly resent until all packets can be extracted from the frames, regardless of out-of-order delivery, and reassembled successfully. An echo check repeats the received data back to its point of origin, comparing it to the original, to confirm transmission success.

   The primary limitation of LANs is that risk increases with each additional device. The more distributed the system (i.e., devices have greater physical or logical separation), the more challenging it is to enforce a consistent control environment. Another limitation is if a key component of the LAN fails, the whole interdependent system can experience data loss or downtime.

   Multiple Choice

   BEC 4-Q72

   1) Client/server applications
   Servers are robust devices that serve as a central repository for applications and data accessible by clients connected via a network. It is common for a LAN to have a client/server architecture. A server is not a special type of hardware; therefore, any device can be configured to be a server. A client is a user device. Client devices include laptops, desktops, tablets (e.g., iPad, Samsung), smartphones (e.g., iPhone, Blackberry).

   Historically, a two-tier client-server architecture was prevalent. In two-tier, a client (tier 1) interacts directly with a server (tier 2). Currently, a three-tiered architecture is more widespread. The client (tier 1), application server (tier 2), and database (tier 3) share the responsibilities for processing. The client's role is to provide a user interface. The client device is often pared down to operate with basic functionality and limited local resources, called a thin client.

The application server provides the logic for processing, and the database server hosts the data. By sharing the responsibilities across multiple machines, it is easier to maintain and update one tier without impacting another tier and to balance the processing load for greater efficiency.

While a three-tier architecture is normal, a network can create additional tiers and have an unlimited number of servers (e.g., print server, mail server, web server) to provide shared services to the network.

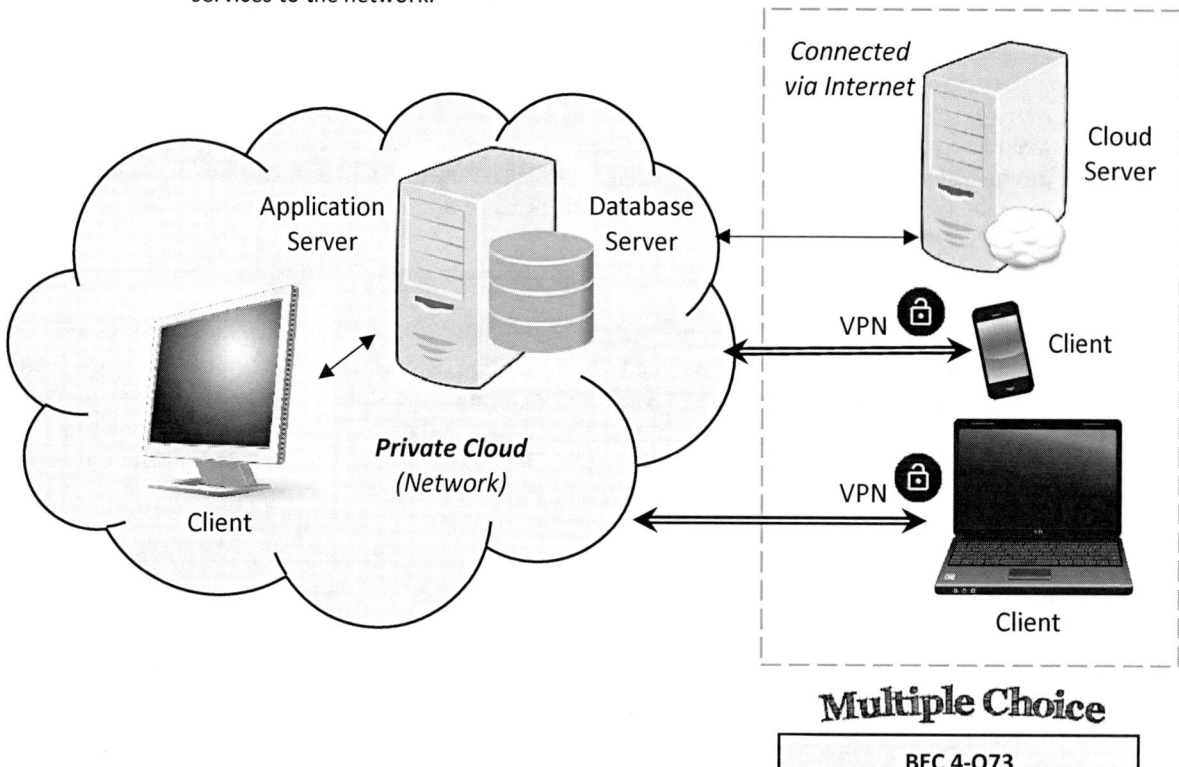

b. Wide area networks (WANs)
Networks spanning an extremely large geographic area utilize a WAN. WANs satisfy the need to connect multiple cities, states, provinces, and even countries within one network. In addition to connecting individual devices, WANs also connect smaller networks, such as LANs. WANs are a secure, cost-effective way to connect geographically-dispersed offices to the organization's headquarters. Publicly owned WANs are available by subscription through a telecommunication provider, or public carrier. The Internet is, in essence, a massive WAN. WANs are connected either point-to-point (e.g., T1, T3) or operate through packet-switched networks (e.g., TCP/IP).

Although less common, privately owned WANs can also be established for greater security; however, a private WAN is very expensive to construct and operate.

c. Metropolitan area network (MAN)
A MAN is a network catering to a city that has the potential to encompass an entire municipality. Generally, a MAN is larger than a LAN, smaller than a WAN.

d. Value-added network (VAN)
A value-added network (VAN) is a privately-owned network for communication by parties conducting business with each other. Because the network is privately owned (instead of public), it provides more security for data transmissions. As with a privately-owned WANs, a VAN can be quite costly. A VAN is an alternative to using the Internet and commonly used for electronic data interchange (EDI).

e. Personal area network (PAN)
As technology becomes more integrated into day-to-day life, each individual is likely to have a collection of electronic devices. A PAN is a network of interconnecting devices (e.g., laptop, phone, wireless printer, wireless speakers) owned or operated by an individual. The main benefit of a PAN is that devices can rapidly transmit data to each other with little effort. Connections can be made using cables (e.g., USB) or with wireless technology (e.g., Bluetooth). All PAN devices must be physically close to one another; standard wireless technology only has a radius of approx. 32-feet.

f. Cloud computing and cloud operations
Cloud computing is a term, circa 2006, that is used to describe a nebulous paradigm of shared computing resources. In 2011, the National Institute of Technology Standards (NIST) defines it as *"a model that is for enabling ubiquitous, convenient, on-demand network access to a shared pool of configurable computing resources (e.g., networks, servers, storage, applications, and services) that can be rapidly provisioned and released with minimal management effort or service provider interaction."*

A cloud has five essential characteristics. First, on-demand cloud services are available self-service, 24/7. Second, a cloud has broad network access meaning devices do not need a special hardware configuration to connect. Third, resources are pooled to serve multiple consumers. A cloud is an appropriate analogy since the customer does not control over the location of the provided resources (e.g., storage, processing). Fourth, rapid elasticity allows customer resource use to scale up or down based on demand. Fifth, cloud computing operates with a metering capability to measure service the amount of the service the customer uses. The customer pays based only on their resource use.

Cloud computing has had rapid growth for a number of reasons. In the past, organizations that were early to adopt new technology bore the full expense. Now, even small business can afford to pay for cloud services without the initial capital expenditure. Expenses occur over time, typically based on usage. Since many organizations share the same computing resources, cloud providers can achieve economies of scale and pass the savings on to their customers. Systems are maintained by skilled professionals that small organizations may not be able to attract and retain. The burden of obsolete equipment shifts to the service provider. Overall, cloud computing decreases IT costs while increasing the quality of the services provided to customers.

The drawback is that security is an ongoing consideration when using cloud-based services. Cloud computing is inherently opaque, and the customer often must relinquish control. Organizations with extremely sensitive data may not be comfortable with cloud technology and are likely to opt for well-established, transparent options. Selecting a reputable cloud service provider with a strong internal control environment is essential; but, no service provider can claim that their system is vulnerability-free or 100 percent secure.

1) Cloud service models
The three service models, also called digital business models, are Software as a Service (SaaS), Platform as a Service (PaaS), and Infrastructure as a Service (IaaS). SaaS allows a customer to share provider-installed applications running on the cloud. PaaS provides the customer with the ability to install consumer-created or acquired applications on the cloud. IaaS provides a customer with cloud-based processing, storage, networks, and other computing resources.

2) Cloud deployment models and data storage
There are generally four deployment models for cloud computing. A private cloud is used exclusively by one organization. A community cloud is shared by a defined group of organizations. A public cloud is open to the general public, assuming they have access. A hybrid cloud is a combination of a private, community, or public cloud.

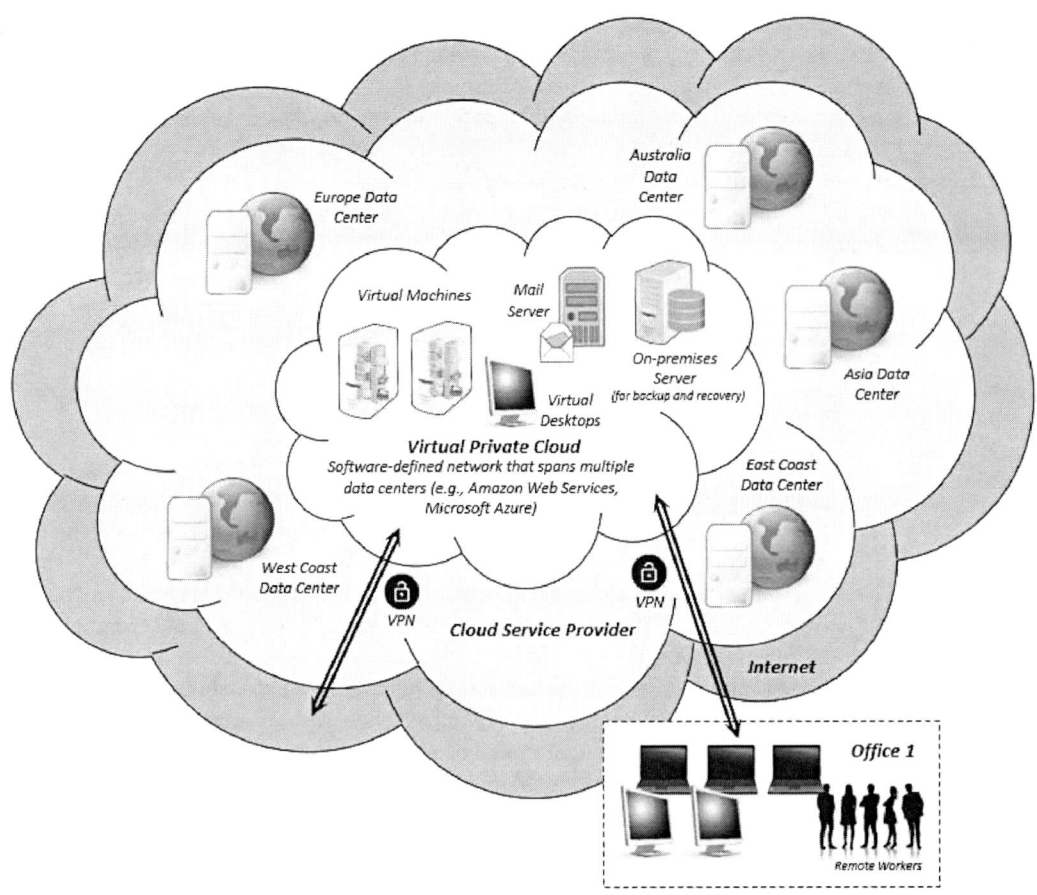

g. Network administration
Network administration involves the maintenance of the computing environment, installation of upgrades, and system monitoring. Job duties of a network administrator range from establishing network specifications and evaluating network performance factors (e.g., availability, utilization, latency) to managing remote access. If problems surface, the network administrator must troubleshoot the problem until it is resolved, or escalate it to the vendor. Small organizations often outsource network administration to third-party service providers. Administrator passwords (e.g., the password for Root account) must be securely guarded and changed regularly.

System software that facilitates network administration is Windows Active Directory (AD). AD is a Windows directory and access control platform that automates network management and can be used to locate and control access to objects on a Window network by providing an authentication framework to restrict the users and devices to those who are authorized to be on the network.

Multiple Choice

BEC 4-Q76

6. Virtualization

    Virtualization is the process of creating multiple hardware independent emulated instances of a computer operating system called "virtual machines" which run on a host server using a special piece of software called a "hypervisor." Virtualization is one of the basic software techniques used to enable cloud computing by allowing network managers to balance the workloads associated with business applications to the available physical hardware.

    Virtual Machine (also called a Guest Machine) is an instance of a computer operating system emulated in software which runs alongside applications or other virtual machines on a server computer. Virtual machines are a key software building block to allow shared workloads in public cloud computing.

    Hypervisor (also called a Virtual Machine Monitor) is a piece of computer software, firmware, or hardware that creates and runs virtual machines on a server computer, also called the "host" computer. The hypervisor emulates in software the physical computer hardware, and interacts with the virtual machines (guest machines) which run custom configurations of computer operating systems and applications. A hypervisor on a single server or cluster of servers may be able to host multiple virtual machines with many different operating systems at the same time. Hypervisors can run as applications on top of a base operating system such as Windows Server 2016 or Linux, or some hypervisors boot directly into the application without a base host operating system. The approach of server virtualization allows network administrators to offset the slack times in one application running on a piece of hardware against spikes in usage in other applications on the same hardware so that the processing capacity is more fully utilized.

7. Internet
    a. Internet

        The internet is a worldwide collection of networks that offers an inexpensive way to communicate at a very high-speed. Internet service providers (ISPs), such as AT&T and Verizon, provide temporary internet connections and are responsible for maintaining net neutrality. Net neutrality is the equal treatment of all internet users and all data on the internet. A router is a type of hardware that allows communication between two networks and is typically how a LAN connects to the internet via an ISP.

        The Transmission Control Protocol and Internet Protocol (TCP/IP) is a protocol for communication over the internet; the IP is a unique address on the internet that is specific to a computer. TCP/IP has two levels. The higher-level breaks data in packets that are transmitted over the internet; the lower level ensures that packets are delivered to the correct computer address.

Multiple Choice

BEC 4-Q77

1) Threats

    Using the internet leaves a system vulnerable to harm. Organizations must be very cognizant that even the most secure system is not completely safe from malicious software, intrusion, and other types of attacks.

    The sole purpose of malicious software, or malware, is to compromise the functionality of a computer system. A worm is a type of software that spreads from computer to computer, destroying data along the way. A virus is a piece of code that infects a program and performs activities not authorized by the user (e.g., delete or change data). A Trojan, or Trojan horse, is a piece of software that tricks a user to think it is legitimate to gain access to a system. Once inside, it causes damage or creates a back door (e.g., an undocumented portal for unauthorized access, bypassing controls). Worms, viruses, and Trojans all have the potential to initiate a denial of service attack that overwhelms a system, making it inoperable. Malware usually infiltrates a system without the user's knowledge. Antivirus software is vital for monitoring a system, notifying the user that an unusual threat is detected, and removing the threat.

In addition to malware, hackers are looking for ways exploit system vulnerabilities to steal data. Hackers often seek personal gain or pleasure from obtaining unauthorized access to a computer network.

Ransomware is another increasingly common threat and cyber liability involving cyber extortion. An attacker uses software to restricts access to sensitive information until the attacker's demands are met (e.g., a ransom payment is received from the targeted victim), or the attacker threatens to delete the data or share it publicly. Once conditions are met, the data is released and access is restored. Ransom payments can be sizable and often require payment in cryptocurrencies.

b. Intranet
A closed, internal network that allows access to parties within a single organization (e.g., corporation, university) owns, operates, and controls their content. An intranet can serve as a digital bulletin board to disseminate information, especially if the organization is large. It is either not connected to the Internet or located behind a firewall. The gateway to accessing the organization's network is called an intranet portal, offering personalized dashboards, custom navigation, and easy access to company information for employees and others inside the company.

c. Extranet
An extranet is an extension of an intranet and provides a collaboration platform for both company employees and specific external parties (e.g., partners, vendors, suppliers, customers). An extranet is basically a web or mobile-based collaboration portal for the company, its employees, its customers, and its vendors/trading partners. The owner of the extranet provides external parties with authentication credentials to access this private network. The external parties are granted controlled access to the organization's intranet via an extranet portal using the provided login credentials, and can only gain access to the limited data related to their work with the company.

8. Firewalls
A firewall is a network security device that isolates a trusted, internal network (e.g., a LAN) from an untrusted, external network (e.g., the internet). A firewall acts as a gatekeeper to control authentication, accept or reject incoming network traffic, and check outgoing traffic. A firewall can be hardware, software, or a combination of both hardware and software. Its primary purpose is to prevent unauthorized access and stop hackers, viruses, and worms from infiltrating the system.

Typically, a firewall is established on the network layer; however, application layer (or proxy) firewalls are configured to provide additional user authentication beyond that of a network firewall. Adding another level of protection, application layer filtering may detect unwanted income traffic that the network layer failed to reject.

Firewalls are not impermeable to vulnerability. Anti-virus software should always be installed in case the firewall fails to block a virus, and it infects the internal network.

Unified threat management (UTM) or unified security management (USM) is the advancement of cybersecurity from traditional firewall protection to all-inclusive security solutions (often called a UTM appliance). Unified threat management appliances perform functions such as:
- Network firewalling
- Network intrusion detection/prevention (IDS/IPS)
- Gateway anti-spam and antivirus

- Virtual private network (VPN)
- Content filtering
- Load balancing
- Data loss prevention
- Real-time reporting and monitoring

Multiple Choice

BEC 4-Q78 through BEC 4-Q80

9. Virtual private networks (VPNs)
   A VPN is a method of securing a network by creating an encrypted connection. Almost like a tunnel, the encrypted connection can provide security to a generally less secure public network (i.e., the Internet). While still providing a reasonable level of security, a VPN is more cost-effective than a privately-owned WAN or VAN. Accounting firms often use a VPN to provide secure, remote access to client documentation that is stored on their private network (e.g., LAN).

10. Artificial intelligence information systems
    As technology continues to advance year after year, artificial intelligence (AI) is becoming less a construct of science fiction and more a reality. Research is underway to develop artificially intelligent machines that are capable of reasoning and learning, exhibit intuition and common sense, and have the ability to emulate human decision-making without intervention. The long-term goal of AI research is to create general-purpose systems with intelligence comparable to that of the human mind.

    Even now, there are an endless variety of uses for AI technology. Current mainstream applications of AI include neural networks, case-based reasoning systems, rules-based expert systems, intelligent agents, and fuzzy logic.

    a. Neural networks
       Modeled after the human brain, a neural network is programmed to learn from experience. For instance, internet giants (e.g., Google, Facebook, etc.) are researching ways to harness a neural network to distinguish between different objects in images and to accurately translate languages.

    b. Case-based reasoning systems
       A case-based reasoning system is programmed to solve a current case based on its experience solving previous cases with similar parameters. The knowledge base encompasses an entire organization's experience and is continuously updated as new cases are stored in a central database.

    c. Rules-based expert systems
       An expert system is based on rules programmed to capture a specialist's expertise using IF-THEN-ELSE logic (e.g., IF X is true, THEN do Y, ELSE do Z). The functionality of a rule-based expert systems is dependent on the overall quality and ongoing maintenance of the programmed rules. An expert system is used to share knowledge across an organization and is a type of computer-based decision support system.

    d. Intelligent agent
       An intelligent agent works independently to collect sensory data and learn from experience to achieve an objective. An intelligent agent is particularly useful for specific and repetitive tasks. Online retailers (e.g., IKEA) use intelligent agents to provide customer service. For example, an intelligent agent called an automated online assistant is programmed to perceive and identify when a customer is in need of assistance on the retailer's website. This automated assistant can provide online sales and customer support.

e. Fuzzy logic

Fuzzy logic is a form of AI that is based on imprecise rules, rather than Boolean logic (e.g., true/false, 1 or 0) or strict IF-THEN rules. Rather than being black or white, fuzziness allows for shades of gray. The rules can use approximate values or ambiguous data. Appliance manufacturers have implemented fuzzy logic in washing machines to detect the contents and adjust the washing strategy (e.g., water level, water temperature, agitation rate) depending on each individual load of laundry.

Example: In the example below, names from two different lists with only one unique possible match are matched by programmatically calculating a "similarity score" for each possible match (where a "zero" represents no similarity, and a one represents an item which is identical to the item in the other list). Accepting the one match with the highest similarity score for each unique item in the list on the left results in obtaining matches for each of these four names.

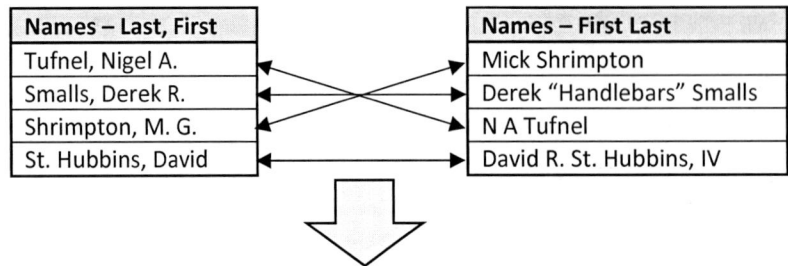

Names – First Last	Names – Last, First	Similarity
Mick Shrimpton	Shrimpton, M. G.	0.2917
Derek "Handlebars" Smalls	Smalls, Derek R.	0.5833
N A Tufnel	Tufnel, Nigel A.	0.5833
David R. St. Hubbins, IV	St. Hubbins, David	0.8667

Multiple Choice

BEC 4-Q81

Glossary: Information Technology

A

Acceptable use policy – guidelines concerning appropriate use of technology and computer equipment at an organization

Accounting information system – a narrow category of information systems reserved for only systems that record financial information about transactions

Active Directory (AD) – Windows directory and access control platform that automates network management and can be used to locate and control access to objects on a Window network by providing an authentication framework to restrict the users and devices to those who are authorized to be on the network

Advanced Encryption Standard (AES) – private-key encryption method, preferred by the U.S. government

Agile system development lifecycle (SDLC) – iterative software development approach focused on flexibility, continuous feedback, and collaboration

Antivirus software – an application that monitors a system for threats, notifies the user when a threat is detected, and removes the threat

Application controls – controls specific to a particular process or subsystem, such as accounts receivable or accounts payable that relate to the use of IT to initiate, record (input), process, and report (output) data

Application software – programs that fulfill a specific user function (e.g., word processing, email)

Arithmetic logic unit (ALU) – component of the CPU that performs all required mathematical computations and logical comparisons

Artificial intelligence – machine that is capable of reasoning and learning, exhibits intuition and common sense, and can emulate human decision-making without intervention

Assembly language – see second generation language (2GL)

Asymmetrical cryptography – public-key encryption technique using a pair of mathematically-related keys to secure data

Attestation engagement – an engagement regarding subject matter other than the fair presentation of financial statements where the practitioner expresses an independent opinion about the subject matter against a set of agreed-upon criteria

Audit trail – automatically recorded system activity, resulting in a comprehensive log file

Authentication – verification that a user is permitted to access a restricted system

Automated control – programmed enforcement of policies and procedures without user intervention

Automated interface – data transfer between systems that do not require human interaction such as manual export or import

Auxiliary storage – see secondary storage

Availability – the system is available for operation and use as committed or agreed; AICPA Trust Services principle

B

Batch processing – processing method that collects and processes transactions in groups (or batches) at a single time

Big data – gigantic stores of raw data differentiated from other data based on its large volume, velocity (i.e., fast, continuous data generation speed), variety, and veracity (i.e., uncertain data accuracy)

Bit (short for binary digit) – basic building block of programming, smallest incremental unit of electronic data; either the digit one (1) or zero (0)

Business information system – a broad category used to describe systems for organizing and integrating information about an organization

Business process reengineering (BPR) – redesigns an organization's workflow to identify inefficiency, eliminate redundancy, and optimize processes using state-of-the-art technology

Business to business (B2B) – transactions between two business organizations for goods and service, rather than the end-user or consumer (e.g., Cisco).

Business to consumer (B2C) – transactions occur between a vendor and the end-user, the consumer, of a product or service (e.g., Amazon, Rakuten)

Byte – string of 8 bits

C

Cardinality – the constraints on relationships (e.g., zero-to-one, one-to-one, one-to-many, many-to-many)

Case-based reasoning systems – artificially intelligent systems programmed to solve a current case based on its experience solving previous cases with similar parameters

Central processing unit (CPU) – a highly complex electronic circuit that functions as the brain and decision-maker for the computer

Centralized processing – processing completed at a single location

Certification Authority (CA) – a digital certificate governance entity that creates, signs, issues, and revokes digital certificates

Check digit – sum or product of a predefined algorithm using digits input by the user that equal the check digit value (e.g., 7 is the check digit for account number 1032017, 1+0+3+2+0+1=7)

Checksum – see check digit

Cipher – a code or algorithm for encrypting sensitive data

Ciphertext – encoded data that is unreadable without decryption

Clock rate – see clock speed

Clock speed – the CPU's internal clock signal that pulses at a fixed rate

Cloud computing – a model for convenient, on-demand network access to a shared pool of configurable computing resources

Cloud-based storage – data storage accessible via the internet, redundantly hosted at multiple off-site locations

COBIT 5 – Control Objective for Information and related Technology; a complete framework of expert-developed, easy-to-use tools for considering IT management and governance holistically within an enterprise

COBIT enabler – the components of an organization that make IT management and governance possible and help the organization achieve its objectives (e.g., processes, information, organizational structure)

COBIT principle – the fundamental propositions that serve as the foundation for the COBIT 5 framework

Cold site – reactive disaster recovery location; dormant shell or physical facility without equipment, waiting for an emergency to occur to activate

Community cloud – computing resources for shared use by a defined group of organizations

Completeness – processing is completed without omission of data

Compromise – a compromise refers to a loss of confidentiality, integrity, or availability of information, including the resultant impairment of processing integrity or availability of systems or the integrity or availability of system inputs or outputs

Confidentiality – information designated as confidential is protected as committed or agreed; AICPA Trust Services principle

Constraint-based logic languages – see fifth generation language (5GL)

Consumer to consumer (C2C) – transactions conducted between two individuals, selling or trading products or services (e.g., eBay, Craigslist, Venmo)

Control – a means to manage risk; synonym for safeguard or countermeasure

Control objectives – overarching aim or purpose of a collection of relevant internal controls, address the risks that the controls are intended to mitigate

Control total – a processing validation technique that confirms the processing was complete and accurate using a meaningful value established prior to the processing of a batch transaction (e.g., total revenue)

Control unit (CU) – component of the CPU that performs the instruction cycle

Corrective control – control that corrects an error or irregularity discovered after the fact

Criteria – the standards used to measure and evaluate the subject matter

Cybersecurity objectives – objectives that the entity establishes to address cybersecurity risks that could otherwise threaten the achievement of the entity's overall business objectives (including compliance, financial reporting, and operational objectives)

D

Data analytics – the science of interpreting raw data to generate accurate, meaningful information to improve decision-making

Data capture – input of data into an information system

Data encryption – a security technique that protects data from unauthorized viewing using a cipher

Data Encryption Standard (DES) – popular private-key (symmetrical) encryption method

Data management architecture – the fundamental design of the technology composed of models, policies, rules, or standards that dictate which data is collected and how it is stored, arranged, integrated, and put to use in systems and in the organization

Database management system (DBMS) – software application that facilitates the administration of a database

Decision support system – a tool that supports day-to-day operating decisions, useful for rapidly changing business conditions

Denial of service attack – a malicious attack that overwhelms a system, making it inoperable

Detective control – control that identifies error or fraud that has previously occurred

Differential backup – copy of only data that has changed since the last full backup

Digital certificate – electronic document that communicates the genuine origin and integrity of data transmitted over the internet

Digital signature – digital equivalent to a handwritten signature that authenticates the origin of a signed message and confirms it has not been altered during transmission

Digital signature acceptance policy – requirements for when a digital signature is permitted as a substitute for a handwritten signature, equivalent in reputability

Direct access processing – see online, real-time processing

Disaster recovery plan – policies and procedures over disaster recovery and business continuity; identification of an alternate processing site; a roster of names, locations, and contact information for key vendors; copies of all insurance policies; a list of current hardware configurations; a list identifying critical applications and priority for recovery

Disaster recovery plan policy – entity requirements over disaster recovery plans

Distributed (decentralized) processing – processing using processing power from multiple computers in the network to process transactions at various locations

Duplicate check – see redundant data check

E

E-commerce – see electronic commerce

Edit check – an input validation technique that compares data to criteria, such as format, and rejects inappropriate data (e.g., a nine-digit social security number must use the XXX-XX-XXX format and only contain numbers)

Electronic commerce – engaging in buying and selling remotely over a network using a computer or other technological device

Electronic data interchange (EDI) – exchange of data electronically between trading partners based on agreed-upon message standards to ensure the data is uniformly structured

Electronic funds transfer (EFT) – electronic transmission of funds-related transactions using a computer-based system that does not require either party to execute a physical exchange of a financial instrument (e.g., cash, checks)

Email policy – acceptable and unacceptable use of the organization's email system

Emergency change – urgent program change governed by modified controls to expedite change implementation procedure

Encryption – see data encryption

Encryption key – cipher or algorithm for scrambling (encrypting) and unscrambling (decrypting) data

Encryption policy – define which encryption algorithms (e.g., DES, AES, and RSA) are acceptable for use within the organization and requirements concerning the management and confidentiality of encryption keys

Enterprise resource planning (ERP) system – integrated set of applications that seamlessly manages business activities; a type of business information system

Entity-relationship diagram (ERD) – a visual depiction of the data and relationships in a relational database

Environmental control – precaution to defend against conditions that might negatively impact computer hardware

Exception – an instance when the criteria established by a control is not met

Executive support system – report and dashboard tool that provides aggregated and summary information geared towards senior-level managers and executives

Expert systems – artificially intelligent systems programmed to capture a specialist's expertise using IF-THEN-ELSE logic (e.g., IF X is true, THEN do Y, ELSE do Z)

Extranet – an extranet is an extension of an intranet, catering both internal and specific external parties (e.g., partners, vendors, suppliers, customers)

F
Fetch-decode-execute (FDX) cycle – see instruction cycle
Field – a collection of bytes
Field check – an input validation technique that restricts user input type (e.g., numerical data only)
Fifth generation language (5GL) – technologically-advanced language that rely on constraints, rather than algorithms
File – a set of records
Firewall – network security device that isolates a trusted, internal network (e.g., a LAN) from an untrusted, external network (e.g., the internet)
First generation language (1GL) – A string of machine-readable code using binary, one (1) or zero (0); also called machine language
Flying start site – turnkey disaster recovery facility with up-to-date, mirrored data
Foreign key – cross-reference of another table's primary key that links the two tables in a relational database
Fourth generation language (4GL) – a computer language that close to natural language, feasibly allowing professionals without extensive computer programming knowledge to write code
Full backup – copy of all data files to date
Fuzzy logic – a form of artificial intelligence that is based on imprecise rules, rather than Boolean logic (e.g., true/false, 1 or 0) or strict IF-THEN rules

G
General controls (ITGC) – controls relevant to an entire processing environment and all of the information systems and applications within it
General ledger system – repository for account balances and source for financial statement information
Governance framework – a set of concepts and practices that provide structure for an organization
Grandfather-father-son backup scheme – backup rotation consisting of a full backup (grandfather), differential backup (father), and incremental backup (son)
Graphical user interface (GUI) – aesthetically pleasing interface that allows the user to interact with a computer using menus and icons

H
Hacker – unauthorized user of a computer system that aim to exploit system vulnerabilities to steal data for personal gain or pleasure
Hard disk drives (HDDs) – a data storage device that features random-access to data using a rewritable rotating magnetic disk
Hardware – the tangible, physical components of a computer or other electronic device
Hash total – an input validation technique that checks for completeness of the input using an otherwise meaningless value (e.g., totaling the employees' identification numbers to ensure that all payroll records have been included in a payroll batch to be processed)
Hertz – measurement of a CPU's clock speed, cycles or oscillations per second
Hierarchical database – organizes data into a tree with relationships between data files that resemble a parent-child relationship
Hot site – proactive disaster recovery location; facilities equipped with redundant hardware and software available for immediate transition compromised processing location
Hybrid cloud – combination of a private, community, or public cloud
Hypervisor – a piece of computer software, firmware, or hardware that creates and runs virtual machines on a server computer, also called the "host" computer; also called a Virtual Machine Monitor

I
Incremental backup – copy of data since the last incremental backup, not including any previous activity
Information security – measures to defend an organization's IT infrastructure from unauthorized access and modification
Information Systems Audit and Control Association (ISACA) – an independent professional association of information security, assurance, risk management, and governance professionals
Infrastructure as a Service (IaaS) – service that offers cloud-based processing, storage, networks, and other computing resources
Input device – hardware component that feeds data into a machine

Input/output (I/O or IO) device – combination or bi-directional devices that can both send (input) and receive (output) information
Instruction cycle – basic operation cycle of a computer (i.e., fetch, decode, and execute) performed by the control unit of a CPU
Intelligent agent – a form of artificial intelligence that independently collects sensory data and learns from experience in order to achieve an objective
Interface – transfer of defined portions of data between two computer systems; see manual interface, automated interface
Internal site – internal backup system that continuously mirrors data allowing for the instantaneous cutover in the event of a disaster
Internet – a worldwide collection of networks that offers an inexpensive way to communicate at a very high-speed
Internet of Things (IoT) – objects (e.g., appliances) have the ability to connect to the internet, enabling object-to-object interaction without human involvement
Intranet – a closed, local network that allows access exclusive to parties within a single organization (e.g., corporation, university)
ISO 27001 – an international specification for an information security management system which involves creating, documenting, and operating processes to manage the organization's security risks and controls; the system's compliance with the standard and its overall effectiveness is often evaluated by an external compliance review

J

Java – a general-purpose object-oriented programming language (3GL)

K

Key – see encryption key, primary key (relational database), or foreign key (relational database)

L

Legacy system – a previous or outdated information system
Limit check – see reasonableness test
Local area network (LAN) – privately owned network that links multiple devices together within close proximity to each other
Logic check – an input validation technique that prevents illogical input based on predefined relationships (e.g., a customer has more than one order, but an order can only have one customer)
Logical access – the ability for a user to connect to a system
Logical access controls – controls to ensure system resources are restricted to authorized individuals

M

Machine language – see first generation language (1GL)
Magnetic tape drives – a cheap, enduring storage device that is often used for archiving data
Main memory – see random access memory
Malicious software (malware) – program that attempts to compromise the functionality of a computer system
Management information system – a system used to analyze financial and nonfinancial data for operation management and decision-making
Management reporting system – organizational monitoring system capable of producing financial reports for internal use
Manual control – a control requiring user execution or review
Manual interface – data transfer that requires the user of the system to facilitate the export and import of data from one system to another
Master file – an aggregated collection of information that serves as a permanent record of all transactions
Metropolitan area network (MAN) – a network catering to a city that has the potential to encompass an entire municipality
Millions of instructions per second (MIPS) – the CPU's performance speed measurement
Missing data check – see null data check
Mobile commerce (m-commerce) – transactions conducted in a wireless environment over mobile devices (e.g., Poshmark, Tradesy, Gilt)
Multitasking – quickly switching between running applications to create the perception of executing more than one application at a time
Mutual aid pact – see reciprocal agreements

N

National Institute of Standards and Technology (NIST) – part of the US Department of Commerce; an organization that issues publications on information technology are often referenced in Federal and state laws and regulations and are thus *de facto* government standards for many areas of basic information security

National Institute of Standards and Technology (NIST) Cybersecurity Framework – a policy framework of security guidance for how private sector businesses can assess and improve their ability to prevent, detect, and respond to cyber-attacks

Net neutrality – the equal treatment of all internet users and all data on the internet

Network – the linkage of two or more computing devices

Network administration – maintenance of the computing environment, installation of upgrades, and system monitoring

Network database – a database that resembles an interconnected web of data

Neural networks – artificially intelligent systems modeled after the human brain and programmed to learn from experience

Non-agile system development lifecycle (SDLC) – see waterfall SDLC

Non-procedural, problem-oriented languages – see fourth generation language (4GL)

Non-repudiation – ability to prove the origin of transmitted data

Normalization – process of organizing data in a database to eliminate redundancy, decrease the required storage space, and simplify file maintenance

Null data check – an input validation technique that prevents the user from submitting a blank field that would result in incomplete records

O

Object-oriented database – a database that integrates object-oriented programming languages, classifying data as objects and structuring relationships based on characteristics (e.g., attributes, operations) of object classes

Online analytical processing (OLAP) – query or request for information that instantaneously extracts data and aggregated information from the system

Online transaction processing (OLTP) – immediate processing of day-to-day transactions, such as journal entries

Online, real-time (OLRT) processing – immediate processing after data is input by a user

Operating effectiveness – evaluation criteria for internal controls to determine adequacy of a control environment

Operating systems (OS) – computer's master control program that schedules tasks, allocates resources, retrieves data, executes applications, and controls peripherals

Optical drives – input/output devices that use a laser beam to read compact discs (CDs), digital video disc (DVDs), and Blu-Ray discs

Out-of-order execution – processing instructions as the information is available rather than in a purely serial or sequential manner

Output device – hardware that allow users to see the electronic data and processing results in human-readable form by displaying text and graphics

P

Parallel conversion – system implementation technique used to launch a new system while continuing to operate the existing system for a period of time

Password policy – standards established by an organization for passwords syntax, change frequency, and rules over password protection and sharing

Peripheral device – see input device, output device, and input/output device

Personal area network (PAN) – network of interconnecting devices (e.g., laptop, phone, wireless printer, wireless speakers) owned or operated by an individual

Personally identifiable information (PXI) – a generic term for personally identifiable information such as name, social security number, address, and telephone number which is covered by restrictive legal or contractual compliance requirements, also referred to Personally Identifiable Information (PII), Protected Healthcare Information (PHI), Sensitive Personal Information (SPI)

Phased launch – system implementation that segments the system in to smaller pieces and installs them one-by-one over a period of time

Physical access – ability to physically touch and interact with an information system

Pilot launch – system implementation technique used to launch a new system in single department or operating division prior to releasing it to the rest of the organization
Platform as a Service (PaaS) – service that offers customer with the ability to install consumer-created or acquired applications on the cloud
Policies – an organization's written guidelines that provide internal control structure
Portal – gateway to accessing the organization's network using login credentials (e.g., username and password)
Preformatting – an input validation technique that forces the user to input data in a specific way, increasing consistency
Preventive control – a control to deter the occurrence of errors and fraudulent activity
Primary key – a unique identifier of a record in a relational database
Primary storage – see random access memory (RAM) and read-only memory (ROM)
Privacy – personal information is collected, used, retained, disclosed and destroyed in conformity with the commitments in the entity's privacy notice and with criteria set forth in Generally Accepted Privacy Principles (GAPP) issued by the AICPA; AICPA Trust Services principle
Private cloud – computing resources for exclusive use by one organization.
Private key – closely guarded encryption key, used to encrypt (symmetrical only) and decrypt (symmetrical and asymmetrical) data and create digital signatures
Private-key encryption – see symmetrical cryptography
Privileged user – powerful administrator access to a system; ability to circumvent controls
Procedural, object-oriented languages – see third-generation language (3GL)
Processing – conversion of data in an information system into meaningful information
Processing integrity – system processing is complete, accurate, timely, and authorized; AICPA Trust Services principle
Processor – see central processing unit (CPU)
Production environment – the live system that hosts all of the organization's actual data
Programming language – vocabulary and syntax needed to instruct a computer to perform a specific task
Public cloud – computing resources open to the general public with access
Public key – widely distributed encryption key, used to encrypt data (asymmetrical only) and validate digital signatures
Public-key encryption – see asymmetrical cryptography
Public-key infrastructure (PKI) – the architecture or framework that provides uniform policies and procedures for the management of public-key encryption, such as the issuance and maintenance of digital certificates

Q

R

Random access memory (RAM) – temporary storage for data currently being processed by the CPU
Ransomware – cyber extortion software that restricts access to sensitive information until the attacker's demands are met (e.g., ransom payment is received from the targeted victim), or the attacker threatens to delete the data or share it publicly
Read-only memory (ROM) – storage for basic startup instructions (e.g., BIOS) and other data (e.g., firmware) that the computer needs to start-up, or boot
Reasonableness test – restriction of values to within a certain upper and lower limit or range (e.g., billable hours per day < 12 hours)
Reciprocal agreements – disaster recovery agreement between two parties that requires either party to come to the other party's aid during a disaster, offering their facilities as an alternative processing site
Record – group of associated fields
Record count – an input validation technique that totals of the number of records processed in a batch
Redundant data check – an input validation technique that prevents duplicate identifiers (e.g., product IDs) from being recorded in the system
Registration Authority (RA) – entity contractually delegated to verify digital certificate registration documents before authorizing the issuance of a digital certificate by Certification Authority
Relational database – a database that organizes data into records of a table focusing on the relationships between each table (e.g., one-to-one, one-to-many, many-to-many)
Reporting – display of information housed in an information system, output function

Resource-event-agent (REA) data model – a diagram that demonstrates resource flows that result from engaging in business transactions (i.e., events) with agents

Risk assessment – evaluation of the impact and likelihood system vulnerabilities could be exploited

Router – a type of hardware that allows communication between two networks

RSA encryption – public-key encryption method that uses prime numbers

S

SANS (System Administration, Audit, Network, and Security) Institute – provider of information security and cybersecurity training

Second generation language (2GL) – low-level programming language that uses rudimentary words and mnemonics to direct computer operations

Secondary storage – a type storage device (e.g., hard drives, optical drives) that saves and retains information, even without being connected to the computer

Security – the system is protected against unauthorized access, use, or modification; AICPA Trust Services principle

Security event – an occurrence due to unauthorized access that impairs the availability, integrity, or confidentiality of information or systems; results in unauthorized disclosure/theft of information or damage to systems

Security incident – event that requires prompt action to protect data or other company assets

Segregation of duties – precautionary technique to provision only system access commensurate with authorized job duties

Service auditor – A practitioner who reports on controls at a service organization

Service organization – An organization that provides services to user entities (e.g., cloud provider)

Service organization control (SOC) report – a report on the internal control over IT-enabled systems; see SOC 1^{SM}, SOC 2^{SM}, or SOC 3^{SM}

Single-sign on (SSO) – a user is prompted to input access credentials (e.g., username and password) one time to gain access to all linked systems without additional prompts

SOC 1^{SM} – an attestation engagement resulting in a restricted use report on the operating effectiveness of a service organization's controls likely to be relevant to user entities' internal control over financial reporting

SOC 2^{SM} – an attestation engagement resulting in a detailed, restricted use report on the operating effectiveness of an entity's controls over a system relevant to one or more Trust Services principles and criteria

SOC 3^{SM} – an attestation engagement resulting in a simple, general use report on the operating effectiveness of an entity's controls over a system relevant to one or more Trust Services principles and criteria

Software – programs that process data, allow a computer to execute commands, and direct a computer's operation

Software as a Service (SaaS) – service that allows a customer to share provider-installed applications running on the cloud

Solid state drives (SSDs) – a fast, reliable data storage device that requires no moving components preferred in portable electronic devices and removable auxiliary storage

SSAE – Statements on Standards for Attestation Engagements promulgated by Auditing Standards Board (ASB) of the AICPA

Structured data – logically organized data housed in a spreadsheet or relational database

Superuser – see privileged user

Symmetrical cryptography – private-key encryption technique using a single key for both encryption and decryption

System – a system refers to infrastructure, software, processes, people, and data that are designed, implemented, and operated to work together to achieve one or more business objectives

System development lifecycle (SDLC) – multi-step process that governs the planning, implementation, and maintenance of a business information system

T

Table – see File

Test environment – a replica of the production environment used for testing and quality assurance of program changes

Test of design (TOD) – evaluation of whether a control is suitably designed to prevent material misstatement or to detect it in a timely manner

Test of operating effectiveness (TOE) – Testing a procedure to verify it is operating as expected, without exceptions.
Third generation language (3GL) – programming language that uses recognizable text and mathematical formulas to convey instructions, it must be translated into machine language (binary) using a compiler or interpreter
Three-way match – verification that an invoice matches accurately to a purchase order and receiving report prior to payment
Transaction file – items that are compiled and used to update a master file (e.g., journal)
Transaction processing system – subsystem of an accounting information system that collects, stores, and retrieves information about routine transactions that impact sales, accounts receivable, and accounts payable
Trojan (or Trojan horse) – a piece of software that tricks a user to think it is legitimate to gain access to a system; once inside, it causes damage or creates a back door (e.g., undocumented portal for unauthorized access, bypassing controls)
Trust services – professional attestation services that provide assurance on the integrity of information stored in a service provider's IT-enabled systems; defined by the AICPA
Two-factor authentication – a combination of two separate techniques to corroborate a user's identify, typically a password and another component

U

Unified security management – see unified threat management
Unified threat management – all-inclusive cybersecurity solutions, often called a UTM appliance that encompasses network firewalling, network intrusion detection/prevention (IDS/IPS), gateway anti-spam and antivirus, virtual private network (VPN), content filtering, load balancing, data loss prevention, and real-time reporting and monitoring
Universal serial bus (USB) – port used to attach a peripheral device to a computer
Unstructured data – unorganized data housed outside of a database (e.g., text, photos, and videos)
User auditor – An auditor who audits and issues an audit opinion on the financial statements of a user entity
User entity – An entity that uses a service organization
Utility program – system software that manages repetitive, housekeeping tasks

V

Validity check – an input validation technique that tests if user input is reasonable (valid) based on a set of programmed conditions (e.g., dates have a feasible day, month, and year)
Value-added network (VAN) – privately owned network for communication by parties conducting business with each other
Virtual machine – an instance of a computer operating system emulated in software which runs alongside applications or other virtual machines on a server computer; also called a Guest Machine
Virtual private network (VPN) – a method of securing a network by creating an encrypted connection which protects data transmission
Virus – a piece of code that infects a program and performs activities not authorized by the user (e.g., delete or change data)
Visitor logs – documents the entry and exit to secure areas, used to identify unauthorized access

W

Warm site – preventive disaster recovery location; pre-installed equipment and hardware ready for the recovery team to import all of the necessary software and data
Waterfall system development lifecycle (SDLC) – sequential approach to system development, each step flowing into each subsequent step
Web 1.0 – first stage of internet development (i.e., the World Wide Web) that is primarily read-only, on-demand content
Web 2.0 – second stage of internet development, shifts focus from static content to interactive user-generated information through social media (e.g., Facebook, YouTube, Twitter, etc.)
Web 3.0 – third stage of internet development, semantic (meaning-centric) web technologies are more personalized and omnipresent
Web 4.0 – fourth stage of internet development, symbiotic web technologies evolve into an Internet of Things (IoT)

WebTrust$^{SM/TM}$ – branded assurance service that assesses the adequacy and effectiveness of the controls employed by Certification Authorities (CAs), developed by the AICPA and CPA Canada
Wide area network (WAN) – a network, often an assortment of connected LANs, that spans an extremely large geographic area (e.g., multiple cities, states, provinces, countries)
Worm – a type of software that spreads from computer to computer, destroying data along the way
X
Z

Multiple Choice – Questions

BEC 4-Q1 B357. Which of the following is an advantage of a computer-based system for transaction processing over a manual system? A computer-based system

A. Does **not** require as stringent a set of internal controls.
B. Will produce a more accurate set of financial statements.
C. Will be more efficient at producing financial statements.
D. Eliminates the need to reconcile control accounts and subsidiary ledgers.

BEC 4-Q2 B70. Which of the following systems assists with non-routine decisions, serves strategic levels of the organization, and helps answer questions regarding what a company's competitors are doing, as well as identifies new acquisitions that would protect the company from cyclical business swings?

A. Executive support system.
B. Decision support system.
C. Transaction processing system.
D. Management information system.

BEC 4-Q3 B239. Which of the following represents the procedure managers use to identify whether the company has information that unauthorized individuals want, how these individuals could obtain the information, the value of the information, and the probability of unauthorized access occurring?

A. Disaster recovery plan assessment.
B. Systems assessment.
C. Risk assessment.
D. Test of controls.

BEC 4-Q4 B172. Which of the following tasks would be included in a document flowchart for processing cash receipts?

A. Compare control and remittance totals.
B. Record returns and allowances.
C. Authorize and generate an invoice.
D. Authorize and generate a voucher.

BEC 4-Q5 B223. ABC, Inc. assessed overall risks of MIS systems projects on two standard criteria: technology used and design structure. The following systems projects have been assessed on these risk criteria. Which of the following projects holds the highest risk to ABC?

	Technology	Structure
A.	Current	Sketchy
B.	New	Sketchy
C.	Current	Well defined
D.	New	Well defined

BEC 4-Q6 B1212. Which of the following is a general use report that considers the operating effectiveness of an entity's controls relevant to the AICPA's Trust Services principles and criteria?

A. SOC 1 report.
B. SOC 2 report.
C. SOC 3 report.
D. WebTrust report.

BEC 4-Q7 B337. Which of the following activities would most likely detect computer-related fraud?

A. Using data encryption.
B. Performing validity checks.
C. Conducting fraud-awareness training.
D. Reviewing the systems-access log.

BEC 4-Q8 B227. An accounts payable clerk is accused of making unauthorized changes to previous payments to a vendor. Proof could be uncovered in which of the following places?

A. Transaction logs.
B. Error reports.
C. Error files.
D. Validated data file.

BEC 4-Q9 B1209. Which of the following does COBIT 5 focus on to address stakeholder needs and achieve enterprise-level goals?

A. Mission statement.
B. Core competencies.
C. Vision statement.
D. Goal cascade.

BEC 4-Q10 B1210. Which of the following is **not** a COBIT 5 enterprise enabler?

A. Culture, ethics, and behavior.
B. People, skills, and competencies.
C. Governance.
D. Information.

BEC 4-Q11 B151. An enterprise resource planning (ERP) system has which of the following advantages over multiple independent functional systems?

A. Modifications can be made to each module without affecting other modules.
B. Increased responsiveness and flexibility while aiding in the decision-making process.
C. Increased amount of data redundancy since more than one module contains the same information.
D. Reduction in costs for implementation and training.

BEC 4-Q12 B116. An enterprise resource planning system is designed to

A. Allow nonexperts to make decisions about a particular problem.
B. Help with the decision-making process.
C. Integrate data from all aspects of an organization's activities.
D. Present executives with the information needed to make strategic plans.

BEC 4-Q13 B53. A client would like to implement a management information system that integrates all functional areas within an organization to allow information exchange and collaboration among all parties involved in business operations. Which of the following systems is most effective for this application?

A. A decision support system.
B. An executive support system.
C. An office automation system.
D. An enterprise resource planning system.

BEC 4-Q14 B1205. A company recently automated a previously manual interface between its outsourced payroll system and its general ledger accounting information system. Which of the following is likely to increase?

A. Failures during data transmission.
B. Manual reconciliations.
C. Interaction with the system by the user.
D. Accurate data transfer.

BEC 4-Q15 B272. What type of computerized data processing system would be most appropriate for a company that is opening a new retail location?

A. Batch processing.
B. Real-time processing.
C. Sequential-file processing.
D. Direct-access processing.

BEC 4-Q16 B67. Credit Card International developed a management reporting software package that enables members interactively to query a data warehouse and drill down into transaction and trend information via various network set-ups. What type of management reporting system has Credit Card International developed?

A. On-line analytical processing system.
B. On-line transaction-processing system.
C. On-line executive information system.
D. On-line information storage system.

BEC 4-Q17 B1232. Real-time processing is most appropriate for which of the following bank transactions?

A. Credit authorizations for consumer loan applicants.
B. Biweekly payroll for bank employees.
C. Purchases of fixed assets.
D. Expiration of prepaid liability insurance.

BEC 4-Q18 B236. Compared to online real-time processing, batch processing has which of the following disadvantages?

A. A greater level of control is necessary.
B. Additional computing resources are required.
C. Additional personnel are required.
D. Stored data are current only after the update process.

BEC 4-Q19 B153. During the annual audit, it was learned from an interview with the controller that the accounting system was programmed to use a batch processing method and a detailed posting type. This would mean that individual transactions were

A. Posted upon entry, and each transaction had its own line entry in the appropriate ledger.
B. Assigned to groups before posting, and each transaction had its own line entry in the appropriate ledger.
C. Posted upon entry, and each transaction group had a cumulative entry total in the appropriate ledger.
D. Assigned to groups before posting, and each transaction group had a cumulative entry total in the appropriate ledger.

BEC 4-Q20 B133. Which of the following transaction processing modes provides the most accurate and complete information for decision making?

A. Batch.
B. Distributed.
C. Online.
D. Application.

BEC 4-Q21 B252. A distributed processing environment would be most beneficial in which of the following situations?

A. Large volumes of data are generated at many locations and fast access is required.
B. Large volumes of data are generated centrally and fast access is **not** required.
C. Small volumes of data are generated at many locations, fast access is required, and summaries of the data are needed promptly at a central site.
D. Small volumes of data are generated centrally, fast access is required, and summaries are needed monthly at many locations.

BEC 4-Q22 B188. Which of the following terms best describes a payroll system?

A. Data base management system (DBMS).
B. Transaction processing system (TPS).
C. Decision support system (DSS).
D. Enterprise resource planning (ERP) system.

BEC 4-Q23 B208. Which of the following is usually a benefit of using electronic funds transfer for international cash transactions?

A. Creation of multilingual disaster recovery plans.
B. Reduction in the frequency of data entry errors.
C. Off-site storage of foreign source documents.
D. Improvement in the audit trail for cash transactions.

BEC 4-Q24 B336. Which of the following statements is correct concerning the security of messages in an electronic data interchange (EDI) system?
A. Removable drives that can be locked up at night provide adequate security when the confidentiality of data is the primary risk.
B. Message authentication in EDI systems performs the same function as segregation of duties in other information systems.
C. Encryption performed by a physically secure hardware device is more secure than encryption performed by software.
D. Security at the transaction phase in EDI systems is **not** necessary because problems at that level will be identified by the service provider.

BEC 4-Q25 B249. Which of the following is usually a benefit of transmitting transactions in an electronic data interchange (EDI) environment?

A. Elimination of the need to continuously update antivirus software.
B. Assurance of the thoroughness of transaction data because of standardized controls.
C. Automatic protection of information that has electronically left the entity.
D. Elimination of the need to verify the receipt of goods before making payment.

BEC 4-Q26 B179. Which of the following best defines electronic data interchange (EDI) transactions?

A. Electronic business information is exchanged between two or more businesses.
B. Customers' funds-related transactions are electronically transmitted and processed.
C. Entered sales data are electronically transmitted via a centralized network to a central processor.
D. Products sold on central web servers can be accessed by users any time.

BEC 4-Q27 B283. Which of the following allows customers to pay for goods or services from a web site while maintaining financial privacy?

A. Credit card.
B. Site draft.
C. E-cash.
D. Electronic check.

BEC 4-Q28 B1230. What should a company do when seeking competitive advantages in planning for the implementation of a new software system?

A. Design an optimal process and then align the software.
B. Design the software to fit the existing processes.
C. Direct manpower to the nonbottleneck process areas.
D. Allow management to dictate processes.

BEC 4-Q29 B1208. An amusement park uses a high-tech wristband to enable patrons to enter the park without a physical ticket, reserve a place in an amusement's queue without standing in line, and purchase merchandise without a wallet. This is an example of which stage in the evolution of the internet?

A. Web 2.0.
B. Web 1.0.
C. Web 3.0.
D. Internet of Things (IoT).

BEC 4-Q30 B351. What is a major disadvantage to using symmetric encryption to encrypt data?

A. Both sender and receiver must have the private key before this encryption method will work.
B. The private key **cannot** be broken into fragments and distributed to the receiver.
C. The private key is used by the sender for encryption but **not** by the receiver for decryption.
D. The private key is used by the receiver for decryption but **not** by the sender for encryption.

BEC 4-Q31 B131. An entity doing business on the Internet most likely could use any of the following methods to prevent unauthorized intruders from accessing proprietary information **except**

A. Password management.
B. Data encryption.
C. Digital certificates.
D. Batch processing.

BEC 4-Q32 B344. A digital signature is used primarily to determine that a message is

A. Unaltered in transmission.
B. Not intercepted en route.
C. Received by the intended recipient.
D. Sent to the correct address.

BEC 4-Q33 B1207. What type of policy expressly prohibits the personal use of the computer resources?

A. Email policy.
B. Acceptable use policy.
C. Disaster recovery plan policy.
D. Password policy.

BEC 4-Q34 B222. Which of the following internal control procedures would prevent an employee from being paid an inappropriate hourly wage?

A. Having the supervisor of the data entry clerk verify that each employee's hours worked are correctly entered into the system.
B. Using real-time posting of payroll so there can be **no** after-the-fact data manipulation of the payroll register.
C. Giving payroll data entry clerks the ability to change any suspicious hourly pay rates to a reasonable rate.
D. Limiting access to employee master files to authorized employees in the personnel department.

BEC 4-Q35 B130. When a client's accounts payable computer system was relocated, the administrator provided support through a dial-up connection to a server. Subsequently, the administrator left the company. No changes were made to the accounts payable system at that time. Which of the following situations represents the greatest security risk?

A. User passwords are **not** required to be in alpha-numeric format.
B. Management procedures for user accounts are not documented.
C. User accounts are **not** removed upon termination of employees.
D. Security logs are **not** periodically reviewed for violations.

BEC 4-Q36 B1211. Which of the following is an example of a control over the systems development lifecycle?

I. Full backups are scheduled daily and monitored for completion.
II. Projects must be approved by senior management prior to implementation.

A. I only.
B. II only.
C. Both I and II.
D. Neither I nor II.

BEC 4-Q37 B43. Which of the following statements presents an example of a general control for a computerized system?

A. Limiting entry of sales transactions to only valid credit customers.
B. Creating hash totals from Social Security numbers for the weekly payroll.
C. Restricting entry of accounts payable transactions to only authorized users.
D. Restricting access to the computer center by use of biometric devices.

BEC 4-Q38 B271. Which of the following configurations of elements represents the most complete disaster recovery plan?

A. Vendor contract for alternate processing site, backup procedures, names of persons on the disaster recovery team.
B. Alternate processing site, backup and off-site storage procedures, identification of critical applications, test of the plan.
C. Off-site storage procedures, identification of critical applications, test of the plan.
D. Vendor contract for alternate processing site, names of persons on the disaster recovery team, off-site storage procedures.

BEC 4-Q39 B260. To prevent interrupted information systems operation, which of the following controls are typically included in an organization's disaster recovery plan?

A. Backup and data transmission controls.
B. Data input and downtime controls.
C. Backup and downtime controls.
D. Disaster recovery and data processing controls.

BEC 4-Q40 B343. Which of the following procedures should be included in the disaster recovery plan for an Information Technology department?

A. Replacement personal computers for user departments.
B. Identification of critical applications.
C. Physical security of warehouse facilities.
D. Cross-training of operating personnel.

BEC 4-Q41 B233. Which of the following best describes a hot site?

A. Location within the company that is most vulnerable to a disaster.
B. Location where a company can install data processing equipment on short notice.
C. Location that is equipped with a redundant hardware and software configuration.
D. Location that is considered too close to a potential disaster area.

BEC 4-Q42 B173. The performance audit report of an information technology department indicated that the department lacked a disaster recovery plan. Which of the following steps should management take first to correct this condition?

A. Bulletproof the information security architecture.
B. Designate a hot site.
C. Designate a cold site.
D. Prepare a statement of responsibilities for tasks included in a disaster recovery plan.

BEC 4-Q43 B175. An information technology director collected the names and locations of key vendors, current hardware configuration, names of team members, and an alternative processing location. What is the director most likely preparing?

A. Data restoration plan.
B. Disaster recovery plan.
C. System security policy.
D. System hardware policy.

BEC 4-Q44 B195. A controller is developing a disaster recovery plan for a corporation's computer systems. In the event of a disaster that makes the company's facilities unusable, the controller has arranged for the use of an alternate location and the delivery of duplicate computer hardware to this alternate location. Which of the following recovery plans would best describe this arrangement?

A. Hot site.
B. Cold site.
C. Back-up site procedures.
D. Hot spare site agreement.

BEC 4-Q45 B154. A company has a significant e-commerce presence and self-hosts its web site. To assure continuity in the event of a natural disaster, the firm should adopt which of the following strategies?

A. Backup the server database daily.
B. Store records off-site.
C. Purchase and implement RAID technology.
D. Establish off-site mirrored web server.

BEC 4-Q46 B135. Which of the following terms refers to a site that has been identified and maintained by the organization as a data processing disaster recovery site but has **not** been stocked with equipment?

A. Hot.
B. Cold.
C. Warm.
D. Flying start.

BEC 4-Q47 B134. Which of the following is considered an application input control?

A. Run control total.
B. Edit check.
C. Report distribution log.
D. Exception report.

BEC 4-Q48 B1255. A customer notified a company that the customer's account did not reflect the most recent monthly payment. The company investigated the issue and determined that a clerk had mistakenly applied the customer's payments to a different customer's account. Which of the following controls would help to prevent such an error?

A. Checksum.
B. Field check.
C. Completeness test.
D. Closed-loop verification.

BEC 4-Q49 B808. An entity has the following sales orders in a batch:

Invoice#	Product	Quantity	Unit Price
101	K 10	50	$ 5.00
102	M 15	100	$10.00
103	P 20	150	$25.00
104	Q 25	200	$30.00
105	T 30	250	$35.00

Which of the following numbers represents a hash total?

A. 5
B. 100
C. 515
D. 750

BEC 4-Q50 B191. An employee mistakenly enters April 31 in the date field. Which of the following programmed edit checks offers the best solution for detecting this error?

A. Online prompting.
B. Mathematical accuracy.
C. Preformatted screen.
D. Reasonableness.

BEC 4-Q51 B274. What should be examined to determine if an information system is operating according to prescribed procedures?

A. System capacity.
B. System control.
C. System complexity.
D. Accessibility to system information.

BEC 4-Q52 B339. Which of the following types of control plans is particular to a specific process or subsystem, rather than related to the timing of its occurrence?

A. Preventive.
B. Corrective.
C. Application.
D. Detective.

BEC 4-Q53 B244. Which of the following is a key difference in controls when changing from a manual system to a computer system?

A. Internal control principles change.
B. Internal control objectives differ.
C. Control objectives are more difficult to achieve.
D. Methodologies for implementing controls change.

BEC 4-Q54 B196. Controls in the information technology area are classified into the preventive, detective, and corrective categories. Which of the following is a preventive control?

A. Contingency planning.
B. Hash total.
C. Echo check.
D. Access control software.

BEC 4-Q55 B232. A fast-growing service company is developing its information technology internally. What is the first step in the company's systems development life cycle?

A. Analysis.
B. Implementation.
C. Testing.
D. Design.

BEC 4-Q56 B150. Which of the following items would be most critical to include in a systems specification document for a financial report?

A. Cost-benefit analysis.
B. Data elements needed.
C. Training requirements.
D. Communication change management considerations.

BEC 4-Q57 B45. Which of the following control activities should be taken to reduce the risk of incorrect processing in a newly installed computerized accounting system?

A. Segregation of duties.
B. Ensure proper authorization of transactions.
C. Adequately safeguard assets.
D. Independently verify the transactions.

BEC 4-Q58 B1254. At what phase in the systems development process is a report generated that describes the content, processing flows, resource requirements, and procedures of a preliminary system design?

A. File and database design.
B. Conceptual systems design.
C. Physical systems design.
D. Procedures design.

BEC 4-Q59 B1256. The most appropriate data-gathering techniques for a system survey include interviews, quick questionnaires, observations, and

A. Prototypes.
B. Systems documentation.
C. PERT charts.
D. Gantt charts.

BEC 4-Q60 B185. To maintain effective segregation of duties within the information technology function, an application programmer should have which of the following responsibilities?

A. Modify and adapt operating system software.
B. Correct detected data entry errors for the cash disbursement system.
C. Code approved changes to a payroll program.
D. Maintain custody of the billing program code and its documentation.

BEC 4-Q61 B132. Which of the following information technology (IT) departmental responsibilities should be delegated to separate individuals?

A. Network maintenance and wireless access.
B. Data entry and antivirus management.
C. Data entry and application programming.
D. Data entry and quality assurance.

BEC 4-Q62 B54. Management of a company has a lack of segregation of duties within the application environment, with programmers having access to development and production. The programmers have the ability to implement application code changes into production without monitoring or a quality assurance function. This is considered a deficiency in which of the following areas?

A. Change control.
B. Management override.
C. Data integrity.
D. Computer operations.

BEC 4-Q63 B44. What is the role of the systems analyst in an IT environment?
A. Developing long-range plans and directs application development and computer operations.
B. Designing systems, prepares specifications for programmers, and serves as intermediary between users and programmers.
C. Maintaining control over the completeness, accuracy, and distribution of input and output.
D. Selecting, implementing, and maintaining system software, including operating systems, network software, and the data base management system.

BEC 4-Q64 B360. Which of the following areas of responsibility are normally assigned to a systems programmer in a computer system environment?

A. Systems analysis and applications programming.
B. Data communications hardware and software.
C. Operating systems and compilers.
D. Computer operations.

BEC 4-Q65 B108. In a large firm, custody of an entity's data is most appropriately maintained by which of the following personnel?

A. Data librarian.
B. Systems analyst.
C. Computer operator.
D. Computer programmer.

BEC 4-Q66 B1206. Which of the following is only an output device?

A. USB flash drive.
B. Speaker.
C. DVD drive.
D. Mouse.

BEC 4-Q67 B338. The computer operating system performs scheduling, resource allocation, and data retrieval functions based on a set of instructions provided by the

A. Multiplexer.
B. Peripheral processors.
C. Concentrator.
D. Job control language.

BEC 4-Q68 B183. Which of the following is a primary function of a database management system?

A. Report customization.
B. Capability to create and modify the database.
C. Financial transactions input.
D. Database access authorizations.

BEC 4-Q69 B152. Which of the following structures refers to the collection of data for all vendors in a relational data base?

A. Record.
B. Field.
C. File.
D. Byte.

BEC 4-Q70 B105. What is the correct ascending hierarchy of data in a system?

A. Character, record, file, field.
B. Field, character, file, record.
C. Character, field, record, file.
D. Field, record, file, character.

BEC 4-Q71 B352. In an accounting information system, which of the following types of computer files most likely would be a master file?

A. Inventory subsidiary.
B. Cash disbursements.
C. Cash receipts.
D. Payroll transactions.

BEC 4-Q72 B374. Jones, an auditor for Farmington Co., noted that the Acme employees were using computers connected to Acme's network by wireless technology. On Jones' next visit to Acme, Jones brought one of Farmington's laptop computers with a wireless network card. When Jones started the laptop to begin work, Jones noticed that the laptop could view several computers on Acme's network and Jones had access to Acme's network files. Which of the following statements is the most likely explanation?

A. Acme's router was improperly configured.
B. Farmington's computer had the same administrator password as the server.
C. Jones had been given root account access on Acme's computer.
D. Acme was not using security on the network.

BEC 4-Q73 B365. Most client/server applications operate on a three-tiered architecture consisting of which of the following layers?

A. Desktop client, application, and database.
B. Desktop client, software, and hardware.
C. Desktop server, application, and database.
D. Desktop server, software, and hardware.

BEC 4-Q74 B240. A value-added network (VAN) is a privately owned network that performs which of the following functions?

A. Route data transactions between trading partners.
B. Route data within a company's multiple networks.
C. Provide additional accuracy for data transmissions.
D. Provide services to send marketing data to customers.

BEC 4-Q75 B155. Which of the following is the primary advantage of using a value-added network (VAN)?

A. It provides confidentiality for data transmitted over the Internet.
B. It provides increased security for data transmissions.
C. It is more cost effective for the company than transmitting data over the Internet.
D. It enables the company to obtain trend information on data transmissions.

BEC 4-Q76 B190. In a large multinational organization, which of the following job responsibilities should be assigned to the network administrator?

A. Managing remote access.
B. Developing application programs.
C. Reviewing security policy.
D. Installing operating system upgrades.

BEC 4-Q77 B263. Which of the following statements is true regarding Transmission Control Protocol and Internet Protocol (TCP/IP)?

A. Every TCP/IP-supported transmission is an exchange of funds.
B. TCP/IP networks are limited to large mainframe computers.
C. Every site connected to a TCP/IP network has a unique address.
D. The actual physical connections among the various networks are limited to TCP/IP ports.

BEC 4-Q78 B250. Which of the following is an electronic device that separates or isolates a network segment from the main network while maintaining the connection between networks?

A. Query program.
B. Firewall.
C. Image browser.
D. Keyword.

BEC 4-Q79 B358. Which of the following risks can be minimized by requiring all employees accessing the information system to use passwords?

A. Collusion.
B. Data entry errors.
C. Failure of server duplicating function.
D. Firewall vulnerability.

BEC 4-Q80 B373. What is the primary advantage of using an application firewall rather than a network firewall?

A. It is less expensive.
B. It offers easier access to applications.
C. It provides additional user authentication.
D. It is easier to install.

BEC 4-Q81 B282. Which of the following artificial intelligence information systems cannot learn from experience?

A. Neural networks.
B. Case-based reasoning systems.
C. Rule-based expert systems.
D. Intelligent agents.

Multiple Choice – Solutions

BEC 4-Q1 B357. The correct choice is C. A computer-based system for transaction processing is more efficient at producing financial statements because the general ledger balances (the end result of transactions processing) can be more quickly and efficiently compiled into financial statements than in a manual system. A computer-based system will also help minimize mathematical errors.

Choice A is not correct because both computer-based systems and manual systems require stringent internal controls, although some of the controls for each system may be different.

Choice B is not correct because a computer-based transactions processing system will not necessarily produce a more accurate set of financial statements; accuracy of the financial statements in a computer-based system relies on accurate transactions, effective software to record the transactions, and effective software to compile the financial statements.

Choice D is not correct because both computer-based systems and manual systems require reconciliations between control accounts and subsidiary ledgers, e.g., reconciling the total in the accounts receivable control account with the total of customers' ending balances in the subsidiary ledger for accounts receivable.

BEC 4-Q2 B70. The correct choice is A. An executive support system is specifically designed to support the information needs of executives in making strategic decisions.

Choice B is not correct because a decision support system assists users at multiple levels of the organization in providing information to support decision making.

Choice C is not correct because a transaction processing system processes routine transactions in applications such as sales, accounts receivable, and accounts payable.

Choice D is not correct because a management information system is a broader concept encompassing numerous types of application systems which are used to support many aspects of the entity's operational needs.

BEC 4-Q3 B239. The correct choice is C. A risk assessment evaluates the likelihood that risks will occur and the effects that the risks will have on the organization. The procedure that managers use to identify unauthorized access and the probability that the unauthorized access will occur is part of the risk assessment. Determining how unauthorized individuals could obtain the information and the value of the information helps management evaluate the inherent risk of such an event.

Choice A is not correct because a disaster recovery plan assessment is an evaluation of the disaster recovery plan and its effectiveness in helping the organization continue operations in the event of a disaster.

Choice B is not correct because a systems assessment evaluates the software, hardware, and infrastructure and its ability to meet the information technology objectives of the organization.

Choice D is not correct because a test of controls evaluates whether controls are properly designed and operating so that the control objectives may be achieved.

BEC 4-Q4 B172. The correct choice is A. Cash receipts occur as a result of collections (also known as remittances) of accounts receivable. Therefore, comparing control and remittance totals would be included in a document flowchart for processing cash receipts.

Choice B is not correct because recording returns and allowances would be part of sales returns and allowances or purchase returns and allowances and not for processing cash receipts.

Choice C is not correct because authorizing and generating an invoice would be part of processing sales and not processing cash receipts.

Choice D is not correct because authorizing and generating a voucher would be part of processing accounts payable and not processing cash receipts.

BEC 4-Q5 B223. The correct choice is B. New technology and a poorly defined design structure are inherently more risky; personnel lack experience with new systems and they will find it more difficult to manage and operate a system with a poorly defined design structure.

Choice A is not correct because a poorly defined design structure is inherently more risky; personnel will find it more difficult to manage and operate a system with a poorly defined design structure.

Choice C is not correct because current systems with a well-defined design structure have lower risk.

Choice D is not correct because new technology is inherently more risky; personnel lack experience with new systems.

BEC 4-Q6 B1212. The correct choice is C. A SOC 3 report is a simple, general use report on the operating effectiveness of an entity's controls over a system relevant to one or more Trust Services principles and criteria.

Choice A is not correct because a SOC 1 is a restricted use report on the operating effectiveness of a service organization's controls likely to be relevant to user entities' internal control over financial reporting. It is not a general use report nor does it use Trust Services principles and criteria.

Choice B is not correct because a SOC 2 is only shared with knowledgeable parties, specified by the auditor. However, a SOC 2 does consider the operating effectiveness of an entity's controls over a system relevant to one or more Trust Services principles and criteria.

Choice D is not correct because the WebTrust Program for Certification Authorities (CAs) assesses the adequacy and effectiveness of a CA's controls using a tailored set of principles and criteria created exclusively for CAs. The result, however, is a general use report.

BEC 4-Q7 B337. The correct choice is D. Reviewing the systems-access log would most likely detect computer-related fraud because the reviewer may notice something out of the ordinary, e.g., the number of attempts to access the system, access during unusual times of the day, and frequent access to sensitive data.

Choice A is not correct because digital encryption is the technique applied to the data in order to encrypt it and a common key must be used by the sender and receiver to encrypt and decrypt the data; encryption is used to prevent computer-related fraud, not detect computer-related fraud.

Choice B is not correct because a validity check is an input control that performs a lookup to confirm that the data entered is a valid input that is included in the universe of valid values for that field.

Choice C is not correct because conducting fraud-awareness training is a preventive control activity, not a detective control activity.

BEC 4-Q8 B227. The correct choice is A. If the accounts payable clerk is making unauthorized changes to previous payments to a vendor, then the current information (as an unauthorized change) could be compared to transaction logs of the original transactions, such as the receipt of the invoice and the creation of the accounts payable. Furthermore, the invoice would be supported by documentation, such as purchase orders and receiving reports.

Choices B and C are not correct because the unauthorized changes to previous payments may not be flagged and reported as errors.

Choice D is not correct because the original payments had already been validated and would have been included in a validated data file. If the amount of the original payment was changed, the payment would still show as being validated.

BEC 4-Q9 B1209. The correct choice is D. The goal cascade is a method for linking stakeholder needs to enterprise goals, IT-related goals, and enabler goals.

Choice A is not correct because a mission statement is a formal description of the organization's values, including its core purpose. It is not a focus of the COBIT 5 principles.

Choice B is not correct because a core competency is a factor or ability that distinguishes the organization from competitors. It is not a focus of the COBIT 5 principles.

Choice C is not correct because a vision statement describes what an organization would optimally like to achieve in the future. It is not a focus of the COBIT 5 principles.

BEC 4-Q10 B1210. The correct choice is C. Governance is an overarching concept in COBIT 5, rather than a specific enabler. Governance is defined, with relation to management, in the fifth COBIT 5 principle (i.e., separating governance from management).

Choice A is not correct because it is a COBIT 5 enabler that relates to individual and collective behavior within an organization, including moral decision-making.

Choice B is not correct because it is a COBIT 5 enabler that relates to staff availability, turnover, education, qualifications, technical skill, and experience.

Choice D is not correct because it is a COBIT 5 enabler that relates to the value creation.

BEC 4-Q11 B151. The correct choice is B. An ERP uses common tables so that data is entered into the system one time and then used in multiple modules. This increases responsiveness and flexibility because the different modules share the same data and multiple modules are updated simultaneously whenever new data is input into the system.

Choice A is not correct because an ERP uses common tables to that data is entered into the system one time and then used in multiple modules. Therefore, modifying data in one module will also modify the data in other modules.

Choice C is not correct because an ERP uses common tables so that data is entered into the system one time and then used in multiple modules. Therefore, a field (e.g., vendor number) will have the same value in the accounts payable module and the master vendor file.

Choice D is not correct because the complexity of an ERP system increases the costs for implementation and training.

BEC 4-Q12 B116. The correct choice is C. An Enterprise Resource Planning (ERP) system integrates numerous functions, such as human resources, payroll, general ledger, fixed assets, sales, production, procurement, accounts payable, and accounts receivable. Therefore, an ERP helps to integrate data from all aspects of an organization's activities.

Choices A and B are not correct because a system that assists in making decisions about a particular problem describes a decision support system.

Choice D is not correct because a system that presents executives with the information needed to make strategic plans describes an executive support system.

BEC 4-Q13 B53. The correct choice is D. An enterprise resource planning (ERP) system integrates numerous functions, such as human resources, payroll, general ledger, fixed assets, sales, production, procurement, accounts payable, and accounts receivable; this allows information exchange and collaboration among all parties involved in business operations.

Choice A is not correct because a decision support system is designed to assist managers in making decisions through user interface to solve novel and unique problems; therefore, it does not allow information exchange and collaboration among all parties.

Choice B is not correct because an executive support system is designed to assist executives in making strategic decisions; therefore, it does not allow information exchange and collaboration among all parties.

Choice C is not correct because an office automation system automates certain manual processes through the use of software tools such as electronic mail, electronic calendars, and spreadsheet and word processing software; these may allow information exchange and collaboration, but not necessarily among all parties.

BEC 4-Q14 B1205. The correct choice is D. An automated interface is more accurate and efficient since the transfer process is configured to execute the exact same procedure every time. With a decrease in the potential for variability, the accuracy of the data transfer is expected to increase.

Choice A is not correct because data transmission failures are more common using a manual interface.

Choice B is not correct because a manual reconciliation is an internal control for a manual interface to ensure accuracy. If a manual reconciliation is still determined by the company to be necessary, it is likely to decrease in frequency.

Choice C is not correct because user interaction will decline once the interface is automated.

BEC 4-Q15 B272. The correct choice is B. A new retail location will require a data communication infrastructure for handling debit and credit card transactions; this type of infrastructure would be best supported by real-time processing so that debit and credit card transactions may be processed as they occur. Real-time processing is required to support real-time approvals and confirmations needed for making in-store sales.

Choices A, B, and C are not correct because these types of processing would not support the debit and credit card transaction requirements of real-time approvals and confirmations needed for making in-store sales.

BEC 4-Q16 B67. The correct choice is A. Querying a data warehouse to drill down into transaction and trend information via various network set-ups is an example of an on-line analytical processing system; the drill down capability allows analysis of the raw data that is summarized at a higher level.

Choice B is not correct because an on-line transaction-processing system deals with applications that process routine transactions, such as sales, accounts receivable, and accounts payable.

Choice C is not correct because an on-line executive information system provides support specifically designed for the information needs of executives in making strategic decisions.

Choice D is not correct because an on-line information storage system deals with secondary storage of data and not with applications which allow users to manipulate and analyze the data.

BEC 4-Q17 B1232. The correct answer is choice A. The benefits of real-time processing include increased security, speed and efficiency, because the processing is done electronically at the same time, and in the same order that activities occur; without manual intervention. For banks, processing credit authorizations in real-time for consumer loan applicants would include such activities as having the applicant's credit history automatically run and added into the loan applicant's electronic file at the bank, which can be immediately reviewed. This leads to a quicker and more efficient approval process for the bank and increased customer satisfaction from receiving a faster decision on the loan application from the bank. In addition, if the loan is approved quicker, the bank will be able to disperse funds and begin receiving interest income sooner.

Choices B, C and D are incorrect because in each of these choices, the bank is making a payment and would be better off to make the payments on the due dates, instead of as the transaction occurs, to have the ability to use those funds for a longer period of time.

BEC 4-Q18 B236. The correct choice is D. Batch processing processes similar transactions together as a batch, usually at pre-set times, such as every day at the same time; the disadvantage of batch processing is that the master files are not updated with the most recent transaction data until the batch is posted.

Choice A is not correct because online real-time processing requires a greater level of control than batch processing because online real-time processing posts transactions to the master files as the transactions occur, so controls must be applied before each transaction is posted.

Choice B is not correct because batch processing requires less computing resources than online real-time processing. The batches in batch processing may be processed during times when computer resources are in low demand, e.g., batches may be run overnight. In contrast, online real-time processing posts transactions as they occur and high user demand may require additional computing resources.

Choice C is not correct because on-line real-time processing requires more personnel than batch processing. Online real-time processing posts transactions as they occur and high user demand may require additional personnel to support the online real-time processing infrastructure.

BEC 4-Q19 B153. The correct choice is B. The batch processing method processes a batch of similar transactions all at the same time during a batch run; the system records are updated once the batch run is complete. Conversely, the real-time processing method processes transactions chronologically as they occur; the system records are updated as each transaction is processed. The detailed posting type means that each transaction in the batch is individually posted in the general ledger. Conversely, a summary posting type means that the batch total is posted instead of the individual lines.

Choice A is not correct because a transaction posted upon entry describes the real-time processing method instead of the batch processing method. But, if each transaction has its own line entry in the appropriate ledger, this describes the detailed posting type as described in the question.

Choice C is not correct because a transaction posted upon entry describes the real-time processing method instead of the batch processing method. Furthermore, posting a cumulative entry total in the appropriate ledger describes the summary posting type instead of the detailed posting type.
Choice D is not correct because posting a cumulative entry total in the appropriate ledger describes the summary posting type instead of the detailed posting type. But, assigning transactions to groups before posting is typically a step in the batch processing method, which is the method described in the question.

BEC 4-Q20 B133. The correct choice is C. The online processing mode provides the most accurate and complete information for decision-making because the data to which management refers in order to make decisions is updated continuously and contains the most complete information.

Choice A is not correct because the batch processing mode provides data that has been updated as of the date of the last batch run and omits data from the last batch run to the present; therefore, batch processing provides incomplete data.

Choice B is not correct because distributed processing refers to processing that occurs at multiple locations (as opposed to a centralized location). Whether processing occurs at multiple locations or a centralized location does not necessarily affect the accuracy and completeness of data.

Choice D is not correct because applications process day-to-day transactions such as sales, accounts receivable, accounts payable, and payroll. Information on which management relies in order to make decisions must be summarized and analyzed at a higher level than the detailed transactions data found in applications.

BEC 4-Q21 B252. The correct choice is A. A distributed processing environment means that processing is handled at multiple locations. The distributed processing environment would be best when there are large volumes of data at many locations and fast access is required. Large volumes of data that require fast access would justify the additional cost of processing at multiple locations, whereas small volumes of data that do not require fast access would not justify the additional cost of processing at multiple locations.

Choice B is not correct because large volumes of data that is generated centrally and which does not require fast access may be processed most economically at a central location.
Choice C is not correct because small volumes of data generated at many locations requiring fast access and prompt summaries at a central site would be processed better at the central location. The small volumes of data at many locations do not justify the additional cost of processing at multiple locations.

Choice D is not correct because small volumes of data generated centrally requiring fast access with summaries needed at many locations would be processed better at the central location. The summaries needed at many locations do not require processing at multiple locations.

BEC 4-Q22 B188. The correct choice is B. A payroll system processes weekly, bi-weekly, semi-monthly, or monthly salary or wage payments to employees. A payroll system is a transaction processing system because its transactions are part of routine accounting and financial operations.

Choice A is not correct because a database management system manages different applications and the database used for processing in the application, for example the accounts payable application and the database of vendor files.

Choice C is not correct because a decision support system (DSS) is designed to assist managers in making decisions through user interface to solve novel and unique problems. Payroll data may be included in a DSS, but at a summarized level and not the detailed transaction level.

Choice D is not correct because an enterprise resource planning (ERP) system integrates numerous functions, such as human resources, payroll, general ledger, fixed assets, sales, production, procurement, accounts payable, and accounts receivable. A payroll system may be included as a function within an ERP.

BEC 4-Q23 B208. The correct choice is B. From the transferor's perspective, electronic funds transfer (EFT) in general reduces errors in payment transactions and in particular for recurring payments of the same amount. Furthermore, because EFT confirms the transmission of transactions, the transferor will be notified more timely if the EFT is rejected so errors can be corrected more quickly. From the recipient's perspective, assuming that the EFT was transmitted correctly, EFT also helps to ensure that the recipient records the correct amount because the amount received appears in the recipient's bank account. If you factor in that international cash transactions may involve payees with names and addresses in a foreign language, EFT helps to reduce data entry errors associated with a different language or even a different alphabet.

Choice A is not correct because, although re-establishing EFT processes may be part of a disaster recovery plan; using EFT for international cash transactions in itself does not create a multilingual disaster recovery plan.

Choice C is not correct because the location where foreign source documents are stored is a policy that is determined independently from the policy to use EFT for international cash transactions.

Choice D is not correct because in some systems, such as electronic data interchange (EDI), the source documents are maintained for a shorter period of time than in manual systems. When using EDI (which incorporates the use of EFT for payments and collections), because the source documents (and therefore the audit trail) may be erased more frequently than in a manual system, auditing must occur more frequently and throughout the accounting cycle.

BEC 4-Q24 B336. The correct choice is C. Electronic Data Interchange (EDI) is the exchange of data electronically between trading partners (typically point-to-point), which reduces the use of paper documents and shortens the cycle time for processing transactions. Encryption is used to secure the data between trading partners and encryption by using hardware that is physically secure provides better security than encryption by software. Encryption using hardware means that in order to circumvent the control you must first gain access to the hardware, whereas software is more easily compromised through modifying the code.

Choice A is not correct because the data on the removable drives is not encrypted. If confidentiality of data is the primary risk, then the data should be encrypted because the drives are locked up at night but not during the day.

Choice B is not correct because message authentication in EDI systems ensures that the message came from a valid trading partner; this is unrelated to segregation of duties in the EDI system.

Choice D is not correct because security at all phases in EDI systems is necessary.

BEC 4-Q25 B249. The correct choice is B. Electronic data interchange (EDI) is the exchange of data electronically between trading partners (typically point-to-point), which reduces the use of paper documents and shortens the cycle time for processing transactions, e.g., the procure-to-pay cycle is shortened so that payments to vendors occur soon after purchases from vendors. Because the data is exchanged electronically between trading partners, this allows controls to be standardized between the two parties and helps assure the thoroughness of transaction data.

Choice A is not correct because EDI does not eliminate the need to continuously update antivirus software. Updating antivirus software should occur in both EDI and non-EDI environments.

Choice C is not correct because EDI does not automatically protect information that has left the entity. EDI helps standardize controls to assure the thoroughness of the data; it does not necessarily protect the data once it has left one trading partner and is transmitted to another trading partner.

Choice D is not correct because EDI reduces the use of paper documents, so receiving reports are electronically generated and the purchasing trading party will still have to verify the receipt of goods before making payment.

BEC 4-Q26 B179. The correct choice is A. Electronic data interchange (EDI) is the exchange of data electronically between trading partners (typically point-to-point), which reduces the use of paper documents and shortens the cycle time for processing transactions, e.g., the procure-to-pay cycle is shortened so that payments to vendors occur soon after purchases from vendors.

Choice B is not correct because electronic transmission of funds-related transactions describes electronic funds transfer (EFT). EFT is one component of EDI.

Choice C is not correct because transmitting sales data electronically using a centralized network to a central processor describes the internal processing of sales.

Choice D is not correct because sales of products on central web server describes internet-based commerce (e.g., on-line shopping).

BEC 4-Q27 B283. The correct choice is C. E-cash maintains financial privacy when customers pay for goods or services from a website. Financial privacy is maintained because the customer's information is located at the e-cash website and not at the website of the retail provider of goods and services.

Choice A is not correct because credit card information about a customer may be maintained at the website of the retail provider of goods and services; therefore, the customer may not maintain financial privacy at the retailer's website.

Choice B is not correct because website draft information about the customer may be maintained at the website of the retail provider of goods and services; therefore, the customer may not maintain financial privacy at the retailer's website. Site drafts generally are used for international transactions.

Choice D is not correct because electronic check (e.g., debit card) information about the customer may be maintained at the website of the retail provider of goods and services; therefore, the customer may not maintain financial privacy at the retailer's website.

BEC 4-Q28 B1230. The correct answer choice is A. The primary goal of business process management (BPM) is to coordinate business functions to best meet customer needs. Business processes are structured activities that organizations use to accomplish their objectives. BPM requires managers to document the existing process architecture, analyze its structure, and determine ways to improve it. BPM activities fit into categories such as design, modeling (pre-testing, "what if" simulations), execution (implementation and post-installation testing), monitoring, and optimization. For a company seeking competitive advantages in planning for the implementation of a new software system, they should first design the optimal process and then align the software to it, for maximum operational effectiveness, efficiency, and customer satisfaction.

Choice B is incorrect because first the company should design an optimal process and then align the software to this process, not the existing one.

Choice C is incorrect because manpower should be directed to the bottleneck process areas to address any issues that need to be resolved. This would be done in the execution and monitoring categories of BPM.

Choice D is incorrect because the process should be dictated by identifying existing processes and areas for process improvement using BPM, and not by management.

BEC 4-Q29 B1208. The correct choice is D. The Internet of Things (IoT) integrates technology into the physical world, creating a symbiotic relationship with humans. The wristband in this example demonstrates internet based, object-to-object interaction and results in a seamless experience for the wristband wearer.

Choice A is not correct because Web 2.0 focuses on interactive sharing.

Choice B is not correct because Web 1.0 is the first generation of the internet, capitalizing on easily accessible static content.

Choice C is not correct because Web 3.0 is a meaning-centric stage in internet evolution that personalizes the web browsing experience. Web 3.0 is bound to traditional devices for human-internet interaction.

BEC 4-Q30 B351. The correct choice is A. Symmetric encryption uses a single private key known only to the sender and the receiver of the data or message that is used to encrypt and decrypt data or a message; this is a major disadvantage because both sender and receiver must have the key.

Choice B is not correct because the private key may be broken down into fragments to be distributed to the receiver. By breaking the private key into fragments, this increases the security of the private key because the receiver must have all fragments in order to decrypt the data or message.

Choices C and D are not correct because both the sender and the receiver must have the private key to encrypt and decrypt the data or message.

BEC 4-Q31 B131. The correct choice is D because e-commerce through the internet uses online real-time processing, not batch processing, and is the exception to methods used to prevent unauthorized access to proprietary information when doing business on the internet.

Choices A, B and C are not correct because they are all valid methods used to prevent unauthorized access to proprietary information when doing business on the internet. Password management ensures strong passwords that are changed periodically so that access to proprietary data is restricted to authorized persons. Data encryption ensures that only authorized persons with the key to encrypt and decrypt data have access to proprietary data. Digital certificates authenticate the identity of persons authorized to access proprietary data.

BEC 4-Q32 B344. The correct choice is A. A digital signature authenticates a message so that the receiver knows who originated the message and that the message has not been altered. Therefore, a digital signature is used primarily to determine that a message was not altered during transmission.

Choice B is not correct because a digital signature does not prevent the message from being intercepted en route to the receiver of the message. A digital signature authenticates a message.

Choice C is not correct because a digital signature does not guarantee that the message will be received by the intended recipient; errors may occur during transmission that would prevent the message from being transmitted properly. A digital signature authenticates the message.

Choice D is not correct because a digital signature does not guarantee that the message was sent to the correct address; a digital signature authenticates the message.

BEC 4-Q33 B1207. The correct choice is B. An acceptable user policy outlines and governs the appropriate use of technology and computer equipment at an organization, including guidelines concerning personal use.

Choice A is not correct because the email policy only outlines the acceptable and unacceptable use of the organization's email system, it does not expressly include personal use of other computer resources.

Choice C is not correct because a disaster recovery plan policy states the requirement to have a disaster recovery plan and does not prohibit computer resource use.

Choice D is not correct because the password policy sets the standards for passwords syntax, change frequency, and rules over password protection and sharing.

BEC 4-Q34 B222. The correct choice is D. By limiting access to employee master files to only authorized employees in the personnel department, very few persons will be able to change an employee's hourly wage rate to an inappropriate rate.

Choice A is not correct because having the supervisor verify hours worked is an internal control on the number of hours worked and not an internal control on the hourly wage rate.

Choice B is not correct because a change in hourly wage rate to an inappropriate wage rate may occur in both batch systems and real-time systems.

Choice C is not correct because giving a payroll data entry clerk the ability to change hourly pay rates would increase the likelihood that an appropriate wage rate may be used due to (1) data entry errors made by the clerk or (2) collusion between the clerk and the employee to change the hourly wage rate to an inappropriate rate.

BEC 4-Q35 B130. The correct choice is C. In this situation, the greatest security risk is unauthorized access to the accounts payable system which could be used to make fraudulent payments to fictitious vendors. If the administrator left the company and the user account was not removed upon the employee's termination, this creates a risk of unauthorized access.

Choice A is not correct because the strength of the password (e.g., lack of alpha-numeric requirements) is not the greatest security risk. The lack of alpha-numeric passwords may make it easier to guess employees' passwords, but this would be true regardless of whether or not the administrator's access was still active.

Choice B is not correct because the lack of documented management procedures for user accounts is not the greatest security risk. The lack of documented procedures for user accounts makes it more likely that the procedures would not be followed, but the procedures could still be omitted even if they were documented. Furthermore, the lack of documented procedures does not necessarily mean that there are no procedures.

Choice D is not correct because the lack of periodic review of security logs for violations is not the greatest security risk. Even if the security logs were periodically reviewed for violations, this control occurs after-the-fact and is a detective control; preventive controls are more effective in mitigating security risks. Furthermore, if the administrator's account was still active, the security log may not flag the administrator's unauthorized access as a security violation.

BEC 4-Q36 B1211. The correct choice is B. The approval by senior management of a project prior to implementation is a control over the systems development lifecycle (SDLC). It relates to the control objective that provides reasonable assurance that new systems (or applications) are authorized, tested, approved, properly implemented, and documented.

Choice A is not correct because the scheduling and monitoring of backups is a control related to computer operations and processing rather than the system development lifecycle.

Choice C is not correct because only one, not both, of the controls relate to the SDLC.

Choice D is not correct because the determination that neither control is an example of a control over the SDLC is inaccurate. Senior management approval of projects prior to implementation relates to the SDLC.

BEC 4-Q37 B43. The correct choice is D. Restricting access to the computer center by use of biometric devices (e.g., by fingerprint or palm print) is a general control because controlling access to programs and data (e.g., controlling access to the computer center) is a general control.

Choice A is not correct because limiting entry of sales transactions to only valid credit customers is an example of a look up control (closed loop verification), which is an input control.

Choice B is not correct because hash totals are an example of an input control.

Choice C is not correct because restricting access to entry of accounts payable transactions is specific to the accounts payable function and is an application control.

BEC 4-Q38 B271. The correct choice is B. The most complete disaster recovery plan will have full implementation and testing. The combination of an existing alternate processing site, backup and off-site storage procedures, identification of critical applications, and finally a test of the plan is the configuration of the most complete disaster recovery plan.

Choices A and D are not correct because a contract for an alternate processing site is less fully implemented that an existing alternative processing site; furthermore, the disaster recovery plan has not been tested.

Choice C is not correct because there is no alternate processing site.

BEC 4-Q39 B260. The correct choice is C. To prevent interrupted information systems operation, the backup and downtime controls are typically included in an organization's disaster recovery plan. The backup controls ensure that data will be available in the event of a disaster because the data has been duplicated at another location. The downtime controls ensure that the disaster recovery plan is activated after a predetermined downtime has occurred because an extended downtime may indicate a disaster has occurred.

Choice A is not correct because data transmission controls should be present in both regular operations and disaster recovery operations, so data transmission controls are not specific to disaster recovery plans.

Choice B is not correct because data input controls should be present in both regular operations and disaster recovery operations, so data input controls are not specific to disaster recovery plans.

Choice D is not correct because data processing controls should be present in both regular operations and disaster recovery operations, so data processing controls should not be specific to disaster recovery plans.

BEC 4-Q40 B343. The correct choice is B. The identification of critical applications should be included in the disaster recovery plan for an Information Technology department because the applications (e.g., accounts receivable and accounts payable) are specific to the IT department.

Choice A is not correct because replacement of personal computers for user departments is specific to the users, not the IT department.

Choice C is not correct because physical security of warehouse facilities is specific to inventories and other items stored in the warehouse facilities, not the IT department.

Choice D is not correct because cross-training of operating personnel is the training of personnel that work in operations, not the training of IT department personnel.

BEC 4-Q41 B233. The correct choice is C. A hot site is a disaster recovery site that already has equipment installed at the site. Therefore, a location that is equipped with redundant hardware and software is a hot site.

Choices A and D are not correct because a hot site is a disaster recovery site that already has equipment installed at the site. A disaster recovery site would be located away from the location within the company that is most vulnerable to a disaster or a location that is considered too close to a potential disaster.

Choice B is not correct because a cold site is a disaster recovery site that is a shell which is ready to receive equipment. Therefore, a location where a company can install data processing equipment on short notice describes a cold site.

BEC 4-Q42 B173. The correct choice is D. The first step management should take with regard to the lack of a disaster recovery plan is to prepare a statement of responsibilities for tasks to be included in the plan. In the event of a disaster, it is important to understand the authorities, roles, and responsibilities associated with each task in the disaster recovery plan.

Choice A is not correct because bulletproofing the information architecture specifically addresses security breaches as opposed to disaster recovery. Bulletproofing the information security architecture could be included in the implementation of a disaster recovery plan, but would not be the first step.

Choices B and C are not correct because management may designate a site as a hot site or cold site as an alternative processing site to help ensure continuity of operations and processing. The designation of a hot site or cold site would be included in the implementation of a disaster recovery plan, but would not be the first step.

BEC 4-Q43 B175. The correct choice is B. A disaster recovery plan documents the steps to be taken to recover from an interruption in operations due to a natural disaster or other adverse event (e.g., civil unrest). By collecting the names and locations of key vendors, the director helps to ensure communication needed to order key services, inventories, materials, equipment, and supplies and pay the vendors. By documenting the current hardware configuration, the director helps to ensure that the configuration can be duplicated. By collecting the names of team members, the director helps to ensure roles and responsibilities are assigned to key individuals. By designating an alternative processing location, the director helps to ensure that operations can re-start in a location unaffected by the disaster.

Choice A is not correct because a data restoration plan restores only the data and not the hardware and personnel as mentioned in the facts. A data restoration plan may be part of a disaster recovery plan.

Choice C is not correct because a system security policy involves security and not vendors as mentioned in the facts. A system security policy, especially for an alternative processing location, may be part of a disaster recovery plan.

Choice D is not correct because a system hardware policy governs only the hardware and not names of team members or an alternative processing location. A system hardware policy, especially for the system configuration, may be part of a disaster recovery plan.

BEC 4-Q44 B195. The correct choice is B. A cold site is a disaster recovery site that is a shell which is ready to receive equipment. The alternate location described in the question is a cold site because the site requires delivery of duplicate computer hardware, so the equipment is not at the location yet.

Choice A is not correct because a hot site is a disaster recovery site that already has equipment installed at the site.

Choice C is not correct because back-up site procedures are procedures included in the disaster recovery plan.

Choice D is not correct because a hot spare site agreement is an agreement with another party that they will provide a facility as a spare hot site in the event that the original hot site is not operational.

BEC 4-Q45 B154. The correct choice is D. A mirrored web server is a copy of the web site. The most comprehensive method for backing up a web site and ensuring business continuity in the event of a natural disaster is to maintain a mirrored web server at an off-site location where the same natural disaster is less likely to have the same adverse impact.

Choice A is not correct because although backing up the server database daily would help to ensure business continuity, the backup should be stored off-site. If both the actual server and backup server were located in the same place, a natural disaster would likely have the same adverse impact on both.

Choice B is not correct because storing records off-site helps protect the records in the event of a natural disaster, but off-site storage of records does not protect the systems that process the records.

Choice C is not correct because RAID (which is an acronym for redundant array of independent disks) technology is the system method that stores and retrieves data on a hard disk. The data is stored in multiple locations (e.g., stored on different disks), which makes the storage "redundant," and helps ensure that the data on the disk is not lost. However, because the disks are stored in the same location, all the disks will be adversely impacted by the natural disaster.

BEC 4-Q46 B135. The correct choice is B. A disaster recovery site that is a shell which is ready to receive equipment is called a cold site.

Choice A is not correct because a disaster recovery site that already has equipment installed is called a hot site.

Choice C is not correct because a warm site has duplicate equipment, although it may not be stocked with the same level of equipment that is found in a disaster recovery hot site and critical applications are not pre-installed.

Choice D is not correct because a flying start site, a type of hot site, is stocked with equipment and has networking and connectivity enabled. A flying start site is a turnkey operation with up-to-date backup data installed on a continuous basis, ready for cutover if disaster occurs.

BEC 4-Q47 B134. The correct choice is B. Edit checks are a type of application control that ensures accurate input of data into the application.

Choices A and D are not correct because a run control total and an exception report are examples of application controls related to processing accuracy and output.

Choice C is not correct because a report distribution log documents the details of when, what, and to whom reports were distributed; report distribution logs are related to output.

BEC 4-Q48 B1255. The correct answer choice is D. Closed-loop verification is an input control that is used to check the input accuracy by taking the inputs and comparing to other related information. In this question, the input error could have been prevented by closed-loop verification. For example, after the clerk applied the payment, the system requires the clerk to verify additional data about the customer, such as the account number, name, address, etc.

Choice A is incorrect because a checksum (or check digit) is the total of a predefined algorithm using digits input by the user that equal the check digit value (e.g., 7 is the check digit for account number 1032017, 1+0+3+2+0+1=7).

Choice B is incorrect because a field check is an input validation technique that restricts user input type (e.g., numerical data only).

Choice C is incorrect because a completeness test only assures that all the inputs were entered and not if they were correctly applied.

BEC 4-Q49 B808. The correct choice is C. A hash total is a total of values, but the value has no meaning; a hash total is used as a control for completeness. By totaling the invoice numbers as a hash total, the value of 515 as a hash total serves as a control that all invoices were included in processing.

Choice A is not correct because it is a record count for the sales orders in a batch; therefore, the record count is 5 invoices.

Choice B is not correct because it adds the product numbers, but omits the alphabet characters. Because of the alphabet characters, the product numbers are less effective (than the invoice numbers which have no alphabet characters) for use as a hash total.

Choice D is not correct because it adds the quantities.

BEC 4-Q50 B191. The correct choice is D. The reasonableness test, also known as a limit test, is a test that ensures that data input into a field complies with certain minimum and maximum requirements, e.g., there can only be 12 months in the year or the date of birth cannot be earlier than a certain date. A reasonableness test would also include the maximum number of days in each month.

Choice A is not correct because online prompting prompts the user to input required fields into a form, e.g., when using the internet, the user may be prompted to enter certain fields, such as an e-mail address, where the user cannot proceed without first inputting data into required fields.

Choice B is not correct because mathematical accuracy checks the correctness of calculations of quantities and dollar amounts.

Choice C is not correct because a preformatted screen allows users to input data into a form designed as a screen, with fields arranged in a logical order to allow for easier input.

BEC 4-Q51 B274. The correct choice is B. System controls would be examined to determine if an information is operating according to prescribed procedures. System controls include general controls and application controls; user controls also operate as system controls. Procedures implementing the general, application, and user controls would be examined to determine if they are operating as prescribed.

Choice A is not correct because system capacity describes the level of activity that the system can accommodate without compromising system speed and availability.

Choice C is not correct because system complexity is a factor which would affect the system control procedures. A more complex system infrastructure would require more complex procedures and controls, but is not the procedures in itself.

Choice D is not correct because accessibility to system information is just one of the types of general controls under system controls. Therefore, system control procedures are more comprehensive and would include procedures to help ensure accessibility to system information.

BEC 4-Q52 B339. The correct choice is C. An application is a specific process or subsystem, such as accounts receivable or accounts payable, and an application control plan would be specific to that process or subsystem.

Choice A is not correct because a preventive control plan helps ensure that errors do not occur.

Choice B is not correct because a corrective control plan helps ensure that errors that have been detected are corrected.

Choice D is not correct because a detective control plan helps ensure that errors that have occurred are detected.

BEC 4-Q53 B244. The correct choice is D. When changing from a manual system to a computer system, key differences are the methodologies used to implement the controls. Certain controls may be automated, such as certain input controls (e.g., hash totals verify completeness, limit/reasonableness tests verify that inputs fall within minimum and maximum criteria, validity checks ensure that customer or vendor numbers are correct). However, in both manual and automated systems, the internal control principles and objectives (e.g., authorizations and approvals, completeness and validity of data, reliable financial reporting, and compliance with laws and regulations) are similar.

Choices A, B, and C are not correct because in both manual and automated systems, the internal control principles and objectives (e.g., authorizations and approvals, completeness and validity of data, reliable financial reporting, and compliance with laws and regulations) are similar. However, the manner in which the controls are applied differs between manual and automated systems. Certain controls may be automated, such as certain input controls (e.g., hash totals verify completeness, limit/reasonableness tests verify that inputs fall within minimum and maximum criteria, validity checks ensure that customer or vendor numbers are correct).

BEC 4-Q54 B196. The correct choice is D. Access control software authenticates the user of the system, such as software to control user identification codes and passwords. The use of access control software is a preventive control because it ensures that only authorized users are using the system.

Choice A is not correct because contingency planning is a general control that covers overall IT operations to ensure continuity if adverse events occur to disrupt operations. Contingency planning could be used as a preventive or corrective control.

Choice B is not correct because a hash total is a total that has no meaning, but checks for completeness of the input; e.g., totaling the employees' identification numbers to ensure that all payroll records have been included in a payroll batch to be processed. A hash total could be used as a preventive or detective control.

Choice C is not correct because an echo check is a hardware check used predominantly in telecommunications and involves repeating the sender's data at the receiving point. An echo check is a detective control.

BEC 4-Q55 B232. The correct choice is A. The systems development life cycle is typically described in seven stages:
(1) planning, (2) analysis, (3) design, (4) development, (5) testing, (6) implementation, and (7) maintenance. Although planning is not one of the answer choices, the analysis stage occurs sooner in the sequence of the seven stages.

Choices B, C and D are not correct because these stages in the systems development life cycle occur after the analysis stage. The seven stages of the systems development life cycle are: (1) planning, (2) analysis, (3) design, (4) development, (5) testing, (6) implementation, and (7) maintenance.

BEC 4-Q56 B150. The correct choice is B. The most critical items to include in a systems specification document for a financial report would be the data elements needed to populate the data and be summarized on the report; deciding on which data elements are needed in the report is integral to the report's design. The data for those data elements are the subject of the report.

Choice A is not correct because performing a cost-benefit analysis would occur before making the decision to create a new report and designing the report.

Choice C is not correct because training requirements for the report are part of the overall implementation of the report once the report is complete and ready for introduction to the users.

Choice D is not correct because communicating the change and change management of the report is part of the overall implementation of the report once the report is complete and ready for introduction to the users.

BEC 4-Q57 B45. The correct choice is D. Independently verifying the transactions by comparing the actual results with the intended results will verify accuracy of the processing and help reduce the risk of incorrect processing in the computerized accounting system.

Choice A is not correct because segregation of duties helps to ensure collusion does not occur; collusion is two or more persons working together to commit fraud. Duties may be properly segregated, but this will not prevent the computerized accounting system from incorrectly processing transactions.

Choice B is not correct because proper authorization of transactions occurs before processing the transactions in the accounting system occurs. Properly authorized transactions may be processed incorrectly in the computerized accounting system.

Choice C is not correct because adequately safeguarding assets consists of activities that are performed both inside and outside the computerized accounting system and helps to ensure that assets are not stolen or misappropriated.

BEC 4-Q58 B1254. The correct answer choice is B. The system development lifecycle (SDLC) is a multi-step process that governs the planning, implementation, and maintenance of a business information system. The conceptual systems design phase would include a report generated that describes the content, processing flows, resource requirements, and procedures of a preliminary system design.

Choice A is incorrect because file and database design would be performed after the conceptual system design phase.

Choice C is incorrect because physical systems design would be performed after the file and database design phase.

Choice D is incorrect because the procedures design phase would be performed once there is a functional system prototype and related procedures can be documented on its intended use and operation.

BEC 4-Q59 B1256. The correct answer choice is B. The system development lifecycle (SDLC) is a multi-step process that governs the planning, implementation, and maintenance of a business information system. A well-designed system starts with clearly defined concept. The planning phase of the SDLC focuses on identifying problems and defining a system to appropriately address them. The plan for the system must consider and incorporate the organization's strategic goals. This is accomplished through data-gathering techniques, such as a system surveys and include interviews, quick questionnaires, observations, and systems documentation.

Choice A is incorrect because prototypes are introduced into the process in the development stage and are not part of a system survey for data gathering.

Choice C is incorrect because a PERT (Program Evaluation Review Technique) chart is used in project management, after a project is in the development stage and is not part of a system survey for data gathering.

Choice D is incorrect because Gantt chart is shows the work performed on a project, compared to the amount that was planned for the same period and is not part of a system survey for data gathering.

BEC 4-Q60 B185. The correct choice is C. An application programmer performs programming functions in applications such as accounts payable, accounts receivable, and payroll. Therefore, coding modifications into the payroll software are appropriate duties for an application programmer.

Choice A is not correct because modifying and adapting operating system software are appropriate duties for a systems programmer. There should be segregation of duties between systems programmers and applications programmers.

Choice B is not correct because correcting detected data entry errors for the cash disbursement system is an appropriate duty for the user of the cash disbursement system. There should be segregation of duties between application users and application programmers.

Choice D is not correct because maintaining custody of the billing program code and its documentation are duties appropriate for the data librarian. There should be segregation of duties between application programmers and the data librarian.

BEC 4-Q61 B132. The correct choice is C. At a minimum, the data entry, programming, and library functions should be segregated in the IT department. Therefore, the data entry (a user function or an operations function) and application programming (a programming function) responsibilities should be delegated to separate individuals.

Choice A is not correct because at a minimum the data entry, programming, and library functions should be segregated in the IT department. Therefore, the network maintenance and wireless access (which are both operations functions) responsibilities do not have to be delegated to separate individuals.

Choice B is not correct because at a minimum the data entry, programming, and library functions should be segregated in the IT department. Therefore, the data entry (a user function or an operations function) and antivirus management (an operations function) responsibilities do not have to be delegated to separate individuals.

Choice D is not correct because at a minimum the data entry, programming, and library functions should be segregated in the IT department. Therefore, the data entry (a user function or an operations function) and the quality assurance (a processing function or an operations function) responsibilities do not have to be delegated to separate individuals.

BEC 4-Q62 B54. The correct choice is A. There should be a segregation of duties between the application programmers and persons whose function is to test the program and also the users whose function is to validate that the modified program meets their needs; these are change control procedures in the applications software environment. Segregated duties in the testing and validation helps to ensure that the applications programmers are not implementing erroneous or fraudulent processing in the applications programs.

Choice B is not correct because management override is one of the reasons why internal controls can provide only reasonable assurance and not absolute assurance; an internal control may be overridden by management and render the control ineffective.

Choice C is not correct because data integrity involves the accuracy of data that is input, processed properly, and output from the system; data integrity involves processing and not necessarily modification to the application programs.

Choice D is not correct because computer operations deal with operations and processing and is a separate function from the applications programming and does not involve the modification of application programs.

BEC 4-Q63 B44. The correct choice is B. The role of the systems analyst is more general in nature and applies to the analysis and recommendation of requirements necessary to modify or design existing or new systems.

Choice A is not correct because developing long-range plans (that are more strategic in nature) is the role of the IT director or the Chief Information Officer; directing application development and computer operations is the role of the systems manager.

Choice C is not correct because maintaining control over the completeness, accuracy, and distribution of input and output is the role of the computer operator.

Choice D is not correct because selecting, implementing, and maintaining system software, network software, and the database management system is the role of the systems programmer.

BEC 4-Q64 B360. The correct choice is C. A systems programmer is responsible for ensuring that the software works effectively in running the hardware in the system. Therefore, a systems programmer is normally assigned responsibility over the operating systems and compilers.

Choice A is not correct because a systems analyst performs systems analysis and an applications programmer is responsible for ensuring that the applications software works effectively.

Choice B is not correct because data communications hardware and software are specialized functions that may be assigned to data communications specialists.

Choice D is not correct because computer operators are responsible for computer operations.

BEC 4-Q65 B108. The correct choice is A. In a large corporation, there is segregation of duties among the various functions in the Information Technology department. In a large corporation, the duties of the Data Librarian are segregated in a manner such that the Data Librarian has custody of the data, programs, and documentation.

Choice B is not correct because the role of the systems analyst is to analyze and recommend requirements necessary to modify or design existing or new systems.

Choice C is not correct because the role of the computer operator is to maintain control over computer operations to help ensure the completeness, accuracy, and distribution of input and output.

Choice D is not correct because the role of the computer programmer is to select, implement, and maintain software.

BEC 4-Q66 B1206. The correct choice is B. A speaker is an output device used to listen to audio files stored in an information system. Headphones could also be used for this purpose.

Choice A is not correct because a USB flash drive, a portable storage device, is an input/output (I/O) device. It can both send and receive information.

Choice C is not correct because a DVD, a removable storage device, is an I/O device. A capable computer can both read (input) data from and write (output) data onto a DVD.

Choice D is not correct because a mouse is an input device.

BEC 4-Q67 B338. The correct choice is D. Job control language provides the instructions for processing jobs by the operating system; jobs could include scheduling, resource allocation and data retrieval functions.

Choice A is not correct because a multiplexer is a device that aids in data communications and does not perform scheduling, resource allocation, and data retrieval functions.

Choice B is not correct because peripheral processors are peripheral equipment; in order for a peripheral computer (as a peripheral processor) to perform scheduling, resource allocation, and data retrieval functions, it would need similar job control language as the job control language of the central computer (the central processor).

Choice C is not correct because a concentrator is a device that aids in data communications and does not perform scheduling, resource allocation, and data retrieval functions.

BEC 4-Q68 B183. The correct choice is B. Primary functions of a database management system (DBMS) include management of data storage, data dictionary, security, back-up and recovery, table creation and modification, transactions processing, and interfaces with other systems. The capability to create and modify the database is a primary function.

Choice A is not correct because report customization is part of reporting, which is not a primary function of a database management system.

Choice C is not correct because financial transactions input is part of overall data input; data input is just one aspect of transactions processing. Managing transactions processing is a primary function of a DBMS.

Choice D is not correct because authorizations and access is part of security; authorizations and access are just one aspect of security. Managing security is a primary function of a DBMS.

BEC 4-Q69 B152. The correct choice is C. The master vendor file is a collection of vendor records in a relational data base.

Choice A is not correct because a vendor record is a collection of fields for a particular vendor. Pertinent information on a vendor includes vendor name, vendor address, and taxpayer identification number.

Choice B is not correct because a field is a collection of characters; e.g., alphabet and numeric characters that compose the vendor's name (e.g., XYZ Company) in the vendor name field.

Choice D is not correct because a byte is a character, such as the letter "X" in the vendor's name of XYZ Company.

BEC 4-Q70 B105. The correct choice is C. From lowest level to highest level of data, it is character, field, record, and file. For example, a numeric character is just one digit in the field for a vendor number. A collection of fields (e.g., vendor number, vendor name, vendor address) forms the vendor record. A collection of vendor records forms the master file of all vendors in the company.

Choices A, B and D are not correct because they do not present the correct hierarchy of data in the system of, from lowest level to highest level, character, field, record, and file.

BEC 4-Q71 B352. The correct choice is A. A control account is the summary for the subsidiary accounts; e.g., the accounts receivable control account is the total of gross accounts receivable, but the individual customer accounts are the subsidiary accounts and the collection of the customer subsidiary accounts is the master file for A/R. Therefore, the inventory control account is the total of the accounts for the inventory items, but the individual accounts for each inventory item are the subsidiary accounts and the collection of the inventory subsidiary accounts is the master file for inventory.

Choice B is not correct because the cash disbursements are the transactions which update the vendor accounts in the accounts payable master file; the cash disbursements are not the master file.

Choice C is not correct because the cash receipts are the transactions which update the customer accounts in the accounts receivable master file; the cash receipts are not the master file.

Choice D is not correct because the payroll transactions that update the employee accounts in the payroll master file; the payroll transactions are not the master file.

BEC 4-Q72 B374. The correct choice is D. Because the auditor was able to view several computers on the company network and access the company network files, the company was not using security to authenticate users before allowing access to the network or to limit users' authorization to view files.

Choice A is not correct because a router is a type of hardware that allows communication between two networks. Improper configuration of the router may not necessarily relate to security.

Choice B is not correct because it is unlikely that the auditor's computer had the same ID and password as the administrator's ID and password.

Choice C is not correct because the network root account has similar authorization to that of the administrator. It is unlikely that the auditor's computer had been given root account access.

BEC 4-Q73 B365. The correct choice is A. A client/server model works between the client (e.g., a desktop) and the service provider (e.g., the server) for an application (e.g., accounts payable). Therefore, there is a three-tiered architecture of desk-top client, application, and database.

Choice B is not correct because software and hardware are both applicable to the client (e.g., a desktop) and the service provider (e.g., the server) and do not describe the three-tiered architecture of client/server applications.

Choice C is not correct because a client/server model works between the client (e.g., a desktop) and the service provider (e.g., the server) for an application (e.g., accounts payable). Therefore, the desktop is, in general, the client and not the server.

Choice D is not correct because a client/server model works between the client (e.g., a desktop) and the service provider (e.g., the server) for an application (e.g., accounts payable). Therefore, the desktop, in general, is the client and not the server. Also, because software and hardware are both applicable to the client and the service provider, software and hardware do not describe the three-tiered architecture of client/server applications.

BEC 4-Q74 B240. The correct choice is A. A value-added network (VAN) is a privately-owned network used for communication by parties conducting business with each other. The owner of the VAN is an entity that specializes in selling and supporting its services. Because the network is privately owned (instead of public), it provides more security for data transmissions.

Choice B is not correct because a VAN is a privately-owned network used for communication between parties conducting business with each other. A VAN does not operate within a single organization's multiple networks.

Choice C is not correct because a VAN is a privately-owned network used for communication by parties conducting business with each other. Because the network is privately owned (instead of public), it provides more security for data transmissions. The VAN does not necessarily provide additional accuracy for data transmissions; accuracy of data transmissions would also depend on the accuracy of the data being transmitted.

Choice D is not correct because a VAN is a privately-owned network used for communication by parties conducting business with each other, e.g., sales and cost of goods sold, accounts receivable and accounts payable between wholesalers and retailers. It is unlikely that trading parties would use a VAN to send marketing data to customers.

BEC 4-Q75 B155. The correct choice is B. A value-added network (VAN) is a privately-owned network used for communication by parties conducting business with each other. The owner of the VAN is an entity that specializes in selling and supporting its services. Because the network is privately owned (instead of public), it provides more security for data transmissions.

Choice A is not correct because a VAN does not transmit data over the internet, which is a public network. A VAN is a privately-owned network.

Choice C is not correct because entities pay more for the more customized value-added services of a VAN; this is more costly than using a public network such as the internet.

Choice D is not correct because the VAN's services may or may not provide statistics to its customers so that customers may determine trends in data transmissions.

BEC 4-Q76 B190. The correct choice is A. The network administrator should be responsible for managing remote access to the network, e.g., employee access to network e-mail via their mobile devices or network access for telework.

Choice B is not correct because an applications programmer or developer should be responsible for developing application programs.

Choice C is not correct because the systems security officer or director should be responsible for reviewing security policy.

Choice D is not correct because installing operating system upgrades should be the responsibility of the system operations staff.

BEC 4-Q77 B263. The correct choice is C. The Transmission Control Protocol and Internet Protocol (TCP/IP) is a protocol for communication over the internet; the IP is a unique address on the internet that is specific to a computer. TCP/IP has two levels. The higher-level breaks data in packets that are transmitted over the internet; the lower level ensures that packets are delivered to the correct computer address.

Choice A is not correct because TCP/IP supports many types of transmissions, not just those that exchange funds.

Choice B is not correct because TCP/IP is a protocol for communication over internet; the IP is a unique address on the internet that is specific to a computer, including a personal computer, so TCP/IP is not limited to large mainframe computers.

Choice D is not correct because TCP/IP is a protocol for communication over the internet; TCP/IP is not the hardware for physical connections among the various networks.

BEC 4-Q78 B250. The correct choice is B. A firewall separates or isolates a network segment from the main network while maintaining the connection between networks. A firewall is typically used as a gateway to entering the network from an external source and prevents unauthorized access into the network.

Choice A is not correct because a query program is a program used to look up information in a database. For example, users may query the vendor database by inputting a vendor number into a field and the query program will retrieve the vendor file for that vendor number.

Choice C is not correct because an image browser is a program that enables the viewing of images, such as charts and graphs.

Choice D is not correct because a keyword is a word that when entered into a search engine, allows the user to obtain search results on topics related to the keyword.

BEC 4-Q79 B358. The correct choice is D. Requiring all employees to access the information by using passwords would minimize firewall vulnerability. Requiring all employees to use passwords will help ensure that only authorized persons will access the system.

Choice A is not correct because collusion is cooperation between two or more persons in order to perpetrate fraud; therefore, collusion may circumvent any control, such as using passwords, when passwords are shared by persons who are colluding.

Choice B is not correct because the use of passwords will not prevent data entry errors; input controls (e.g., reasonableness checks and hash totals) will help prevent data entry errors.

Choice C is not correct because the failure to duplicate the server function may result in unavailability of the server; therefore, discontinuity of services will not be prevented by using passwords.

BEC 4-Q80 B373. The correct choice is C. A firewall separates or isolates a network segment from the main network while maintaining the connection between networks. A firewall is typically used as a gateway to entering the network from an external source and prevents unauthorized access into the network. The primary advantage of using an application firewall is that it provides additional user authentication to the application after the user has provided authentication to enter the network.

Choice A is not correct because using an application firewall requires a firewall for each application, which increases the expense.

Choice B is not correct because if a user has authority to access multiple applications, then the user will have to provide authentication for each application, making access to applications more difficult for the user.

Choice D is not correct because using an application firewall requires a firewall for each application; this increases the complexity for installing the firewall because each application may require a customized firewall.

BEC 4-Q81 B282. The correct choice is C. Rule-based expert systems are based on rules that have been programmed to reflect the expert's experience. Rule-based expert systems do not improve unless the rules are updated based on the expert's experience.

Choices A is not correct because a neural network is based on the human brain. Neural networks are programmed to learn from experience.

Choice B is not correct because case-based reasoning systems are programmed to solve current cases based on experience with solving previous cases. As the number of cases increase, case-based reasoning systems are better able to find similarities between the current case and previous cases, meaning that case-based reasoning systems can learn from experience based on the previous cases' solutions.

Choice D is not correct because intelligent agents work independently to collect sensory data and learn from experience with the sensory data in order to help people achieve an objective.

This page is intentionally left blank.

BEC 5 – Operations Management

A. Financial and Non-Financial Measures of Performance Management		**5A-1 – 5A-22**
	1. Financial measures and value-based metrics	1
	2. Non-financial measures	18
	3. Quality of earnings	20
	4. Incentive compensation	20
	5. Benchmarking	21
	6. Cost of quality	22
B. Cost Accounting		**5B-1 – 5B-31**
	1. Cost measurement concepts, methods and techniques	1
	2. Variance analysis	27
C. Process Management		**5C-1 – 5C-9**
	1. Approaches, techniques, measures, benefits to process management driven businesses	1
	2. Management philosophies and techniques for performance and quality improvement	3
D. Planning Techniques		**5D-1 – 5D-20**
	1. Budgeting and analysis	2
	2. Forecasting and projection	6
Glossary: Operations Management		**Glossary 5-1 – 5-7**
Multiple Choice – Questions		**MCQ 5-1 – 5-21**
Multiple Choice – Solutions		**MCQ 5-22 – 5-54**

Operations Management

Operations management refers to the activities and administrative techniques companies use to improve the efficiency of the production process (i.e., converting materials and labor into finished goods and services). Operations management is worthwhile and should be a consideration for all companies, both large and small. It is a means to improve profitability, the ratio of outputs divided by inputs, and increase shareholder wealth, the primary goal of a business endeavor. Managers who can generate the greatest output with the least input are the most competitive in the marketplace.

As managers strive for efficiency by carefully monitoring operations, the production process becomes more effective – requiring fewer resources to deliver goods and services to customers.

Superior operations management not only adds value to companies with regard to profitability, but it also adds value in other ways too. For example, managers gather and use information about operations to assist with decision-making and to develop new or bolster existing relationships with stakeholders.

With regard to the CPA exam, the operations management topic is divided into (a) performance measures, (b) cost accounting, (c) process management, and (d) planning techniques. Assuming the BEC section of the exam is the fourth and final section, the performance measure ratios discussed here will be familiar. These ratios are also covered to varying degrees in FAR and AUD.

A. Financial and Non-Financial Measures of Performance Management

Performance management is a mechanism that organizations use to achieve their objectives through the identification of improvement areas using financial and non-financial performance indicators. Financial measures are numerical indicators (e.g., quantities, percentages, ratios) that are dependent on an entity's books and records. They typically quantify factors such as profitability and resource utilization.

Non-financial measures, such as customer satisfaction and product quality, are not captured directly by an entity's basic financial statements. Nevertheless, non-financial indicators are also important and should be included for a thorough analysis of performance. In addition to performance management, financial and non-financial measures assist managers with decision-making and strategy execution. CPAs must understand both types (financial and non-financial) and be able to determine the most appropriate measure to analyze specific aspects of an entity's performance.

CPA Exam Blueprint Representative Task
Calculate financial and non-financial measures appropriate to analyze specific aspects of an entity's performance (e.g., Economic Value Added, Costs of Quality-Prevention vs. Appraisal vs. Failure, etc.).
Determine which financial and non-financial measures are appropriate to analyze specific aspects of an entity's performance and risk profile (e.g., Return on Equity, Return on Assets, Contribution Margin, etc.).

1. Financial measures and value-based metrics
   Theoretically, financial measurements are more objective than non-financial (i.e., qualitative) measurements and enable internal and external comparative analysis. Financial measures are useful for determining resource allocation (budgeting), incentive compensation, and business unit evaluation.

   Value-based metrics (a category of financial measures) are indicators of economic profitability. Value-based metrics include return on investment (ROI), residual income, economic-value added (EVA), cash flow ROI, profitability index, and economic rate of return on common stock.

a. Consolidated balance sheet and multi-step income statement refresher

Yaeger Emporium, Inc.*
CONSOLIDATED BALANCE SHEETS
December 31, 20X4 and 20X5
($000,000, except per share data)

ASSETS	20X5	20X4
Current assets		
Cash and cash equivalents	$660	$363
Trading securities	10	14
Accounts receivable	60	46
Inventory	1,438	1,200
Prepaid expenses and other	87	132
Deferred income taxes	13	10
Total current assets	2,268	1,765
Fixed assets		
Property, plant, and equipment, gross	4,035	3,470
Less accumulated depreciation and amortization	(1,780)	(1,606)
Long-term investments	2	5
Other long-term assets	163	151
TOTAL ASSETS	**$4,688**	**$3,785**
LIABILITIES & STOCKHOLDER'S EQUITY		
Current liabilities		
Accounts payable	928	690
Accrued expenses and other	385	360
Accrued payroll and benefits	256	200
Income taxes payable	16	18
Total current liabilities	1,585	1,268
Long-term debt	398	150
Other long-term liabilities	260	300
Deferred income taxes	87	59
TOTAL LIABILITIES	2,330	1,777
Stockholders' equity		
Common stock, par value $.0 1per share, authorized 600,000,00 shares, issued and outstanding 207,470,000 and 213,420,000 shares, respectively	2	2
Additional paid-in capital	1,016	936
Treasury stock	(160)	(121)
Accumulated other comprehensive income	0	0
Retained earnings	1,500	1,191
TOTAL EQUITY	2,358	2,008
TOTAL LIABILTIES AND STOCKHOLDERS' EQUITY	**$4,688**	**$3,785**

Adapted from Ross Stores, Inc. 2015 10-K

Yaeger Emporium, Inc.*
CONSOLIDATED INCOME STATEMENT
For year-ended December 31, 20X5
($000,000, except share data)

INCOME STATEMENT	20X5
Sales	$11,000
Cost of goods sold	7,800
Gross profit	3,200
Selling, general and administrative	1,635
Operating income	1,565
Interest expense (income), net	3
Total costs and expenses	9,438
Earnings before taxes	1,562
Provision for taxes on earnings	560
Net earnings	$1,002
Earnings per share	
Basic	$4.85
Diluted	$4.79
Weighted average common shares outstanding	
Basic	206,777,000
Diluted	209,039,000

*Adapted from Ross Stores, Inc. 2015 10-K

> **Hint:** Cut off the last three zeros as appropriate (e.g., 1,000 / 2,000 = 1 / 2)! Smaller numbers are easier to calculate on the exam. This financial statement is in millions, unless otherwise specified.

> **Hint:** What good is memorizing an equation if you don't know where to find the numbers?

b. Accounting equation refresher

Assets = Liabilities + Equity

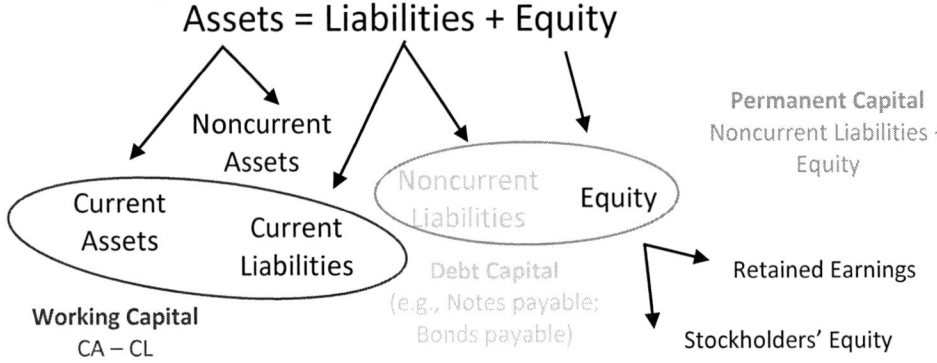

Working Capital
CA – CL

Permanent Capital
Noncurrent Liabilities + Equity

Debt Capital
(e.g., Notes payable;
Bonds payable)

Retained Earnings

Stockholders' Equity

c. Percentage change refresher

$$\text{Percentage change} = \frac{\text{Year 2 balance} - \text{Year 1 balance}}{\text{Year 1 balance}}$$

> **Hint:** Memorize the phrase "percentage change is new minus old, over old."

Multiple Choice

BEC 5-Q1

d. Return on investment (ROI)
ROI measures the financial benefit of investing resources by computing the benefits (i.e., the return) in relation to the outlay of resources (i.e., the investment). Variations of the generic ROI ratio include return on assets (ROA), income divided by average total assets, or return on equity (ROE), income divided by shareholders' equity.

$$ROI = \frac{Income}{Investment\ capital}$$

$$ROA = \frac{Net\ income}{Average\ total\ assets}$$

$$ROE = \frac{Net\ income}{Average\ shareholders'\ equity}$$

Alternatively, ROI can be calculated by multiplying the return on sales or profit margin by asset turnover (see DuPont ROI analysis).

ROI is a popular metric but is not without its potential limitations. First, ROI ignores future cash flows and may lead to rejection of projects that yield positive cash flows over time. Second, ROI may be positive, but still not cover the cost of capital. This makes ROI more difficult to evaluate as a performance measurement. Management should evaluate the performance of investment center managers as poor if the ROI does not attain a minimum percentage to cover the cost of the investment. Conversely, if a positive ROI exceeds the cost of capital, then management should undertake the project because it will increase shareholder wealth. Because the ROI does not incorporate the cost of capital, it is a performance measure that is more difficult to evaluate.

> *Hint*: Equivalent terms for ROI calculations include average total assets, investment, capital, and invested capital. Income is typically net income after interest and tax, but this amount can be substituted with operating income (EBIT) or operating income after taxes if net income is not available.

e. DuPont analysis
The DuPont analysis, developed by the DuPont Company in 1914, is a technique of separating return on equity (ROE) into its components, including profit margin (or return on sales), asset turnover, and financial leverage ratio (or equity multiplier). By disaggregating ROE using the DuPont analysis, analysts can determine differences between companies with equivalent overall returns calculated by dividing net income by average total shareholders' equity.

$$ROA = Profit\ margin \times Asset\ turnover$$

$$ROA = \frac{Net\ Income}{Net\ sales\ revenue} \times \frac{Net\ sales\ revenue}{Average\ total\ assets}$$

$$ROE = Profit\ margin \times Asset\ turnover \times Equity\ multiplier$$

$$ROE = \frac{Net\ income}{Net\ sales\ revenue} \times \frac{Net\ sales\ revenue}{Average\ total\ assets} \times \frac{Average\ total\ assets}{Average\ shareholders'\ equity}$$

> *Hint*: Forget the _____ turnover equation? Turn it over, the _____ becomes the denominator (e.g., total asset turnover = sales / average total assets).

Gross sales
− Sales discounts
− Sales returns or allowances
Net sales (Net sales revenue)

> **Hint:** Don't forget 0.10 is 10% not 0.10%.

f. Residual income
Residual income is a performance metric that managers often use to evaluate departments or projects. The interest on an investment in a department (project) is subtracted from the net income attributable to that department (or project). The calculation can also be used to evaluate the entity as a whole by subtracting interest on the average total assets from net operating profit after tax.

$$\text{Residual income} = \text{Net income} - (\text{Interest on investment})$$

Entity-wide:

$$\text{Residual income} = \text{NOPAT} - (\text{Required rate of return} \times \text{Average total assets})$$

Department:

$$\text{Residual income} = \text{Net income of division} - (\text{Required rate of return} \times \text{Average total assets of division})$$

> **Hint:** Equivalent terms for residual income calculations include average total assets, investment, capital, and invested capital.

1) Residual income profile
Residual income can be shown graphically, the interest rate on the x-axis and residual income, in dollars, on the y-axis. The x-intercept is the ROI (e.g., required rate of return as a percentage) and the y-intercept is net income. The difference between the ROI and the cost of capital represents the spread, or increase in shareholder wealth as a result of the investment.

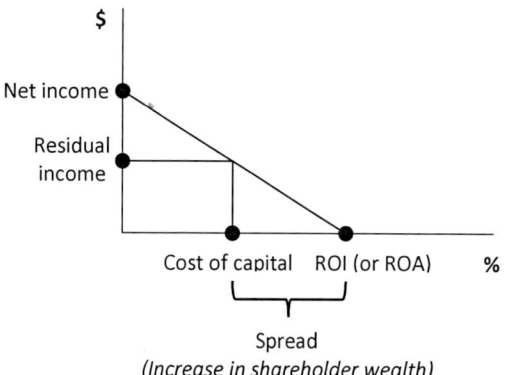

> **Hint:** The likelihood of being asked to label a graph on the exam is low; however, be prepared to answer questions about how the elements labeled on the graph relate to each other.

For example, let's determine if a project should be accepted using the graph.

Assume Division A has an ROI of 12% with a weighted average cost of capital (WACC) of 5%, resulting in a 7% spread. The company is considering a $500,000 project that has projected income of $45,000. This project has an ROI of 9% ($45,000 / $500,000), leaving a 4% spread above the WACC.

Although the project with a 9% ROI is less than the Division A's departmental average ROI of 12%, it still has the potential to increase shareholder wealth since the return is greater than the cost of capital (assuming the company's capacity is sufficient to complete the project.) The residual income is $20,000 [$45,000 − (5% * $500,000)].

Example:

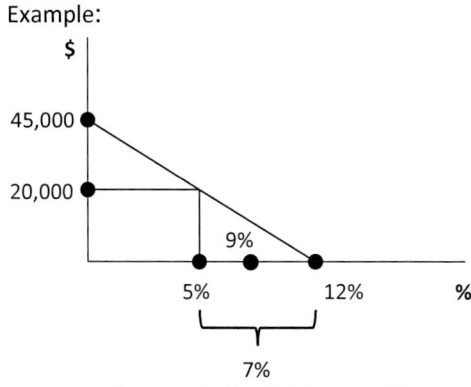

(Increase in shareholder wealth)

Focusing on ROI could cause management to reject the project because it will lower the division's average ROI. Evaluating the project using residual income can help limit self-serving management decisions, especially if ROI is one of the division manager's compensation-determining performance measures. Assuming no additional information is available, the project should be accepted because the ROI (9%) is greater than the WACC (5%) and it has a positive residual income ($20,000).

Multiple Choice

BEC 5-Q2 through BEC 5-Q5

g. Economic profit
Economic profit is the profit remaining after subtracting implicit costs from accounting profit.

$$\text{Economic profit} = \underset{(\text{Revenue} - \text{Explicit costs})}{\text{Accounting profit}} - \text{Implicit costs}$$

Explicit costs are recognizable accounting expenses (e.g., rent, labor) that result from a transaction. Accountants are familiar with explicit costs since GAAP only deals with explicit costs, disregarding implicit costs in most situations.

Implicit costs quantify the benefits foregone when choosing one alternative over another alternative, also known as opportunity costs. Implicit costs do not involve a payment or transaction but do decrease economic profit.

Examples of implicit costs include the potential salary an owner could earn if he or she chose to work outside the company rather than run the company. Or, the interest that could be earned if capital currently held as inventory was instead invested in securities. Accountants do not recognize implicit costs in financial statements.

Due to the structure of the equation, economic profit is typically less than accounting profit. Economic loss (or negative economic profit) occurs when implicit costs are greater than the accounting profit. For instance, assume a company earns accounting profit (or net income) of $10,000 during the period. If the company had purchased equity securities rather than inventory, it could have generated earnings of $15,000 during the same period.

The result is an economic loss of $5,000 ($10,000 - $15,000 = -$5,000). Purchasing inventory in this example is not economically lucrative, even though the company is profitable from an accounting standpoint. Economists argue that owners will ultimately leave the marketplace to invest in securities rather than operating the business (i.e., purchasing inventory) if they experience consistent economic losses.

h. Economic Value Added (EVA)
Economic value added is the economic profit or residual value a company creates in excess of the capital employed (total assets minus current liabilities) multiplied by the weighted average cost of capital (WACC).

$$EVA = NOPAT - [\ WACC \times (\ Total\ assets - Current\ liabilities\ )\ ]$$

> *Hint:* To memorize, match it up to residual income equation. NOPAT is calculated by subtracting taxes from net operating profit (or earnings before interest and taxes, EBIT). WACC is the weighted average cost of capital.
>
> $$NOPAT = EBIT \times (\ 1 - Tax\ rate\ )$$

One of the disadvantages of EVA is a bias towards "low hanging fruit" in decision-making. Put another way, EVA encourages managers to select the course of action that is easiest to achieve. For example, cost reduction by increasing fixed assets utilization. The entity reduces capital outlay for fixed assets by foregoing maintenance or replacement costs, overusing the property, plant, and equipment. Managers should be aware of this tendency to prevent inappropriate decisions.

Multiple Choice
BEC 5-Q6 through BEC 5-Q7

i. Free cash flow (FCF)
Free cash flow is the amount of cash a company can generate to sustain operations after deducting equipment and other capital expenditures. Cash is "free" to be used at the manager's discretion. For example, managers may use this cash to retire debt, invest in trading securities, or purchase treasury stock.

```
   Net operating profit after taxes (NOPAT)
 + Depreciation expense or amortization expense
 - Capital expenditures
 - Change in working capital requirements
   Free cash flow (FCF)
```

> *Hint:* Add or subtract the change in working capital requirements based on the direction of change. Increase in working capital requirements are subtracted; decreases are added.

> *Hint:* There are multiple ways of calculating free cash flow, and it is not uncommon to find that a finance or managerial accounting textbook has a different variation of the calculation. The calculation above is appropriate for the CPA exam.

Investors find it particularly useful to take a step back from the financial statements (and accrual accounting) and look at a company's cash flow. A positive FCF is favorable and typically indicative of a healthily operating company. Consistently negative FCF can indicate mismanagement or financial distress. Sporadically negative FCF is a sign of capital investment and a sign of growth; therefore, negative FCF must be evaluated within the context of the company over time.

j. Cash flow ROI (CFROI)
CFROI is computed by dividing the company's cash flow by its invested capital to determine the rate of return generated by all of its operating assets. This rate of return approximates the firm's internal rate of return (IRR).

$$CFROI = \frac{Cash\ flow}{Invested\ capital}$$

Remember, as discussed in BEC 3C, under Capital Budgeting, the IRR is the discount rate needed to calculate a net present value equal to zero. Or, put another way, the IRR is the required rate of return necessary to ensure the present value of future cash inflows exactly equal the present value of future cash outflow (e.g., PV inflow = PV outflow).

k. Profitability index
A profitability index is a technique to make capital budgeting decisions based on the initial outlay of capital (or initial investment) compared to the present value of future cash inflows. In an environment where there is a limit on the funds available to invest, management may prioritize projects accordingly from highest to lowest profitability index; this invests scarce resources in those projects with the highest return and maximizes shareholder wealth.

$$Profitability\ index = \left(\frac{PV\ of\ future\ cash\ inflows}{Initial\ investment}\right) \times 100$$

A limitation of the profitability index is that it requires projections of future cash inflows that may require detailed analysis for the long-term.

Multiple Choice
BEC 5-Q8 through BEC 5-Q9

l. Economic rate of return on common stock
In general, the rate of return on common stock is the earnings and change in market value of the common stock divided by its price.

$$\text{Economic rate of return on common stock} = \frac{(Dividends + change\ in\ price)}{Beginning\ price}$$

The economic rate of return accounts for both dividend yield and capital gain/loss from the change in stock price.

> *Hint*: Recall that the dividend yield ratio is:
> $$Dividend\ yield\ ratio = \frac{Dividends\ per\ common\ share}{Market\ price\ per\ common\ share}$$

Multiple Choice
BEC 5-Q10 through BEC 5-Q12

m. Financial statement ratios by category
Ratios used for financial analysis are classified as profitability, liquidity, solvency (debt utilization), activity (asset utilization), and market ratios.

> *Hint:* You must memorize the formulas for the exam!

1) Profitability ratios
Profitability ratios indicate how effectively a firm is able to generate earnings from business activities. The higher the ratio, the higher the firm's overall profitability. The goal is to maximize these ratios since investors often monitor and analyze these calculations when making investment decisions.

   i. Gross margin or gross profit ratio:

$$\text{Gross margin} = \frac{\text{Gross profit}}{\text{Net sales}} = \frac{\$3,200}{\$11,000} = 29.1\%$$

Gross margin demonstrates a company's pricing strategy (or markup) compared to its inventory costs. A company can improve (increase) its gross margin percentage by increasing prices or implementing cost reduction techniques such as finding less expensive raw materials or labor.

```
  Gross sales
− Sales discounts
− Sales returns or allowances
  Net sales
− COGS
  Gross profit
```

Multiple Choice
BEC 5-Q13

   ii. Operating profit margin ratio:

$$\text{Operating profit margin} = \frac{\text{Operating profit}}{\text{Net sales}} = \frac{\$1,565}{\$11,000} = 14.2\%$$

Operating profit margin demonstrates the percentage of each sales dollar that a company is earning by operating its primary business. In this example, the company has operating income of $0.14 out of every $1.00 of sales.

Operating profit margin is an indication of a company's pricing and costing strategies. A large operating profit margin likely indicates that the company has effective pricing strategies and/or initiatives to manage product and overhead costs.

   iii. Profit margin ratio:

$$\text{Profit margin ratio} = \frac{\text{Net income after interest and taxes}}{\text{Net sales}} = \frac{\$1,002}{\$11,000} = 9.1\%$$

The profit margin ratio shows the percentage of net sales (total revenue) available to shareholders after all expenses are deducted. Using this example, $0.09 of every $1.00 of sales is left as income after deducting operating expenses, interest, and taxes.

Multiple Choice
BEC 5-Q14

i. Return on assets (ROA)

$$\text{ROA} = \frac{\text{Net income}}{\text{Average total assets}} = \frac{\$1,002}{\$4,237} = 24\%$$

$$\text{Average total assets} = \frac{(\$4,688 + \$3,785)}{2} = \$4,237$$

A large ROA is favorable, indicating that a company generates additional earnings by managing its assets effectively. ROA significantly varies by industry due to differences in asset requirements.

> *Hint*: Whenever ratios "mix" a balance sheet item and an income statement item, always take the average of the balance sheet item. Why? The income statement covers an entire period, such as a full year, and the balance sheet is as of a certain date or a single point in time. Averaging eliminates the mismatch, converting the balance sheet item from a single point in time (i.e., the balance sheet date) to an entire period (i.e., the beginning of the period to the end).

Simply take the balance at the balance sheet date, plus the balance at the previous balance sheet date, and divide the sum by 2.

Multiple Choice
BEC 5-Q15 through BEC 5-Q17

ii. Return on equity (ROE):

$$\text{ROE} = \frac{\text{Net income after interest and taxes}}{\text{Average common shareholders' equity}} = \frac{\$1,002}{\$2,183} = 46\%$$

$$\text{Average common shareholders' equity} = \frac{(\$2,358 + \$2,008)}{2} = \$2,183$$

ROE measures how well stockholder funds are used to generate profits. Profits are more promising when the return on equity is larger than the company's cost of equity capital.

To calculate common shareholders' equity, deduct everything that belongs to preferred stockholders.

    Total shareholders' equity
− Preferred stock (P/S), par value
− P/S liquidation premium
− P/S dividends
    Common shareholders' equity

> *Hint*: Return on equity requires subtracting preferred dividends from numerator (net income after interest and taxes), if applicable.

iii. Dividend payout ratio:

$$\text{Dividend payout ratio} = \frac{\text{Cash dividend per common share}}{\text{Earnings per common share}} = \frac{\$0.44^*}{\$4.85} = 9.1\%$$

Assume Yaeger Emporium, Inc. paid out cash dividends of $0.44 per common share during the period.

Investors like to see relatively high, consistent dividend payout ratios. Conversely, if a company experiences steady decreases in its dividend payout ratios over a period of time, it could indicate financial difficulties.

> *Hint*: If in doubt, use basic earnings per share (EPS) for the exam. Recall that basic EPS is calculated:
>
> $$\text{Basic EPS} = \frac{\text{Net income} - \text{Current year preferred dividends}}{\text{Weighted average number of common shares outstanding}}$$

Multiple Choice
BEC 5-Q18 through BEC 5-Q20

2) Liquidity ratios

Liquidity ratios gauge a company's ability to fulfill short-term obligations (e.g., current liabilities) when they come due, which is typically within one year.

i. Current ratio (working capital ratio):

$$\text{Working capital} = \text{Current assets} - \text{Current liabilities} = \$2,268 - \$1,585 = \$683$$

$$\text{Current ratio} = \frac{\text{Current assets}}{\text{Current liabilities}} = \frac{\$2,268}{\$1,585} = 1.43$$

Current assets	Current liabilities
Reasonably expect to convert to cash in one year (or the operating cycle) or less	Due within one year (or the operating cycle)
Cash and Cash equivalents Short-term investments Marketable securities, current portion Accounts receivable, net Inventories Prepaid expenses	Accounts payable Short-term notes payable Accrued expenses Accrued payroll and benefits Current portion of long-term debt Unearned revenue Income taxes payable

The current ratio illustrates the number of times a company's current assets would cover its current liabilities. A ratio of less than 1 is a red flag, indicating the company may be unable to pay short-term debt as it is due.

Multiple Choice
BEC 5-Q21 through BEC 5-Q24

ii. Quick ratio (acid-test ratio):
The quick ratio (or acid-test) is a gauge of a company's ability to fulfill its short-term obligations with liquid or near liquid assets. Compared to the current ratio, by excluding inventories and other current (albeit less liquid) assets, the quick ratio is more conservative.

$$\text{Quick ratio} = \frac{\text{Cash and cash equivalents} + \text{Marketable securities} + \text{A/R, net}}{\text{Total current liabilities}} = \frac{\$730}{\$1,585} = 0.46$$

Multiple Choice

BEC 5-Q25 through BEC 5-Q31

3) Solvency ratios (debt utilization)
Solvency ratios measure a company's ability to meet long-term financial obligations to operate as a going concern, including the company's use of financial leverage (e.g., debt financing).

i. Debt to total assets:

$$\text{Debt to total assets} = \frac{\text{Total liabilities}}{\text{Total assets}} = \frac{\$2,330}{\$4,688} = 0.497$$

A higher ratio is less favorable, indicating higher risk and more leverage.

> **Hint**: If the calculation does not "mix" a balance sheet item and an income statement item, no average of the balance sheet item is required. Just remember, "No mix, no average" as demonstrated by this equation of two balance sheet items.

ii. Debt to equity:

$$\text{Debt to equity} = \frac{\text{Total liabilities}}{\text{Total equity}} = \frac{\$2,330}{\$2,358} = 0.988$$

A lower ratio is more favorable and indicates less risk. A higher ratio is unfavorable as it indicates there is more reliance on external factors, leading to higher risk (higher interest rates). The numerator can also be expressed equivalently as total debt and the denominator as total stockholders' equity.

iii. Times interest earned:

$$\text{Times interest earned} = \frac{\text{EBIT}}{\text{Interest expense}} = \frac{\$1,565}{\$3} = 521.7$$

A higher value is favorable, showing the company is able to pay the interest due on its debt many times over. A low value is a red flag, signaling that the company might be headed toward bankruptcy if it is consistently unable to pay interest on its debt.

```
  Gross sales
− Sales discounts
− Sales returns and allowances
  Net sales
− COGS
  Gross profit or gross margin
− Operating expenses (SG&A)
− R&D, organizational costs
  Operating income or operating profit (EBIT)
```

4) Activity ratios (asset utilization)
Activity ratios gauge how efficiently a company uses its resources, translating business activities into sales (and cash).

i. Receivable turnover:

$$\text{Receivables turnover} = \frac{\text{Net credit sales}}{\text{Average accounts receivable, net}} = \frac{\$700}{\$53} = 13.21$$

*Assume Yaeger Emporium, Inc. had $700,000,000 credit sales of during the period.

$$\text{Average accounts receivable, net} = \frac{(\$60 + \$46)}{2} = \$53$$

Managers use this ratio to evaluate how efficiently accounts receivable are collected and how well working capital is managed by the company. For this example, the receivables turned over 13.21 times during the year. A higher ratio is favorable indicating receivables are more liquid and quickly convert to cash. A lower ratio could signal a collection problem.

Accounts receivable, gross
− Allowance for doubtful accounts
Accounts receivable, net

Multiple Choice

BEC 5-Q32

ii. Average collection period:

$$\text{Average collection period in days} = \frac{365 \text{ days}}{\text{Accounts receivable turnover}} = \frac{365}{13.21} = 27.61 \text{ days}$$

In this example, the company will collect on a credit sale after approximately one month (27.64 days). This measure is also called days sales outstanding.

Multiple Choice

BEC 5-Q33 through BEC 5-Q37

iii. Inventory turnover:

$$\text{Inventory turnover} = \frac{\text{Cost of goods sold}}{\text{Average inventory}} = \frac{\$7,800}{\$1,319} = 5.91$$

This ratio is an asset utilization measurement to judge how efficient a company is at managing their inventory.

Net sales
− COGS
Gross profit or gross margin

Gross purchase
− Purchase discounts
− Returns and allowances
Net purchases
+ Freight-in or transportation-in
COGS purchases

Inventory, beginning balance
+ COGS purchase
Cost of goods available for sale
− Inventory, ending balance
COGS

Multiple Choice

BEC 5-Q38 through BEC 5-Q41

iv. Days in inventory:

$$\text{Days in inventory} = \frac{365 \text{ days}}{\text{Inventory turnover}} = \frac{365}{5.91} = 61.7 \text{ days}$$

The inventory in this example is sold and replaced every 61.7 days.

v. Total asset turnover:

$$\text{Total asset turnover} = \frac{\text{Net sales}}{\text{Average total assets}} = \frac{\$11,000}{\$4,237} = 2.6$$

Multiple Choice

BEC 5-Q42 through BEC 5-Q43

5) Market ratios
Market ratios evaluate the company from an investor's perspective, applicable to a company that is publicly traded and has a market value for its stock.

i. Price-earnings (P/E) ratio:

$$\text{PE ratio} = \frac{\text{Stock price per share}}{\text{Basic EPS}} = \frac{\$50^*}{\$4.85} = 10.31$$

*Assume Yaeger Emporium, Inc. has a $50 share price.

A lower ratio is favorable (greater than zero), indicating the company needs fewer years to earn the amount investors paid per share (assuming the PE ratio and earnings remains constant). For example, if the company earns $4.85 per share and the price per share is $50, it will take about 10.32 years for the company to earn the $50 paid for the stock.

Multiple Choice

BEC 5-Q44 through BEC 5-Q48

ii. Book value per share:

$$\text{Book value per share} = \frac{\text{Common shareholders' equity}}{\text{Number of shares of common stock outstanding}} = \frac{\$2,358,000,000}{206,777,000} = \$11.40$$

To calculate common shareholders' equity, deduct everything that belongs to preferred stockholders. This is the amount that the common shareholders are entitled to if the company files for liquidating bankruptcy.

```
  Total shareholders' equity
− Preferred stock (P/S), par value
− P/S liquidation premium
− P/S dividends, including all preferred dividends in arrears
  Common shareholders' equity
```

Hint: Denominator excludes treasury stock (treasury stock is not outstanding).

n. Summary of financial ratios

Financial Ratio	Numerator	Denominator
Profitability ratios		
Gross margin or gross profit	Gross profit	Net sales
Operating profit margin	Operating profit	Net sales
Profit margin	Net income after interest and tax	Net sales
Return on assets	Net income after interest and tax	Average total assets
Return on equity	Net income after interest and tax	Average common shareholders' equity
Dividend payout ratio	Cash dividend per common share	Basic EPS
Liquidity ratios		
Current ratio (Working capital ratio)	Current assets	Current liabilities
Quick ratio (Acid-test ratio)	Cash/cash equivalents + marketable securities + A/R, net	Total current liabilities
Solvency / Debt utilization / Coverage ratios		
Debt to total assets	Total liabilities	Total assets
Debt to equity	Total liabilities	Total equity
Times interest earned	EBIT	Interest expense
Free cash flow	NOPAT + Depreciation − Capital expenditures − Change in working capital	
Activity / Asset utilization ratios		
Receivable turnover	Net credit sales	Average accounts receivable, net
Average collection period	365	Accounts receivable turnover
Inventory turnover	COGS	Average inventory
Days in inventory	365	Inventory turnover
Total asset turnover	Net Sales	Average total assets
Market ratios		
Price/Earnings (PE) ratio	Stock price per share	Basic EPS
Book value per share	Common shareholders' equity	Number shares of stock outstanding

o. Analysis of financial statements
Financial statement comparability is one of the primary benefits of using accounting standards (e.g., GAAP, IFRS) for financial reporting. Financial statement analysis involves using the data found in financial statements to determine trends and other decision-useful information. It is commonly grouped as horizontal, cross-sectional, or vertical analysis.

1) Horizontal (or time series) analysis
The horizontal analysis examines trends within the same company over time. Multiple accounting periods can be compared to highlight positive and negative trends. For example, steadily increasing revenue figures over multiple periods demonstrates a positive growth trend.

For accurate comparisons, the accounting periods must have equivalent attributes such as length and period-end date. The analyst must also account for any significant accounting policy changes. If an accounting change occurs during the period, all comparisons must be adjusted to eliminate variances that result solely from the change.

2) Cross-sectional analysis
Cross-sectional analysis studies two or more comparable companies (i.e., similar size and equivalent industry) during identical accounting periods. This information is useful for benchmarking, or optimizing performance by identifying a company's strengths and weaknesses in relation to other companies. Accurate analysis requires companies to be as similar as possible, especially in terms of accounting policies (e.g., inventory valuation methods).

3) Vertical analysis
Vertical analysis eliminates financial statement size differences and facilitates straightforward comparisons by converting each financial statement line item into a percentage, or a common size. Analysts typically divide by gross sales on the income statement or total assets on the balance sheet. The primary advantage of using a common-size statement is that it is easier to identify and interpret relative similarities and differences year-to-year or company-to-company.

Yaeger Emporium, Inc.
COMMON-SIZE INCOME STATEMENT
For year-ended December 31, 20X5

INCOME STATEMENT	20X5 Amount	% of Sales
Sales	$11,000	100.00%
Cost of goods sold	7,800	70.91%
Gross profit	3,200	29.09%
Selling, general and administrative	1,635	14.86%
Operating income	1,565	14.23%
Interest expense (income), net	3	0.03%
Total costs and expenses	9,438	85.80%
Earnings before taxes	1,562	14.20%
Provision for taxes on earnings	560	5.09%
Net earnings	$1,002	9.11%

p. Limitations of financial ratios
Even though ratio analysis is a popular technique, it is not without limitations. Not surprisingly, miscalculation and misinterpretation are always potential pitfalls when using ratio analysis. On top of that, analysts must consider the comparability of data, the reliability of industry averages, and the potential for overreliance on financial ratios when making decisions.

First, analysts must be mindful to compare only companies that are similar. Comparing companies of drastically different sizes or from different industries provide relatively little value for decision-making. Additionally, even if companies are similar in size, it is important to evaluate the comparability of financial information from each company. Current accounting standards allow managers to estimate certain amounts (e.g., impairment loss, bad debt expense). Depending on the company, these estimates may vary in conservativeness and could distort findings if company policies are not the same.

Second, analysts often compare a company's financial ratios to the industry average to determine relative performance (e.g., what might be a good debt to equity ratio in one industry may be poor in another industry). It is crucial that they use a reliable industry average. The analyst must perform the calculation using the same methodology for all companies. Variations between input values can lead to a skewed industry average and result in misleading findings.

Third, analysts need to be wary of an overreliance on ratios. Ratios alone offer only a narrow view of a company's operations and performance. That being said, it is important to evaluate non-financial measures to obtain a complete and balanced picture of a company's standing in the marketplace.

q. Relationship between numerator and denominator refresher
What happens when you add or subtract an equal amount to the numerator and denominator? It depends. Let's try it.

Numerator > Denominator

$$\frac{200}{100} = 2.0$$

Add 50: $\quad \dfrac{200 + 50}{100 + 50} = \dfrac{250}{150} = 1.67 \quad$ = Decrease

Subtract 50: $\quad \dfrac{200 - 50}{100 - 50} = \dfrac{150}{50} = 3.0 \quad$ = Increase

Numerator < Denominator

$$\frac{100}{200} = 0.5$$

Add 50: $\quad \dfrac{100 + 50}{200 + 50} = \dfrac{150}{250} = 0.60 \quad$ = Increase

Subtract 50: $\quad \dfrac{100 - 50}{200 - 50} = \dfrac{50}{150} = 0.33 \quad$ = Decrease

> *Hint*: You don't have to memorize this relationship, just replicate it on the exam's scratch paper. Do one relationship, and the other will be the opposite!

> *Hint*: Historically the CPA exam does not include "none of the above" as an answer choice. However, "All of the above" or "Both (a) and (c)" are potential multiple-choice answer options. Be sure to read all answer choices carefully.

2. Non-financial measures
   "Cash is king" in business, right? It depends. Nonmonetary factors (e.g., satisfaction) can be just as, if not more important. For example, winning a Top 10 Best Employers award is intangibly valuable for employee recruitment, satisfaction, and retention. This is true regardless of whether the company is an average performer or industry all-star based on financial measures.

   a. Balanced Score Card (BSC)
      The primary purpose of the balanced score card (BSC) is to measure operations in a holistic (i.e., balanced, hence the name) manner by evaluating all aspects of a company's performance. The benefit of using a BSC is that it considers both traditional financial performance measures in addition to relevant non-financial measures.

      Strategy-focused, a BSC clearly outlines targets for performance. The BSC uses four different perspectives to translate the mission and vision of the company into something measurable. The four perspectives are financial, customer, internal business process, learning and growth (innovation). It is imperative to effectively link each objective with appropriate performance measures to implement a company's strategy.

      1) Financial perspective
         The financial perspective uses the most traditional approach to judging a company's performance. Financial ratios using various financial statement items are computed to determine if a company is attaining its targets. Companies typically monitor metrics like ROI, cash flow, and cost of sales to determine improvement strategies. Financial performance can be enhanced by generating additional revenue (e.g., diversifying products, acquiring customers, and expanding markets) or improving productivity (e.g., decreasing expense or increasing efficiency of asset utilization).

      2) Customer perspective
         The customer perspective considers attributes related to the delivery of products and services to targeted market segments. Highlighted in this category are aspects of the customer relationship (e.g., satisfaction, loyalty) and the reputation of the company. Examples include customer satisfaction, customer retention, and percentage of business from customer referrals. Customer surveys are often used to gather this type of information.

         > *Hint*: As silly as it sounds, customer perspective measurements usually include the word "customer" in them.

      3) Internal business processes perspective
         The internal business processes perspective is a broad category covering operations, innovation (read: short-term innovation), and regulatory compliance. Specifically, measures consider product quality, on-time delivery, inventory cost (e.g., cost per unit), order backlog, defects, cycle-time, safety incidents and so forth.

         > *Hint*: Consider this the "catch-all" category. If it doesn't obviously fit elsewhere, put it here.

      4) Learning and growth (innovation) perspective
         The learning and growth perspective focuses on improving and engaging people (and systems) that have a long-term impact on the company. For example, employee satisfaction and employee training are commonly measured. Occasionally, this perspective is called innovation (read: long-term innovation) and growth. Automation or other technology implementation that enhances the longevity of the organization can be included here too.

> *Hint*: Keep an eye out for "employee" and "R&D" when classifying measurements. It is likely those items will fit in this perspective.

The BSC is depicted as a chart with columns for perspective, strategic objective, measure, and target. The frequency of measurement may also be included as applicable. A strategic objective in the balanced scorecard framework is a statement identifying the high-level goals and how success, as defined by the organization, can be achieved. A performance measure is a defined metric for evaluation. A target is a desired result or outcome, whether a goal for performance or improvement.

BSC performance metrics can be classified as either leading or lagging indicators. Leading indicators show future performance and lagging indicators highlight past performance. The classification is fully dependent on context. The same performance measure might be a lagging indicator for one activity and a leading indicator for another activity.

To demonstrate this concept, consider customer retention at a shipping company as both a leading and lagging indicator. On-time delivery directly impacts customer retention. It is, therefore, a leading indicator (or driver) of customer retention (the lagging indicator). On the other hand, customer retention leads to revenue growth. In this case, customer retention is the leading indicator while revenue growth is the lagging indicator.

> *Hint*: Be familiar with which types of measures fall under each different perspective. Be able to classify a list of measures appropriately into their respective categories.

Multiple Choice

BEC 5-Q49 through BEC 5-Q51

Perspective	Strategic Objectives	Measures	Targets	Frequency
Financial Ensure products and services are offered at a competitive price	Benchmark products and services to ensure pricing is competitive	1. Average product prices 2. Sales margin	1. Average price no more than 10% over online retailers' average price 2. 60% or more	1. Quarterly 2. Annually
Customer Ensures service satisfies customer and faculty expectation	Provide above average service to customers and faculty	1. Ratings on customer satisfaction survey 2. Customer queuing time at register during holiday season 3. Hours open per week 4. Repeat sales to customers	1. 4.0 or better on a scale of 5.0 Maximum 2. 90% or better have less than 3 minutes to wait 3. Industry Standard or better 4. 40% of customers make more than one purchase per year	1. Annually 2. Quarterly 3. Weekly 4. Annually
Internal business processes Ensure staff is knowledgeable and	Properly train employees on customer service and store knowledge	1. Customer survey at the register on employee helpfulness and product knowledge	1. 90% employee effectiveness rate 2. Rating of 85 or better on mystery	1. Quarterly 2. Quarterly 3. Weekly

Perspective	Strategic Objectives	Measures	Targets	Frequency
provides an exceptional level of service		2. Mystery shopper rating 3. Customer return process time	shopper checklist (e.g., store cleanliness, employee helpfulness) 3. Average of less than 4 minutes to process customer return transaction	
Learning and growth Seek to provide products and services that meet future needs of customers	Provide products and services that are innovative, or provide current products in innovative ways	1. Employee training on new products and services	1. 80% of employees attend and complete an 8-hour training program	1. Annually

3. Quality of earnings
   The maxim "quality over quantity" is still applicable to corporate earnings although it might seem counterintuitive in a profit-maximizing, competitive marketplace. High-quality earnings are stable, predictable, and indicative of future earnings levels. Earnings that exhibit a high-quality signal that a company is in good operating health and it is likely to have long-term profitability.

   For example, companies that primarily rely on recurring revenue-generating transactions demonstrate high-quality earnings. Inconsistent, one-off transactions have lower earnings quality since there is no guarantee the company will benefit from any future payments and securing each new transaction requires additional resources and effort. Additionally, companies that have a shorter collection period (e.g., converting receivables into cash sooner) have a higher quality of earnings.

   Within the confines of US GAAP, a company's bottom line earnings amount (e.g., net income) depends on the accounting policies the company selects to use for its financial statements. Consistent and conservative policies result in higher quality earnings. Abusing accounting policies to increase earnings not only decreases earnings quality, but it is unethical and could result in disciplinary actions.

   > *Hint:* Even if two companies generate exactly same amount of earnings during the accounting period, the quality of their earnings might not be equal.

4. Incentive compensation
   Companies use incentive compensation to motivate employees, linking pay and other perks directly to desired performance. Incentive compensation typically consists of offering bonuses (temporary) or merit pay (permanent) on top of an employee's base pay or fixed salary when an employee achieves a performance goal.

   Ideally, they should be based on measures that are within the employee's area of responsibility and can be directly controlled by the employee. The incentive program should also align with the company's goals and objectives.

   The program can either focus on individual or group performance, and managers can evaluate one or more performance measures. In practice, many employers award incentive compensation using a balanced scorecard approach, rewarding employees for achieving a combination of financial and non-financial target goals.

Cash bonuses, stock options, and other non-salary related perks are all common incentives. Cash bonuses can be paid out to a single employee, a group, or even the whole company on a specific date if performance targets exceed expectations. Stock options grant employees the right to purchase a specified number of shares at a predetermined purchase price. Options encourage employees to have an interest in the company's stock market performance and behave in ways that will increase the stock's market value. By design, this employee incentive only exists when the stock price is greater than the predetermined purchase price of the stock. Non-salary perks include extra vacation days, personal use of corporate assets (e.g., corporate jet), or public recognition of an achievement.

Employers implement incentive programs to motive employees, encouraging each employee to match his or her values to the company's goals. Some companies use sizable incentives as a technique to attract and retain talented employees. Plus, companies enjoy the variable nature of these incentives. Since incentives are only paid for strong performance, they can help manage labor costs in difficult economic times.

Incentive programs are not without disadvantages. Too much emphasis on incentives could (and often does) cause unethical behavior. For example, managers might be tempted to participate in earnings management or engage in earnings smoothing techniques to earn a bonus based on a financial performance measure (e.g., EPS).

Poorly designed incentive plans have the potential to cause managers to make decisions that improve short-term individual performance without regard for the long-term impact on the company. Additionally, incentives could fail to change employee behavior resulting in a waste of resources or cause resentment within the company if employees perceive incentives are inequitable or awarded unfairly.

5. Benchmarking
    Benchmarking is a way to objectively evaluate a company's performance in relation to other companies or business units. Although a relatively simple technique, benchmarking can be a powerful tool to optimize performance by identifying a company's strengths and weaknesses. The technique can utilize both external and internal comparison data depending on the manager's intent.

    To perform external benchmarking, managers typically collect published information about similar companies from like industries. Industry benchmarking analysis produces a set of comparison data or benchmarks. Managers use these benchmarks to identify ways to emulate the industry's best performer. It is important to note that benchmarks can include both financial and non-financial performance measures.

    By pinpointing only competitor data, as long as it is publicly available, managers can use benchmarking as a strategy to gain market share. This technique is called competitive benchmarking. Or, on the opposite end of the spectrum, generic benchmarking can also be useful in certain situations such as optimizing the company's order fulfillment procedures or improving its recruiting processes. Generic benchmarking involves collecting benchmark data across unrelated industries. It assumes that the benchmark data is universally applicable regardless of the industry.

    Shifting the focus from external to internal analysis, companies can also use internal benchmarking to drive process improvement and performance optimization. Managers identify in-house best practices and use this knowledge to improve efficiency in other business units or departments within the organization.

Multiple Choice

BEC 5-Q52

6. Cost of quality
   The cost of quality is the added expense a company incurs to prevent or handle low-quality products. The cost of quality is made up of prevention costs, appraisal costs, internal failure costs, and external failure costs, with each being categorized as either a cost of conformance or a cost of nonconformance.

   Costs of conformance are the costs incurred to ensure the product conforms to the quality requirements for the "avoidance of failure," where the goal is to prevent defects from happening in the first place. These are "costs of quality."

   a. Prevention costs
      Costs to reduce the potential for defective goods or services (e.g., training, quality improvement initiatives, system audits, preventative maintenance, and product redesign).

   b. Appraisal (detection) costs
      Costs to evaluate and detect items that do not conform to specifications (e.g., quality assurance (QA) testing inspection, statistical defect sampling, and laboratory tests). Costs accumulate prior to completing the final product.

   Costs of nonconformance are the costs incurred for not conforming to the quality requirements. These are "costs for non-quality."

   a. Internal failure costs
      Costs related to goods or services that fail to meet the usual or required standard identified *before* transfer to the consumer (e.g., spoilage, rework, scrap, disposal, debug software).

   b. External failure costs
      Costs related to goods or services that fail to meet the usual or required standard identified *after* transfer to the consumer (e.g., handling complaints, product returns, product recall, warranty repairs, liability lawsuits, tarnished reputation, lost sales). Consequences of failures are the most severe after the customer receives the product or service. These costs may be hard to quantify and are often underestimated.

Multiple Choice

BEC 5-Q53

B. Cost Accounting
1. Cost measurement concepts, methods and techniques

> Apply cost accounting concepts, terminology, methods and measurement techniques within an entity.

The primary objective of the cost accountant is to compute the product cost for financial statement presentation of cost of goods sold (COGS) on the income statement and ending inventories on the balance sheet.

a. Definitions and flow of costs

1) Cost
   A cost is the amount of resources that an entity must forgo to achieve a specific objective. Measured in a monetary unit, costs can be either actual or budgeted. Actual costs are observable (past). Budgeted costs must be predicted by management (future).

2) Cost object
   A cost object is anything for which a manager can compute and assign a cost (e.g., products, services, customers, activities, departments, and facilities). Each cost object represents a separate cost measurement.

   As resources are consumed, the costs are assigned to the appropriate cost object. This is done in two ways: tracing and allocating. Tracing costs involve assigning costs to a cost object using some type of direct relationship. Allocating costs (the emphasis of cost accounting) involves assigning costs using a rational and systematic method since no direct relationship exists.

   > *Hint*: Cost objects can have different cost computations depending on the purpose of measurement (e.g., internal recordkeeping, financial reporting, and taxes).

3) Direct costs
   Direct costs are easy to assign to a cost object and include direct materials (DM) and direct labor (DL). The relationship clear and indisputable. It is economically feasible (cost-effective) to trace the amount used to the cost object. Direct costs are usually variable in nature, displayed graphically as a linear equation.

   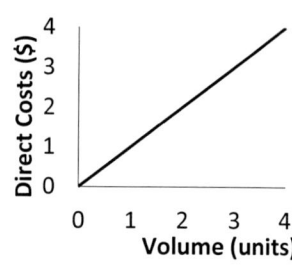

4) Indirect costs
   Indirect costs do not have an obvious relationship with a cost object and must be allocated in a systematic, cost-effective manner. Indirect costs include overhead costs such as indirect materials, indirect labor, and factory costs (e.g., rent, machinery depreciation). Overhead costs typically have both fixed and variable components. Indirect costs are accumulated in a cost pool and allocated using an allocation base (e.g., units produced, direct labor hours).

5) Manufacturing costs
   Manufacturing costs are all of the costs attributed to producing a product. These costs are product costs (capitalized) rather than period costs (expensed immediately). These are costs that could be called factory or inventoriable costs.

The three components of manufacturing costs are:
  i. **Direct materials (DM)** – materials which become part of the product
  ii. **Direct labor (DL)** – employees who work on the product
  iii. **Overhead or factory overhead (OH)** – all other MANUFACTURING costs, including normal spoilage
     (a) Variable overhead (Variable OH)
     (b) Fixed overhead (Fixed OH)

Total cost of cost object

```
         DM
   DL ↘  ↓         
       Direct | Indirect  → Fixed OH
       costs  | costs    ↘
                          Variable OH
```

6) Period costs
Period costs are considered non-manufacturing or office costs which are not associated with manufacturing (factory) costs. Typically, these costs are expensed in the period incurred. Examples include costs related to selling, general, and administrative expenses (SG&A) and certain research and development costs.

7) Prime and conversion costs
Prime costs are a combination of direct material used and direct labor used. Conversion cost are the total direct labor used plus any overhead applied (variable and fixed).

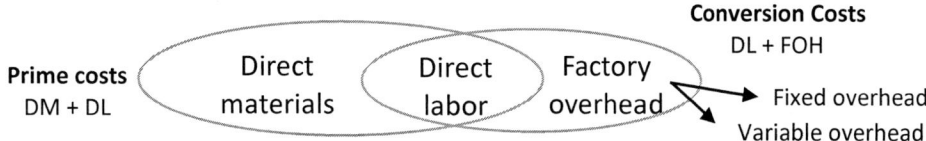

Prime costs
DM + DL

Conversion Costs
DL + FOH
→ Fixed overhead
Variable overhead

8) Flow of costs
Costs flow through the accounting system in a way that faithfully represents the underlying activity. The production process starts out with input resources (DM, DL, and OH). When these inputs reach production, the costs are transferred into work-in-process. Once finished the costs are transferred to finished goods inventory. When the products are sold the associated costs are debited to costs of goods sold. The result of the process is the capitalization of product costs on the balance sheet until the period of sale.

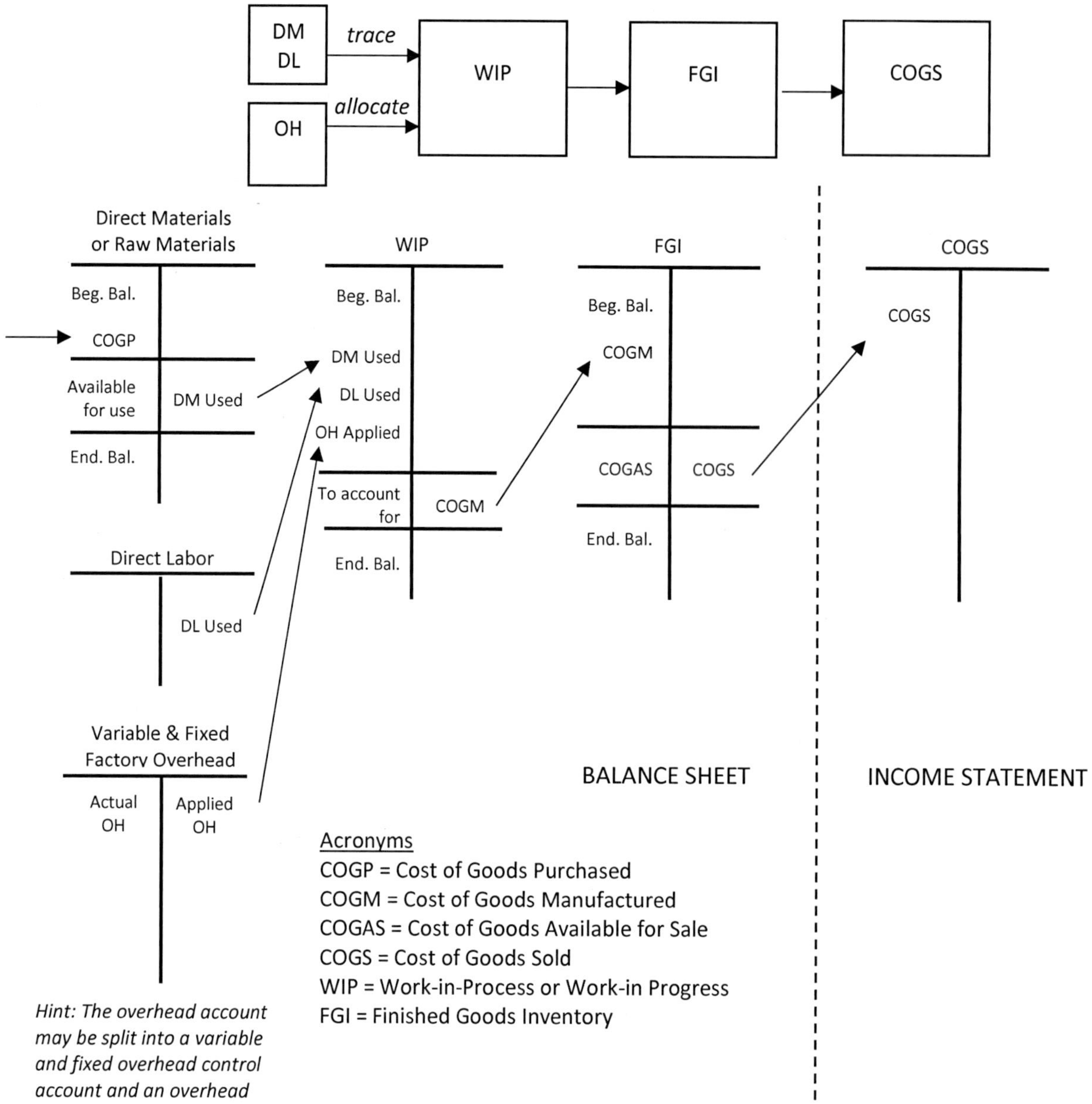

[Cost flow diagram showing DM, DL traced to WIP and OH allocated to WIP, flowing to FGI, then to COGS]

[T-accounts for Direct Materials or Raw Materials, Direct Labor, Variable & Fixed Factory Overhead, WIP, FGI, and COGS showing cost flows across Balance Sheet and Income Statement]

Acronyms
COGP = Cost of Goods Purchased
COGM = Cost of Goods Manufactured
COGAS = Cost of Goods Available for Sale
COGS = Cost of Goods Sold
WIP = Work-in-Process or Work-in Progress
FGI = Finished Goods Inventory

Hint: The overhead account may be split into a variable and fixed overhead control account and an overhead applied or allocated contra account.

b. Traditional costing

Compare and contrast the different costing methods such as absorption vs. variable and process vs. job order costing.

Traditional costing is made of job-order costing, process costing, and operation (hybrid) costing.

1) Job-order costing
   Job-order costing, or simply job costing, is a costing system that accumulates and expenses costs for each individual job. Jobs are unique and distinct products or services with units that are easy to identify (e.g., car repairs at a car repair shop). Although individual jobs each use a different amount of resources, tracking costs for each job is a straightforward process.

Examples of companies that are likely to use job costing are audit firms (for each audit engagement), airline manufacturers (for each airplane), and interior designers (for each room or house).

Multiple Choice

BEC 5-Q54 through Q64

i. Job-order journal entries

Assume Alpha Company is recording the journal entries for job #128, a custom-order motorcycle. For simplicity, #128 is the only job Alpha performs in January. Once Alpha receives the order and specifications for the motorcycle, the journal entries follow the underlying activities.

Purchase of materials (direct and indirect) for cash:
Dr. Materials – Job #128 $XX
   Cr. Cash $XX

Use direct and indirect materials in production:
Dr. Work-in-process (direct) – Job #128 $XX
Dr. Overhead (indirect) $XX
   Cr. Materials – Job #128 $XX

Accrue payroll for manufacturing employees:
Dr. Work-in-process (direct) – Job #128 $XX
Dr. Overhead (indirect) $XX
   Cr. Wages payable $XX

Record actual overhead incurred during the period:
Dr. Overhead $XX
   Cr. Cash $XX
   Cr. Rent payable $XX
   Cr. Insurance payable $XX
   Cr Depreciation $XX

Allocation or application of overhead (indirect) costs to work-in-process based on predetermined rate:
Dr. Work-in-process – Job #128 $XX
   Cr. Overhead applied or allocated $XX

> *Hint:* The overhead is applied based on the actual activity multiplied by the predetermined rate.

Finish job and transfer to finished goods:
Dr. Finished goods inventory– Job #128 $XX
   Cr. Work-in-process $XX

Product (motorcycle) sold, paid for on credit, and picked up by the customer:
Dr. Cost of goods sold $XX
   Cr. Finished goods inventory– Job #128 $XX

Dr. Accounts receivable $XX
   Cr. Revenue $XX

Option 1: Adjusting entry for *immaterial* overhead over- or under-applied using write-off approach (see discussion below):

Dr. Cost of goods sold (under-applied)	$XX	
Dr. Overhead applied or allocated (balance)	$XX	
Cr. Overhead (balance)		$XX

OR

Dr. Overhead applied or allocated (balance)	$XX	
Cr. Overhead (balance)		$XX
Cr. Cost of goods sold (over-applied)		$XX

Option 2: Adjusting entry for *material* overhead over- or under-applied using proration approach (see discussion below):

Dr. Work-in-process (% of under-applied)	$XX	
Dr. Finished goods (% of under-applied)	$XX	
Dr. Cost of goods sold (% of under-applied)	$XX	
Dr. Overhead applied or allocated (balance)	$XX	
Cr. Overhead applied or allocated (balance)		$XX

OR

Dr. Overhead applied or allocated (balance)	$XX	
Cr. Overhead (balance)		$XX
Cr. Work-in-process (% of over-applied)		$XX
Cr. Finished goods (% of over-applied)		$XX
Cr. Cost of goods sold (% of over-applied)		$XX

ii. Indirect cost allocation using normal costing
As indirect costs are grouped into a cost pool. This cost pool is allocated in a systematic way using a cost allocation base. A cost allocation base is simply a metric to assign indirect costs to a cost object (e.g., units produced, direct labor hours).

$$\text{Predetermined or budgeted overhead rate} = \frac{\text{Budgeted or estimated annual costs}}{\text{Budgeted or estimated annual quantity of cost allocation base}}$$

This overhead rate is then multiplied by the actual activity (e.g., direct labor hours for the job) for normal costing. The resulting product is the amount the company records in the journal entry to allocate overhead costs to work-in-process inventory by debiting work-in-process and crediting overhead applied (a contra account to overhead).

Multiple Choice

BEC 5-Q65

Hint: US GAAP (ASC 330-10-30) requires companies to use normal capacity to allocate fixed overhead. Normal capacity is not 100% theoretical capacity. It is the capacity expected to be achieved over a number of periods or seasons under normal circumstances, adjusted for downtime due to planned maintenance.

iii. Overhead accounting and over- and under-applied overhead
Remember that overhead must be allocated or applied since it cannot be directly traced to a final product. At the end of a period, overhead may be over- or under-applied due to the use of predetermined overhead rates. Predetermined rates are based on historical data and information on future estimated activity and are applied using the

actual activity for the job (e.g., budgeted rate * actual hours). Adjusting journal entries must be made to reconcile the over- or under-applied amounts once actual rates are determinable or at the end of the period based on actual overhead incurred.

The difference is accounted for using the (a) adjusted allocation-rate approach, (b) proration approach, or (c) the write-off approach. The adjusted allocation-approach re-calculates allocation of overhead and adjust the journal entries to reflect actual overhead rates. The proration approach debits (or credits) cost of goods sold, work-in-process, and finished goods inventory based on their relative size to clear the net overhead account to zero. Proration is appropriate for material amounts of misallocation. If differences are immaterial, the write-off approach debits (or credits) the cost of goods sold for the appropriate amount to clear the net overhead account to zero.

Analogy: The overhead account is a water glass. Actual overhead "fills the water glass," each time the company incurs overhead costs by debiting overhead and credit the other account (e.g., cash, accounts payable). The company removes water from the glass by applying overhead to WIP (based on a predetermined rate). It does this by crediting the overhead applied contra account and debiting WIP. At the end of the period, we either have too much or not enough "water" in the overhead account, net of overhead applied.

(a) Remaining water (debit balance) – under-applied
When a company under-applies overhead it means that less overhead is applied than incurred. The company has *underestimated* overhead cost and actual overhead costs were more than expected.

(b) Not enough water (credit balance) – over-applied
When a company over-applies overhead it means that more overhead is applied than incurred. The company *overestimated* overhead costs and actual overhead costs were less than expected.

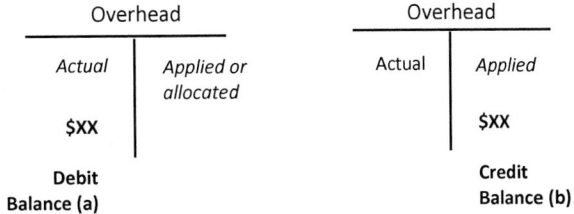

2) Process costing
Process costing is the opposite of job costing, and it is ideal for homogeneous products (i.e., identical or extremely similar products). In process costing, the total cost of producing the product or service is divided it the total by number of units to get an average rate.

Companies that mass produce products are likely to use process costing. Examples include beverage producers, newspaper publishers, and paper manufacturers.

> *Hint*: Process costing has the nickname "peanut butter costing" because it uses a single allocation base (e.g., total labor hours) to calculate the allocation rate. These broad averages spread the costs evenly to the cost objects, like peanut butter. Process costing can inaccurately cost products that use more (under-cost) or less (over-cost) resources than the average.

i. Process costing steps

Process costing is a sequential process that involves determining the number of units and total costs. The units are measured in terms of equivalent units of production (EUP) or by another term; equivalent finished units (EFU). Unfinished units are converted into the quantity of equivalent finished units that could have been produced with the same quantity of input. For example, four units that are 25% complete are equivalent to one finished unit.

Costs associated with direct materials (DM) and conversion costs (CC) remain separate during the calculations since direct materials are added at the beginning of the production process (i.e., the units are 100% complete right away with regard to materials), and conversion costs are added equally during the production processes.

The four steps of process costing are:
   (1) Calculate number of units shipped/transferred out/completed (in whole units).
   (2) Calculate the equivalent units of production (EUP).
   (3) Calculate the cost per EUP.
   (4) Complete the WIP T account.

Step 1. Calculate the number of units shipped/transferred out/completed.
   Beginning inventory
   + Units started
   = Units to be accounted for
   − Ending inventory
   = Units shipped (or completed and transferred out)

Step 2. Calculate the EUPs. The two methods used are FIFO and weighted-average.

A. FIFO			B. Weighted-Average		
	DM	CC		DM	CC
Units shipped			Units shipped		
+ End. Inv. (EUPs)			+ End. Inv. (EUPs)		
− Beg. Inv. (EUPs)			= W/A EUPs		
= FIFO EUPs					

Step 3. Calculate the cost per EUP.
   A. FIFO
   Cost per EUP = $\dfrac{\text{Current Costs Only}}{\text{EUPs}}$

   B. Weighted-Average
   Cost per EUP = $\dfrac{\text{Beg. Inv. + Current Costs}}{\text{EUPs}}$

Step 4. Complete the WIP T account.
   Using the number of Ending Inventory EUPs from Step 2 and Cost per EUP in Step 3, calculate the dollar value of ending inventory in WIP and plug COGM.

> *Hint:* The weighted average method equals the FIFO method when the company has no beginning inventory.

Multiple Choice

BEC 5-Q66 through BEC 5-Q69

ii. Process costing equations

Applicable to:	Equations	
FIFO & Weighted-Average Method	Units Started, Completed, and Transferred "Units S,C,T" =	Units Started – Ending WIP Units* *all units in ending WIP.
	Ending WIP Units =	Units Started – Units S,C,T
	Units Completed and Transferred** = **Same as "units shipped"	Units in Beginning WIP + Units S,C,T
Weighted-Average	Equivalent Units Produced "EUPs" =	All Units in Beginning WIP + Units S,C,T + Equivalent units produced in Ending Inventory* *Equivalent Units Produced in Ending WIP = Ending WIP units x % completed
	Cost per Equivalent Unit =	(Costs in Beg. WIP + Costs added during the period) divided by EUPs
	Cost of Ending WIP =	Cost per Equivalent Unit x Equivalent units produced in Ending Inventory
FIFO	Equivalent Units Produced "EUPs" =	Equivalent units needed to complete for Beg. WIP* + Units S,C,T + Equivalent units produced in Ending Inventory** *Equivalent units needed to complete for Beg. WIP = Beg. WIP units x % needed to complete **Equivalent Units Produced in Ending WIP = Ending WIP units x % completed
	Cost per Equivalent Unit =	Costs added during the period divided by EUPs
	Cost of Ending WIP =	Cost per Equivalent Unit x Equivalent units produced in Ending Inventory

3) Operation (hybrid) costing
Operation costing is a hybrid or blend of process and job-order costing. It is typically found in organizations that repeat the same basic process over and over on different materials to produce different finished goods or services. Examples include clothing, jewelry, and appliance manufacturers.

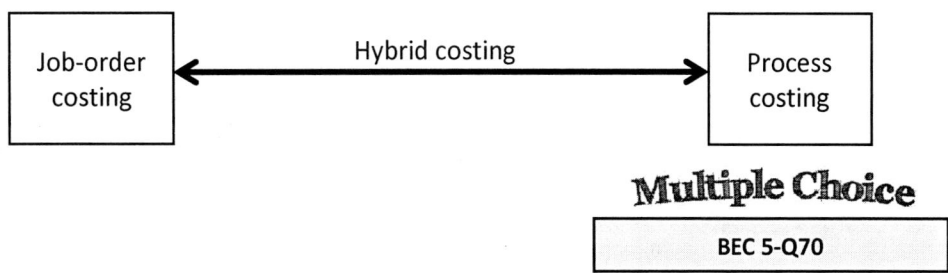

Multiple Choice

BEC 5-Q70

c. Activity-based costing (ABC)
Simple methods of costing (e.g., traditional costing) can be inaccurate and lead to poor decisions. Using a single cost allocation rate (traditional costing) leads to cost subsidization, the result of over- and under-costing. This is most pronounced in companies with diverse product mixes where each product requires different activities and uses a different amount of resources. More complex methods of costing, such as activity-based costing (ABC), can lead to more accurate decisions.

ABC assigns costs to activities using multiple activity cost pools. Allocation rates are determined by dividing the cost pools by cost drivers. Cost drivers are precise metrics for allocation with clear cause and effect relationship to the long-run behavior of the cost. For example, if the company is costing the machine configuration activity, all of the machine configuration costs are gathered into a single cost pool, then an appropriate cost driver (e.g., machine setup labor hours) is used to determine an allocation rate. Machine setup labor hours are appropriate cost drivers because an increase in the hours would directly impact the cost of the machine configuration activity.

ABC supplements traditional costing and the activity-based methodology can be applied to both job-order and process costing.
1) Cost hierarchy
    i. Unit-level costs – costs of activities for individual products or services (e.g., machine maintenance costs)
    ii. Batch-level costs – costs of activities related to groups of products or services (e.g., setup or configuration costs)
    iii. Product-sustaining costs – cost of activities to support products or service without regard for units produced or sold (e.g., design costs)
    iv. Facility-sustaining costs – costs of activities that are not traced to products or services (i.e., lack cause and effect relationship) but are necessary to operate the facility (e.g., rent, administration, insurance, property tax).

ABC is ideal for minimizing non-value added activities such as inventory storage and addressing the costs of quality. These costs are highlighted in ABC rather than smoothed into the product cost, as is the norm with traditional costing.

> *Hint*: A cost driver does not need to be a financial measure. For example, direct labor hours or machine hours are both popular cost drivers for ABC costing.

Multiple Choice
BEC 5-Q71 through BEC 5-Q74

d. Spoilage, rework, and scrap
   1) Spoilage
      Spoilage includes any units that do not meet the specifications for sale. These units can be sold at a discount or discarded.

      Spoilage can be classified as either normal or abnormal.
         i. Normal spoilage
            Normal spoilage is the result of efficient operations and is a *product cost* since it is unavoidable. The costs of the spoiled units are spread across all of the good units and are inventoriable (capitalized) on the balance sheet. Costs usually are recorded as a part of overhead (OH), applied to the appropriate work-in-process inventory account (depending on if the company uses job or process costing). Over time, the company expenses the costs associated with normal spoilage when good units are sold.

ii. Abnormal spoilage
Abnormal spoilage is the result of poor quality production. It is both avoidable and can be controlled by management. Abnormal Spoilage is a *period cost* and is expensed immediately in the income statement (e.g., loss on abnormal spoilage).

> *Hint*: Do not include abnormal spoilage in work-in-process (WIP) inventory.

iii. Treatment of spoilage in job order costing
In job costing, normal spoilage is attributable to a single job or all jobs. If one job causes the normal spoilage, that individual job is assigned the whole cost, and the spoilage is not factored into the predetermined overhead calculation. If the normal spoilage is common to all jobs, the cost is allocated as a manufacturing overhead cost and spread across every job.

Abnormal spoilage is expensed to loss on abnormal spoilage in the period incurred and it is not relevant if the cost is attributable to a single job or common to all jobs.

iv. Treatment of spoilage in process costing
In process costing, normal and abnormal spoilage that occurs during production is included in the number of completed units' calculation (Step 1). The cost per EFU includes the spoiled EFU in the denominator (Step 3). Costs are assigned to completed units, spoiled units, and ending work-in-process.

Abnormal spoilage is expensed to loss on abnormal spoilage in the period incurred.

> *Hint*: Abnormal spoilage is accounted for the same under both job-order costing and process costing.

2) Rework
Rework is a defective product that is repaired to meet the specifications for sale.
3) Scrap
Scrap is a byproduct of the production process that has low or zero sales value.

> *Example*: A glass fabrication plant produces glass bottles for a soda company. Glass is poured into molds to create the desired bottle shape.
> Spoilage: Flawed glass bottles with permanent defects (e.g., wrong color)
> Rework: Pours that fail to fill the entire mold but the glass can be melted again and remolded
> Scrap: Extra glass beads or broken glass (called cullet in the glass industry) that the company can no longer use to make bottles.

e. Joint products and byproducts
   1) Joint costing
      Joint product costing is necessary when two or more products (with relatively high sales value) are produced together, and costs are difficult to differentiate and assign to each individual product. Joint costs include materials, labor, and indirect manufacturing overhead of the joint production process.

      An important juncture during the joint production process is the point when two or more products are separately identifiable. This point is called the split-off point. Joint products processed further after the split-off point are directly assigned any separable costs incurred during separate processing.

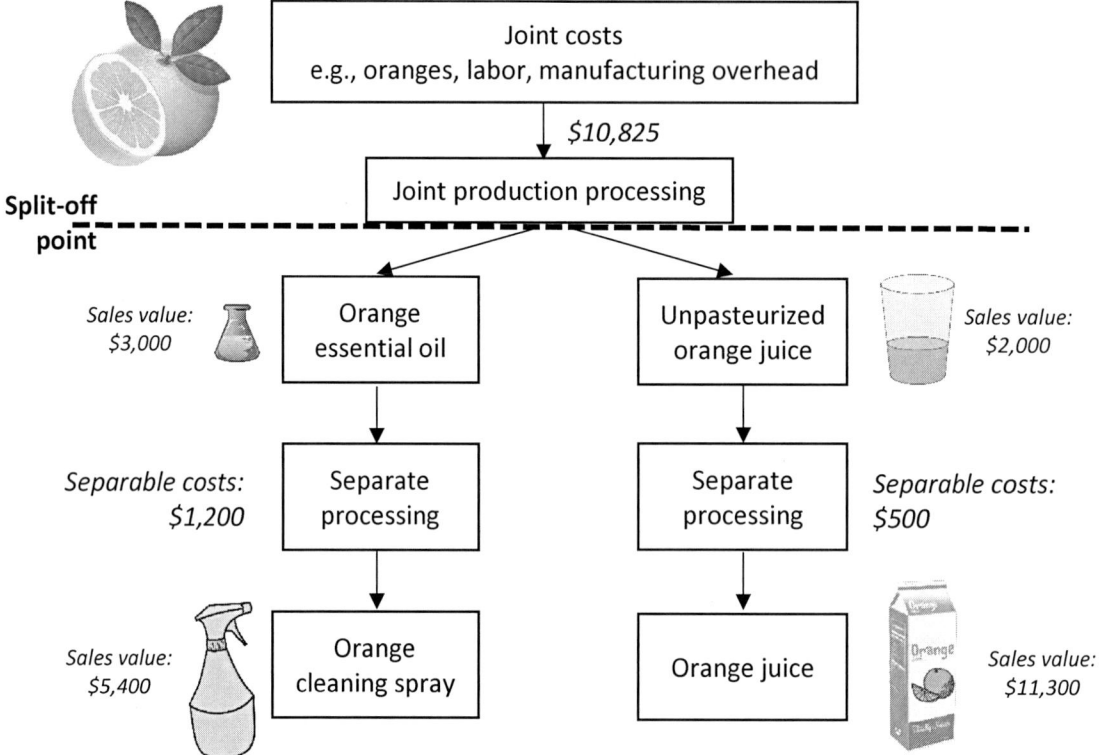

      Various methods may be used to allocate joint costs, including the value at split-off method, the physical measure method, the estimated net realizable value method or the constant gross margin percentage net realizable value method.

      i. Sales value at split-off method
         The sales value at split-off method allocates and assigns costs based on the relative sales value of each separately identifiable product at the split-off point. For example, the joint costs to process the unpasteurized orange juice and orange essential oil would be allocated based on the sales value of each of those products without further processing.

         > *Hint:* This method must be used if a sales value at split-off point exists. It is the best measure of the benefits received from joint processing and does not factor in uncertain future business decisions or market conditions. It is also preferred due to its simplicity compared to other acceptable calculations (e.g., estimated NRV).

	Orange Essential Oil	Orange Juice	Total
Sales value at split-off	$3,000	$2,000	$5,000
Weighting ratio	$3,000 / $5,000 = 0.6	$2,000 / $5,000 = 0.4	1.0
Joint costs allocated	$10,825 * 0.6 = **$6,495**	$10,825 * 0.4 = **$4,330**	**$10,825**

Multiple Choice

BEC 5-Q75

ii. Physical measure method
The physical measure method allocates costs based on a comparable physical measure of products at the split-off point. The measure must apply to both joint products or the calculation is not possible. Physical measures include product weights or volumes.

> *Hint:* This method is least desirable because physical measures are not directly tied to the benefits received from joint processing and can be misleading.
>
> For example, assume managers measure and allocate costs to orange essential oil and orange juice in terms of a liquid pint. One orange can produce more juice than oil. As such, the physical measure method would allocate fewer costs to the oil than to the juice. Assuming essential oil sold for more per pint than orange juice, allocation of a smaller percentage of joint costs is misleading because the profit margin for the oil would be deceptively large. The orange juice, on the other hand, would have a smaller profit margin than it would use a different joint cost allocation method (e.g., sales value at split-off).

Multiple Choice

BEC 5-Q76

iii. Estimated net realizable value (NRV) method
The estimated NRV method allocates the joint costs of production using the relative estimated net realizable value (final sales value minus separable costs). This method assumes that the products are processed separately; otherwise, the net realizable value would be identical to the sales-value at split-off.

	Orange Essential Oil	Orange Juice	Total
Final sales value of total production	$5,400	$11,300	$16,700
Deduct: Separable costs	($1,200)	($500)	($1,700)
Net realizable value (NRV) at split-off	$4,200	$10,800	$15,000
Weighting ratio	$4,200 / $15,000 = 0.28	$10,800 / $15,000 = 0.72	1.0
Joint costs allocated	$10,825 * 0.28 = **$3,031**	$10,825 * 0.72 = **$7,794**	**$10,825**

> *Hint:* This method is appropriate when the sales value at split-off not readily available.

iv. Constant gross margin percentage NVR method
The constant gross margin percentage NRV method assumes each product has the same gross margin percentage and allocates joint costs to maintain this relationship. To achieve a consistent gross margin percentage:
   a. Calculate a combined gross margin percentage.
   b. Deduct each product's gross margin dollar amount from the sales value, which results in the total production costs for each product.
   c. Then, deduct separable costs to arrive at joint costs allocated.

Again, the objective is to assign joint costs such that the gross margin for each product is equal.

Final sales value of total production	$16,700
Deduct:	
Joint costs	($10,825)
Separable costs	($1,700)
Gross margin	$4,175
Gross margin percentage	**25%**

Gross margin / Final sales value of total production = $4,175 / $16,700 = 0.25 or 25%

	Orange Essential Oil	Orange Juice	Total
Final sales value of total production	$5,400	$11,300	$16,700
Deduct: Gross margin	$5,400 * 25% = $1,350	$11,300 * 25% = $2,825	$4,175
Total production costs	$4,050	$8,475	$12,525
Deduct: Separable costs	$1,200	$500	$1,700
Joint costs allocated	**$2,850**	**$7,975**	**$10,825**

Multiple Choice

BEC 5-Q77

2) Byproducts
Byproducts are goods generated in a joint process that have low total sales value in relation to the main product. A main product is the primary, high sales value product produced during a joint production process in relation to all other simultaneously produced products. For example, in the production of orange juice, the peel and pulp of the orange are byproducts. These byproducts can be sold as cattle feed for a low sales value compared to the sales value of the orange juice, the main product.

If the pulp is discarded, it would be considered scrap and accounted for using appropriate accounting procedures to handle spoilage depending on its nature (i.e., normal or abnormal).

> *Hint*: In practice, it may be hard to distinguish between main products, joint products, and byproducts. Joint costs are not allocated to byproducts.

Accounting for byproducts is achieved using the production method or the sales method.

i. Production method
The production method offsets the net realizable value (NRV) of the byproduct against the costs of the main product.

Record purchase of materials and conversion costs:
Dr. Work-in-process $20
  Cr. Accounts payable* $5
  Cr. Wages payable* $10
  Cr. Accumulated depreciation* $5
  *Hint: Accounts may vary depending on the situation.

Record completion of main product and byproduct:
Dr. Byproduct inventory $2 *(NRV of byproduct)*
Dr. Finished goods $18
  Cr. Work-in-Process $20

Record cost of main product at time of sale:
Dr. Cost of goods sold $18*
  Cr. Finished goods $18
  *Cost of goods sold is less than it would have been if the byproduct was not recorded on the balance sheet at the time of production ($20 - $2 = $18).

Record revenue of main product at time of sale:
Dr. Cash $30
  Cr. Revenue – main product $30

Record the byproduct transaction at time of sale:
Dr. Cash $2
  Cr. Byproduct inventory $2

> *Hint:* This scenario assumes no ending inventory.

ii. Sales method
The sales method recognizes the byproduct revenues in the period of sale and no journal entries are recorded prior to its sale.

Record purchase of materials and conversion costs:
Dr. Work-in-process $20
  Cr. Accounts payable* $5
  Cr. Wages payable* $10
  Cr. Accumulated depreciation* $5
  *Hint: Accounts may vary depending on the situation.

Record completion of main product:
Dr. Finished goods $20
  Cr. Work-in-Process $20

Record cost of main product at time of sale:
Dr. Cost of goods sold $20
  Cr. Finished goods $20

Record revenue of main product at time of sale:
Dr. Cash $30
    Cr. Revenue – main product $30

Record the revenue of byproduct at time of sale:
Dr. Cash $2
    Cr. Revenue – byproduct $2

> *Hint:* This scenario assumes no ending inventory.

f. Departmental cost allocation and common costs
   1) Departmental cost allocation methods
      Companies are made up of operating departments and support departments. Operating departments add value to product or service (e.g., production). Support (or service) departments provide internal services (e.g., HR, IT, marketing) to operating departments.

      Support department costs can be allocated using the direct method, the step-down method, or the reciprocal method.

      Example scenario: A bookstore and coffee shop consists of two operating departments: (1) books sales and (2) coffee. It also has two support departments: (A) warehousing and (B) maintenance.

Department	Budgeted costs	Budgeted warehouse sq. ft.	Budgeted maintenance hours
1. Book sales	$110,000	900	600
2. Coffee	$175,000	600	1,000
A. Warehousing	$350,000	N/A	400
B. Maintenance	$150,000	300	N/A
TOTAL	**$785,000**	**1,800**	**2,000**

   i. Direct method
      The direct method is the simplest cost allocation approach because it ignores service to service department costs. Support department costs are allocated only to operating departments.

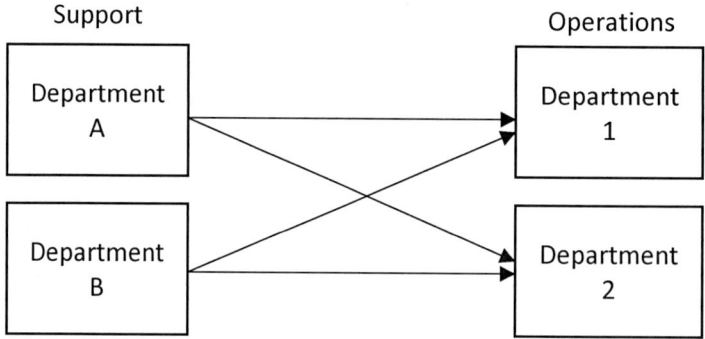

Department	Budgeted costs	Allocation of A	Allocation of B	TOTAL
1. Book sales	$110,000	$350,000 * (900/1500) = $210,000	$150,000 * (600/1600) = $56,250	$376,250
2. Coffee	$175,000	$350,000 * (600/1500) = $140,000	$150,000 * (1000/1600) = $93,750	$408,750
A. Warehousing	$350,000	($350,000)	-	$0
B. Maintenance	$150,000	-	($150,000)	$0
TOTAL	$785,000	$0	$0	$785,000

ii. Step-down (sequential) method

The step-down method allocates support department costs to other departments sequentially, starting by allocating costs to all other departments. Service departments are eliminated one by one as their cost are allocated (i.e., no costs are allocated back to a previously allocated support department).

Departments are ranked to determine which one to allocate first. The ranking is based on percentage services rendered to other service departments, from most to least. This method ignores the mutual benefit support departments experience in relation to one another.

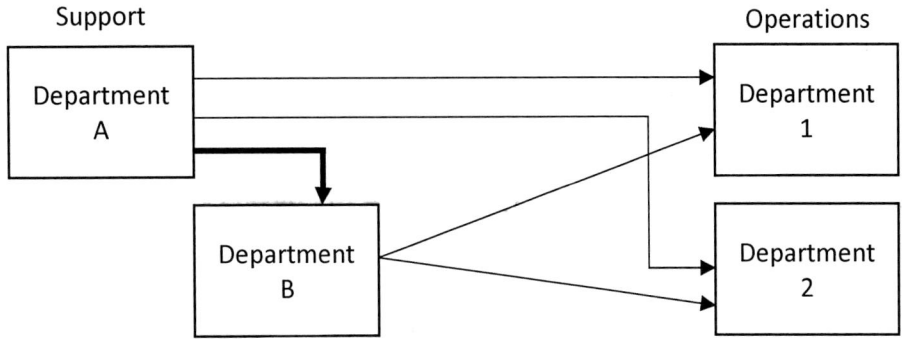

Ranking of services rendered to other service departments:
1. Maintenance provides 20% of its services to warehousing.
   400 / (600 + 1000 + 400) = 20%

2. Warehousing provides 16.67% of its services to maintenance.
   300 / (900 + 600 + 300) = 16.67%

Department	Budgeted costs	Rank 1: Allocation of B (20%)	Rank 2: Allocation of A	TOTAL
1. Book sales	$110,000	$150,000 * (600/2000) = $45,000	$380,000 * (900/1500) = $228,000	$383,000
2. Coffee	$175,000	$150,000 * (1000/2000) = $75,000	$380,000 * (600/1500) = $152,000	$402,000
A. Warehousing	$350,000	$150,000 * (400/2000) = $30,000	($380,000)	$0
B. Maintenance	$150,000	($150,000)	-	$0
TOTAL	$785,000	$0	$0	$785,000

iii. Reciprocal method
The reciprocal method allocates each support department's costs to every other support department, fully adjusting each support department's costs for mutual services.

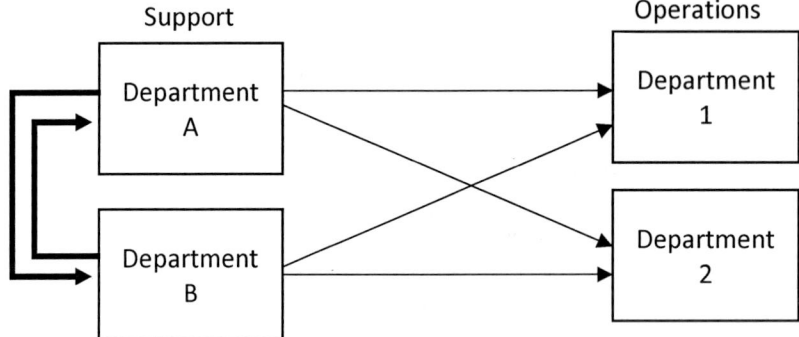

This technique requires managers to express each support department linear relationship as an equation and solve using substitution. This will mathematically determine the reciprocated costs. The more complex the organization, the more difficult the reciprocal method is to calculate.

Warehousing:
A = $350,000 + (400/2,000)*B
A = $350,000 + 0.2*B

Maintenance:
B = $150,000 + (300/1,800)*A
B = $150,000 + 0.1667*A

Solve using substitution:
        A = $350,000 + 0.2*B
        A = $350,000 + 0.2*($150,000 + 0.1667A)
        A = $350,000 + $30,000 + 0.0333A
        1.0A = $380,000 + 0.0333A
        1.0A - 0.0333A = $380,000 + 0.0333A - 0.0333A
        .9667A = $380,000
        A = $393,103.45

        B = $150,000 + 0.1667*A
        B = $150,000 + 0.1667*($393,103.45)
        B = $150,000 + $65,517.24
        B = $215,517.24

Department	Budgeted costs	Allocation of A	Allocation of B	TOTAL
1. Book sales	$110,000	$393,103.45 * (900/1800) = $196,551.72	$215,517.24 * (600/2000) = $64,655.17	$371,206.90
2. Coffee	$175,000	$393,103.45 * (600/1800) = $131,034.48	$215,517.24 * (1000/2000) = $107,758.62	$413,793.10
A. Warehousing	$350,000	($393,103.45)	$215,517.24 * (400/2000) = $43,103.45	$0
B. Maintenance	$150,000	$393,103.45 * (300/1800) = $65,517.24	($215,517.24)	$0
TOTAL	$785,000	$0	$0	$785,000

2) Single-rate and dual-rate method of allocating costs
   i. Single-rate
   The single-rate method for allocating costs uses the same cost pool for both variable and fixed costs. By using only one allocation rate per cost pool (e.g., support department), both fixed and variable costs are allocated based on actual usage.

   The primary advantage of the single-rate method is that it is less expensive to implement than the dual-rate method. Yet, the single-rate method is not without fault. Using a single-rate causes fixed costs to appear variable and may lead to inappropriate outsourcing decisions. Also, this method's dependence on actual usage increases the amount of control managers have over costs. This may encourage managers to make decisions in their own best interest and not in the best interest of the company as a whole.

   ii. Dual-rate
   The dual-rate method for allocating costs distinguishes between variable and fixed cost pools, assigning costs using different cost allocation bases as appropriate. Support department costs are allocated based on two different rates, one rate associated with the variable cost pool and one with the fixed cost pool. Managers assign variable costs using actual usage and fixed costs using budgeted practical capacity.

   Although more expensive than the single-rate method, the dual-rate is less subject to manipulation by department managers, and the allocation of fixed costs using budgeted capacity is more timely.

   Criticism of the dual-rate method stems from using budgeted capacity to allocate fixed costs, regardless of its timeliness. First, managers may be tempted to underestimate their budgeted fixed costs during planning to ultimately appear more profitable. Second, operating managers may never have a clear understanding of their departments' fair share of allocated fixed costs based on actual usage.

g. Common costs and bundled product revenue allocation
Common costs are any costs shared by one or more users. The term common cost is not interchangeable with joint cost. A joint cost only relates to the simultaneous processing costs of joint products. The term common cost is broader, although a joint cost could be considered a common cost. It is important to determine separate costs for each distinct product, even if the costs are shared.

Similar to common costs, it is also necessary to allocate bundled product revenue. A bundled product is a package deal of two or more products sold for one price, often discounted.

There are two methods managers typically often use to handle common costs and allocate revenue from bundled products: the stand-alone method and the incremental method.

1) Stand-alone method
   The stand-alone method determines each item's stand-alone cost or price and assigns the common (shared) cost or bundled revenue using a stand-alone ratio.

$$\text{Cost assigned to Product A} = \frac{\text{Product A Stand-alone cost}}{\text{Total stand-alone cost Product A + Product B}} \times \text{Common cost}$$

$$\text{Revenue assigned to Product A} = \frac{\text{Product A Stand-alone revenue}}{\text{Total stand-alone revenue Product A + Product B}} \times \text{Bundled selling price}$$

Example:
Common cost or bundled revenue (A+B) = $28
Cost of Product A = $10
Cost of Product B = $30

$$\text{Product A} = \frac{\$10}{\$40} \times \$28 = \$7 \text{ assigned}$$

$$\text{Product B} = \frac{\$30}{\$40} \times \$28 = \$21 \text{ assigned}$$

2) Incremental method
   The incremental method uses a ranking system to determine which product is primary and assigns that product the cost or revenue first. The second product is called the first incremental (secondary) product, and so forth. The primary product is based on manager judgment. The reasoning for the primary product of a common cost is that it is often the most responsible for generating the cost. For revenue, it may be the product with higher stand-alone unit sales.

   An extension of the incremental method is called the Shapley method, named for Lloyd Shapley. To use this technique, all variations of the incremental method are performed, and the results are averaged to eliminate bias and improve fairness.

   Example:
   Common cost or bundled revenue (A+B) = $28
   Cost of Product A = $10
   Cost of Product B = $30

   Option 1, Product A is the primary product:
   Product A = $10 ($28 - $10 = $18 remaining to assign)
   Product B = $18

   Option 2, Product B is the primary product:
   Product B = $28 ($28 - $30 = $0 remaining to assign)
   Product A = $0

Shapley method, uses an average:
Product A: $10 + $28 / 2 = $19
Product B: $18 + $0 / 2 = $9

h. Backflush costing

Backflush costing is a non-GAAP technique for costing. Companies with a just-in-time (JIT) inventory structure may elect to use backflush costing internally for recordkeeping. The technique is ideal for companies that hold little or no inventory. Rather than recording estimated costs prior to production, actual costs are recorded when the goods are completed (Method I) or when the goods are sold (Method II). The term "backflush" originates from the idea that costs are "flushed backwards" from final products, eliminating the tedious task of tracking of costs throughout the production process.

Under both methods, the WIP inventory account is eliminated and direct labor (DL) and manufacturing overhead (OH) are combined into a conversion cost control account.

1) Refresher of traditional cost flows (GAAP), for comparison

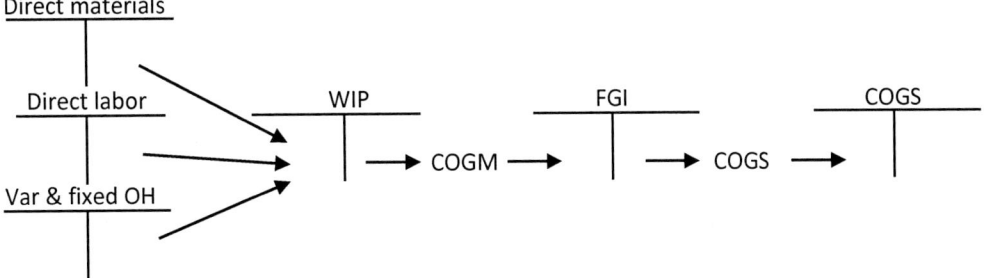

2) *Backflush Costing Method I* – JIT inventory methods with vendors/suppliers
As demonstrated below, combine DM + WIP (materials & in-process) and DL + OH (conversion cost control) to simplify the cost flow.

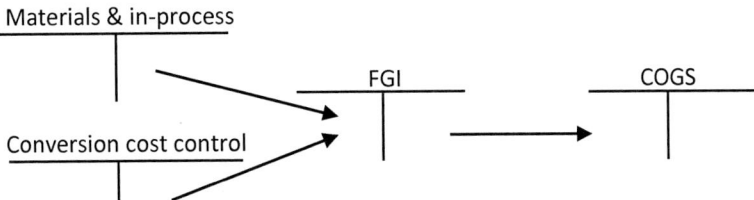

3) *Backflush Costing Method II* – JIT inventory methods with vendors/suppliers *and* customers
Method II, an extension of method I, eliminates FGI. Costs flow directly from the combined accounts on the balance sheet to income statement. Once combined, account balances and inventory records are difficult to disaggregate. This is one reason that backflush costing is not acceptable under GAAP.

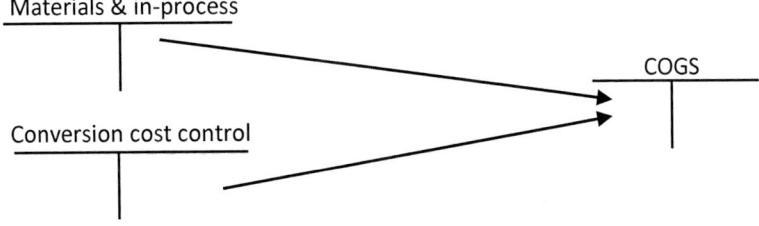

	Traditional (GAAP)	Backflush method I JIT – w/ vendors (or suppliers)	Backflush method II JIT – w/ vendors and customers
1. Purchase raw materials			

	Materials DR
	  A/P CR
		Materials & in-process DR
		  A/P CR
			Same as I

2. Issue materials to production			
	WIP DR Materials CR	None	None
3. Incur direct labor costs			
	WIP DR Payroll CR	See next entry	See next entry
4. Incur overhead costs			

	Variable OH control DR
	Fixed OH control DR
	  A/P, etc. CR
		Conversion cost ctrl DR
		  Payroll CR
		  A/P, etc. CR
			Same as I

5. Apply overhead			

	WIP DR
	  Variable OH control CR
	  Fixed OH control CR
		None	None

6. Complete goods			**6 & 7. Complete and sell goods**

	FGI DR
	  WIP CR
		FGI DR
		  Conversion cost ctrl CR
		  Materials & in process CR
			COGS DR
			  Conversion cost ctrl CR
			  Materials & in-process CR

7. Sell goods			
	COGS DR FGI CR	Same as traditional	
8. Recognize overhead variance (under-applied)			

	COGS DR
	  Overhead control CR
		COGS DR
		  Conversion cost ctrl CR
			Same as I

i. Target costing

Target costing is a costing technique that managers implement to reduce costs. It involves first determining an estimated price the customer will pay for a particular product and then working backwards to determine the maximum costs allowable to achieve a desired profit margin. If the actual costs are expected to exceed the maximum target costs, the production process is redesigned to reduce costs.

j. Estimating cost functions

Differentiate the characteristics of fixed, variable and mixed costs within an entity.

An activity's total cost consists of variable costs (VC), fixed costs (FC), or a combination of both types of costs (mixed/semi-variable costs).

Managers rely on cost functions to estimate the total cost associated with an activity at any production volume. A cost function is a mathematical formula, typically linear, that in generic form is defined as:

$$y = a + bx$$

y = dependent variable = total costs = VC + FC
x = independent variable = production volume = number of units
a = constant (or, the intercept value) = FC **in total**
b = coefficient or slope = VC **per unit**

Variable cost y = $1x	Proportional change **in total**	Constant cost **per unit**
Fixed cost y = $1,000	Constant **in total** (within relevant range)	Inversely proportional **per unit**
Mixed cost (semi-variable) y = $1,000 + 1x	Combination of variable and fixed	Combination of variable and fixed

1) Variable cost
   Variable costs can be traced to a cost object and **total** variable costs change proportionately as activity levels fluctuate, increasing as activity increases and decreasing as activity decreases during a period. This relationship means that **per unit** variable costs are constant, such that each additional unit costs an equal amount.

   The most basic variable cost function is y = $1x. For every additional unit, it will cost the company $1 more (assuming the variable cost does not fluctuate during the period).

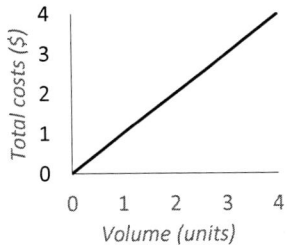

2) Fixed cost
   Total fixed costs are constant **in total** within a specific relevant range. The relevant range is a span of normal activity or production volume that has a constant relationship with the fixed cost.

   The cost function below is y = $1000. For every additional unit, the cost **in total** is constant ($1000) and the cost **per unit** decreases proportionally (inverse relationship). For instance, the fixed cost **per unit** is $500 at 2 units ($1000/2 units = $500) and $250 at 4 units ($1000/4 units = $250).

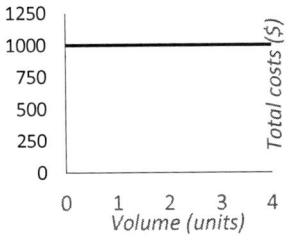

   If the relevant range is narrow, the fixed cost could appear stepped graphically or semi-fixed. The cost is still considered fixed **in total** within each relevant range. In the example below, the total fixed cost is $500 for 0-2 units and $750 for 2+ units.

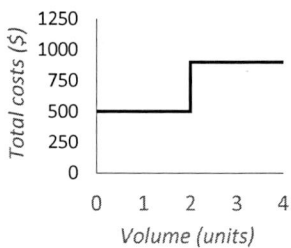

3) Mixed costs (semi-variable cost)
A mixed or semi-variable cost has a combination of characteristics of both a variable and fixed cost. For example, if a bandana costs $1 per unit and the fixed costs to set up the equipment cost $1000, regardless of the units produced, the appropriate cost function is y = $1X + $1,000.

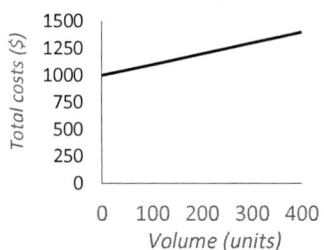

4) Scattergraph or scatter diagram method
The scattergraph is a technique to estimate a cost function by finding a line of "best fit" (regression line) for a particular data set. The dataset, consisting of multiple observations, is plotted on a graph with the independent variable on the x-axis (e.g., number of units, production volume) and the dependent variable on the y-axis (e.g., total cost). Ideally, the line selected should minimize the distance vertically to each point. The line drawn on a scattergraph is an estimation based on visual inspection of data set represented by the points on the graph.

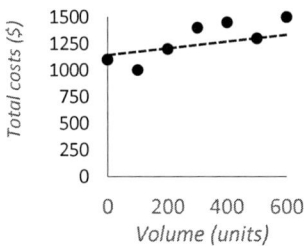

To improve accuracy, regression analysis is used to numerically measure the vertical distance between the line and each point. To eliminate positive and negative values, the distance from point to line is measured and squared. The sum of the squared distances is minimized to find the line of best fit. The accuracy of the line is measured and this value is called the standard error.

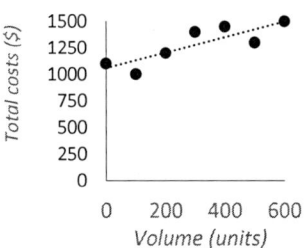

Multiple Choice

BEC 5-Q78

5) Correlation analysis
Managers use correlation analysis to determine if two variables are related statistically. Correlations help managers make predictions as to the impact one variable will have on the other. For example, correlation analysis could tell an outerwear retailer that a customer is likely to purchase a hat and a coat at the same time if the two are highly correlated.

> *Hint*: Keep in mind that correlation does not indicate or imply a causal relationship. Therefore, while customers purchasing a hat and coat may be correlated, it would be inaccurate to imply that purchasing a hat would cause a customer also to purchase a coat.

Correlations can either be positive or negative. A positive correlation indicates there is a direct relationship between the variables, as one variable increases the other will also increase and vice versa. A negative correlation describes an inverse relationship, as one variable increases the other will decrease and vice versa.

Statisticians communicate correlations using a correlation coefficient ranging from -1 to 1. A perfectly negative correlation is -1, a perfectly positive correlation is +1, and a coefficient of zero indicates there is no correlation. The closer the coefficient is to 1 (positive or negative) the stronger the two variables are correlated.

$$-1 < r < +1$$

r = correlation coefficient

6) High-low method
The high-low method is a way to compute a cost equation using a highest and lowest observed unit volume (independent variable) and total cost (dependent variable).

> *Hint*: The highest and lowest observation is based on the activity volume, not dollar value.

$$\text{Slope} = \frac{\text{Change in Y}}{\text{Change in X}} = \frac{\text{Change in total cost}}{\text{Change in activity or unit volume}}$$

1) Step 1: Determine the highest and lowest observed unit volume and total cost.

Observation	Activity (Number of Units)	Total Cost ($)	Highest/ Lowest
1	47,000	$65,000	-
2	50,000	$80,000	Highest
3	31,000	$62,000	-
4	10,000	$20,000	Lowest
5	22,000	$56,000	-

2) Step 2: Compute the slope.

Observation	Total Cost ($)	Activity (Number of Units)
Highest	$80,000	50,000
Lowest	$20,000	10,000
Change	$60,000	40,000
	Y	X

$$\text{Slope} = \frac{\text{Change in Y}}{\text{Change in X}} = \frac{\$60,000}{40,000} = \$1.5 \text{ per unit}$$

3) Step 3: Compute the fixed cost or y-intercept.

Lowest
$1.5 per unit * 10,000 unit = $15,000 total variable cost
$20,000 - $15,000 = $5,000 fixed cost

Check: Total cost = 1.5x + $5,000
Total cost = 1.5(10,000) + $5,000
Total cost = $15,000 + $5,000
Total cost = $20,000

OR

Highest
$1.5 *50,000 = $75,000 total variable cost
$80,000 - $75,000 = $5,000 fixed cost

Check: Total cost = 1.5x + $5,000
Total cost = 1.5(50,000) + $5,000
Total cost = $75,000 + $5,000
Total cost = $80,000

4) Step 4 (optional): Graph the cost function:

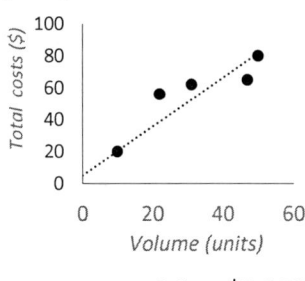

y = 1.5x + $5,000

k. Variable and absorption costing
Variable (direct) costing and absorption costing are techniques to compute a company's product costs and ultimately cost of goods sold. Selecting either variable or absorption costing changes the presentation of the income statement.

Variable costing, a non-GAAP costing method, treats all variable product costs (DM, DL, & VOH) as costs that are attached to inventory (capitalized as product costs) and treats fixed manufacturing overhead (FMOH) as a period cost, expensing FMOH immediately. Selling, general, and administrative costs are still considered period costs under variable costing. This method is only appropriate for internal financial reporting and is also called direct costing. Companies use the contribution format income statement under variable costing.

The alternative is absorption costing, a GAAP costing technique, which treats all variable product costs (DM, DL, VOH) and fixed overhead (FOH) as a product cost. The period costs are only the costs associated with selling, general, and administrative costs. Absorption costing is used for external financial reporting and companies use the traditional or functional income statement.

Direct or Variable Costing	**Absorption or Full Costing**
Not GAAP	GAAP
Used for internal decision making.	Used for external financial reporting.
Treats FMOH as a PERIOD cost.	Treats FMOH as a PRODUCT cost.
Income Statement:	Income Statement:
Sales	Sales
– Variable COGS (DM, DL, VMOH)	– COGS (DM, DL, VMOH, FMOH)
= Manufacturing Contribution Margin	= Gross Profit or Gross Margin
– Variable Period Costs	– Period Costs (Fixed & Variable)
= Contribution Margin	= Net Income
– Fixed Costs (FMOH as Period Cost)	
= Net Income	

Direct or Variable Costing	Absorption or Full Costing
If Production > Sales, then ending inventory **increases**	
Lower NI	Higher NI
If Production < Sales, then ending inventory **decreases**	
Higher NI	Lower NI
If Production = Sales, then Ending inventory does **not change**	
Same NI for both	

Hint: To calculate the difference in the net income between the two methods, multiply the change in ending inventory (in units) by the fixed manufacturing overhead rate per unit.

Multiple Choice

BEC 5-Q79 through BEC 5-Q82

2. Variance analysis

> Determine the appropriate variance analysis method to measure the key cost drivers by analyzing business scenarios.

a. Standard costs
A standard cost is a carefully predetermined cost per unit of output under normal circumstances. Managers base standard costs on historical data adjusted to eliminate past cost abnormalities and to anticipate future market conditions. Standard costs are preferred over actual costs because managers do not need to delay costing a product until actual costs are available. Standard costs are crucial in the budgeting process and are the foundation for variance analysis.

b. Variance analysis
The term variance simply describes the difference between actual and expected results. Variances often help managers prioritize their attention on poorly performing areas or areas that fail to achieve target performance level. This is called management by exception.

Variance analysis starts with a master budget. Created at the beginning of the period, a master budget is a static snapshot of the future using standard costs and anticipated sales figures. Using the master budget for reference, variances can be determined related to direct material (DM), direct labor (DL), and variable overhead (OH). For each of these items, variances can relate to price and efficiency (e.g., number of units). When the actual quantity (AQ) or actual price (AP) is different than the standard quantity (SQ) or standard price (SP), it indicates either a favorable or unfavorable variance.

Favorable (F) variances exist when operating income increases compared to the budget, namely actual revenues are more, or costs are less than anticipated. Unfavorable (U) variances occur when operating income decreases compared to the budget.

1) Direct materials (DM)
   i. Price variance
      Price variance, also called purchase price variance, is the difference between actual input price and a standard input price.

      $$\text{Price variance} = (AP - SP) \times AQ_{\text{Purchased}}$$

      > *Hint:* For direct materials, the AQ is recognized at the time of purchase rather than when the materials are used.

      This equation can also be adapted to determine selling price variance by substituting the actual quantity purchased with the actual quantity sold.

   ii. Efficiency variance
      Efficiency variance, sometimes called usage or volume or quantity variance for DM, is the difference between the actual input quantity and the standard quantity allowed based on the units produced.

Multiple Choice
BEC 5-Q83 through BEC 5-Q85

$$\text{Efficiency variance} = (AQ_{Used} - SQ_{Allowed\ based\ on\ units\ produced}) \times SP$$

Multiple Choice
BEC 5-86 through BEC 5-Q87

2) Direct manufacturing labor (DL)
   i. Price variance
   Price variance is also called the rate variance with respect to DL. It is the difference between actual labor rate (e.g., hourly pay rate) and a standard rate.

   ii. Efficiency variance
   Efficiency or usage variance is the difference between the actual input quantity and the standard quantity allowed based on the units produced.

   > *Hint*: The calculation for price and efficiency variance is the same for DM and DL, although the names sometimes vary slightly.

   > *Hint*: Both price variance and efficiency variance for DM and DL are controllable and impacted by managers' decisions over time.

Multiple Choice
BEC 5-Q88 through BEC 5-Q89

3) Variable manufacturing overhead (VOH)
   i. Spending variance
   The variable manufacturing overhead spending variance is the difference between actual OH costs per unit of the allocation base (e.g., machine hours) and standard cost per unit of the allocation base.

   $$\text{Spending variance} = (AP - SP) \times AQ_{Used}$$

Multiple Choice
BEC 5-Q90

   ii. Efficiency variance
   The variable manufacturing overhead efficiency variance is the difference between the actual quantity of the allocation base used and the standard quantity of the allocation base that should have been used.

   $$\text{Efficiency variance} = (AQ_{Used} - SQ_{Allowed\ based\ on\ units\ produced}) \times SP$$

Hint: Calculate these variances using the following matrix:

```
                                              *** Sales Price Variance ***
AQPurchased/Used    *   AP   = [     ]        DM purchase price variance; DM price variance
                                              DL Rate Variance
                                              ***Variable OH Spending Variance***

AQPurchased/Used    *   SP   = [     ]
                                              DM Quantity/Usage Variance
                                              DL Efficiency/Usage Variance
SQAllowed           *   SP   = [     ]        ***Variable OH Efficiency Variance***
(Based on Units Produced)                     *** Sales Volume Variance ***
```

Acronyms
AQ = Actual quantity
AP = Actual price
SQ = Standard quantity
SP = Standard price

For DM, DL, and VOH variances, as you go UP the matrix, if the numbers are going UP (increasing), then the variances are UNFAVORABLE.

** For sales variances, as you go UP the matrix, if the numbers are going UP (increasing), then the variances are FAVORABLE. Remember that these are REVENUES and not COSTS. **

4) Fixed manufacturing overhead (Fixed OH)
   i. Spending (budget) variance
   Fixed OH budget variance is the difference between actual fixed overhead and fixed overhead in the budget. This is also called the flexible-budget variance.

   Budget variance = (AQ * AP) − BUDGET

   Hint: There is no fixed overhead efficiency variance because overhead is unaffected by changes in quantity within a relevant range.

   ii. Production-volume variance
   Fixed OH production-volume variance is the difference between budgeted fixed costs and fixed overhead allocated based on the number of units produced. A favorable (unfavorable) variance indicates that overhead was over-allocated (under-allocated).

   Production-volume variance = BUDGET − (SQAllowed based on units produced * SP)

   It is important to understand that production-volume variance is not-controllable. It is an indication of how much of the company's capacity is being used. It is also only applicable to fixed overhead.

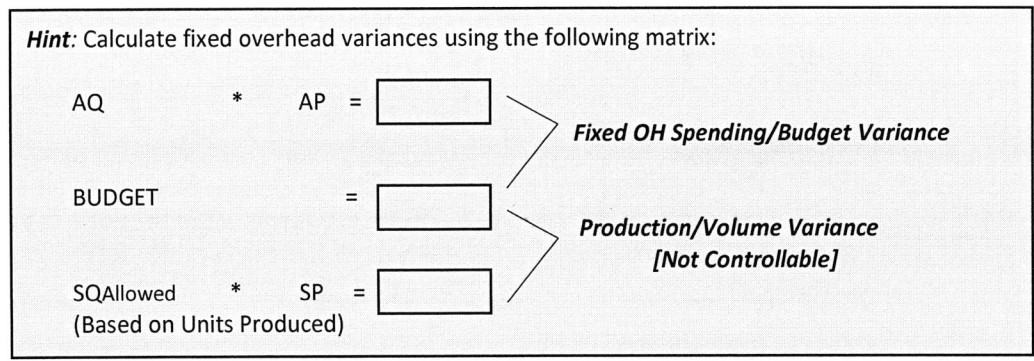

5) Variance analysis calculation summary
   <u>4-Way OH Variance Analysis:</u>
   (1) Variable OH Spending Variance
   (2) Variable OH Efficiency Variance
   (3) Fixed OH Spending/Budget Variance
   (4) Production/Volume Variance [NOT CONTROLLABLE]

   <u>3-Way OH Variance Analysis:</u>
   (a)   (1) + (3) above together are the OH Spending Variance
   (b)   (2) above becomes the OH Efficiency Variance (drop the word Variable)
   (c)   (4) above is the Production/Volume Variance [NOT CONTROLLABLE]

   <u>2-Way OH Variance Analysis:</u>
   (I)   (1) + (2) + (3) above together are the Controllable Variance
   (II)   (4) above is the Production/Volume Variance [NOT CONTROLLABLE]

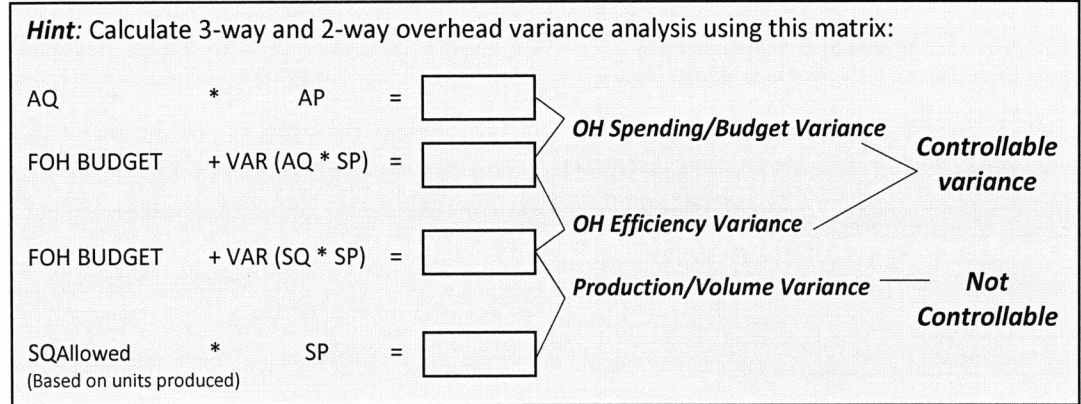

Multiple Choice

BEC 5-Q91 through BEC 5-Q92

6) Variance equation summary

	UNFAVORABLE	FAVORABLE
DM Price Variance = AQ Purchased x (Actual Price – Standard Price)	Actual Price > Standard Price	Actual Price < Standard Price
DM Efficiency or Quantity Variance = Standard Price x (Actual Quantity Used in Production – SQ*) *SQ is the standard quantity of DM allowed for actual production	Actual Qty > Standard Qty	Actual Qty < Standard Qty
DL Rate or Price Variance = Actual Hours Worked x (Actual Rate – Standard Rate)	Actual Rate > Standard Rate	Actual Rate < Standard Rate
DL Efficiency Variance = Standard Rate x (Actual Hours Worked – SH's allowed for actual output) SH = Standard Hours	Actual Hours > Standard Hours	Actual Hours < Standard Hours
VOH Rate or Spending Variance = Actual Qty of Activity Used x (Actual Rate – Standard Rate)	Actual Rate > Standard Rate	Actual Rate < Standard Rate
VOH Efficiency Variance = Standard Rate x (Actual Qty of Activity Used – SQ*) *SQ is the standard qty of activity allowed for actual output	Actual Quantity > Standard Quantity	Actual Quantity < Standard Quantity
Fixed OH Spending or Budget Variance = Actual Fixed OH Costs – Budgeted Fixed OH Costs	Actual Fixed OH > Standard Fixed OH	Actual Fixed OH < Standard Fixed OH
Hint: Notice that on all the variances so far, if the "actual" is greater than the "standard" than the variance is UNFAVORABLE and if "actual" is less than the "standard" than the variance is FAVORABLE.		
Fixed OH Production-Volume Variance = Budgeted Fixed OH – (SQ* x Standard Price) *Standard Quantity allowed based on units produced.	Budget > (SQ x Standard Price)	Budget < (SQ x Standard Price)
Sales Price Variance = Actual Quantity Sold x (Actual Price – Standard or Budgeted Price)	Actual Selling Price < Standard Price	Actual Selling Price > Standard Price
Sales Quantity Variance = Standard or Budgeted Price x (Actual Quantity Sold – Budgeted or Standard Quantity Sold)	Actual Qty < Standard or Budgeted Qty	Actual Qty > Standard or Budgeted Qty
Hint: Notice with the two sales variances that if "actual" is greater than "standard" than it is FAVORABLE and if "actual" is less than "standard" than it is UNFAVORABLE. The sales variances are opposite of that of the other variances since sales is dealing with a "revenue" item and the "DM, DL, VOH, & Fixed OH" are dealing with "cost or expense" items.		

C. Process Management
1. Approaches, techniques, measures, benefits to process management driven businesses

> **Identify commonly used operational management approaches, techniques and measures within the context of business process management.**

The primary goal of business process management (BPM) is to coordinate business functions to best meet customer needs. Business processes are structured activities that organizations use to accomplish their objectives. A robust set of business processes should be seen as an enterprise asset, although it is intangible.

Process managers continuously tailor business processes for maximum operational effectiveness and efficiency using a variety of process management philosophies and techniques. Management philosophies include just-in-time (JIT), total quality management (TQM), and lean (as well as several others discussed below). Regardless of the specific management philosophy adopted, BPM requires managers to document the existing process architecture, analyze its structure, and determine ways to improve it.

Business process management activities fit into categories such as design, modeling (pre-testing, "what if" simulations), execution (implementation and post-installation testing), monitoring, and optimization. These five categories are often referred to as the BPM lifecycle.

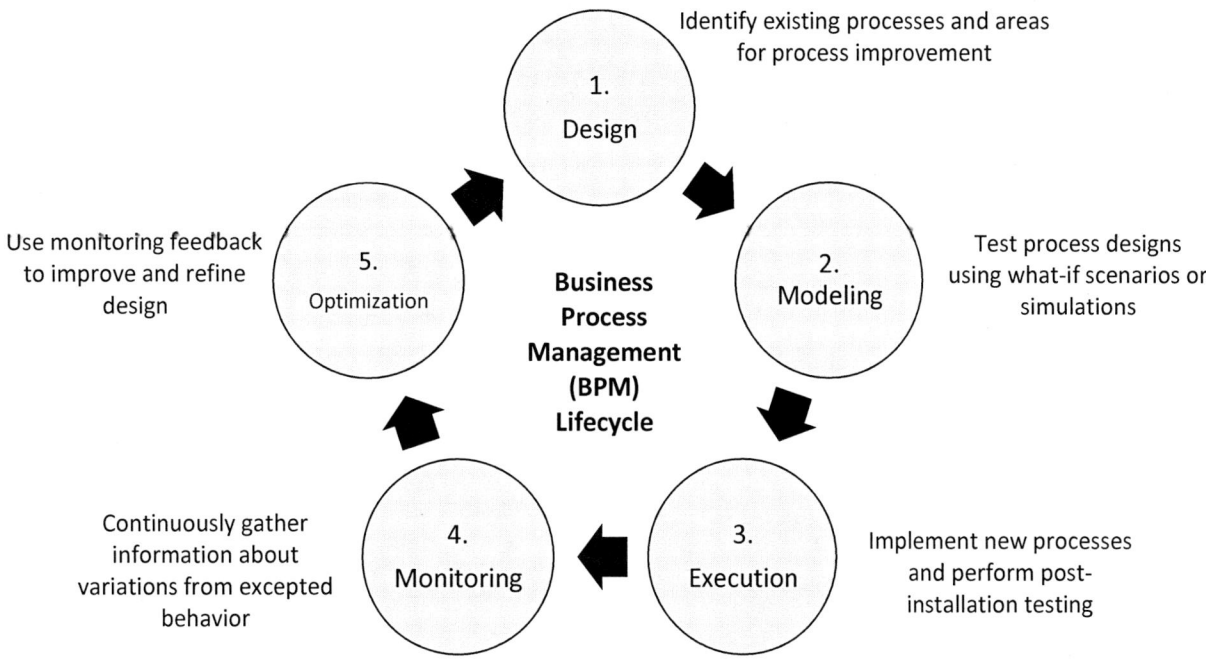

BPM in highly IT-dependent and automated environments may focus on optimizing human-technology interactions. Highly effective BPM initiatives often consider ways to improve the consistency, adaptability, and execution of existing processes.

a. Roles of shared services, outsourcing, and off-shore operations, and their implications on business risks and controls

1) Shared services
Shared services eliminate redundancy by combining and consolidating departments and duplicative processes within a company. An entity-wide information technology help desk

and human resources service center are two common shared service groups. Economies of scale can be achieved due to the increased volume of shared service use over operating independent service groups.

   i. Risks of shared services
      a) Capacity unable to meet demand – limited resources could be unable to handle the demand at peak times
      b) Delays – shared services can experience congestion due to a finite capacity

2) Outsourcing
   Outsourcing is contracting with an external provider to obtain goods or services rather than completing the job in-house. Examples include outside payroll, information technology, or virtual bookkeeping services. Companies opt to outsource specific processes to free up capacity, reduce internal headcount, or obtain unusual expertise when internal manufacturing or service capabilities are insufficient to do the job. Outsourced services may provide cost savings compared to executing the same process in-house and can be easier to scale as the company grows over time.

   i. Risks of outsourcing
      Due to the many risks, companies that decide to outsource should exercise caution when contracting outside parties. Risks include:
      a) Diminished quality – defects or manufacturing errors cannot be caught immediately and may result in entire batches that are unusable or impact customer satisfaction
      b) Data security vulnerability – outsourced information has an increased potential for unauthorized access due to more widely distributed access points and additional users
      c) Supply interruption risk – external provider could experience financial difficulties (e.g., reduce capacity or go out of business) and be unable to perform contracted services according to service agreement specifications
      d) Intellectual property exposure – contractors have access to proprietary information and other intellectual property which could be disturbed without authorization
      e) Negative public opinion – the word outsourcing carries a negative connotation since outsourcing leads to relocation of jobs and layoff potential
      f) Diminished productivity – highly technical processes could have a long learning curve, decreasing initial output
      g) Social responsibility risk – ethical employment practices are under the stewardship of a different company and out of the company's direct control
      h) Inconsistent staffing – contractors may experience high turnover and have an inexperienced team completing the job

3) Off-shore operations
   Off-shore operations involve outsourcing services to a foreign country.

   i. Risks of off-shore operations
      In addition to all of the risks associated with outsourcing, off-shore operations have a handful of additional considerations:
      a) Security concerns – international locations could have less stringent physical access controls, and the information is, therefore, less safe
      b) Transportation challenges – distance between the domestic location and the off-shore location adds complexity and room for delays (e.g., shipping holdup, port closures)

c) Language barriers – Communicating with foreign employees and contractors can be challenging
d) Training and qualification mismatch – Different countries have varying standards when it comes to training and qualifications for certain jobs, it is important the these align with the job requirements

a. Selecting and implementing improvement initiatives
Each step of a process must add value to the organization; if not, there is room for improvement. Improvement initiatives should consider if any steps in the process do not add value, are not contributing to the organization's strategic competitive advantage (e.g., product differentiation, cost leadership), and do not maximize customer satisfaction.

Before an organization can select and implement an initiative, it must document the existing process architecture. Flow or workflow diagrams, visual depictions of the conversion of inputs to outputs, are helpful tools for communicating business processes. Managers analyzing the workflows can determine which steps add value and suggest eliminating steps that do not add value.

Managers will likely select initiatives for which the benefits outweigh the costs to implement and are likely to improve the operational efficiency and effectiveness within the organization.

b. Business process reengineering
Business process reengineering is a complete process overhaul. Starting with a clean slate, managers rethink and redesign entire business processes to be more effective. Reengineering is the primary way to convert manual processes into automated processes. Core business processes (e.g., production, order fulfillment, customer service) are typically the subject of this type of radical redesign.

Reengineering has a potentially negative connotation due to its aggressive nature. Rather than continuously improving and tweaking processes to adapt them slowly (referred to as business process management), reengineering changes are sweeping and abrupt.

2. Management philosophies and techniques for performance and quality improvement

Identify commonly used management philosophies and techniques for performance and quality improvement within the context of business process management.

a. Just-in-time (JIT)
Just-in-time, or JIT systems obtain and deliver goods exactly as-needed, delivering no more or less than the quantity demanded. JIT principles can be applied to purchasing (procurement) and manufacturing (production).

A JIT system is a demand-pull system; therefore, the purchasing and the manufacturing processes are initiated only when a customer orders a product. This is opposite of a demand-push system, where inventory is purchased based on a manager's forecast of future demand.

JIT increases efficiency and reduces waste. Companies that decrease on-hand inventory are able to eliminate most, if not all of the costs associated with storing inventory. Equally important, companies limit their exposure to inventory obsolescence and any potential write-offs associated with inventory impairment.

Timing is extremely important for JIT. If too much of an item is delivered, the company must pay to store the extra stock in inventory. If too little, rush delivery may be needed to meet the demands of production. When companies execute JIT successfully, they receive all inputs exactly as-needed during the production process.

For JIT to function properly the supplier-manufacturer relationship must be stable, with clear roles and responsibilities. Frequent communication between the manufacturer and supplier is a must. Miscommunications, errors, and delays all have the potential to add additional, avoidable costs and reduce the savings associated with JIT.

b. Quality control principles and practices
   1) Total quality management (TQM)
      TQM is a management approach that focuses on improving product and service quality by refining operations incrementally, in response to feedback.

      This diagram demonstrates how the concepts typically relate to one another. TQM is the broadest of the four. Activity-based costing and backflush costing are discussed in the Cost Accounting section of Operations Management (above).

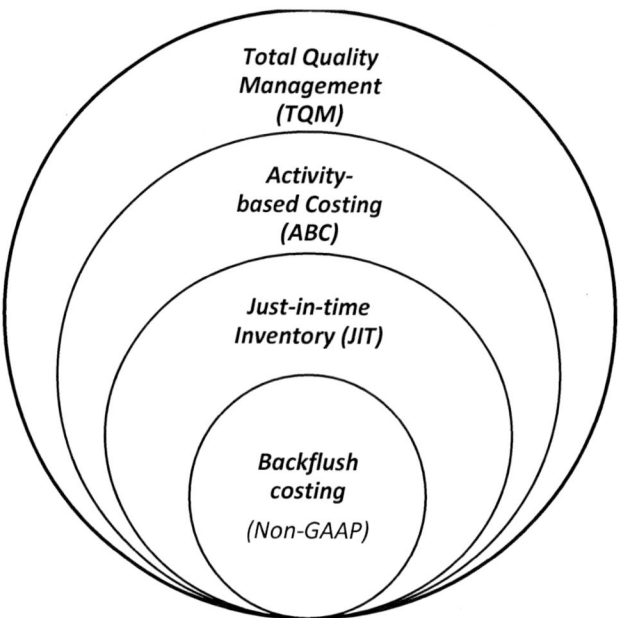

   2) Continuous improvement (e.g., Kaizen)
      As the name suggests, continuous improvement is a non-stop effort to determine ways to improve and perfect an activity. Kaizen, a Japanese word, is another name for this approach. Managers that implement continuous improvement as a management approach disagrees with the idea "if it's not broken, don't fix it" and, as a result, are never done striving for perfection. Managers are open to recommendations and encourage employees and customers to communicate their ideas.

      > *Hint:* The alternative to continuous improvement is to initiate initiatives for improvement only at scheduled intervals, such as following an audit or review. If feasible, continuous improvement is more beneficial since changes can be made in a timely manner.

3) Cause-and-effect analysis

A cause-and-effect analysis helps identify quality issues and determine what is causing each issue. This technique is best performed using an Ishikawa (or fishbone) diagram, with each "bone" of the chart identifying one potential cause of the problem listed on the far right, or the "head" of the fish. Although variations of the diagram exist, causes typically stem from categories including manpower, methods, materials, or machinery/equipment. Individual causes are grouped into one of the main categories and are drawn as a smaller "bone" connecting to the existing skeleton of the fish. This type of diagram is great for group brainstorming.

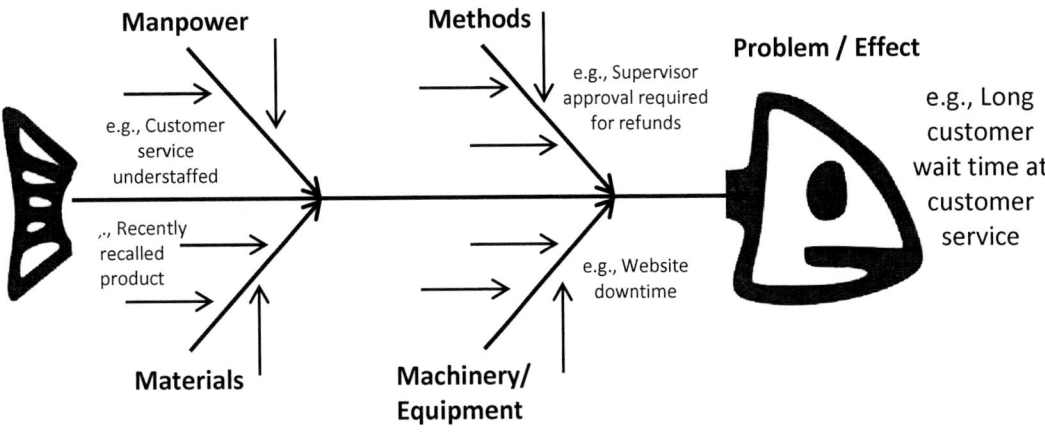

Hint: In practice, the fish head and tail are excluded. These visual elements are included to help make this example memorable.

A Pareto diagram is a bar graph that managers use to visualize data about the frequency of complaints, defects, or process problems. It lists the type of complaint or defect from most frequent to least frequent along the x-axis. For each item on the x-axis, managers plot the cumulative sum as a percentage of the total and connect each dot with a line.

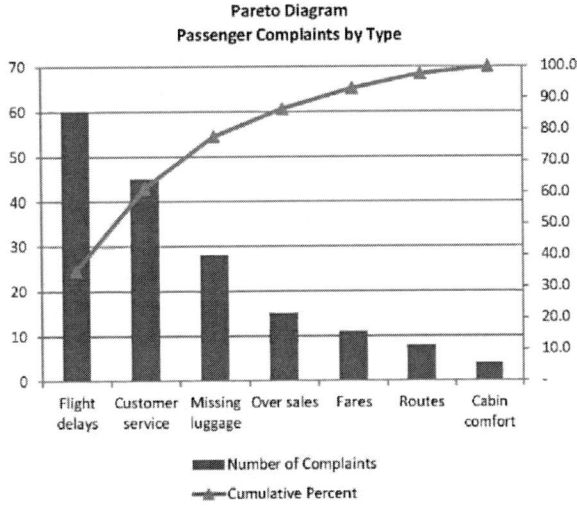

The 80-20 rule, developed by Joseph Juran, is often seen reflected in Pareto diagrams. The 80-20 rule suggests that 80% of a company's outcomes stem from only 20% the applicable causes. It is theorized that this distribution is a natural, universally applicable phenomenon.

A control chart is a graph that shows actual results plotted in relationship to upper and lower acceptable tolerances. Control charts help detect trends that could signal problems by detecting when outputs are in danger of crossing outside normal limits and would be marked defective.

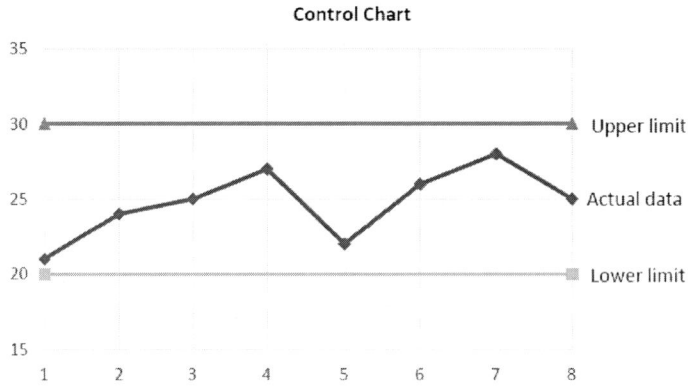

4) Plan-Do-Check-Act (PDCA) cycle

The PDCA cycle, or Deming wheel, identifies the four iterative steps of continuous improvement. The cycle repeats infinitely since continuous improvement is an ongoing approach to management. One notable variation of the cycle is to replace the "check" step with "study" to emphasise the inquisitive, analytical nature of the third step rather than inspection.

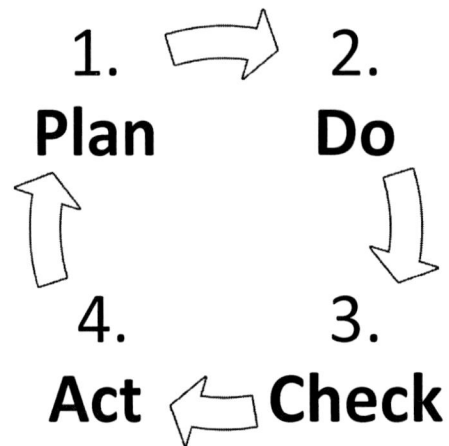

c. Lean

Lean is a minimalistic approach to manufacturing that maximizes value while minimizing waste. Initiatives to reduce waste take precedence over initiatives to improve quality. Managers holistically trim down extraneous processes and continuously search for ways to reduce costs. Lean is likely to employ continuous improvement (Kaizen) techniques.

In practice, managers attempt to decrease the amount of time between the customer order and product shipment (cycle time) and the time needed to convert raw materials into finished goods (manufacturing throughput time). Reducing both cycle time and manufacturing throughput time eliminates waste. Managers also examine resource utilization. Their goal is to only invest resources in activities that clearly create customer value and eliminate all nonessential activities along the value stream.

A side effect of implementing lean is that employees have a more direct line of sight to customer outcomes and satisfaction. Employees perceive more meaning in their everyday work because they are more able to connect to the big picture, which in turn increases their morale.

The distinction between lean and JIT is minor; the terms are used interchangeably in colloquial English. The main difference is that JIT emphasizes continuous improvement and lean emphasizes waste elimination and customer understanding.

d. Demand flow
Demand flow is the term for customer-driven supply chain management. The customer's needs ultimately determine the organization's allocation of resources and priorities.

Demand flow is similar and interrelated to just-in-time and lean methodology, since all three aim to manage resources efficiently and reduce waste. Sometimes a demand flow system will utilize a Kanban (a Japanese word), or instruction card that communicates the customer requests (e.g., quantities and other specifications) to the production line. Demand flow is the opposite of management based on forecasts.

e. Supply chain management
The term supply chain refers to the generic steps of the manufacturing process, which will vary from company to company. Typically, the supply chain begins with raw materials, flows through production and distribution, and finally arrives at the end customer who consumes the goods or services. The steps of the supply chain either occur within a single entity or require several entities working together.

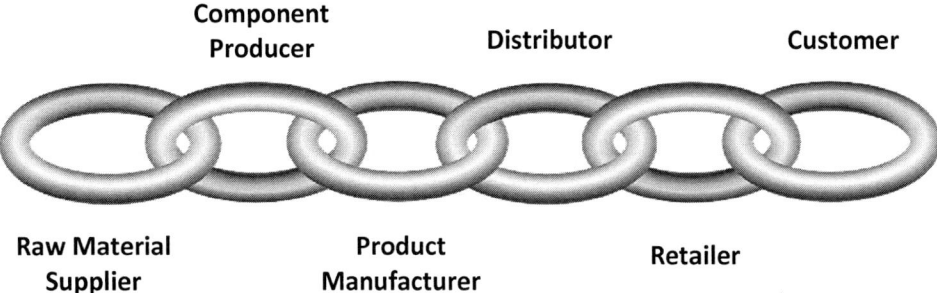

Supply chain management aims to reduce costs by improving the efficiency of each link in the chain, especially with regard to transitions from one link to another (e.g., manufacturer to distributor).

Communication, both forward and backward along the supply chain, helps companies to avoid bottlenecks and to improve product quality. For example, information about defects identified by retailers can help the manufacturers improve products prior to sale; as such, the company is able to rework defective products that are still in production sooner, hopefully avoiding the possibility of more expensive external failure costs (e.g., product recalls or lawsuits).

Additionally, sales forecasting is much easier when all parties share information along the supply chain. Strong relationships and frequent exchanges of quantity data ensure that an appropriate amount of a particular good or service is ready to meet the expected customer demand.

f. Theory of constraints (TOC)
   The theory of constraints is a set of principles that address the limitations and obstructions that impede an entity from achieving its objectives. Constraints are delays to throughput and can be physical (e.g., resource availability) or nonphysical (e.g., procedures), internal or external. The objective is to avoid or leverage a constraint to increase throughput. Eliminating one or more constraints increases profitability if costs are reasonable.

   The theory identifies five steps to increase throughput and handle constraints. The five steps are:
   1) Identify the constraint
   2) Develop a plan to avoid or leverage the constraint
   3) Focus resources to execute the plan (developed in step 2)
   4) Reduce impact of constraint by adding capacity or decreasing workload
   5) Repeat

   The theory uses terminology such as bottleneck, buffer, and drum. A bottleneck is an activity that has less capacity than the demand. A buffer helps managers deal with bottlenecks. A buffer is a resource that ensures the constraint is operating at capacity, managing the flow of resources in and out of the bottleneck to eliminate congestion of throughput before and after the constraint. The drum is the constraint or weakest link. The name is symbolic of the fact that production follows the "beat" of the drum.

g. Six Sigma
   In operations management, Six Sigma is a total quality management (TQM) methodology and framework used to reduce the number of manufacturing defects. The term six sigma originates from a statistical quality goal of 99.99966% accuracy or only 3.4 defects per million opportunities (DPMO). For comparison, one sigma has 68% accuracy, and three sigma has 99.7%.

   The methodology uses a formal Six Sigma process improvement model. The acronym is DMAIC – define, measure, analyze, improve, and control. It is applicable to existing processes (i.e., continuous improvement).

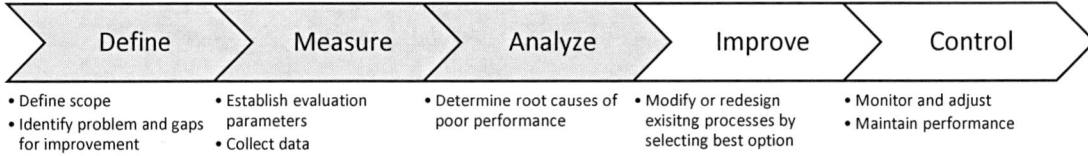

- Define scope
- Identify problem and gaps for improvement
- Establish evaluation parameters
- Collect data
- Determine root causes of poor performance
- Modify or redesign exisitng processes by selecting best option
- Monitor and adjust
- Maintain performance

The DMAIC model can be modified for new processes (i.e., reengineering and innovation) using the DMADV acronym – define, measure, analyze, *design*, and *verify/validate*.

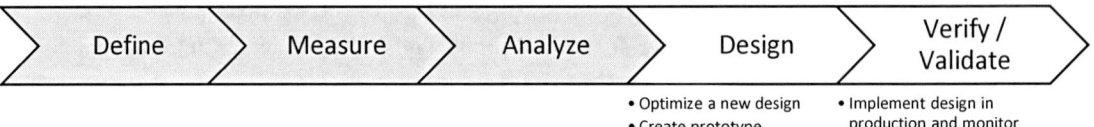

- Optimize a new design
- Create prototype
- Implement design in production and monitor

Professionals who understanding of all aspects of the DMAIC/DMADV model and Six Sigma principles are eligible for certification as a Six Sigma black belt.

h. International quality standards

The International Organization for Standardization (ISO) is an independent body that develops voluntary standards to support product and service quality across the globe. The ISO 9000 series, an internationally recognized set of quality standards published in 1987, addresses quality management and provides guidance to ensure products and services consistently meet customer expectations. The ISO 9000 family of standards is one of the most widely-accepted resources for quality management systems, reaching over 1 million certified ISO 9001 companies to date.

The ISO 14000 series of standards provide techniques for entities to address environmental impact and sustainability. ISO 14001 defines the requirements for an environmental management system to reduce waste and conserve resources through efficient use.

Multiple Choice

BEC 5-Q93

D. Planning Techniques

Strategies are high-level plans that companies use to seize opportunities in the marketplace and create value for customers. Strategies determined during the strategic planning process implement the firm's current and future objectives, outlined in short-run operational plans.

Proper plans guide decision-making and help managers coordinate their actions across departments or subunits. The importance of planning is summarized with the adage "failing to plan is planning to fail." Budgeting and forecasting techniques of strategic planning assist managers by anticipating future operating performance.

Multiple Choice
BEC 5-Q94

The steps, at a high level, in the strategic planning process are:

Step 1: Compose the mission and vision statement.
   The mission statement briefly outlines and communicates the purpose of the organization. The vision statement declares the organization's direction and focus for the future.

Step 2: Conduct a SWOT analysis (strengths, weaknesses, opportunities, and threats).
   A SWOT analysis helps determine positive/negative and internal/external factors that could impact the organization.

	Positive	Negative
Internal	Strengths 1. Competitive advantages 2. Intellectual property rights 3. Skilled labor	Weaknesses 1. Cash flow 2. Brand recognition 3. Employee turnover
External	Opportunities 1. Untapped foreign market 2. Technology advancements 3. Marketing campaign	Threats 1. Competitors 2. Substitute products 3. Regulations

Step 3: Develop strategies consistent with a mission statement and address SWOT analysis.
   Strategies fall into two main categories: cost leadership and differentiation. As defined and illustrated by Michael Porter, these two strategies can be further classified as having either a broad or narrow scope.

		Competitive advantage	
		Cost	Differentiation
Scope	Broad	Cost leadership (e.g., Walmart)	Differentiation (e.g., Nordstrom)
	Narrow	Cost focus (e.g., H&M)	Differentiation focus (e.g., Lululemon Athletica)

Step 4: Implement the strategies.
Step 5: Measure effectiveness of the strategies; adjust accordingly.

Multiple Choice
BEC 5-Q95

1. Budgeting and analysis

CPA Exam Blueprint Representative Task

Prepare a budget to guide business decisions.

Reconcile results against a budget or prior periods and perform analysis of variances as needed.

Budgets are vital planning tools that quantify a proposed plan of action. Budgets guide business decisions by offering a comprehensive look at anticipated operating performance. Not only do budgets communicate goals, but they can also be used to judge performance and motivate employees.

Hint: Budgets and other managerial (internal) accounting figures are not required to comply with U.S. GAAP or IFRS.

Multiple Choice
BEC 5-Q96

a. Master budget
A master budget is a static snapshot of the future using standard costs and anticipated sales figures. A master budget is prepared for a set time frame (e.g., 1 year). Created at the beginning of the period, a master budget includes pro forma (budgeted) financial statements and an operating budget for the period.

The master budget has two main components: a financial budget and an operating budget. Together, these budgets help managers determine how to allocate resources for capital projects, obtain financing, and make day-to-day decisions.

Hint: In practice, accountants are likely to see companies that use a rolling master budget (e.g., add 1 month, drop last month)

1) Financial budget
The financial budget establishes the cash and financing needs of the company. Although the master budget is typically only relevant to a 12-month period, the financial budget considers multi-year capital expenditure projects including long-term asset purchase and disposal.

The financial budget has four parts, including:
i. Capital expenditures budget
ii. Cash budget
iii. Budgeted balance sheet
iv. Budgeted statement of cash flow

2) Operating budget
The operating budget consists of a budgeted income statement along with all of the supporting schedules necessary to prepare the income statement.

The supporting schedules typically include budgets for sales, production, direct materials (DM), direct labor (DL), and manufacturing overhead (OH), cost of goods sold (COGS) and nonmanufacturing period costs. These supporting schedules quantify all of the elements in the value chain.

b. Budgeting steps
At the beginning of the period, managers collaborate to prepare the master budget according to the following steps.
i. Prepare the sales forecast and **sales budget**. The sales budget determines how many units will be sold.
ii. Develop **production budget** based on units to be sold, the beginning inventories, and the desired ending inventories.
iii. Prepare the **direct materials (DM), direct labor (DL), and manufacturing overhead (OH) budgets** using the production budget.
iv. Calculate the **cost of goods sold budget**.
v. Create **nonmanufacturing period cost budgets** (e.g., selling, general and administrative and/or research and development). These budgets support sales and production.
vi. Prepare the **capital expenditures budget**. This is the acquisition of additional fixed assets to increase productivity and efficiency; this budget supports current production and future production.
vii. Prepare the **cash budget**. The cash budget incorporates cash collections from sales and cash disbursements for the cost budgets.
viii. Develop the **pro forma financial statements** in the following order: budgeted income statement, budgeted balance sheet, and budgeted statement of cash flow.

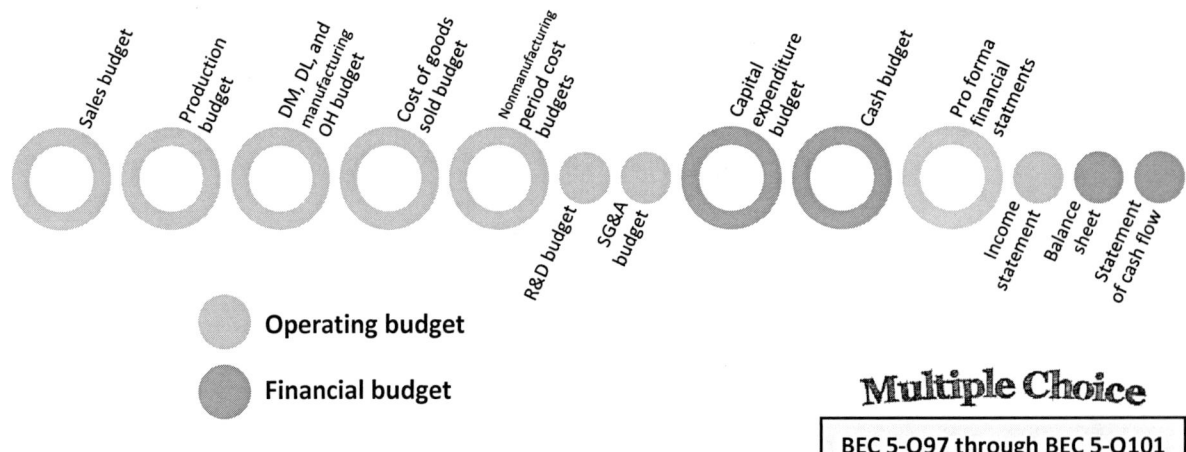

BEC 5-Q97 through BEC 5-Q101

c. Budget planning process
   Budget planning can be initiated from a top-down or a bottom-up perspective.

   1) Top-down
      Top-down budgeting starts with senior, upper-level management mandating high-level budget parameters with allocations for each department. The allocations are passed down along the employee hierarchy structure, and lower level managers fill in the details of the budget.

      The advantages of the top-down method are that a budget can be prepared quickly, with little argument, and the budget sets clear expectations for each department or subunit.

      The main disadvantage is that the budget may be perceived negatively and have limited buy-in from frontline managers.

   2) Bottom-up (participative) budgeting
      Participative budgeting is a bottom-up approach to budgeting. The company develops a budget after consulting lower level managers and employees for input.

      The advantages of this technique are that by increasing input of frontline employees the budget is potentially more accurate. This is because frontline employees are more knowledgeable about the day-to-day operational details of the company. Also, if implemented properly, participative budgeting can increase motivation and bolster morale. Employees have a greater sense of commitment and more accountability to their expectations and evaluation criteria.

      On the contrary, the budgeting process is time-consuming and the budget is susceptible to padding. Budget padding, also called budgetary slack, is the deliberate underestimation of revenue and overestimation of expenses to make a budget easier to achieve. While some padding is inherent, aggressive slack can impact productivity and profitability. Due to its disadvantages, participative budgeting is perceived as more idealistic and less practical than top-down budgeting.

Multiple Choice
BEC 5-Q102

d. Static budget
   A static budget presents budgeted production and costs for one level of activity.

Multiple Choice
BEC 5-Q103

e. Flexible budget and variances
   A flexible budget is a static budget adapted to demonstrate the actual levels of activity (e.g., production quantities) based on standard costs. While a master budget shows only one specific level of activity, a flexible budget is designed to exhibit any level of activity within a relevant range.

   Managers use flexible budgets to restate the original static budget to come up with the hypothetical budget they would have created at the beginning of the period if their estimates of activity level were perfect. Flexible budgets can be used to determine flexible-budget variances (differences between flexible budgets and actual results) and sales-volume variances (differences between static and flexible budgets).

	Static budget	Flexible budget	Actual
Activity level (units sold)	1,000	1,500	1,500
Sales ($110 per unit)	$110,000	$165,000	$165,000
Variable costs			
Direct materials [1]	20,000	30,000	33,000
Direct labor [2]	30,000	45,000	43,500
Variable OH [3]	12,000	18,000	21,000
Contribution margin	48,000	72,000	67,500
Fixed manufacturing costs	16,000	16,000	16,000
Operating income	$32,000	$56,000	$51,500

	Sales-volume variance	Flexible-budget variance
	$24,000 (favorable)	$4,500 (unfavorable)

[1] *Direct material standard cost: $20 per unit; actual cost: $22 per unit*
[2] *Direct labor standard cost: $30 per unit; actual cost: $29 per unit*
[3] *Variable OH standard cost: $12 per unit; actual cost: $14 per unit*

> **Hint**: In this example, all levels of activity (1,000, 1,500, and 2,000) are within the relevant range with regard to fixed manufacturing costs.

Multiple Choice
BEC 5-Q104

f. **Activity-based budgeting**
In activity-based budgeting (ABB) an operating budget is developed for each activity rather than each functional category (e.g., R&D, SG&A). Similar to activity-based costing (ABC), the budget is developed by multiplying the budgeted activity level of a cost driver by the standard or budgeted cost. The cost of each activity is then assigned the appropriate functional category for internal reporting. By basing operating budgets on cost drivers first, managers are able to clearly identify actions that directly influence the costs for each activity and have more information to control budget variances.

g. **Kaizen budgeting**
Kaizen budgeting, a technique for continuous improvement, incorporates expectations for improvement (e.g., cost reductions) into the budget to encourage managers to strive to achieve the budgeted targets during the period.

Multiple Choice
BEC 5-Q105

h. **Zero-based budgeting**
Zero-based budgeting is a budgeting technique that rejects same-as-last-year methodology and requires a fresh budget each year, reevaluating all line items without focusing on past assumptions or variances.

2. Forecasting and projection

Use forecasting and projection techniques to model revenue growth, cost and expense characteristics, profitability, etc.

Prepare and calculate metrics to be utilized in the planning process such as cost benefit analysis, sensitivity analysis, breakeven analysis, economic order quantity, etc.

a. Basic planning techniques and metrics

Hint: Emphasize using and understanding the following formulas during your studies. There is an extremely high probability they will appear on your exam.

1) Cost per unit
The cost per unit is calculated by dividing the total costs (variable costs plus fixed costs) by the total number of units.

$$\text{Cost per unit} = \frac{\text{Variable cost} + \text{Fixed cost}}{\text{Total number of units}}$$

Multiple Choice

BEC 5-Q106

2) Cost-volume-profit (CVP) analysis
CVP analysis explores the interaction between a company's revenue, costs, and operating income by highlighting the impact that changes in cost and volume have on profit (hence, cost-volume-profit). The CVP equation defines the number of units sold, selling price per unit, variable costs per unit, and total fixed costs.

$$\text{Revenue} - \text{Variable costs} - \text{Fixed costs} = \text{Profit}$$

$$(\text{Selling price} \times \text{Quantity of units sold}) - (\text{Variable cost per unit} \times \text{Quantity of units sold}) - \text{Fixed costs} = \text{Profit}$$

Hint: The CVP equation should seem familiar. It is the same as the direct (variable) costing calculation.

i. CVP within the relevant range
Due to the nature of variable and fixed costs, fixed costs **in total** are constant within the relevant range, and variable costs **in total** are proportional based on activity. Further, variable costs **per unit** are constant and fixed cost **per unit** are inversely proportional.

Multiple Choice

BEC 5-Q107 through BEC 5-Q108

ii. Assumptions of CVP
The CVP equation is a simplistic calculation and therefore is reliant on a number of assumptions. The primary assumptions are:
   a) The CVP equation is linear (a straight line).
   b) Selling price is constant and does not vary with sales volume.
   c) Total costs consist of variable and fixed costs.

d) Variable cost **per unit** is constant. For example, a more complex calculation is needed to handle oil and other fossil fuels costs due to their volatile variable prices.
e) Fixed costs **in total** are constant (within the relevant range)
f) In a multi-product firm, the relative sales proportion (sales mix) is known and constant.
g) Interest (time-value of money) is ignored.
h) Ending inventory is constant (e.g., units produced equal units sold)

Hint: Sometimes is it easier to visualize a calculation using a variable costing income statement instead of using the horizontal CVP formula.

Multiple Choice

BEC 5-Q109

iii. CVP relationship graph

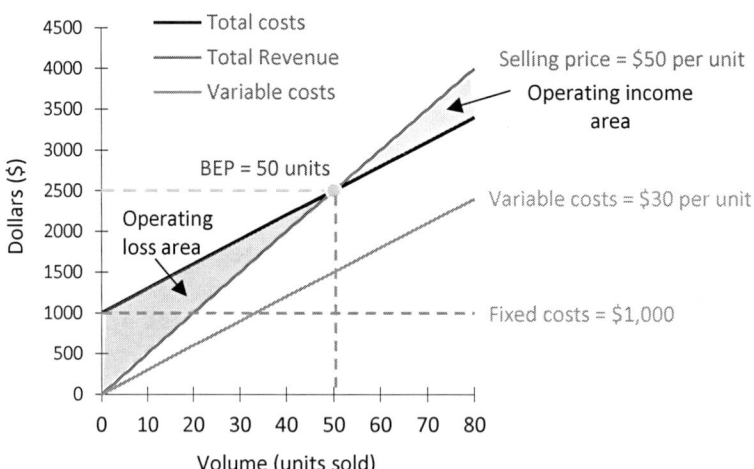

3) Contribution margin (CM) analysis
The contribution margin represents the amount of revenue available to cover the company's fixed costs and return a profit after subtracting variable costs.

CM = Revenue – Total variable costs

CM/unit = Selling price per unit – Variable costs per unit

An alternative way to calculate contribution margin per unit is to divide the net income by the margin of safety in units. The margin of safety is the excess revenue over the breakeven point.

$$\text{CM/unit} = \frac{\text{Net income}}{\text{Margin of safety (in units)}}$$

Multiple Choice

BEC 5-Q110

i. Contribution margin ratio (CMR)
Contribution margin can also be expressed as a percentage of the selling price. The CMR is the percentage of every sales dollar that is available after variable costs are subtracted.

$$CMR = \frac{SP - VC}{SP}$$

SP = Selling price
VC = Variable costs

$$CMR = \frac{Net\ Income}{Margin\ of\ safety\ (in\ \$)}$$

$$CMR = \frac{CM}{Sales}$$

4) **Breakeven point (BEP) analysis**
The breakeven point is the quantity of units sold at which operating income/profit is zero (i.e., the sales revenue exactly covers all fixed and variable costs with no excess). The breakeven point can be expressed in units or sales dollars.

   i. **Breakeven units**
   The breakeven point in units is determined by dividing the total fixed costs by the contribution margin (CM) per unit.

   The breakeven point calculation can be extended to determine the quantity of units required to achieve a particular before-tax profit.

   $$BEP_{Units} = \frac{Total\ fixed\ costs}{CM\ per\ unit} \quad OR \quad BEP_{Units} = \frac{Total\ fixed\ costs + before\ tax\ profit}{CM\ per\ unit}$$

   Hint: Be sure to memorize the calculation for before and after-tax profit. Examiners may provide the after-tax profit, and you will have to convert it.

   $$After\ tax\ profit = (Before\ tax\ profit) * (1 - Tax\ rate)$$

   $$Before\ tax\ profit = \frac{After\text{-}tax\ profit}{(1 - Tax\ rate)}$$

   Multiple Choice
   BEC 5-Q111 through BEC 5-Q114

   ii. **Breakeven sales dollars**
   By substituting the contribution margin ratio in for the contribution margin in the breakeven equation, managers can calculate the breakeven point in sales rather than units. Conceptually, this is the amount of revenue the company must generate to prevent an operating loss.

   $$BEP_{Sales\ \$} = \frac{Total\ fixed\ costs}{CMR} \quad OR \quad BEP_{Sales\ \$} = \frac{Total\ fixed\ costs + before\ tax\ profit}{CMR}$$

   $$BEP_{Sales\ \$} = BEP_{units} \times Selling\ price\ per\ unit$$

   Multiple Choice
   BEC 5-Q115

iii. **Multi-product company (product sales mix/composite units)**
It is unlikely a company will only produce one product. To determine the breakeven point when there is a known ratio of sales for each product, the company divides the total costs by the contribution margin **per composite unit**. A contribution margin per composite unit is a theoretical single product contribution margin determined by multiplying each products' separate contribution margin proportionately by the company's sales mix.

Example: A company sells 5 jump ropes for every 2 kettlebells. A jump rope sells for $15, and variable costs are $8 per unit. A kettlebell sells for $40, and variable costs are $24 per unit. Fixed cost are $187,600.

Product	Sales mix	Selling price (SP)	Variable cost (VC)	Contribution margin (SP – VC = CM)	Proportionate Contribution margin (CM * Sales mix)
Jump rope	5	$15	$8	$7	$35 (5 * $7)
Kettlebell	2	$40	$24	$16	$32 (2 * $16)
				CM **per composite unit**	$67

$$BEP_{Units} = \frac{\text{Total fixed costs}}{\text{CM per composite unit}}$$

$$BEP_{Units} = \frac{\$187,600}{\$67}$$

BEP_{Units} = 2,800 **composite units**

Hint: Do not stop here! In multi-product questions, make sure to extend BEP according to the proper product mix.

Jump rope = 2,800 * 5 units = <u>14,000</u> units

Kettlebell = 2,800 * 2 units = <u>5,600</u> units

Multiple Choice

BEC 5-Q116

5) **Margin of safety**
Margin of safety is the excess revenue over the breakeven point and is a technique to perform sensitivity analysis. Managers perform sensitivity analysis to gauge how changes in CVP variables (e.g., selling price, quantity of units sold, costs) affect profitability. Conceptually, the margin of safety communicates the amount the company's sales could decline before the company becomes unprofitable.

Margin of safety (in units or $) = Current sales level (units or $) – BEP (units or $)

Hint: Margin of safety can be expressed in units, dollars, or as a percentage.

6) Cash collections
A cash budget shows all of the sources (e.g., receipts from collections, financing) and uses (e.g., payments) of cash to reconcile the beginning and ending cash balance.

During the preparation of the cash budget, it is important to consider the payment terms (e.g., 2/10 net 30) and historical collection rates to estimate cash that is likely to be collected during the period.

Hint: Depreciation is a non-cash expense.

Multiple Choice

BEC 5-Q117 through BEC 5-Q119

b. Sales forecasting

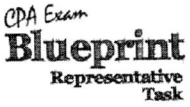

CPA Exam Blueprint Representative Task

Analyze results of forecasts and projections using ratio analysis and explanations of correlations to, or variations from, key financial indices.

Sales forecasting is the first step of the budgeting process and is necessary to project how many units will be sold during the period. The forecast developed during this process is then captured in the sales budget. Due to its foundational importance, the sales forecast is based on both quantitative and qualitative techniques.

1) Quantitative
Sales forecasts developed using quantitative methods typically rely on historical trend data, observations, and predictions about consumer behavior.

i. Moving average
A moving average is the statistical mean of historical sales performance which is updated on a rolling basis each month by including the most recent month and dropping the oldest month.

ii. Exponential smoothing
Exponential smoothing is an extension of the moving average technique that assigns more weight to recent sales and less to older observations.

iii. Decomposition of time series
The decomposition of time series technique evaluates historical sales data for trends such as seasonality or cyclical buying patterns. The trends identified are used to adjust future sales forecasts.

Multiple Choice

BEC 5-Q120

iv. Regression analysis
Linear regression is a statistical process of showing the relationship between an independent and dependent variable. Multiple regression determines a relationship among a dependent variable and one or more independent variables.

Assuming that future sales are dependent on observed relationships with the independent variable, regression analysis can help predict future sales. Correlations are measured using the correlation coefficient (r) and the coefficient of determination (r^2), a measurement of how much of the variation in sales is explained by the independent variable. The higher the coefficient of determination (r^2), the greater the goodness of fit (e.g., more of the sales variation is explained by the independent variable).

$$0 < r^2 < 1$$

r^2 = coefficient of determination

> *Hint*: Regression analysis is also discussed above on page 5B-23.

    v. Percentage of sales method
The percentage of sales method uses the premise that most income statement and balance sheet accounts fluctuate with sales. A common-sized income statement sets net sales at 100 percent and divides each line item on the income statement by net sales so that each line item is expressed as a percentage of net sales. After management has analyzed a number of periods of common-sized income statements, management is able to budget the expense line items on the income statement as a percentage of net sales. Therefore, management is basing budgeted product and period expenses on budgeted sales revenue.

Limitations of the percentage of sales method include:
- Usually lacks detailed analysis because forecasts are based on the applicable financial statement line item's percentage of sales.
- It forecasts the future based on past performance, especially with fluctuations in the economy and demand from year to year.

    vi. Markov technique
The Markov technique is a probabilistic model for forecasting that assumes historical occurrences do not predict future occurrences and instead focuses on the current state of consumer behavior (e.g., brand loyalty, tendency to brand-switch) to determine future purchase patterns. The probability a customer will purchase one product over another is the basis for developing the sales forecast.

Once managers agree on a sales forecast for the upcoming period, other budgeted income statement information is developed based on each items percentage of sales.

Multiple Choice
BEC 5-Q121

2) Qualitative
In addition to the mathematical techniques to determine a sales forecast, it is important for managers to consider reasonableness of the predictions using qualitative methods. Structured questionnaires and customer surveys are beneficial when evaluating if the sales forecast is appropriate. Management's professional judgment and executive opinions are just as beneficial.

    i. Delphi forecasting method
The Delphi method is qualitative in nature and uses a series of questionnaires to achieve consensus among the members of a group. It relies primarily on judgment and is iterative (i.e., each round of questions helps the participants' forecasts converge, resulting in consensus).

Multiple Choice
BEC 5-Q122

c. Relevant costs and decision-making

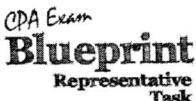

Compare and contrast alternative approaches (such as system replacement, make vs. buy, and cost/benefit) proposed to address business challenges or opportunities for a given entity.

Not every cost is relevant when making a decision, and it is important to be able to distinguish between relevant and irrelevant costs. Relevant cost must occur in the future and differ between two alternatives. Relevant costs are sometimes called incremental costs, or the additional total (relevant) cost incurred by selecting a single alternative out of two or more. Differential cost is the total cost difference between two alternatives. The terms incremental and differential can also be applied to revenues.

Past costs are irrelevant (unless there are future tax consequences) and are considered sunk costs.

Example:	Option 1: Romantic dinner	Option 2: Basketball game
Taxi to dinner/game	$35	$35
Dinner at 5-star restaurant	$150	-
Wine/beer	$35	$20
Basketball tickets	-	$200
Taxi to home	$35	$35
Total cost	$255	$290
Relevant costs (or incremental costs)	$185	$220
Difference (or differential cost)	$35	

Hint: What is a relevant? Anything that is different between the two alternatives.
Relevant = Different

Opportunity costs are benefits foregone when choosing one alternative over another alternative. Opportunities costs are relevant in certain situations such as when there is no excess capacity and producing one product would mean forgoing the contribution margin of the other.

Hint: Be able to identify relevant cost, sunk costs, opportunity costs.

Multiple Choice
BEC 5-Q123 through BEC 5-Q126

3) System or equipment replacement decisions
The decision to replace a piece of equipment involves determining which alternative (e.g., continuing to maintain old equipment or replacing the old equipment with something new) is expected to generate the highest operating income. Equipment replacement decisions assume revenues are constant unless specified.

Example:
A company can replace an existing machine for $275,000. The new machine has an expected useful life of 5 years, and annual operating costs are $15,000. The old machine originally cost $400,000 and has 20% left of its 10-year useful life. The old machine is depreciated using straight-line depreciation and annual costs to operate the machine are $125,000. The salvage value of the old machine with 20% useful life remaining is $25,000. Assume the

product quality is identical and revenue would not vary based on the machine utilized for production.

	Old	New
Historical cost	$400,000	$275,000
Useful life	10 years	5 years
Remaining useful life	20%	100%
Accumulated depreciation (straight-line)	$320,000	-
Book carrying value	$80,000	-
Current salvage value (less costs for disposal)	$25,000	-
Salvage value at the end of useful life	$0	$0
Annual operating cost	$125,000	$15,000

Relevant costs	Keep	Replace
Machine cost[1]	Not relevant	$275,000
Operating cost[2]	$250,000	$30,000
Current salvage value (old machine)[3]	-	($25,000)
Total relevant costs	**$250,000**	**$280,000**

[1] Expensed periodically as depreciation to reduce the carrying value.
[2] Annual costs multiplied by 2 years remaining useful life.
[3] The current salvage value is a future cash inflow that differs between the two alternatives; it is, therefore, relevant if the old machine is replaced.

The analysis of relevant costs suggests keeping the old machine until the end of its useful life. This alternative increases operating income based on the information provided by $30,000 ($280,000 - $250,000).

> *Hint:* Equipment cost, accumulated depreciation, and carrying value are irrelevant. Gain (loss) on the sale (disposal) of equipment are typically not considered since gains and losses are the dependent on depreciation method and have no future relevance. The exception is when the gain or loss prompts future tax consequence.

Multiple Choice

BEC 5-Q127

4) Make vs. buy (outsourcing) decisions
The make vs. buy decision is an outsourcing decision that compares the costs to produce the good or provide a service internally vs. procuring it externally. The objective is to select the alternative that has the lowest cost, thus maximizing operating income.

Example:
A company can purchase 20,000 widgets for $10/unit. For the company to make the widget internally, direct materials (DM) are $3/unit, direct labor (DL) is $5 per unit, and variable manufacturing overhead (variable OH) is $2 per unit. The company allocates $10,000 fixed cost to the project that is independent of the decision and has $5,000 setup costs if it makes the widget. The company has sufficient capacity to produce the widget.

	Units	20,000	Buy	Make
	Purchase cost ($10/unit)	$200,000	$200,000	
	DM ($3/unit)	$60,000	-	$60,000
	DL ($5/unit)	$100,000	-	$100,000
	Variable OH ($2/unit)	$40,000	-	$40,000
	Setup - avoidable[1]	$5,000	-	$5,000
	Allocated fixed - unavoidable	$10,000	Not Relevant	Not Relevant
	Total relevant costs		**$200,000**	**$205,000**

[1] *Avoidable costs are variable and can be controlled by management's decisions to choose one alternative over another alternative.*

The company will buy the widget since the relevant costs are $200,000 rather than $205,000, a differential cost savings of $5,000.

Qualitative factors to consider in a make vs. buy decision include reputation of the outsourcee (e.g., the vendor selling the widget), loss of control, quality concerns, employee morale due to concerns about layoffs, and the logistics of transportation if the outsourcee is geographically separated from the outsourcer.

5) Discontinue operations decisions

The decision to discontinue operations (e.g., close a department or segment) follows the same methodology as other relevant costs decisions. Costs, especially fixed costs, must be evaluated to see if they can be avoided if the department is closed. All avoidable costs are relevant. Any costs that cannot be avoided are irrelevant.

Relevant costs are compared to the revenue that will be eliminated if the operations are discontinued. The objective is to select the alternative which maximizes operating income for the company as a whole.

Example: A company has three departments (A, B, and C) and must determine if it is appropriate to discontinue operations in any of its departments. Of the total $12,000 fixed costs allocated to each department, $8,000 is avoidable.

	Department		
	A	B	C
Revenue	$20,000	$80,000	$5,000
Variable costs	($10,000)	($25,000)	($1,000)
Contribution margin	$10,000	$55,000	$4,000
Direct fixed costs – avoidable	($8,000)	($8,000)	($8,000)
Allocated fixed costs – unavoidable	($4,000)	($4,000)	($4,000)
Operating income	*($2,000)*	*$43,000*	*($8,000)*

	Department		
	A	B	C
Revenue foregone	($20,000)	($80,000)	($5,000)
Relevant costs			
Variable costs	$10,000	$25,000	$1,000
Avoidable fixed costs	$8,000	$8,000	$8,000
Change in operating income if department is discontinued	($2,000)	($47,000)	$4,000

The company will keep department A and B and discontinue department C.

6) Sell or process further decisions
   Sell or process further decisions rely on determining if the separable costs after the split-off point exceed the increase in incremental (relevant) revenue.

   In a sell or process further decision, all joint costs are considered sunk costs and are irrelevant to the sell or process further decision.

   Hint: Recall the joint cost orange example from joint costing:

    Sales value: $3,000   Separable cost: $1,200    Sales value: $5,400

   The incremental costs are $1,200 based on the separable cost after split-off. The incremental revenue is $1,400 ($5,400 – $3,000). The company will decide to process the orange essential oil since relevant revenues exceed relevant costs by $200.

   > *Hint*: The incremental revenue is the difference between the sales values of the orange essential oil and the cleaning spray because the $3,000 revenue from the orange essential oil is expected to be realized under both alternatives. Since it doesn't differ, it is not relevant, and only the $1,400 incremental revenue is relevant.

7) Cost/benefit decisions (special orders)
   Special order situations often arise when there is extra (unused) capacity. A company considers the additional costs versus the additional benefits (e.g., increase in operating income).

   In special order decisions when there is no extra capacity (e.g., the plant is operating at 100% capacity), the contribution margin forgone is a relevant opportunity cost and must be added to the calculation.

   In addition to financial ramifications of a decision, managers must also evaluate the long-run implications and qualitative costs and benefits. Considerations include the possible negative effect on customer existing relationships and additional wear and tear on property, plant, and equipment.

   > *Hint*: At full capacity, be able to calculate the minimum price a customer would have to pay for the special order. The minimum price is calculated by adding the relevant costs per unit to the opportunity costs per unit (i.e., the contribution margin forgone).

   Example: A company gets a special order for 1,000 widgets. If the customer pays $30 per widget, should the company accept the order? Determine the answer with and without unused capacity. Assuming production capacity is full, what is the lowest price the company would be willing accept to proceed with the special order? The company typically sells the product for $38 per widget. The cost per unit amounts are based on normal capacity (see table below).

Special order with unused capacity:

	$ per unit	1,000 units	
Revenue	$30	$30,000	
DM	$18	($18,000)	
DL	$6	($6,000)	
Variable OH	$2	($2,000)	
Fixed OH	$1	-	Not relevant
Setup cost	$3	($3,000)	
Fixed advertising cost	$4	-	Not Relevant
Increase in operating income		**$1,000**	

The company should **accept** the special order.

Special order at 100% capacity:

	$ per unit	1,000 units	
Revenue	$30	$30,000	
DM	$18	($18,000)	
DL	$6	($6,000)	
Variable OH	$2	($2,000)	
Fixed OH	$1	-	Not relevant
Setup cost	$3	($3,000)	
Fixed advertising cost	$4	-	Not Relevant
Opportunity cost: contribution margin forgone[1]	$9	($9,000)	
Decrease in operating income		**($8,000)**	

[1] *Contribution* margin foregone = Selling price – variable costs
= SP – DM – DL – Var. OH – Setup
= $38 – $18 – $6 – $2 – $3
= $9 per unit

The company should **reject** the special order if the revenue is based on a special order selling price of $30 per unit.

Minimum special order pricing:

	$ per unit	1,000 units
Relevant costs	$29	$29,000
Opportunity cost: contribution margin forgone	$9	$9,000
Minimum special order price	**$38**	**$38,000**

The company would accept the order if the price the customer is willing to pay is $38 or more.

Hint: Some variable costs are unavoidable, when specified, making them irrelevant. Read each question carefully. For example, variable selling expenses might not apply to a special order. When variable costs are irrelevant, the minimum special order pricing will be less than the pricing for regular customers.

Multiple Choice

BEC 5-Q128 through BEC 5-Q129

d. Responsibility accounting
Responsibility accounting systems are often found in decentralized organizations. With a structure based on delegated authority and control, the company is divided into responsibility centers. There are four types of responsibility centers:
1) Cost center – managers are responsible and held accountable for only expenses.
2) Revenue center – managers are responsible and held accountable for only revenues.
3) Profit center – managers are responsible and held accountable for both revenues and expenses.
4) Investment center – managers are responsible and held accountable for revenues, expenses and investment in assets (e.g., capital expenditures).

Hint: Responsibility equals control. If a manager does not have control over something, he or she cannot be held accountable for it.

Responsibility accounting is a favorable structure for decentralized organizations due to the quality of evaluation metrics and perceived fairness, especially in terms of incentive compensation. Managers are only judged on performance targets that they can directly control. Managers have a greater sense of ownership and autonomy in an entity that uses responsibility accounting.

Hint: A cost center with respect to external parties may be treated as a profit center due to internal transactions with other departments or subunits.

e. Product and service pricing
Pricing is the determination of how much to charge for a given product or service. Pricing should always consider costs, customer preferences, competitor prices, and economic conditions. Pricing decisions require a substantial amount of judgment.

1) Consumer pricing
Consumer pricing describes the process of assigning a price to goods or services sold to external customers. Managers must evaluate all of the market factors (e.g., consumer preferences, competition, economic conditions) to determine a price that will yield the greatest long-term profitability.

i. Target contribution margin (variable costing) or gross margin (full costing) pricing
Pricing a product using a target margin involves determining the relevant costs (depending on variable or full costing) and solving for the selling price.

Example: A company's target contribution margin is 30%. The product's variable costs are $56.00.

Selling price (SP)	$80.00	(100%)
Variable costs	- 56.00	(70%)
Contribution margin	$24.00	(30%)

SP – $56.00 = .30SP
SP = 0.30SP + $56.00
SP – 0.30SP = $56.00
0.70SP = $56.00
SP = $56.00 / 0.70
SP = $80.00

Multiple Choice

BEC 5-Q130

ii. Cost-plus pricing
Cost-plus pricing is a cost-based approach to pricing. Cost-plus prices are the result of adding a markup to cost per unit (e.g., variable cost or full cost) of a good or service. While the markup could be an arbitrary percentage, more likely it will be based on the target return on investment (ROI) per unit. The target ROI is the target annual operating income divided by the invested capital (e.g., total assets).

Basic markup example:
If a product's cost is $28.00 and the markup is 11.25%, the selling price is $31.15.

Base cost (full cost)	$ 28.00
Mark-up (11.25%)	+ 3.15
Selling price	$ 31.15

Target ROI example: Assume the company's capital investment is $300,000 and the target (pretax) rate of return is 21%. During the year, the company sells 20,000 units.

Invested capital (total assets)	$300,000
Target ROI	x 21%
Target annual operating income	$63,000

Target operating income per unit = $63,000 / 20,000 units
= $3.15

Base cost (full cost)	$ 28.00
Target operating income per unit	+ 3.15
Selling price	$31.15

Hint: The selling price for both examples is $31.15. Remember, the target ROI percentage (21%) does not equal the markup (11.25%). The target ROI represents the annual operating income divided by the invested capital ($63,000 / 300,000 = 21%). The markup is operating income per unit divided by base cost ($3.15 / $28.00 = 11.25%).

iii. Target pricing
Target pricing is a market-based pricing approach for estimating the price a customer is willing to pay for a good or service according to its perceived value. Since products are sold to prospective customers in a competitive marketplace, competitor prices are also subject to consideration when evaluating what a customer would be willing to pay.

Once a target price is determined managers derive the target cost per unit that would allow them to achieve the target price. The target cost is the remainder of target price less target operating income per unit.

Target costs are often lower than the full cost of a good or service. Managers strive to increase efficiency using value engineering to attain a target cost. Value engineering is a technique of carefully reducing costs at various stages of the value chain (e.g., design, production) while still maintaining equivalent quality standards.

2) Transfer pricing
Determining the price when one subunit (e.g., department) sells goods or services to another subunit of a decentralized organization is called transfer pricing. Once the price is set, it is used for all internal transfers of goods or services. The department selling the good or service records revenue. The department purchasing the good or service records a cost.

To establish a transfer price, a decentralized entity will use a:

i. Cost-based price – price is based on the cost of a product or service such as the full cost, variable and fixed costs, or just variable costs. Full costs include all production costs plus nonproduction functions (e.g., research and development, marketing). The cost used can be actual or budgeted as long as it is applied consistently.

ii. Market price – external market price reduced by cost saving by selling internally (e.g., selling expenses).

iii. Prorated difference between maximum and minimum price – hybrid of the market price and the variable cost-based price, setting the transfer price in the middle of the maximum and minimum using relative subunit costs.

iv. Negotiated price – price agreed upon by all subunits.

v. Dual price – two transfer prices are used to record an internal transaction (e.g., selling subunit credits the full cost-base price and the buying subunit pays market price) and to balance the difference between the two prices is cleared to a corporate cost account. If subunits are geographically separated, dual pricing could result in difficulty computing taxable income.

> *Hint:* The perfect transfer price, in theory, would account for opportunity cost in addition to cost outlay. Managers do not typically consider opportunity cost since it is nearly impossible to determine accurately.

Transfer prices should maximize profit for the entire company and not a single subunit and support goal congruence and constancy. By preventing subunits from establishing their own price, organizations are less susceptible to subunits acting self-interestedly to make their own performance appear better.

Certain transfer prices (e.g., full cost) can lead to sub-optimization when unused capacity is present. For example, one subunit may inappropriately source a service externally rather than procure it internally since the transfer price is greater than the external price. However, if the service had been obtained internally, it would have benefited the entity as a whole by contributing to entity-level fixed costs.

> *Hint:* Be familiar with the terms and concepts regarding transfer pricing for the exam.

Multiple Choice

BEC 5-Q131

3) Unethical or illegal pricing
Pricing practices that prey on consumers to increase profitability are not only unethical; they can also be illegal. Illegal pricing practices vary by country.

i. Dual pricing or product dumping
Dual pricing is the practice of selling identical products for different prices in different markets. In general, dual pricing is acceptable. For example, companies often introduce products at lower penetration prices to establish them in untapped foreign markets. Companies increase prices once products obtain sufficient brand recognition.

On the contrary, dual pricing has the potential to be illegal. For instance, it is illegal for a company to export and sell products to a foreign market for significantly less in the foreign market than if they were sold domestically. Referred to as product dumping, this practice can cause economic injury to the importing country (e.g., bankrupt local manufacturers and suppliers).

ii. Collusive pricing
Collusive pricing is when two or more competitors manipulate product prices by signing an agreement to artificially fix or rig a price. Engaging in this dishonest practice on a large scale can disrupt the market's equilibrium price; therefore, it is illegal in most countries.

iii. Predatory pricing
Predatory pricing is when a company establishes below-cost prices to force their competitors into bankruptcy. Maliciously undercutting prices is illegal under antitrust law because it results in a less diverse competitive marketplace and more monopolies.

This page is intentionally left blank.

Glossary: Operations Management

A

Abnormal spoilage – spoiled units that exist due to poor quality production processes which managers have the ability to control and avoid

Absorption costing – a GAAP costing technique that treats fixed manufacturing overhead as a product cost and is used for external financial reporting

Activity-based budgeting (ABB) – a budgeting technique that involves developing an operating budget each activity rather than each functional category

Activity-based costing (ABC) – a precise costing technique that assigns cost to activities using multiple activity cost pools and cost drivers

Actual activity level – observable or past output (e.g., actual direct labor hours)

Appraisal costs – costs to evaluate and detect items that do not conform to specifications prior to completing the final product

Avoidable costs – costs that are variable and can be controlled by management's decisions to choose one alternative over another alternative

B

Backflush costing – a non-GAAP (internal) costing technique that uses actual costs at completion or sale of a good; ideal for companies that use JIT or hold little inventory

Balanced scorecard – holistic measure of operations that evaluates all aspects of a company's performance and considers financial and non-financial measures

Benchmarking – way to objectively evaluate a company's performance in relation to other companies or business units

Bottleneck – activity that has less capacity than the demand; relates to the theory of constraints (TOC)

Bottom-up budgeting – see participative budgeting

Breakeven point (BEP) – quantity of units sold at which operating income/profit is zero (i.e., the sales revenue exactly covers all fixed and variable costs with no excess)

Budget – an estimate or monetary plan for operations for a defined period of time

Budgetary slack – cushion for extra expenditure produced by underestimating income or overestimating expenses in a budget

Buffer – a resource that ensures the constraint is operating at capacity, managing the flow of resources in and out of the bottleneck to eliminate congestion of throughput before and after the constraint; relates to the theory of constraints (TOC)

Byproducts – Goods generated in a joint process that have low total sales value in relation to the main product(s)

C

Cash flow ROI (CFROI) – company's cash flow divided by its invested capital; the rate of return generated by all of its operating assets

Cause-and-effect analysis – method of identifying quality issues and determine what is causing each issue

Coefficient of determination – a measurement of how much of the variation in sales is explained by the independent variable

Collusive pricing – two or more competitors illegally manipulate product prices by signing an agreement to artificially fix or rig a price

Composite unit – theoretical single product based on proportionate sales mix

Conformance costs – costs to avoid failure; also see prevention costs and appraisal costs

Constant gross margin percentage net realizable value (NVR) method – a joint cost allocation technique that assumes each product has the same gross margin percentage and allocates joint costs to maintain this relationship

Consumer pricing – the process of assigning a price to goods or services sold to external customers

Continuous improvement – a non-stop effort to determine ways to improve and perfect an activity; also see Kaizen

Contribution margin (CM) – amount of revenue available to cover the company's fixed costs and return a profit after subtracting variable costs

Control chart – graph that shows actual results plotted in relationship to upper and lower acceptable tolerances

Conversion costs – total direct labor used plus any overhead applied (variable and fixed); all manufacturing costs other than direct material costs

Cost allocation – assigning indirect costs in a systematic way to a cost object

Cost center – a responsibility center where managers are responsible and held accountable for only expenses

Cost driver – precise metric for allocation with a clear cause and effect relationship to the long-run behavior of the cost

Cost leadership strategy – a company's strategy obtain market share by offering lower costs than competitors

Cost management – management activities over resource usage

Cost object – anything to which a manager can compute and assign a cost

Cost of quality (COQ) – added expense a company incurs to prevent or handle low-quality products (e.g., prevention costs, appraisal costs, internal failure costs, external failure costs)

Cost pools – accumulated indirect costs

Cost tracing – assignment of direct costs to a cost object

Cost/benefit decisions – consideration if additional costs outweigh the additional benefits (e.g., increase in operating income)

Cost-based transfer price – price based on the cost of a product or service such as the full cost, variable and fixed costs, or just variable costs

Cost-plus pricing – consumer price determined by adding a markup to cost per unit (e.g., variable cost or full cost) of a good or service

Cost-volume-profit (CVP) analysis – relationship between revenue, costs, and operating income based on the units sold, selling price per unit, variable costs per unit, and total fixed costs

Cross-sectional analysis – study of two or more comparable companies (i.e., similar size and equivalent industry) during identical accounting periods

Cycle time – amount of time between the customer order and product shipment

D

Decomposition of time series – evaluation of historical sales data for trends such as seasonality or cyclical buying patterns

Delphi forecasting method – iterative forecasting using a series of questionnaires to achieve consensus among the members of a group

Demand flow – customer-driven supply chain management

Deming wheel – see Plan-Do-Check-Act (PDCA) cycle

Detection costs – see appraisal costs

Differential cost – total cost difference between two alternatives; also see incremental cost

Differentiation strategy – a company's competitive advantage is to obtain market share by offering a unique or different product perceived as better than a lower cost option

Direct allocation method – cost allocation approach that ignores service to service department costs and allocates department costs only to operating departments

Direct costing – see variable costing

Direct manufacturing labor costs – compensation cost that can be traced to cost object by means of a clear, economically feasible relationship

Direct materials – purchase and acquisition cost of raw materials that can be traced the salable cost object by means of a clear, economically feasible relationship

Drum – constraint or weakest link in the theory of constraints; the name is symbolic of the fact that production follows the "beat" of the drum

Dual price – two transfer prices are used to record an internal transaction (e.g., selling subunit credits the full cost-base price and the buying subunit pays market price) and to balance the difference is cleared to a corporate cost account

Dual pricing – practice of selling identical products for different prices in different markets

Dual-rate method – allocation method that distinguishes between variable and fixed cost pools, assigning costs using different cost-allocation bases as appropriate

DuPont analysis – a technique of separating return on equity (ROE) into its components, including profit margin (or return on sales), asset turnover, and financial leverage ratio (or equity multiplier)

E

Economic profit – residual profit remaining after subtracting implicit costs from accounting profit (revenue less explicit costs)

Economic value added – The economic profit or residual value a company creates in excess of the capital employed (total assets minus current liabilities) multiplied by the weighted average cost of capital (WACC).

Efficiency variance – difference between the actual input quantity and the standard quantity allowed based on the units produced

Eighty-twenty (80-20) rule – hypothesis suggests that 80% of a company's outcomes stem from only 20% the applicable causes

Equipment replacement decisions – determining whether continuing to maintain old equipment or replacing the old equipment with something new is expected to generate the greatest operating income

Equivalent units – quantity of finished units theoretically equal (in terms of inputs) to quantity of unfinished units

Estimated net realizable value (NRV) method – joint cost allocation technique that allocates the joint costs using the relative estimated net realizable value (final sales value minus separable cost)

Explicit costs – recognizable accounting expenses (e.g., rent, labor) that result from a transaction; opposite of implicit costs

Exponential smoothing – weighted average of historical sales performance that assigns more weight to recent sales and less to older observations

External failure costs – costs of related to goods of services that fail to meet the usual or required standard identified after transfer to the consumer

F

Factory overhead costs – see indirect manufacturing costs

Favorable (F) variance – operating income increases compared to the budget, actual revenues are more or costs are less than anticipated

Financial budget – Component of the master budget addressing cash and capital expenditures, includes cash budget, capital budget, budgeted balance sheet, and budgeted statement of cash flows

Finished goods inventory (FGI) – inventory of completed goods prior to sale

Fishbone diagram – chart that resembles a fish that identifies potential causes (fish bones) of the problem on the far right of the diagram (fish head)

Fixed costs – costs constant (in total) within a relevant range and a specific time period

Flexible budget – budget that can be adjusted to reflect any output volumes within a relevant range often adapted to demonstrate the actual levels of activity (e.g., production quantities) based on standard costs

Flexible-budget variance – the difference between the flexible budget and actual result

Free cash flow – amount of cash a company is able to generate to sustain operations after deducting equipment and other capital expenditure

Full costing – see absorption costing

G

H

High-low method – method to compute a cost equation using a highest and lowest observed unit volume (independent variable) and total cost (dependent variable)

Horizontal analysis – study of trends within the same company over time

I

Implicit costs – benefits foregone when choosing one alternative over another alternative; also called opportunity costs

Incremental cost – additional total cost incurred by selecting a single alternative out of two or more

Indirect manufacturing costs – manufacturing costs with no obvious, economically feasible relationship to cost object

Indirect manufacturing labor – compensation cost with no obvious, economically feasible relationship to cost object

Indirect materials – purchase and acquisition cost of raw materials no obvious, economically feasible relationship to cost object

Internal failure costs – costs of related to goods of services that fail to meet the usual or required standard identified before transfer to the consumer

Investment center – a responsibility center where managers are responsible and held accountable for revenues, expenses, and investment in assets (e.g., capital expenditures)

Ishikawa diagram – see fishbone diagram

J

Job – distinct products or services with units that are easy to identify

Job costing – see job-order costing

Job-order costing – costing system that accumulates and expenses costs for each individual job

Joint costing – costing technique to determine difficult to differentiate costs when two or more products are produced together

Joint costs – costs shared in the simultaneous production of multiple outputs with the same inputs

Joint products – two or more high sales value products produced simultaneously

Just-in-time (JIT) – obtain and deliver goods exactly as-needed, delivering no more or less than the quantity demanded; a demand-pull manufacturing system

K

Kaizen – Japanese name for continuous improvement; a non-stop effort to determine ways to improve and perfect an activity

Kaizen budgeting – technique for continuous improvement that incorporates expectations for improvement (e.g., cost reductions) into the budget to encourage managers to strive to achieve the budgeted targets during the period

L

Lean – minimalistic approach to manufacturing that maximizes value while minimizing waste

M

Main product – primary, high sales value product produced during a joint production process in relation to all other simultaneously produced products

Make-or-buy decision – determine if managers will produce a product internally (insource) or acquire it externally (outsource)

Management by exception – prioritization of management's attention on poorly performing areas or areas that fail to achieve target performance level

Margin of safety – excess revenue over the breakeven point; the amount the company's sales could decline before the company becomes unprofitable

Market transfer price – external market price reduced by cost saving by selling internally (e.g., selling expenses).

Markov technique – a probabilistic model for forecasting that assumes historical occurrences do not predict future occurrences and instead focuses on the current state of consumer behavior (e.g., brand loyalty, tendency to brand-switch) to determine future purchase patterns

Master budget – static snapshot of the future using standard costs and anticipated sales figures including a pro forma financial statements and operating budget for a period

Mission statement – brief statement that outlines and communicates the purpose of the organization

Mixed costs – a cost that blends characteristics of both fixed and variable costs, also referred to as semi-variable

Moving average – statistical mean of historical sales performance which is updated on a rolling basis each month by including the most recent month and dropping the oldest month

Multiple regression – statistical process of determining a relationship among a dependent variable and one or more independent variables

N

Negative correlation – an inverse relationship, as one variable increases the other will decrease and vice versa.

Negotiated transfer price – price agreed upon by all subunits

Nonconformance costs – consequences of failure; also see internal failure costs and external failure costs

Non-value added costs – costs that add no actual or perceived value to a product or service (e.g., costs of quality and inventory storage costs)

Normal activity level – capacity utilization that satisfies the average demand during a defined period

Normal spoilage – spoiled units that are unavoidable and the result of efficient operations

O

Operating budget – future period forecast addressing revenue and expenses; budgeted income statement along with all of the supporting schedules necessary to prepare the income statement

Operating department – department that adds value to product or service (e.g., production)
Opportunity cost – benefits (e.g., operating income) forgone when choosing one alternative over another alternative
Outlay costs – a capital expenditure or cash disbursement; also called out-of-pocket costs
Out-of-pocket costs – see outlay costs
Outsourcing – contracting with an external provider to obtain goods or services rather than completing the job in-house (e.g., outside payroll, information technology, or virtual bookkeeping services)
Over-allocated overhead – see over-applied overhead
Over-applied overhead – more overhead is applied than incurred because the company overestimated overhead costs and actual overhead costs were less than expected; also called over-allocated overhead

P

Pareto chart – bar graph that managers use to visualize data about the frequency of complaints, defects, or process problems
Participative budgeting – budget after consulting lower level managers and employees for input
Past costs – see sunk costs
Period costs – all costs expensed in the current period except cost of goods sold (e.g., selling, general, and administrative expenses)
Physical measure method – joint cost allocation technique that allocates costs based on a comparable physical measure of products at the split-off point
Plan-Do-Check-Act (PDCA) cycle – four iterative steps of continuous improvement
Positive correlation – direct relationship between the variables
Predatory pricing – establishing below-cost prices to force competitors into bankruptcy
Predetermined allocation rates – rate used to apply overhead calculated using historical data and future estimated activity
Prevention costs – costs to reduce the potential for a defective goods or services
Price variance – difference between actual input price and a standard input price
Prime costs – combined total of direct material used and direct labor used
Process costing – costing method that divides the total cost of producing the product or service by the total by number of units to get an average rate; ideal for homogeneous products (i.e., identical or extremely similar)
Product costs – total amount of costs assigned to a product and capitalized on the balance sheet until the product is sold
Product dumping – illegal practice of exporting and selling products to a foreign market for significantly less in the foreign than if they were sold domestically
Production-volume variance – the difference between budgeted fixed costs and fixed overhead allocated based on the number of units produced
Product-mix decision – determination of the most profitable mix of product type and quantity
Profit center – a responsibility center where managers are responsible and held accountable for both revenues and expenses

Q

Quantity variance – see efficiency variance

R

Rate variance – see price variance
Regression analysis – statistical process of showing the relationship between independent and dependent variables
Relevant costs – anticipated future costs that vary when choosing one alternative over another alternative
Relevant range – a span of normal activity or production volume that has a constant relationship with the fixed cost
Relevant revenues – anticipated future revenues that vary when choosing one alternative over another alternative
Residual income – a performance metric that managers often use to evaluate departments or projects by subtracting the interest on an investment in a department/project from the net income attributable to that department/project
Residual income profile – graphical representation of residual income showing interest rate on the x-axis and residual income, in dollars, on the y-axis

Responsibility accounting – reporting system that considers the ability for managers of responsibility centers (departments or subunits) to control and achieve budgetary targets
Responsibility center – delegated authority and control in a decentralized organization
Return on investment (ROI) – measurement of the financial benefit of investing resources (e.g., income divided by investment)
Revenue center – a responsibility center where managers are responsible and held accountable for only revenues
Rework – a defective product that is repaired with to meet the specifications for sale

S

Sales budget – the budget that determines how many units will be sold
Sales forecasting – the first step of the budgeting process necessary to project how many units will be sold during the period
Sales mix – blend of product type and quantity to describe total sales
Sales value at split-off method – joint costs allocation technique that allocates and assigns costs based on the sales value of each product at the split-off point
Sales-volume variance – the difference between a static and flexible budget adapted for actual levels of activity
Scrap – byproduct of the production process that has low or zero sales value
Sell or process further decisions – determining if the separable costs after the split-off point exceed the increase in incremental (relevant) revenue
Semi-fixed costs – see stepped cost
Semi-variable costs – see mixed costs
Sequential allocation method – see step-down method
Service department – see support department
Single-rate method – allocation method that uses the same cost pool for both variable and fixed costs
Special orders decisions – see cost/benefit decisions
Split-off point – moment in time when joint products become separately identifiable and are sold or proceed to independent manufacturing processes
Spoilage – product units that do not meet the specifications for sale
Standard costs – a carefully predetermined cost of a unit of output under normal circumstances
Static budget – budgeted production and costs for one level of activity
Step-down allocation method – cost allocation method that allocates support department costs to other departments sequentially, starting by allocating costs to all other departments and eliminated each department one by one as their cost are allocated (i.e., no costs are allocated back to a previously allocated support department)
Stepped costs – a fixed cost that appears stepped graphically because the relevant range is narrow; also called semi-fixed costs
Strategy – high level plan a company uses to seize opportunities in the marketplace and create value for customers
Sunk costs – unavoidable, past costs that cannot be reversed or changed by managers
Support department – department that provides internal services (e.g., HR, IT, marketing); also called service department
Supporting schedules – supplementary budgets that quantify elements of value chain which are needed to develop the income statement
SWOT analysis – exploration of the positive/negative and internal/external factors that could impact the organization

T

Target contribution margin pricing – a way to determine a consumer price solving for the selling price based on a specified contribution margin and relevant costs
Target costing – a costing technique managers implement to reduce costs by first determine the estimated price the customer will pay and working backward to determine the maximum costs allowable to achieve a desired profit margin
Target pricing – market-based pricing approach for estimating the price a customer is willing to pay for a good or service according to its perceived value
Target return on investment (ROI) – target annual operating income divided by the invested capital (e.g., total assets)

Throughput time – time needed to convert raw materials to finished goods
Time series analysis – see horizontal analysis
Top-down budgeting – budget that starts with senior, upper-level management mandating parameters and lower level managers filling in the details
Total quality management (TQM) – management approach that focuses on improving product and service quality by refining operations incrementally, in response to feedback.
Transfer pricing – determination of price when one department provides goods or services to another department
U
Under-allocated overhead – see under-applied overhead
Under-applied overhead – less overhead is applied than incurred because the company has underestimated overhead costs and actual overhead costs were more than expected; also called under-allocated overhead
Unfavorable (U) variance – operating income decreases compared to the budget
Usage variance – see efficiency variance
V
Value chain – the series of activities (inbound logistics, operations, outbound logistics, marketing/sales, and service) that add value (e.g., usefulness) to a product or service
Value-added costs – costs that add actual or perceived value to a product or service
Value-based management – management technique that focuses on indicators of economic profitability to maximize value
Variable costing – a non-GAAP costing method that treats all variable costs as product costs (capitalized) and only treats fixed manufacturing overhead as a period cost (expensed immediately); also called direct costing
Variable costs – costs that are traceable to a cost object and change proportionately with activity
Variance – difference between actual and expected results
Vision statement – declaration of the organization's direction and focus for the future
Volume variance – see efficiency variance
W
Weighted-average process costing – method of process costing that assigns the cost per equivalent unit based on all units, disregarding costs specific to a certain accounting period
Work-in-process (WIP) inventory – account of partially finished goods awaiting completion at the report date
Work-in-progress – see work-in-process inventory
X
Y
Z
Zero-based budgeting – a budgeting technique that rejects same-as-last-year methodology and requires a fresh budget each year, reevaluating all line items without focusing on past assumptions or variances

This page is intentionally left blank.

Multiple Choice – Questions

BEC 5-Q1 B62. The controller of Gray, Inc. has decided to use ratio analysis to analyze business cycles for the past two years in an effort to identify seasonal patterns. Which of the following formulas should be used to compute percentage changes for account balances for year 1 to year 2?

A. (Prior balance - current balance) / current balance.
B. (Prior balance - current balance) / prior balance.
C. (Current balance - prior balance) / current balance.
D. (Current balance - prior balance) / prior balance.

BEC 5-Q2 B145. SkBound Airlines provided the following information about its two operating divisions:

	Passenger	Cargo
Operating profit	$40,000	$50,000
Investment	250,000	500,000
External borrowing rate	6%	8%

Measuring performance using return on investment (ROI), which division performed better?

A. The Cargo division, with an ROI of 10%.
B. The Passenger division, with an ROI of 16%.
C. The Cargo division, with an ROI of 18%.
D. The Passenger division, with an ROI of 22%.

BEC 5-Q3 B201. A company has two divisions. Division A has operating income of $500 and total assets of $1,000. Division B has operating income of $400 and total assets of $1,600. The required rate of return for the company is 10%. Division B's residual income would be which of the following amounts?

A. $40
B. $240
C. $400
D. $640

BEC 5-Q4 B303. A company has two divisions. Division A has operating income of $500 and total assets of $1,000. Division B has operating income of $400 and total assets of $1,600. The required rate of return for the company is 10%. The company's residual income would be which of the following amounts?

A. $0
B. $260
C. $640
D. $900

BEC 5-Q5 B350. A divisional manager receives a bonus based on 20% of the residual income from the division. The results of the division include: Divisional revenues, $1,000,000; divisional expenses, $500,000; divisional assets, $2,000,000; and the required rate of return is 15%. What amount represents the manager's bonus?

A. $200,000
B. $140,000
C. $100,000
D. $40,000

BEC 5-Q6 B273. Which of the following terms represents the residual income that remains after the cost of all capital, including equity capital, has been deducted?

A. Free cash flow.
B. Market value-added.
C. Economic value-added.
D. Net operating capital.

BEC 5-Q7 B348. Zig Corp. provides the following information:

Pretax operating profit	$ 300,000,000
Tax rate	40%
Capital used to generate profits 50% debt, 50% equity	$1,200,000,000
Cost of equity	15%
Cost of debt (after-tax)	5%

What of the following represents Zig's year-end economic value-added amount?

A. $0
B. $60,000,000
C. $120,000,000
D. $180,000,000

BEC 5-Q8 B86. Which of the following is a limitation of the profitability index?

A. It uses free cash flows.
B. It ignores the time value of money.
C. It is inconsistent with the goal of shareholder wealth maximization.
D. It requires detailed long-term forecasts of the project's cash flows.

BEC 5-Q9 B125. What is the formula for calculating the profitability index of a project?

A. Subtract actual after-tax net income from the minimum required return in dollars.
B. Divide the present value of the annual after-tax cash flows by the original cash invested in the project.
C. Divide the initial investment for the project by the net annual cash inflow.
D. Multiply net profit margin by asset turnover.

BEC 5-Q10 B275. Which of the following formulas should be used to calculate the economic rate of return on common stock?

A. (Dividends + change in price) divided by beginning price.
B. (Net income - preferred dividend) divided by common shares outstanding.
C. Market price per share divided by earnings per share.
D. Dividends per share divided by market price per share.

BEC 5-Q11 B1015.* Selected information regarding Dyle Corporation's outstanding equity is shown below.

Common stock, $10 par value, 350,000 shares outstanding	$3,500,000
Preferred stock, $100 par value, 10,000 shares outstanding	1,000,000
Preferred stock dividend paid	60,000
Common stock dividend paid	700,000
Earnings per common share	3
Market price per common share	18

Dyle's dividend yield on common stock is

A. 11.11%
B. 16.66%
C. 16.88%
D. 20.00%

---

* CMA adapted.

BEC 5-Q12 B1019.* The following information concerning Arnold Company's common stock was included in the company's financial reports for the last two years.

	Year 2	Year 1
Market price per share on December 31	$60	$50
Par value per share	10	10
Earnings per share	3	3
Dividends per share	1	1
Book value per share on December 31	36	34

Arnold's dividend yield in Year 2

A. Increased compared to Year 1.
B. Indicative of the company's failure to provide a positive return to the investors.
C. Is the same as Year 1.
D. Declined compared to Year 1.

BEC 5-Q13 B129. Which of the following ratios would be used to evaluate a company's profitability?

A. Current ratio.
B. Inventory turnover ratio.
C. Debt to total assets ratio.
D. Gross margin ratio.

BEC 5-Q14 B997.* Douglas Company purchased 10,000 shares of its common stock at the beginning of the year for cash. This transaction will affect all of the following except the

A. Debt-to-equity ratio
B. Earnings per share
C. Net profit margin
D. Current ratio

BEC 5-Q15 B962.* The owner of a chain of grocery stores has bought a large supply of mangoes and paid for the fruit with cash. This purchase will adversely impact which one of the following?

A. Working capital
B. Current ratio
C. Quick or acid test ratio
D. Price earnings ratio

BEC 5-Q16 B340. Minon, Inc. purchased a long-term asset on the last day of the current year. What are the effects of this purchase on return on investment and residual income?

	Return on investment	Residual income
A.	Increase	Increase
B.	Decrease	Decrease
C.	Increase	Decrease
D.	Decrease	Increase

BEC 5-Q17 B347. Vested, Inc. made some changes is operations and provided the following information:

	Year 2	Year 3
Operating revenues	$ 900,000	$1,100,000
Operating expenses	650,000	700,000
Operating assets	1,200,000	2,000,000

What percentage represents the return on investment for year 3?

A. 28.57%
B. 25%
C. 20.31%
D. 20%

BEC 5-Q18 B1006.* Selected financial data for ABC Company is presented below.
- For the year just ended ABC has net income of $5,300,000.
- $5,500,000 of 7% convertible bonds were issued in the prior year at a face value of $1,000. Each bond is convertible into 50 shares of common stock. No bonds were converted during the current year.
- 50,000 shares of 10% cumulative preferred stock, par value $100, were issued in the prior year. Preferred dividends were not declared in the current year, but were current at the end of the prior year.
- At the beginning of the current year 1,060,000 shares of common stock were outstanding.
- On June 1 of the current year 60,000 shares of common stock were issued and sold.
- ABC's average income tax rate is 40%.

ABC Company's basic earnings per share for the current fiscal year is

A. $3.67
B. $4.29
C. $4.38
D. $4.73

* CMA adapted.

BEC 5-Q19 B1011.* Collins Company reported net income of $350,000 for the year. The company had 10,000 shares of $100 par value, non-cumulative, 6% preferred stock and 100,000 shares of $10 par value common stock outstanding. There were also 5,000 shares of common stock in treasury during the year. Collins declared and paid all preferred dividends as well as a $1 per share dividend on common stock. Collins' basic earnings per share for the year was

A. $3.50
B. $3.33
C. $2.90
D. $2.76

BEC 5-Q20 B1014.* Roy company had 120,000 common shares and 100,000 preferred shares outstanding at the close of the prior year. During the current year Roy repurchased 12,000 common shares on March 1, sold 30,000 common shares on June 1, and sold an additional 60,000 common shares on November 1. No change in preferred shares outstanding occurred during the year. The number of shares of stock outstanding to be used in the calculation of basic earnings per share at the end of the current year is

A. 100,000
B. 137,500
C. 198,000
D. 298,000

BEC 5-Q21 B128. Which of the following ratios would most likely be used by management to evaluate short-term liquidity?

A. Return on total assets.
B. Sales to cash.
C. Accounts receivable turnover.
D. Acid test ratio.

BEC 5-Q22 B964.* When reviewing a credit application for a corporation, the credit manager should be most concerned with the applicant's

A. Profit margin and return on assets
B. Price-earnings ratio and current ratio
C. Working capital and return on equity
D. Working capital and current ratio

BEC 5-Q23 B969.* If a company has a current ratio of 2.1 and pays off a portion of its accounts payable with cash, the current ratio will

A. Decrease
B. Increase
C. Remain unchanged
D. Move closer to the quick ratio

BEC 5-Q24 B958.* Davis Retail Inc. has current assets of $7,500,000 and a current ratio of 2.3 times before purchasing $750,000 of merchandise on credit for resale. After this purchase, the current ratio will

A. Remain at 2.3 times
B. Be higher than 2.3 times
C. Be lower than 2.3 times
D. Be exactly 2.53 times

BEC 5-Q25 B55. A company has cash of $100 million, accounts receivable of $600 million, current assets of $1.2 billion, accounts payable of $400 million, and current liabilities of $900 million. What is its acid-test (quick) ratio?

A. 0.11
B. 0.78
C. 1.75
D. 2.11

BEC 5-Q26 B83. Farrow Co. is applying for a loan in which the bank requires a quick ratio of at least 1. Farrow's quick ratio is 0.8. Which of the following actions would increase Farrow's quick ratio?

A. Purchasing inventory through the issuance of a long-term note.
B. Implementing stronger procedures to collect accounts receivable at a faster rate.
C. Paying an existing account payable.
D. Selling obsolete inventory at a loss.

BEC 5-Q27 B1071.* A credit manager considering whether to grant trade credit to a new customer is most likely to place primary emphasis on

A. Profitability ratios
B. Debt utilization ratios
C. Market ratios
D. Liquidity ratios

---

* CMA adapted.

BEC 5-Q28 B957.* Shown below are beginning and ending balances for certain of Grimaldi Inc.'s accounts.

	January 1	December 31
Cash	$48,000	$62,000
Marketable securities	42,000	35,000
Accounts receivable	68,000	47,000
Inventory	125,000	138,000
Plant & equipment	325,000	424,000
Accounts payable	32,000	84,000
Accrued liabilities	14,000	11,000
7% bonds payable	95,000	77,000

Grimaldi's acid test ratio or quick ratio at the end of the year is

A. 0.83
B. 1.02
C. 1.15
D. 1.52

BEC 5-Q29 B961.* Garstka Auto Parts must increase its acid test ratio above the current 0.9 level in order to comply with the terms of a loan agreement. Which one of the following actions is **most** likely to produce the desired results?

A. Expediting collection of accounts receivable.
B. Selling auto parts on account.
C. Making a payment to trade accounts payable.
D. Purchasing marketable securities for cash.

BEC 5-Q30 B967.* All of the following are included when calculating the acid test ratio except

A. six-month treasury bills
B. prepaid insurance
C. accounts receivable
D. 60-day certificates of deposit

BEC 5-Q31 B965.* Both the current ratio and the quick ratio for Spartan Corporation have been slowly decreasing. For the past two years, the current ratio has been 2.3 to 1 and 2.0 to 1. During the same time period, the quick ratio has decreased from 1.2 to 1 to 1.0 to 1. The disparity between the current and quick ratios can be explained by which one of the following?

A. The current portion of long-term debt has been steadily increasing.
B. The cash balance is unusually low.
C. The accounts receivable balance has decreased.
D. The inventory balance is unusually high.

BEC 5-Q32 B194. A company has the following information in its financial records:

	Beginning balance	Ending balance
Cash	$ 3,900	$ 3,000
Marketable securities	3,800	4,400
Accounts receivable	14,600	12,900
Total current assets	$22,300	$20,300
Net sales		$103,200
Expenses		20,430
Net income		$ 82,770

What is the company's receivable turnover ratio?

A. 6.0
B. 7.1
C. 7.5
D. 8.0

BEC 5-Q33 B149. Green, Inc., a financial investment-consulting firm, was engaged by Maple Corp. to provide technical support for making investment decisions. Maple, a manufacturer of ceramic tiles, was in the process of buying Bay, Inc., its prime competitor. Green's financial analyst made an independent detailed analysis of Bay's average collection period to determine which of the following?

A. Financing.
B. Return on equity.
C. Liquidity.
D. Operating profitability.

---

* CMA adapted.

BEC 5-Q34 B258. Super Sets, Inc. manufactures and sells television sets. All sales are finalized on credit with terms of 2/10, n/30. Seventy percent of Super Set customers take discounts and pay on day 10, while the remaining 30% pay on day 30. What is the average collection period in days?

A. 10
B. 16
C. 24
D. 40

BEC 5-Q35 B307. Which of the following ratios is appropriate for the evaluation of accounts receivable?

A. Days sales outstanding.
B. Return on total assets.
C. Collection to debt ratio.
D. Current ratio.

BEC 5-Q36 B316. Amicable Wireless, Inc. offers credit terms of 2/10, net 30 for its customers. Sixty percent of Amicable's customers take the 2% discount and pay on day 10. The remainder of Amicable's customers pay on day 30. How many days' sales are in Amicable's accounts receivable?

A. 6
B. 12
C. 18
D. 20

BEC 5-Q37 B986.* Maydale Inc.'s financial statements show the following information.

Accounts receivable, end of Year 1	$320,000
Credit sales for Year 2	3,600,000
Accounts receivable, end of Year 2	400,000

Maydale's accounts receivable turnover ratio is

A. 0.10
B. 9.00
C. 10.00
D. 11.25

BEC 5-Q38 B78. The following information was taken from the income statement of Hadley Co.:

Beginning inventory	17,000
Purchases	56,000
Ending inventory	13,000

What is Hadley Co.'s inventory turnover?

A. 3
B. 4
C. 5
D. 6

BEC 5-Q39 B189. To measure inventory management performance, a company monitors its inventory turnover ratio. Listed below are selected data from the company's accounting records:

	Current year	Prior year
Annual sales	$2,525,000	$2,125,000
Gross profit percent	40%	35%

Beginning finished goods inventory for the current year was 15% of the prior-year's annual sales, and ending finished goods inventory was 22% of the current-year's annual sales. What was the company's inventory turnover at the end of the current period?

A. 1.82
B. 2.31
C. 2.73
D. 3.47

BEC 5-Q40 B376. Green Co. has an inventory conversion period of 80 days and annual revenue of $4,200,000. How many times per year (360 days) does Green turn over its inventory?

A. 2.25
B. 4.30
C. 4.50
D. 9.00

BEC 5-Q41 B987. * Zubin Corporation experiences a decrease in sales and the cost of goods sold, an increase in accounts receivable, and no change in inventory. If all else is held constant, what is the total effect of these changes on the receivables turnover and inventory ratios?

	Inventory Turnover	Receivables Turnover
A.	Increased	Increased
B.	Increased	Decreased
C.	Decreased	Increased
D.	Decreased	Decreased

BEC 5-Q42 B156. Wexford Co. has a subunit that reported the following data for year 1:

Asset (investment) turnover	1.5 times
Sales	$750,000
Return on sales	8%

The imputed interest is 12%. What is the division residual income for year 1?

A. $60,000
B. $30,000
C. $20,000
D. $0

BEC 5-Q43 B158. Galax, Inc. had operating income of $5,000,000 before interest and taxes. Galax's net book value of plant assets at January 1 and December 31 were $22,000,000 and $18,000,000, respectively. Galax achieved a 25 percent return on investment for the year, with an investment turnover of 2.5. What were Galax's sales for the year?

A. $55,000,000
B. $50,000,000
C. $45,000,000
D. $20,000,000

BEC 5-Q44 B176. A company currently has 1,000 shares of common stock outstanding with zero debt. It has the choice of raising an additional $100,000 by issuing 9% long-term debt, or issuing 500 shares of common stock. The company has a 40% tax rate. What level of earnings before interest and taxes (EBIT) would result in the same earnings per share (EPS) for the two financing options?

A. An EBIT of $27,000 would result in EPS of $10.80 for both.
B. An EBIT of $27,000 would result in EPS of $7.20 for both.
C. An EBIT of -$18,000 would result in EPS of ($7.20) for both.
D. An EBIT of -$10,800 would result in EPS of ($7.92) for both.

BEC 5-Q45 B1007. * Devlin Inc. has 250,000 shares of $10 par value common stock outstanding. For the current year, Devlin paid a cash dividend of $3.50 per share and had earnings per share of $4.80. The market price of Devlin's stock is $34 per share. Devlin's price/earnings ratio is

A. 2.08
B. 2.85
C. 7.08
D. 9.71

BEC 5-Q46 B1008. * At year-end, Appleseed Company reported net income of $588,000. The company has 10,000 shares of $100 par value, 6% preferred stock and 120,000 shares of $10 par value common stock outstanding and 5,000 shares of common stock in treasury. There are no dividend payments in arrears, and the market price per common share at the end of the year was $40. Appleseed's price-earnings ratio is

A. 9.47
B. 9.09
C. 8.50
D. 8.16

---

* CMA adapted.

BEC 5-Q47 B1009. * Archer Inc. has 500,000 shares of $10 par value common stock outstanding. For the current year, Archer paid a cash dividend of $4.00 per share and had earnings per share of $3.20. The market price of Archer's stock is $36 per share. The average price-earnings ratio for Archer's industry is 14.00. When compared to the industry average, Archer's stock appears to be

A. Overvalued by approximately 25%
B. Overvalued by approximately 10%
C. Undervalued by approximately 10%
D. Undervalued by approximately 25%

BEC 5-Q48 B1010. * A steady drop in a firm's price-earnings ratio could indicate that

A. Earnings per share has been increasing while the market price of the stock has held steady.
B. Earnings per share has been steadily decreasing.
C. The market price of the stock has been steadily rising.
D. Both earnings per share and the market price of the stock are rising.

BEC 5-Q49 B98. Which of the following is one of the four perspectives of a balanced scorecard?

A. Just in time.
B. Innovation.
C. Benchmarking.
D. Activity-based costing.

BEC 5-Q50 B342. Under the balanced scorecard concept developed by Kaplan and Norton, employee satisfaction and retention are measures used under which of the following perspectives?

A. Customer.
B. Internal business.
C. Learning and growth.
D. Financial.

BEC 5-Q51 B308. Which of the following balanced scorecard perspectives examines a company's success in targeted market segments?

A. Financial.
B. Customer.
C. Internal business process.
D. Learning and growth.

BEC 5-Q52 B202. The management of a company would do which of the following to compare and contrast its financial information to published information reflecting optimal amounts?

A. Budget.
B. Forecast.
C. Benchmark.
D. Utilize best practices.

BEC 5-Q53 B80. To evaluate its performance, the Blankie Co. is comparing its costs of quality from one year to the next. The relevant costs are as follows:

	First Year	Second Year
Prevention	$45,000	$60,000
Appraisal	25,000	35,000
Internal failure	80,000	50,000
External failure	75,000	65,000

Which of the following conclusions can Blankie draw about its quality program?

A. It has been a failure, because conformance costs decreased by $40,000 while nonconformance costs increased by $25,000.
B. It has been a success, because conformance costs decreased by $40,000 and nonconformance costs increased by $25,000.
C. It has been a failure, because conformance costs increased by $25,000 while nonconformance costs decreased by $40,000.
D. It has been a success, because conformance costs increased by $25,000 while nonconformance costs decreased by $40,000.

---

* CMA adapted.

BEC 5-Q54 B315. Which of the following is assigned to goods that were either purchased or manufactured for resale?

A. Relevant cost.
B. Period cost.
C. Opportunity cost.
D. Product cost.

BEC 5-Q55 B330. In the past, four direct labor hours were required to produce each unit of product Y. Material costs were $200 per unit, the direct labor rate was $20 per hour, and factory overhead was three times direct labor cost. In budgeting for next year, management is planning to outsource some manufacturing activities and to further automate others. Management estimates these plans will reduce labor hours by 25%, increase the factory overhead rate to 3.6 times direct labor costs, and increase material costs by $30 per unit. Management plans to manufacture 10,000 units. What amount should management budget for cost of goods manufactured?

A. $4,820,000
B. $5,060,000
C. $5,200,000
D. $6,500,000

BEC 5-Q56 B65. If a product required a great deal of electricity to produce, and crude oil prices increased, which of the following costs most likely increased?

A. Direct materials.
B. Direct labor.
C. Prime costs.
D. Conversion costs.

BEC 5-Q57 B267. The following is selected information from the records of Ray, Inc.:

Purchases of raw materials	$ 6,000
Raw materials, beginning	500
Raw materials, ending	800
Work-in-process, beginning	0
Work-in-process, ending	0
Cost of goods sold	12,000
Finished goods, beginning	1,200
Finished goods, ending	1,400

What is the total amount of conversion costs?

A. $5,500
B. $5,900
C. $6,100
D. $6,500

BEC 5-Q58 B355. Which of the following types of costs are prime costs?

A. Direct materials and direct labor.
B. Direct materials and overhead.
C. Direct labor and overhead.
D. Direct materials, direct labor, and overhead.

BEC 5-Q59 B42. Based on the following data, what is the gross profit for the company?

Sales	$1,000,000
Net purchases of raw materials	600,000
Cost of goods manufactured	800,000
Marketing and administrative expenses	250,000
Indirect manufacturing costs	500,000

	Beginning inventory	Ending inventory
Work in process	$500,000	$400,000
Finished goods	100,000	500,000

A. $200,000
B. $400,000
C. $600,000
D. $900,000

BEC 5-Q60 B262. What is the cost of ending inventory given the following factors?

Beginning inventory	$ 5,000
Total production costs	60,000
Cost of goods sold	55,000
Direct labor	40,000

A. $5,000
B. $10,000
C. $45,000
D. $50,000

BEC 5-Q61 B318. What is the required unit production level given the following factors?

	Units
Projected Sales	1,000
Beginning inventory	85
Desired ending inventory	100
Prior-year beginning inventory	200

A. 915
B. 1,015
C. 1,100
D. 1,215

BEC 5-Q62 B251. Card Bicycle Co. has prepared production and raw materials budgets for next year. At the end of this year, the finished product inventory is expected to include 2,000 bicycles, and raw material inventory is expected to include 3,000 bicycle tires. Each finished bicycle requires two tires. The marketing department provided the following data from the sales budget for the first quarter:

	January	February	March
Expected bicycle sales (units)	12,000	16,000	18,000

The company inventory policy is to have finished product inventory equal to 20% of the following month's sales requirements, and raw material equal to 10% of the following month's production requirements. In the January budget for raw materials, how many tires are expected to be purchased?

A. 24,200
B. 26,120
C. 26,600
D. 26,680

BEC 5-Q63 B266. Crisper, Inc. plans to sell 80,000 bags of potato chips in June, and each of these bags requires five potatoes. Pertinent data includes:

	Bags of potato chips	Potatoes
Actual June 1 inventory	15,000 bags	27,000 potatoes
Desired June 30 inventory	18,000 bags	23,000 potatoes

What number of units of raw material should Crisper plan to purchase?

A. 381,000
B. 389,000
C. 411,000
D. 419,000

BEC 5-Q64 B323. Jonathan Mfg. adopted a job-costing system. For the current year, budgeted cost driver activity levels for direct labor hours and direct labor costs were 20,000 and $100,000, respectively. In addition, budgeted variable and fixed factory overhead were $50,000 and $25,000, respectively. Actual costs and hours for the year were as follows:

Direct labor hours	21,000
Direct labor costs	$110,000
Machine hours	35,000

For a particular job, 1,500 direct labor hours were used. Using direct labor hours as the cost driver, what amount of overhead should be applied to this job?

A. $3,214
B. $5,357
C. $5,625
D. $7,500

BEC 5-Q65 B199. Merry Co. has two major categories of factory overhead: material handling and quality control. The costs expected for these categories for the coming year are as follows:

Material handling	$120,000
Quality inspection	200,000

The plant currently applies overhead based on direct labor hours. The estimated direct labor hours are 80,000 per year. The plant manager is asked to submit a bid and assembles the following data on a proposed job:

Direct materials	$4,000
Direct labor (2,000 hours)	6,000

What amount is the estimated product cost on the proposed job?

A. $ 8,000
B. $10,000
C. $14,000
D. $18,000

BEC 5-Q66 B100. A company uses process costing to assign product costs. Available inventory information for a period is as follows:

	Inventory (in units)	Material cost	Conversion cost
Beginning	0		
Started during the period	15,000	$75,000	$55,500
Transferred out	13,500		
End of period	1,500		

The ending inventory was 25% complete as to the conversion cost. 100% of direct material was added at the beginning of the process. What was the total cost transferred out?

A. $130,500
B. $126,973
C. $121,500
D. $117,450

BEC 5-Q67 B203. Weighted average and first in, first out (FIFO) equivalent units would be the same in a period when which of the following occurs?

A. No beginning inventory exists.
B. No ending inventory exists.
C. Beginning inventory units equal ending inventory units.
D. Both a beginning and an ending inventory exist but are **not** necessarily equal.

BEC 5-Q68 B298. During the current year, the following manufacturing activity took place for a company's products:

Beginning work-in-process, 70% complete	10,000 units
Units started into production during the year	150,000 units
Units completed during the year	140,000 units
Ending work-in-process, 25% complete	20,000 units

What was the number of equivalent units produced using the first-in, first-out method?

A. 138,000
B. 140,000
C. 145,000
D. 150,000

BEC 5-Q69 B332. Black, Inc. employs a weighted average method in its process costing system. Black's work in process inventory on June 30 consists of 40,000 units. These units are 100% complete with respect to materials and 60% complete with respect to conversion costs. The equivalent unit costs are $5.00 for materials and $7.00 for conversion costs. What is the total cost of the June 30 work in process inventory?

A. $200,000
B. $288,000
C. $368,000
D. $480,000

BEC 5-Q70 B370. Which of the following is a disadvantage of using a process costing system versus job-order costing?

A. It is difficult to determine cost of goods sold when partial shipments are made before completion.
B. It is difficult to ensure that material and labor are accurately charged to each specific job.
C. It involves the calculation of stage of completion of goods-in-process and the use of equivalent units.
D. It is expensive to use as a good deal of clerical work is required.

BEC 5-Q71 B99. The New Wave Co. is considering a new method for allocating overhead to its two products, regular and premium coffee beans. Currently New Wave is using the traditional method to allocate overhead, in which the cost driver is direct labor costs.

However, it is interested in using two different drivers: machine hours (MH) for separating and roasting beans, and pounds of coffee for packing and shipping. Machine hours for the current month are 700 hours, direct labor cost per pound of coffee is $1.25, and direct materials cost per pound of coffee is $1.50. There are 1,000 pounds of coffee packed and shipped for the current month.

The following data are also available:

		Regular	Premium
Overhead for the current month	$5,000.00		
Cost pool for separating and roasting beans	3,500.00	150 MH	550 MH
Cost pool for packing and shipping	1,500.00	500 pounds	500 pounds

What is the total cost per pound for the premium coffee using the new activity-based costing method?

A. $5.00
B. $5.75
C. $7.75
D. $9.75

BEC 5-Q72 B139. A CPA would recommend implementing an activity-based costing system under which of the following circumstances?

A. The client is a single-product manufacturer.
B. Most of the client's costs currently are classified as direct costs.
C. The client produced products that heterogeneously consume resources.
D. The client produced many different products that homogeneously consume resources.

BEC 5-Q73 B160. Boyle, Inc. makes two products, X and Y, that require allocation of indirect manufacturing costs. The following data was compiled by the accountant before making any allocations:

	Product X	Product Y
Quantity produced	10,000	20,000
Direct manufacturing labor hours	15,000	5,000
Setup hours	500	1,500

The total cost of setting up manufacturing processes and equipment is $400,000. The company uses a job-costing system with a single indirect cost rate. Under this system, allocated costs were $300,000 and $100,000 for X and Y, respectively. If an activity-based system is used, what would be the allocated costs for each product?

	Product X	Product Y
A.	$100,000	$300,000
B.	$150,000	$250,000
C.	$200,000	$200,000
D.	$250,000	$150,000

BEC 5-Q74 B269. Which of the following nonvalue-added costs associated with manufactured work in process inventory is most significant?

A. The cost of materials that cannot be traced to any individual product.
B. The cost of labor that cannot be traced to any individual product.
C. The cost of moving, handling, and storing any individual product.
D. The cost of additional resources consumed to produce any individual product.

BEC 5-Q75 B331. Mighty, Inc. processes chickens for distribution to major grocery chains. The two major products resulting from the production process are white breast meat and legs. Joint costs of $600,000 are incurred during standard production runs each month, which produce a total of 100,000 pounds of white breast meat and 50,000 pounds of legs. Each pound of white breast meat sells for $2 and each pound of legs sells for $1. If there are **no** further processing costs incurred after the split-off point, what amount of the joint costs would be allocated to the white breast meat on a relative sales value basis?

A. $120,000
B. $200,000
C. $400,000
D. $480,000

BEC 5-Q76 B324. A company manufactures two products, X and Y, through a joint process. The joint (common) costs incurred are $500,000 for a standard production run that generates 240,000 gallons of X and 160,000 gallons of Y. X sells for $4.00 per gallon, while Y sells for $6.50 per gallon. If there are **no** additional processing costs incurred after the split-off point, what is the amount of joint cost for each production run allocated to X on a physical-quantity basis?

A. $200,000
B. $240,000
C. $260,000
D. $300,000

BEC 5-Q77 B200. Which of the following is **not** a basic approach to allocating costs for costing inventory in joint-cost situations?

A. Sales value at split-off.
B. Flexible budget amounts.
C. Physical measures such as weights or volume.
D. Constant gross margin percentage net realizable value method.

BEC 5-Q78 B335. A management accountant performs a linear regression of maintenance cost vs. production using a computer spreadsheet. The regression output shows an "intercept" value of $322,897. How should the accountant interpret this information?

A. Y has a value of $322,897 when X equals zero.
B. X has a value of $322,897 when Y equals zero.
C. The residual error of the regression is $322,897.
D. Maintenance cost has an average value of $322,897.

BEC 5-Q79 B50. Which of the following statements is correct regarding the difference between the absorption costing and variable costing methods?

A. When production equals sales, absorption costing income is greater than variable costing income.
B. When production equals sales, absorption costing income is **less** than variable costing income.
C. When production is greater than sales, absorption costing income is greater than variable costing income.
D. When production is **less** than sales, absorption costing income is greater than variable costing income.

BEC 5-Q80 B268. Which of the following costing methods provide(s) the added benefit of usefulness for external reporting purposes?

I. Variable.
II. Absorption.

A. I only.
B. II only.
C. Both I and II.
D. Neither I nor II.

BEC 5-Q81 B334. Waldo Company, which produces only one product, provides its most current month's data follows:

Selling price per unit	$80
Variable costs per unit:	
Direct materials	$21
Direct labor	10
Variable manufacturing overhead	3
Variable selling and administrative	6
Fixed costs:	
Manufacturing overhead	$76,000
Selling and administrative	58,000
Units:	
Beginning inventory	0
Month's production	5,000
Number sold	4,500
Ending inventory	500

Based upon the above information, what is the total contribution margin for the month under the variable costing approach?

A. $46,000
B. $180,000
C. $207,000
D. $226,000

BEC 5-Q82 B345. At the end of a company's first year of operations, 2,000 units of inventory are on hand. Variable costs are $100 per unit, and fixed manufacturing costs are $30 per unit. The use of absorption costing, rather than variable costing, would result in a higher net income of what amount?

A. $60,000
B. $140,000
C. $200,000
D. $260,000

BEC 5-Q83 B333. Virgil Corp. uses a standard cost system. In May, Virgil purchased and used 17,500 pounds of materials at a cost of $70,000. The materials usage variance was $2,500 unfavorable and the standard materials allowed for May production was 17,000 pounds. What was the materials price variance for May?

A. $17,500 favorable.
B. $17,500 unfavorable.
C. $15,000 favorable.
D. $15,000 unfavorable.

BEC 5-Q84 B306. Central Winery manufactured two products, A and B. Estimated demand for product A was 10,000 bottles and for product B was 30,000 bottles. The estimated sales price per bottle for A was $6.00 and for B was $8.00. Actual demand for product A was 8,000 bottles and for product B was 33,000 bottles. The actual price per bottle for A was $6.20 and for B was $7.70. What amount would be the total selling price variance for Central Winery?

A. $3,700 unfavorable.
B. $8,300 unfavorable.
C. $3,700 favorable.
D. $14,100 favorable.

BEC 5-Q85 B311. To meet its monthly budgeted production goals, Acme Mfg. Co. planned a need for 10,000 widgets at a price of $20 per widget. Acme's actual units were 11,200 at a price of $18.50 per widget. What amount reflected Acme's selling price variance?

A. $7,200 unfavorable.
B. $15,000 favorable.
C. $16,800 unfavorable.
D. $24,000 unfavorable.

BEC 5-Q86 B63. For the current period production levels, XL Molding Co. budgeted 8,500 board feet of production and used 9,000 board feet for actual production. Material cost was budgeted at $2 per foot. The actual cost for the period was $3 per foot. What was XL's material efficiency variance for the period?

A. $1,000 favorable.
B. $1,000 unfavorable.
C. $1,500 favorable.
D. $1,500 unfavorable.

BEC 5-Q87 B136. Relevant information for material A follows:

Actual quantity used	6,500 lbs.
Standard quantity allowed	6,000 lbs.
Actual price	$3.80
Standard price	$4.00

What was the direct material quantity variance for material A?

A. $2,000 favorable.
B. $1,900 favorable.
C. $1,900 unfavorable.
D. $2,000 unfavorable.

BEC 5-Q88 B159. Management has reviewed the standard cost variance analysis and is trying to explain an unfavorable labor efficiency variance of $8,000. Which of the following is the most likely cause of the variance?

A. The new labor contract increased wages.
B. The maintenance of machinery has been inadequate for the last few months.
C. The department manager has chosen to use highly skilled workers.
D. The quality of raw materials has improved greatly.

BEC 5-Q89 B296. A company produces widgets with budgeted standard direct materials of 2 pounds per widget at $5 per pound. Standard direct labor was budgeted at 0.5 hour per widget at $15 per hour. The actual usage in the current year was 25,000 pounds and 3,000 hours to produce 10,000 widgets. What was the direct labor usage variance?

A. $25,000 favorable.
B. $25,000 unfavorable.
C. $30,000 favorable.
D. $30,000 unfavorable.

BEC 5-Q90 B85. A company has gathered the following information from a recent production run:

Standard variable overhead rate	$10
Actual variable overhead rate	8
Standard process hours	20
Actual process hours	25

What is the company's variable overhead spending variance?

A. $50 unfavorable.
B. $50 favorable.
C. $40 unfavorable.
D. $40 favorable.

BEC 5-Q91 B82. Which of the following types of variances would a purchasing manager most likely influence?

A. Direct materials price.
B. Direct materials quantity.
C. Direct labor rate.
D. Direct labor efficiency.

BEC 5-Q92 B137. Smart Co. uses a static budget. When actual sales are **less** than budget, Smart would report favorable variances on which of the following expense categories?

	Sales commissions	Building rent
A.	Yes	Yes
B.	Yes	No
C.	No	Yes
D.	No	No

BEC 5-Q93 B1258. Which of the following terms refers to a willing adoption of one organization's culture over the other after a merger or acquisition?

A. Integration.
B. Separation.
C. Assimilation.
D. Deculturation.

BEC 5-Q94 B279. What is strategic planning?

A. It establishes the general direction of the organization.
B. It establishes the resources that the plan will require.
C. It establishes the budget for the organization.
D. It consists of decisions to use parts of the organization's resources in specified ways.

BEC 5-Q95 B349. Which of the following steps in the strategic planning process should be completed first?

A. Translate objectives into goals.
B. Determine actions to achieve goals.
C. Develop performance measures.
D. Create a mission statement.

BEC 5-Q96 B197. Which of the following topics is the focus of managerial accounting?

A. Financial statements and other financial reports.
B. Historical cost principles.
C. The needs of creditors.
D. The needs of the organization's internal parties.

BEC 5-Q97 B364. Which of the following inputs would be most beneficial to consider when management is developing the capital budget?

A. Supply/demand for the company's products.
B. Current product sales prices and costs.
C. Wage trends.
D. Profit center equipment requests.

BEC 5-Q98 B56. Which of the following types of budgets is the last budget to be produced during the budgeting process?

A. Cash.
B. Capital.
C. Cost of Goods Sold.
D. Marketing.

BEC 5-Q99 B257. Which of the following budgets provides information for preparation of the owner's equity section of a budgeted balance sheet?

A. Sales budget.
B. Cash budget.
C. Capital expenditures budget.
D. Budgeted income statement.

BEC 5-Q100 B276. Fargo, Mfg., a small business, is developing a budget for next year. Which of the following steps should Fargo perform first?

A. Forecast Fargo's sales volume.
B. Determine the price of Fargo's products.
C. Identify costs of Fargo's forecasted sales volume.
D. Compute the dollar amount of Fargo's forecasted sales.

BEC 5-Q101 B329. Johnson Co. is preparing its master budget for the first quarter of next year. Budgeted sales and production for one of the company's products are as follows:

Month	Sales	Production
January	10,000	12,000
February	12,000	11,000
March	15,000	16,000

Each unit of this product requires four pounds of raw materials. Johnson's policy is to have sufficient raw materials on hand at the end of each month for 40 percent of the following month's production requirements. The January 1 materials inventory is expected to conform with this policy.

How many pounds of raw materials should Johnson budget to purchase for January?

A. 11,600
B. 46,400
C. 48,000
D. 65,600

BEC 5-Q102 B254. Which of the following is a disadvantage of participative budgeting?

A. It is more time consuming.
B. It decreases motivation.
C. It decreases acceptance.
D. It is **less** accurate.

BEC 5-Q103 B52. A static budget contains which of the following amounts?

A. Actual costs for actual output.
B. Actual costs for budgeted output.
C. Budgeted costs for actual output.
D. Budgeted costs for budgeted output.

BEC 5-Q104 B287. Quick Co. was analyzing variances for one of its operations. The initial budget forecast production of 20,000 units during the year with a variable manufacturing overhead rate of $10 per unit. Quick produced 19,000 units during the year. Actual variable manufacturing costs were $210,000. What amount would be Quick's flexible budget variance for the year?

A. $10,000 favorable.
B. $20,000 favorable.
C. $10,000 unfavorable.
D. $20,000 unfavorable.

BEC 5-Q105 B51. Johnson Co., distributor of candles, has reported the following budget assumptions for year 1: No change in candles inventory level; cash disbursement to candle manufacturer, $300,000; target accounts payable ending balance for year 1 is 150% of accounts payable beginning balance; and sales price is set at a markup of 20% of candle purchase price. The candle manufacturer is Johnson's only vendor, and all purchases are made on credit. The accounts payable has a balance of $100,000 at the beginning of year 1. What is the budgeted gross margin for year 1?

A. $60,000
B. $70,000
C. $75,000
D. $87,500

BEC 5-Q106 B141. A delivery company is implementing a system to compare the costs of purchasing and operating different vehicles in its fleet. Truck 415 is driven 125,000 miles per year at a variable cost of $0.13 per mile. Truck 415 has a capacity of 28,000 pounds and delivers 250 full loads per year. What amount is the truck's delivery cost per pound?

A. $0.00163 per pound.
B. $0.00232 per pound.
C. $0.58036 per pound.
D. $1.72000 per pound.

BEC 5-Q107 B138. An increase in production levels within a relevant range most likely would result in

A. Increasing the total cost.
B. Increasing the variable cost per unit.
C. Decreasing the total fixed cost.
D. Decreasing the variable cost per unit.

BEC 5-Q108 B168. Which of the following costs would decrease if production levels were increased within the relevant range?

A. Total fixed costs.
B. Variable costs per unit.
C. Total variable costs.
D. Fixed costs per unit.

BEC 5-Q109 B140. A company that produces 10,000 units has fixed costs of $300,000, variable costs of $50 per unit, and a sales price of $85 per unit. After learning that its variable costs will increase by 20%, the company is considering an increase in production to 12,000 units. Which of the following statements is correct regarding the company's next steps?

A. If production is increased to 12,000 units, profits will increase by $50,000.
B. If production is increased to 12,000 units, profits will increase by $100,000.
C. If production remains at 10,000 units, profits will decrease by $50,000.
D. If production remains at 10,000 units, profits will decrease by $100,000.

BEC 5-Q110 B71. Brewster Co. has the following financial information:

Fixed costs	$20,000
Variable costs	60%
Sales price	$50

What amount of sales is required for Brewster to achieve a 15% return on sales?

A. $33,333
B. $50,000
C. $80,000
D. $133,333

BEC 5-Q111 B49. A ceramics manufacturer sold cups last year for $7.50 each. Variable costs of manufacturing were $2.25 per unit. The company needed to sell 20,000 cups to break even. Net income was $5,040. This year, the company expects the following changes: sales price per cup to be $9.00; variable manufacturing costs to increase 33.3%; fixed costs to increase 10%; and the income tax rate to remain at 40%. Sales in the coming year are expected to exceed last year's sales by 1,000 units. How many units does the company expect to sell this year?

A. 21,000
B. 21,600
C. 21,960
D. 22,600

BEC 5-Q112 B68. State College is using cost-volume-profit analysis to determine tuition rates for the upcoming school year. Projected costs for the year are as follows:

Contribution margin per student	$ 1,800
Variable expenses per student	1,000
Total fixed expenses	360,000

Based on these estimates, what is the approximate break-even point in number of students?

A. 129
B. 200
C. 360
D. 450

BEC 5-Q113 B165. Wren Co. manufactures and sells two products with selling prices and variable costs as follows:

	A	B
Selling price	$18.00	$22.00
Variable costs	12.00	14.00

Wren's total annual fixed costs are $38,400. Wren sells four units of A for every unit of B. If operating income last year was $28,800, what was the number of units Wren sold?

A. 5,486
B. 6,000
C. 9,600
D. 10,500

BEC 5-Q114 B192. A ceramics manufacturer sold cups last year for $7.50 each. Variable costs of manufacturing were $2.25 per unit. The company needed to sell 20,000 cups to break even. Net income was $5,040. This year, the company expects the price per cup to be $9.00; variable manufacturing costs to increase 33.3%; and fixed costs to increase 10%. How many cups (rounded) does the company need to sell this year to break even?

A. 17,111
B. 17,500
C. 19,250
D. 25,667

BEC 5-Q115 B247. Pinecrest Co. had variable costs of 25% of sales, and fixed costs of $30,000. Pinecrest's break-even point in sales dollars was

A. $24,000
B. $30,000
C. $40,000
D. $120,000

BEC 5-Q116 B93. A company produces and sells two products. The first product accounts for 75% of sales and the second product accounts for the remaining 25% of sales. The first product has a selling price of $10 per unit, variable costs of $6 per unit, and allocated fixed costs of $100,000. The second product has a selling price of $25 per unit, variable costs of $13 per unit, and allocated fixed costs of $212,000. At the break-even point, what number of units of the first product will have been sold?

A. 52,000
B. 39,000
C. 25,000
D. 14,625

BEC 5-Q117 B256. Ryan Co. projects the following monthly revenues for next year:

January	$100,000	July	$250,000
February	500,000	August	275,000
March	425,000	September	300,000
April	450,000	October	350,000
May	575,000	November	400,000
June	300,000	December	525,000

Ryan's terms are net 30 days. The company typically receives payment on 80% of sales the month following the sale, and 17% is collected two months after the sale. Approximately 3% of sales are deemed bad debt. What amount represents the expected cash collection in the second calendar quarter of next year?

A. $1,450,000
B. $1,393,750
C. $1,325,000
D. $1,234,250

BEC 5-Q118 B286. On June 30, 20X3, a company is preparing the cash budget for the third quarter. The collection pattern for credit sales has been 60% in the month of sale, 30% in the first month after sale, and the rest in the second month after sales. Uncollectible accounts are negligible. There are cash sales each month equal to 25% of total sales. The total sales for the quarter are estimated as follows: July, $30,000; August, $15,000; September, $35,000. Accounts receivable on June 30, 20X3, were $10,000. What amount would be the projected cash collections for September?

A. $21,375
B. $28,500
C. $30,125
D. $37,250

BEC 5-Q119 B77. A company forecast first quarter sales of 10,000 units, second quarter sales of 15,000 units, third quarter sales of 12,000 units and fourth quarter sales of 9,000 units at $2 per unit. Past experience has shown that 60% of the sales will be in cash and 40% will be on credit. All credit sales are collected in the following quarter, and none are uncollectible. What amount of cash is forecasted to be collected in the second quarter?

A. $8,000
B. $18,000
C. $26,000
D. $30,000

BEC 5-Q120 B280. The following table contains Emerald Corp.'s quarterly revenues, in thousands, for the past three years. During that time, there were no major changes to Emerald's selling strategies and total capital investment.

Year	1st Qtr.	2nd Qtr.	3rd Qtr.	4th Qtr.
Year 1	500	500	550	750
Year 2	525	550	600	800
Year 3	550	525	625	850

Which of the following statements best describes the likely cause of the fluctuations in Emerald's revenues and the best response to those fluctuations?

A. The fluctuations are from changes in the economy, and Emerald should examine its cost structure for potential changes.
B. The fluctuations are from changes in the economy, and Emerald should manage its inventories and cash flow to match the cycle.
C. The fluctuations are from the seasonal demand for Emerald's products, and Emerald should examine its cost structure for potential changes.
D. The fluctuations are from the seasonal demand for Emerald's products, and Emerald should manage its inventories and cash flow to match the cycle.

BEC 5-Q121 B295. Which of the following would be most impacted by the use of the percentage of sales forecasting method for budgeting purposes?

A. Accounts payable.
B. Mortgages payable.
C. Bonds payable.
D. Common stock.

BEC 5-Q122 B353. Which of the following forecasting methods relies mostly on judgment?

A. Time series models.
B. Econometric models.
C. Delphi.
D. Regression.

BEC 5-Q123 B124. Carter Co. paid $1,000,000 for land three years ago. Carter estimates it can sell the land for $1,200,000, net of selling costs. If the land is not sold, Carter plans to develop the land at a cost of $1,500,000. Carter estimates net cash flow from the development in the first year of operations would be $500,000. What is Carter's opportunity cost of the development?

A. $1,500,000
B. $1,200,000
C. $1,000,000
D. $500,000

BEC 5-Q124 B146. Egan Co. owns land that could be developed in the future. Egan estimates it can sell the land for $1,200,000, net of all selling costs. If it is not sold, Egan will continue with its plans to develop the land. As Egan evaluates its options for development or sale of the property, what type of cost would the potential selling price represent in Egan's decision?

A. Sunk.
B. Opportunity.
C. Future.
D. Variable.

BEC 5-Q125 B198. Which of the following statements is true regarding opportunity cost?

A. Opportunity cost is recorded in the accounts of an organization that has a full costing system.
B. The potential benefit is **not** sacrificed when selecting an alternative.
C. Idle space that has **no** alternative use has an opportunity cost of zero.
D. Opportunity cost is representative of actual dollar outlay.

BEC 5-Q126 B300. The CPA reviewed the minutes of a board of director's meeting of LQR Corp., an audit client. An order for widget handles was outsourced to SDT Corp. because LQR couldn't fill the order. By having SDT produce the order, LQR was able to realize $100,000 in sales profits that otherwise would have been lost. The outsourcing added a cost of $10,000, but LQR was ahead by $90,000 when the order was completed. Which of the following statements is correct regarding LQR's action?

A. The use of resource markets outside of LQR involves opportunity cost.
B. Accounting profit is total revenue minus explicit costs and implicit costs.
C. Implicit costs are **not** opportunity costs because they are internal costs.
D. Explicit costs are opportunity costs from purchasing widget handles from resource market.

BEC 5-Q127 B41. Management at MDK Corp. is deciding whether to replace a delivery van. A new delivery van costing $40,000 can be purchased to replace the existing delivery van, which cost the company $30,000 and has accumulated depreciation of $20,000. An employee of MDK has offered $12,000 for the old delivery van. Ignoring income taxes, which of the following correctly states relevant costs when making the decision whether to replace the delivery vehicle?

A. Purchase price of new van, disposal price of old van, gain on sale of old van.
B. Purchase price of new van, purchase price of old van, gain on sale of old van.
C. Purchase price of new van, disposal price of old van.
D. Purchase price of new van, purchase price of old van, accumulated depreciation of old van, gain on sale of old van, disposal price of old van.

BEC 5-Q128 B161. A company is offered a one-time special order for its product and has the capacity to take this order without losing current business. Variable costs per unit and fixed costs in total will be the same. The gross profit for the special order will be 10%, which is 15% less than the usual gross profit. What impact will this order have on total fixed costs and operating income?

A. Total fixed costs increase, and operating income increases.
B. Total fixed costs do not change, and operating income increases.
C. Total fixed costs do not change, and operating income does not change.
D. Total fixed costs increase, and operating income decreases.

BEC 5-Q129 B293. Rodder, Inc. manufactures a component in a router assembly. The selling price and unit cost data for the component are as follows:

Selling Price	$15
Direct materials cost	3
Direct labor cost	3
Variable overhead cost	3
Fixed manufacturing overhead cost	2
Fixed selling and administration cost	1

The company received a special one-time order for 1,000 components. Rodder has an alternative use for production capacity for the 1,000 components that would produce a contribution margin of $5,000. What amount is the lowest unit price Rodder should accept for the component?

A. $9
B. $12
C. $14
D. $24

BEC 5-Q130 B164. A company's target gross margin is 40% of the selling price of a product that costs $89 per unit. The product's selling price should be

A. $124.60
B. $142.40
C. $148.33
D. $222.50

BEC 5-Q131 B326. Spring Co. had two divisions, A and B. Division A created Product X, which could be sold on the outside market for $25 and used variable costs of $15. Division B could take Product X and apply additional variable costs of $40 to create Product Y, which could be sold for $100. Division B received a special order for a large amount of Product Y. If Division A were operating at full capacity, which of the following prices should Division A charge Division B for the Product X needed to fill the special order?

A. $15
B. $20
C. $25
D. $40

This page is intentionally left blank.

Multiple Choice – Solutions

BEC 5-Q1 B62. The correct choice is D. When calculating the percentage change from Year 1 to Year 2, use the following formula:

(Year 2 balance – Year 1 balance)/Year 1 balance

Choices A, B, and C are not correct because the correct formula for calculating the percentage change from Year 1 to Year 2 is
(Year 2 balance – Year 1 balance)/Year 1 balance.

BEC 5-Q2 B145. The correct choice is B. The Return on Investment (ROI) is calculated as Net Income/Average Total Assets. In this case, operating profit will be used instead of Net Income (because Net Income is not available in this question) and Average Total Assets is the Investment. The ROI for both operating divisions is calculated below.

Passenger ROI = $40,000/$250,000 = 0.16 or 16%
Cargo ROI = $50,000/$500,000 = 0.10 or 10%

Therefore, the Passenger division ROI of 16% performed better. Note: The data regarding external borrowing rate was not needed to solve this question.

BEC 5-Q3 B201. The correct choice is B. The formula for calculating residual income is:

Residual Income = Net Income – (Required rate of return x Average Total Assets)

Operating income is used instead of net income because information to calculate the net income is not provided in the question.

Residual Income = $400 – (0.10 x $1,600)
Residual Income = $400 – $160
Residual Income = $240

Note: The question asked for Division B's residual income. Therefore, the information about Division A was not needed to solve the question.

BEC 5-Q4 B303. The correct choice is C. The formula for residual income is:

Residual Income = Net Income – (interest rate x average total assets), where the interest rate is either the weighted-average cost of capital or the required rate of return.

Total operating income = Division A $500 + Division B $400
Total operating income = $900

Total average assets = Division A $1,000 + Division B $1,600
Total average assets = $2,600

Residual Income = $900 – (0.10 x $2,600)
Residual Income = $900 – $260
Residual Income = $640

Note that operating income was used instead of net income because net income was not provided; also, we assume that the total assets are average total assets because average total assets was not provided.

BEC 5-Q5 B350. The correct choice is D.
The formula for residual income is:

Residual Income = Net Income – (Required Rate of Return x Invested Capital)
Residual Income = (Revenues $1,000,000 – Expenses $500,000) – (0.15 x $2,000,000)
Residual Income = $500,000 – $300,000
Residual Income = $200,000

Bonus = 0.20 x Residual Income $200,000
Bonus = $40,000

BEC 5-Q6 B273. The correct choice is C. The economic value-added formula is:

EVA = Net Operating Profit After Taxes – [(Total Assets – Current Liab.) x Weighted-Avg. Cost of Capital
or
EVA = NOPAT – [(Total Assets – CL) x WACC
Therefore, the assets net of current liabilities, then multiplied by the WACC, accounts for the dollar value of the cost of capital. This dollar value of the cost of capital is subtracted from NOPAT to calculate a residual that remains after the cost of capital.

Choice A is not correct because the free cash flow is calculated as:
NOPAT
+ Depreciation and amortization
− Capital expenditures
− Change in working capital requirements
= Free cash flow

The formula for free cash flow does not deduct the cost of capital.

Choice B is not correct because market value-added is the fair value of the corporation, less the capital that has been contributed by the shareholders. The calculation for market value- added does not deduct the cost of capital.

Choice D is not correct because net operating capital is very similar to working capital. The formula for net operating capital is operating current assets less operating current liabilities. Operating current assets and operating current liabilities are the types of items whose change would be included as adjustments in the operating section of the statement of cash flows using the indirect method of presentation.

BEC 5-Q7 B348. The correct choice is B.

The economic value-added (EVA) is calculated as:

EVA = NOPAT − [WACC x (Total Assets − Current Liabilities)]
EVA = $180,000,000 − (0.10 x $1,200,000,000 capital)
EVA = $180,000,000 − $120,000,000
EVA = $60,000,000

Where:
 NOPAT = Net Operating Profit After Taxes
 NOPAT = $300,000,000 x (1 − 0.40)
 NOPAT = $300,000,000 x 0.60
 NOPAT = $180,000,000

 WACC = Weighted-Average Cost of Capital, where
  0.50 weight x 0.15 = 0.075 for equity
  0.50 weight x 0.05 = 0.025 for debt
  WACC   = 0.10 or 10 percent

BEC 5-Q8 B86. The correct choice is D. The Profitability Index is calculated as follows:

Profitability Index = (PV of future cash inflows/Initial Investment) x 100

In an environment where there is a limit on the funds available to invest, management may prioritize projects accordingly from highest to lowest profitability index; this invests scarce resources in those projects with the highest return and maximizes shareholder wealth.

Therefore, a limitation of the profitability index is that it requires projections of future cash inflows that may require detailed analysis for the long-term.

Choice A is not correct because free cash flow is calculated as:

 Net Operating Profit After Taxes (NOPAT)
+ Depreciation Expense or Amortization Expense
− Capital Expenditures
− Change in Working Capital Expenditures
= Free Cash Flow

Free cash flow is not included in the calculation of Profitability Index.

Choice B is not correct because the Profitability Index uses the time value of money when discounting the future cash inflows.

Choice C is not correct because in an environment where there is a limit on the funds available to invest, management may prioritize projects accordingly from the highest to lowest profitability index; this invests scarce resources in those projects with the highest return and maximizes shareholder wealth.

BEC 5-Q9 B125. The correct choice is B. The formula for the profitability index is:

Present Value of Future Net Cash Inflows/Initial Investment

The index may or may not be multiplied by 100 to convert to a percentage.

Choice A is not correct because this formula describes in dollars the change in shareholders' wealth.

Choice C is not correct because this formula describes the payback period.

Choice D is not correct because this formula describes the Return on Assets (also known as the Return on Investment).

BEC 5-Q10 B275. The correct choice is A. In general, the rate of return on common stock is the earnings and change in market value of the common stock, then divided by its price. The formula for the economic rate of return on common stock is

Economic rate of Return on C/S = (Dividends + change in price)/beginning price

The economic rate of return accounts for both dividend yield and capital gain/loss from the change in stock price.

Choice B is not correct because the formula closely resembles the formula for basic earnings per share (EPS), which is:

EPS (basic) = (Net Income – Curr. Year P/S Dividends)/Weighted Avg number of C/S shares outstanding

Choice C is not correct because the formula closely resembles the formula for the price to earnings ratio, which is:

Price/Earnings Ratio = Market Price per share/basic EPS

Choice D is not correct because this is the formula for the dividend yield. The dividend yield is not the economic rate of return on common stock because it does not include the capital gain/loss from the change in stock price.

BEC 5-Q11 B1015. The correct answer is A. The dividend yield ratio is:
Dividends per common share / Market price per common share

Dyle's yield on common stock is calculated as follows:
Dividends per common share / Market price per common share
($700,000 / 350,000) / $18
11.11%

BEC 5-Q12 B1019. The correct answer is D. The dividend yield ratio is:

Dividends per common share / Market price per common share

Arnold's dividend yield for years 1 and 2 are calculated as follows:
Year 1
Dividends per common share / Market price per common share
$1 / $50 = 2.00%

Year 2
Dividends per common share / Market price per common share
$1 / $60 = 1.67%

Arnold's dividend yield has declined in Year 2 when compared to Year 1.

BEC 5-Q13 B129. The correct choice is D. The formula for the gross margin ratio is:

(Gross Margin, which is Net Sales – Cost of Goods Sold)/Net Sales

The gross margin ratio is a financial statement ratio used to evaluate profitability; the gross margin ratio shows the percentage of each sales dollar that remains after covering cost of goods sold.

Choice A is not correct because the current ratio is a financial statement ratio used to evaluate short-term liquidity.

Choice B is not correct because inventory turnover is a financial statement ratio used to evaluate the efficiency of inventory management and working capital management.

Choice C is not correct because debt to total assets is a financial statement ratio used to evaluate the company's use of debt to finance its assets; debt to total assets is a measure of financial leverage.

BEC 5-Q14 B997. The correct answer is C. The only measure not affected by the purchase of its own common stock is Douglas' net profit margin. Both the debt/equity ratio and the earnings per share are affected by the number of outstanding shares of common stock, while the current ratio is affected by the amount of cash held.

BEC 5-Q15 B962. The correct answer is C. The quick (acid test) quick ratio is:

Quick (acid test) ratio = (Current assets – Inventory) / Current liabilities

The quick ratio will be adversely affected by the decrease in the cash balance. Inventory is not included in the quick ratio, so the change in inventory will not offset the reduction in cash.

BEC 5-Q16 B340. The correct choice is B.

The formula for return on investment (ROI) is:

ROI = Net Income/Average Total Assets

The purchase of a long-term asset on the last day of the current year will increase the average total assets (the denominator) and decrease the ROI.

The formula for residual income is:

Residual Income = Net Income – (Required Rate of Return x Invested Capital)

The purchase of a long-term asset on the last day of the current year will increase the invested capital and increase the amount subtracted from net income; this will decrease residual income.

Therefore, the correct answer is ROI will decrease and residual income will decrease.

BEC 5-Q17 B347. The correct choice is B. The return on investment (ROI) for Year 3 is calculated below:

ROI = Net Income/Average Total Assets
ROI = $400,000/$1,600,000
ROI = 0.25 or 25%

where:
Net Income = $1,100,000 Year 3 Revenues – $700,000 Year 3 Expenses
Net Income = $400,000

Average Total Assets = (Beg. Assets, Year 3 $1,200,000 + Ending Assets, Year 3 $2,000,000)/2
Average Total Assets = $3,200,000/2
Average Total Assets = $1,600,000

BEC 5-Q18 B1006. The correct answer is C. The formula for calculating basic earnings per share is:

Basic EPS = Net income available to common shareholders / Weighted average number of common shares outstanding

Net income available to common shareholders is determined by taking the net income and subtracting the preferred dividends. The preferred dividends are $500,000 (10% x $100 par x 50,000 shares of preferred stock).

The weighted average number of common shares outstanding is calculated as follows:

Beginning number of
common shares outstanding   1,060,000
June 1: (60,000 additional
shares sold x 7/12)   35,000
Total number of
weighted average
common shares
outstanding   1,095,000

The basic earnings per share is calculated as follows:
(Net income – Preferred dividends) / Weighted average shares
($5,300,000 – $500,000) / 1,095,000
$4,800,000 / 1,095,000
$4.38

BEC 5-Q19 B1011. The correct answer is C. The formula for calculating basic earnings per share is:

Basic EPS = Net income available to common shareholders / Weighted average number of common shares outstanding

Net income available to common shareholders is determined by taking the net income and subtracting the preferred dividends. Collins' preferred dividends are $60,000 ($100 x .06 x 10,000).

The weighted average number of common shares outstanding is 100,000 as provided in the question. There were no other transactions affecting the number of common shares outstanding during the year.

The basic earnings per share is calculated as follows:

(Net income − Preferred dividends) / Weighted average shares
($350,000 - $60,000) / 100,000
$2.90

BEC 5-Q20 B1014. The correct answer is B. Roy Company's weighted average number of shares for calculating earnings per share is determined as follows.

Beginning number of common shares outstanding	120,000
March 1: Repurchased 12,000 common shares x 10/12	(10,000)
June 1: 30,000 additional shares sold x 7/12	17,500
November 1: 60,000 additional shares sold x 2/12	10,000
Total number of weighted average common shares outstanding	137,500

BEC 5-Q21 B128. The correct choice is D. The formula for the acid-test ratio (also known as the quick ratio) is:

(Quick Assets, which are Cash + Marketable Securities + A/R, net)/Current Liabilities

The acid-test ratio is a financial statement ratio that management uses to evaluate short-term liquidity; the acid-test ratio is used to evaluate the company's ability to cover payment of its current liabilities with its quick assets.

Choice A is not correct because return on total assets is a financial statement ratio that management uses to evaluate profitability.

Choice B is not correct because sales to cash is a financial statement ratio that management uses to evaluate the ability to generate sales revenues.

Choice C is not correct because accounts receivable turnover is a financial statement ratio that management uses to evaluate how efficiently accounts receivable are collected and how well working capital is managed.

BEC 5-Q22 B964. The correct answer is D. The comparison of current assets with current liabilities provides an indication of the ability for the corporation to pay its short-term debt. Both working capital and the current ratio compare current assets with current liabilities and therefore, measure credit worthiness.

BEC 5-Q23 B969. The correct answer is B. The current ratio formula is:

Current assets/Current liabilities

Given the 2.1 current ratio, the payment will have a proportionally greater affect on current liabilities than on current assets and as a result, the current ratio will increase.

BEC 5-Q24 B958. The correct answer is C. The current ratio formula is:
Current assets/Current liabilities

The current liabilities are not provided in the question. Substituting the information provided in the question, the current liabilities before the additional purchase are calculated as follows:

Before purchase:
$7,500,000 / Current liabilities = 2.3
Current liabilities = $3,260,870

After purchase:
($7,500,000 + $750,000)/($3,260,870 + $750,000) = 2.05

After the purchase, Davis' current ratio is 2.05 and is lower than the current ratio before the purchase of 2.3.

BEC 5-Q25 B55. The correct choice is B. The acid test (or quick) ratio is calculated as follows:

Acid test (or quick ratio) = (Cash + Marketable Securities + A/R, net)/Total Current Liabilities
Numerator: Cash $100 million + Marketable Securities $0 + A/R, net $600 million = $700 million
Denominator: $900 million
Acid test (or quick ratio) = $700 million/$900 million
Acid test (or quick ratio) = approximately 0.78

BEC 5-Q26 B83. The correct choice is D. The formula for calculating the quick ratio (also known as the acid-test ratio) is:

(Cash + Marketable Securities + A/R, net)/Current Liabilities.

Using an example where the numerator (the quick assets) is $80 and the denominator (the current liabilities) is $100, this is a quick ratio of 0.80. When selling obsolete inventory at a loss, this would increase cash (assume cash increases by $5) so that the quick ratio would be calculated as:

($80 + $5)/$100 = $85/$100 = 0.85, which is an increase over 0.80.

Choice A is not correct because purchasing inventory through the issuance of a long-term note would not affect the numerator (the quick assets) or the denominator (the current liabilities); inventory is not a quick asset and a long-term note is not a current liability.

Choice B is not correct because collecting accounts receivable faster merely increases cash and decreases A/R, net for the same amount, meaning that one quick asset is substituted for another quick asset and the numerator of the quick ratio is unaffected; the denominator is likewise unaffected.

Choice C is not correct because paying an existing account payable decreases the numerator and the denominator by equal amounts and makes the quick ratio lower, not higher. For example, assuming that the A/P paid was $10:

Numerator: $80 – $10 = $70
Denominator: $100 – $10 = $90
Quick Ratio = $70/$90 = approximately 0.78, which is lower than the original 0.80 in our example.

BEC 5-Q27 B1071. The correct answer is D. A credit manager considering whether to grant trade credit to a new customer is most likely to place primary emphasis on liquidity ratios because they measure a company's ability to convert assets to cash, so it can meet its short-term obligations as they come due.

Answer A is incorrect because profitability ratios measure how effective a firm is generating profit from operations.

Answer B is incorrect because debt utilization ratios measure the effectiveness of how assets are financed and are used to evaluate financial leverage.

Answer C is incorrect because market ratios utilize the market value of the company's common stock.

BEC 5-Q28 B957. The correct answer is D. Grimaldi's quick (acid test) ratio is calculated as follows:

(Current assets – Inventory)/Current liabilities

($62,000 + $35,000 + $47,000)/($84,000 + $11,000) = 1.52

BEC 5-Q29 B961. The correct answer is B. The quick (acid test) quick ratio is:

Quick (acid test) ratio = (Current assets – Inventory) / Current liabilities

If Garstka sells the parts on account, it will increase its acid test ratio because the transaction will increase accounts receivable, which will increase the numerator of the ratio. Inventory is not included in the ratio so the change in inventory will not affect the ratio.

BEC 5-Q30 B967. The correct answer is B. The quick (acid test) ratio is:

Quick (acid test) ratio = (Current assets – Inventory) / Current liabilities

Another way of stating the quick (acid teat) ratio is:

Quick (acid test) ratio = (Cash + Cash Equivalents + Marketable equity securities) / Current liabilities

The quick (acid test) ratio measures debt-paying ability using assets that are highly liquid, such as six-month treasury bills, accounts receivable and 60-day certificates of deposit. Prepaid insurance is excluded because they do not represent a current cash flow.

BEC 5-Q31 B965. The correct answer is D. Both the current ratio and the quick ratio compare components of current assets with current liabilities. The quick ratio does not include inventory in current assets because it may not be readily converted into cash. The disparity between the current and quick ratios can be explained by the high level of inventory.

BEC 5-Q32 B194. The correct choice is C. The accounts receivable turnover ratio is calculated as follows:

A/R Turnover = Net Sales/Average accounts receivable, net

Average A/R, net = (Beginning A/R, net + Ending A/R, net)/2
Average A/R, net = ($14,600 + $12,900)/2
Average A/R, net = $27,500/2
Average A/R, net = $13,750

A/R Turnover = $103,200/$13,750
A/R Turnover = 7.5

BEC 5-Q33 B149. The correct choice is C. The average collection period (of accounts receivable) is a measure of how quickly the accounts receivable are converted into cash. Both cash and accounts receivable are quick assets used in financial statement ratios on liquidity, such as the quick ratio (also known as the acid-test ratio) and current ratio.

Choice A is not correct because a company's financing is based on the mix of liabilities and shareholders' equity used to finance the assets. Financing could also be based on the mix of short-term and long-term debt in the liabilities.

Choice B is not correct because return on equity (ROE) is a financial statement ratio that measures profitability and is based on Net Income and Shareholders' Equity. The ROE ratio does not include the average collection period (of accounts receivable).

Choice D is not correct because operating profitability is based on sales and expenses and does not include the average collection period (of accounts receivable).

BEC 5-Q34 B258. The correct choice is B. The average collection period in days is calculated as follows:

7 days	0.70 of customers x 10 days
9 days	0.30 of customers x 30 days
16 days	average collection period

Note that the formula for the average collection period in days of:

Average Collection Period in Days = 365 days/Accounts Receivable Turnover

could not be used because the information to calculate the accounts receivable turnover (which is net sales divided by the average accounts receivable, net) was not provided.

BEC 5-Q35 B307. The correct choice is A. The days sales outstanding ratio measures the average time needed to collect the receivables and is calculated as:

Days Sales Outstanding = 365 days/Accounts Receivable Turnover

The accounts receivable turnover ratio measures how many times a year the A/R revolves (i.e., is collected) and is calculated as:

Accounts Receivable Turnover = Net Credit Sales/Average Accounts Receivable, Net

Both these measures are appropriate for the evaluation of accounts receivable because they measure the efficiency of how accounts receivable are turned into cash.

Choice B is not correct because the return on assets (ROA) is a measure of profitability and is calculated as:

ROA = Net Income/Average Total Assets

Choice C is not correct because collections of accounts receivable are generally not compared to debt outstanding.

Choice D is not correct because the current ratio measures the firm's liquidity (i.e., the ability of the firm to pay its current liabilities are they come due) and is calculated as:

Current Ratio = Current Assets/Current Liabilities

BEC 5-Q36 B316. The correct choice is C. The number of day's sales in accounts receivable is calculated below:

6.0 days = (0.60 of customers that take the discount)(10 days)
12.0 days = (0.40 of customers that do not take the discount)(30 days)

18.0 days for days' sales in accounts receivable

Note that the typical formula for the number of days' sales in accounts receivable of:

Number of days' sales in accounts receivable = 365 days/Accounts Receivable turnover

is not used because the information to calculate the A/R turnover is not provided in the question (i.e., values for net credit sales and beginning and ending accounts receivable, net. The formula for the A/R turnover is:

Accounts Receivable Turnover = Net credit Sales/Average accounts receivable, net

BEC 5-Q37 B986. The correct answer is C. The formula for the accounts receivable turnover ratio is:

Credit sales/Average accounts receivable

Maydale's accounts receivable turnover ratio is calculated as follows:
Credit sales/Average accounts receivable
$3,600,000/(($320,000 + $400,000)/2)
$3,600,000/$360,000
10.00

BEC 5-Q38 B78. The correct choice is B. The first step to solve this problem is to calculate the cost of goods sold (COGS) using the periodic system inventory formula:

$17,000	Beginning Inventory	
+ 56,000	Cost of Goods Purchased	
= 73,000	Cost of Goods Available for Sale	
− 13,000	Ending Inventory	
= $60,000	Cost of Goods Sold	

The inventory turnover ratio is calculated as Cost of Goods Sold/Average Inventory.

Numerator: Cost of Goods Sold $60,000
Denominator: (Beginning Inventory $17,000 + Ending Inventory $13,000)/2 = $15,000

Inventory Turnover = $60,000/$15,000 = 4

BEC 5-Q39 B189. The correct choice is D. The question is solved in three steps. In step 1, solve for the average inventory:

Average Inventory = (Beginning Inventory + Ending Inventory)/2
Average Inventory = [(0.15 x Prior year's sales $2,125,000) + (0.22 x Current year's sales $2,525,000)]/2
Average Inventory = ($318,750 + $555,500)/2
Average Inventory = $874,250/2
Average Inventory = $437,125

In step 2, solve for cost of goods sold in the current year:

$2,525,000	Sales
− 1,515,000	Cost of Goods Sold (0.6 x $2,525,000)
= $1,010,000	Gross Profit (0.4 x $2,525,000)

In step 3, solve for inventory turnover:

Inventory Turnover = Cost of Goods Sold/Average Inventory
Inventory Turnover = $1,515,000/$437,125
Inventory Turnover = 3.47

BEC 5-Q40 B376. The correct choice is C. The inventory conversion period is the number of days needed to manufacture the product and sell it, from inputs to final product to sale. The inventory turnover is the number of times per year that the inventory is sold. The number of times per year (360 days) that Green turns over its inventory is calculated as:

Inventory turnover = Days in the year/Inventory conversion period
Inventory turnover = 360 days/80 days
Inventory turnover = 4.5 times

BEC 5-Q41 B987. The correct answer is D. The formula for the inventory turnover ratio is:
Cost of goods sold/Average inventory

The formula for the accounts receivable turnover ratio is:
Credit sales/Average accounts receivable

Both Zubin's inventory turnover and accounts receivable turnover ratios will decrease under these scenarios. If cost of goods sold and credit sales both decline, the value of both ratios will decline.

BEC 5-Q42 B156. The correct choice is D. The formula for Residual Income is:

Residual Income = NOPAT – (interest rate x Investment)

where NOPAT = Net Operating Profit After Taxes, but we will use Net Income instead of NOPAT to solve this question because NOPAT is not available.

The first step in solving this question is to use the Asset Turnover formula to derive the Average Total Assets (also known as the amount of the investment).

Asset Turnover = Net Sales/Average Total Assets
1.5 = $750,000/Average Total Assets
1.5 x Average Total Assets = $750,000
Average Total Assets = $750,000/1.5
Average Total Assets = $500,000

The second step in solving this question is to use the Return on Sales formula to derive the Net Income.

Return on Sales = Net Income/Net Sales
0.08 = Net Income/$750,000
0.08 x $750,000 = Net Income
$60,000 = Net Income

The last step in solving this question is to plug in the values for Average Total Assets (also known as Investment) and Net Income (used instead of NOPAT because NOPAT is not available) to solve for Residual Income:

Residual Income = Net Income $60,000 – (0.12 x $500,000)
Residual Income = $60,000 – $60,000
Residual Income = $0

BEC 5-Q43 B158. The correct choice is B. Yearly sales are calculated below using the Asset (or Investment) Turnover. The Asset Turnover formula is:

Asset Turnover = Net Sales/Average Total Assets

The Average Total Assets is the average of the beginning and ending balances of the plant assets' book values, which is ($22 million + $18 million)/2 = $40 million/2 = $20 million.

2.5 = Net Sales/$20,000,000
2.5 x $20,000,000 = Net Sales
$50,000,000 = Net Sales

BEC 5-Q44 B176. The correct choice is A. The first step is to solve for EBIT, by setting the two scenarios equal to each other.

Scenario of issuing $100,000 debt at 9%:
Net Income, which is [EBIT x (1 – 0.40 tax rate)] – Interest Expense $9,000, net of tax (1 – 0.40 tax rate)
Weighted-average number of common shares outstanding 1,000

equal to

Scenario of issuing 500 shares of common stock:
Net Income, which is [EBIT x (1 – 0.40 tax rate)]
Wtd avg # c/s shares o/s 1,000 + 500

So, to solve:
$$\frac{0.60 \text{ EBIT} - \$5,400}{1,000} = \frac{0.60 \text{ EBIT}}{1,500}$$

1,500 (0.60 EBIT – $5,400) = 1,000 (0.60 EBIT)
900 EBIT – $8,100,000 = 600 EBIT
300 EBIT = $8,100,000
EBIT = $8,100,000/300
EBIT = $27,000

The second step is to plug EBIT of $27,000 into the earnings per share formula:

$$\text{EPS} = \frac{0.60 \text{ EBIT}}{1,500}$$

$$\text{EPS} = \frac{0.60(\$27,000)}{1,500}$$

EPS = $16,200/1,500
EPS = $10.80

BEC 5-Q45 B1007. The correct answer is C. The price/earnings ratio formula is:
Stock price per share / Earnings per share

Devlin's price/earnings ratio is calculated as follows:
Market price per share ÷ Earnings per share
$34 / $4.80
7.08

BEC 5-Q46 B1008. The correct answer is B. The price-earnings ratio is:
Price-earnings ratio = Market price per share / Earnings per share

Earnings per share:
(Net income − Preferred dividends)/ Common shares outstanding
($588,000 − ($6 x 10,000)) / 120,000
$528,000 / 120,000
$4.40

Price-earnings ratio:
Market price per share/Earnings per share
$40 / $4.40
9.09

BEC 5-Q47 B1009. The correct answer is D. To determine how Archer's stock compares to the average price/earnings ratio for the industry of 14.00, calculate Archer's price-earnings ratio. The price-earnings ratio is:

Price-earnings ratio = Market price per share / Earnings per share

Archer's price-earnings ratio is 11.25 ($36/$3.20), which represents an undervaluation of 2.75 (14.00 − 11.25), or 24.4% (2.75/11.25).

BEC 5-Q48 B1010. The correct answer is A. The price-earnings ratio (also referred to as the multiple), measures the relationship between the price of a company's stock related to the company's earnings per share. The price earnings ratio formula is:

Price-earnings ratio = Market price per share / Earnings per share

Because earnings per share is the denominator, an increase in earnings per share compared to no change in the numerator (market price per share), will result in a decrease of the overall ratio.

BEC 5-Q49 B98. The correct choice is B. The four perspectives in the Balanced Scorecard framework of performance measurement are the financial perspective, customer perspective, internal business processes perspective, and learning and growth perspective. The learning and growth perspective may also be called the innovation perspective because the learning and growth perspective measures research and development, which deal with innovation.

Choice A is not correct because just in time inventory methods implement activity-based costing principles to reduce the non-value added costs of inventory.

Choice C is not correct because benchmarking is the performance measurement technique of comparing your actual performance measures against ideal measures or "benchmarks."

Choice D is not correct because ABC is a costing methodology that is based on two principles: reducing or eliminating non-value added activities and allocating overhead costs based on the consumption of cost drivers in accordance with a cause-and-effect relationship.

BEC 5-Q50 B342. The correct choice is C. The learning and growth perspective of the balanced scorecard focuses on measures with regard to employee satisfaction and research and development, e.g., employee retention, employee training, and research and development expenditures per employee.

Choice A is not correct because the customer perspective of the balanced scorecard focuses on measures with regard to customers and markets, not employee satisfaction and retention measures.

Choice B is not correct because the internal business process perspective of the balanced scorecard focuses on measures with regard to operational effectiveness and efficiency, e.g., percentage of defective units, factory rework, and cycle time, not employee satisfaction and retention measures.

Choice D is not correct because the financial perspective of the balanced scorecard focuses on measures with regard to financial statements, e.g., profitability and asset utilization, not employee satisfaction and retention measures.

BEC 5-Q51 B308. The correct choice is B. In general, the customer perspective of the balanced scorecard focuses on measures with regard to customers and markets. Therefore, the customer perspective of the balanced scorecard examines a company's success in targeted market segments.

Choice A is not correct because the financial perspective of the balanced scorecard focuses on measures with regard to financial statements, e.g., profitability and asset utilization.

Choice C is not correct because the internal business process perspective of the balanced scorecard focuses on measures with regard to operational effectiveness and efficiency, e.g., percentage of defective units, factory rework, and cycle time.

Choice D is not correct because the learning and growth perspective of the balanced scorecard focuses on measures with regard to employee satisfaction and research development, e.g., employee retention, employee training, and research and development expenditures per employee.

BEC 5-Q52 B202. The correct choice is C. A benchmark involves comparisons between current performance and optimum performance. Management of a company could compare and contrast its financial information (current performance) to published information reflecting optimal amounts (optimum performance, e.g., the financial statements of a publicly traded competitor with the largest market share).

Choice A is not correct because a budget is a forecast of the company's future financial performance, often expressed as a master budget that encompasses the entire operations of the company, including sales forecasts, beginning and ending inventory levels, production costs, capital expenditures, operating expenses (e.g., selling, general and administrative, and research and development expenses), cash inflows and outflows, and budgeted financial statements (income statement, balance sheet, and statement of cash flows).

Choice B is not correct because a forecast predicts a company's future performance with regard to future financial or non-financial performance or future economic conditions, e.g., number of motor vehicles sold or interest rates on loans used to finance purchases of motor vehicles.

Choice D is not correct because applying best practices to the company's operations is a method used to help achieve benchmarks.

BEC 5-Q53 B80. The correct choice is D. Prevention costs and appraisal costs are conformance costs; conformance costs in the first year increased $25,000 from $70,000 to $95,000. Internal failure costs and external failure costs are nonconformance costs; nonconformance costs decreased $40,000 from $155,000 to $115,000. The quality program has been a success because conformance costs increased only $25,000, but nonconformance costs decreased $40,000, resulting in a $15,000 savings.

Choices A and B are not correct because conformance costs increased $25,000 and nonconformance costs decreased $40,000.

Choice C is not correct because the quality program has been a success; if conformance costs increased $25,000 and nonconformance costs decreased $40,000, there has been a savings of $15,000.

BEC 5-Q54 B315. The correct choice is D. Product costs are the costs that are inventoriable as inventory in a retail firm or work-in-process and finished goods inventory in a manufacturing firm; the product costs (inventoriable costs) are eventually transferred to cost of goods sold at the time the goods are sold. The accounting for product costs presented on the financial statements must comply with U.S. GAAP and IFRS.

Choice A is not correct because relevant costs are considered in differential cost decisions where the relevant costs are those costs that would differ between two alternatives; costs that do not differ between two alternatives are not relevant to the differential cost decision.

Choice B is not correct because period costs are costs such as selling expenses, general and administrative expenses, and research and development expenses. Period costs are not inventoriable. The accounting for period costs presented on the financial statements must comply with U.S. GAAP and IFRS.

Choice C is not correct because opportunity cost is the cost of benefits forgone when choosing one alternative versus another alternative. Opportunity costs are not considered as product/inventoriable costs.

BEC 5-Q55 B330. The correct choice is B.

The amount that management should budget for cost of goods manufactured (COGM) is calculated below:

$230 per unit	DM/unit, revised ($200 + $30)
60 per unit	DL/unit, revised (4 DL hours/unit x 0.75 x $20/hour)
216 per unit	Manufacturing OH, revised (DL costs $60 x 3.6)
$506 per unit	Cost per unit

COGM = $506/unit x 10,000 units
COGM = $5,060,000

BEC 5-Q56 B65. The correct choice is D. Electricity is a utility cost; utilities are a type of manufacturing overhead. Conversion costs consist of direct labor used and manufacturing overhead applied. Therefore, if utilities costs increased, then conversion costs would likely increase.

Choices A and B are not correct because an increase in utilities costs, a manufacturing overhead cost, will not likely increase direct materials costs and direct labor costs.

Choice C is not correct because direct materials used and direct labor used are prime costs; an increase in utilities costs, a manufacturing overhead cost, will not likely increase direct materials costs and direct labor costs.

BEC 5-Q57 B267. The correct choice is D. Conversion costs consist of direct labor used and manufacturing overhead. To solve this question, use the T accounts from the flow of costs, but start with the finished goods inventory T account and solve for cost of goods manufactured (COGM) of $12,200. Then put COGM of $12,200 into the work-in-process (WIP) T account. Then, solve for direct materials used of $5,700 in the direct materials T account. Note that WIP has beginning and ending balances of zero. Finally, solve for conversion costs by subtracting the DM used of $5,700 from the total production costs of $12,200.

Finished Goods			
Begin.	1,200		
COGM	12,200		
COGAS	13,400	12,000	COGS
Ending	1,400		

Work-In-Process			
Begin.	0		
DM Used	5,700		
CC (plug)	6,500		
Total	12,200		
To a/c for	12,200	12,200	COGM
Ending	0		

Direct Materials			
Begin.	500		
Purchases	6,000		
DM (plug)	6,500		DM (plug)
Ending	800		

BEC 5-Q58 B355. The correct choice is A. Production costs are direct materials used, direct labor used, and manufacturing overhead. Prime costs are direct materials used and direct labor used; conversion costs are direct labor used and manufacturing overhead.

Choice B is not correct because prime costs are direct materials used and direct labor used; prime costs do not include manufacturing overhead.

Choice C is not correct because prime costs are direct materials used and direct labor used; conversion costs are direct labor used and manufacturing overhead.

Choice D is not correct because production costs are direct materials used, direct labor used, and manufacturing overhead; prime costs are direct materials used and direct labor used.

BEC 5-Q59 B42. The correct choice is C. Gross profit (or gross margin) is calculated as Net Sales – Cost of Goods Sold (COGS). To calculate gross profit, we must first calculate COGS. The calculation of COGS using T accounts in the flow of costs (in 000's of dollars) is presented below.

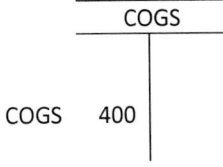

	WIP				FGI		
Beg.	500			Beg.	100		
	700			COGM	800		
S/T	1200	800	COGM	COGAS	900		
						400	COGS
End.	400			End.	500		

COGS	
COGS 400	

Gross Profit is calculated as Net Sales of $1,000,000 – COGS of $400,000 = $600,000.

Note that in WIP, the subtotal of $700,000 consists of the current period's Indirect manufacturing costs of $500,000 and $200,000 (plugged) of DM and DL used. Therefore, answer A is not correct because it is the DM and DL used.

Answer B is not correct because it is COGS.

Answer D is not correct because it is Cost of Goods Available for Sale (COGAS).

BEC 5-Q60 B262. The correct choice is B. The ending inventory is calculated in the T account for work in process (WIP) below. Note that the direct labor of $40,000 is already included in the total production costs of $60,000. Also, because cost of goods manufactured (COGM, the credit to WIP and debit to finished goods inventory) is not provided, we assume that cost of goods manufactured is the same as cost of goods sold (COGS).

Work in Process			
Beginning Bal.	5,000		
Total Production Costs	60,000		
Costs to a/c for	65,000	55,000	COGM or COGS
Ending Bal. (plug)	10,000		

BEC 5-Q61 B318. The correct choice is B. The question is solved below using the T account for finished goods inventory. However, the T account is in units of inventory instead of dollars.

Finished Goods Inventory			
Beg. Inventory	85		
Units manufactured (plug)	1,015		
Units available for sale (plug)	1,100	1,000	Units sold
End. Inventory	100		

Note that the prior-year beginning inventory was not needed to solve the question.

BEC 5-Q62 B251. The correct choice is D. A good way to solve budgeting problems is to use the T accounts from the flow of costs, but instead of dollars, use units of finished goods and units of direct materials. Because the problem does not mention work-in-process inventories, we may assume that beginning and ending WIP inventories are zero and omit WIP from the solution.

Note that the January 31 DM ending balance of 3,280 tires is based on 10 percent of the February production of 16,400 bikes (16,400 x 0.10 x 2 tires/bike) and that the February production of 16,400 bikes requires two months of analysis for the FGI T account.

Finished Goods (Bikes)

Begin. Jan. 1	2,000		
Production and DM Used (plug)	13,200		
		12,000	COGS Jan. Sales
COGAS (plug)	15,200		
Ending Jan. 31 20% x 16,000	3,200		
Production and DM Used (plug)	16,400		
		16,000	COGS Feb. Sales
COGAS (plug)	19,600		
Ending Feb. 28 20% x 18,000	3,600		

Finished Goods (Bags)

Begin. June 1	15,000		
Production and DM Used (plug)	83,000		
		80,000	COGS June Sales
COGAS (plug)	98,000		
Ending June 30	18,000		

Direct Materials (Potatoes)

Begin. June 1	27,000		
Purch. (plug)	411,000		
DM Available	438,000	415,000	DM Used 83,000 x 5
Ending June 30	23,000		

Direct Materials (Tires)

Begin. Jan. 1	3,000		
Purch. (plug)	26,680		
DM Available (plug)	29,680	26,400	DM Used 13,200 x 2
Ending Jan. 31 10% x 16,400 x 2/bike	3,280		

BEC 5-Q63 B266. The correct choice is C. A good way to solve budgeting problems is to use the T accounts from the flow of costs, but instead of dollars, use units of finished goods and units of direct materials. Because the problem does not mention work-in-process inventories, we may assume that beginning and ending WIP inventories are zero and omit WIP from the solution.

Note that it takes 5 units of DM (5 potatoes) to create one unit of FGI (1 bag of chips).

BEC 5-Q64 B323. The correct choice is C. The amount of overhead that should be applied to this job is calculated in two steps. First, calculate the overhead rate per direct labor hour. Second, apply the overhead rate based on the actual 1,500 direct labor hours used.

Step 1. Calculate the overhead rate per direct labor hour.

($25,000 Budg. Fixed Manuf. OH + $50,000 Budg. Variable Manuf. OH)/20,000 Budgeted DL hours

= $75,000/20,000 DL hours
= $3.75 per DL hour

in this question, we assume that the 20,00 budgeted DL hours is the normal capacity for fixed manufacturing overhead and the estimated actual activity level for variable manufacturing overhead.

Step 2. Apply the overhead rate based on the actual 1,500 DL hours used.

1,500 DL hours x $3.75 per DL hour = $5,625

BEC 5-Q65 B199. The correct choice is D. The estimated product cost of the proposed job is calculated below.

Materials handling = $120,000 expected costs/80,000 estimated DL hours
= $1.50/DL hour
Quality inspection = $200,000 expected costs/80,000 estimated DL hours
= $2.50/DL hour

$4,000	Direct materials
6,000	Direct labor
3,000	Materials handling (2,000 DL hours x $1.50/DL hour)
5,000	Quality inspection (2,000 DL hours x $2.50/DL hour)
$18,000	Estimated product cost

BEC 5-Q66 B100. The correct choice is C. The problem may be solved using the four steps for EFUs/Equivalent Finished Units (also known as EUPs/Equivalent Units of Production) in process costing. Note that there is no beginning inventory; therefore, it does not matter which method is used to solve the problem and either FIFO or weighted-average methods will yield the same results.

Step 1. Calculate the number of units shipped/transferred out/completed (in whole units).

Beginning Inventory	0
+ # Started	15,000
= # to account for	15,000
− Ending Inventory	1,500
= # of units shipped	13,500

Step 2. Calculate the number of EFUs.

		DM		CC	
# of units shipped	(100%)	13,500		13,500	(100%)
+ Ending Inventory	(100%)	1,500		375	(25%)
= # EFUs (wtd avg)		15,000		13,875	

Step 3. Calculate the Cost per EFU.

	DM	CC
Beginning + Current Costs	$0 + $75,000	$0 + $55,500
Divided by # EFUs	15,000	13,875
= Cost per EFU (wtd avg)	$5.00/EFU	$4.00/EFU

Step 4. Complete the WIP T Account.

		Work in Process	
Begin. Inv.	DM	$0	
	CC	0	
Curr. Costs	DM	$75,000	
	CC	55,500	
Costs to a/c for		$130,500	COGM (Plugged) $121,500
Ending Inv.	DM	$7,500	
	CC	$1,500	
Total End		$9,000	

Ending Inventory for DM is calculated as 1,500 EFUs x $5.00/EFU = $7,500.
Ending Inventory for CC is calculated as 375 EFUs x $4.00/EFU = $1,500.

This is a total of $9,000 for Ending Inventory, which is subtracted from $130,500 of costs to account for to arrive at Cost of Goods Manufactured (COGM) of $121,500, which is also the costs transferred out of WIP.

BEC 5-Q67 B203. The correct choice is A. When computing the number of equivalent units in process costing, the formulas for the first and second steps of process costing when applying the FIFO and weighted-average methods are described below.

Step 1. Calculate, in whole units, the number of units shipped (also known as units completed or units transferred out

Beginning Inventory
+ Number of units started
= Number of units to account for
− Ending Inventory
= Number of units shipped (or completed or transferred out)

Step 2. Calculate the number of equivalent units of production (EUPs)

FIFO method
Number of units shipped (100% complete)
+ Ending inventory (X% complete)
− Ending inventory (X% complete)
= FIFO EUPs

Weighted-average method
Number of units shipped (100% complete)
<u>+ Beginning inventory (X% complete)</u>
= Weighted-average EUPs

The starting point for step 2 is the number of units shipped (or completed or transferred out) from step 1. As can be seen from the FIFO versus weighted-average formulas for calculating the number of EUPs (step 2), the FIFO method subtracts the beginning inventory, whereas the weighted-average method does not. Therefore, if beginning inventory is zero, then FIFO EUPs will equal weighted-average EUPS.

Choice B is not correct because both FIFO and the weighted-average methods include ending inventory in their calculation of EUPs; a zero ending inventory will not render the same number of EUPs under both methods if a beginning inventory exists.

Choices C and D are not correct because the FIFO method subtracts the beginning inventory, whereas the weighted-average method does not subtract the beginning inventory when calculating the number of EUPs. Therefore, if beginning inventory and ending exist, then the FIFO method will yield a lower number of EUPs than the weighted-average method.

BEC 5-Q68 B298. The correct choice is A. The number of equivalent finished units (EFUs) using the first-in, first-out method (FIFO) is calculated below.

Step 1. Calculate the number shipped (or completed or transferred out, in whole units)

10,000 units	Beginning inventory
+ 150,000 units	Units started
= 160,000 units	Units to be accounted for
− 20,000 units	Ending inventory
= 140,000 units	Units shipped

Step 2. Calculate the EFUs (FIFO Method)

140,000 units	Units shipped (from Step 1)
+ 5,000 units	Ending inventory (20,000 units x 0.25 complete)
= 145,000 units	Subtotal (the correct answer if using weighted average method)
− 7,000 units	Beginning inventory (10,000 units x 0.70 complete)
138,000 units	EFUs, FIFO method

BEC 5-Q69 B332. The correct choice is C. Ending inventory consists of both direct materials and conversion costs. The total cost of the June 30 work in process inventory is calculated below:

$200,000   DM costs (40,000 x 100% complete with respect to materials x $5/EFU)
 168,000   CC costs (40,000 x 60% complete with respect to conversion x $7/EFU)
$368,000   Total cost of the June 30 WIP inventory

Note: EFU is equivalent finished unit.

BEC 5-Q70 B370. The correct choice is C. A disadvantage of using a process costing system is that it must calculate the number of equivalent units of production based on the units' stage of completion and the stage of completion may differ between materials and conversion cost (e.g., units may be 100 percent complete as to materials, but only 50 percent complete as to conversion). The determination of the completeness of the units is a disadvantage of the process costing system when compared to the job-order costing system.

Choice A is not correct because cost of goods sold consists of completed units and the cost of completed units has already been calculated in both the process costing and job-order costing systems by the time the goods are sold. Therefore, at the stage when goods are sold, neither method has advantages or disadvantages.

Choice B is not correct because both the process costing system and the job-order costing system accurately charge materials and labor to units produced; both systems use full costing as required by U.S. GAAP.

Choice D is not correct because both the process costing system and the job-order costing system require recordkeeping (e.g., percentage of completion in the process costing system and job cost sheets in the job-order costing system); however, the recordkeeping used in both systems may be automated and reduce the clerical work level.

BEC 5-Q71 B99. The correct choice is D. The calculation for price per pound for premium coffee using the new ABC method is presented below.

	Overhead for the current month	Cost pool for separating and roasting beans	Cost pool for packing and shipping
	$5,000.00	$3,500.00	$1,500.00
Regular		150 MH	500 pounds
Premium		550 MH	500 pounds
Total		700 MH	1,000 pounds
Unit cost		$5.00/MH	$1.50/pound

Premium Coffee, 500 pounds:

DM: 500 pounds x $1.50/pound = $750.00
DL: 500 MH x $1.25 = $625.00

Roasting:
550 MH x $5.00/MH = $2,750.00
Packing/Shipping:
500 pounds x $1.50/pound = $750.00

Total costs, 500 pounds: $4,875.00
Cost per pound: $4,875.00/500 pounds = $9.75

BEC 5-Q72 B139. The correct choice is C. Activity-based costing (ABC) allocates costs based on a cause and effect relationship between cost pools and the cost drivers that increase costs in the cost pools. Therefore, if the client produces different types of products which consume resources in a different manner, an ABC system would allocate the costs in each cost pool to each product type based on its consumption of the cost driver, resulting in a more accurate cost allocation based on cause and effect factors.

Choice A is not correct because if the client produces only one type of product, then the allocation of costs among different product types is not required.

Choice B is not correct because if most of the client's costs are classified as direct costs, then the direct costs may be traced directly to the products; therefore, indirect costs (e.g., manufacturing overhead) are less material and their method of allocation (an ABC system versus a traditional system) will have less of an impact.

Choice D is not correct. An ABC system would allocate the costs in each cost pool to each product type based on its consumption of the cost driver, resulting in a more accurate cost allocation based on cause and effect factors. However, because the client produces the types of products that consume resources in the same manner, an ABC system would produce fewer benefits.

BEC 5-Q73 B160. The correct choice is A. The allocated costs using an activity-based system are calculated below.

Total Setup Hours = 500 for X + 1,500 for Y = 2,000 setup hours

Ratio of hours = 500/2,000 for X and 1,500/2,000 for Y, which is 0.25 for X and 0.75 for Y

Allocation of costs:
  $400,000 setup costs to be allocated x 0.25 for X = $100,000 allocated to X
  $400,000 setup costs to be allocated x 0.75 for Y = $300,000 allocated to Y

BEC 5-Q74 B269. The correct choice is C. In activity-based costing, the most significant nonvalue-added costs are associated with inventory and costs associated with poor quality. Therefore, the cost of moving, handling and storing individual products are costs associated with inventory.

Choice A is not correct because the cost of materials that cannot be traced to any individual product are indirect materials; indirect materials is a type of manufacturing overhead and is considered a product cost (a value-added cost), not a nonvalue-added cost.

Choice B is not correct because the cost of labor that cannot be traced to any individual product is indirect labor; indirect labor is a type of manufacturing overhead and is considered a product cost (a value-added cost), not a nonvalue-added cost.

Choice D is not correct because additional resources consumed to produce any individual product are variable product costs, such as direct materials used, direct labor used, and variable manufacturing overhead applied; these product costs are value-added, not nonvalue-added.

BEC 5-Q75 B331. The correct choice is D.

The amount of the joint costs that would be allocated to the white breast meat on a relative sales value basis is calculated below: below:

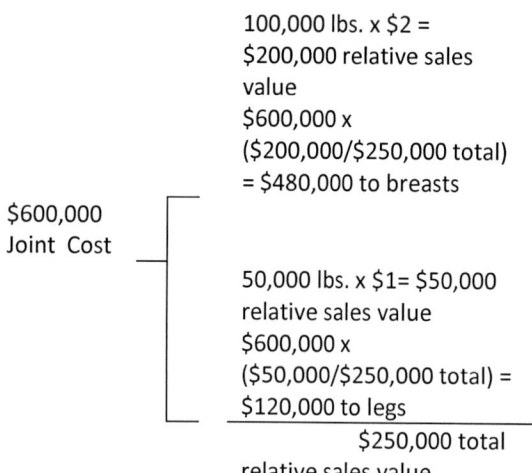

$600,000 Joint Cost

100,000 lbs. x $2 = $200,000 relative sales value
$600,000 x ($200,000/$250,000 total) = $480,000 to breasts

50,000 lbs. x $1= $50,000 relative sales value
$600,000 x ($50,000/$250,000 total) = $120,000 to legs

$250,000 total relative sales value

Therefore, $480,000 of the $600,000 joint cost is allocated to white breast meat.

BEC 5-Q76 B324. The correct choice is D. The amount of joint cost for each production run allocated to Product X on a physical quantity basis is calculated below:

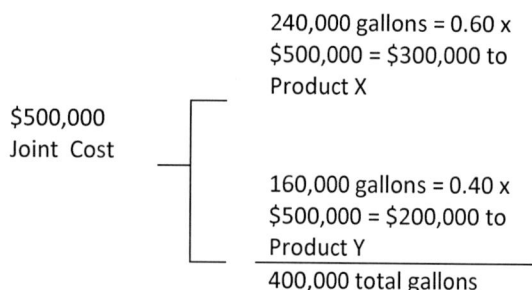

$500,000 Joint Cost

240,000 gallons = 0.60 x $500,000 = $300,000 to Product X

160,000 gallons = 0.40 x $500,000 = $200,000 to Product Y

400,000 total gallons

Therefore, $300,000 of the $500,000 joint cost is allocated to Product X.

BEC 5-Q77 B200. The correct choice is B. When costing inventory, joint costing involves allocating a common cost that must be incurred in order to produce multiple types of products; e.g., a barrel of oil is a common cost to producing gasoline, kerosene, and heating oil. Various methods may be used to allocate the common cost, including the sales value at split-off method (this method must be used if a sales value at split-off exists), physical measures, or a constant gross margin percentage of net realizable value. Using flexible budget amounts is not a basic approach for allocating costs in joint cost situations.

Choices A, C, and D are not correct because using flexible budget amounts is not a basic approach to allocating costs for costing inventory in joint cost situations. When costing inventory, joint costing involves allocating a common cost that must be incurred in order to produce multiple types of products; e.g., a barrel of oil is a common cost when producing gasoline, kerosene, and heating oil from the same barrel of oil. Various methods may be used to allocate the common cost, including the sales value at split-off method (this method must be used if a sales value at split-off exists), physical measures, or a constant gross margin percentage of net realizable value.

BEC 5-Q78 B335. The correct choice is A.

Using the regression formula of
y = a + bx

or

Total costs = Total fixed costs + total variable costs

where
y = the dependent variable, the total costs
a = the constant, the total fixed costs
b = the slope, or the variable cost per unit
x = the independent variable, the number of units within the relevant range
bx = total variable costs

If x equals zero, then

y = $322,897 + $b(0)
y = $322,897

Choice B is not correct because $322,897 as the intercept value is the constant, or total fixed costs.

Choice C is not correct because the residual error is disregarded in the cost formula using regression.

Choice D is not correct because y represents the total cost, not the average cost; $322,897 as the intercept value is the constant, or total fixed costs.

BEC 5-Q79 B50. The correct choice is C. The difference between absorption costing and variable costing is that absorption costing treats fixed manufacturing overhead as a product cost, whereas variable costing treats fixed manufacturing overhead as a period cost. Therefore, whenever production exceeds sales, ending inventories increase and in absorption costing, the fixed manufacturing overhead is inventoried into finished goods inventory and causes FGI to increase; because FGI increases, COGS decreases, and income increases. An easier way to think about this is that in absorption costing, the income follows the ending inventory. So, when production > sales, ending inventories increase, and income under absorption costing increases and is higher than income under variable costing.

Choices A and B are not correct because when production equals sales, absorption costing income equals variable costing income.

Choice D is not correct because when production is less than sales, ending inventories decrease and absorption costing income is less than variable costing income.

BEC 5-Q80 B268. The correct choice is B. Absorption costing (also known as full costing) is used for external financial reporting and is required for compliance with U.S. GAAP. Variable costing (also known as direct costing) is used for internal decision making; variable costing is not allowed for external financial reporting because it does not comply with U.S. GAAP. Therefore, only absorption costing is useful for external reporting purposes.

Choice A is not correct because variable costing (also known as direct costing) is used for internal decision making; variable costing is not allowed for external financial reporting because it does not comply with U.S. GAAP.

Choice C is not correct because only absorption costing (also known as full costing) is used for external financial reporting and is required for compliance with U.S. GAAP. Variable costing (also known as direct costing) is not allowed for external financial reporting because it does not comply with U.S. GAAP.

Choice D is not correct because absorption costing (also known as full costing) is used for external financial reporting and is required for compliance with U.S. GAAP.

BEC 5-Q81 B334. The correct choice is B. The total contribution margin for the month under the variable costing approach is calculated in two steps.

Step 1. Calculate the contribution margin per unit
$80   Sales price per unit
− 40   VC per unit (variable costs only: $21 + $10 + $3 + $6)
= $40 CM per unit

Step 2. Using the number of units sold of 4,500 units, calculate the total contribution margin for the month
$40 CM/unit x 4,500 units = $180,000 total contribution margin

BEC 5-Q82 B345. The correct choice is A. The difference between absorption costing and variable costing is the treatment of the fixed manufacturing overhead (FMOH); both include the other production costs of direct materials used, direct labor used, and variable manufacturing overhead (VMOH) in the inventory accounts.

Absorption costing includes FMOH in work-in-process and finished goods inventories; variable costing treats FMOH as a period cost, not a product cost. When ending inventories increase, absorption costing ending inventory costs will be higher (due to including FMOH), cost of goods sold will be lower, and absorption costing will show a higher net income than variable costing. When ending inventories decrease, absorption costing ending inventories will be lower, cost of goods sold will be higher, and absorption costing will show lower net income than variable costing. Therefore, the difference between absorption costing and variable costing is the

Change in ending inventory x FMOH/unit
2,000 units increase in ending inventory x $30 = $60,000 higher net income in absorption costing

BEC 5-Q83 B333. The correct choice is A.

The calculation of the direct materials price variance is presented below. Because the SP/lb. is unknown, we solve algebraically as the difference between the second and third lines of the matrix:

second line: AQ Used 17,500 lbs. x SP ? = $?
third line: SQ Allow 17,000 lbs. x SP ? = $?

and we subtract the third line from the second line, keeping in mind that the difference is $2,500 to get:

```
  AQ Used 17,500 lbs. x SP ? = $ ?
- SQ Allow 17,000 lbs. x SP ? = $ ?
             500 lbs. x SP ? = $2,500
```
SP ? = $2,500/500 lbs.
SP ? = $5.00/lb.

Once the SP of $5.00/lb. is input into the matrix, we can solve as:

```
AQused     x    AP      = $70,000
17,500         $4.00/lb.
lbs.                      (given)      DM Price
                                       Variance
               (plug)                  $17,500
                                       Favorable
AQused     x    SP      = $87,500
17,500         $5.00/lb.
lbs.
                                       DM
                                       Quantity/Usage
                                       Variance
SQ         x    SP      = $85,000      $2,500
Allowed                                Unfavorable
Based on
Units
Produced

17,000         $5.00/lb.
lbs.
```

Note: This same matrix may also be used to calculate DL and VMOH variances.

BEC 5-Q84 B306. The correct choice is B. The total selling price variance for Central Winery is calculated below:

```
AQ              X    AP    = $303,700
A  8,000 units      $6.20    $49,600    Sales Price
B 33,000 units      $7.70    $254,100   Variance
                                        $8,300
                                        Unfavorable

AQ              X    SP    = $312,000
A  8,000 units      $6.00    $48,000
B 33,000 units      $8.00    $264,000
                                        Sales Volume
SQ Allowed      X    SP    =
Based on Units
Produced
```

The same matrix may be used to calculate direct materials, direct labor, and variable manufacturing overhead variances. However, the sales variances are variances in revenues and the DM, DL, and VMOH variances are variances in product costs. In DM, DL, and VMOH variances, as you go up the matrix, if the numbers are going up, then the variance is unfavorable; however, in sales variances, as you go up the matrix, if the numbers are going up, then the variance is favorable.

BEC 5-Q85 B311. The correct choice is C. The selling price variance is calculated below:

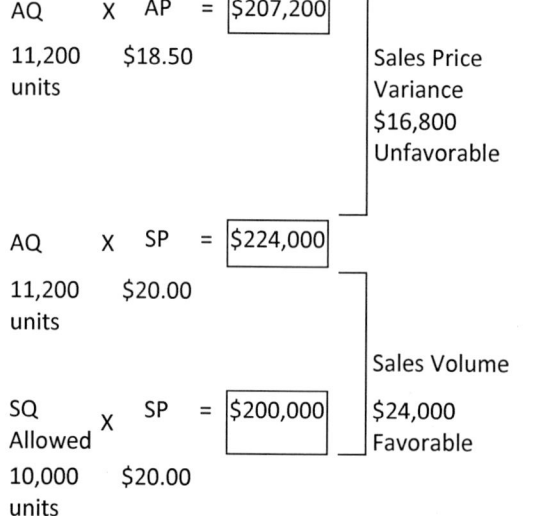

The same matrix may be used to calculate direct materials, direct labor, and variable manufacturing overhead variances. However, the sales variances are variances in revenues and the DM, DL, and VMOH variances are variances in product costs. In DM, DL, and VMOH variances, as you go up the matrix, if the numbers are going up, then the variance is unfavorable; however, in sales variances, as you go up the matrix, if the numbers are going up, then the variance is favorable.

BEC 5-Q86 B63. The correct choice is B. The DM efficiency variance may be calculated using the following matrix:

```
AQ Used   x   AP      = $27,000
9,000 ft.     $3.00/ft.
                                  DM Price
                                  Variance
                                  $9,000
                                  Unfavorable

AQ Used   x   SP      = $18,000
9,000 ft.     $2.00/ft.
                                  DM Quantity
                                  or Usage
                                  Variance

SQ        x   SP      = $17,000   $1,000
Allowed                           Unfavorable
Based on
Units
Produced
8,500 ft.     $2.00/ft.
```

The same matrix also be used to calculate the direct labor and variable manufacturing overhead variances.

BEC 5-Q87 B136. The correct choice is D. The direct material quantity variance may be calculated using the following matrix:

```
AQ         x   AP      = $24,700
6,500 lbs.     $3.80/lb.
                                   DM Price
                                   Variance
                                   $1,300
                                   Favorable

AQ         x   SP      = $26,000
6,500 lbs.     $4.00/lb.
                                   DM Usage or
                                   Efficiency
                                   Variance
SQ Allowed x   SP      = $24,000   $2,000
                                   Unfavorable
Based on
Units
Produced
6,000 lbs.     $4.00/lb.
```

The same matrix may also be used to calculate the direct labor and variable overhead variances.

BEC 5-Q88 B159. The correct choice is B. The direct labor (DL) efficiency (or usage) variance may be calculated using the following matrix:

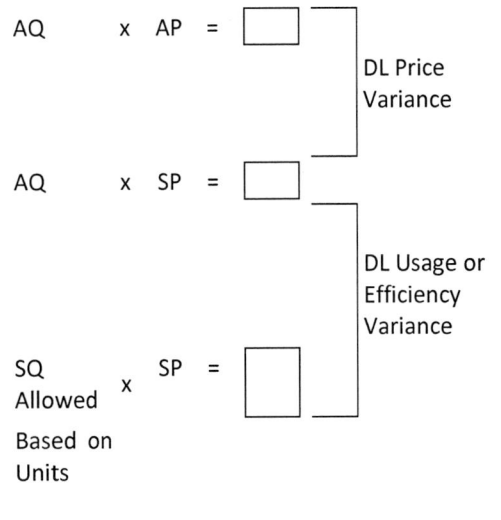

The difference between the middle and bottom lines of the matrix is the DL efficiency variance. When referring to the middle and bottom lines of the matrix, the SP (standard price or standard rate) is the same for both lines, but the quantities are different (AQ, actual quantity versus SQ allowed, standard quantity allowed). Therefore, the correct answer will involve differences in quantity. Because the DL efficiency is unfavorable, the AQ of DL hours used will be greater than the SQ allowed. Poorly maintained machinery will cause labor hours to increase because the machinery will either break down or be more difficult to use.

Choice A is not correct because an increase in wages will affect the AP (actual price or actual rate), not the number of DL hours used. The DL efficiency variance is based on the difference between the AQ (actual quantity) of DL hours and the SQ allowed (standard quantity allowed).

Choice C is not correct because highly skilled workers are more efficient and effective and will likely work fewer DL hours. The DL efficiency variance is based on the difference between the AQ (actual quantity) of DL hours and the SQ allowed (standard quantity allowed). If the AQ DL hours are less than the SQ allowed, then this would result in a favorable DL efficiency variance instead of an unfavorable variance.

Choice D is not correct because high quality materials are easier to work with and will likely result in fewer actual DL hours used. The DL efficiency variance is based on the difference between the AQ (actual quantity) of DL hours and the SQ allowed (standard quantity allowed). If the AQ DL hours are less than the SQ allowed, then this would result in a favorable DL efficiency variance instead of an unfavorable variance.

The same matrix may also be used to calculate the direct material and variable overhead variances.

BEC 5-Q89 B296. The correct choice is C. The calculation of the direct labor usage variance is presented below.

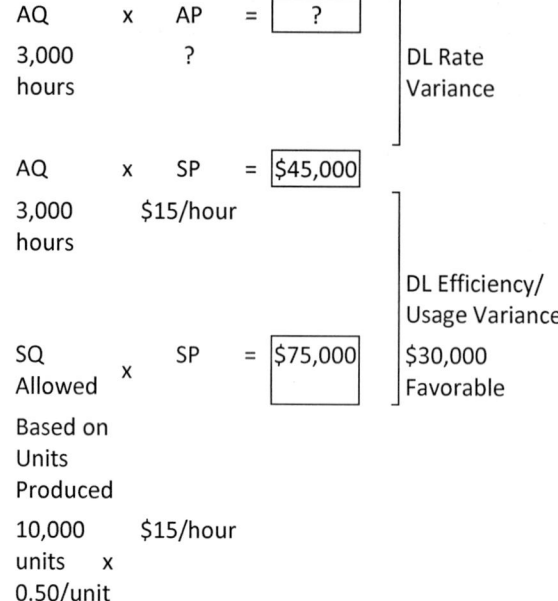

The DL rate variance could not be calculated because the actual labor costs or actual direct labor rate per hour was not provided. Note: This same matrix may also be used to calculate the direct materials and variable manufacturing overhead variances.

BEC 5-Q90 B85. The correct choice is B. The variable overhead spending variance may be calculated using the following matrix:

AQ	x	AP	= $200
25 hours		$8.00/hour	

VOH Spending Variance
$50 Favorable

AQ	x	SP	= $250
25 hours		$10.00/hour	

VOH Efficiency Variance

SQ Allowed Based on Units Produced	x	SP	= $200
20 hours		$10.00/hour	

$50 Unfavorable

The same matrix may also be used to calculate the direct materials and direct labor variances.

BEC 5-Q91 B82. The correct choice is A. The purchasing manager controls the actual cost of the direct materials purchased. Therefore, it is most likely that the purchasing manager would influence the direct materials price variance.

Choices B, C and D are not correct because the direct materials quantity variance, direct labor rate variance, and direct labor efficiency variance are variances most likely influenced by the production manager instead of the purchasing manager.

BEC 5-Q92 B137. The correct choice is B. Sales commissions are a variable expense based on sales. When actual sales are less than budget, then sales commissions would likewise be lower than budget, resulting in a favorable variance. However, building rent is likely to be a fixed cost; therefore, building rent expense would remain unchanged and would not result in a favorable budget.

Choice A is not correct because building rent is likely to be a fixed cost; therefore, expense for building rent would remain unchanged and would not result in a favorable budget.

Choice C is not correct because sales commissions are a variable expense based on sales. When actual sales are less than budget, then sales commissions would likewise be lower than budget, resulting in a favorable variance. Also, building rent is likely to be a fixed cost; therefore, expense for building rent would remain unchanged and would not result in a favorable budget.

Choice D is not correct because sales commissions are a variable expense based on sales. When actual sales are less than budget, then sales commissions would likewise be lower than budget, resulting in favorable variance.

BEC 5-Q93 B1258. The correct answer choice is C. Assimilation takes place in an acquisition when the acquired company accepts and adopts the acquiring company's culture. Assimilation assumes that one organization's culture is superior, and after a merger or acquisition, the superior culture is willingly adopted by all employees regardless of their former employer prior to the merger.

Choice A is incorrect because integration occurs when merged companies combine both of their cultures into a new overall culture applicable for the new merged entity. Integration assumes that the two entities join together as equals. Each organization is represented in the new combined culture without labeling either former culture as superior.

Choice B is incorrect because separation is where the two merged companies are managed as two entities which are legally affiliated, but, both continue separate operations and each entity maintains a distinct culture identity.

Choice D is incorrect because deculturation occurs when the acquiring company forces its culture onto the acquiring company. The prompt suggest that the organization adopts a new culture willingly, so assimilation is a better choice.

BEC 5-Q94 B279. The correct choice is A. Strategic planning establishes the general direction of the organization because strategic planning is the process which will implement the firm's current and future objectives.

Choices B, C and D are not correct because a budget establishes the type, amount, and cost of resources that will be needed in its operations. Choices B, C, and D also describe capital budgeting, which is the process of gathering information about a project or investment, including the types of resources required, the budget for those resources, and the management decision to undertake a project or investment.

BEC 5-Q95 B349. The correct choice is D. The steps, at a high level, in the strategic planning process are:
1. Compose the mission statement.
2. Conduct a SWOT analysis (strengths, weaknesses, opportunities, and threats).
3. Develop strategies consistent with the mission statement that also address the SWOT analysis.
4. Implement the strategies.
5. Measure effectiveness of the strategies; adjust accordingly.

Therefore, the step that should be completed first in the strategic planning process is to create a mission statement.

Choice A is not correct because translating the objectives into goals is part of step 3 to develop strategies consistent with the mission statement that also address the SWOT analysis; therefore, choice A is not the first step.

Choice B is not correct because determining actions to achieve goals is part of step 3 to develop strategies consistent with the mission statement that also address the SWOT analysis; therefore, choice B is not the first step.

Choice C is not correct because developing performance measures is part of step 5 to measure the effectiveness of the strategies; therefore, choice C is not the first step.

BEC 5-Q96 B197. The correct choice is D. Managerial accounting is the use of accounting and non-accounting information in order to make a management decision. The accounting information does not have to comply with U.S. GAAP or IFRS; the decisions are made internal to the organization. Therefore, managerial accounting focuses on the needs of the organization's internal parties.

Choice A is not correct because financial accounting uses accounting information (that must comply with U.S. GAAP or IFRS) in order to prepare financial statements and other financial reports for the use of external parties (e.g., current or potential shareholders, owners, and creditors).

Choice B is not correct because managerial accounting often focuses on cash-basis accounting information and may consider historical cost to be a sunk cost (a cost that will not change based on the alternative selected) and a sunk cost is not relevant in making a management decision.

Choice C is not correct because a creditor is an external party. Managerial accounting focuses on the needs of the organization's internal parties.

BEC 5-Q97 B364. The correct choice is D. The capital budget is one of the budgets that is prepared when preparing the master budget. The capital budget is a plan for allocating resources to capital investments, such as new plant, property and equipment (PP&E). Therefore, information with regard to PP&E would be most beneficial to consider when management is developing the capital budget, e.g., profit center equipment requests.

Choice A is not correct because the demand for the company's products would assist in preparing the sales budget, which is the mix and number of products that will be produced; the sales budget would be the first step in preparing the master budget and only indirectly affects the preparation of the capital budget, which is a subsequent step.

Choice B is not correct because the current product sales prices and costs would assist in preparing the budgeted income statement; the preparation of the financial statements in the master budget occurs after preparing the capital budget.

Choice C is not correct because the wage trends would assist in preparing the direct labor budget when preparing the master budget; the preparation of production budgets for direct materials, direct labor, and manufacturing overhead occurs before preparing the capital budget. The preparation of the production budgets only indirectly affects the preparation of the capital budget, which is a subsequent step.

BEC 5-Q98 B56. The correct choice is A because the cash budget is prepared subsequent to the capital, COGS, and marketing (a selling expense) budgets. The order of the budgeting process is described below.
1. Sales budget; determines how many units will be sold.
2. Production Budget, Period Costs Budget, and Capital Budget
　2a. Production budget; based on how many units to be sold and desired ending inventories.
　2b. Period costs budgets: selling expense, general & administrative expense, research & development expense; these budgets support sales and production.
　2c. Capital budget: this is the acquisition of additional fixed assets to increase productivity and efficiency; this budget supports current production and future production.
3. Direct Materials, Direct Labor, and Manufacturing Overhead budgets; based on the number of units to be produced (these are the product costs).
　3a. COGS budget, which is the component of DM used, DL used, and MOH applied that is associated with the units that are sold.
　3b. DM purchases budget, which is based on the desired ending inventory for DM and the DM used.

4. Cash budget: incorporates cash collections from sales and cash disbursements for the cost budgets listed above.
5. Budgeted Financial Statements
   5a. Budgeted Income Statement
   5b. Budgeted Balance Sheet
   5c. Budgeted Statement of Cash Flows

Choices B, C, and D are not correct because the cash budget (item 4) is prepared subsequent to the capital (item 2c.), COGS (item 3a.), and marketing (a selling expense, item 2b.) budgets.

BEC 5-Q99 B257. The correct choice is D. A master budget is a budget prepared for one level of activity. The master budget is prepared in the following steps:

(1) Prepare the sales forecast and the sales budget.
(2) Based on the number of units to be sold, the beginning inventories, and the desired ending inventories, prepare the production budget.
(3) Based on the production budget, prepare the direct materials, direct labor, and manufacturing overhead budgets.
(4) Prepare the budgets for period costs, e.g., selling, general and administrative, and research and development expenses.
(5) Prepare the capital expenditures budget.
(6) Prepare the cash budget based on (1) through (5) above.
(7) Prepare the budgeted financial statements: Income statement, balance sheet, and statement of cash flows.

The preparation of the budgeted balance sheet is in step (7) above; the budgeted financial statements are prepared in the order of the income statement, then balance sheet, and then statement of cash flows. The budgeted income statement provides the net income or net loss. The budgeted net income/loss is included in budgeted retained earnings; then, the budgeted retained earnings is included in the owner's equity section of the balance sheet.

Choice A is not correct because the sales budget is prepared in step (1); the owner's equity section of a budgeted balance sheet is prepared in step (7) from information provided by the budgeted income statement in step (7). The budgeted income statement prepared in step (7) provides information for the preparation of the owner's equity section of the budgeted balance sheet in step (7). The budgeted income statement provides the net income or net loss; then, the budgeted net income/loss is included in budgeted retained earnings; then, the budgeted retained earnings is included in the owner's equity section of the balance sheet.

Choice B is not correct because the cash budget is prepared in step (6). The budgeted income statement prepared in step (7) provides information for the preparation of the owner's equity section of the budgeted balance sheet in step (7). The budgeted income statement provides the net income or net loss; then, the budgeted net income/loss is included in budgeted retained earnings; then, the budgeted retained earnings is included in the owner's equity section of the balance sheet.

Choice C is not correct because the capital expenditures budget is prepared in step (5). The budgeted income statement prepared in step (7) provides information for the preparation of the owner's equity section of the budgeted balance sheet in step (7). The budgeted income statement provides the net income or net loss; then, the budgeted net income/loss is included in budgeted retained earnings; then, the budgeted retained earnings is included in the owner's equity section of the balance sheet.

BEC 5-Q100 B276. The correct choice is A. The master budget is prepared according to the following steps:
(1) Prepare the sales forecast and the sales budget.
(2) Based on the number of units to be sold, the beginning inventories, and the desired ending inventories, prepare the production budget.
(3) Based on the production budget, prepare the direct materials, direct labor, and manufacturing overhead budgets.
(4) Prepare the budgets for period costs, e.g., selling, general and administrative, and research and development expenses.
(5) Prepare the capital expenditures budget.
(6) Prepare the cash budget based on (1) through (5) above.
(7) Prepare the budgeted financial statements: Income statement, balance sheet, and statement of cash flows.

Therefore, a forecast of sales volume is the first item prepared in step (1) for developing a budget.

Choice B is not correct because the sales forecast is prepared before determining the price of the products. Once the sales forecast is complete, the sales prices may be determined, and the sales budget may be prepared.

Choice C not correct because identifying the costs associated with forecasted sales volume would be part of steps (3) and (4).

Choice D is not correct because in step (1) computing the dollar amount of the forecasted sales (the sales budget) occurs after the sales forecast is complete.

BEC 5-Q101 B329. The correct choice is B. The question is solved below using the T account for direct materials inventory. However, the T account is in pounds of direct materials inventory instead of dollars.

Direct Materials Inventory

Debit		Credit	
Beg. Inv. 0.40 x Jan. Prod. 12,000 units x 4 lbs./unit	19,200		
DM lbs. purchased (plug)	46,400		
		DM used Jan. Prod. 12,000 units x 4 lbs./unit	48,000
DM lbs. available for use (plug)	65,600		
End. Inv. 0.40 x Feb. Prod. 11,000 units x 4 lbs./unit	17,600		

Note that the sales information was not needed to solve the question.

BEC 5-Q102 B254. The correct choice is A. Participative budgeting is a bottom-up approach to budgeting because the budget is based on input from employees and management at lower levels of the organization. Because of the number of employees and management involved and the distributed nature of participative budgeting, the process is more time consuming.

Choices B, C, and D are not correct because participative budgeting is based on input from employees and management at lower levels of the organization. When employees and management at lower levels of the organization are consulted about the budget, this increases the morale and motivation of the employees and management and their acceptance of the budget's requirements. Participative budgeting is also more accurate because it is based on input from employees and management at lower levels of the organization who are more knowledgeable in the details of the budgeted activities.

BEC 5-Q103 B52. The correct choice is D. A static budget presents budgeted production and costs for one level of activity. Therefore, a static budget will have budgeted costs for budgeted output.

Choices A, B, and C are not correct because a static budget does not have actual costs or actual output.

BEC 5-Q104 B287. The correct choice is D. The calculation of the flexible budget variance may be solved by using the variable manufacturing overhead variance matrix. We may use this matrix because the fixed costs are not a factor; only variable manufacturing overhead costs are mentioned in the MCQ.

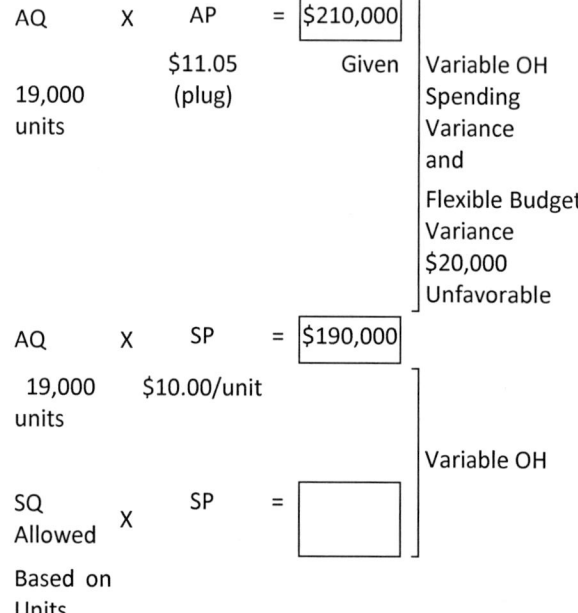

BEC 5-Q105 B51. The correct choice is B. To solve this problem, use a T account for Accounts Payable to calculate the inventory purchased; because the inventory of candles did not change, this means that all purchases were sold and purchases equals cost of goods sold (COGS).

Accounts Payable			
		100,000	Beginning
Disbursements	300,000		
Subtotal	200,000		
		350,000	Purchases (plug)
		150,000	Ending @ 150% of Beg.

Now that purchases of $350,000 are known, gross margin (also known as gross profit) is calculated as:

Sales @ 120% of purchase price $420,000
Less: COGS (same as purchases)   (350,000)
Gross Margin $70,000

BEC 5-Q106 B141. The correct choice is B. This question omits total fixed costs. The first step is to calculate the total variable costs per year, which is 125,000 miles x $0.13 per mile = $16,250. The second step is to calculate the total number of pounds per year, which is 28,000 pounds x 250 loads per year = 7,000,000 pounds. The third step is to divide the total variable costs per year by the number of pounds per year:

$16,250 total variable costs/7,000,000 pounds = $0.00232 delivery cost per pound

BEC 5-Q107 B138. The correct choice is A. The cost formula is:

  Total Fixed Costs, which remain fixed over the relevant range
  + Total Variable Costs, which is # of units x variable cost per unit
  = Total Costs

An increase in production levels within the relevant range would most likely result in an increase in total variable costs, resulting in an increase in total costs. However, because the production levels remain within the relevant range, total fixed costs would remain unchanged.

Choices B and D are not correct because the variable cost *per unit* would remain unchanged as long as production levels remain within the relevant range. However, *total* variable costs would change proportionately with the change in the number of units as long as production levels remain within the relevant range.

Choice C is not correct because *total* fixed costs remain unchanged within the relevant range. However, because *total* fixed costs remain unchanged and are spread over a greater number of units, the fixed cost *per unit* would decrease.

BEC 5-Q108 B168. The correct choice is D. As long as production levels remain within the relevant range, total fixed costs will remain fixed and the variable cost per unit will remain constant; because total variable costs will increase by the change in # units x variable cost per unit, then total costs (total costs = total fixed costs + total variable costs) will also increase. Because total fixed costs remain fixed over the relevant range and additional units are produced, this will decrease the fixed cost per unit.

Choice A is not correct because as long as production levels remain within the relevant range, total fixed costs will remain fixed.

Choices B and C are not correct because as long as production levels remain within the relevant range, the variable cost per unit will remain constant; however, total variable costs will increase by the change in # units x variable cost per unit.

BEC 5-Q109 B140. The correct choice is D. The change in profits is calculated below for 10,000 units before VC/unit increases; for 10,000 units after VC/unit increases by 20 percent; and for 12,000 units after VC/unit increases by 20 percent. Note: Sometimes it is easier to use the variable costing income statement instead of the cost-volume-profit (CVP or break-even point) formulas.

	10,000 before	10,000 after	12,000 After
Sales, 10,000; 10,000; 12,000 @ $85	$850,000	$850,000	$1,020,000
Less: VC, 10,000 @$50; 10,000 @ $60 [$50 x $1.20]; 12,000 x $60	(500,000)	(600,000)	(720,000)
Contribution Margin	350,000	250,000	300,000
Less: Total Fixed Costs	(300,000)	(300,000)	(300,000)
Profit Before Income Taxes	$50,000	($50,000)	$0

As calculated above, if production remains at 10,000 units and VC/unit increase by 20%, then profits will decrease from $50,000 to ($50,000), a decrease of $100,000.

Choices A and B are not correct because if production is increased to 12,000 units and VC/unit increase by 20%, then profits will decrease from $50,000 to $0, a decrease of $50,000.

Choice C is not correct because if production remains at 10,000 units and VC/unit increase, then profits will decrease from $50,000 to ($50,000), a decrease of $100,000.

BEC 5-Q110 B71. The correct choice is C. This problem may be solved using the variable costing income statement as presented below.

Sales	1.00x
− Variable Costs	0.60x
= Contribution Margin	0.40x
− Total Fixed Costs	20,000
= Net Income before Taxes	0.15x

Solving as an equation:

$0.40x - \$20,000 = 0.15x$
$0.40x - 0.15x = \$20,000$
$0.25x = \$20,000$
$x = \$20,000/0.25$
$x = \$80,000$

BEC 5-Q111 B49. The correct choice is D. To solve this problem, use the BEP formula in units to calculate the total fixed costs as follows:

BEP in units = Total Fixed Costs/(Sales Price per unit − Variable Cost per unit)
20,000 = Total Fixed Costs/($7.50 − $2.25)
20,000 = Total Fixed Costs/$5.25
20,000 x $5.25 = Total Fixed Costs
Total Fixed Costs = $105,000

Remember that fixed costs remain fixed as long as production stays within the relevant range. Now that the Total Fixed Costs of $105,000 are known, use the same BEP in units formula, but add the profit to the numerator. The profit is $5,040, but this is a net of tax amount. The profit in the BEP formula in units must be before tax. To convert from after-tax profit of $5,040 to the before tax profit, divide $5,040 by 0.60 (which is 1 − 0.40 tax rate) = $8,400 before tax profit.

BEP in units = (Total Fixed Costs + Profit)/(Sales Price per unit − Variable Cost per unit)
BEP in units = (105,000 + $8,400)/($7.50 −$2.25)
BEP in units = $113,400/$5.25
BEP in units = 21,600 units, which is the current operating level

Because the manufacturer expects sales to exceed last year's sales by 1,000 units:
21,600 units at the current level + 1,000 additional units = 22,600 units

BEC 5-Q112 B68. The correct choice is B. The calculation for BEP in units is presented below.

BEP in units = Total Fixed Costs/Contribution Margin per unit
BEP in units = $360,000/$1,800
BEP in units = 200 students

BEC 5-Q113 B165. The correct choice is D. In order to calculate the number of units that Wren sold, first determine the contribution margin as follows:

Operating income + fixed costs = Contribution margin
$28,800 + $38,400 = $67,200

Next, calculate the contribution margin for each composite unit of A:B, which is 4:1.

Product A CM = SP $18 – VC $12 = $6 per unit x 4 = $24
Product B CM = SP $22 – VC $14 = $8 per unit x 1 = $8
Total CM per composite units of 4A:1B = $32

Using the CVP formula: BEP units = Total contribution margin/CM per composite unit
BEP units = ($28,800 + $38,400)/$32
BEP units = 2,100 composite units of which
Product A, 2,100 x 4 = 8,400 units of A
Product B, 2,100 x 1 = 2,100 units of B
Total units sold   10,500 units of A and B

Another way to solve this question is to use the formula:

($6 x 4B) + ($8 x B) = $67,200
$24B + $8B = $67,200
$32B = $67,200
B = 2,100 units

A = 4 x B
A = 4 x 2,100
A = 8,400 units
A + B = 10,500 units

BEC 5-Q114 B192. The correct choice is C. The question is solved in two steps. In step 1, solve for total fixed costs using the break-even point (BEP) formula:

BEP in units = Total Fixed Costs /Contribution margin per unit, which is sales price – variable costs
20,000 = Total Fixed Costs /($7.50 – $2.25)
20,000 = Total Fixed Costs/$5.25
20,000 x $5.25 = Total Fixed Costs
$105,000 = Total Fixed Costs

In step 2, using the total fixed costs from step 1, solve for the new BEP in units.

The facts have changed so that
Total Fixed Costs = $105,000 x 1.10 = $115,500
Sales Price = $9.00 per unit
Variable Costs = $2.25 x 1.333 = $3.00 per unit
Contribution margin = $9.00 –$3.00 = $6.00 per unit

BEP in units = Total Fixed Costs/CM per unit
BEP in units = $115,500/$6.00
BEP in units = 19,250 units

BEC 5-Q115 B247. The correct choice is C. The break-even point in sales dollars is calculated below.

BEP, sales dollars = Total Fixed Costs/Contribution Margin Ratio
BEP, sales dollars = $30,000/(Sales Price 100% – Variable Costs 25%)
BEP, sales dollars = $30,000/0.75
BEP, sales dollars = $40,000

BEC 5-Q116 B93. The correct choice is B. This question involves the break-even point in a multi-product firm; e.g., Product A and Product B. The ratio is 3 units of Product A to 1 unit of Product B. The contribution margin per unit is:
  Product A: Sales Price $10 – Variable Cost $6 = $4
  Product B: Sales Price $25 – Variable Cost $13 = $12

The contribution margin for each package of 3:1 of Product A:
Product B is:
  Product A: Contribution Margin $4 x 3 units/package = $12
  Product B: Contribution Margin $12 x 1 unit/package = $12
  Total Contribution Margin per package = $24

The break event point in units (or packages in a multi-product firm) is calculated as:
  BEP in packages = Total Fixed Costs/CM per package
  Numerator = $100,000 + 212,000 = $312,000
  Denominator = $24
  BEP in packages = $312,000/$24
  BEP in packages = 13,000 packages

The 13,000 packages must then be extended to Product A and Product B:
  Product A: 13,000 packages x 3 units/package = 39,000 units of Product A
  Product B: 13,000 packages x 1 unit/package = 13,000 units of Product B.

Note: In a multi-product question, make sure that you extend the BEP of 13,000 packages to the products in accordance with the proper product mix.

BEC 5-Q117 B256. The correct choice is B. The second calendar quarter is April, May, and June. The expected cash collections in the second calendar quarter of the next year is calculated as follows:

April cash collections:
$ 85,000	February sales collected in 2 months, $500,000 x 0.17
340,000	March sales collected in 1 month, $425,000 x 0.80
$425,000	Total April cash collections

May cash collections:
$ 72,250	March sales collected in 2 months, $425,000 x 0.17
360,000	April sales collected in 1 month $450,000 x 0.80
$432,250	Total May cash collections

June cash collections:
$ 76,500	April sales collected in 2 months, $450,000 x 0.17
460,000	May sales collected in 1 month, $575,000 x 0.80
$536,500	Total June cash collections

Total cash collections in the second calendar quarter = $425,000 + $432,250 + $536,500 = $1,393,750

BEC 5-Q118 B286. The correct choice is C. The amount of projected cash collections for September is presented as the third calculation. The calculations for July collections and August collections are provided as solutions in case a similar question asked for just July collections, just August collections, or collections for the quarter ended September 30. Note that the June 30, 20X3 accounts receivable balance of $10,000 is split between 30% for first month collections and 10% for second month collections for credit sales made prior to July.

July collections:
  $7,500 ¾ (30% of 40%) x $10,000 June 30 A/R
   7,500 July cash sales, 0.25 x $30,000 total sales
  13,500 July credit sales, same month, 0.60 x ($30,000 total sales – $7,500 cash sales)
  $28,500 Total July collections

August collections:
  $2,500 ¼ (10% of 40%) x $10,000 June 30 A/R
   6,750 July credit sales, 1 month, 0.30 x ($30,000 total sales – $7,500 cash sales)
   3,750 August cash sales, 0.25 x $15,000 total sales
   6,750 August credit sales, same month, 0.60 x ($15,000 total sales – $3,750 cash sales)
  $19,750 Total August collections

September collections:
  $2,250 July credit sales, two months, 0.10 x ($30,000 total sales – $7,500 cash sales)
   3,375 August credit sales, 1 month, 0.30 x ($15,000 total sales – $3,750 cash sales)
   8,750 September cash sales, 0.25 x $35,000 total sales
  15,750 September credit sales, same month, 0.60 x ($35,000 total sales – $8,750 cash sales)
  $30,125 Total September collections; the correct choice is C.

BEC 5-Q119 B77. The correct choice is C. Calculating cash to be collected in the second quarter is described below.

	First Quarter	Second Quarter
Sales	10,000 units x $2/unit = $20,000	15,000 units x $2/unit = $30,000
Cash Sales are 60%	$12,000	$18,000
Credit Sales are 40% collected in the next quarter	Not applicable	$20,000 Q1 Sales x 0.40 = $8,000
Total Cash Collected	Not applicable	$18,000 + $8,000 = $26,000

BEC 5-Q120 B280. The correct choice is D. In the three years presented, quarterly revenues increase in the third quarter and then peak in the fourth quarter. This pattern indicates a seasonal increase in demand in the third quarter and a peak in seasonal demand in the fourth quarter, with a decline in demand in the first quarter of the following year. Therefore, due to the seasonal demand for its products, Emerald should manage its inventories and cash flows to match the seasonal pattern of demand.

Choices A and B are not correct because changes in the economy are more gradual and longer-lasting and would span multiple years instead of a pattern that repeats each year and at the same time during the year (a yearly pattern indicates the seasonality of demand).

Choice C is not correct because the cost structure would impact expenses, such as cost of goods sold and operating expenses, which in turn would affect gross profit, operating income, and net income; the cost structure would not affect revenues.

BEC 5-Q121 B295. The correct choice is A. The percentage of sales forecasting method is a budgeting technique based on the common-sized income statement. A common-sized income statement sets net sales at 100 percent and divides each line item on the income statement by net sales so that each line item is expressed as a percentage of net sales. After management has analyzed a number of periods of common-sized income statements, management is able to budget the expense line items on the income statement as a percentage of net sales. Therefore, management is basing budgeted product and period expenses on budgeted sales revenue. Accounts payable is a liability associated with product and period expenses.

Choices B, C and D are not correct because these are long-term liabilities and contributed capital associated with financing the firm with debt and equity and are not associated with product and period expenses as budgeted using the percentage of sales forecasting method.

BEC 5-Q122 B353. The correct choice is C. The Delphi forecasting method is qualitative in nature and uses a series of questionnaires to achieve consensus among the members of a group. Because the Delphi forecasting model is qualitative, it relies on judgment in the design of the questionnaires.

Choice A is not correct because time series models are quantitative in nature and extrapolate past results for the same item to future outcomes for the same item.

Choice B is not correct because econometric models are quantitative in nature and try to predict the effects of different variables on a forecasted result.

Choice D is not correct because regression is quantitative in nature; based on past observations, regression expresses the linear relationship between fixed and variable components and their effects on the dependent variable.

BEC 5-Q123 B124. The correct choice is B. The opportunity cost is the cost of benefits forgone when choosing one alternative versus another alternative. Therefore, if Carter Co. chooses to keep and develop the land, then Carter Co. foregoes any benefits derived from the next best use of the land (e.g., net proceeds from selling the land for $1,200,000).

Choice A is not correct because $1,500,000 is the cost to develop the land, which is a cost of pursuing the alternative to develop the land.

Choice C is not correct because $1,000,000 is the net cash outflow in the first year of operations (cash outflow of $1,500,000 less $500,000 cash inflow) when pursuing the alternative to develop the land.

Choice D is not correct because $500,000 is the cash inflow when pursing the alternative to develop the land.

BEC 5-Q124 B146. The correct choice is B. The opportunity cost is the cost of benefits forgone when choosing one alternative versus another alternative. Therefore, if Egan Co. chooses to develop the land, then it forgoes the proceeds from selling the land for $1,200,000, which is the opportunity cost.

Choice A is not correct because a sunk cost represents a cost that has already been incurred. A sunk cost is not relevant to the decision because the sunk cost remains the same regardless of which alternative is selected. An example of a sunk cost would be the price Egan Co. paid to purchase the land.

Choice C is not correct because a future cost (e.g., a future cash outflow) would be netted with a future benefit (e.g., a future cash inflow) to calculate the difference (e.g., a future net cash inflow). A future net cash inflow from the land development would be an example of an opportunity cost if Egan chooses to sell the land instead of develop the land.

Choice D is not correct because a variable cost is a cost that remains constant on a per unit basis when operating within the relevant range of activity. Variable costs are not applicable to the scenario presented in the question.

BEC 5-Q125 B198. The correct choice is C. Opportunity cost is the cost of benefits forgone when choosing one alternative versus another alternative. If idle space has no alternative use, then no benefit is forgone and the opportunity cost would be zero.

Choice A is not correct because opportunity cost is the cost of benefits forgone when choosing one alternative versus another alternative. Any benefit forgone when selecting between alternatives is not recorded in a full costing system because a full costing system must comply with U.S. GAAP and IFRS; opportunity cost is not a cost recognized under U.S. GAAP or IFRS.

Choice B is not correct because opportunity cost is the cost of benefits forgone when choosing one alternative versus another alternative. Therefore, the potential benefit that *is* sacrificed is the opportunity cost.

Choice D is not correct because opportunity cost is the cost of benefits foregone when choosing one alternative versus another alternative. Because the benefits are forgone, opportunity cost is not representative of an actual dollar outlay.

BEC 5-Q126 B300. The correct choice is A. Opportunity cost is the cost of benefits forgone when choosing one alternative versus another alternative. If LQR Corp. had chosen to forego filling the order, the opportunity cost would have been $90,000, the additional profit which would have been earned if the order were fulfilled by outsourcing the order to SDT.

Choice B is not correct because accounting profit is total revenue minus explicit costs. Opportunity cost, an implicit cost, is not included in accounting profit as measured by U.S. GAAP.

Choice C is not correct because implicit costs include opportunity costs. Opportunity cost is the cost of benefits forgone when choosing one alternative versus another alternative.

Choice D is not correct because explicit costs are not opportunity costs. Explicit costs are costs that result in cash outflows. Opportunity cost is the cost of benefits forgone when choosing one alternative versus another alternative.

BEC 5-Q127 B41. The correct choice is C. Remember that past costs already incurred are sunk costs and are not relevant, unless there is a tax consequence associated with the sunk cost, such as additional taxes owed on a taxable gain or a decrease in taxes owed on a tax-deductible loss. However, the problem requires that we ignore income taxes. The relevant costs consist of those cash inflows and cash outflows that would occur as a result of replacing the delivery van; in this case, the relevant cash outflow is the purchase of the new van of $40,000 and the relevant cash inflow is the proceeds from disposal of the old van of $12,000.

Choice A is not correct because the gain on sale of the old van is not relevant; the additional taxes owed on a taxable gain would be relevant, but the problem requires that we ignore income taxes.

Choice B is not correct because the purchase price of the old van is not relevant. The purchase price of the old van and its corresponding accumulated depreciation would be used to calculate the carrying value of the old van; then, the carrying value would be compared to the proceeds from disposal to calculate the taxable gain or tax deductible loss. It is the increase in taxes owed on the taxable gain or the decrease in taxes owed on the tax deductible loss that would be relevant; however, the problem requires that we ignore income taxes.

Choice D is not correct because the purchase price of the old van, the accumulated depreciation on the old van, and the gain on sale of the old van are not relevant. The purchase price of the old van and its corresponding accumulated depreciation would be used to calculate the carrying value of the old van; then, the carrying value would be compared to the proceeds from disposal to calculate the taxable gain or tax deductible loss. It is the increase in taxes owed on the taxable gain or the decrease in taxes owed on the tax deductible loss that would be relevant; however, the problem requires that we ignore income taxes.

BEC 5-Q128 B161. The correct choice is B. Fixed costs remain fixed within the relevant range. Because the company has the capacity to take the special order and production levels remain within the relevant range, the fixed costs will remain fixed. Also, because the special order earns gross profit of 10%, the operating income will increase.

Choice A is not correct because fixed costs remain fixed within the relevant range; the company has the capacity to take the special order, so production levels will remain within the relevant range and fixed costs will not increase.

Choice C is not correct because the special order earns gross profit of 10%; therefore, operating income will increase due to higher gross profit.

Choice D is not correct because fixed costs remain fixed within the relevant range; the company has the capacity to take the special order, so production levels will remain within the relevant rage and fixed costs will not increase. Furthermore, because the special order earns gross profit of 10%, the operating income will increase instead of decrease.

BEC 5-Q129 B293. The correct choice is C. Rodder should accept the special one-time order as long as the sales price per unit covers the variable costs per unit; fixed costs are disregarded because the fixed costs will not change as a result of accepting the special one-time order. Calculations for the lowest unit price that Rodder should accept for the component are presented below.

The variable costs per unit would be direct materials, direct labor, variable manufacturing overhead per unit, and the opportunity cost of $5,000 (as spread over the 1,000 units in the special one-time order, which is $5 per unit):

$ 3	DM
3	DL
3	VMOH
5	Opportunity cost
$14	Total variable costs

BEC 5-Q130 B164. The correct choice is C.
Using the formula:
  Sales
 – Cost of Goods Sold
 = Gross Profit

Set sales as X, COGS as $89 and gross profit as 0.40X, solving algebraically as:

$X - 89 = 0.40X$
$X = 0.40X + 89$
$0.60X = 89$
$X = 89/0.60$
$X = 148.33$

BEC 5-Q131 B326. The correct choice is C.

If Division A manufactured Product X and sells to outsiders, the contribution margin would be:
$25	Sales price per unit
– 15	Variable cost per unit
$10	Contribution margin per unit

If Division B manufactured Product Y (using Product X purchased from Division A) and paid the same sales price for Product X that outsiders pay, the contribution margin for Division B would be:
$100	Sales price per unit
– 65	Variable cost per unit ($25 for Product X + $40 additional costs)
$ 35	Contribution margin

When selling to Division B, by setting the sales price as $25 for Product X, Division A would earn the same $10 CM as if it sold Product X to outsiders.

Choice A is not correct because at a sales price of $15 for Product X, Division A would earn a $0 CM, which is less than the $10 CM from selling to outsiders.

Choice B is not correct because at a sales price of $20 for Product X, Division A would earn a $5 CM, which is less than the $10 CM from selling to outsiders.

Choice D is not correct because at a sales price of $40 for Product X, this sales price is greater than the $25 sales price to outsiders; therefore, Division B would purchase Product X from another manufacturer for less than $40 instead of purchasing Product X from Division A.

This page is intentionally left blank.

BEC 6 - Task-based Simulations and Written Communication

Task-based Simulation – Questions   6-2
    BEC 6-SIMQ1 SIM3   6-2
    BEC 6-SIMQ2 SIM6   6-3

Written Communication – Prompts   6-4
    BEC 6-WCQ1 WC4   6-4
    BEC 6-WCQ2 WC28   6-5

Task-based Simulation – Solutions   6-6
    BEC 6-SIMQ1 SIM3   6-6
    BEC 6-SIMQ1 SIM6   6-7

Written Communication – Example Responses   6-8
    BEC 5-WCQ1 WC4   6-8
    BEC 5-WCQ2 WC28   6-9

Task-based Simulation – Question

Remember: The icons and buttons below are not functional. The formatting in this chapter mirrors the CPA exam. It is intended to familiarize you with the look and feel of the exam.

BEC 6-SIMQ1 SIM3

System and Organization Control (SOC) Reports | Help | Authoritative Literature | Submit Testlet

For each item listed below, determine the corresponding System and Organization Control (SOC) report to which it applies by checking the box(es) in the proper column(s). Each item may apply to one or more report.

Item	SOC 1	SOC 2	SOC 3
1. Reports are prepared in accordance with AICPA standard AT-C 105 and AT-C 205.			
2. Controls relate to security, availability, confidentiality, processing integrity, and/or privacy.			
3. The use of the report is restricted, and only the user auditor, management of service organization, and management of user may rely on the report.			
4. The report is based on the Trust Services categories and criteria.			
5. Reports are for public use.			
6. Reports are prepared in accordance with AICPA standard AT-C 320 based on SSAE 18.			
7. Controls relate to the financial statements of user entities and a user entity's internal control over financial reporting.			
8. The use of the report is limited to knowledgeable parties, specified by the auditor.			

⚑ = Reminder   Directions | 1 | 2 | 3 | 4 | 5   ◀ Previous | Next ▶

BEC 6-SIMQ2 SIM6

Process Costing | Help | Authoritative Literature | Submit Testlet

Brown Box Company uses weighted-average process costing to assign product costs. Inventory information for the period is as follows:

	Inventory (in units)	Material cost	Conversion cost
Beginning of period	3,000	$ 3,000	$ 6,000
Started during the period	5,000	$ 10,000	$ 7,500
Transferred out	4,000		
End of period	4,000		

Note:
- 100% of the direct materials cost and 40% of the conversion cost for beginning inventory was incurred in last period on these units.
- The ending inventory was 40% complete as to the conversion cost.
- 100% of direct material was added at the beginning of the process.
- Conversion costs are added evenly during the process.

How many units were shipped/transferred out/completed (in whole units)?

Calculate the number of equivalent finished goods for material costs

Calculate the number of equivalent finished goods for conversion costs

Calculate the cost per equivalent finished goods for material costs

Calculate the cost per equivalent finished goods for conversion costs

= Reminder   Directions | 1 | 2 | 3 | 4 | 5   ◀ Previous | Next ▶

Written Communication – Prompts

Remember: The icons and buttons below are **not** functional. The formatting in this chapter mirrors the CPA exam. It is intended to familiarize you with the look and feel of the exam.

BEC 6-WCQ1 WC4

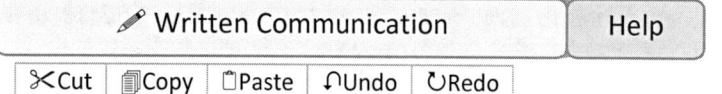

Authoritative Literature

Submit Testlet

Joe Candle, the accounting manager of Zain Company, is confused as to when to use a risk-adjusted discount rate and a time-adjusted discount rate. He has asked you to write a memorandum to him explaining the use of each one.

Type your communication in the response area below the horizontal line using the word processor provided.

REMINDER: Your response will be graded for both technical content and writing skills. Technical content will be evaluated for information that is helpful to the intended reader and clearly relevant to the issue. Writing skills will be evaluated for development, organization, and the appropriate expression of ideas in professional correspondence. Use a standard business memo or letter format with a clear beginning, middle, and end. Do not convey information in the form of a table, bullet point list, or other abbreviated presentation.

> To: Joe Candle, Accounting Manager, Zain Company
> Re: Risk-Adjusted Discount Rate and Time-Adjusted Discount Rate
>
> *Type your response here.*

*Remember: The icons and buttons below are **not** functional. The formatting in this chapter mirrors the CPA exam. It is intended to familiarize you with the look and feel of the exam.*

BEC 6-WCQ2 WC28

During a meeting with the accounting manager of a client, Best Meat Products, you are discussing general economic conditions related to demand for your client's products. The conversation included that the demand curve is downward sloping and that a movement along the demand curve is caused by a change in price. The accounting manager wasn't as comfortable discussing what happens to cause a shift in the demand curve, as he was in discussing a movement along the demand curve. The accounting manager asked you to write a memorandum describing the 2-3 main factors that would have a direct relationship in shifting the demand curve.

Type your communication in the response area below the horizontal line using the word processor provided.

REMINDER: Your response will be graded for both technical content and writing skills. Technical content will be evaluated for information that is helpful to the intended reader and clearly relevant to the issue. Writing skills will be evaluated for development, organization, and the appropriate expression of ideas in professional correspondence. Use a standard business memo or letter format with a clear beginning, middle, and end. Do not convey information in the form of a table, bullet point list, or other abbreviated presentation.

To: Accounting Manager
Re: Direct Relationship Factors that Shift Demand Curve

Type your response here.

Task-based Simulation – Solution

BEC 6-SIMQ1 SIM3

Item	SOC 1	SOC 2	SOC 3
1. Reports are prepared in accordance with AICPA standard AT-C 105 and AT-C 205.		✓	✓
2. Controls relate to security, availability, confidentiality, processing integrity, and/or privacy.		✓	✓
3. The use of the report is restricted, and only the user auditor, management of service organization, and management of user may rely on the report.	✓		
4. The report is based on the Trust Services categories and criteria.		✓	✓
5. Reports are for public use.			✓
6. Reports are prepared in accordance with AICPA standard AT-C 320 based on SSAE 18.	✓		
7. Controls relate to the financial statements of user entities and a user entity's internal control over financial reporting.	✓		
8. The use of the report is limited to knowledgeable parties, specified by the auditor.		✓	

BEC 6-SIMQ1 SIM6

How many units were shipped/transferred out/completed (in whole units)?	4,000
Calculate the number of equivalent finished goods for material costs	8,000
Calculate the number of equivalent finished goods for conversion costs	5,600
Calculate the cost per equivalent finished goods for material costs	1.63
Calculate the cost per equivalent finished goods for conversion costs	2.41

Calculations:
How many units were shipped/transferred out/completed (in whole units)? **4,000**

Beginning Inventory	3,000
+ # Started	5,000
= # to account for	8,000
− Ending Inventory	4,000
= # of units shipped	**4,000**

Calculate the number of equivalent finished goods for material costs: **8,000 (4,000 + 4,000)**
Calculate the number of equivalent finished goods for conversion costs: **5,600 (4,000 + 1,600)**

	Physical units	DM Equivalent units	CC Equivalent units
WIP, beginning (given)	3,000		
Started during the current period (given)	5,000		
# to account for	8,000		
Completed and transferred out during the current period	4,000	4,000	4,000
WIP, ending (given)	4,000	4,000[a]	1,600[b]
# to account for	8,000		
Equivalent units of WIP (weighted-average)		**8,000**	**5,600**

[a] 4,000 * 100% complete = 4,000
[b] 4,000 * 40% complete = 1,600

Calculate the cost per equivalent finished goods for material costs: **1.63 ($13,000 / 8,000)**
Calculate the cost per equivalent finished goods for conversion costs: **2.41 ($13,500 / 5,600)**

	DM	CC
Beginning + Current Costs	$13,000	$13,500
Divided by # EFUs	8,000	5,600
	1.63	2.41

Written Communication – Example Responses

BEC 5-WCQ1 WC4

Example response.

> To: Joe Candle, Accounting Manager, Zain Company
> Re: Risk-Adjusted Discount Rate and Time-Adjusted Discount Rate

Dear Mr. Candle,

As you requested, here is an explanation of a risk-adjusted discount rate and a time-adjusted discount rate.

Risk-adjusted discount rates are used to account for the riskiness of a project. It adjusts for risk by applying different discount rates based on the level of risk involved in a given project. Typically, a project with a normal level of risk would be discounted at Zain's cost of capital. Likewise, projects with higher levels of risk would be discounted at higher rates. A method of applying a risk-adjusted discount rate is to establish a rate hierarchy depending on the risk. For example, low risk projects (replace old machinery) would have a discount rate of 4%, medium risk projects (launch new product) would have a discount rate of 8% and high risk projects (open a new facility in a foreign country) would have a discount rate of 15%.

Time-adjusted discount rates are used to take into consideration the accuracy of forecasting financial information. For example, cash flows are much more difficult to forecast the further out in time. So, cash flows in the later years of a project's life are less likely to be as accurate as the cash flows in the earlier years. Because many variables can occur over time such as, inflation, interest rates and other economic conditions, cash flows in later years should be discounted at higher rates. For example, Zain might establish bench mark rates for specific time frames such as, 8% for years 1 through 3, 10% for years 4 through 7 and 12% for years 8 through 10.

Keep in mind the purpose of discounting the project or investment. If you are looking at it from a risk management standpoint, you might consider a risk-adjusted discount rate. If you are looking to take into consideration various economic conditions in the future, the time-adjusted discount rate might be more appropriate.

If you have any other questions or require more information, please let me know.

Sincerely,
CPA Candidate

BEC 5-WCQ2 WC28

Example response.

    To: Accounting Manager
    Re: Direct Relationship Factors that Shift Demand Curve

Dear Accounting Manager,

This memorandum is in response to your request of me to describe the 2-3 main factors that would have a direct relationship in shifting the demand curve.

In reviewing any product and the economic environment it is sold in, it is important to consider the amount of products produced compared to the actual market demand for those products. A shift in the demand curve occurs when there are changes in demand variable, other than price. There are economic conditions that have a direct relationship in shifting the demand curve for a product including, the size of the market, expectations of a price increase, and the price of other substitute products.

The size of the market has a direct relationship in shifting the demand curve because as the size of the market increases, the demand for the product will increase. For example, this may occur when there is an increase in population or when the size of the typical customer base increases due to customers gaining wealth and moving up in the class scale.

I am available if you would like to discuss this in more detail. Thank you and please let me know if you have any questions or need additional information.

Sincerely,
CPA Candidate

This page is intentionally left blank.